EYEWITNESS TRAVEL
RUSSIA
DK

LONDON, NEW YORK,
MELBOURNE, MUNICH AND DELHI

Managing Editor MadhuMadhavi Singh
Senior Editorial Manager Savitha Kumar
Senior Manager Design and Cartography Priyanka Thakur
Editors Shreya Sarkar, Vatsala Srivastava
Project Designer Stuti Tiwari Bhatia
Designer Aradhana Gupta
Senior Cartographic Manager Uma Bhattacharya
Cartography Manager Suresh Kumar
Senior Cartographer Hassan Mohammmad
Senior DTP Designer Azeem Siddiqui
DTP Designer Rakesh Pal
Picture Research Manager Taiyaba Khatoon
Senior Picture Researcher Sumita Khatwani

Contributors
Catherine Phillips, Christopher Rice, Melanie Rice,
Daniel Richardson, Matt Willis

Photographers
Matt Willis, Katerina Zaharieva

Illustrators
Stephen Conlin, Richard Draper, Stephen Gyapay, Claire Littlejohn,
Chris Orr & Associates, Maltings Partnership,
Arun Pottirayil, Paul Weston

Printed and Bound by
L. Rex Printing Co. Ltd, China

First published in Great Britain in 2013
by Dorling Kindersley Limited
80 Strand, London WC2R 0RL, UK

14 15 16 10 9 8 7 6 5 4 3 2

A CIP catalogue record is available from the British Library.

ISBN 978 1 4093 8665 0

The information in this DK Eyewitness Travel Guide is checked regularly.

Every effort has been made to ensure that this book is as up-to-date as possible at the time of going to press. Some details, however, such as telephone numbers, opening hours, prices, gallery hanging arrangements and travel information are liable to change. The publishers cannot accept responsibility for any consequences arising from the use of this book, nor for any material on third party websites, and cannot guarantee that any website address in this book will be a suitable source of travel information. We value the views and suggestions of our readers very highly. Please write to: Publisher, DK Eyewitness Travel Guides, Dorling Kindersley, 80 Strand, London WC2R 0RL, UK, or email: travelguides@dk.com.

Front cover main image: Gilded onion domes, Cathedral of the Annunciation, the Kremlin

◀ St Basil's Cathedral at twilight, Red Square

Contents

The colourful domes of St Basil's Cathedral, Red Square, Moscow

Introducing Russia

Ballet troupe performing *Swan Lake* at the Mikhailovskiy Theatre, St Petersburg

Moscow Area by Area

Detailed mosaic work in the Small Throne Room at the Hermitage, St Petersburg

St Petersburg Area by Area

A herd of reindeer migrating, northern Kamchatka

Russia Region by Region

Travellers' Needs

Survival Guide

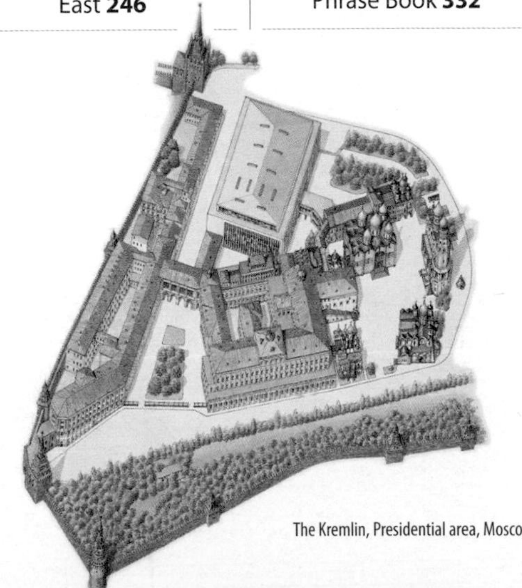

The Kremlin, Presidential area, Moscow

HOW TO USE THIS GUIDE

This Dorling Kindersley Travel Guide helps you get the most from your visit to Russia. It provides detailed practical information and expert recommendations. *Introducing Russia* maps the country and its regions, sets them in their historical and cultural context and describes events through the year. *Russia Region by Region* is the main sightseeing section, which covers all the important sights, with photographs, maps and illustrations. Information on hotels, restaurants, shops, entertainment and sports is found in *Travellers' Needs*. The *Survival Guide* has advice on everything from travel to medical services, banks and communications.

Moscow and St Petersburg Area By Area

Russia's main cities have been dealt with in their respective sections. Both sections have been divided into six sightseeing areas. Each area has its own chapter, which opens with an introduction and a list of the sights described. All sights are plotted on an *Area Map*. The key to the map symbols is on the back flap.

All pages relating to St Petersburg have green thumb tabs.

A locator map shows where the area is in relation to other parts of the city.

1 Area Map *For easy reference, the sights are numbered and located on a map. Sights in each area are also shown on the Moscow and St Petersburg Street Finder maps on pages 126–9 and 196–9 respectively.*

Sights at a Glance lists the chapter's sights by category: Churches, Museums and Galleries, Historic Buildings, Parks and Gardens, and so on.

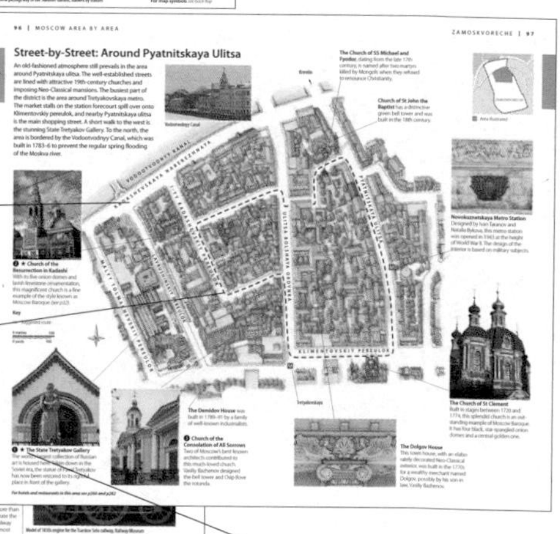

All pages relating to Moscow have red thumb tabs.

2 Street-by-Street Map *This gives a bird's-eye view of a key area in each chapter.*

A suggested route for a walk is shown with a dotted red line.

Stars indicate the sights that no visitor should miss.

3 Practical information *The main sights in both cities are described individually with addresses, websites and information on opening hours and admission charges.*

Story boxes explore specific subjects further.

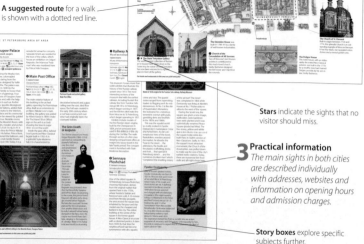

Northern Russia
Pages 204–211

SIBERIA AND THE FAR EAST

Magadan

Kamchatka

Krasnoyarsk

Irkutsk

Sakhalin Island

Vladivostok

Central and Southern Russia
Pages 220–235

Siberia and the Far East
Pages 246–259

EYEWITNESS TRAVEL

RUSSIA

6/6/14

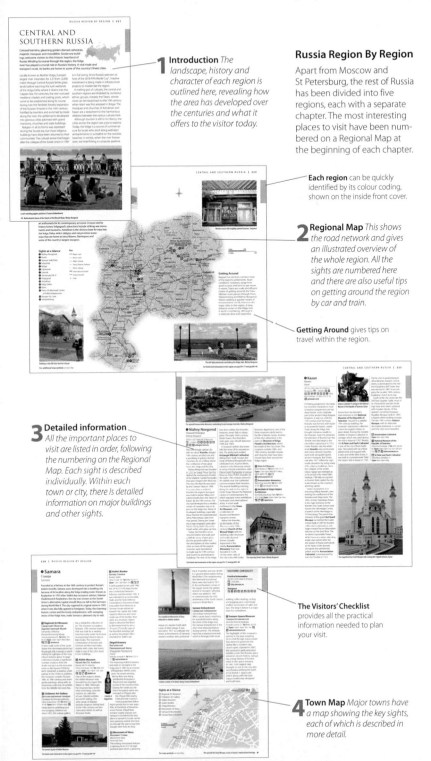

Russia Region By Region

Apart from Moscow and St Petersburg, the rest of Russia has been divided into five regions, each with a separate chapter. The most interesting places to visit have been numbered on a Regional Map at the beginning of each chapter.

1 Introduction *The landscape, history and character of each region is outlined here, revealing how the area has developed over the centuries and what it offers to the visitor today.*

Each region can be quickly identified by its colour coding, shown on the inside front cover.

2 Regional Map *This shows the road network and gives an illustrated overview of the whole region. All the sights are numbered here and there are also useful tips on getting around the region by car and train.*

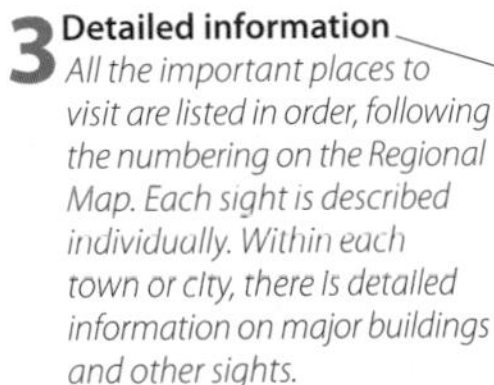

Getting Around gives tips on travel within the region.

3 Detailed information *All the important places to visit are listed in order, following the numbering on the Regional Map. Each sight is described individually. Within each town or city, there is detailed information on major buildings and other sights.*

The Visitors' Checklist provides all the practical information needed to plan your visit.

4 Town Map *Major towns have a map showing the key sights, each of which is described in more detail.*

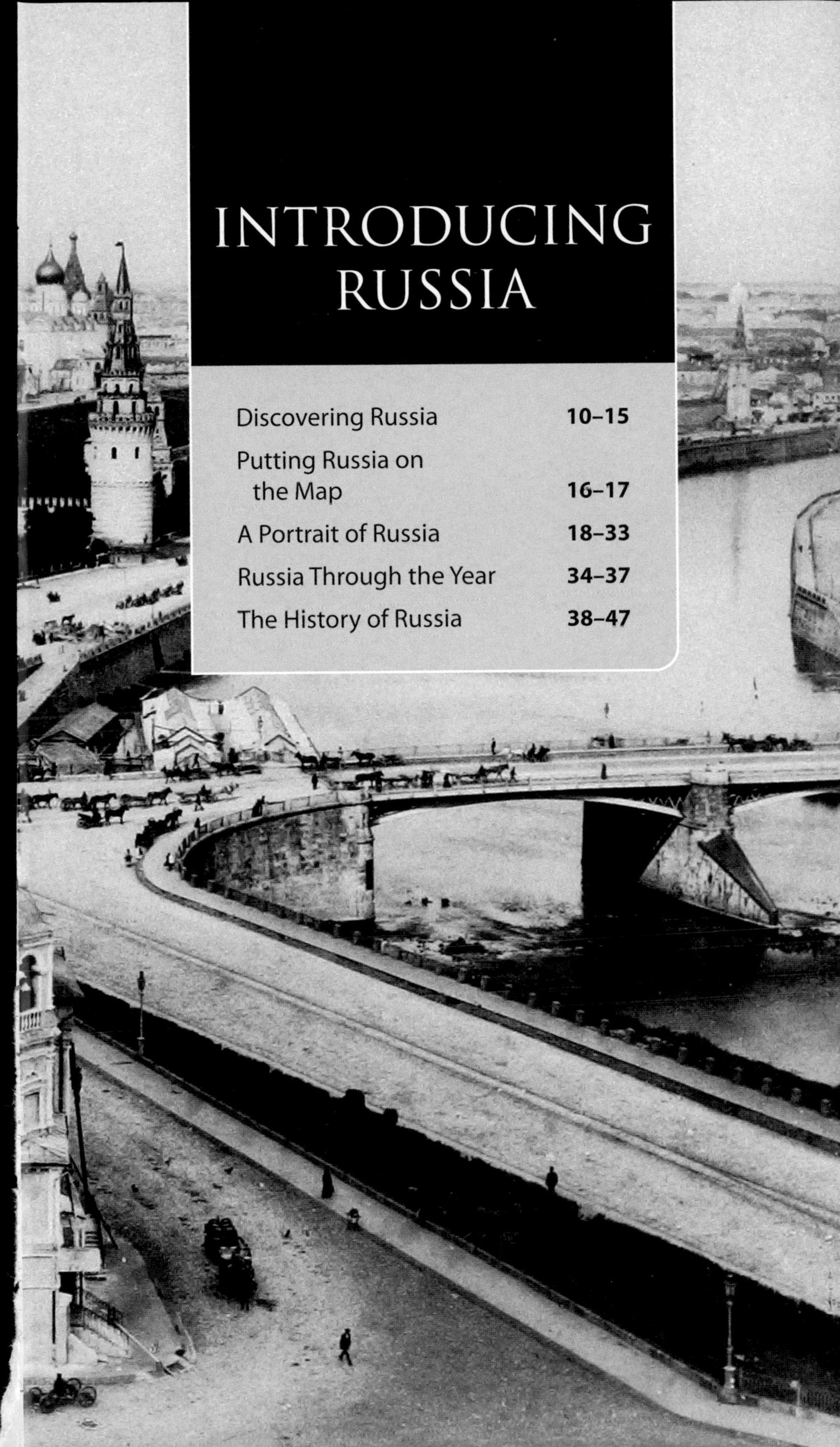

INTRODUCING RUSSIA

DISCOVERING RUSSIA

The following tours have been designed to take in as many of the country's highlights as possible, while keeping long-distance travel manageable. The first tours outlined here are two 2-day tours of Russia's historic capitals: Moscow and St Petersburg. These itineraries can be followed individually or combined to form a week-long tour, which can commence in either city. There is also a two-week tour that follows the mighty Volga river by boat all the way from the beautiful city of Nizhny Novgorod to the Caspian Sea. Finally, there is a seven-day tour of the Lake Baikal region with the option of adding three days to include the 5,000-km (3,110-mile) Trans-Siberian rail journey from Irkutsk to Moscow. Choose and combine tours or dip in and out and be inspired.

Volga and Oka rivers, Nizhy Novgorod
In the Tsarist era, the Volga and Oka rivers formed a natural moat around Nizhny Novgorod and protected it from invasions. Today, the dynamic city and its ancient Kremlin rise over the rivers' banks.

Two weeks on the Volga river

- Marvel at the sheer size of the Volga from the Kremlin in **Nizhny Novgorod**. The city rises above the strategic confluence of the Oka and Volga rivers.
- Be awed by **Kazan's** illuminated Kremlin complex, which looks particularly striking at night.
- Join a boat trip to visit the pretty medieval churches in **Sviyazhsk**.
- Descend 30 m (100 ft) into Stalin's intriguing secret bunker in **Samara**.
- Stand in deferential silence beneath one of the world's largest freestanding statues at the Mamayev Kurgan war memorial complex in **Volgograd**.
- Allow time to visit **Volgograd's** superb Battle of Stalingrad Panorama Museum.
- Explore at leisure the glorious medieval churches and cathedrals within the formidable white-walled Kremlin in **Astrakhan**.

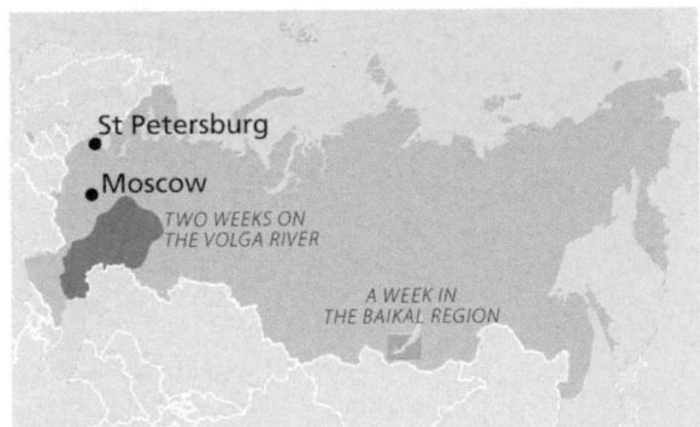

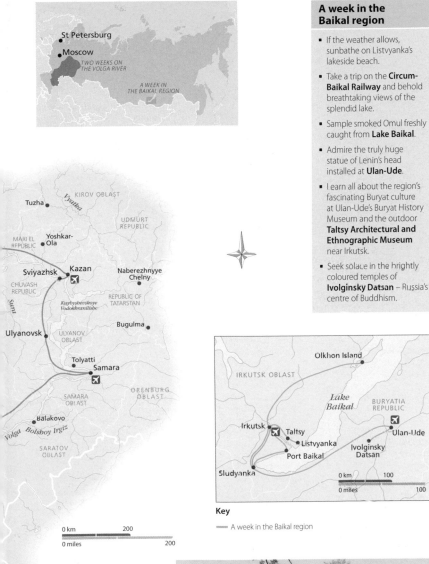

A week in the Baikal region

- If the weather allows, sunbathe on Listvyanka's lakeside beach.
- Take a trip on the **Circum-Baikal Railway** and behold breathtaking views of the splendid lake.
- Sample smoked Omul freshly caught from **Lake Baikal**.
- Admire the truly huge statue of Lenin's head installed at **Ulan-Ude**.
- Learn all about the region's fascinating Buryat culture at Ulan-Ude's Buryat History Museum and the outdoor **Taltsy Architectural and Ethnographic Museum** near Irkutsk.
- Seek solace in the brightly coloured temples of **Ivolginsky Datsan** – Russia's centre of Buddhism.

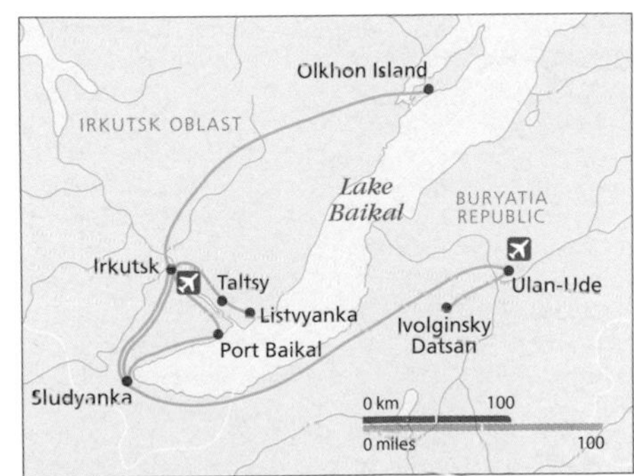

Key

A week in the Baikal region

Taltsy Architectural and Ethnographic Museum This delightful open-air museum displays preserved Siberian folk architecture and is the perfect place to experience the colourful culture of the people of Siberia.

Two days in Moscow

Russia's capital is a riveting blend of old and new, where onion-domed churches jostle for space with glass-fronted blocks and Communism's red stars still adorn many buildings.

- **Arriving** Moscow's largest airport, Domodedovo, is located 42 km (26 miles) southeast of the city centre. Aeroexpress trains run from 6am till midnight and take around 45 minutes to reach Moscow's metro system.
- **Moving on** Moscow to St Petersburg by Sapsan train takes about 4 hours.

The remarkable skyline of Moscow, with St Basil's Cathedral dominating Red Square

Day 1

Morning Whatever the weather, head straight for **Red Square** *(p68)* to marvel at the iconic gilded onion domes of **St Basil's Cathedral** *(pp70–71)*. Queue outside the **Lenin Mausoleum** *(p69)* for a brief glimpse of the great leader's embalmed remains. From here, head for the **GUM** shopping mall *(p69)*, commissioned by Catherine the Great in the late 19th century. Next, visit the **Historical Museum** *(p68)* that faces Red Square. A proud statue of World War II hero Marshal Georgi Zhukov stands in front of the museum beside Kilometre Zero, the point from where all distances in Russia are measured – line up with visiting Russian tourists to have your picture taken here as a keepsake.

Afternoon Dedicate the afternoon to a thorough exploration of the Kremlin. Among the highlights are the glorious **Cathedral of the Assumption** *(p57)* where Ivan the Terrible was crowned in 1547 and the exquisitely decorated **Patriarch's Palace** *(p56)*. Be sure to check out the giant 16th-century **Tsar Cannon** *(p56)* and the 200-tonne (221-ton) Tsar Bell, the heaviest bell in the world. Save plenty of time for the **Armoury Chamber** *(pp62–3)*; star exhibits include Tsar Alexis's 17th-century diamond throne and a glittering selection of Fabergé eggs.

Portraits of notable Russians on display at Moscow's Historical Museum

Day 2

Morning Start off with a spell of art appreciation by paying a visit to the world's largest collection of Russian art at the **State Tretyakov Gallery** *(pp98–9)*. Then, tour the **Pushkin State Museum of Fine Arts** *(pp90–91)* – its superb collection includes the **Gallery of 19th- and 20th- Century European and American Art** *(p88)*. Be prepared for a long visit as there is plenty to see.

Evening Explore the cavernous interior of the nearby **Cathedral of Christ the Saviour** *(p89)*, rebuilt in 2000 to replace the original that was demolished on Stalin's orders in 1931 to make way for the unrealized Palace of Soviets. From here take the metro to Arbatskaya to arrive at the busy **Arbat Square** *(p89)*. Stroll along the popular ulitsa Arbat where buskers perform outside the many shops, cafés and bars. Do not miss the intimidating Gothic **Ministry of Foreign Affairs** building *(p93)* that towers over the end of the street.

To extend your trip...
Spend a day at the **Trinity Monastery of St Sergius** *(p114)*, 75 km (47 miles) north of Moscow and another at the UNESCO-listed settlement of **Suzdal** *(p116)*.

Two days in St Petersburg

Founded by Peter the Great in the early 18th century, St Petersburg was Russia's capital from 1732 to 1918. Much of its stunning architectural heritage has been remarkably well preserved.

- **Arriving** Pulkovo 2 is St Petersburg's main international airport, located 17 km (11 miles) south of the city. Buses link the airport to Moskovskaya metro station between 6am and 12:30am.
- **Moving on** Moscow is an hour and 20 minutes away by air, or approximately 4 hours by Sapsan train.

Stunning murals portraying the symbols of Orthodox Christianity, Church on Spilled Blood

Day 1

Morning Get a feel of both contemporary and historic St Petersburg with a stroll along **Nevskiy prospekt** *(p166)*, the main street since the city was founded in the 18th century. Covering a length of 5 km (3 miles), it is jammed with monuments, churches and exquisite buildings. Look out for the **Cathedral of Our Lady of Kazan** *(p168)*, a statue of Catherine the Great and the **Church on Spilled Blood** *(p162)*, which was built as a memorial to Alexander II on the spot where he was assassinated. Its quintessentially Russian onion domes are reminiscent of Moscow's St Basil's Cathedral.

Gilded golden domes adorning the grand palace at Peterhof

Afternoon Arrive at the vast **Palace Square** *(p152)* that is dominated by the monumental **Hermitage** *(pp154–5)*. Spend time exploring the luxurious former residence of the tsars that now houses one of the world's largest and most illustrious art collections. Start with a tour of the magnificent interiors of the **Winter Palace** *(pp156–7)* to get a feel of the museum before progressing further. It is impossible to see everything in an afternoon, so choose one or two collections to focus on. Later, head to the well-manicured gardens in front of the nearby **Admiralty** building *(p148)* for a relaxing evening stroll.

Day 2

Morning Begin the day with a hydrofoil trip to **Peterhof** *(pp186– 7)*, Peter the Great's magnificent complex of palaces and gardens that was built to rival the Gardens of Versailles in Paris. Spend the morning soaking up the imperial atmosphere – highlights include the opulent Throne Room, the Grand Cascade of bronze sculptures, fountains and water jets, and the Imperial Suite featuring original 18th-century oak panelling.

Afternoon Wander through the historic **Peter and Paul Fortress** *(pp136–7)* that faces the Hermitage across the Neva river. The main attraction here is the **Cathedral of SS Peter and Paul** *(p134)* where the Romanov family are buried. If the weather is suitable, consider joining the locals to sunbathe on the riverside beach. Afterwards, pay a late afternoon visit to the colossal **St Isaac's Cathedral** *(pp150–51)*, Russia's largest church that took 40 years to construct and was finally opened in 1858. Round of the day with an evening ballet or opera performance at the renowned **Mariinskiy Theatre** *(p174)*.

To extend your trip...

Take a day trip to the peaceful 18th-century palace at **Pavlovsk** *(pp190–91)*. Located 26 km (16 miles) south of St Petersburg, it is refreshingly free of crowds.

Two weeks on the Volga river

- **Airports** Fly from Moscow's Sheremetyevo Airport to Nizhny Novgorod International Airport and depart from Astrakhan's Narimanovo Airport.
- **Transport** Organized cruises run the length of the Volga from May till September. While it is possible to join shorter cruises between cities during the same period, services are unpredictable so it is best to seek out the latest information at local river terminals or travel agencies. It may be necessary to travel by train when riverboats are unavailable for any part of the journey.

The exquisite Kul Sharif Mosque located within the Kremlin, Kazan

Day 1: Nizhny Novgorod

The perfect preamble to this itinerary, **Nizhny Novgorod** offers many attractions. Devote a morning to exploring its Kremlin *(p224)*, which occupies a superb vantage point overlooking the confluence of the Oka and Volga rivers. Visit the Church of the Blessed Virgin *(p224)*, one of the many churches scattered around the city, and marvel at its multicoloured domes.

Days 2 and 3: Kazan

From Nizhny Novgorod, take the riverboat (24 hours) to **Kazan**. Spend time in its historic centre where the riverside Kremlin *(p225)* is the main attraction. The nearby National Museum of the Republic of Tatarstan *(p225)* provides a fascinating insight into the region's complex history.

Days 4 and 5: Sviyazhsk

Travel to **Sviyazhsk** on a riverboat (3 hours) to visit the meticulously restored Assumption Monastery *(p225)* that once served as a stronghold for Ivan the Terrible. Head back to Kazan and, in the evening, take the riverboat (24 hours) to Ulyanovsk.

Day 6: Ulyanovsk

Most famous for being Lenin's birthplace, **Ulyanovsk** has several museums dedicated to the renowned Soviet leader, notable among which is the Lenin Memorial Centre *(p227)*. Take time out to appreciate the town's well-preserved old quarter of 19th-century wooden houses.

Days 7 and 8: Samara

Travel by boat (24 hours) to **Samara**. Wander through the atmospheric centre and pretty embankment of this city. Soak up some history at Stalin's Bunker *(p229)* and browse the exhibits at the splendid Samara Space Museum *(p229)*. Consider joining a rafting trip to the Samara Bend.

Days 9, 10 and 11: Volgograd

Take the riverboat (2½ days) to **Volgograd**. Visit the many memorials and museums dedicated to the Battle of Stalingrad, which destroyed the city during World War II. Behold the awe-inspiring statue of Mother Russia at the Mamayev Kurgan memorial complex *(p232)*.

Giant Soyuz rocket on display at the entrance of the Samara Space Museum

Days 12 and 13: Astrakhan

Travel by riverboat (around 24 hours) to **Astrakhan** where the Volga river meets the Caspian Sea. Spend time touring the city's splendid Kremlin *(p233)* and surveying its quarter of faded wooden Tatar houses.

Day 14: Volga Delta

Join a boat tour of the labyrinthine **Volga Delta**, home to countless endemic and endangered species of wildlife. Spend a memorable night at one of the delta's floating wooden hotels.

The lovely Church of the Blessed Virgin and its pleasing environs, Nizhny Novgorod

For practical information on travelling around Russia, see pp314–15

A week in the Baikal region

- **Airports** Fly from Moscow's Sheremetyevo Airport to Irkutsk International Airport and depart from Ulan-Ude International Airport.
- **Transport** Take the 6-hour flight from Moscow to Irkutsk. The city makes the perfect base for day trips around the region. Local buses and the Circum-Baikal Railway serve destinations around Lake Baikal. The journey from Irkutsk to Ulan-Ude is 7 hours by train.

Rock projection from the amazing blue expanse of Lake Baikal

Day 1: Irkutsk

Roughly halfway between Moscow and Vladivostok on the Trans-Siberian Railway is **Irkutsk**, a thoroughly enjoyable city to wander. Start at the Museum of City Life *(p252)* and the complex of preserved wooden mansions of Irkutsk's 19th-century Decembrist aristocrats. From here, follow the curve of the Angara river to ploshchad Kirova where the city's oldest churches stand side by side. Don't miss the brightly painted façade of the Epiphany Cathedral *(p252)*.

Day 2: Taltsy and Listvyanka

Take the minibus from Irkutsk to Listvyanka, which stops halfway at the **Taltsy Architectural and Ethnographic Museum** *(p253)*. This museum offers an insight into Siberian culture and architecture. The wooded grounds of the museum are filled with traditional Buryat dwellings. Of special note are a complex of wooden Cossack homes and stalls selling traditional crafts. Continue to the lakeside village of Listvyanka in the afternoon and to the banks of Lake Baikal *(p253)*. Sunbathe on the beach if the weather permits and sample freshly smoked Omul – Lake Baikal's most famous fish. Head back to Irkutsk via minibus in the evening.

Day 3: Circum-Baikal Railway

Catch the early morning minibus to Sludyanka. From here a local train operates daily on the Circum-Baikal Railway *(p253)* along the rocky shore of Lake Baikal. Enjoy the scenic views and quaint stations en route, but fight back the hunger pangs as refreshments won't be available until the train arrives at Port Baikal several hours later. Return to Irkutsk to catch the minibus to Olkhon Island the next morning.

Day 4: Olkhon Island

Spend the day investigating this peaceful island *(p253)* dotted with ancient shamanic monuments and wooden houses. A day trip can easily be extended to an overnight stay at one of the island's many guesthouses.

Day 5: Irkutsk to Ulan-Ude

Travel by train to Ulan-Ude and enjoy the stunning vistas the journey offers. The railway skirts the edge of Lake Baikal for more than a 100 km (62 miles), passing picturesque wooden cottages and offering stunning views of the lake to the north. Look out for the peaks of the Ardaban Mountains to the southeast as the train nears Ulan-Ude.

Day 6: Ulan-Ude

Visit the world's largest statue of Lenin's head in the modern city centre of **Ulan-Ude** before inspecting the region's fascinating past at the Buryat History Museum *(p256)*. Next, stop by the Ethnographic Museum *(p256)* to explore the nomadic roots and shamanic beliefs of the indigenous Buryats.

Day 7: Ivolginsky Datsan

Minibuses regularly take tourists and locals out of Ulan-Ude and into the featureless plains beyond in the direction of **Ivolginsky Datsan** *(p256)*. Visit the Buddhist monastery complex here that forms the spiritual heart of Russian Buddhism. The monastery's colourful temples make for a meditative day trip. Return to Ulan-Ude in the evening.

To extend your trip...
Catch the overnight train from Ulan-Ude to Irkutsk and then spend three days travelling to Moscow on the **Trans-Siberian Railway**, converting this into a 10-day itinerary.

Devotee practicing temple rites at the Ivolginsky Datsan monastery complex

Putting Russia on the Map

With an area of 17 million sq km (6.6 million sq miles), the Russian Federation was the greatest of the USSR's 15 republics and is now the world's largest country, almost twice the size of the US. Moscow, the capital with 12 million inhabitants, is the biggest city, followed by St Petersburg. At its widest point along a geodesic line, Russia measures 8,000 km (4,971 miles) from east to west, including the Kaliningrad region, an extraterritorial enclave on the Baltic.

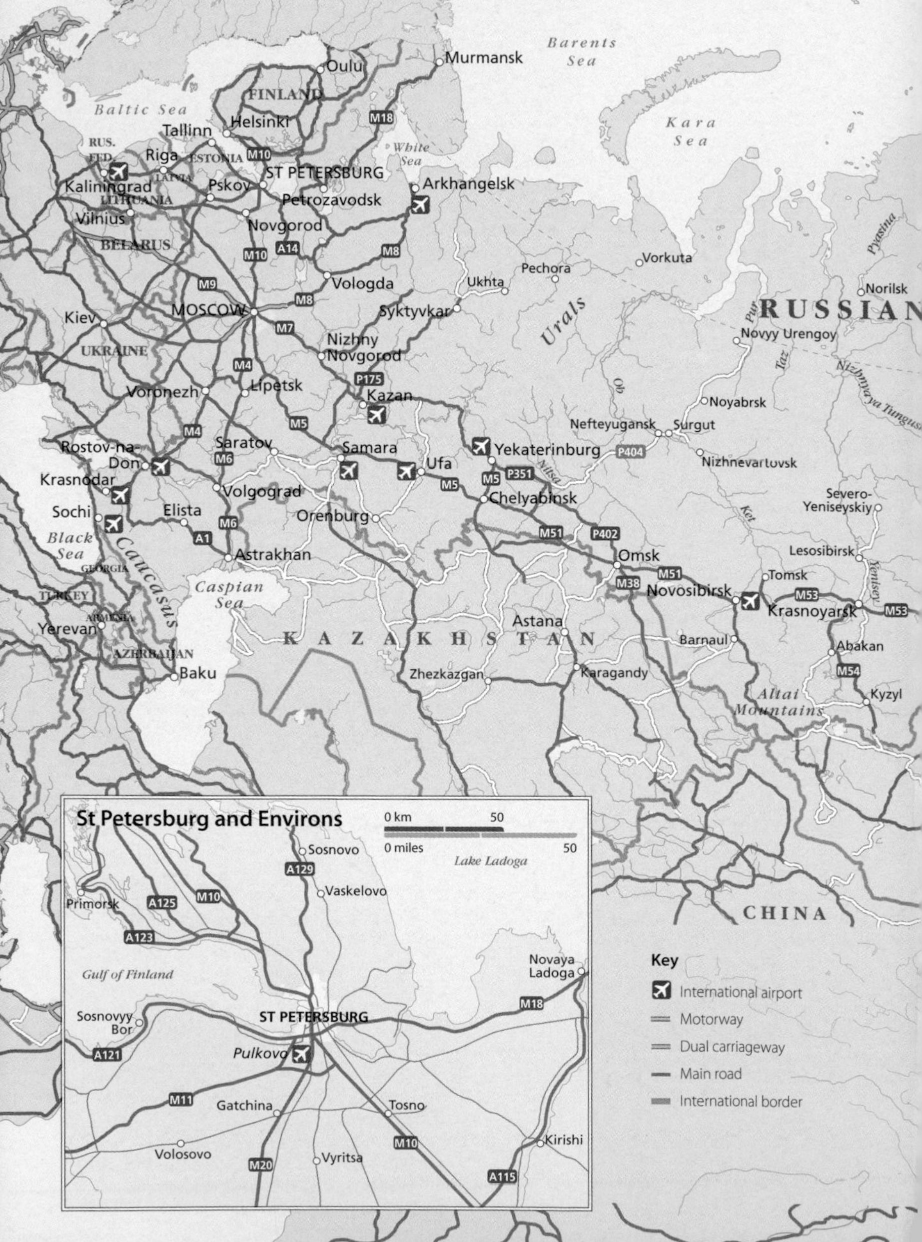

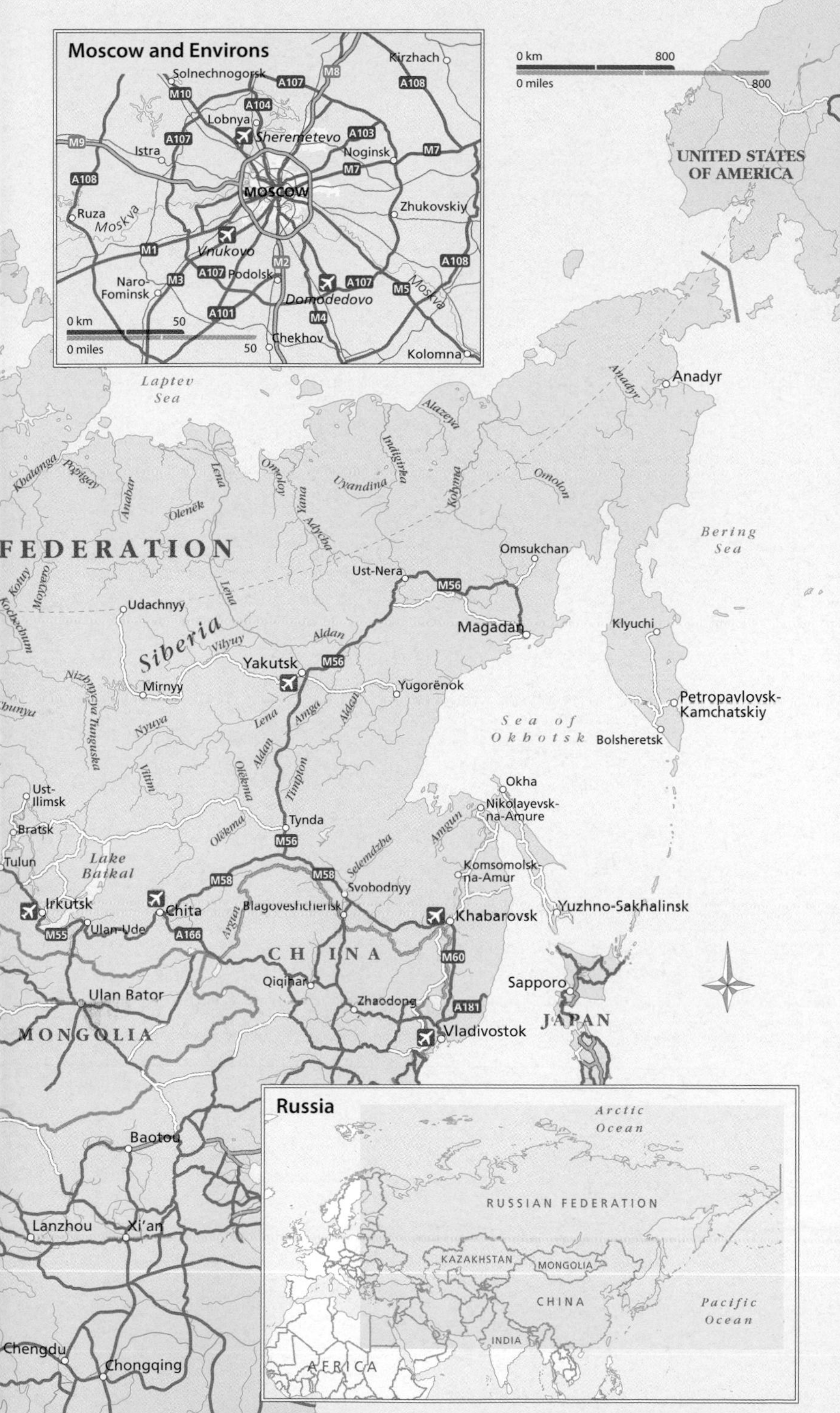
Moscow and Environs
Solnechnogorsk
Kirzhach
Lobnya
Sheremetevo
Istra
Noginsk
MOSCOW
Ruza
Moskva
Zhukovskiy
Vnukovo
Naro-Fominsk
Podolsk
Domodedovo
Chekhov
Kolomna
M10
M9
M8
M7
M1
M3
M2
M4
M5
A107
A108
A104
A103
A101
0 km 50
0 miles 50
0 km 800
0 miles 800
UNITED STATES OF AMERICA
Laptev Sea
Bering Sea
Sea of Okhotsk
FEDERATION
Siberia
Anadyr
Omsukchan
Ust-Nera
Magadan
Klyuchi
Udachnyy
Yakutsk
Mirnyy
Yugorënok
Petropavlovsk-Kamchatskiy
Bolsheretsk
Okha
Nikolayevsk-na-Amure
Ust-Ilimsk
Bratsk
Tynda
Tulun
Lake Baikal
Komsomolsk-na-Amur
Svobodnyy
Irkutsk
Chita
Blagoveshchensk
Khabarovsk
Yuzhno-Sakhalinsk
Ulan-Ude
CHINA
Qiqihar
Sapporo
Ulan Bator
Zhaodong
Vladivostok
JAPAN
MONGOLIA
Baotou
Lanzhou
Xi'an
Chengdu
Chongqing
M56
M58
M55
A166
M60
A181
Russia
Arctic Ocean
RUSSIAN FEDERATION
KAZAKHSTAN
MONGOLIA
CHINA
Pacific Ocean
INDIA
AFRICA

A PORTRAIT OF RUSSIA

Straddling the vast Eurasian landmass, from the Baltic to the Pacific and the Arctic to the Caucasus, Russia is the world's largest nation, with an unparalleled ethnic and geographical diversity. The country's epic history is reflected in its rich culture of arts, literature, music, ballet and drama. The bustling cities of Moscow and St Petersburg are vanguards of Russian culture as well as being home to iconic onion-domed cathedrals, stunning imperial palaces and superb museums.

The low-lying Urals separate European Russia from the enormity of Siberia and the Far East. Split between Europe and Asia, Russia has an extraordinary diversity of indigenous people. In fact, the Russian language is the only element that unites the multi-ethnic society.

At the heart of most old Russian cities is a kremlin (fortress), a reminder of the land's many invasions and conquests. With a glittering skyline of gilded cupolas and red stars symbolizing the fusion of Holy Russia and Soviet power, Moscow's Kremlin serves as the seat of the Russian government. For over 200 years, however, the Tsarist Empire was ruled from St Petersburg, a splendid city aptly described as the Venice of the North. The decline of the Tsarist Empire marked the beginning of the Soviet era, with Russia as the leading constituent of the Soviet Union born of the October Revolution of 1917. As the world's first socialist state, it boasted of overthrowing capitalism and establishing a classless Communist utopia. However, the Soviet system failed to satisfy its citizens' material aspirations and fell behind its Western and Asian competitors. Its dissolution in 1991 led to Russia's transition from Communism to capitalism. Today's Russia comprises three-quarters of the territory of the former Soviet Union, whose legacy is manifest in everything from architecture to local slang.

Outside the booming urban hubs of Moscow and St Petersburg are charming historic cities, spa towns and a diverse landscape of great lakes, beaches, rolling plains and icy wastes. This vibrant mix of mesmerizing attractions, amazing landscapes and fascinating culture makes a visit to Russia a truly enriching experience.

View of the golden-domed St Isaac's Cathedral – one of St Petersburg's most iconic landmarks – from the Mojka Canal

◄ Traditional dancers in lavish costumes performing at ulitsa Arbat, Moscow

Rolling grasslands against a backdrop of the snow-capped peaks of the western Caucasus

Land and Ecology

With an area of 17 million sq km (6.6 million sq miles), stretching from Europe to the Pacific Ocean, Russia is the world's largest country. Constituting 33 per cent of this total area, European Russia stretches south to the Caucasus and the Caspian Sea, and is flanked by Georgia, Armenia and Azerbaijan. Extending beyond the Urals, Asian Russia forms the larger half of the territory and shares borders with Kazakhstan, China, Mongolia and North Korea. Sandwiched between Poland and Lithuania, the Kaliningrad region is an extraterritorial enclave of Russia.

Due to its vast extent, Russia features a wide variety of terrain, distinguished by their different climates and vegetation. The far north is dominated by the tundra, which is characterized by moss, lichen and permafrost. Stunted trees mark the transition of these barren flatlands to the taiga forests. Covering most of Northern Russia, these dense coniferous forests account for a fifth of the world's forest reserves. Watered by the mighty Don and Volga rivers that flow into the Black and Caspian seas, southern Russia is the nation's granary. Dominated by steppes, or undulating grasslands, this region consists of fertile *chernozem* (black earth) or semi-arid salt-marshes. The rugged far east lays claim to being the wildest and most remote region, with taiga forests inhabited by a variety of fauna, notably tigers.

Russia's seemingly infinite resources have long encouraged rampant environmental exploitation. The country saw some of the worst ecological disasters during the Soviet era, when preservation of the environment was thought to be a hindrance to economic advancement. As a result, extensive oil and gas drilling activities in the Arctic and Siberian regions eventually led to the destabilization of the tundra ecosystem. In addition, water pollution caused by industrial and chemical waste contributed to the decimation of fish species in the Black and Caspian seas. Fortunately, the government of Russia today has recognized these problems and has made significant efforts to establish 101 *zapovedniki* (nature reserves) and 38 national parks to protect the country's ecosystem.

Economy

Since the dissolution of the Soviet Union, Russia has moved from a largely isolated, centrally planned economy to a more market-based, globally integrated one.

Typical snow-covered Siberian landscape

Façade of the skyscraper housing Gazprom's headquarters, Moscow

Although the country is rich in natural resources such as oil, gas, coal and precious metals, most of these reserves are in inhospitable regions, requiring huge investments in infrastructure. Multinational corporations have been instrumental in developing new oil- and gasfields in joint ventures. However, their operations have often run into problems resulting from takeover bids by the Russian energy giants Gazprom and Sibneft.

In 2011, Russia became the world's largest producer of natural gas and the second-largest producer of crude oil, with proven reserves of 60 billion barrels. State levies on oil and gas exports account for nearly half of Russia's revenue, making the economy critically dependent on commodity prices. Other sectors of the economy have seen rapid or fitful growth since the 1990s, notably services, industry and agriculture, which accounted for 58, 32 and 10 per cent of the national economy, respectively, in 2011. One-fifth of manufacturing jobs are in the defence sector, making Russia the world's second-largest exporter of weapons.

For a majority of Russians, life for the past 10 years has been better than before. The average monthly salary has increased eight-fold and the percentage of people living below the poverty line has fallen from 30 to 14 per cent.

Politics and Government

Since the overthrow of Communism in 1991, Russia has experienced rapid change and bewildering dislocations. The break-up of the Soviet Union left Russia beset by hyper-inflation, mass unemployment and rampant criminality, with millions of ethnic Russians facing an uncertain future in newly independent states. Under President Boris Yeltsin, state assets, including oilfields, were privatized at knockdown rates, creating a new class of wealthy oligarchs, in league with organized crime, corrupt bureaucrats and politicians.

After the wild capitalism of the 1990s, Yeltsin's successor, Vladimir Putin, experienced a sweeping victory in the 2000 presidential elections. In contrast to Yeltsin, Putin consolidated the mafia-state and by curbing the oligarchs he convinced a majority of Russians that he was a man of the people. His second term in office saw Russia enriched by petrodollars with improved living standards in cities besides Moscow and St Petersburg.

In small towns across Russia, people are grateful for stability, and influenced by pro-regime TV. However, in major cities, the fact that wages and pensions are paid on time is no longer enough. Growing disparities between the super rich and the majority of the population continue to breed resentment in Russian society.

President Vladimir Putin speaking on the Day of Russia, Moscow

Graceful ballet dancers performing *The Sleeping Beauty* at the Bolshoi Theatre, Moscow

Culture and Arts

Russians are intensely proud of their culture, language and arts. This pride stems from the Slavophile movement of the 19th century, which emphasized belief in the uniqueness of Russian traditions and culture. The movement included the composers Modest Mussorgsky and Alexander Borodin as well as the writers Nikolai Gogol and Fyodor Dostoevsky. For Slavophiles, Russia's Orthodox Church, mysticism and the concept of *sobornost*, which advocated cooperation between opposing ideas in favour of the ultimate, holy good, were infinitely superior to the Western values of rationalism, materialism and individualism. It is a view that still resonates today, much to the chagrin of the liberal-minded minority who cherish democracy and secularism.

Russian despotism, xenophobia and corruption have long been ascribed to the three centuries that the country spent under the Mongol yoke while Europe underwent the Renaissance. These political and social themes depicted in the Russian arts are a distinct mix of Western and indigenous styles. Although most Russians regard themselves as Europeans, they acknowledge an Asian dimension to their national identity that sets them apart from their Western neighbours.

A symphony orchestra performing at the Mariinskiy Theatre, St Petersburg

The psychological realism of Dostoevsky's novels, the naturalistic dialogue in Anton Chekhov's plays, the poet masterpieces of Alexander Pushkin, and Konstantin Stanislavskiy's method acting are all highly regarded around the world. The legacy of Russian creativity is further manifested in film maker Sergei Eisenstein's jump-cuts, Pyotr Tchaikovsky's symphonies and Vasily Kandinsky's abstract art.

Visitors to Russia can enjoy world-class ballet, opera and classical music in Moscow's Bolshoi Theatre *(see pp82–3)* and St Petersburg's Mariinskiy Theatre *(see p174)*. Both cities have a thriving theatre scene too, with the Moscow Arts Theatre *(see p84)* and the Mikhaylovskiy Theatre *(see p163)* in St Petersburg staging the works of contemporary Russian playwrights. The cities are also at the cutting edge of Russian nightlife and fashion. Other urban locations such as Sochi, Yekaterinburg and Vladivostok host festivals that showcase contemporary culture not only from all over the country but also from around the world.

People and Society

Russia's population has been declining. The 2010 census recorded a population of nearly 143 million, around 2 million fewer than 10 years earlier. Some trace the country's stunted demography back to the scores of people who died in wars, famines and purges during the 20th century, others to a plummeting birth rate, endemic alcoholism and poor healthcare.

Despite the break-up of the Soviet Union, Russia is home to a great diversity of ethnic minorities, from camel-riding Kalmyks in southern Russia and reindeer-herding Nenets in Siberia to Tatars fishing on the Volga and Sakha in the Far East. Of the country's 160 recognized ethnic groups, nearly 81 per cent of citizens identify themselves as Russians. Tartars (4 per cent), Ukrainians (1 per cent), Bashkir (1 per cent), Chechens (1 per cent) and Armenians (1 per cent) form the largest minorities, amounting to two-thirds of the total ethnic-minority population.

While over 100 languages are spoken across the country, many are on the verge of extinction, particularly among the indigenous peoples of the far north. If anything unites this multicultural society it is the Russian language, which is universally understood. Religion comes a poor second, with some 100 million citizens considering themselves Orthodox Christians. Muslims number between 9 and 20 million, but are undoubtedly the nation's fastest growing demographic. As Orthodoxy has grown more assertive in Russia and Islam in the Caucasus, secularists, liberals, feminists and gays have been stigmatized and assaulted.

Beautifully carved wooden handicrafts on sale

A Nenet man with his herd of reindeer in northwestern Siberia

Russia has seen rapid urbanization over the last century, with around three-quarters of its population now living in cities and towns. The life of most Russians has also vastly improved in contrast to Soviet times, or even the 1990s, when millions of families still struggled to make a living. Today, even provincial school teachers can afford a holiday abroad besides owning a car and a computer. Despite these advancements, Russian society is not devoid of disparities. At the start of this century, Moscow boasted more billionaires than any city in the world, while thousands of towns and villages languished in poverty. Such polarities exist in the societies of many countries, but are magnified in Russia due in part to the vast distances and climactic extremes.

Tourism is now a major industry in Russia. Although renowned for its cultural and historical attractions, the country is fast emerging as a prime destination for adventure sports enthusiasts, with activities ranging from pony trekking and caving to volcano-watching. Russia is also famous for its ornate folk arts and artisan crafts, such as amber jewellery, lacquered boxes, glazed earthenware and wood carvings. However, caviar, vodka and Soviet memorabilia remain the most sought-after souvenirs.

Landscape and Wildlife

Russia comprises nearly every kind of natural environment found in the northern hemisphere. From the windswept southern grasslands and the densely forested north to the cold seas and barren tundra bordering the Arctic coastline, the world's largest country is a land of incredible contrasts. This vast landmass is divided into European Russia and Siberia by the Ural Mountains, beyond which the great rivers of Siberia flow northwards into the Arctic Ocean. With one of the largest forest reserves in the world, Russia is home to diverse ecosystems. Notable among the many animal species found here are the Siberian tiger, Amur leopard, sturgeon and brown bear.

Snow-covered fir trees in the southern Ural region

Steppe and Desert

The Eurasian steppes, or grasslands, extend from Hungary to Mongolia and are largely treeless lands. Some areas are semi-arid, merging into desert. Desertification of the Kalmyk Steppe and soil erosion in the *chernozem* belt of southern Russia are problems for these areas.

Steppe marmots are a common sight in the grasslands. They graze on the steppe's vegetation cover and have served as a natural food "reservoir", saving many Russians from starving to death during famines in the 20th century.

The steppe eagle breeds in southern Russia and winters in Africa. Its diet includes carrion of all kinds, but it also hunts rodents and other small mammals.

Purple pasqueflowers bloom on the steppes of the black-earth zone in mid-April when the snow melts.

Rivers and Lakes

Of Russia's 10,000 rivers, the Volga is the longest in Europe, and the Siberian Ob, Yenisei, Lena and Amur are among the longest rivers in the world. Besides this, Russia also has Lake Baikal, the world's largest, deepest and purest fresh-water lake – home to several unique species.

Sturgeon is the common name for some 26 species of fish prized for their roe, or caviar. Most are critically endangered due to over-fishing or pollution of the Caspian Sea, the Volga river and other breeding grounds.

Nerpas are the only freshwater seals in the world, unique to Lake Baikal. Their main breeding colony lies on the lake's western shores.

The Sacred Lotus blossoms on a bed of white water lily pads. It is chiefly found in the Astrakhan Biosphere Reserve *(see p233)* of the Volga Delta.

Saving the Siberian Tiger

Also known as the Amur tiger, this is the world's largest sub-species of tiger, weighing up to 300 kg (160 lb). It is a critically endangered feline species: the Sikhote-Alin Mountains, to the northeast of Vladivostok, account for 90 per cent of the population in the wild, with an estimated 350–500 surviving adults. Under the Species Survival Plan of 1981, thousands of tigers have been bred in zoos in order to achieve maximum genetic diversity and stabilize their dwindling numbers. Their survival is also dependent on conserving prey such as roe, sika deer, wild boar and brown bear. Adult tigers are seasoned hunters and have been known to imitate bear calls to lure them into an ambush, springing from a rock or fallen tree to seize the bear's throat and sever its spinal column with a single bite.

The majestic Siberian tiger – the largest living felid in the world

Forests and Tundra

Forests cover over half the territory of Russia, forming a great belt across Eurasia. The northern coniferous forest, or taiga, merges into mixed woodlands towards the south. To the north it is bounded by the treeless tundra, which is populated by reindeer, arctic foxes and wolves.

The brown bear is the national animal of Russia. The country boasts a robust population of approximately 120,000 bears.

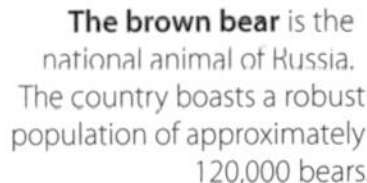

Wolves were once found throughout Russia. Today there are perhaps 30,000 left nationwide, with relatively few in central Russia but growing numbers in Chechnya and Kalmykia.

Amur leopards are critically endangered by poaching and logging. Having lost 80 per cent of their habitat since the 1970s, leopards are now confined to the temperate forests between Vladivostok and the Chinese border.

Mountains and Coasts

The Caucasus boasts both alpine and sub-tropical flora and fauna around Sochi and Mount Elbrus, while Kamchatka is famed for its volcanoes and mud-geysers. Russia's 37,000-km (22,991-mile) long coastline borders the Arctic and Pacific oceans, and no fewer than nine seas.

The pincushion flower turns alpine meadows violet-blue by the end of summer. Over 13,000 plant species have been identified within the Teberdinsky Nature Reserve near Dombay, 190 of them endemic to the Caucasus.

The Pacific walrus weighs over a ton and measures up to 4-m (13-ft) long. During the mating season, 80,000 walruses pack the coast of Wrangel Island, using their tusks to anchor themselves to ice floes.

The polar bear is the world's largest land carnivore and the walrus's only natural predator. Subsistence hunting was made legal for Chukotka natives in 2007 and has threatened the bear population in Russia.

Russian Orthodox Church

In 988, Prince Vladimir made Byzantine Rite Christianity the official religion of the Kievan Rus. The newly created Russian Orthodox Church was subordinate to the Patriarch of Constantinople, who appointed its archbishop. Having gained autonomy a few years before the fall of Constantinople in 1453, the church saw itself as the rightful head of Eastern Orthodoxy. Moscow was heralded as the Third Rome, in accordance with a prophecy by the monk Philotey of Pskov, "two Romes have already fallen but the third remains standing and a fourth there will not be".

Prince Vladimir the Great, canonized as an Orthodox saint

Early History

Christianity is said to have been brought to Russia by the Apostle Andrew, who foretold the founding of a great Christian city where Kiev stands today. Princess Olga of Kiev was the first Russian ruler to convert to Christianity. Her grandson Vladimir made the Kievan Rus a Christian state.

Cyril and Methodius were 9th-century Greek monks who tried to convert the Slavs. The Cyrillic script is named after St Cyril, who laid the foundation for the Cyrillic alphabet.

Candles are symbolic of the faith of the worshippers and the light of knowledge.

Monasteries, like the one at Suzdal *(see p116)*, doubled as strategic fortifications. They were built overlooking a river or as part of a chain blocking an invasion route across the plain. Under the Mongol yoke *(see p40)*, they became important repositories of Russian culture and faith.

Warrior saints such as Dmitri Donskoy (1350–89) embody the Church's historic association with the Russian nation state. In the post-Communist era, the church has exploited its constitutional status as one of the four "recognized" faiths (the other three being Islam, Judaism and Buddhism) to discourage other Christian denominations from evangelizing.

Iconostasis

The iconostasis is a screen on which icons of saints are displayed. It separates the nave from the sanctuary and symbolizes the division between Earth and Heaven. It is usually made of wood, delicately carved with natural motifs and gilded.

Icons of Christ and the saints play a major role in the Orthodox Church. The icon is a sanctified object that helps the faithful sense God's presence. This is why icons have always been highly stylized.

Parts of a Church

Orthodox churches are usually oriented on an east-west axis. Worshippers enter the church from the west (associated with sin) and head up the aisle towards the light of Truth (in the east). The plan of a church is often rectangular like a ship (or Ark) or cruciform (like the Cross). Inside, the main space is the nave, with walls usually decorated with frescoes and icons. The altar, in the sanctuary, is hidden from the worshippers behind the iconostasis, but is visible during services, when the Royal Doors are opened.

Beautiful frescoes cover the walls of Russian churches. This one, adorning the Cathedral of the Annunciation *(see p57)* in Moscow, dates from the 16th century. A popular subject on the west walls of churches is the Apocalypse.

The cross is an important symbol of the Church and has been described as the joining of the heavenly and the earthly. The three-armed cross, found in Slavic countries, has an upper bar that represents the inscription over Christ's head, while the lower slanting bar represents the foot rest.

Orthodox Worship

Orthodox services can be very moving as the church is lit mainly by candles and the air is heavy with incense. The whole service is sung, as the human voice is believed to be the finest medium for praising the Lord. The service forms a sung dialogue between the clergy and the congregation. Traditionally, there are no chairs and everyone is expected to stand as a mark of respect.

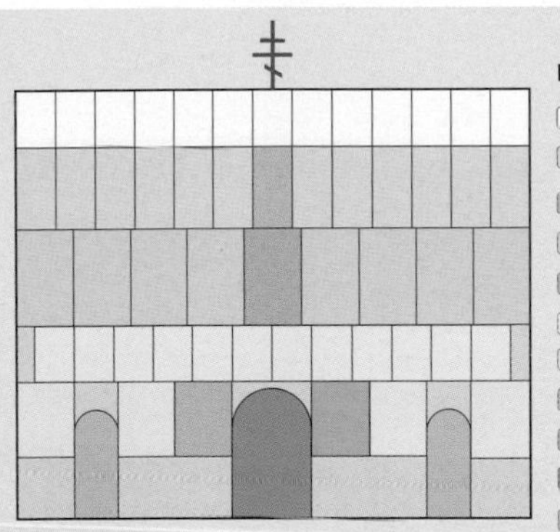

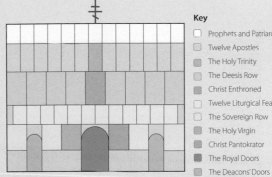

Key

- Prophets and Patriarchs
- Twelve Apostles
- The Holy Trinity
- The Deesis Row
- Christ Enthroned
- Twelve Liturgical Feasts
- The Sovereign Row
- The Holy Virgin
- Christ Pantokrator
- The Royal Doors
- The Deacons' Doors

The order of icons on an iconostasis is not rigid although it keeps roughly to the plan above. Rows may not follow the same sequence, and all five are not always featured. An icon of one of the church's patron saints sometimes takes the place of the icon of Christ Pantokrator.

Mary has always been venerated by the Orthodox Church. Russians refer to her as the *Bogomateri* or *Bogroditsa* (Mother of God).

The Arts

Russia has made a vast contribution to the arts including music, drama, ballet, painting and cinema, not to mention literature, where the contribution of its poets and novelists is particularly remarkable. These cultural triumphs are all the more impressive for having frequently been made in the face of official repression under Tsarist or Soviet regimes. Artistes who were accused of subversion often suffered terrible persecution and exile.

Anton Chekhov with members of the Moscow Arts Theatre, 1899

Drama

Medieval Russia was noted for its *skomorokhi* (minstrels), who recited fables, sang and danced at harvest festivals. Unfortunately, the Orthodox Church abhorred such pagan traditions and encouraged performances of biblical stories instead. These were staged at Russia's first ever theatre, established at the court of Tsar Alexis in 1672. His son, Peter the Great, had the first public theatre built on Moscow's Red Square in 1702, but it was in his new capital St Petersburg that European drama took root. During the late 18th and early 19th centuries, theatrical troupes comprising serfs were established in aristocratic estates in St Petersburg, Moscow and the provinces.

The mid-19th century saw Alexander Griboedov, Nikolai Gogol and Nikolai Ostrovsky create a distinctively Russian canon, but the most significant development was the foundation of the Moscow Arts Theatre (1898) by Konstantin Stanislavskiy and Vladimir Nemirovich-Danchenko. It was this theatre that successfully staged Anton Chekhov's naturalistic drama *The Seagull* *(see p84)* after it had flopped in St Petersburg. Subsequently, director Stanislavskiy's theories of method acting became hugely influential abroad and inspired Hollywood actors such as Marlon Brando and Dustin Hoffman.

Music and Ballet

Russian classical music began with Mikhail Glinka, whose *Life for the Tsar* (1836) and *Ruslan and Ludmila* (1842) initiated the genres of musical drama and folk opera, drawing on Orthodox chant and folk melodies. Glinka inspired the next generation of composers known as The Mighty Five, which included Modest Mussorgsky, famous for *Pictures at an Exhibition* (1874), and Alexander Borodin, known for the opera *Prince Igor* (1887).

A scene from *Swan Lake*, Mikhailovskiy Theatre, St Petersburg

Pyotr Tchaikovsky *(see p115)* established Russian music on the world stage with his ballets *Swan Lake* (1876) and *The Nutcracker* (1892), performed at the Bolshoi and Mariinskiy. His successors included the experimentalist composers Alexander Scriabin and Igor Stravinsky, and Sergei Rachmaninov. The last two left Russia after the Revolution. Composers who remained in, or returned to the USSR risked ideological criticism. After Shostakovich's opera *Lady Macbeth of Mtensk* (1934) was condemned by the newspaper *Pravda*, he could only redeem himself with the *Leningrad Symphony* (1941), which had patriotic overtones. Sergei Prokofiev was more adept in pleasing the authorities with his composition *Peter and the Wolf* (1936).

Ballet moved from imitating foreign forms to becoming a national art of surpassing

Premiere of Glinka's opera *Ruslan and Ludmila* at the Bolshoi Theatre, Moscow

Fifteenth-century icons painted by Andrei Rublev on display in the State Tretyakov Gallery, Moscow

brilliance. Its heritage and hopes are embodied in two great rival institutions, the Bolshoi Theatre *(see pp82–3)* and the Mariinskiy Theatre *(see p174)*.

Painting

Russia's steppe cultures had no tradition of painting, until Prince Vladimir's adoption of Orthodox Christianity introduced the Byzantine art of icon painting. As individual principalities became more independent, different schools developed in Vladimir, Suzdal, Novgorod and Pskov. Theophanes the Greek (around 1340–1405) was the first artist to imbue his subjects with human emotions, but it was only with Andrei Rublev (around 1360–1430) that a truly Russian school was created.

By the end of the 17th century, icon painting began to lose its significance, superseded by European portraiture. Peter the Great and his successors promoted the training of Russian artists abroad and established an Academy of Arts in St Petersburg. The academic style that developed here set the tone for Russian art until the middle of the 19th century.

After 14 of the academy's most talented students rebelled and launched themselves as a travelling art exhibition known as *Peredvizhniki* (The Wanderers) in 1870, Russian art changed irrevocably. Realist works such as *Barge-Haulers on the Volga* (1873) by Ilya Repin excoriated the ills of Tsarist society, while Symbolist and Primitivist paintings by the likes of Mikhail Vrubel and Natalya Goncharova challenged every tenet of the academic style.

The five years before and after the Revolution saw the rise and fall of Futurism – a radical experiment in new forms of the visual arts, architecture and design, by Kazimir Malevich, Vasily Kandinsky and Vladimir Tatlin. While Kandinsky left Russia in 1921 to teach at the Bauhaus school, Malevich and Tatlin remained in Russia long after the regime had rejected Futurism for socialist realism, which was Stalin's version of the academic style.

Cinema

Russian cinema came of age after the Revolution, when the Soviet state recognized the genius of Sergei Eisenstein (1898–1948). His silent masterpieces *Battleship Potemkin* (1925) and *October* (1927) pioneered the jump-cut, which has been used in movies ever since. Eisenstein's historical epics *Alexander Nevsky* (1938) and *Ivan the Terrible* (1944, 1958) were overseen by Stalin, who rewrote the script to make Ivan's speeches more laconic, like his own.

A poster of Eisenstein's masterpiece *Battleship Potemkin*

The Brezhnev era was the heyday of slapstick comedies such as *Operation Y*, the romantic *Irony of Fate* (still shown every New Year's day on TV) and *White Sun of the Desert* (a Soviet "Eastern" set in Central Asia). Andrey Tarkovsky's *Andrey Rublev* and Sergei Bondarchuk's *War and Peace* won prizes abroad.

Films long hidden in the archives, such as Aleksandr Askoldov's *The Commissar* (1967), were released during Gorbachev's reign, before the collapse of state funding and a flood of Hollywood imports left Russia's film industry in dire straits. Directors had to master new genres and find investors in order to survive; only Nikita Mikhalkov, whose *Burnt by the Sun* (1994) won an Oscar, got state funding. Alexei Balabanov's gangster movie *Brother* (1997) was the first domestic blockbuster, followed by the supernatural thrillers *Night Watch* (2004) and *Day Watch* (2006), directed by Timur Bekmambetov. Alexander Sokurov's *Russian Ark* (2003) has the distinction of being filmed in a single 96-minute shot, the longest in the history of cinematography.

Russian Literature

For a country where most of the population was illiterate before the October Revolution and where French was the *lingua franca* of the aristocracy, Russia has made a remarkable contribution to world literature. With its supple inflections, Russian is ideally suited to poetic and psychological expression – a trait brilliantly exploited by great writers such as Pushkin, Dostoevsky and Tolstoy. Often criticizing the draconian policies of the regime, poets and novelists have been regarded as the conscience of the nation in both Tsarist and Soviet times.

Leo Tolstoy (1828 – 1910) with his wife Sonya in the garden of their Russian home

Early Russian Literature

Russian literature is suffused with an oral heritage of folk mythology, ballads and slang. The tradition of *byliny*, or folk tales, told by minstrels in the courts of the Kievan Rus *(see p39)* over a millennium ago is preserved in the 12th-century epic poem *The Lay of Igor's Host*. The only manuscript of the poem was discovered in 1795. Excavations in Veliky Novgorod have unearthed love letters and poems written on birchbark dating from around 1400, implying that literacy was widespread here. After the Mongol invasion *(see p40)*, hagiographies of Orthodox saints became virtually the only form of literature besides the Gospels. Printing presses were initially regarded by the majority of Muscovites as satanic and printing output remained constrained.

Pushkin, Lermontov and Gogol

Russian literature came of age with Alexander Pushkin *(see p93)*, whose work ranged from short stories to poetry and even a novel in verse, *Yevgeny Onegin* (1832). Pushkin created a Russian literary idiom, expanding the language to explore nuances of feeling and sensation. His writing invited harsh censorship by Tsar Nicholas I, thus setting the precedent for dissent by future writers in opposition to autocracy.

Mikhail Lermontov expressed the existential angst of a generation that felt both impotent and ignored in *A Hero for Our Time* (1841). Like Pushkin, Lermontov was exiled to the Caucasus and killed in a duel.

Nikolai Gogol was a master of the grotesque, satirizing the snobbery and corruption of St Petersburg society in short stories. His novel *Dead Souls* (1842) was written as he lapsed into religious melancholia. He burned the second part in the fireplace. Afflicted by cataleptic fits, Gogol was allegedly buried alive in a Moscow cemetery.

Street scene from a 1997 film version of Tolstoy's eponymous novel *Anna Karenina*

Turgenev, Tolstoy and Dostoevsky

The next generation of writers was also dominated by a trio of titans. Ivan Turgenev made his name with short stories about the lives of serfs and went on to write *Fathers and Sons* (1892). The novel explores the conflict between generations and the dilemmas of liberals in an autocratic state. Leo Tolstoy *(see p106)* presented the stoical humility of the peasantry in sharp contrast to the decadence and hypocrisy of the nobility and bourgeoisie in his epic works *War and Peace* (1869) and *Anna Karenina* (1877). He was expelled from the Orthodox Church for espousing Christian anarchism.

On the other hand, Fyodor Dostoevsky *(see p177)* renounced his socialist ideals after exile in Siberia. He became a fervent upholder of autocracy and a savage critic of Russia's revolutionaries in such masterpieces as *Crime and Punishment* (1866), *The Devils* (1872) and *The Brothers Karamazov* (1880). The psychological insights that these works offer had a lasting influence on Western literature.

Chekhov

Dostoevsky's psychological realism was echoed in the works of playwright and novelist Anton Chekhov *(see p86)*. His collaboration with the director of the Moscow Arts Theatre, Konstantin Stanislavskiy, gave rise to the first "modern" plays, namely *The Seagull* (1896) and *Uncle Vanya* (1899). The characters' silences and non sequiturs conveyed their inner natures and feelings more effectively than conventional dialogue, while simultaneously presenting a subtle critique of social values.

Poster of Anton Chekhov, a dramatist associated with the Moscow Arts Theatre

The Silver Age

The beginning of the 20th century was the Silver Age of Russian poetry. Unfortunately, the abundance of artistic talent was significantly reduced by the Revolution. Emotional honesty was the ethos of the Acmeist movement, advocated by Anna Akhmatova *(see p182)* and Osip Mandelstam. Both produced their greatest work in Soviet times. Subsequently Akhmatova endured the purges, which have been recounted in her famous poem *Requiem* (1935–40), while Mandelstam died in the Gulag for lampooning Stalin. Marina Tsvetaeva was another "spiritual exile" in Soviet Russia. Her works were banned by the regime but circulated clandestinely, along with those of Alexander Blok, who had heralded the Revolution with his poem *The Twelve* (1918).

Actors rehearsing a scene from *The Master and Margarita* by Mikhail Bulgakov

Soviet and Émigré Writers

The Futurist Vladimir Mayakovsky *(see p75)* and the peasant poet Sergei Yesenin were supporters of the Bolshevik movement and their agitational propaganda was promulgated via their art. Unfortunately, both of them committed suicide in the 1920s. Isaac Babel's *Red Cavalry* (1924) enraged Marshal Budyonny to such an extent that Babel was later tortured to death. Stalin saw writers as "engineers of the human soul" and decreed socialist realism obligatory. The genre was epitomized by Nikolai Ostrovsky's *How the Steel was Tempered* (1936), but Mikhail Sholokhov's Cossack epic *And Quiet Flows the Don* (1940) is better known abroad.

Among the host of writers who fled Russia in the 1920s, Ivan Bunin became the first Russian ever to be awarded a Nobel Prize for Literature in 1933. Vladimir Nabokov wrote with equal brilliance in English, becoming famous the world over for *Lolita* (1955). Another novel that had a lasting impact abroad was Yevgeny Zamyatin's *We* (1927), which inspired George Orwell's *Nineteen Eighty-Four* and Aldous Huxley's *Brave New World*.

In Stalinist Russia, expulsion from the Writers' Union meant loss of privileges, arrest or even death. So harsh were the conditions that Mikhail Bulgakov worked in a theatre while secretly writing *The Master and Margarita* (1937) and Boris Pasternak eschewed poetry for translation work. His novel *Dr Zhivago* (1965) was written "for the desk drawer" and was only published during Khrushchev's reign. This was also the time when the literary magazine *Noviy Mir* serialized Alexander Solzhenitsyn's *One Day in the Life of Ivan Denisovich*, which is about life in the Gulag.

After ideological conformity was re-imposed in the 1960s, the work of dissident writers could only be circulated as *samizdat* (clandestine copies) or smuggled abroad for publication. Solzhenitsyn was expelled from Russia in 1974 for his work *The Gulag Archipelago*. The poet Joseph Brodsky suffered a similar fate after a grotesque trial where the judge asked him, "Who has recognized you to be a poet?"

Vladimir Mayakovsky in Yalta in 1926, four years before he committed suicide

Russian Architecture

The architectural landscape of Russia borrows elements from several different styles. While the architecture of the Kievan Rus was influenced by the Byzantine style, the medieval Novgorod and Pskov schools developed their own distinct features such as the onion dome. As the might of the Russian state grew, Ivan the Great invited Italian masters to build structures with Renaissance motifs. In the 18th century, Elizabeth favoured Bartolomeo Rastrelli and his Baroque style. A Russian version of Art Nouveau flourished before the Revolution, while postwar Constructivism influenced Modernist architecture worldwide.

Intricate wrought-iron Baroque gate of the Winter Palace, St Petersburg

Early Russian Architecture

Russia's earliest buildings were constructed entirely from wood. The Kizhi *pogost (see p208)*, a complex with a pair of domed wooden churches, is a prime example of sophisticated wooden architecture. Although stone and brick began to be used to construct important buildings around the 14th century, wood continued to be the main building material. This practice continued until the 1812 Great Fire of Moscow *(see p42)* burnt the city to the ground.

Churches constitute a majority of Russia's oldest surviving buildings. One of the earliest among these is Vladimir's 12th-century Cathedral of the Assumption *(see p116)* in Moscow. Its namesake in the Kremlin *(see pp58–9)* dates from the 14th century and is a fusion of the early-Russian style and Italian Renaissance features. This architectural confluence during the 15th and 16th centuries was a result of the imperial practice of inviting talented Italian architects to Russia. The Italian masters were assigned the task of constructing prestigious buildings befitting the reputation and stature of the ever-expanding Russian Empire.

Another architectural innovation in the 16th century was the spire-like tent roof, apparent in St Basil's Cathedral *(see pp70–71)* in Moscow. In the mid-17th century, Patriarch Nikon (1665–81) banned its use, insisting that plans for new churches must be based on ancient Byzantine designs.

Multi-domed wooden churches in Kizhi, an example of early Russian architecture

Although most secular buildings from this period have not survived, Moscow's Palace of the Romanov Boyars *(see p72)* remains a notable exception.

Baroque

The magnificent gate churches at the Novodevichiy Convent *(see pp104–105)* and the Upper Monastery of St Peter *(see pp84–5)* are representative of the Moscow Baroque, or Naryshkin, style of architecture. The filigree limestone trimmings and pilasters set against a redbrick background embody a fusion of early-Russian and European Baroque motifs.

European Baroque reached its apogee in St Petersburg under Empress Elizabeth. The Winter Palace *(see pp156–7)*, the Great Palace at Peterhof *(see pp186–7)* and the Catherine Palace at Tsarskoe Selo *(see pp188–9)* are the creations of her favourite architect, the Italian maestro Bartolomeo Rastrelli *(see p157)*. His flamboyant style was later superseded by Neo-Classical designs in St Petersburg and Moscow. However, archetypal Baroque features such as stucco mouldings and vibrantly coloured façades remained the leitmotif of architecture in provincial towns, as evinced by 19th-century merchants' villas in the old quarter of Ulyanovsk *(see p227)* in the Volga region.

Neo-Classicism

The accession of Catherine the Great to the throne in 1762 gave a new direction to Russian architecture. She favoured the Neo-Classical style, which derives from the architecture of Classical Greece and Rome. This style has been used to great effect in Moscow's Pashkov House *(see p88)*, thought to have been designed by Vasily Bazhenov.

Bazhenov's assistant, the prolific Matvei Kazakov, demonstrated the flexibility of Neo-Classicism in his designs for a range of buildings, including churches, hospitals and the Moscow Old University *(see p81)*. The huge fire that followed Napoleon's brief occupation of Moscow led to a wholesale reconstruction of the city in the fashionable Empire style, a grandiose form of Neo-Classicism typified by the work of Osip Bove and Carlo Rossi. Both architects created monumental public spaces, namely Bove's Theatre Square *(see p80)* in Moscow, and Rossi's General Staff Building *(see p152)* and Ostrovskiy Square *(see p167)* in St Petersburg.

Historicism and Style-Moderne

Historicism replaced Neo-Classicism in the mid 19th century. It arose from a desire to create a national style by reviving architectural movements from the past. Moscow's Grand Kremlin Palace *(see p60)* and Armoury Chamber *(see pp62–3)*, designed by Konstantin Ton in the 1840s, combine features from various erstwhile styles including Renaissance, Classical and Baroque. Ton also designed the Byzantine-style Cathedral of Christ the Saviour *(see p89)*, which was finished in 1883 and rebuilt between 1994–7.

Traditional Russian wooden architecture and folk art were rich sources of inspiration for the architects that formulated the Russian-Revival style. Moscow's Historical Museum *(see p68)* and the magnificent Church on Spilled Blood *(see p162)* in St Petersburg are outstanding examples of this genre.

Church on Spilled Blood exemplifying the Russian-Revival style, St Petersburg

Another radical architectural style that developed during this time was Style-Moderne, akin to Art Nouveau. Its greatest exponents were Fyodor Shekhtel in Moscow, who designed the extraordinary mansion that is now the Gorky House-Museum *(see p86)*, and the St Petersburg architect Fyodor Livdal, whose Kshesinskaya Mansion *(see p141)* uses mosaic friezes, glazed brick and stained glass to stunning effect.

Architecture after the Revolution

Constructivism was a novel attempt to combine form and function in the decade after the October Revolution. Although many visionary projects were never realized, Moscow has two outstanding buildings by the architect Konstantin Melnikov: the Bakhmetevsky Bus Garage that is now the Jewish Museum and Tolerance Centre, and the Melnikov House *(see p92)* that he built for himself shortly before his career stalled.

In the 1930s, Stalin decreed a plan to rebuild large areas of Moscow. Constructivism was abandoned in favour of a grand Soviet version of Neo-Classicism. Many of Moscow's metro stations are superb examples of design from this era. More obtrusive are the Stalin-Gothic skyscrapers known as the Seven Sisters, including the Ministry of Foreign Affairs *(see p93)* and the Moscow State University *(see p108)*.

The Stalin-Gothic Ministry of Foreign Affairs building, Moscow

RUSSIA THROUGH THE YEAR

Russians love to celebrate and take their public holidays seriously. Almost all official holidays as well as local ones are marked with concerts and fireworks. Music, whether classical, folk or contemporary, is the central theme of many festivals, bringing in talent from all over the world. Flowers play a particularly important role in Russian society. Mimosas symbolize International Women's Day when men present women with flowers, whereas lilacs herald the advent of summer. Even without an official holiday, Russians love to get outdoors, whether to ski or ice-skate in winter, or gather mushrooms in late summer and autumn.

Spring

When rooks appear, usually in late March, and snowdrops bloom, spring is reckoned to have arrived. To warm themselves up after the months of cold, locals celebrate *maslenitsa*, the feast of pancake-making before Lent. Once the snow has melted, city-dwellers make a visit to their *dacha* (country cottage) to put the garden in order.

March

Maslenitsa *(end Feb–early Mar)*, nationwide. Pancake week heralds spring with events such as concerts and carnivals.

International Women's Day, *Mezhdunarodnyy den zhenshchin, (8 Mar)*, nationwide. Men buy gifts for their womenfolk and congratulate them on the holiday with the words *"S prazdnikom"*, meaning "best wishes".

Easter Sunday, *Paskha, (Mar–early May, following the Orthodox calendar)*, nationwide. Churches throng with chanting devotees. After the greeting *Khristos voskres* (Christ is risen) and the reply *Voistine voskres* (He is truly risen) are exchanged, people kiss one another three times.

April

Musical Spring in St Petersburg, *Muzikalnaya Vesna v Sankt-Peterburge, (mid-Apr)*. Concert halls host musical programmes.

May

Labour Day, *Den truda, (1 May)*, nationwide. In the Soviet era, parades lined Moscow's Red Square *(see p68)*. Today, the festivities are rather low-key, with concerts and fireworks.

Victory Day, *Den pobedy, (9 May)*, nationwide. Wreath are laid at war memorials in memory of the 1945 Nazi surrender. A parade, with soldiers in historic uniforms, takes place in Red Square.

Peterhof Fountains, *Fontany v Petergofe, (weekend in mid-May)*, St Petersburg. Bands and orchestras accompany the switching on of the fountains at Peterhof *(see pp186–7)* under a colourful fireworks display.

Day of Slav Culture, *Den Slavyanskoe Kultury, (24 May)*, nationwide. Religious processions are held in honour of the saints Cyril and Methodius, the "apostles of the Slavs".

City Day, *Den goroda, (last week of May)*, St Petersburg. Events, mainly taking place around the Peter and Paul Fortress *(see pp136–7)*, mark the founding of the city on 27 May 1703.

Soldiers in uniform at the Victory Day parade on Red Square, Moscow

Moscow Stars, *Moskovskyy Zvezdy, (throughout May)*. Conductors, soloists and ensembles from around the world perform at Moscow's Conservatory *(see p87)* and Tchaikovsky Concert Hall.

SKIF Festival *(May)*, St Petersburg. Indie and avant-garde musicians, DJs and performance artists from Russia and abroad delight audiences at clubs and other venues.

Stars of the White Nights, *Zvezdy Belykh nochi, (late May–early Jul)*, St Petersburg. First-class opera, classical music and ballet performances across the city during the famous White Nights, when the sun hardly sets.

Cossack Fairs, *Kazachi yarmarki, (May–Sep, last Sun of the month)*, Starocherkassk. Horse-riding, singing, dancing and merry-making takes place in this Cossack village.

Easter celebrations outside the Cathedral of Our Lady of Kazan, Moscow

Summer

Throughout summer, cities are almost empty during weekends, when people visit their *dachas*.

Crowds at the delightful hot-air balloon festival, Kungur

Despite this, there are several major music festivals and other events, including an air show outside Moscow and a hot-air balloon festival in the Urals.

June

Trinity Sunday, *Troitsa, (50 days after Easter Sunday, according to the Orthodox calendar),* nationwide. Believers and atheists alike go to the graves of their loved ones and raise a toast for their souls.

Moscow International Film Festival *(Jun).* A glamorous event attended by both celebrities and the general public, and featuring the latest releases from all over the world.

Sadko Folklore Festival, *Mezhdunarodnyy folklore festival Sadko, (7–10 Jun),* Veliky Novgorod. An international festival of folklore and crafts that starts with a parade from the Kremlin to Yaroslav's Court *(see p210).*

St Petersburg Palaces, *Dvortsy Sankt-Peterburga, (early Jun–early Jul).* An international festival of chamber music and fireworks at the imperial summer palaces of Peterhof, Tsarskoe Selo *(see pp188–9)* and Pavlovsk *(see pp190–91).*

Day of Russia, *Den Rossii, (12 Jun),* nationwide. This official holiday marks the day when Russia became "independent" of the Soviet Union in 1991. It is celebrated with a fireworks display in cities across the country.

Tsarskoe Selo Carnival, *Tsarskoselskiy karnaval, (last weekend of Jun).* Funny costumes, music and mayhem fill the centre of Pushkin, the town surrounding the imperial palace of Tsarskoe Selo.

Tales of the Boy Onfim, *Skazi malchika Onfima, (Jun, Jul and Sep),* Veliky Novgorod. Russian fairy-tale heroes, show puppets and age-old myths come to life in the medieval Kremlin.

July

Sky Fair of the Urals, *Nebesnaya yarmarka Urala, (early Jul),* Kungur. A week-long international hot-air balloon festival held near the Kungur Ice Cave *(see p235).*

Young boys at the Night of Ivan Kupala near Veliky Novgorod

US Independence Day *(4 Jul),* Moscow. Celebrated with rock bands, fashion shows and fireworks in the grounds of Kuskovo Palace *(see p109).*

Night of Ivan Kupala, *Noch Ivana Kupala, (around 6 Jul),* near Veliky Novgorod. Ostensibly dedicated to St John the Baptist, this nocturnal pagan fertility rite, marked by youths leaping over bonfires, is held beside Lake Ilmen.

Grushinsky Festival, *Vserossiyskiy festival avtorskoy pesni, (first weekend of Jul),* Samara. Two rival festivals devoted to Bard music, a Soviet genre of acoustic ballads. One is held by the Mastryukovskie lakes near Samara *(see pp228–9)*, and the other outside Tolyatti, in the Samara region.

Amber Beach *(mid-Jul),* Kaliningrad. A Baltic pop festival held in the Kaliningrad region.

Kizhi Volost Festival *(mid–Jul),* Kizhi. Folk music, dancing and a handicrafts display on the remote island in Lake Onega *(see p208).*

Navy Day, *Den voenno-morskovo flota, (last Sun in Jul),* port cities. Naval regattas of warships and submarines are held in St Petersburg's Neva basin and Vladivostok's harbour, plus there are celebrations in many other cities that have a waterfront.

Kamwa Festival, *Etnofuturisticherskiy festival* KAMWA, *(late Jul–early Aug),* Perm. Russia's answer to WOMAD, this ethno-futuristic festival brings together ancient Ugric traditions and modern art, music and fashion.

Aircraft trailing the colours of the Russian national flag, MAKS Air Show 2009

August

MAKS Air Show *(mid-Aug),* Zhukovskiy Airbase, 20 km (13 miles) southeast of Moscow. Aerial displays by Russia's latest and vintage warplanes.

Novorossiysk Bikers' Festival *(last weekend of Aug).* This Black Sea port hosts Russia's biggest bikers' festival, which President Putin has attended in 2010, riding a Harley Davidson.

Autumn

City life begins to gain pace as people return from their *dachas* and families begin to prepare for the start of school. In September, when theatres re-open after the summer break, cultural life resumes. October marks the beginning of the festival season in Moscow and St Petersburg, with musicians and theatre groups from all over the world taking part. Autumn is ideal for gathering mushrooms in the forests. Locals are skilled at identifying edible mushrooms, but amateur pickers should beware the dangers of poisonous ones.

President Putin laying a wreath in memory of victims of the Siege of Leningrad

September

Knowledge Day, *Den znaniy, (1 Sep)*, nationwide. Children and parents celebrate the start of the new academic year by bringing flowers to teachers.

Knowledge Day celebrated with balloons and flowers at a school in Vladimir

Battle of Borodino, *Borodinskaya bitva, (first Sun of Sep)*, Borodino. A re-enactment of the famous 1812 battle.
City Day, *Den goroda, (first weekend of Sep)*, Moscow. A carnival on ulitsa Tverskaya and a pageant at the royal estate of Kolomenskoe are organized.
Peterhof Fountains *Fontany v Petergofe, (second weekend of Sep)*, St Petersburg. Celebrations with fireworks mark the switching off of the famous fountains.
Siege of Leningrad Day, *Den Blokady Leningrada, (8 Sep)*, St Petersburg. Commemorated by a parade of war veterans along Nevskiy prospekt and wreath-laying ceremonies at the Piskarevskoe Memorial Cemetery.
International Early Music Festival, *Mezhdunarodnyy festival Early Music, (late Sep–mid-Oct)*, St Petersburg, Moscow, Nizhny Novgorod, Yekaterinburg, Perm and Novosibirsk. Soloists and ensembles perform music from the Middle Ages, Baroque, Renaissance and Classical times.

October

Baltic House, *Baltiyskiy dom, (Oct)*, St Petersburg. Actors, clowns and pantomime artists from the Baltic countries perform in theatres and on the streets for over two weeks.
Autumn Rhythms, *Osenie Ritmy, (mid-Oct–mid-Nov)*, St Petersburg. A month-long international festival that segues from Ballroom and Latin dancing into jazz, held at clubs and concert halls.
Halloween Night *(31 Oct)*, nationwide. Despite Halloween being anathematized by the Russian Orthodox Church as a pagan celebration, the country's

Climate Of Russia

Russia experiences climatic extremes. Most of European Russia, southwestern Siberia and the southern Pacific coast have a continental climate, with cold winters and hot summers. Extremely severe winters characterize Russia's sub-arctic and polar regions, while the Black Sea coast has a humid subtropical climate with wet winters.

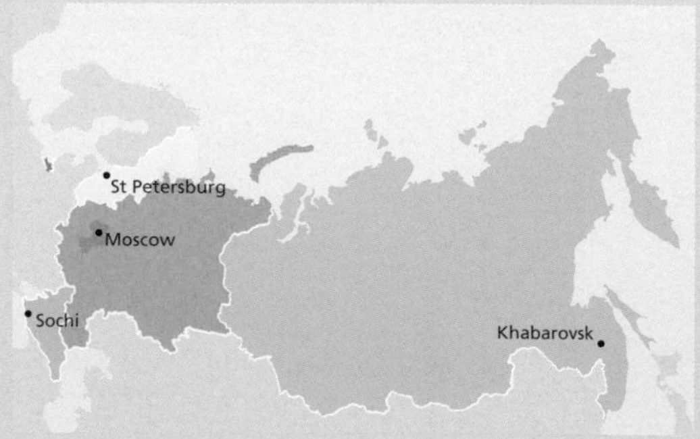

Moscow has a continental climate, characterized by cold winters, and warm, often hot summers. During heat waves, daytime temperature exceeds 30°C (86°F). In the winter months precipitation falls mainly as snow.

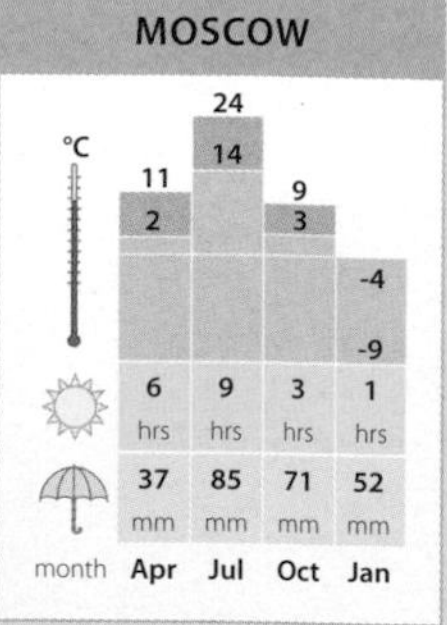

youth enjoy dressing up as vampires and werewolves for a night's clubbing.

November

Day of National Unity, *Den' narodnogo yedinstva, (4 Nov)*, nationwide. Originally meant to commemorate the liberation of the country, when all members of Russian society united to expel the Polish-Lithuanian forces in 1612, this official holiday has now been hijacked by far-right groups that proclaim "Russia is for Russians".

Winter

As the ice thickens on the waters and the snow deepens, Russians head for the outdoors. Sledging, ice-skating and cross-country skiing are popular wherever the topography allows. Hardy "Walruses" breaking the ice to take an early morning dip and fishermen sitting over holes drilled in the ice are a common sight.

A Russian Orthodox archbishop performing the evening service on Christmas Eve

December

Four Nations Tournament, *Turnir chetiryy natsyy, (mid-Dec)*, Moscow, Podolsk and other cities. Ice-hockey teams from Russia, Sweden, Finland and the Czech Republic compete.

Moscow Forum, *Moskovskyy Forum, (Dec or Jan)*. Annual festival of contemporary music held at various venues.

New Year's Eve *Novyy god, (31 Dec)*, nationwide. New Year's Eve is a family celebration, with visitors dressed as *Ded Moroz* (Grandfather Frost, the Russian equivalent of Santa Claus) or his sidekick *Snegurochka* (Snow Maiden), the bearer of gifts.

Russian Winter Festival *(mid-Dec–early Jan)*, Moscow. Folk music performances and *troika* (sleigh) rides can be enjoyed at Izmaylovo Park, with plenty of vodka to keep one warm amid the freezing temperatures.

January

Russian Orthodox Christmas, *Rozhdestvo, (7 Jan)*, nationwide. Christmas is celebrated in a quieter fashion than Easter, with attendance at the evening service on Christmas Eve a tradition.

Old New Year, *Staryy Novyy god, (night of 13 Jan)*, nationwide. Orthodox Christians and die-hard party-goers welcome the New Year according to the defunct Julian calendar.

Svyatki Masquerades, *Svyatki, (Sun nearest 19 Jan)*, Moscow. Bell-ringing and the blessing of the water at Kolomenskoe.

February

Defender of the Fatherland Day, *Den zashchitnika Otechestva, (23 Feb)*, nationwide. Men are given flowers and presents, and Russia's armed forces are honoured.

Buddhist New Year *Tsagaalgan, (late Feb-early Mar)*, Siberia. A 16-day festival marking the lunar New Year, with offerings at Buddhist temples and family feasting. The festival is known as *Shagaa* here.

Public Holidays

New Year (1–8 Jan)
Russian Orthodox Christmas (7 Jan)
Defender of the Fatherland Day (23 Feb)
International Women's Day (8 Mar)
Labour Day (1 May)
Day of Russia (12 Jun)
Day of National Unity (4 Nov)

St Petersburg enjoys a mild maritime climate. Summers are warm and humid, particularly during the White Nights (mid-Jun–mid-Jul). In winter the Neva river freezes over, not thawing until late March or April.

ST PETERSBURG

month	Apr	Jul	Oct	Jan
°C (max)	9	23	9	-3
°C (min)	1	15	4	-8
sunshine	6 hrs	9 hrs	2 hrs	2 hrs
rainfall	33 mm	78 mm	67 mm	40 mm

Sochi, on the Black Sea coast, is on the same latitude as Nice in France, with a humid subtropical climate. However, winters are colder due to chill winds from Asia, and the temperature can even drop below freezing point.

SOCHI

month	Apr	Jul	Oct	Jan
°C (max)	16	27	20	10
°C (min)	9	19	12	3
sunshine	5 hrs	9 hrs	6 hrs	3 hrs
rainfall	116 mm	124 mm	167 mm	181 mm

Khabarovsk boasts of being the world's coldest city, with a population of over half a million people. Winter temperatures can approach -30°C (-22°F), with the lowest temperature recorded at -41°C (-42°F).

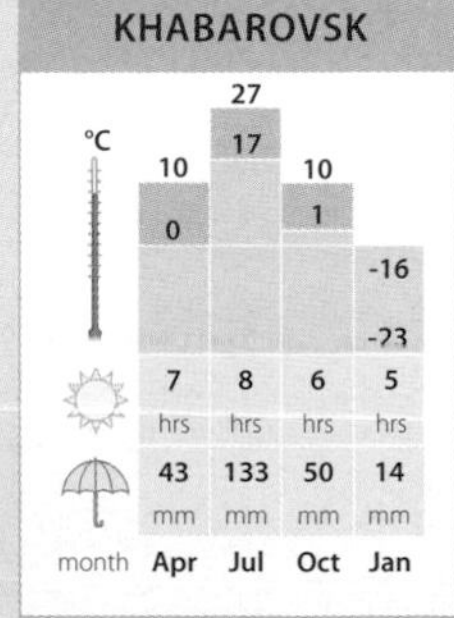

KHABAROVSK

month	Apr	Jul	Oct	Jan
°C (max)	10	27	10	-16
°C (min)	0	17	1	-23
sunshine	7 hrs	8 hrs	6 hrs	5 hrs
rainfall	43 mm	133 mm	50 mm	14 mm

THE HISTORY OF RUSSIA

From a few medieval principalities based around European Russia's inland waterways, Russia has grown to encompass one-sixth of the world. The story of its rise is marked by triumphs and tragedies on an epic scale, including such historic watersheds as the Mongol invasion that laid waste to its medieval civilization, and the creation and collapse of the Soviet Union. Modern-day Russia continues to surge ahead with a flourishing economy and achievements in science and industry.

According to Herodotus's *The Histories*, nomadic tribes known as the Scythians made the steppes of southern Russia their home between the 9th and 3rd centuries BC. Frozen tombs in the permafrost of the Altai Mountains and *kurgans* (burial mounds) on the steppes have yielded mummified humans and horses as well as magnificent gold jewellery. The Scythian empire stretched from southern Russia to the borders of Persia. Despite being scorned as barbarians by outsiders, the Scythians cross-fertilized numerous civilizations. They settled on the northern shores of the Black Sea, but were eventually displaced or absorbed by later nomadic invaders such as the Sarmatians, Huns, Goths and Khazars. The Khazar state, which ruled the lower Volga basin from the 5th to the 11th centuries AD, was a vital link in the Silk Road from Asia to Europe.

The Slavs were relative latecomers from the Pripet Marshes of what is now Belarus. They spread eastwards after the 7th century. Early Slav pottery in Moscow's Historical Museum suggests a primitive peasant culture, but the Slavs proved to be enduring and adaptable on the Eurasian landmass.

Kievan Rus

In the mid-9th century, a Scandinavian people known as the Varangians (Vikings) ventured along inland waterways from the Baltic to the Black and Caspian seas, where they came in contact with the Slavs of Novgorod. Constant in-fighting between the Slavic tribes was quelled when the Varangian prince Rurik took control of the region in 860. His successor Oleg took Kiev, a Slavic city, and made it his capital, creating an alliance of principalities controlling the river trade routes for furs and slaves between Scandinavia and Byzantium. Kievan Rus' absorbed the Viking minority into a Slavic alliance, ruled by feuding *boyars* (nobles).

In 988, Prince Vladimir of Kiev (r.980–1015) took the historic step of adopting Byzantine Orthodox Christianity and imposing it on his pagan subjects by mass baptism. This move deeply affected the future of Russia, whose main religion continues to be Orthodox Christianity. The Kievan state flourished under Vladimir's son Yaroslav the Wise (r.1019–54). But feuding among his successors weakened the state just as a deadly threat emerged from the east in 1223.

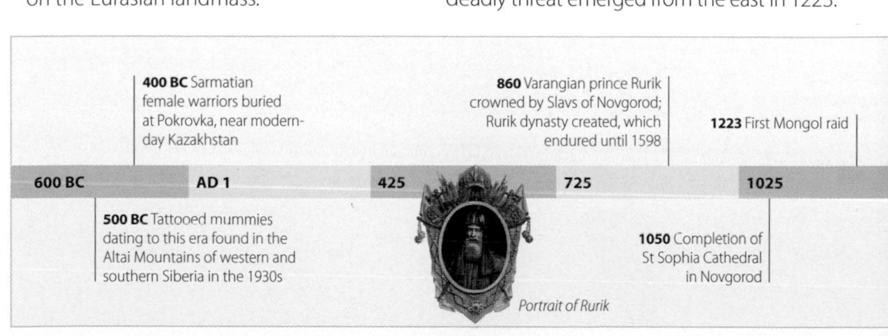

400 BC Sarmatian female warriors buried at Pokrovka, near modern-day Kazakhstan
860 Varangian prince Rurik crowned by Slavs of Novgorod; Rurik dynasty created, which endured until 1598
1223 First Mongol raid
600 BC
AD 1
425
725
1025
500 BC Tattooed mummies dating to this era found in the Altai Mountains of western and southern Siberia in the 1930s
1050 Completion of St Sophia Cathedral in Novgorod

Portrait of Rurik

◄ A 1901 painting depicting Russians fighting off Tartars during one of their numerous clashes

The Mongol Yoke

Between 1237 and 1240, Russia was invaded from the east by the fearsome Mongol horde led by Genghis Khan's grandson Batu Khan. They swept across the steppe destroying everything in their path.

While Batu later withdrew to Central Asia, he left behind a detachment known as the Golden Horde that dominated Russia for the next 250 years, exacting tribute in the form of gold, furs and slaves. In the 14th century, the Mongols chose Grand Prince Ivan I of Muscovy (as the principality of Moscow was known) to collect tributes from all their conquered principalities, giving the city supremacy over its neighbours.

Muscovy owed its rise not just to bribery, but to its position at the centre of Russia's river trade routes. In 1380, an army led by Prince Dmitri Donskoy won a victory, the first of its kind, over the Mongols at Kulikovo on the Don river, and the idea of a Russian nation was born. The Orthodox monk Sergius of Radonezh (c.1319–92) was instrumental in uniting the *boyars* behind this patriotic crusade, cementing the Church's place at the heart of the Russian nation state.

The people of Kazan submitting to Ivan the Terrible, the first tsar of Russia

Ivan the Great and Ivan the Terrible

During the long reign of Ivan III, known as "the Great" (r.1462–1505), the Mongols were forced back to the lower Volga region. Even independent Novgorod was forced to submit to Muscovy's authority. Furthermore, Ivan the Great's marriage to the niece of the last emperor of Byzantium increased Moscow's prestige, particularly her claim to being the last defender of true Orthodoxy.

Ivan the Great's grandson, Ivan IV "the Terrible" (r.1533–84) was the first to be called "Tsar of All the Russias". It was during his reign that the Mongol strongholds of Kazan and Astrakhan were captured. Russia expanded beyond the Urals into Siberia and strong trade links were established with England. The power of the *boyars* was broken by exiling them to remote provinces. But after killing his son and intended heir in a fit of rage, Ivan the Terrible's dynastic hopes rested on a retarded elder son, Fyodor, and an infant, Dmitri.

The Time of Troubles

For 14 years, Fyodor (r.1584–98) ruled under the guidance of Boris Godunov, a former much-hated member of the *oprichniki* (state police). After Fyodor died childless, bringing the Rurik dynasty to an end, Godunov staged his own accession, but his wiles were no match for a run of disasters after 1601.

Two imposters claiming to be Tsarevich Dmitri invaded Russia one after the other. The first "False Dmitri" invaded

1325–40 Ivan I rules Moscow and strengthens its position

1380 Dmitri Donskoy defeats the Mongols at the Battle of Kulikovo

Statue of Dmitri Donskoy

1453 Constantinople, previously Moscow's Orthodox ally, falls to the Ottomans; emperor of Byzantium flees the city

1462–1505 Reign of Ivan the Great

1476 Ivan the Great stops paying tribute to the Mongols

1478 Ivan the Great revokes Novgorod's charter of independence

1533–84 Reign of Ivan the Terrible

1350 | 1400 | 1450 | 1500

Coronation of Ivan V and Peter I as co-tsars in 1682

Russia with Polish help and was crowned in 1605, but soon alienated Muscovites and was torn to pieces by a mob. In 1607, the second "False Dmitri", backed by a Polish-Lithuanian army, began five years of invasions, civil war and banditry. This period came to be known as the Time of Troubles.

Only after the abbot of the Trinity Monastery of St Sergius declared a holy war to liberate Moscow did the *boyars* rally behind Prince Pozharskiy of Suzdal, and Kuzma Minin, a butcher from Nizhny Novgorod. They led an army that expelled the Poles in 1612. A monument in Moscow's Red Square commemorates the event.

The First Romanovs

To avert further strife among the *boyars*, the abbot of the Trinity Monastery proposed Mikhail Romanov (r.1613–45), brother of Ivan the Terrible's first wife, as tsar, thus initiating the 300-year rule of the Romanovs. Under Mikhail, Moscow made a dramatic recovery with a spate of new stone churches in the tent-roofed style, symbolizing the unity of Church and State. His successor, Alexis (r.1645–76), took the first steps to modernizing Russia by bringing in foreign soldiers, doctors and other professionals.

Alexis was succeeded by his sickly son Fyodor (r.1676–82), whose demise left his 10-year-old half-brother, Peter, heir to the throne. The powerful Miloslavskiy family along with Peter's half-sister Sophia instigated the 1682 Streltsy Revolt of Kremlin musketeers to force Peter's retarded other half-brother Ivan V to be recognized as co-tsar, under the regency of Sophia.

Peter the Great

By the time Ivan V died in 1696, Peter had grown into a 24-year-old giant with willpower and energy to match. In 1697, he went on a European tour to study shipbuilding and other technological advances. On returning to Russia, he lost no time in enforcing Westernized reforms, using his fledgling Guards regiments to crush the Streltsy when they revolted again in 1698.

Tsar Peter I, known as "the Great" (r.1682–1725)

It was Peter's determination to establish a northern port with an unrestricted passage to the Baltic that led to war with Sweden. In 1703, he began to fortify the Neva delta and founded the city of St Petersburg. After victory at Poltava in 1709 diminished the Swedish threat, St Petersburg was proclaimed the capital of Russia. By the time of Peter's death it had 40,000 inhabitants.

1552 Mongol capital of Kazan captured; Ivan the Terrible builds St Basil's Cathedral to celebrate

1584 Ivan the Terrible dies and is succeeded by his son Fyodor

1598–1605 Reign of Boris Godunov

1610 Moscow falls to the Poles but they are driven out two years later

1613 Coronation of Mikhail Romanov marks the end of the Time of Troubles and the birth of the Romanov dynasty

1654–67 Second war with Poland

Mikhail Romanov

1682 The Streltsy Revolt; Peter I and his half-brother Ivan V become co-tsars with Sophia as regent

1700–21 Great Northern War against Sweden

1712 St Petersburg becomes the Russian capital

1725 Peter the Great is succeeded by his widow Catherine I

1550 | 1600 | 1650 | 1700

The Petticoat Period

For most of the rest of the 18th century Russia was ruled by women, whose taste did much to set the celebrated architectural tone of St Petersburg.

During the brief reigns of Peter's widow Catherine I (r.1725–7) and his grandson Peter II (r.1727–30), the court abandoned this frontier city for Moscow. But when the throne passed to Anna Ioannovna (r.1730–40), the daughter of Ivan V, she set about creating a European court in St Petersburg. Fashion was imported from France and opera from Italy. Many of her ministers were German, including her lover, Count Biron.

In 1741 Peter the Great's daughter, Elizabeth I was crowned tsarina after she staged a coup backed by the Imperial Guards. Her chief legacy is the splendid architecture she commissioned, mainly by her favourite architect, Bartolomeo Rastrelli.

Elizabeth was also responsible for choosing a German princess, Catherine, as wife for her heir, Peter III. By the time Peter III became tsar in 1761, Catherine had lived in Russia for 18 years, spoke fluent Russian and was steeped in Russian culture – unlike her husband, who alienated the nobility with his Germanic ways. Six months into Peter's reign, Catherine and her allies in the guards deposed the tsar, who was murdered within days of her coronation as Catherine II.

Portrait of Catherine II by Alexander Roslin

Catherine II, known as "the Great", was an enlightened ruler who reformed the legal system and built hospitals and schools. By the end of her reign, she had left Russia vastly enlarged after successful campaigns against Turkey and Poland, and donated a superb art collection that formed the basis of the Hermitage *(see pp154–5)*.

Napoleon and Alexander I drawing up the Treaty of Tilsit in 1807

War and Peace

Under Catherine II's grandson Alexander I, Russia finally took her place alongside the great European powers during the Napoleonic wars. Alexander I's first campaign against Napoleon was a disaster, leading to the Treaty of Tilsit in 1807, which divided Europe into French and Russian spheres. In 1812, Napoleon advanced on Moscow with a Grande Armée of 600,000 men. However, the Russian Army evacuated, set fire to the city and fled. In just four days, two-thirds of the city burnt down leaving the French Army without shelter or provisions. Facing winter without supplies, the army began its retreat in October. In celebration, Alexander I commissioned imposing public edifices in the Empire style, which became the dominant movement during the reconstruction of Moscow.

Russian officers who had witnessed the freedom of democratic Europe were frustrated by Alexander I's refusal to consider constitutional reform. When his autocratic

1741 Elizabeth I takes power, supported by the Imperial Guards

1750

Elizabeth I of Russia

1762 Catherine II deposes her husband and is coronated in Moscow

1768–74 First Russo-Turkish War

1773 Pugachev Rebellion begins

1775

1787–92 Second Russo-Turkish War

1796 Paul, son of Catherine II, becomes tsar

1800

1801 Paul is murdered; Alexander I becomes tsar

1805–7 War with France: Russia is defeated at battles of Austerlitz and Friedland

1825 Nicholas I becomes tsar; the Decembrist Rebellion is crushed

1825

brother Nicholas I was declared tsar in December 1825, they rallied their troops in revolt in what is now Senate Square in St Petersburg. This Decembrist Rebellion was rapidly crushed and Nicholas personally sentenced five ringleaders to death by hanging and over a hundred rebels to exile in Siberia.

Bloody Sunday depicted in a painting by Vladimir Makovsky

Progress and Reaction

After the unrelenting autocracy of Nicholas I, liberals welcomed the reign of his enlightened son Alexander II (r.1855–81). In 1861, the tsar passed the Edict of Emancipation, abolishing serfdom, but requiring peasants to buy their land at rates that proved ruinous. Industrialization took off as peasants flocked to the big cities to work in factories.

As reforms faltered, revolutionary groups known as Nihilists waged a campaign of terror, killing state officials and, in 1881, Alexander II himself. He was succeeded by Alexander III, an iron-fisted reactionary who forced the revolutionaries underground. As Russia industrialized at breakneck speed, his ministers diverted popular discontent by staging anti-Semitic pogroms. Nobody anticipated that the tsar would die at the age of 47, leaving Alexander II's son Nicholas II (r.1894–1917) to inherit the throne.

The Death of Tsarist Russia

Nicholas II was chronically indecisive and unfit to rule. An unsuccessful war with Japan (1904–5) was followed by the massacre of Bloody Sunday. On 9 January 1905, peaceful demonstrators were killed in St Petersburg, sparking strikes and uprisings across Russia. To avert further disaster, Nicholas promised an elected Duma (Parliament), which convened in 1906. However, the tsar simply dissolved the Duma whenever it displeased him and fired ministers at whim. Furthermore, society was scandalized by lurid rumours about the friendship between the royal family and Rasputin *(see p176)*. However, the regime might have survived had Nicholas not committed Russia to war against Germany in 1914.

By late 1916, Russia had lost 3.5 million men, morale at the front was low and food supplies at home, scarce. In February 1917, strikes broke out in St Petersburg, then called Petrograd. The tsar was forced to abdicate, bringing 300 years of Romanov rule to an inglorious end, and a provisional government of liberals was formed.

The provisional government decreed human rights for all, but fatally undermined its popularity by continuing the war. Its authority was challenged by the Petrograd Soviet of Soldiers, Workers and Peasants, whose "Order No.1", authorizing the formation of *soviets* (local revolutionary councils) throughout the army, threatened what discipline remained. By the autumn of 1917, the provisional government was ripe to be overthrown by more radical revolutionaries.

Alexander Pushkin

1833 Pushkin publishes *The Bronze Horseman*

1850

1853 Crimean War begins

1855 Death of Nicholas I; Alexander II succeeds him

1861 Emancipation of serfs

1875

1881 Alexander II is assassinated by terrorists; Alexander III becomes tsar

Tsar Nicholas II

1894 Alexander III dies; throne passes to Nicholas II

1900

1914 Outbreak of World War I; St Petersburg changes name to Petrograd

1917 Tsarist regime falls in February

February 27, 1917, a painting by Boris Kustodiev

Revolution and Civil War

The Bolsheviks were an extreme faction of Russian Marxists, who had split from the more moderate Mensheviks at the party's 1902 congress in Brussels. Under their leader-in-exile, Vladimir Lenin, the Bolsheviks built up an underground network of activists in Russia that awaited Lenin's return following the overthrow of tsarism in February 1917. Lenin lost no time in denouncing the provisional government for its continuation of the war against Germany and in October 1917 the Bolsheviks were able to stage a coup in Petrograd under the slogan "All power to the Soviets".

The October Revolution was the harbinger of a savage Civil War (1918–21) that engulfed all Russia from the Polish border to the Pacific coast of Siberia. The Reds (Bolsheviks) were opposed by a diverse coalition of anti-revolutionary groups that came to be known as the Whites, initially supported by foreign intervention.

By the time the Whites were beaten by the Red Army, Soviet Russia was devastated by years of conflict and Lenin's policy of War Communism, whereby crops were seized from the peasantry to feed the urban proletariat who laboured under military discipline. To revive the shattered economy, Lenin introduced the New Economic Policy, allowing limited private enterprise while retaining state control over the "commanding heights" of the economy. Enfeebled by strokes, Lenin died in 1924, when the Soviet state was still in its infancy.

The Stalin Years

In the first five years after Lenin's death, Joseph Stalin used his position as General Secretary of the Communist Party to eliminate all rivals and establish a brutal dictatorship that utterly transformed Soviet society, dragging a nation still using horse-drawn ploughs into the nuclear age.

The collectivization of agriculture under the first Five-Year Plan (1928–33) forced peasants to surrender all livestock, machinery and land to collective farms. Up to 10 million peasants are thought to have died during the famine of 1931–2, or in the slave-labour camps of the Gulag, building such "hero projects" as the White Sea Canal. In December 1934, the assassination of the Bolshevik leader Sergei Kirov gave Stalin the pretext for a nationwide purge lasting five years. During this

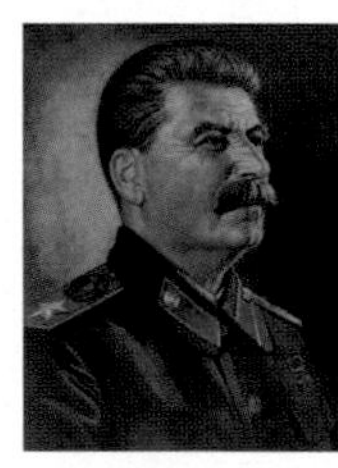

Portrait of Joseph Stalin (1879–1953)

1917 The October Revolution

Lenin (1874–1924)

1924 Lenin dies; Petrograd is named Leningrad

1934 Assassination of Party Secretary Kirov triggers the Great Terror

1942 Shostakovich's *Leningrad Symphony* is broadcast while the city is besieged

1920 | 1930 | 1940 | 1950

1918 Civil War begins; the capital moves to Moscow

1929 Collectivization of private land begins

1941 Nazi Germany invades Russia; Siege of Leningrad begins

1945 The Red Army captures Berlin

1947 The term "Cold War" is coined

Soldiers commemorating their victory over Nazi Germany

period (known as the Great Terror), some 15 million people were arrested, over a million executed and the rest sent to the Gulag.

In 1937–8, the Red Army was included in this purge, which left it ill-prepared for the Nazi invasion of Russia in June 1941. Within months, the Germans had encircled Leningrad, subjecting the city to a 900-day siege that killed 670,000 citizens. The tide turned only at Stalingrad, where the Russians trapped the German Sixth Army in 1943. When the Soviet people celebrated victory over Nazi Germany in 1945, they also mourned 27 million dead and the devastation of much of western Russia, whose cities lay in ruins.

Stalin's iron grip now held Eastern Europe as well as the Soviet Union, as the Cold War with the West began. A new wave of purges was only halted by Stalin's death in 1953.

Thaw and Stagnation

Stalin's successor, Nikita Khrushchev, denounced Stalin's crimes at the 20th Party Congress – initiating what Russians call "the Thaw". Political prisoners were released and Aleksandr Solzhenitsyn's book, *One Day in the Life of Ivan Denisovich*, about life in the Gulag, was published. The launch of Sputnik in 1957 and Yuri Gagarin's pioneering journey into space four years later made Khrushchev's boast that Russia would overtake the West sound credible, and new housing and consumer goods seemed a foretaste of future prosperity for Soviet citizens.

However, Khrushchev's decision in 1962 to station nuclear missiles in Cuba brought the world to the brink of nuclear war. In 1964, Khrushchev was deposed by politburo rivals, but was allowed to live on in obscurity rather than being shot, as disgraced leaders had been previously – a sign of how much had changed since Stalin's time.

When Leonid Brezhnev took over, the intellectual climate froze once more and the persecution of dissidents was stepped up. The first decade of Brezhnev's rule was a time of relative plenty, but beneath the surface a vast black market and network of corruption was growing. Party *apparatchiks* (functionaries), who benefited most from the corruption, had no interest in rocking the boat. When Brezhnev died in 1982, the politburo's choice of two geriatric leaders in succession, Yuri Andropov and Konstantin Chernenko, confirmed that Russia was living in an Era of Stagnation.

Sputnik I in the Soviet pavilion at Brussels World's Fair in 1958

1953 Stalin dies

Yuri Gagarin

1960

1961 Cosmonaut Yuri Gagarin becomes the first man in space

1964 Khrushchev ousted; Brezhnev becomes General Secretary

1968 Soviet troops enter Czechoslovakia to suppress the "Prague Spring"

1970

1970 Solzhenitsyn wins the Nobel Prize for Literature for *One Day in the Life of Ivan Denisovich*

Aleksandr Solzhenitsyn

1980

1979 Soviet forces invade Afghanistan

1982 Brezhnev dies and is replaced by Yuri Andropov

Glasnost and Perestroika

When 53-year-old Mikhail Gorbachev announced his policies of *glasnost* (openness) and *perestroika* (restructuring) after taking over in 1985, he had no idea of what would follow. The elections for the Congress Peoples' Deputies in 1989 were the first free elections in the Soviet Union since 1917 and contained an element of genuine choice, with rebels such as Boris Yeltsin winning seats.

Mikhail Gorbachev

It was 1989 onwards that local elections brought nationalist candidates to power in the Soviet republics, and democrats to the major Russian city councils. By 1991, the Baltic Republics and a number of other republics had seceded from the Soviet Union. Economic crisis and rising criminality due to slack Soviet law and order led to Communist hardliners pressing for radical reforms to save the country.

In August 1991, die-hard Communists staged a coup against Gorbachev while he was on holiday in Crimea. Military tanks reached the Russian Parliament building in Moscow, declaring a state of emergency. But Yeltsin, then the President of the Russian Republic, led the popular protest against the coup along with the presidents of other Soviet republics. After three days of confrontation, the coup collapsed with the retreat of the Communist hardliners. Upon Gorbachev's return from house arrest in the Crimea, Yeltsin forced him to outlaw the Communist Party, and in December, the secession of Ukraine and Belarus marked the break-up of the Soviet Union. On December 25, Gorbachev resigned as president of a state which no longer existed; that evening, the Soviet flag was lowered over the Kremlin and replaced by the Russian tricolour.

Boris Yeltsin (1931–2007) defying the August Coup

Wild Capitalism

In January 1992, President Yeltsin lifted price controls on subsidized products, sending inflation soaring. Sixteen thousand state enterprises were privatized and citizens given vouchers to "invest" in them, even as wages went unpaid for months. This enabled speculators to buy vouchers for a pittance, thereby gaining ownership of invaluable assets. In Moscow, shoot-outs and car-bombings became common as rival mafia gangs battled over territory.

The social and economic meltdown of "wild capitalism" was exacerbated by a political deadlock between Yeltsin's arch-reformers in the Kremlin and the "red-brown" coalition of Communists and radical nationalists in parliament. The conflict

Chernobyl Nuclear Power plant

1985 Gorbachev becomes Soviet leader, espousing *glasnost* and *perestroika*

1986 Chernobyl reactor fire contaminates 1 million hectares of Belarus and Ukraine

1988 Estonia declares independence from the USSR, followed by Latvia and Lithuania

1989 First multi-candidate elections for Congress of People's Deputies

1990

1990 Boris Yeltsin declares Russian independence from the USSR

1991 Boris Yeltsin elected President of Russia; dissolution of the Soviet Union

1993 Conflict between Yeltsin and parliament climaxes in the bombardment of the Russian White House

1995

1996 Yeltsin re-elected president

2000 Vladimir Putin becomes President of Russia

2000

Vladimir Putin

climaxed in October 1993 when demonstrators descended on the Russian White House and took over the Mayor's offices. The army, on Yeltsin's orders, stormed the building and arrested the ringleaders bringing an end to the conflict.

In December 1994, the Kremlin embarked on a war in Chechnya to subdue the breakaway republic. This left the Chechen capital, Grozny, in ruins with 120,000 dead – including thousands of Russian conscripts. Yeltsin looked set to be defeated in the 1996 presidential election until Russia's financiers and journalists united behind him.

Once the Communist threat was dispelled, the financial oligarchs behind Yeltsin's re-election fell out over the spoils. Vladimir Potanin acquired 30 per cent of the world's nickel reserves for a mere US$70 million, while Boris Berezovsky, Vladimir Gusinsky, Roman Abramovich and Mikhail Khodorkovsky made similar fortunes from oil, gas, telecoms and the media.

Managed Democracy

By the late 1990s, the ailing Yeltsin needed a successor who could guarantee his family's security and wealth. His chosen heir was Vladimir Putin, an ex-KGB officer made acting prime minister shortly before a wave of apartment-block bombings that killed over 300 people in September 1999. Most Russians readily believed that Chechen terrorists were responsible and applauded Putin's vow to "wipe out terrorists wherever we find them – even on the toilet".

Within weeks, Russia launched a second war on Chechnya as Berezovsky's media empire went into overdrive, casting Putin as the resolute leader that Russia needed. Yeltsin's surprise resignation during his New Year message to the nation on the last night of the old millennium set the stage for Putin's inauguration as president in May 2000. Putin advocated a "strong vertical", appointing governors and mayors from the senior ranks of the armed forces and security services. He slaked the public thirst for vengeance against the oligarchs by forcing two into exile and sending another to a labour camp – but allowed the others to continue enriching themselves provided they courted his favour. The nexus of power and corruption forged in the 1990s reached its zenith in a "mafia state".

Vladimir Putin and Dmitri Medvedev at the Kremlin on 7 May 2008

Barred by the constitution from a third consecutive term, Putin became prime minister under a new president, Dmitri Medvedev, who pledged to make Russia "a law-based state", but nothing really changed. While Putin's decision to run again as president was expected, the blatantly rigged parliamentary elections of 2011 provoked a wave of protests that caught the Kremlin by surprise.

Although Putin claimed victory in the 2012 election, his "managed democracy" looked threadbare and few believe that another, fourth term as president is feasible.

2004 Chechen separatists seize school in Beslan; more than 300 left dead after special forces storm the building

Protests against election rigging

2005

2008 Putin becomes prime minister and Dmitri Medvedev president

2010

2011 Rigged elections provoke protests in major cities

2012 Putin claims victory in presidential election; ascribes protests to "foreign meddling"

2014 Winter Olympics in Sochi and Krasnaya Polyana

2015

2018 Russia to host the FIFA World Cup™

MOSCOW AREA BY AREA

Moscow at a Glance

The capital city of Russia, Moscow, lies at the heart of European Russia. Spread over an area of 2,510 sq km (970 sq miles), the city grew up around a hilltop citadel, or Kremlin. In medieval times, the adjacent quarter of Kitay Gorod was Moscow's commercial hub. In 1812, almost the entire city was burnt to the ground in a great fire, lit deliberately by Muscovites to deny Napoleon possession of the city. Home to around 10 million today, Moscow is a melange of beautiful pre-Revolutionary architecture and Communist landmarks from the Soviet era. Most of the sights are situated in the city centre, within the area bounded by the Garden Ring and the Boulevard Ring.

Locator Map

Bolshoi Theatre *(see pp82–3)* is Moscow's most iconic cultural landmark. Founded in 1776, the grand six-tiered auditorium stages excellent ballet and opera performances.

Garden Ring
(see pp76–93)

Pushkin State Museum of Fine Arts *(see pp90–91)* is renowned for its impressive collection of art. In addition to altarpieces by Botticelli and biblical scenes by Rembrandt, the museum houses German archaeologist Heinrich Schliemann's *Treasures of Troy* artifacts.

◀ Bronze monument to Minin and Pozharskiy at the entrance to St Basil's Cathedral, Moscow

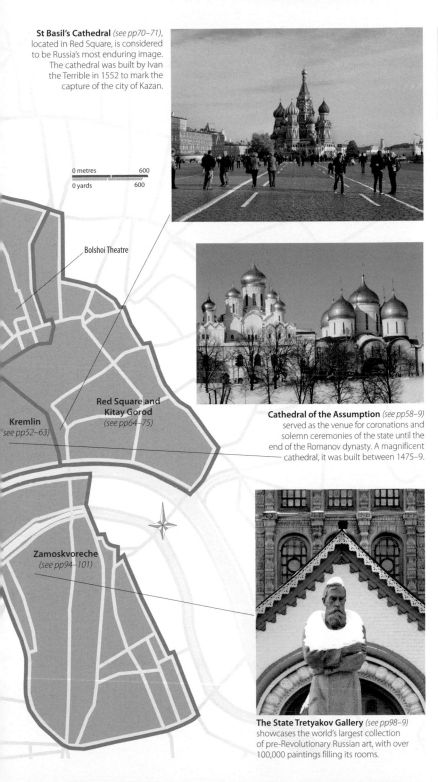

St Basil's Cathedral *(see pp70–71)*, located in Red Square, is considered to be Russia's most enduring image. The cathedral was built by Ivan the Terrible in 1552 to mark the capture of the city of Kazan.

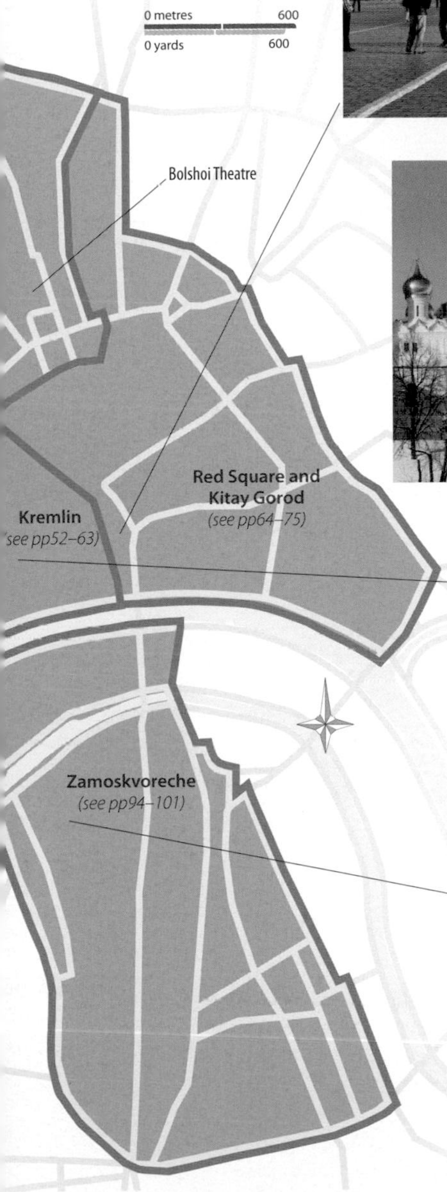

0 metres 600

0 yards 600

Bolshoi Theatre

Red Square and Kitay Gorod
(see pp64–75)

Kremlin
(see pp52–63)

Cathedral of the Assumption *(see pp58–9)* served as the venue for coronations and solemn ceremonies of the state until the end of the Romanov dynasty. A magnificent cathedral, it was built between 1475–9.

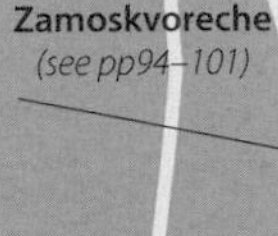

Zamoskvoreche
(see pp94–101)

The State Tretyakov Gallery *(see pp98–9)* showcases the world's largest collection of pre-Revolutionary Russian art, with over 100,000 paintings filling its rooms.

THE KREMLIN

Citadel of the tsars, headquarters of the Soviet Union and now residence of the Russian president, the Kremlin has been a symbol of the power of the State for centuries. In 1156, Prince Yuri Dolgorukiy chose the confluence of the Moskva and Neglinnaya rivers as the site for the first wooden kremlin (*kreml* means fortress). Later, in the 15th century, Tsar Ivan the Great organized a large-scale reconstruction project, inviting several Italian masters to build a sumptuous new complex. They designed the present magnificent ensemble of cathedrals and the Faceted Chamber, among other buildings, in a fascinating fusion of early-Russian and Renaissance styles. Unfortunately, the Kremlin could not escape the architectural vandalism of the 1930s, when it was closed and several of its churches and palaces were destroyed on Stalin's orders. Only in 1955, two years after his death, was the Kremlin partially reopened to the public.

Sights at a Glance

Churches and Cathedrals

6 *Cathedral of the Assumption pp58–9*
7 Cathedral of the Archangel
8 Cathedral of the Annunciation
10 Church of Laying Our Lady's Holy Robe

Museums

3 Patriarch's Palace
13 *Armoury Chamber pp62–3*

Historic Buildings and Monuments

1 Trinity Tower
2 State Kremlin Palace
4 Tsar Cannon
5 Ivan the Great Bell Tower
9 Grand Kremlin Palace
11 Terem Palace
12 Faceted Chamber

Gardens

14 Alexander Gardens

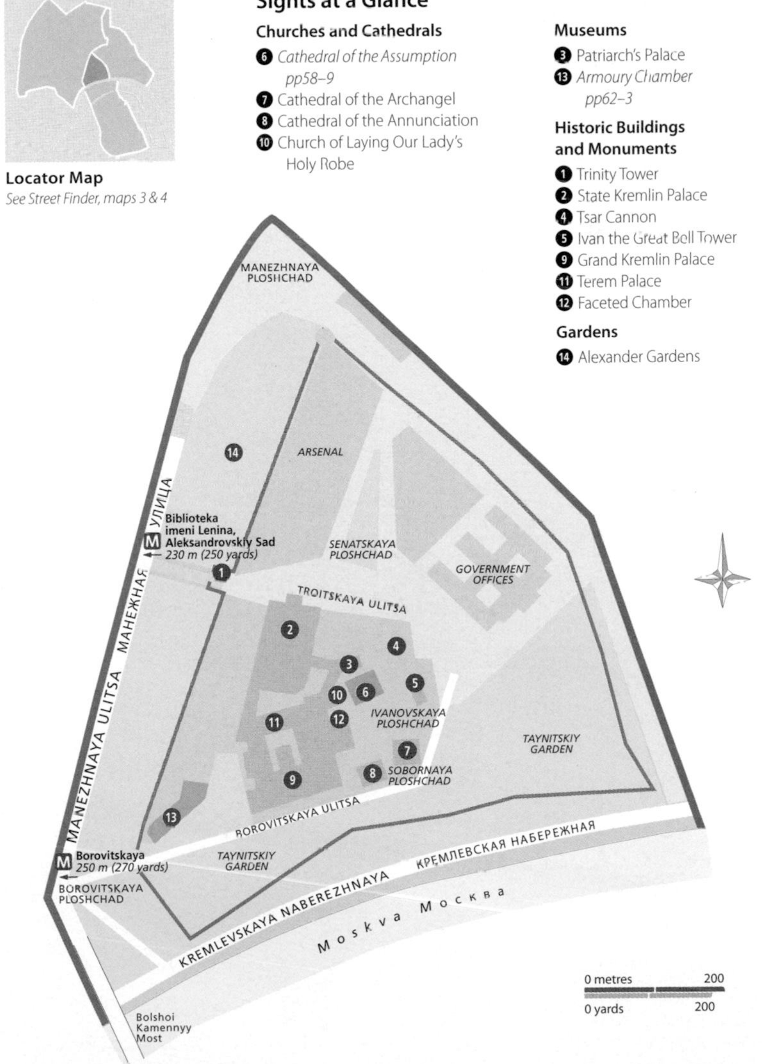

Locator Map
See Street Finder, maps 3 & 4

For map symbols *see back flap*

Street by Street: The Kremlin

The Kremlin is home to the Russian president and is the seat of his administration. As a result, less than half of it is accessible to the public, but highlights including the Armoury Chamber, the Patriarch's Palace and the churches in Cathedral Square are open to visitors. Christians have worshipped at this site for more than eight centuries, but their early stone churches were demolished in the 1470s to make way for the present magnificent ensemble of cathedrals. In imperial times, these were the settings for great state occasions such as coronations, baptisms and burials.

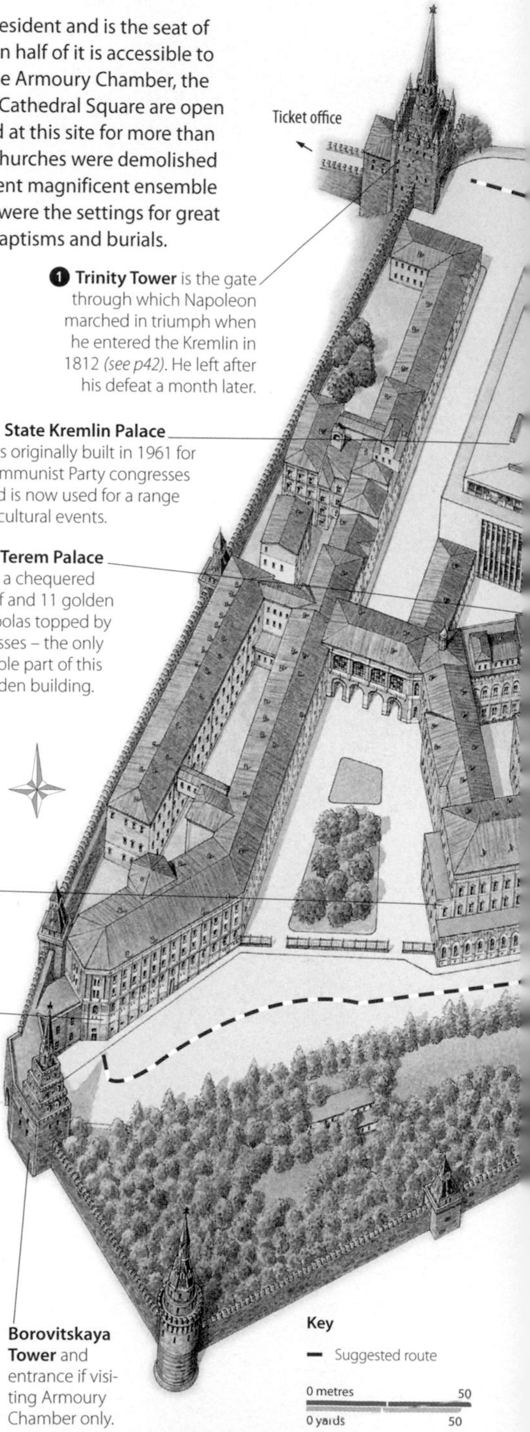

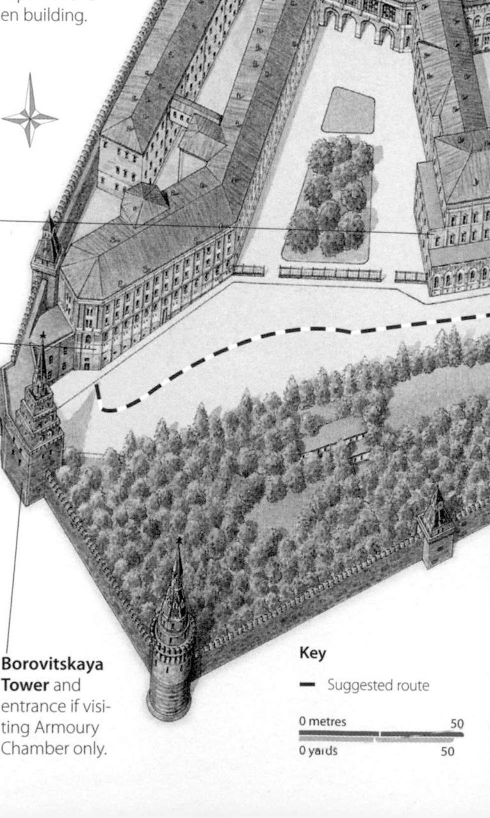

❶ Trinity Tower is the gate through which Napoleon marched in triumph when he entered the Kremlin in 1812 *(see p42)*. He left after his defeat a month later.

❷ State Kremlin Palace was originally built in 1961 for Communist Party congresses and is now used for a range of cultural events.

⓫ Terem Palace has a chequered roof and 11 golden cupolas topped by crosses – the only visible part of this hidden building.

❾ Grand Kremlin Palace
The palace contains several vast ceremonial halls. The sumptuous stucco work of St George's Hall provides a magnificent backdrop for state receptions. Its marble walls are inscribed with the names of military heroes.

⓭ ★ Armoury Chamber
The Armoury Chamber was designed by Konstantin Ton to complement the Grand Kremlin Palace. Constructed in 1844–51, the building is now a museum. It houses the stunning imperial collections of decorative and applied art and the priceless State Diamond Fund.

Borovitskaya Tower and entrance if visiting Armoury Chamber only.

Key

— Suggested route

0 metres 50

0 yards 50

⑩ Church of Laying Our Lady's Holy Robe
This served as the domestic church of the metropolitans and patriarchs.

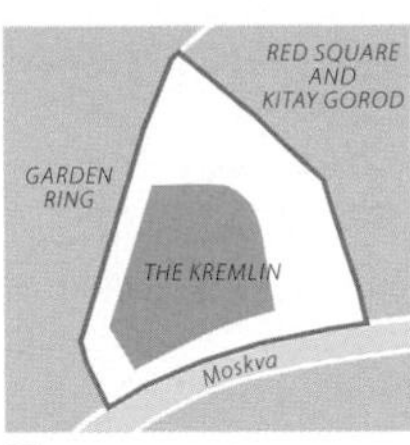

Area illustrated

③ Patriarch's Palace was rebuilt for Patriarch Nikon in 1652–6, and now houses the Museum of 17th-century Life and Applied Art.

Church of the Twelve Apostles *(see p56)*

④ Tsar Cannon, cast in 1586, weighs a massive 40 tonnes (44 tons).

⑤ Ivan the Great Bell Tower became the tallest building in Russia after a third storey was added to this beautiful octagonal tower in 1600.

⑥ ★ Cathedral of the Assumption
This 12th-century painting of St George the Warrior is one of the oldest surviving Russian icons. It forms part of the iconostasis in the cathedral's richly decorated interior.

⑦ Cathedral of the Archangel has many elaborate tombs including that of Tsarevich Dmitri, the younger son of Ivan the Terrible.

Cathedral Square

⑫ Faceted Chamber was constructed by two Italian architects, Marco Ruffo and Pietro Solario, between 1485 and 1491.

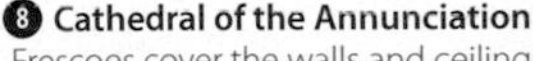

⑧ Cathedral of the Annunciation
Frescoes cover the walls and ceiling of this cathedral. In the dome above the iconostasis is a painting of Christ Pantokrator, above tiers of pictures of angels, prophets and patriarchs.

❶ Trinity Tower

Троицкая башня
Troitskaya bashnya

The Kremlin. **Map** 3 C1.

This tower is named after the Trinity Monastery of St Sergius *(see p114)*. The tower's Trinity Gate was once the entrance for patriarchs and the tsars' wives and daughters. At 76 m (249 ft), the Trinity Tower is the Kremlin's tallest. Built in 1495–9, it was linked by a bridge over the Neglinnaya river to the Kutafya Tower – the sole survivor of the circle of towers that was originally built to defend the Kremlin walls. In September 1812, Napoleon marched his army into the Kremlin through the Trinity Gate – they left only a month later when the Russians set fire to the city.

The seven-storey Trinity Tower, the tallest tower in the Kremlin

❷ State Kremlin Palace

Государственный Кремлёвский дворец
Gosudarstvennyy Kremlevskiy dvorets

The Kremlin. **Map** 3 C1. **Open** for performances only.

Sunk 15 m (49 ft) into the ground so as not to dwarf the surrounding buildings, the State Kremlin Palace is the Kremlin's only modern building. It was built in 1961 to host Communist Party conferences. Today, its 6,000-seat auditorium is a venue for operas and rock concerts.

❸ Patriarch's Palace

Патриарший дворец
Patriarshiy dvorets

The Kremlin. **Map** 4 D1. **Open** 10am–5pm Fri–Wed.

The metropolitans of the Russian Orthodox Church lived on the site of the current Patriarch's Palace for many years. When Nikon became the patriarch in 1652, he had the residence extended and renovated to create the Patriarch's Palace, with its integral Church of the Twelve Apostles. The palace now houses the Museum of 17th-century Life and Applied Art, displaying more than 1,000 exhibits drawn from the Armoury Chamber collection *(see pp62–3)* and from churches and monasteries that were destroyed by Stalin in the 1930s.

Entry to the museum is up a flight of stairs. To the left is the Cross Chamber; when built, it was the largest room in Russia without columns supporting its roof. Consecrated oil called *miro* was produced here and the silver vats and ornate stove used in its production can still be seen.

Located to the right of the stairs, the Church of the Twelve Apostles houses some brilliant icons, including works by Simon Ushakov (1626–86). The iconostasis dates from around 1700 and was brought to the church from the Kremlin Convent of the Ascension before it was demolished in 1929.

The Gala Antechamber has a dazzling array of 17th-century patriarchs' robes, including some of Nikon's own vestments as well as regalia.

The grandiose Patriarch's Palace, former residence of Patriarch Nikon (1605–81)

❹ Tsar Cannon

Царь-пушка
Tsar-pushka

The Kremlin. **Map** 4 D1.

Cast in 1586, the Tsar Cannon is one of the largest cannons ever made; its bronze barrel weighs 40 tonnes (44 tons) and has a calibre of 89 cm (35 inches). It was originally intended to guard the Saviour's Tower, but has only ever been used to blast the ashes of the False Dmitri *(see p40)* back towards Poland.

❺ Ivan the Great Bell Tower

Колокольня Ивана Великого
Kolokolnya Ivana Velikovo

The Kremlin. **Map** 4 D1.

Built to a design by Marco Bon Friazin, this 16th-century bell tower takes its name from the Church of St Ivan Climacus, which stood here in the 14th century. It became the tallest building in Moscow in 1600 when Tsar Boris Godunov added a third storey, extending it to a height of 81m (266 ft).

The massive Tsar Cannon, decorated with reliefs

Beside the tower rises the Assumption Belfry, with its single gilded dome, built in 1532–43. It holds 21 bells, the largest of which, the 64-tonne (71-ton) Assumption Bell, was traditionally tolled three times when the tsar died.

Tsar Bell, the largest bell in the world

The colossal Tsar Bell, weighing over 200 tonnes (221 tons), stands at the foot of the bell tower. When the original bell fell from the tower and shattered in a fire in 1701, the fragments were used in a second bell, which was still in its casting pit when the Kremlin caught fire again in 1737. When cold water was poured over the hot bell, a large piece, displayed beside the bell, broke off.

❻ Cathedral of the Assumption

See pp58–9.

❼ Cathedral of the Archangel

Архангельский собор

Arkhangelskiy sobor

The Kremlin. **Map** 4 D1.

Commissioned by Ivan the Great shortly before his death in 1505, this was the last of the great cathedrals to be built in the Kremlin. Its Venetian architect, Aleviz Novyy, incorporated elements from early-Russian and Italian Renaissance architecture in its design. The cathedral served as the burial place for Moscow's tsars, whose white stone sarcophagi with bronze covers fill the nave. The tsars were no longer buried here after the capital city was moved to St Petersburg in 1712, with the exception of Peter II, who died of smallpox in Moscow in 1730.

The walls, pillars and domes of the cathedral are covered with frescoes painted in 1652–66 by a team of artists led by Simon Ushakov. There are over 60 full-length portraits of Russian rulers, and some images of the Archangel Michael, traditionally the protector of the early Muscovite rulers. The fresco in the central cupola depicts the triune God. The Father holds the Son on his lap and the Holy Spirit, in the form of a white dove, hovers nearby. The cathedral's four-tiered iconostasis was built in 1680–81.

❽ Cathedral of the Annunciation

Благовещенский собор

Blagoveshchenskiy sobor

The Kremlin. **Map** 4 D1.

Unlike the other Kremlin cathedrals, which were created by Italians, this cathedral is a wholly Russian affair. Ivan the Great commissioned it in 1484 as a royal chapel. It originally had open galleries on all sides but, after a fire in 1547 the corner chapels were added and the galleries were enclosed. On the south façade is the Groznenskiy Porch, from which Ivan the Terrible watched religious services through a grille. He was barred from attending them, having contravened church law by marrying for the fourth time.

The interior of the cathedral is painted with frescoes in warm colours, creating an atmosphere of intimacy. The vertical thrust of the pillars draws the eye upwards to the cupola and its awe-inspiring painting of Christ Pantokrator (Christ as Ruler of All). Three of Russia's greatest icon painters contributed to the iconostasis. Theophanes the Greek painted the images of Christ, the Virgin and the Archangel Gabriel; Andrey Rublev, *The Icon of the Archangel Michael*, *The Annunciation* and *The Nativity*; and Prokhor Gorodetskiy, *The Last Supper* and *The Crucifixion*.

The golden onion-shaped domes of the Cathedral of the Annunciation

❻ Cathedral of the Assumption

Успенский собор

Uspenskiy sobor

From the early 14th century, the Cathedral of the Assumption was the most important church in Moscow. It was here that princes were crowned and the metropolitans and patriarchs of the Orthodox Church were buried. In the 1470s, Ivan the Great decided to build a cathedral to reflect the growing might of the nation during his reign. When the first version collapsed, possibly in an earthquake, Ivan summoned the architect Aristotele Fioravanti to Moscow, who designed a spacious masterpiece in the spirit of the Renaissance.

★ Frescoes
In 1642–4, a team of artists headed by Sidor Pospeev and Ivan and Boris Paisein painted these frescoes. The walls of the cathedral were first gilded to give the look of an illuminated manuscript.

KEY

① **The tabernacle** contains holy relics including the remains of Patriarch Hermogen, who starved to death in 1612 during the Polish invasion.

② **Metropolitans' and patriarchs' tombs** line the walls of the nave and the crypt. Almost all the leaders of the Russian Orthodox Church are buried in the cathedral.

③ **The Tsarina's Throne** (17th–19th centuries) is gilded and has a double-headed eagle crest.

④ **The iconostasis** dates from 1652. The haunting 14th-century *Icon of the Saviour Not Made With Hands* is one of several icons forming part of the glorious iconostasis.

⑤ **Orthodox cross**

⑥ **The golden domes** stand on towers inset with windows, which allow light to flood into the interior of the cathedral.

⑦ **Frescoes in the central dome**

⑧ **The pillars** that stand in the centre of the cathedral are painted with over 100 figures of canonized martyrs and warriors.

⑨ **Royal gate**

⑩ **The Harvest Chandelier** contains silver recovered from the French after their occupation of the city in 1812 *(see p42)*.

⑪ **The Patriarch's Seat** was carved from white stone in 1653 for use by the head of the Russian Orthodox Church.

⑫ **Monomakh Throne**

★ Scenes from the Life of Metropolitan Peter
This 15th-century icon was made in the workshop of the artist Dionysius, albeit not by the master himself. Located on the cathedral's southern wall, it depicts events in the life of the religious and political leader.

VISITORS' CHECKLIST

Practical information
The Kremlin.
Map 4 D1.
kreml.ru
Open 10am–5pm Fri–Wed. religious holidays.

Transport
6, K. Alexandrovskiy sad, Biblioteka imeni Lenina, Borovitskaya. 1, 2, 12, 16, 33.

The Monomakh Throne

The royal seat of Ivan the Terrible is decorated with carvings relating the exploits of Prince Vladimir Monomakh (1053–1125). The panels depict his military campaigns and one shows him receiving the crown from the Byzantine Emperor Constantine Monomachus. This legend was used to confer legitimacy to the idea that the Russian monarchs were the heirs to Byzantium.

Inscribed legend of Prince Vladimir

Panels depicting scenes from Vladimir's life

7 8 9 10 11 12

South Portal
This splendid arched portal, decorated with 17th-century frescoes, was the entrance used for royal processions. Brought to Moscow from Suzdal *(see p116)* in 1401, the door's reverse side is engraved with scenes from the Bible.

❾ Grand Kremlin Palace

Большой Кремлёвский дворец
Bolshoy Kremlyovskiy Dvorets

The Kremlin. **Map** 3 C1. **Closed** to public.

The grand 125-m (410-ft) façade of this yellow-and-white palace is best admired from the Kremlin embankment. Built to replace an 18th-century palace that previously stood on the site, the Grand Kremlin Palace became the Moscow residence of the royal family. Built between 1837 and 1849, it was designed by a team of architects led by Konstantin Ton *(see p33)*. Ton's design integrated the Terem Palace and Faceted Chamber with the new palace, creating a single complex.

On the ground floor are the private rooms of the royal family, which are offered to visiting heads-of-state. The first-floor state chambers include many ceremonial halls. The St George's Hall has white walls engraved in gold with the names of those awarded the Order of St George, one of Russia's highest military decorations. Grander still is the green and gold St Andrew's Hall, named after the supreme award in the Tsarist Empire, bestowed in post-Soviet times on the Nobel Laureate Alexander Solzhenitsyn, and the inventor of the AK-47 rifle, Mikhail Kalashnikov. Today, the palace serves as the Russian President's residence.

Four of the eleven ornate domes of the Terem Palace churches

❿ Church of Laying Our Lady's Holy Robe

Церковь Ризоположения
Tserkov' Rizopolozheniya

The Kremlin. **Map** 4 D1.

Crowned by a single golden dome, this church was built in 1484–5 by architects from Pskov *(see pp210–11)*. It is named after a Byzantine feast day that celebrates the arrival, in Constantinople, of a robe supposed to have belonged to the Virgin Mary. The robe is believed to have saved the city from invasion several times.

The church's exterior has distinctive ogee arches shaped like the cross-section of an onion, a feature of many Russian churches from this period and a favourite device of the Pskov school of architecture. Inside the church, the walls and columns are covered with 17th-century frescoes depicting scenes from the lives of the Virgin, Christ, the prophets, royalty and the Moscow metropolitans. The impressive iconostasis created by Nazariy Istomin dates from 1627. To the left of the royal gate is a splendid image of the Trinity, and the *Icon of the Laying of the Virgin's Holy Robe* is to the right.

⓫ Terem Palace

Теремной дворец
Teremnoy dvorets

The Kremlin. **Map** 3 C1. **Closed** to public.

Built beside the Faceted Chamber in 1635–6, at the behest of Tsar Mikhail Romanov, the palace takes its name from the *terem*, a pavilion-like structure with a red-and-white chequered roof atop the main building. Here, royal wives and concubines were secluded in small, low-vaulted, simply furnished rooms. The tsar had five sumptuous rooms situated on the third floor of the palace, where he selected his bride from a group of virgins ostensibly asleep on eiderdowns, in a ritual known as the *smotriniy* (viewing).

Impressive façade of the Grand Kremlin Palace, as seen from the Kremlin walls

Magnificent vaulted ceiling of the main hall, Faceted Chamber

The anteroom, where *boyars* and foreign dignitaries waited to be received, leads into the council chamber, where the tsar held these meetings. Beyond this are the throne room, the tsar's bedchamber and a small prayer room.

As a constituent building of the Grand Kremlin Palace, the Terem Palace is part of the residence of the Russian President. Most of the spectacular palace is not visible from the areas of the Kremlin to which the public have access. The eleven ornately decorated, gilded onion domes of the four palace churches, at one end of the palace, are all that can be seen.

⓬ Faceted Chamber

Грановитая палата

Granovitaya palata

The Kremlin. **Map** 4 D1. **Closed** to public.

Named after its distinctive stonework façade, the Faceted Chamber is all that is left of a larger 15th-century royal palace. It was commissioned by Ivan the Great in 1485, designed by two Italian architects, Marco Ruffo and Pietro Solario, and built over a period of six years. The chamber's first floor comprises the vaulted main hall and adjoining Sacred Vestibule, both decorated with rich frescoes and gilded carvings. With an area of about 500 sq m (5,380 sq ft), the main hall was the tsars' throne room and banquet hall. Today, it serves as a venue for diplomatic receptions.

On the chamber's southern façade is the Red Staircase. Monarchs passed down this ceremonial staircase en route to the Cathedral of the Assumption *(see pp58–9)* for their coronations. The last such procession was at the coronation of Nicholas II in 1896. During the Streltsy Revolt of 1682 *(see p41)*, many of Peter the Great's relatives were hurled down the Red Staircase on to the pikes of the Streltsy guard. Demolished by Stalin in the 1930s, the staircase was rebuilt in 1994 at great expense.

⓭ Armoury Chamber

See pp62–3.

⓮ Alexander Gardens

Александровский сад

Aleksandrovskiy sad

The Kremlin. **Map** 3 C1.

These gardens are named after Tsar Alexander I, who presided over the restoration of the city after the Napoleonic Wars. Before they were laid out in 1821, the Neglinnaya river, part of the Kremlin moat, was channelled underground. The only reminder of its presence is a stone bridge linking the Kremlin's Kutafya and Trinity towers.

An obelisk erected in 1913 in the Upper Garden marks 300 years of the Romanov dynasty. After the 1917 October Revolution, its imperial eagle was removed and the inscription was replaced by the names of thinkers such as Karl Marx and Friedrich Engels.

A short distance away is the marble Tomb of the Unknown Soldier, unveiled in 1967. Its eternal flame, lit with a torch kindled at the Field of Mars in St Petersburg, burns for all the Russians who died in World War II. The body of a nameless soldier is buried beneath the monument, which is inscribed with the words, "Your name is unknown, your deeds immortal".

To the north of the gardens, whimsical statues based on Russian fairy tales such as the *The Frog Princess* welcome visitors to an underground shopping mall. It was opened in 1996 as part of Mayor Yuri Luzhkov's campaign to re-brand Moscow as an affluent, fun-loving metropolis.

Relaxing in Alexander Gardens, one of the first public parks in Moscow

⓭ Armoury Chamber

Оружейная палата

Oruzheynaya palata

The collection of the Armoury Chamber represents the wealth accumulated by Russian princes and tsars over many centuries. The first mention of a state armoury occurs in 1508, but there were forges in the Kremlin producing weapons and armour as early as the 13th century. Later, gold- and silversmiths, workshops producing icons and embroidery and the Office of the Royal Stables all moved into the Kremlin. The original armoury was demolished in 1960 to make way for the State Kremlin Palace. The current state armoury was built as a museum on the orders of Nicholas I. It was designed by Konstantin Ton in 1844 and completed in 1851.

★ Fabergé Eggs
This egg, also a musical box, was made in 1904 in the St Petersburg workshops of the famous House of Fabergé. The egg forms part of a stylized model of the Kremlin.

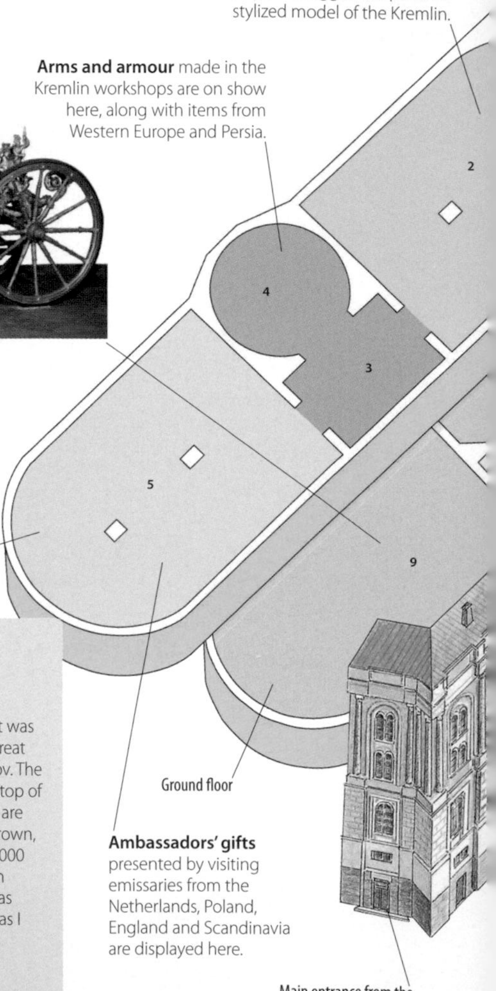

Arms and armour made in the Kremlin workshops are on show here, along with items from Western Europe and Persia.

Carriages and Sledges
This magnificent collection includes the beautiful gilded summer carriage presented to Catherine the Great by Count Orlov. The oldest carriage displayed in this collection was a gift from King James I of England to Boris Godunov.

2

4

3

5

9

First floor

Ground floor

Ambassadors' gifts presented by visiting emissaries from the Netherlands, Poland, England and Scandinavia are displayed here.

Main entrance from the Kremlin grounds

The State Diamond Fund

This dazzling exhibition of diamonds, crowns, jewellery and state regalia includes the famous Orlov Diamond. Taken from an Indian temple, it was one of many presents given to Catherine the Great by her lover Count Grigori Orlov. The tsarina had it mounted at the top of her sceptre. Also on show are Catherine's imperial crown, inset with almost 5,000 gems, and the Shah Diamond, which was given to Tsar Nicholas I by Shah Mirza.

Great Imperial Crown, made for Catherine the Great's coronation

★ Crown of Monomakh
Emperor Constantine Monomachus was said to have given this 13th- or 14th-century gold crown to Vladimir Monomakh. Decorated with sable and gems, it was used at royal coronations until 1682.

Catherine the Great's Coronation Dress is among the many richly decorated clothes from the royal court on display. An ornate brocade gown embroidered with double-headed eagles in gold thread, it was made in 1762 for the queen's coronation.

VISITORS' CHECKLIST

Practical information
The Kremlin.
Map 3 C1.
Tel (495) 697 03 49.
Open admittance at 10am, noon, 2:30pm and 4:30pm Fri–Wed.
English, call (495) 697 41 15 to book.
State Diamond Fund: **Tel** (495) 621 86 20. **Open** 10am–1pm and 2–5pm Fri–Wed.
English.

Transport
M Alexandrovskiy sad, Biblioteka imeni Lenina, Borovitskaya.

Stairs to first floor

Stairs to ground floor

1

6

Precious fabrics encrusted with jewels and garments worn by the tsars are on display here.

★ Anna of Russia's Coronation Dress
It was in this dress that Anna Ioannovna, niece of Peter the Great, was crowned the Empress of Russia in 1730. Although the original pink colour of the dress has faded due to exposure to light over time, it remains preserved in the folds.

State Diamond Fund entrance

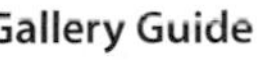

Gallery Guide

Tickets for the Armoury Chamber are sold at the Kremlin's main ticket office near Trinity Tower. If visiting in conjunction with other sights in the Kremlin, continue through the Trinity Tower. If only visiting the Armoury Chamber halls, entry is via the Borovitskaya Tower. The State Diamond Fund, a separate museum, is housed within this building.

Key to Floorplan

- Russian gold and silver
- Arms and armour
- Works by European craftsmen
- Russian dress and fabrics
- Carriages and harnesses
- State regalia
- Non-exhibition space

Harnesses and other equipment, originally produced for the Office of the Royal Stables, can be seen here.

Diamond Throne
Made in Persia in 1659, this throne was presented to Tsar Alexis by an Armenian trading company. It is encrusted with 900 diamonds and turquoises and is the most valuable throne in the collection.

ΜΡ ΘΥ

RED SQUARE AND KITAY GOROD

Moscow's first suburb, Kitay Gorod was settled in the 12th century by tradesmen and artisans employed by the tsar. In fact, the word *kitay* is thought to refer to the wattle used to build the ramparts around the suburb. Red Square was created as a market square beside the Kremlin in the late 15th century. Behind it, trading rows were set up, each line of wooden cabins specializing in a particular item, such as icons, pans or hats. In the 16th century, a number of *boyars*, including the Romanovs, built their estates nearby, while the presence of merchants from Novgorod and as far away as England was actively encouraged. Later, in the 19th century, Kitay Gorod became Moscow's financial district, home to the city's first stock exchange and major banks.

Sights at a Glance

Churches and Cathedrals

3 Kazan Cathedral
6 *St Basil's Cathedral pp70–71*
10 Church of the Trinity in Nikitniki

Museums

4 Lenin Mausoleum
9 Palace of the Romanov Boyars
14 Polytechnical Museum
15 Mayakovsky Museum

Streets and Squares

1 Red Square
7 Ulitsa Varvarka
11 Ulitsa Ilinka
12 Nikolskaya Ulitsa
13 Lubyanka Square

Historic Buildings and Monuments

2 Resurrection Gate
5 GUM
8 Old English Court
16 Sandunovskiy Baths

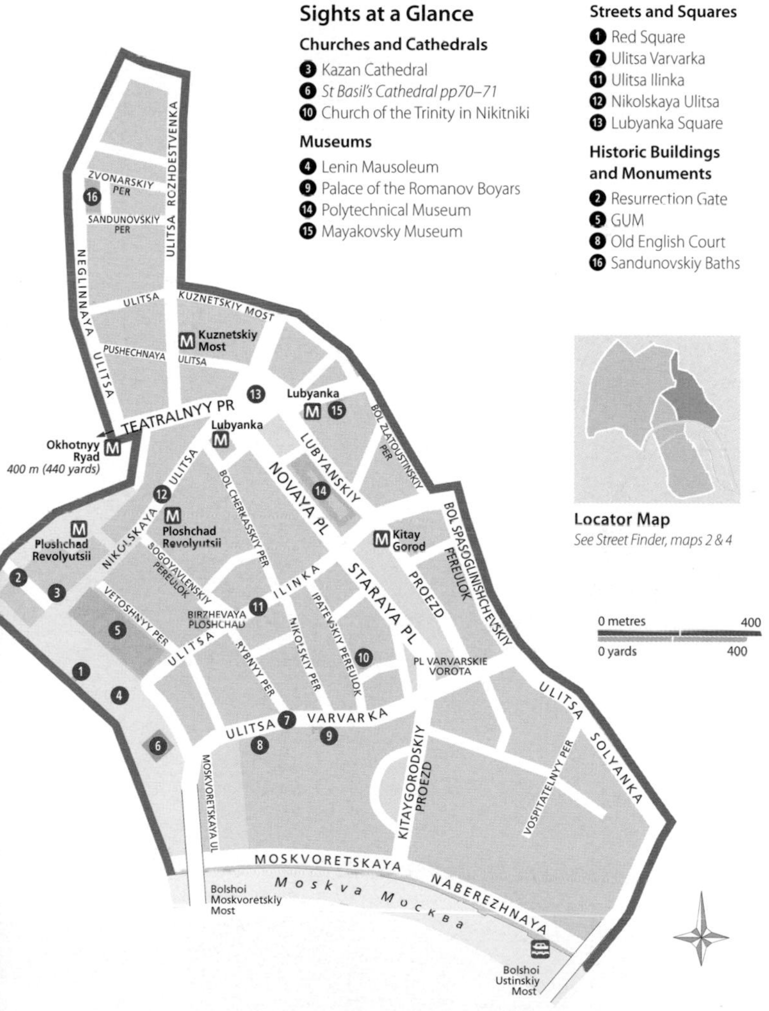

◀ *Kokoshniki* (tiered gables) adorning the façade of Kazan Cathedral, Red Square

Street-by-Street: Kitay Gorod

Commerce and religion go hand-in-hand in this ancient part of the city. The heart of Moscow's financial district is Birzhevaya ploshchad, and the surrounding area has been home to traders for centuries. Among the banks and offices are numerous upmarket stores, especially lining Nikolskaya ulitsa, and the area now rivals Russia's best-known shopping arcade, GUM. At one time there were more than 40 churches and monasteries dotted about these narrow streets. Only around a dozen have survived and most of these are now undergoing painstaking restoration.

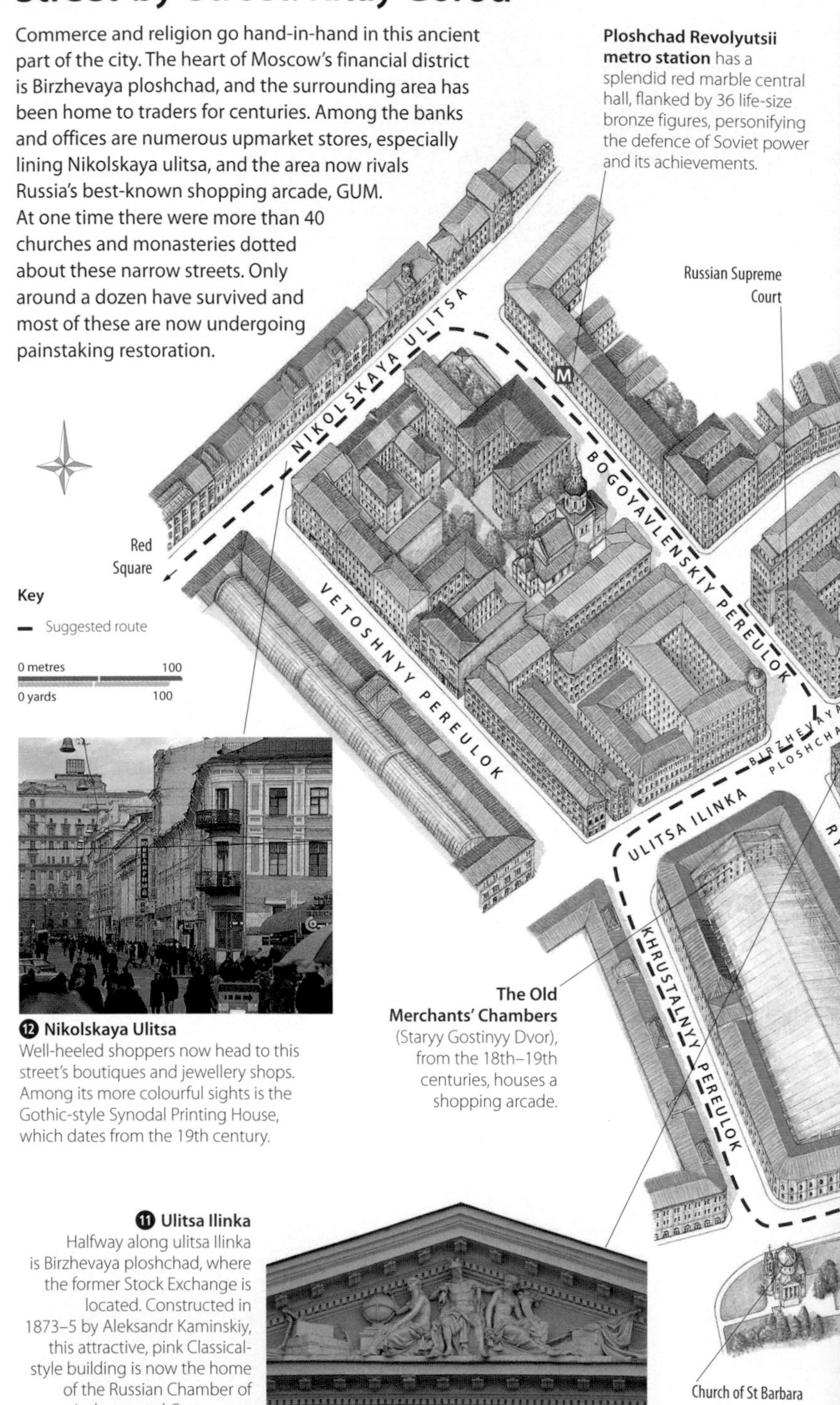

Ploshchad Revolyutsii metro station has a splendid red marble central hall, flanked by 36 life-size bronze figures, personifying the defence of Soviet power and its achievements.

Key

— Suggested route

0 metres 100

0 yards 100

⓬ Nikolskaya Ulitsa
Well-heeled shoppers now head to this street's boutiques and jewellery shops. Among its more colourful sights is the Gothic-style Synodal Printing House, which dates from the 19th century.

The Old Merchants' Chambers (Staryy Gostinyy Dvor), from the 18th–19th centuries, houses a shopping arcade.

⓫ Ulitsa Ilinka
Halfway along ulitsa Ilinka is Birzhevaya ploshchad, where the former Stock Exchange is located. Constructed in 1873–5 by Aleksandr Kaminskiy, this attractive, pink Classical-style building is now the home of the Russian Chamber of Industry and Commerce.

For hotels and restaurants in this area see p266 and p280

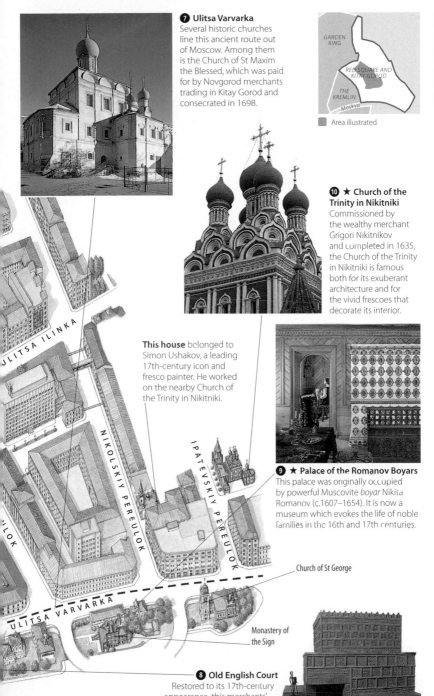

7 Ulitsa Varvarka
Several historic churches line this ancient route out of Moscow. Among them is the Church of St Maxim the Blessed, which was paid for by Novgorod merchants trading in Kitay Gorod and consecrated in 1698.

Area illustrated

10 ★ Church of the Trinity in Nikitniki
Commissioned by the wealthy merchant Grigori Nikitnikov and completed in 1635, the Church of the Trinity in Nikitniki is famous both for its exuberant architecture and for the vivid frescoes that decorate its interior.

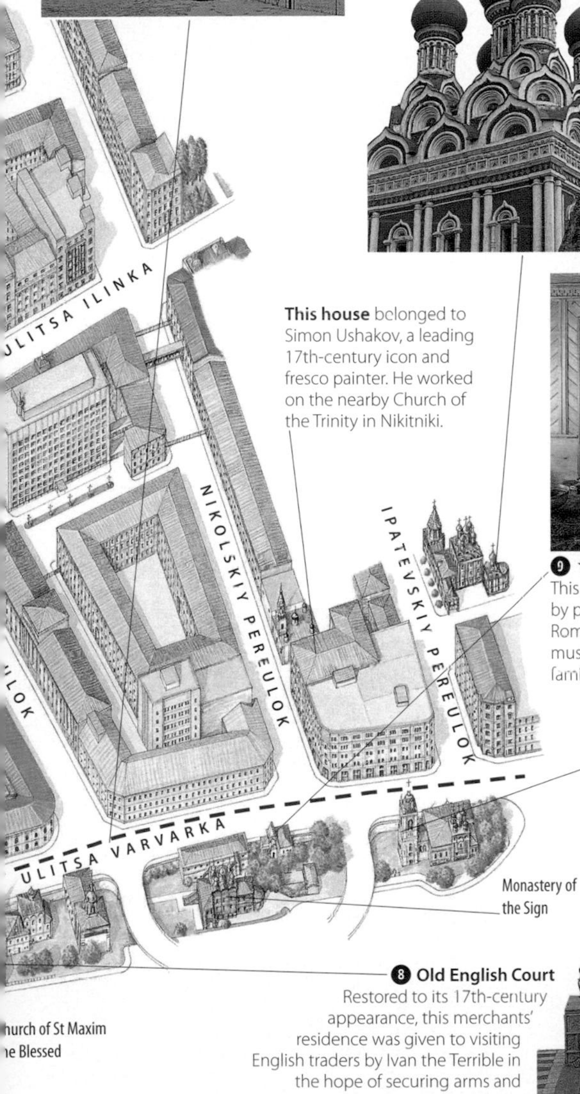

This house belonged to Simon Ushakov, a leading 17th-century icon and fresco painter. He worked on the nearby Church of the Trinity in Nikitniki.

9 ★ Palace of the Romanov Boyars
This palace was originally occupied by powerful Muscovite *boyar* Nikita Romanov (c.1607–1654). It is now a museum which evokes the life of noble families in the 16th and 17th centuries.

Church of St George

Monastery of the Sign

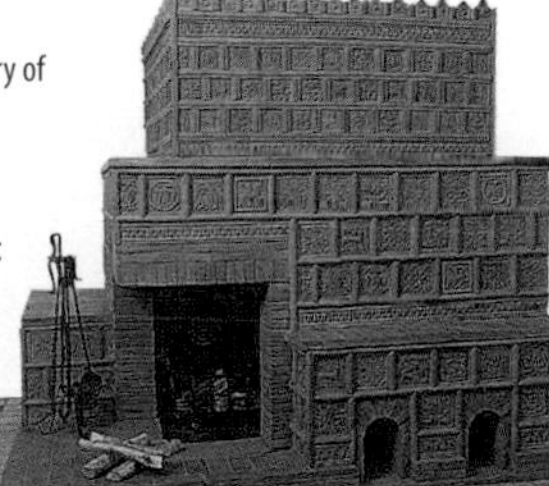

8 Old English Court
Restored to its 17th-century appearance, this merchants' residence was given to visiting English traders by Ivan the Terrible in the hope of securing arms and other goods from them.

hurch of St Maxim
he Blessed

Krasnaya ploshchad, or Red Square, with the Historical Museum at its far end

❶ Red Square

Красная площадь

Krasnaya ploshchad

Map 4 D1. Ⓜ Ploshchad Revolyutsii, Okhotnyy Ryad. Historical Museum: **Tel** (495) 692 40 19. **Open** 10am–6pm Mon, Wed & Fri–Sun, 11am–8pm Thu. **Closed** first Mon of the month.

Originally a marketplace, this area was popularly known as Fire Square due to frequent fires in its wooden stalls. The current name, Krasnaya ploshchad, dates from the 17th century and derives from the Russian word *krasnyy*, which originally meant "beautiful" but later came to denote "red". The coincidental association between the colour and Communism was fortuitous for Russia's Soviet rulers.

The square is approximately 500 m (1,600 ft) in length, with a slight curvature from one end to another, as it slopes towards the river. From the 14th century onwards, this was the setting for public announcements and executions, which were staged on a stone dais called the Lobnoe Mesto.

Red Square

Resurrection Gate
Kazan Cathedral
Red Square
GUM
Lenin Mausoleum
Lobnoe Mesto
St Basil's Cathedral

It was from this dais that tsars addressed the people, and patriarchs blessed the faithful on Palm Sunday. In the Soviet era, however, religious processions were abolished and military parades were staged instead. On May Day and the anniversary of the Revolution, the line-up of Soviet leaders atop the Lenin Mausoleum was studied by foreign "kremlinologists", trying to work out the pecking order within the regime. During the revolutionary utopianism of the 1920s, Futurists dreamt of erecting a 396-m (1,300-ft) high Monument to the Third International on the square, while Stalin later envisaged destroying its most famous landmark, St Basil's Cathedral *(see pp70–71)*.

Today, the square is used for a variety of cultural events, concerts, firework displays and other public occasions. At its northern end is the redbrick **Historical Museum**, built by Vladimir Sherwood in the Russian-Revival style. Among its exhibits are a 5,000-year-old oak longboat, Scythian goldwork and Siberian funerary masks. Behind the museum on Manezhnaya ploshchad is an equestrian statue of Marshal Georgi Zhukov, the great Soviet commander. It was erected on the 50th anniversary of Russia's victory in World War II.

❷ Resurrection Gate

Воскресенские ворота

Voskresenskie vorota

Krasnaya ploshchad. **Map** 2 D5. Ⓜ Okhotnyy Ryad, Ploshchad Revolyutsii.

This gateway, with its twin red towers topped by green tent spires, is a copy of the 17th-century original, which Stalin demolished to make Red Square more accessible for tanks and marchers. Rebuilt in the 1990s, the gateway is notable for both its mosaic icons – one of which depicts Moscow's patron saint, St George, slaying the dragon – and the colourful Chapel of the Iverian Virgin inside. Whenever the tsar came to Moscow, he would visit this shrine before entering the Kremlin. Visitors should try to see the gate at night, when it is impressively lit up.

❸ Kazan Cathedral

Казанский собор

Kazanskiy sobor

Nikolskaya ulitsa 3. **Map** 2 D5. Ⓜ Okhotnyy Ryad.

Besides the Resurrection Gate, Stalin also demolished the 17th-century Kazan Cathedral. A heroic architect, Pyotr Baranovskiy secretly made plans to rebuild it even as it was being pulled down. He is also known for saving St Basil's from a similar fate. Decades later, his detailed plans were used to faithfully reconstruct the cathedral, which was reconsecrated by Patriarch Aleksey II in 1993. The original cathedral housed the *Icon of the Kazan Virgin*, revered because it had accompanied Prince Dmitri Pozharskiy during his victorious campaign against the invading Poles in 1612. When the sacred icon was stolen in 1904, the Russians saw it as a bad omen. The icon that is now on display in the cathedral is a copy.

Icon of the Kazan Virgin, Kazan Cathedral

❹ Lenin Mausoleum

Мавзолей ВИ Ленина

Mavzoley VI Lenina

Krasnaya ploshchad. **Map** 4 D1. Ⓜ Ploshchad Revolyutsii, Okhotnyy Ryad. **Open** 10am–1pm Tue–Thu, Sat & Sun.

Following Lenin's death in 1924, and against his wishes, it was decided to preserve the former Soviet leader's body for posterity. The body was embalmed and placed in a temporary wooden mausoleum in Red Square. Once it became clear that the embalming process had worked, Aleksey Shchusev designed the current mausoleum of a pyramid of cubes cut from red granite and black labradorite.

Paying one's respects to Lenin's remains was once akin to a religious experience and queues used to trail all over Red Square. Since 1993, however, a lone militiaman guards the mausoleum and it now attracts mostly tourists. Rumours that Lenin might be moved from the mausoleum have proved to be unfounded.

Behind the mausoleum at the foot of the Kremlin Wall are the graves of other famous Communists. They include Joseph Stalin, Leonid Brezhnev and Yuri Andropov. Lenin's wife and sister are also buried here, as are the first man in space, Yuri Gagarin, the novelist Maxim Gorky and the American journalist John Reed, honoured for his sympathetic account of the October Revolution in *Ten Days that Shook the World*.

Lenin Mausoleum, final resting place of the Russian leader

The impressive wrought-iron railings and walkways at GUM

❺ GUM

ГУМ

GUM

Krasnaya ploshchad 3. **Map** 4 D1. **Tel** (495) 788 43 43. Ⓜ Ploshchad Revolyutsii, Okhotnyy Ryad. **Open** 10am–10pm daily. **gum.ru**

Before the Revolution, this building was known as the Upper Trading Rows after the covered market that used to stand on the site. In fact, lines of stalls used to run all the way from here to the Moskva river. The store's name, Gosudarstvennyy Universalnyy Magazin, dates from its nationalization in 1921. The building was designed by Aleksandr Pomerantsev in 1889–93 in the Russian-Revival style, and the archways, wrought-iron railings and stuccoed galleries inside are especially impressive when sunlight streams through the glass roof.

There were once more than 1,000 shops here, selling goods ranging from furs and silks to humble candles. Nowadays, Western firms such as Armani, Max Mara and Dior dominate the ground floor along with a variety of cafés and restaurants.

Embalming Lenin

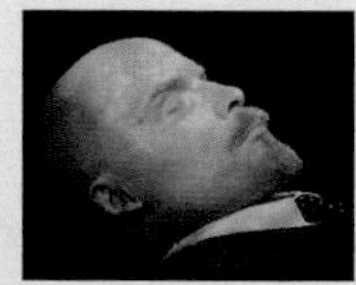

Preserved body of Lenin

"Do not raise monuments to him, or palaces to his name, do not organize pompous ceremonies in his memory." Such were the words of Lenin's widow, Krupskaya. Despite this, Lenin's body was embalmed by two professors and, after a delay to see if the process had worked, put on display. A laboratory is dedicated to preserving the body, which needs regular applications of special fluids. Rumours that parts of the body have been replaced with wax substitutes are denied. Besides Lenin, the laboratory has also embalmed such Communist leaders as Ho Chi Minh (1890–1969) and Kim Il Sung (1912–94).

❻ St Basil's Cathedral

Собор Василия Блаженного

Sobor Vasiliya Blazhennovo

Commissioned in 1552 by Ivan the Terrible to celebrate the capture of the Mongol stronghold of Kazan, and completed in 1561, this cathedral is reputed to have been designed by the architect Postnik Yakovlev. According to legend, Ivan was so amazed at the beauty of Postnik's work that he had him blinded so that he would never be able to design anything as exquisite again. The church was officially called the Cathedral of the Intercession because the final siege of Kazan began on the Feast of the Intercession of the Virgin. However, it is usually known as St Basil's after the "holy fool" Basil the Blessed whose remains are interred within. The cathedral's design, which was inspired by traditional Russian timber architecture, is a riot of gables, tent roofs and twisting onion domes.

★ Domes
Following a fire in 1583 the original helmet-shaped cupolas were replaced by ribbed or faceted onion domes. It is only since 1670 that the domes have been painted in bright colours; at one time St Basil's was white with golden domes.

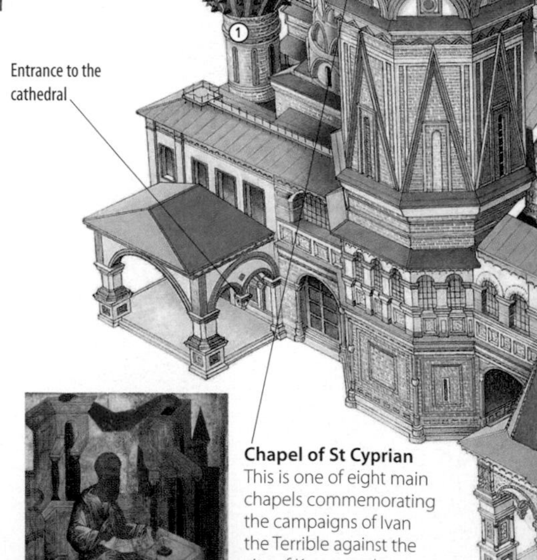

Entrance to the cathedral

Chapel of St Cyprian
This is one of eight main chapels commemorating the campaigns of Ivan the Terrible against the city of Kazan, to the southeast of Moscow. It is dedicated to St Cyprian, whose feast is on 2 October, the day after the last attack.

KEY

① **The Chapel of St Basil**, the ninth chapel to be added to the cathedral, was built in 1588 to house the remains of the "holy fool", Basil the Blessed.

② **Chapel of the Three Patriarchs**

③ **Chapel of the Trinity**

④ **Bell tower**

⑤ **Tent roof on the Central Chapel**

⑥ **Chapel of St Nicholas**

⑦ **Chapel of St Varlaam of Khutynskiy**

⑧ **Tiered gables**

⑨ **The Chapel of the Entry of Christ into Jerusalem** was used as a ceremonial entrance during the annual Palm Sunday procession. On this day the patriarch rode from the Kremlin to St Basil's Cathedral on a horse dressed up to look like a donkey.

⑩ **Chapel of Bishop Gregory**

Central Chapel of the Intercession
Light floods in through the windows of the tent-roofed central church, which soars to a height of 61 m (200 ft).

VISITORS' CHECKLIST

Practical information
Krasnaya ploshchad 2.
Map 4 D1.
Tel (495) 698 33 04.
saintbasil.ru
Open May–Oct: 10am–6pm daily; Nov–Apr: 10am–5pm daily. English.

Transport
25. Okhotnyy Ryad, Ploschad Revolyutsii. 8.

★ Main iconostasis
The Baroque-style iconostasis in the Central Chapel of the Intercession dates from the 19th century. However, some of the icons housed inside were painted much earlier.

Minin and Pozharskiy

A bronze statue by Ivan Martos depicts two heroes from the Time of Troubles *(see p40)*, the butcher Kuzma Minin and Prince Dmitri Pozharskiy. They raised a volunteer force to fight the invading Poles and, in 1612, led their army to victory when they drove the Poles out of the Kremlin. The statue was erected in 1818, in the triumphal afterglow of the Napoleonic Wars. Originally placed in the centre of Red Square facing the Kremlin, it was moved to its present site in front of St Basil's during the Soviet era.

Monument to Minin and Prince Pozharskiy

★ Gallery
The gallery runs around the outside of the Central Chapel and connects it to the other eight chapels. It was roofed over at the end of the 17th century and the walls and ceilings were decorated with floral tiles in the late 18th century.

7 Ulitsa Varvarka

Улица Варварка

Ulitsa Varvarka

Map 4 D1. Ⓜ Kitay Gorod.

Leading eastwards from St Basil's, ulitsa Varvarka is one of Moscow's oldest streets and the heart of the former merchants' quarter of Zaryade. It is named after the medieval Church of St Barbara (Varvara) the Martyr, which was demolished in 1796 to make way for a Neo-Classical church of the same name.

Further along is the Church of St Maxim the Blessed, built in 1698 by traders from Novgorod to house St Maxim's bones. Sandwiched between the two churches is the Old English Court, while across the road stand the Old Merchants' Chambers (Staryy Gostinyy Dvor), a market designed by Giacomo Quarenghi, an Italian architect, in 1790. Today, exhibitions and performances are held in its covered yard.

A little ahead, beside the Palace of the Romanov Boyars is the 17th-century Monastery of the Sign, whose redbrick cathedral is adorned with *kokoshniki* (tiered gables) and four onion domes covered in green-and-red shingles. The last in the row of historic churches is the Church of St George, built in 1657–8 by merchants from Pskov *(see p210)*. A surviving section of Kitay Gorod's medieval walls can be seen in the subway entrance to the Kitay Gorod metro.

Domes of the historic Church of St George, ulitsa Varvarka

8 Old English Court

Старый английский двор

Staryy angliyskiy dvor

Ulitsa Varvarka 4a. **Map** 4 D1. **Tel** (495) 698 39 52. Ⓜ Ploshchad Revolyutsii, Kitay Gorod. **Open** 10am–6pm Tue, Wed, Fri–Sun & 1–9pm Thu. **Closed** last Fri of the month. English, book in advance.

This building is Moscow's earliest known diplomatic mission. In 1553, while searching the northern coast of Russia for a passage to the east, the English merchant-adventurer Richard Chancellor was shipwrecked. He was taken to Moscow and received by Ivan the Terrible, whose desire to trade with England later led him to propose marriage to Queen Elizabeth I. On returning to Russia in 1556, Chancellor and his trading mission were given this property in Zaryade to serve as a depot, trading house and lodgings for English merchants. The company exported furs, caviar and honey until it was expelled from Russia in 1649 by Tsar Alexis, who was enraged by the execution of Charles I. Pyotr Baranovskiy, who recognized the building's medieval origins, saved it from demolition in the 1960s and it reopened as a museum during the state visit of Queen Elizabeth II to Russia in 1994.

The exhibits here are not as interesting as the house itself. Stone staircases lead down to the official chamber once used for negotiations and functions. English merchants fitted the Russian stove with an open hearth as a reminder of home.

Ornate dining room in the Palace of the Romanov Boyars

9 Palace of the Romanov Boyars

Дворец бояр Романовых

Palaty Boyar Romanovikh

Ulitsa Varvarka 10. **Map** 4 E1. **Tel** (495) 698 12 56. Ⓜ Kitay Gorod. **Open** 10am–6pm Thu–Mon, 11am–7pm Wed. **Closed** first Mon of the month.

Only the upper storeys of this palace can be seen from ulitsa Varvarka, since it is built on a steep slope that descends from the street towards the Moskva river. Originally built by the *boyar* Nikita Romanov in the 16th century, it was home to the Romanovs until 1613 when Mikhail Romanov *(see p41)* became tsar and the family moved to the Kremlin. The palace was restored on the orders of Nicholas I and has been protected as a museum since 1859.

A frozen ulitsa Varvarka, with the Old English Court in the background

Magnificent gilded iconostasis in the Church of the Trinity in Nikitniki

A double-headed eagle, the Romanov family crest, adorns the archway leading to the courtyard via which visitors enter the palace. The ground and first floors probably date from the 17th century. In the painted hall, personal effects of the early Romanovs are displayed, including gold dishes, ancient title deeds, ledgers inlaid with precious gems and the robes of Nikita's eldest son, Patriarch Fyodor Filaret. The rooms have been refurbished in the lavish style of the period, with walls covered in gilt embossed leather or painted in accents of red, green and gold.

In the 16th and 17th centuries even the richest families had to tolerate rather cramped and dim conditions. The portals in the palace are so low that a man of average height has to stoop; and the windows let in little light because they are made of mica, a translucent mineral, rather than glass. After a fire in 1674, a light and airy wooden upper storey was added to the palace, where the Romanov womenfolk occupied their lives with weaving. The main hall on this level has a beautifully carved wooden ceiling.

❿ Church of the Trinity in Nikitniki

Храм Святой Троицы в Никитниках

Khram Svyatoy Troitsy v Nikitnikakh

Nikitnikov pereulok 3. **Map** 4 E1. **Tel** (495) 698 34 51. Ⓜ Kitay Gorod. **Closed** to public. Ⓦ **nikitniki.ru**

This splendid church is dwarfed by ugly 1970s buildings that were once Communist Party offices. When it was founded in 1635 by Grigori Nikitnikov, a wealthy merchant, the church would have dominated the local skyline with its five green domes, its profusion of decoration and painted tiles, and its tiers of *kokoshniki*. The equally elaborate tent-roofed bell tower, linked to the main building by an enclosed gallery, was added shortly after construction was finished in 1653.

The church's frescoes were completed three years later, shortly before Nikitinikov died from the plague, which remained a scourge in Moscow until well into the 18th century. Many of the frescoes, such as *The Parable of the Rich Man*, portray scenes from the Gospels in direct, emotional terms, and are credited to the great fresco and icon painter Simon Ushakov (1626–86). He also painted several panels in the splendid gilded iconostasis, including *The Annunciation of the Virgin*, to the left of the Royal Gate *(see pp26–7)*.

The pediment of the Russian Chamber of Industry and Commerce, ulitsa Ilinka

⓫ Ulitsa Ilinka

Улица Ильинка

Ulitsa Ilinka

Map 4 D1. Ⓜ Kitay Gorod.

Before the Revolution, this narrow street running alongside GUM was home to many banks and trading offices. Their colourful façades remain the highlight of a stroll along the street even today. Several important institutions are still located here, despite a wholly new financial district having sprung up a mile upriver from the Kremlin in the past two decades.

Russia's previous surge of capitalism – at the turn of the 19th and 20th centuries – was notable for its God-fearing entrepreneurs known as *Kuptsy*. When Moscow's first stock exchange opened in 1836, many merchants still wore long patriarchal beards and the traditional kaftan, and were used to dealing with one another in the street. They had to be coerced by the police to do business in the new premises on the corner of Birzhevaya ploshchad. The building now houses the Russian Chamber of Industry and Commerce. Across the street, a Russian-Revival-style pile built in 1876 is home to the Supreme Court, which has ruled on many disputes between oligarchs in the capitalist free-for-all of post-Communist Russia.

Gothic-style façade of the Synodal Printing House, Nikolskaya ulitsa

⓬ Nikolskaya Ulitsa

Никольская улица
Nikolskaya ulitsa

Map 2 D5. Ⓜ Lubyanka, Ploshchad Revolyutsii.

Named after the Kremlin's Nicholas's Tower, this street was settled by merchants and traders from the 12th century onwards. Long characterized by its shops, stalls and monasteries, Nikolskaya ulitsa underwent decades of dowdiness under Communism before reasserting its commercial vigour in the 1990s, when many designer clothes stores and jewellers opened up here.

Through the courtyard at No. 7 is a gateway leading into the Zaikonospasskiy Monastery, which was founded in the 15th century or earlier. The name means Saviour Beyond the Icons and recalls the time when there was a brisk trade in icons here. From 1687–1814 the monastery also housed Moscow's first institute of higher education, the Slavic Greek Latin Academy, whose pupils included the future founder of Moscow University, Mikhail Lomonosov.

At No. 15 are the Gothic-style spires of the Synodal Printing House. The pale blue building, with a lion and unicorn sculpted over its central window, dates from 1810–14. Its courtyard is enhanced by a colourful chequered roof and walls of blue and white tiles. In the chambers previously on this site Ivan Fyodorov produced Russia's first printed book, *The Acts of the Apostles* (1564), before being forced to flee by superstitious Muscovites incensed by what they saw as "Satan's work".

Next door, in the courtyard of No. 17, is the Slavyanskiy Bazaar restaurant, founded in 1870. Its former patrons include the theatre directors Konstantin Stanislavskiy and Vladimir Nemirovich-Danchenko, whose legendary 18-hour-long discussion led to the founding of the Moscow Arts Theatre *(see p84)*. The restaurant obligingly stayed open until two o'clock in the morning, when they finished talking.

⓭ Lubyanka Square

Лубянская площадь
Lubyanskaya ploshchad

Map 2 D5. Ⓜ Lubyanka.

For generations of Soviet citizens, the name Lubyanka was synonymous with the Communist secret police, which began life as the Cheka and evolved into the KGB of Cold War notoriety, before being renamed the Federal Security Service (FSB) in post-Communist Russia. The institution is inseparable from its headquarters in the former Rossiya Insurance building, taken over in 1918 by the Cheka's founder, "Iron" Feliks Dzerzhinskiy. His statue loomed over Lubyanka Square until it was toppled by a cheering crowd following the unsuccessful coup against President Gorbachev in 1991 *(see p46)*.

While Dzerzhinskiy's statue has been relegated to the Muzeon *(see p107)*, the secret police are still ensconced in the Lubyanka, which was enlarged in the 1930s and 40s to include an underground prison where thousands of people were interrogated, tortured and killed. The only monument to their fate is a boulder from the Solovetskiy concentration camp, embedded on the edge of Lubyanka Square near the Polytechnical Museum.

Far more prominent is the nation's largest toyshop, Detskiy Mir (Children's World), which the Soviet authorities chose to build just across from the Lubyanka in 1957 – supposedly as a tribute to Dzerzhinskiy, who chaired a committee on children's welfare after the Revolution.

The formidable FSB headquarters on Lubyanka Square

For hotels and restaurants in this area see p266 and p280

Sophisticated waiting area inside the plush Sandunovskiy Baths

Polytechnical Museum, at the southern end of Lubyanka Square

⓮ Polytechnical Museum

Политехнический музей

Politekhnicheskiy muzey

Novaya ploshchad 3/4. **Map** 2 E5. **Tel** (495) 625 06 14. Ⓜ Kitay Gorod, Lubyanka. **Open** 10am–6pm Tue–Sun. **Closed** last Fri of the month. W **polymus.ru**

The southern end of Lubyanka Square is dominated by the Polytechnical Museum, built in the 1870s. Many of its exhibits were originally assembled for an exhibition staged to mark the 200th anniversary of the birth of Peter the Great, but its collection has been expanded to trace the development of Russian science and technology from the 19th century onwards. Every two hours there are demonstrations of devices such as robots, sound equipment and working models.

⓯ Mayakovsky Museum

Музей-квартира ВВ Маяковского

Muzey-kvartira VV Mayakovskovo

Lubyanskiy proezd 3/6. **Map** 2 E5. **Tel** (495) 621 93 87. Ⓜ Lubyanka. **Open** 10am–5pm Fri–Tue, 1–8pm Thu. **Closed** last Fri of the month. W **mayakovsky.info**

Poet, iconoclast and self-publicist, Vladimir Mayakovsky gave voice to the Revolution in his verses, plays, film scripts and poster art. Mayakovsky's provocative persona is reflected in this museum where artworks mingle with his belongings. Huge frameworks of metal bars lean at fantastic angles, providing a backdrop to chairs, old boots, typewriters, posters, sewing machines, photomontages and manuscripts.

Room designed to symbolize Mayakovsky's poetic origins

Mayakovsky actually lived in this block from 1919 until his death in 1930 – a single room on the fourth floor has been furnished to look as it would have done when he moved in. While living here, Mayakovsky continued his long-running love affair with Lilya Brik, the wife of his friend Osip Brik. The last part of the exhibition deals with Mayakovsky's suicide at the age of 37, following which Stalin praised him as the greatest of Soviet poets and continued to use his work for propaganda purposes.

⓰ Sandunovskiy Baths

Сандуновские бани

Sandunovskie bani

Neglinnaya ulitsa 14, building 3–7. **Map** 2 D4. **Tel** (495) 625 46 31. Ⓜ Kuznetskiy Most, Trubnaya. **Open** 8am–10pm daily (last adm: 8pm). W **sanduny.ru**

The back streets beyond Lubyanka harbour Moscow's famous Sandunovskiy Baths, founded in 1808 by the actor Sila Sandunov. A Beaux-Arts façade hides a sumptuous interior decorated in a mix of styles, inspired by the Alhambra Palace in Spain. The best, most expensive facilities are located on the first floor. Thrashing yourself with birch branches is an integral part of the Russian *banya* (steam bath) experience.

GARDEN RING

The Garden Ring *(Sadovoye Koltso)* marks the limit of what used to be the fortifications encircling the Kremlin and Kitay Gorod in the 17th century. After the 1812 Great Fire of Moscow destroyed the city centre, it was rebuilt in a predominantly Neo-Classical style, in a patchwork of mansions and orchards, with a network of boulevards and side streets running its perimeter. In Soviet times this leafy periphery was turned into a ring road dominated by Stalin-Gothic skyscrapers. The juxtaposition of Soviet gigantism and pre-Revolution elegance lends a unique character to this area. Alongside cultural landmarks such as the Bolshoi Theatre and Pushkin State Museum of Fine Arts is the grand Cathedral of Christ the Saviour. The atmospheric backstreets between the cathedral and the Old Arbat area, with its historic churches and early 19th-century mansions, make for a rewarding walk.

Sights at a Glance

Churches and Cathedrals

- 25 Cathedral of Christ the Saviour

Museums

- 10 Gulag History Museum
- 13 Museum of Contemporary History
- 14 Bulgakov House and Museum
- 16 Chekhov House-Museum
- 17 Gorky House-Museum
- 18 Stanislavskiy House-Museum
- 22 *Pushkin State Museum of Fine Arts pp90–91*
- 23 Gallery of 19th- and 20th-Century European and American Art
- 24 Glazunov Picture Gallery
- 27 Lermontov House-Museum
- 28 Skryabin House-Museum
- 31 Pushkin House-Museum
- 33 Shalyapin House-Museum

Streets and Squares

- 2 Theatre Square
- 6 Manège Square
- 7 Tverskaya Ulitsa
- 9 Bryusov Pereulok
- 12 Pushkin Square
- 20 Bolshaya Nikitskaya Ulitsa
- 26 Arbat Square
- 29 Spasopeskovskiy Pereulok

Historic Buildings and Monuments

- 1 Hotel Metropol
- 4 House of Unions
- 5 Hotel National
- 11 Upper Monastery of St Peter
- 15 Patriarch's Pond
- 21 Pashkov House
- 30 Melnikov House
- 32 Ministry of Foreign Affairs

Theatres and Concert Halls

- 3 *Bolshoi Theatre pp82–3*
- 8 Moscow Arts Theatre
- 19 Moscow Conservatory

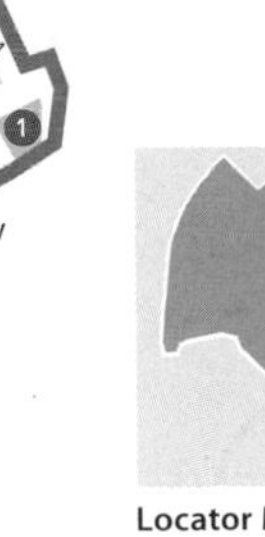

Locator Map

See Street Finder, maps 1, 2 & 3

0 metres 600

0 yards 600

◀ The Patriarchal Bridge over Moskva river leading to the Cathedral of Christ the Saviour

For map symbols *see back flap*

Street-by-Street: Around Theatre Square

Moscow's theatreland is centred, quite appropriately, around Theatre Square (Teatrelnaya ploshchad). Dominating the square is one of the most famous opera and ballet stages in the world, the Bolshoi Theatre. The Malyy (Small) Theatre is on the east side of the square, while the Russian Academic Youth Theatre is on the west. Further to the west is the city's main shopping street, Tverskaya ulitsa, and two more theatres, the Yermolova Theatre and the Moscow Arts Theatre. There are also several excellent restaurants and bars in this neighbourhood.

Yuri Dolgorukiy, Moscow's founder, is depicted in this statue. It was unveiled in 1954, seven years after the city's 800th anniversary.

Pushkin Square

TVERSKAYA PLOSCHAD

STOLESHNIKOV PEREULO

ULITSA

KAMERGERSKIY PEREULO

TVERSKAYA ULITSA

9 Bryusov Pereulok
A granite archway leads from Tverskaya ulitsa to this quiet lane, once home to director Vsevolod Meyerhold. The 17th-century Church of the Resurrection is visible further down the lane.

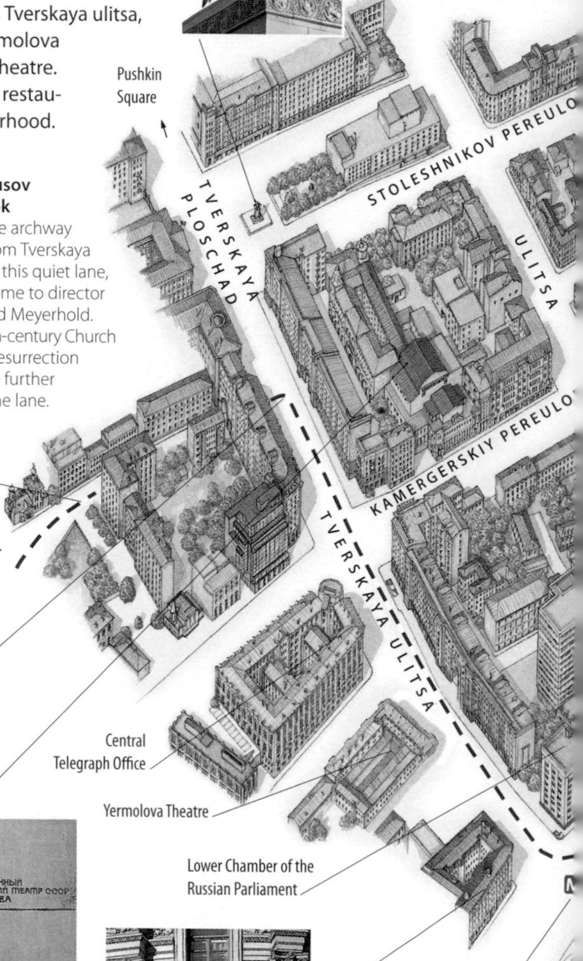

Bolshaya Nikitskaya ulitsa

7 Tverskaya Ulitsa is Moscow's main shopping street. Most of the imposing Stalinist blocks here date from the 1930s, but a few older buildings survive.

Central Telegraph Office

Yermolova Theatre

Lower Chamber of the Russian Parliament

Okhotnyy Ryad

8 Moscow Arts Theatre
This famous theatre will always be associated with the dramatist Anton Chekhov *(see p31)*. Several of his plays, including *The Cherry Orchard*, were premiered here.

5 Hotel National
The National is a mix of Style-Moderne and Classical styles. Now restored, its decor is as impressive as it was before the Revolution, when it was Moscow's finest hotel.

For hotels and restaurants in this area see p266 and pp280–82

3 ★ Bolshoi Theatre
Two earlier theatres on this site, including the first Bolshoi, were destroyed in fires. The current building was completed by Albert Kavos in 1856.

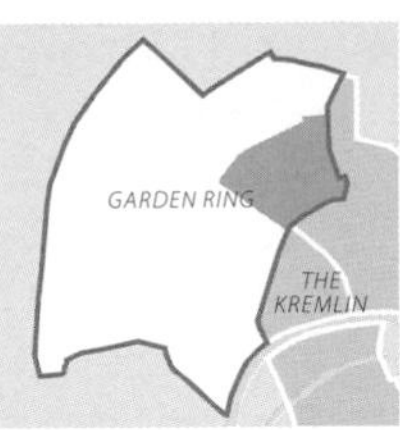

Area illustrated

Key

— Suggested route

0 metres 150

0 yards 150

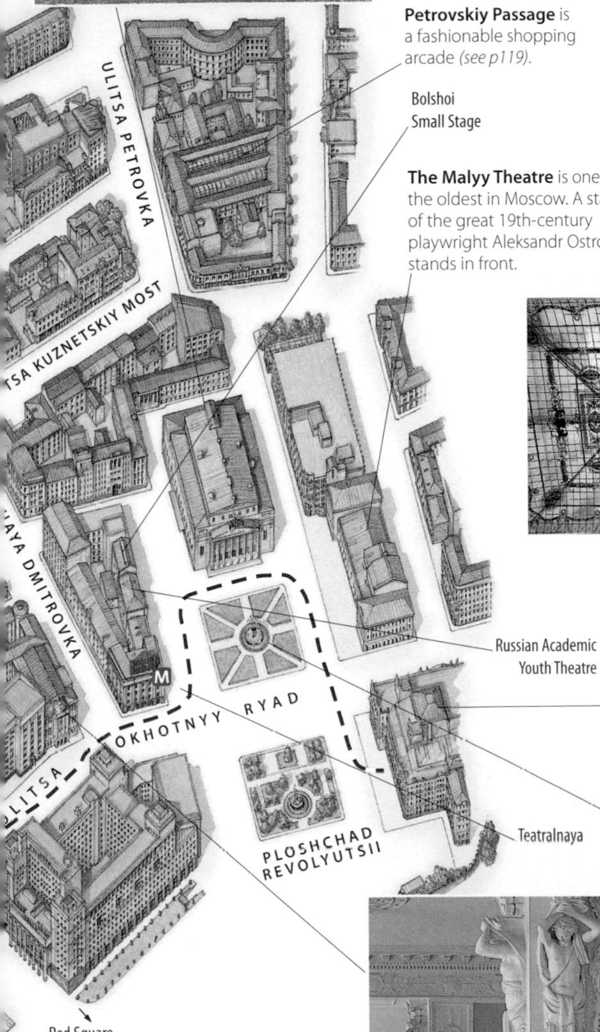

Petrovskiy Passage is a fashionable shopping arcade *(see p119)*.

Bolshoi Small Stage

The Malyy Theatre is one of the oldest in Moscow. A statue of the great 19th-century playwright Aleksandr Ostrovskiy stands in front.

ULITSA PETROVKA

ULITSA KUZNETSKIY MOST

BOLSHAYA DMITROVKA

OKHOTNYY RYAD

ULITSA

PLOSHCHAD REVOLYUTSII

Russian Academic Youth Theatre

Teatralnaya

Red Square

1 Hotel Metropol
Built in 1899–1905 by Englishman William Walcot, the Metropol is one of Moscow's grandest hotels. This painted, glazed ceiling is the outstanding feature of the main dining room.

7 Theatre Square
Laid out in its present form in the 1820s, Theatre Square served as a military parade ground between 1839–1911. Playbills around the city advertise performances in the theatres on the square.

4 ★ House of Unions
In the 1780s, architect Matvey Kazakov converted this Neo-Classical mansion into a noblemen's club. The trade unions took it over in the Soviet era, when it hosted Stalin's infamous show trials.

❶ Hotel Metropol

Гостиница Метрополь
Gostinitsa Metropol

Teatralnyy proezd 2. **Map** 2 D5. **Tel** (499) 501 78 00. Ⓜ Teatralnaya.

Built in 1899–1905, the Hotel Metropol is a fine example of Style-Moderne architecture *(see p33)* by William Walcot. *The Daydreaming Princess*, a large ceramic panel by Mikhail Vrubel, crowns its façade, and the hotel has a superb painted glass roof in its Metropol Zal restaurant. Its celebrity guests have included Irish dramatist George Bernard Shaw and Michael Jackson.

❷ Theatre Square

Театральная площадь
Teatralnaya ploshchad

Map 2 D5. Ⓜ Teatralnaya, Ploshchad Revolyutsii, Okhotnyy Ryad.

This elegant square is named after the theatres on three of its sides. Originally this area was marshy ground; in the 1820s the square was laid out to a design by Osip Bove. Today, Theatre Square is dominated by the Bolshoi Theatre. On the square's eastern side is the Malyy (Small) Theatre, where Aleksandr Ostrovskiy's satirical plays were staged. The Russian Academic Youth Theatre, with its elaborate Neo-Classical porch, stands on the square's western side, beside the Bolshoi Theatre's small stage.

To the northwest of Theatre Square is the Operetta Theatre. In the 1890s, the private opera company of the wealthy industrialist and arts patron Savva Mamontov (1842–1914) performed here. The opera singer Fyodor Shalyapin *(see p93)* and the famous pianist and composer Sergei Rachmaninov began their careers with Mamontov's company.

In the centre of the square is a granite statue of Karl Marx, erected in 1961, bearing the words "Workers of the world unite!"

❸ Bolshoi Theatre

See pp82–3.

❹ House of Unions

Дом Союзов
Dom Soyuzov

Bolshaya Dmitrovka ulitsa 1. **Map** 2 D5. **Tel** (495) 692 07 36. Ⓜ Teatralnaya, Okhotnyy Ryad. **Open** for performances only. **W domsojuzov.ru**

This green and white Neo-Classical mansion built in the first half of the 18th century was converted into a noblemen's club in the early 1780s by architect Matvei Kazakov *(see p33)*, who added a number of rooms including a magnificent ballroom known as the Hall of Columns. It was here, in 1856, that Tsar Alexander II addressed the Russian nobility on the need to emancipate the serfs.

The well-proportioned Hall of Columns in the elegant 18th-century House of Unions

After the Revolution, trade unions took over the building; in 1924 the hall was used for the lying in state of Lenin's body, when over a million citizens filed past his open coffin. Many of his closest colleagues, who formed the guard of honour, were later tried here during the infamous show trials of 1936–8 staged by Stalin, who lay in state here himself in 1953. Nowadays, the House of Unions is used for concerts and public meetings.

The luxurious Metropol Zal restaurant with its painted glass roof, inside the Hotel Metropol

❺ Hotel National

Гостиница Националь
Gostinitsa Natsional

Mokhovaya ulitsa 15/1. **Map** 1 C5. **Tel** (495) 258 70 00. Ⓜ Okhotnyy Ryad.

The Hotel National is an eclectic mixture of Style-Moderne and Classical-style architecture. Its façade is topped by a mosaic from the Soviet era featuring factories belching smoke, oil derricks, railway engines and tractors.

Lenin stayed in Room 107 at the National for a week, in March 1918, before moving into the Kremlin. In the early 1990s, the hotel was totally refurbished and its Style-Moderne interiors were restored to their original splendour.

The ornately painted façade and mosaic of the Hotel National

❻ Manège Square

Манежная площадь
Manezhnaya ploshchad

Map 1 C5. Ⓜ Biblio-teka imeni Lenina, Okhotnyy Ryad. Manège: **Tel** (495) 645 92 77. **Open** exhibitions only.

The square is named after the Tsarist military riding school, **Manège**, situated at its southern end. Built in 1817 to a design by General Augustin de Béthencourt, the Manège's 45-m (148-ft) wide roof had no supporting columns, leaving an uninterrupted floor space large enough for a squadron of cavalry to manoeuvre. In 1957, it became the Central Exhibition Hall, where Nikita Khrushchev *(see p45)* condemned abstract art at an exhibition in 1962. Khrushchev posthumously made amends to the sculptor Ernst Neizvestniy – whose work he had lambasted – by specifying in his will that Neizvestniy should design his tombstone. Fire partly destroyed the building in 2004, but it was swiftly rebuilt and is still used to house exhibitions.

The Manège, designed by Augustin de Bethencourt in 1817, lit up at night

The square itself underwent substantial renovation in the 1990s. Mayor Yuri Luzhkov had a shopping mall constructed beneath the square in an effort to humanize the bleak space.

The Moscow Old University is another principal landmark here. Founded by the polymath Mikhail Lomonosov in 1755, the university moved into this building in 1793. Designed by Matvei Kazakov in 1782, it was rebuilt by Domenico Gilardi after the 1812 Great Fire and is an excellent example of Neo-Classical architecture.

❼ Tverskaya Ulitsa

Тверская улица
Tverskaya ulitsa

Map 1 B3. Ⓜ Okhotnyy Ryad, Tverskaya, Pushkinskaya.

During the 19th century, Tverskaya ulitsa was the grandest thoroughfare in Moscow, renowned for its restaurants, theatres, hotels and purveyors of French fashions. Stalin's reconstruction of Moscow in the 1930s resulted in the road being widened by 42 m (138 ft) and renamed after the writer Maxim Gorky. Many buildings were torn down to make way for apartment blocks to house party bureaucrats, and others were rebuilt further back on the wider road. Now called Tverskaya ulitsa again, the street and surrounding area are among Moscow's most popular places to eat out and shop.

Elegant boutique lining Tverskaya ulitsa, Moscow's prominent shopping street

At No. 7 is the Central Telegraph Office, a severe grey edifice with an illuminated globe outside, designed by Ilya Rerberg in 1927. Through the arch on the far side of the road is a green-tiled building with floral friezes and tent-roofed turrets, built in 1905 as the Moscow mission of the Savvinskiy Monastery; it now contains luxury flats and offices.

Further up the street, Tverskaya Square is dominated by the red-and-white Mayor's office, designed in 1782 by Matvei Kazakov as the residence of Moscow's Tsarist governor-general. After the Revolution, it became the Moscow City Soviet or town hall.

Beyond Tverskaya Square, at No. 14, is Moscow's pre-eminent delicatessen, Yeliseyevsky Food Hall. In the 1820s, this building was the home of Princess Zinaida Volkonskaya, whose soirées were attended by great figures of the day, including Alexander Pushkin *(see p93)*. In 1898, Grigori Yeliseev bought the building and had it lavishly redecorated with stained-glass windows, crystal chandeliers, polished wood counters and huge mirrors.

❸ Bolshoi Theatre

Большой театр

Bolshoy teatr

Established in 1776, the Bolshoi ballet and theatre companies are among the oldest in the world. The first theatre building opened in 1780, but was razed by fire in 1805, forcing the company to perform at the Petrovsky Theatre. Soon this building too was consumed by fire during Napoleon's invasion. Its successor was completed in 1825 to a design by Osip Bove and Andrei Mikhaylov. However, the building was once again claimed by fire, in 1853, and was reconstructed by Albert Kavos in 1856. The building was closed for six years of renovations in 2005. It finally reopened in 2011.

Elegant ballet dancers performing Victor Hugo's *Esmeralda*, Bolshoi Theatre

★ Apollo in the Chariot of the Sun

This eye-catching sculpture by Pyotr Klodt, part of the original 1825 building, was retained by Albert Kavos. It depicts Apollo driving the chariot on which he carried the sun across the sky.

KEY

① **Eight-columned portico**

② **The Neo-Classical pediment** boasts a relief depicting a pair of angels bearing aloft the lyre of Apollo, the Greek god of music and light. The relief was an addition by Albert Kavos during his reconstruction of the theatre.

③ **The auditorium** has six tiers and a seating capacity of 1,740. When Kavos rebuilt it he modified its shape to improve the acoustics.

④ **Main stage**

⑤ **The upper stage** is where the ballet dancers rehearse and perfect their technique.

⑥ **Artists' dressing rooms**

⑦ **The exhibition foyer** extends around the whole of the front of the building on the first floor and hosts temporary exhibitions that are open to the public during performances.

New Beethoven Concert Hall is an impressive 300-seat hall that lies beneath Teatralnaya ploshchad *(see p79)*. It was added during the recent renovation work and is accessed from inside the Bolshoi Theatre. The hall features moveable sections of floor that can be lowered or raised to transform it into an amphitheatre.

Entrance

Vestibule

Patrons entering the theatre find themselves in this grand, grey and white tiled vestibule. Magnificent staircases, lined with white marble, lead up from either side of the vestibule to the spacious exhibition foyer.

Small Imperial Foyer
This ornately decorated room was known as the Beethoven Hall in the Soviet era. It is now used for occasional exhibitions. The stuccoed decoration on the ceiling includes about 3,000 rosettes and the walls are adorned with delicately embroidered panels of crimson silk.

VISITORS' CHECKLIST

Practical information
Teatralnaya ploshchad 1.
Map 2 D5.
Tel (495) 455 55 55.
bolshoi.ru
Open Tue–Sun for performances.
Closed every year in August and reopens in the second week of September.
in auditorium.

Transport
12. Teatralnaya. 2, 12.

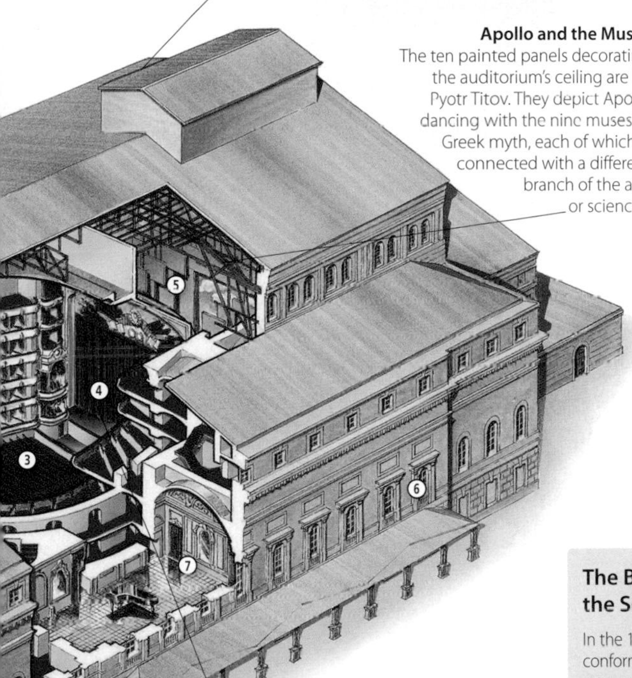

Apollo and the Muses
The ten painted panels decorating the auditorium's ceiling are by Pyotr Titov. They depict Apollo dancing with the nine muses of Greek myth, each of which is connected with a different branch of the arts or sciences.

The Bolshoi Ballet in the Soviet Era

In the 1920s and 30s, new ballets conforming to revolutionary ideals were created for the Bolshoi, but the company's heyday was in the 1950s and 60s. Ballets were produced and the dancers toured abroad for the first time to widespread acclaim. The distinguished Soviet choreographer Yuri Grigorovich staged a number of productions for the Bolshoi, including *Spartacus*, *Ivan the Terrible* and *Golden Age*.

The Bolshoi Ballet Company's production of *Spartacus* (1954)

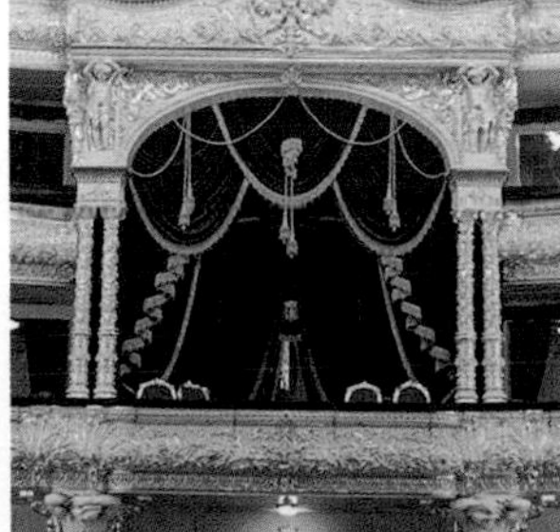

★ Royal Box
Situated at the centre of the gallery, the royal box, hung with crimson velvet, is one of over 120 boxes. The imperial crown on its pediment was removed in the Soviet era but has now been restored.

❽ Moscow Arts Theatre

МХАТ имени АП Чехова

MKhAT imeni AP Chekhova

Kamergerskiy pereulok 3. **Map** 1 C5. **Tel** (495) 629 87 60/67 48. Ⓜ Teatralnaya, Okhotnyy Ryad. **Open** performances only. **W mxat.ru**

The Moscow Arts Theatre (MKhAT) was founded by a group of young enthusiasts, led by the directors Konstantin Stanislavskiy and Vladimir Nemirovich-Danchenko and the first ever performance took place in 1898. The theatre made a name for itself with a production of Anton Chekhov's play *The Seagull* in its first year. When staged three years earlier in St Petersburg it was a disastrous flop, but performed using Stanislavskiy's new method acting *(see p28)*, it was rapturously received.

In 1902, architect Fyodor Shekhtel *(see p33)* reconstructed the theatre's interior, adding innovations such as a central lighting box and a revolving stage. The auditorium was sparsely decorated so that audiences were forced to concentrate on the performance.

The theatre's repertoire was restricted after the Revolution by state censorship. Most of the plays produced were written by Maxim Gorky, whose work was in favour with the regime. The frustrations and compromises of the period were satirized in the 1930s by Mikhail Bulgakov in his novel *Teatralnyy Roman*.

The Moscow Arts Theatre entrance with *The Wave* bas-relief above

There were still problems and in the 1980s part of the company moved to the Gorky Arts Theatre on Tverskoy bulvar.

Today, a variety of productions are staged at the Moscow Arts Theatre, including many of Chekhov's plays.

❾ Bryusov Pereulok

Брюсов переулок

Bryusov pereulok

Map 1 C5. Ⓜ Okhotnyy Ryad, Arbatskaya.

A granite arch on Tverskaya ulitsa marks the entrance to this side street, named after the Bruces, a Scottish family who were involved with the Russian court.

In the 1920s, new apartments here were assigned to the staff of the Moscow state theatres. No. 12 was home to the avant-garde director Vsevolod Meyerhold, who lived here from 1928 until his arrest in 1939 at the height of Stalin's Great Terror. Next door, Nos. 8–10 were the headquarters of the Composers' Union, where composers Sergei Prokofiev and Dmitri Shostakovich were forced to read an apology for works that deviated from socialist realism *(see p107)*.

About halfway along Bryusov pereulok is the 17th-century single-domed Church of the Resurrection, one of the few churches to remain open during the Soviet era.

Arch at the entrance to Bryusov Pereulok, a street where artists lived in the 1920s

❿ Gulag History Museum

Музей истории ГУЛАГа

Muzey istorii GULAGa

Ulitsa Petrovka 16. **Map** 2 D4. **Tel** (495) 621 73 10. Ⓜ Kuznetskiy Most. **Open** 11am–7pm Tue–Wed & Fri–Sun, noon–8pm Thu. **Closed** last Fri of the month. Russian only. **W gmig.ru**

Tucked away in a courtyard, approached by a barbed-wire fenced walkway, this museum recounts the grim history of Soviet prisons and labour camps (collectively known by their Russian acronym, GULAG). Prisoners' clothing, eating utensils, handmade chess sets, paintings, drawings and photos show how millions suffered in the "white hell" of Kolyma in Siberia and other infamous sites across the Soviet Union. There were hundreds of prisons and camps, constituting what the writer Aleksandr Solzhenitsyn called the "Gulag Archipelago".

⓫ Upper Monastery of St Peter

Высоко-Петровский монастырь

Vysoko-Petrovskiy monastyr

Ulitsa Petrovka 28/2. **Map** 2 D4. **Tel** (495) 694 64 37. Ⓜ Pushkinskaya, Chekhovskaya. **Open** 8am–7pm daily. book in advance.

Founded in the reign of Ivan I, this monastery was rebuilt in the late 17th century with

Iconostasis in the bell tower, Upper Monastery of St Peter

funding from the Naryshkin family, relatives of Peter the Great. Its six churches include the Church of the Metropolitan Peter, after which the monastery is named. It was built in 1514–17 to a design by Aleviz Novyy. The Church of the Icon of the Virgin of Bogolyubovo commemorates three of Peter the Great's uncles killed in the 1682 Streltsy Revolt. The Refectory Church of St Sergius has five cupolas and scallop-shell decoration. The complex includes a green-domed bell tower and monks' cells.

⓬ Pushkin Square

Пушкинская площадь

Pushkinskaya ploshchad

Map 1 B4. Ⓜ Pushkinskaya, Tverskaya, Chekhovskaya.

The square is named for a bronze statue of poet Alexander Pushkin, sculpted by Alexander Opekushin. It was unveiled in the presence of two other Russian literary giants, Fyodor Dostoevsky and Ivan Turgenev, in 1880. Pushkin has long epitomized the spirit of freedom in Russia, and, since the 1960s, his statue has been a rallying point for demonstrations, which have usually been broken up by the police.

The Rossiya Musical Theatre behind the statue is the venue for Moscow's International Film Festival and Russia's equivalent of the Oscars. It stands on the site of the 17th-century Convent of the Passion, which was demolished in 1935.

Beyond the theatre, at the beginning of Malaya Dmitrovka ulitsa, is the Church of the Nativity of the Virgin in Putinki. Built between 1649–52, this attractive church has clustered tent roofs, tiered *kokoshniki* and blue onion domes.

On the northeast corner of the square stand the offices of the newspaper *Izvestiya*, once an official mouthpiece of the Soviet government and now one of Russia's independent daily newspapers.

⓭ Museum of Contemporary History

Музей современной истории

Muzey sovremennoy istorii

Tverskaya ulitsa 21. **Map** 1 B4. **Tel** (495) 699 67 24. Ⓜ Pushkinskaya, Tverskaya. **Open** check website for timings. English, book in advance. **sovr.ru**

A pair of stone lions guards this elegant red mansion, built in the late 18th century. In 1831, the mansion became the English Club, where the Muscovite aristocracy drank and gambled until 1917, after which it ironically – or fittingly – became the Museum of the Revolution. Since the break-up of the Soviet Union in 1991, its exhibits have reflected a more objective view of 20th-century Russian history, and the museum's name has been changed to reflect this shift.

Laid out chronologically, the exhibits cover 1900–91. They include home-made grenades, a Maxim gun on a converted carriage (used in the Civil War), sweet wrappers depicting Marx and Lenin and former premier Nikita Khrushchev's camera from his 1959 trip to the United States. The so-called propaganda porcelain and gifts presented to Soviet rulers are also interesting.

Model of the five-pointed red star at the centre of the exhibition hall in the Museum of Contemporary History

⓮ Bulgakov House and Museum

Дом и музей Булгаков

Dom i Muzey Bulgakova

Bolshaya Sadovaya ulitsa 10. **Map** 1 A4. Ⓜ Mayakovskaya. Bulgakov Museum: **Tel** (495) 699 53 66. **Open** noon–7pm Tue, Wed & Fri–Sun, 2–9pm Thu. **W bulgakovmuseum.ru/en**. Bulgakov House: **Tel** (495) 970 06 19. **Open** 1pm–1am Fri & Sat, 1–11pm Sun–Thu. **W dombulgakova.ru**

Mikhail Bulgakov (1891–1940) wrote his classic satire of Stalinist Russia, *The Master and Margarita*, knowing that it would never be published in his lifetime. Although typed copies circulated on the black market, it was only published in Russia in the 1980s. Today, there are two museums in Bulgakov's honour, in the building where many surreal scenes from his novel are set.

An official **Bulgakov Museum** occupies Flat 50, where the author set portions of his novel while nearby is the rival **Bulgakov House**. Both museums organize performances, lectures and excursions. A memorable experience is the Bulgakov House's night-ride around central Moscow in a converted trolleybus with its own buffet.

⓯ Patriarch's Pond

Патриаршие пруды

Patriarshie prudy

Map 1 A4. Ⓜ Pushkinskaya.

Just a few minutes' walk south from the Bulgakov Museum is a leafy, secluded square with the Patriarch's Pond at its heart. The pond was dug by a 16th-century patriarch to drain a reputedly haunted swamp. This association with evil spirits and Christianity inspired Bulgakov to make it the setting for the opening scene in *The Master and Margarita*, in which the Devil appears in Moscow and causes havoc. Locals have prevented the installation of giant sculptures illustrating Bulgakov's novel, preferring instead to keep a bronze statue of the 19th-century writer of fables, Ivan Krylov, surrounded by creatures from his stories.

Picture of Chekhov (left) with Leo Tolstoy, in the Chekhov House-Museum

⓰ Chekhov House-Museum

Дом-музей АП Чехова

Dom-muzey AP Chekhova

Sadovaya-Kudrinskaya ulitsa 6. **Map** 1 A5. **Tel** (495) 691 38 37. Ⓜ Barrikadnaya, Krasnopresnenskaya. **Open** 11am–6pm Tue & Sat, 2pm–8pm Wed & Fri, 2pm–9pm Thu. **Closed** last day of the month. book in advance.

Author Anton Chekhov (1860–1904) lived in this two-storey house in 1886–90. It was later refurbished in consultation with his widow, actress Olga Knipper-Chekhova, and opened as a museum in 1954. A brass plate by the door testifies to Chekhov's medical profession. Writing in his spare time, it was here that he created his first major play, *Ivanov*, and wrote many short stories.

In the study, exhibits include his doctor's bag, manuscripts and pictures. Upstairs, Chekhov's sister Mariya's room is the most attractive in the house.

⓱ Gorky House-Museum

Дом-музей АМ Горького

Dom-muzey AM Gorkovo

Malaya Nikitskaya ulitsa 6/2. **Map** 1 B5. **Tel** (495) 690 05 35. Ⓜ Pushkinskaya. **Open** 11am–5:30pm Wed–Sun. **Closed** last Thu of the month. English.

A frieze of irises against a background of blue and purple clouds runs around the top of the yellow glazed-brick walls of this mansion, a masterpiece of Style-Moderne architecture designed in 1900. In 1931, Stalin presented the mansion as a gift to the esteemed socialist writer Maxim Gorky,

The spectacular Style-Moderne staircase in the Gorky House-Museum

For hotels and restaurants in this area see p266 and pp280–82

who never got used to its luxury, nor produced much work while living here. However, Gorky's pre-revolutionary fame and support for the Bolshevik Party made him a useful propaganda tool for the Soviet government.

The interior of the house features ceilings with elaborate mouldings, stained-glass windows and carved door frames. The *pièce de résistance* is the staircase of polished Estonian limestone, which ends in a lamp resembling a jellyfish. On display are Gorky's hat, overcoat and walking stick, his collection of Japanese netsuke carvings and many of his letters and books.

Stunning stained-glass window in the Gorky House-Museum

⑱ Stanislavskiy House-Museum

Дом-музей КС Станиславского

Dom-muzey KS Stanislavskovo

Leontevskiy pereulok 6. **Map** 1 B5. **Tel** (495) 629 24 42. M Arbatskaya, Tverskaya. **Open** noon–7pm Wed & Fri, 11am–8pm Thu, 11am–6pm Sat & Sun. **Closed** last Thu of the month.

This 18th-century mansion was the home of the great director and actor Konstantin Stanislavskiy. Disillusionment with the conservative ethos of the old Moscow Theatre School led Stanislavskiy to found the Moscow Arts Theatre (MKhAT) in 1898 *(see p84)*. After moving into this flat, he converted its ballroom into a makeshift theatre where he rehearsed his experimental Opera Dramatic Group. The actors would step on stage from the adjacent Red Room, which served as a make-up studio.

Stanislavskiy was indifferent to his surroundings and, for most of his life, slept in his study. He died here in 1938.

The opulent Bolshoi Zal in the Moscow Conservatory

⑲ Moscow Conservatory

Московская консерватория

Moskovskaya Konservatoriya

Bolshaya Nikitskaya ulitsa 13/6. **Map** 1 B5. **Tel** (495) 629 94 01. M Arbatskaya, Pushkinskaya. **Open** performances only. W **mosconsv.ru**

Russia's premier music school was founded in 1866 by Nikolai Rubinstein, the brother of pianist and composer Anton Rubinstein. One of the Conservatory's teachers was the young Pyotr Tchaikovsky. In the forecourt is his statue wielding a baton, and the railings are patterned with the opening notes of his symphonies.

Portraits of famous composers adorn the walls of the light, airy Bolshoi Zal (Great Hall), which hosts the prestigious Tchaikovsky International Competition. A museum that is open during performances celebrates alumni such as the pianist-composers Sergei Rachmaninov and Dmitri Shostakovich.

Globe-shaped sign outside the ITAR-TASS news agency, Bolshaya Nikitskaya ulitsa

⑳ Bolshaya Nikitskaya Ulitsa

Большая Никитская улица

Bolshaya Nikitskaya ulitsa

Map 1 B5. M Arbatskaya, Okhotnyy Ryad, Biblioteka imeni Lenina.

This street, once the main road to Novgorod, is named after the 16th-century Nikitskiy Convent, demolished in the 1930s. Prominent aristocratic families built their palaces here in the 18th century. The finest among them is the former residence of Prince Sergei Menshikov, with its pale blue façade, reconstructed after the 1812 Great Fire of Moscow.

Opposite the Moscow Conservatory is the Church of the Little Ascension. Behind it is the Gothic tower of St Andrew's Anglican Church, built for the city's English community in 1882.

The heavily ornamented red-brick building at Nos. 19–20 is the Mayakovsky Theatre, which premiered Mayakovsky's plays *Bath House* and *The Bed Bug* in 1928–9. Both were staged by the great avant-garde director Vsevolod Meyerhold, who was tortured and executed by the Soviet regime in 1940.

About halfway along the road is Nikitskie Vorota ploshchad, named after the medieval gate that used to stand here. The building with a sign in the shape of a large globe is the ITAR-TASS news agency, Russia's main news agency.

Opposite is the Church of the Great Ascension. Alexander Pushkin married Natalya Goncharova here in 1831.

The imposing Pashkov House perched on its enormous stone base

㉑ Pashkov House

Дом Пашкова

Dom Pashkova

Ulitsa Znamenka 6. **Map** 3 C2. Ⓜ Borovitska, Biblioteka imeni Lenina. **Closed** to public.

This mansion built in the Neo-Classical style between 1784–8 was once the finest private house in Moscow and enjoys a hilltop location overlooking the Kremlin. The mansion's height was achieved by placing it on an enormous stone base. The building is surmounted by a perfectly proportioned rotunda. The most impressive façade is at the rear of the building, which originally led to a garden. The Moscow Institute for Nobles occupied the house from 1839 to 1861, when it was taken over by the Rumyantsev Museum. Once part of the National State Library, the restored building can be hired for special events.

㉒ Pushkin State Museum of Fine Arts

See pp90–91.

㉓ Gallery of 19th- and 20th-Century European and American Art

Музей Галерея искусства стран Европы и Америки XIX–XX веков

Galeryeya Iskusstva Stran Evropi I Ameriki X1X–XX Vekov

Ulitsa Volkhonka 14. **Map** 3 C2. **Tel** (495) 697 15 46. Ⓜ Kropotkinskaya. **Open** 10am–7pm Tue, Wed & Fri–Sun, (till 9pm Thu). **W** **newpaintart.ru**

Before the Revolution, this building housed the Kanyazhiy Dvor Hotel, whose guests included Maxim Gorky and Ilya Repin. Now it is a museum displaying Impressionist and post-Impressionist paintings that were previously shown in the Pushkin State Museum of Fine Arts next door, plus works from the Hermitage in St Petersburg.

The first of the three floors displays mainly European oil paintings from the first half of the 19th century, but the real masterpieces are upstairs. On the second floor are paintings by Vincent van Gogh, including *The Red Vineyard at Arles* (1888) and *Prisoners Exercising* (1890) as well as Pierre Auguste Renoir's *Nude* (1876) and *Bathing on the Seine* (1879). The same floor also holds Paul Cézanne's *Mont Ste Victoire* (1905) and a series of paintings by Paul Gauguin.

The third floor features works by Henri Matisse, including *Goldfish* (1911–12), and Pablo Picasso's *Girl Standing on a Ball* (1905). Russia is also represented, with paintings by Vasily Kandinsky, including *Improvisation No. 20a* (1911).

㉔ Glazunov Picture Gallery

Картинная галерейя Илйи Глазунова

Kartinnaya galereya Ilyi Glazunova

Ulitsa Volkhonka 13. **Map** 3 C2. **Tel** (495) 691 69 49. Ⓜ Kropotkinskaya. **Open** 11am–7pm Tue, Wed & Fri–Sun, 11am–9pm Thu. **W** **glazunov.ru**

This gallery showcases the work of Russia's most famous living artist, Ilya Glazunov. His fascination for Orthodox and Tsarist culture led to him being exiled to the provinces in the 1970s. His dissident mystique was enhanced by tales of a giant painting called *The Mystery of the Twentieth Century*, and senior Communists were said to secretly collect his work. Glazunov's retro-patriotism is typified by a picture called *Eternal Russia*, and his scathing view of Russian capitalism by another canvas, *The Market of Our Democracy*. His polemical art resonates with many Russians even if Moscow's intelligentsia despise it.

The well-lit façade of the Glazunov Picture Gallery

For hotels and restaurants in this area see p266 and pp280–82

Frescoes adorning the central dome of the Cathedral of Christ the Saviour

㉕ Cathedral of Christ the Saviour

Храм Христа Спасителя

Khram Khrista Spasitelya

Ulitsa Volkhonka 15. **Map** 3 C2

Ⓜ Kropotkinskaya.

The rebuilding of this vast cathedral in the late 1990s was the most ambitious of the construction projects undertaken by Moscow's then mayor, Yuri Luzhkov. The project courted controversy from the start, both on grounds of taste and cost. A presidential decree declared that no taxpayers' money should be spent on it – funds were to be raised through donations from the public, the Orthodox Church, foreign corporations and local oligarchs. In reality, the better part of the total bill of over US$200 million came from the state budget at a time when many Russians were suffering extreme poverty.

The original cathedral was built to commemorate Russia's victory over Napoleon's Grande Armée *(see p42)*, by architect Konstantin Ton. When completed in 1883 it was the tallest building in Moscow, its 103-m (338-ft) high gilded dome dominating the skyline. The cathedral was blown up on Stalin's orders in 1933 to make way for the never-built Palace of Soviets that was eventually superseded by an outdoor swimming pool in 1959.

In 2007, the rebuilt cathedral hosted the lying in state of former president Boris Yeltsin. The dome proffers spectacular views of Moscow.

㉖ Arbat Square

Арбатская площадь

Arbatskaya ploshchad

Map 3 B1. Ⓜ Arbatskaya.

A chaotic mass of traffic and underpasses, Arbat Square is the link between the vividly contrasting areas of Old (ulitsa Arbat) and New Arbat (ulitsa Novy Arbat). Beneath the square, the underpasses contain a society of their own. Expect to come across an impromptu rock concert, kittens and puppies for sale and, in late summer, pensioners selling wild mushrooms, though these are not always safe to buy.

Old Arbat street, a narrow thoroughfare that was once the heart of bohemian Moscow is celebrated in a famous ballad by Bulat Okudhava. Today, it lures tourists with its street-performers, portrait artists and souvenir stalls. New Arbat street was built in the 1960s on an inhuman scale. One side is lined with 24-storey apartment complexes, once awarded to People's Artists. The other side features office blocks overlaid by a synchronized neon light display that visitors can view from aboard trolleybus 2.

Stalin's Plan for a Palace of Soviets

The original Cathedral of Christ the Saviour was to have been replaced by a Palace of Soviets – a tower, 315 m (1,034 ft) high, topped by a 100-m (328-ft) statue of Lenin. It was designed as the highlight of Stalin's reconstruction of Moscow, much of the rest of which was realized: skyscrapers, boulevards and the metro system are now familiar features of the city. In the process, many supposedly unnecessary buildings were destroyed, but the intended centrepiece of Stalin's plan was never built due to the swampy subsoil in this locality. Devout Russians whispered that it was God's vengeance that thwarted Stalin's "Tower of Babel".

Palace of Soviets as envisioned by an artist

㉒ Pushkin State Museum of Fine Arts

Музей изобразительных искусств имени АС Пушкина
Muzey izobrazitelnykb iskusstv imeni AS Pushkina

Founded in 1898, the Pushkin State Museum houses a fine collection of works from antiquity to the early 19th century. Following the collapse of the Soviet Union, the curators admitted that they had countless works of art hidden away. Some of these are now on show, including Heinrich Schliemann's *Treasures of Troy* excavations, which were taken from the Museum of Ancient History in Berlin by Soviet military authorities in 1945. The building was designed by Roman Klein. It was first built to house plaster casts of Classical sculptures for Moscow University art students to use for research. The museum remains open while undergoing a major renovation programme, which includes plans to open new galleries and an exhibition hall.

Museum Building
The design of the building borrows from Ancient Greece, Italy, France and Germany to create a suitably impressive façade and interior.

Room 23 houses mostly 18th–19th-century French paintings.

Stairs to ground floor

First floor

★ Annunciation
Painted around 1490 by Italian artist Sandro Botticelli, this work was originally part of a large altarpiece. It shows the angel Gabriel telling the Virgin Mary that she is to bear the Son of God.

Room 3 houses Schliemann's *Treasures of Troy*.

Key to Floorplan

- Collection of plaster casts
- Art of ancient civilizations
- Italian art of 13th–16th centuries
- 15th–17th-century German, Dutch, and Flemish art
- 17th–18th-century Spanish and Italian art
- 17th–early 19th-century French art
- Temporary exhibition space

Gallery Guide

The ticket office is in the entrance hall. The displays are spread over two floors. Although the museum halls are numbered, the layout is not strictly chronological. The ground floor houses all of the works from ancient civilizations as well as Byzantine art and Italian, Dutch and Flemish art from the 13th to the 17th centuries. Spanish, Italian and French art from the 17th to the early 19th centuries is upstairs. The cloakroom and toilets are in the basement.

For hotels and restaurants in this area see p266 and pp280–82

Bucentaur's Return to the Pier by the Palazzo Ducale (1729–30)
Venetian landscape painter, Canaletto, was known for his bold use of colour, exemplfied in this scene of the Grand Canal.

VISITORS' CHECKLIST

Practical information
Ulitsa Volkhonka 12.
Map 3 C2.
Tel (495) 697 95 78.
W arts-museum.ru
Open 10am–7pm Tue–Sun (till 9pm Thu). English.

Transport
M Kropotkinskaya.

Ahasuerus, Haman and Esther (1660)
In this biblical scene by Rembrandt, the Persian king, Ahasuerus, is flanked by his Jewish wife and his minister, Haman. Esther, lit by a single ray of light, accuses Haman of plotting to destroy the Jews.

Room 10
is dedicated to Rembrandt and his school and includes drawings, etchings and six paintings by the great master.

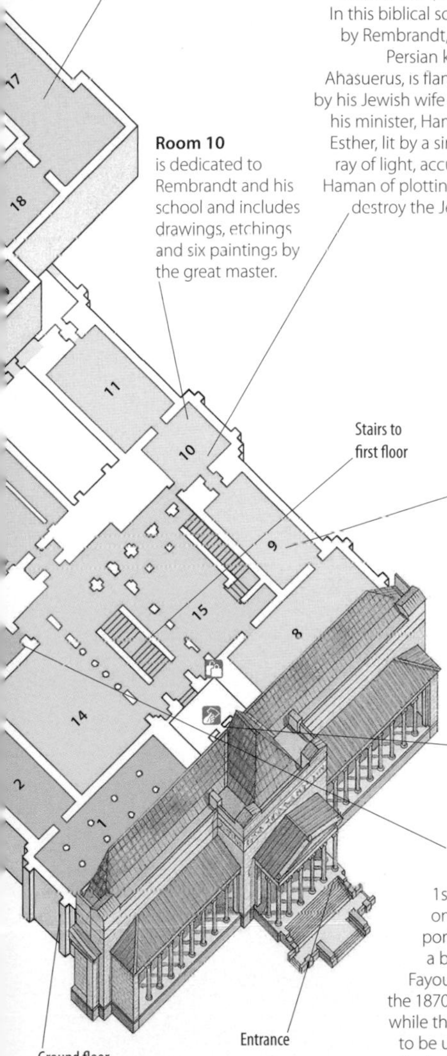

Stairs to first floor

★ **Bacchanalia** (around 1615)
Based on the myth of the god of nature, vegetation and viniculture, Dionysus-Bacchus, this splendidly exuberant, sensual painting was in the possession of its artist, Peter Paul Rubens, his entire life.

Tickets and information

★ **Fayoum Portrait**
Painted in the 1st century AD, this is one of a collection of portraits discovered at a burial ground at the Fayoum oasis in Egypt in the 1870s. They were painted while the subjects were alive, to be used as death masks on their mummies when they died.

Entrance

Ground floor

㉗ Lermontov House-Museum

Дом-музей МЮ Лермонтова

Dom-muzey MYu Lermontova

Ulitsa Malaya Molchanovka 2. **Map** 3 B1. **Tel** (495) 691 52 98. Ⓜ Arbatskaya. **Closed** for renovation.

Tucked away behind the tower blocks of the New Arbat is the house where the Romantic poet and novelist Mikhail Lermontov lived with his grandmother from 1829–32, when he was a student at Moscow University.

More interested in writing poetry than in his studies, Lermontov left university without graduating, becoming a guardsman. In 1937, he was exiled to the Caucasus for criticizing the authorities in a poem about the death of Pushkin. This marked a turning point in Lermontov's writing, presaging his most famous work, the novel *A Hero of our Time*, written in 1840. He was killed in a duel the next year, when he was only 26.

There are five rooms in the museum, and each bears testament to Lermontov's intellectual gifts and zest for life. In the study he would play the guitar, piano and violin, and compose music, while the drawing room was often the site of dancing, singing and masquerades. Many of his manuscripts are displayed downstairs, together with watercolours of the Caucasus, some by Lermontov himself.

The elegant drawing room in the Lermontov House-Museum

Sitting room with one of Skryabin's pianos, Skryabin House-Museum

㉘ Skryabin House-Museum

Дом-музей АН Скрябина

Dom-muzey AN Skryabina

Bolshoi Nikolopeskovskiy pereulok 11. **Map** 3 A1. **Tel** (499) 241 19 01. Ⓜ Smolenskaya, Arbatskaya. **Open** 11am–6pm Tue, Wed & Fri–Sun, 1–9pm Thu. **Closed** last Fri of the month.

Pianist and composer Aleksandr Skryabin (1872–1915) lived in this apartment from 1912 until his death at the age of 43. A graduate of the Moscow Conservatory with an international reputation as a concert pianist, he was also a composer and theorist, best known for orchestral works such as *Prometheus*.

Although Skryabin spent much of his time abroad giving concerts, he paid considerable attention to the decor of his apartment. The lofty rooms house his pianos, autographed manuscripts and Style-Moderne furniture. The museum also houses his original colour organ, with which he used to combine musical notes with colours. Regular concerts are held in the rooms on the ground floor.

㉙ Spasopeskovskiy Pereulok

Спасопесковский переулок

Spasopeskovskiy pereulok

Map 3 A1. Ⓜ Smolenskaya.

The charms of the Old Arbat have been preserved in this secluded lane and the adjoining square, Spasopeskovskaya ploshchad. In 1878, Vasiliy Polenov painted *A Moscow Courtyard*, depicting the square as a bucolic haven in the midst of the city.

At the centre of Polenov's picture, now in the State Tretyakov Gallery *(see pp98–9)*, is the white bell tower of the Church of the Saviour on the Sands (Tserkov Spas na Peskakh) from which the lane gets its name. This 18th-century church still dominates the square, which is otherwise known as the site of Spaso House. This Classical-style mansion has been the home of US ambassadors since 1933.

㉚ Melnikov House

Дом Мельникова

Dom Melnikova

Krivoarbatskiy pereulok 10. **Map** 3 A2. Ⓜ Smolenskaya. **Closed** to public.

This unique Modernist house was designed by Konstantin Melnikov, one of Russia's greatest Constructivist architects *(see p33)*, in 1927. Made from brick overlaid with stucco, it consists of two interlocking cylinders studded with hexagonal windows, creating a honeycomb effect. A spiral staircase rises through the space where the cylinders overlap, linking the airy living spaces.

Though it was built for Melnikov's family, it was meant as a prototype for future housing developments, until Stalin encouraged architects to adopt a new monumental style. Although he had won the Gold Medal at the 1925 Paris World

Fair, Melnikov's work was later ignored. However, he lived in this house for the rest of his life, one of the few residents of central Moscow allowed to live in a privately built dwelling.

㉛ Pushkin House-Museum

Музей-квартира АС Пушкина

Muzey-kvartira AS Pushkina

Ulitsa Arbat 53. **Map** 3 A2. **Tel** (499) 241 92 95. Ⓜ Smolenskaya. **Open** 10am–6pm Wed & Fri–Sun, noon–9pm Thu. **Closed** last Fri of the month. English (book in advance).

Alexander Pushkin rented this elegant Empire-style flat for the first three months of his marriage to Natalya Goncharova. Soon, however, Pushkin tired of life in Moscow and the couple moved to St Petersburg, where gossip began to circulate that Pushkin's brother-in-law, a French officer, was making advances to Natalya. Pushkin challenged him to a duel, was mortally wounded, and died two days later.

The fascinating exhibition on the museum's ground floor gives an idea of what Moscow would have been like before the Great Fire. On display are wax figures of a serf orchestra that belonged to the Goncharova family. Pushkin and Natalya lived upstairs. There are few personal possessions other than Pushkin's writing bureau and some family portraits, but the atmosphere is reverential.

Detail of a plaque outside Pushkin House-Museum

㉜ Ministry of Foreign Affairs

Министерство Иностранных дел

Ministertsvo Inostrannikh del

Smolenskaya ploshchad X. **Map** 3 A2. Ⓜ Smolenskaya. **Closed** to public.

Old Arbat meets the Garden Ring at Smolenskaya ploshchad, a wide expanse dominated by a Stalin-Gothic "skyscraper". Built between 1948 and 1953 to house the Soviet Foreign Ministry (known to Russians as "MID"), the 27-storey central block is crowned by a spire, taking it to a height of 172 m (564 ft). The original design was without a spire; when Stalin remarked on this a metal spire was hastily added, painted to match the rest of the building.

The Ministry of Foreign Affairs building, an example of Stalin-Gothic architecture

㉝ Shalyapin House-Museum

Дом-музей Ф.И. Шаляпина

Dom-muzey FI Shalyapina

Novinskiy bulvar 25. **Map** 1 A5. **Tel** (495) 605 62 36. Ⓜ Smolenskaya, Barrikadnaya. **Open** check website for timings. book in advance. **shalyapin-museum.org**

The renowned Russian bass, Fyodor Shalyapin, occupied this mansion from 1910 until he emigrated from Soviet Russia in 1922. Born in Kazan in 1873, he worked as a stevedore on the *Volga* before his unique vocal talent was discovered. He went on to sing such great operatic bass roles as *Don Quixote*, *Ivan the Terrible* and *Boris Godunov*. He died in Paris in 1938, but his remains were later returned to Russia for reburial in the Novodevichiy Cemetery *(see p105)*.

Shalyapin rehearsed with renowned musicians and composers in the concert room, where visitors can now listen to recordings of the master at work. There is also a Bachstein grand piano, which was presented to Shalyapin in 1913.

Items on display in the house include the singer's much treasured velvet armchair. A selection of his playing cards are laid out on a side table. The mementoes on the second floor include amusing portraits of the singer in his various operatic roles, as well as a collection of theatrical costumes.

Alexander Pushkin

Born in 1799 into Russia's aristocracy, Alexander Pushkin had established a reputation as both a poet and a rebel by the time he was 20. In 1820, he was exiled by the state for his liberal verse, but eventually allowed back to Moscow. Following early narrative poems such as *The Robber Brothers* (1821), he created his famous novel in verse, *Eugene Onegin* (1823–30). Later he wrote mostly prose, developing a unique style in pieces such as *The Queen of Spades* (1834). He is revered for giving Russian literature its own identity.

ZAMOSKVORECHE

First settled in the 13th century, Zamoskvoreche (literally "beyond the Moscow river") acted as an outpost against the Mongols. The district's main road, Bolshaya Ordynka, was the route to the *Orda*, or Golden Horde, the Mongol headquarters on the Volga river. Later, under Ivan the Terrible, the Streltsy (royal guard) was stationed here. Artisans serving the court also moved in, living in areas according to their trade, each of which sponsored a church. These historic churches, now in varying states of repair, and the fact that the district was almost untouched by the replanning of the 1930s, give it a more old-fashioned atmosphere than the centre, which is dominated by massive Soviet architecture. In the 19th century, wealthy merchants settled here, many of whom, such as Aleksey Bakhrushin and Pavel Tretyakov, were patrons of the arts. Today, the State Tretyakov Gallery, home to its founder's collection, is the nation's most important collection of Russian art.

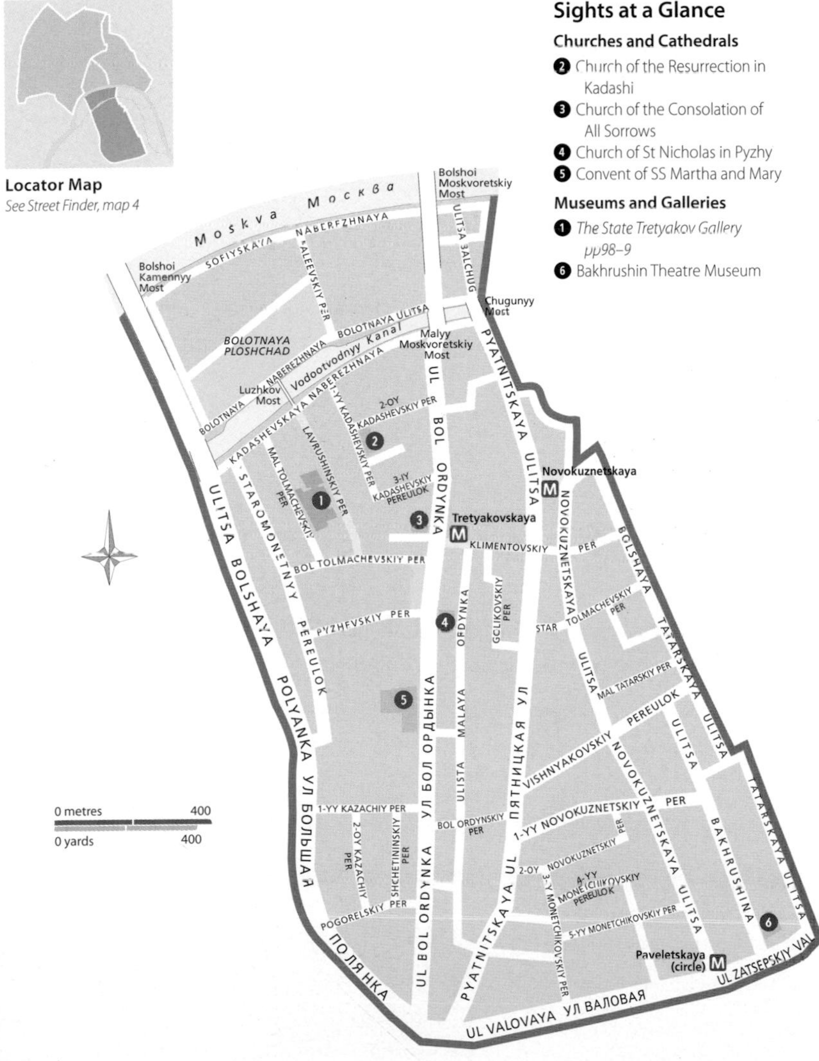

Locator Map
See Street Finder, map 4

Sights at a Glance

Churches and Cathedrals

2. Church of the Resurrection in Kadashi
3. Church of the Consolation of All Sorrows
4. Church of St Nicholas in Pyzhy
5. Convent of SS Martha and Mary

Museums and Galleries

1. *The State Tretyakov Gallery pp98–9*
6. Bakhrushin Theatre Museum

◀ *The Appearance of Christ to the People* by Alexander Ivanov in the State Tretyakov Gallery

For map symbols *see back flap*

Street-by-Street: Around Pyatnitskaya Ulitsa

An old-fashioned atmosphere still prevails in the area around Pyatnitskaya ulitsa. The well-established streets are lined with attractive 19th-century churches and imposing Neo-Classical mansions. The busiest part of the district is the area around Tretyakovskaya metro. The market stalls on the station forecourt spill over onto Klimentovskiy pereulok, and nearby Pyatnitskaya ulitsa is the main shopping street. A short walk to the west is the stunning State Tretyakov Gallery. To the north, the area is bordered by the Vodootvodnyy Canal, which was built in 1783–6 to prevent the regular spring flooding of the Moskva river.

Vodootvodnyy Canal

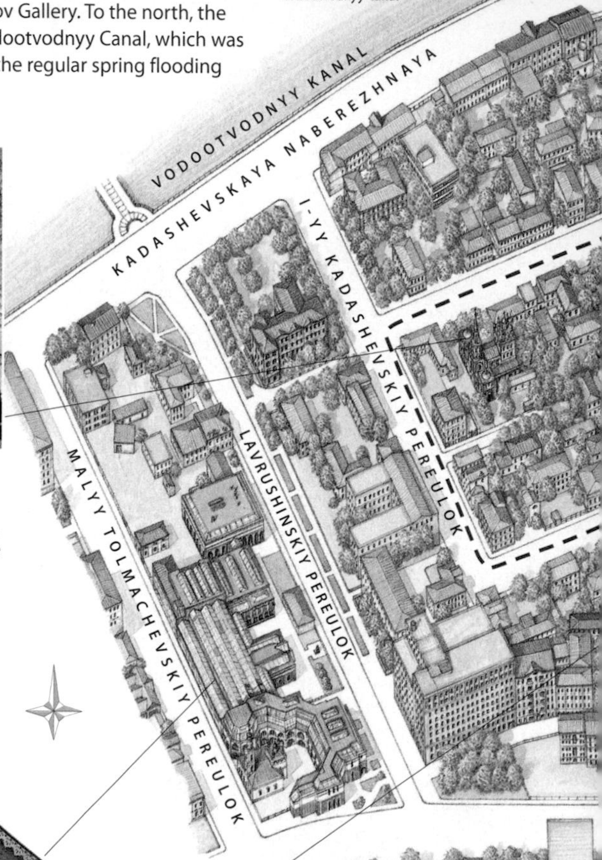

VODOOTVODNYY KANAL

KADASHEVSKAYA NABEREZHNAYA

1-YY KADASHEVSKIY PEREULOK

LAVRUSHINSKIY PEREULOK

MALYY TOLMACHEVSKIY PEREULOK

2 ★ Church of the Resurrection in Kadashi
With its five onion domes and lavish limestone ornamentation, this magnificent church is a fine example of the style known as Moscow Baroque *(see p32)*.

Key

– Suggested route

0 metres 100

0 yards 100

1 ★ The State Tretyakov Gallery
The world's largest collection of Russian art is housed here. Taken down in the Soviet era, the statue of Pavel Tretyakov has now been restored to its rightful place in front of the gallery.

The Demidov House was built in 1789–91 by a family of well-known industrialists.

3 Church of the Consolation of All Sorrows
Two of Moscow's best-known architects contributed to this much-loved church. Vasiliy Bazhenov designed the bell tower and Osip Bove the rotunda.

For hotels and restaurants in this area see p266 and p282

Moskva
ZAMOSKVORECHE

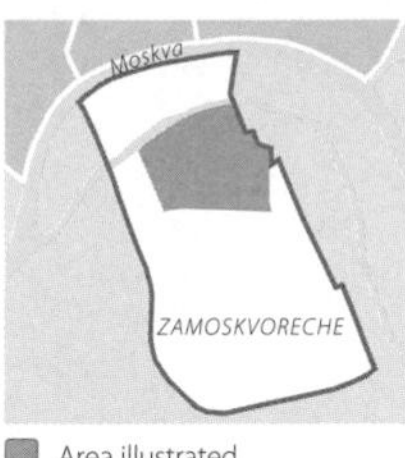

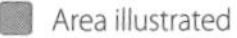

Area illustrated

The Church of SS Michael and Fyodor, dating from the late 17th century, is named after two martyrs killed by Mongols when they refused to renounce Christianity.

Church of St John the Baptist has a distinctive green bell tower and was built in the 18th century.

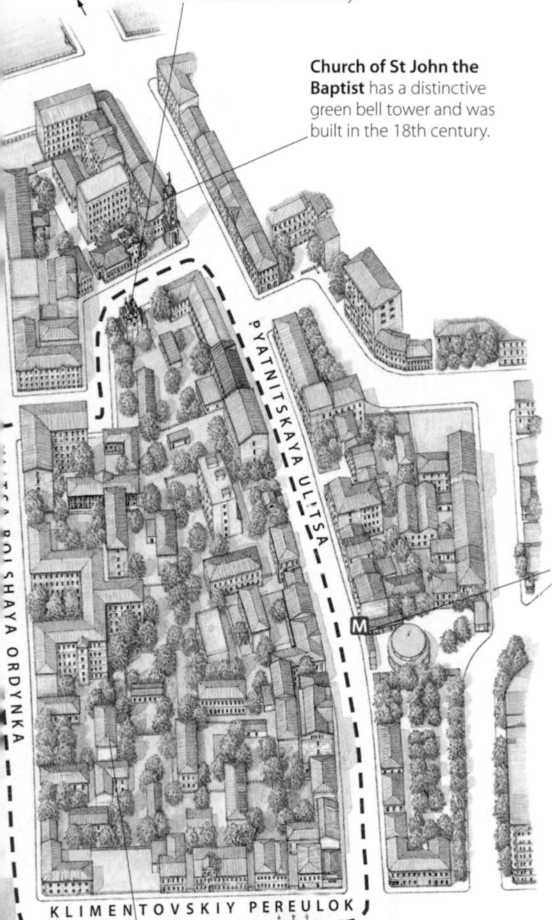

Kremlin
PYATNITSKAYA ULITSA
KLIMENTOVSKIY PEREULOK
ULITSA BOLSHAYA ORDYNKA
M
Tretyakovskaya

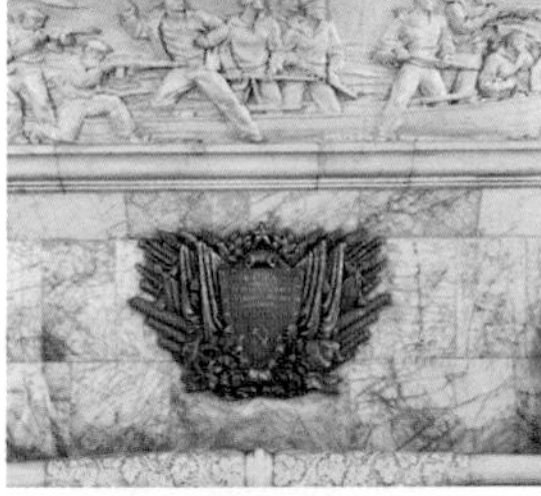

Novokuznetskaya Metro Station
Designed by Ivan Taranov and Natalia Bykova, this metro station was opened in 1943 at the height of World War II. The design of the interior is based on military subjects.

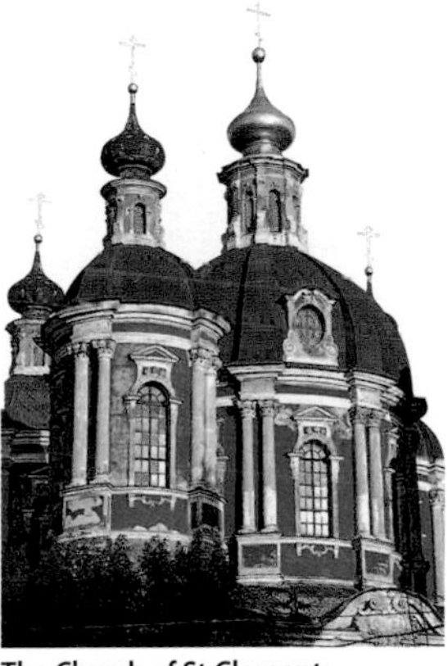

The Church of St Clement
Built in stages between 1720 and 1774, this splendid church is an outstanding example of Moscow Baroque. It has four black, star-spangled onion domes and a central golden one.

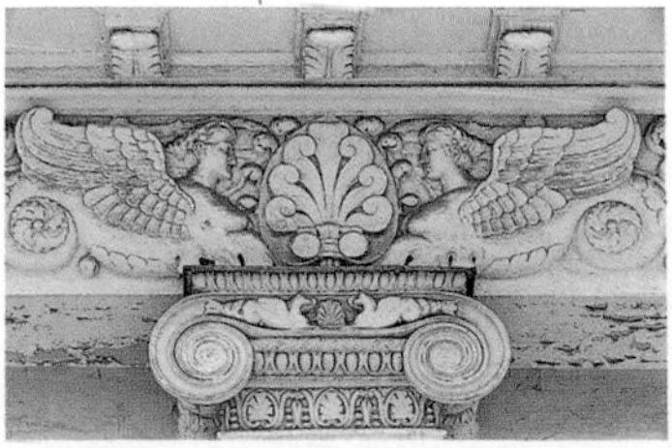

The Dolgov House
This town house, with an elaborately decorated Neo-Classical exterior, was built in the 1770s for a wealthy merchant named Dolgov, possibly by his son-in-law, Vasiliy Bazhenov.

❶ The State Tretyakov Gallery

Третьяковская галерея

Tretyakovskaya galereya

The Tretyakov Gallery was founded in 1856 by the wealthy merchant Pavel Tretyakov who presented his private museum of Russian art to the city in 1892. His brother Sergei also donated a number of works and the gallery's collection has been expanding ever since. Today, the Tretyakov has the largest collection of Russian art in the world. The building has a striking façade, designed by artist Viktor Vasnetsov, with a bas-relief of St George and the dragon at its centre. Many of the early 20th-century works from the collection are now housed in the State Tretyakov Gallery on Krymsky Val.

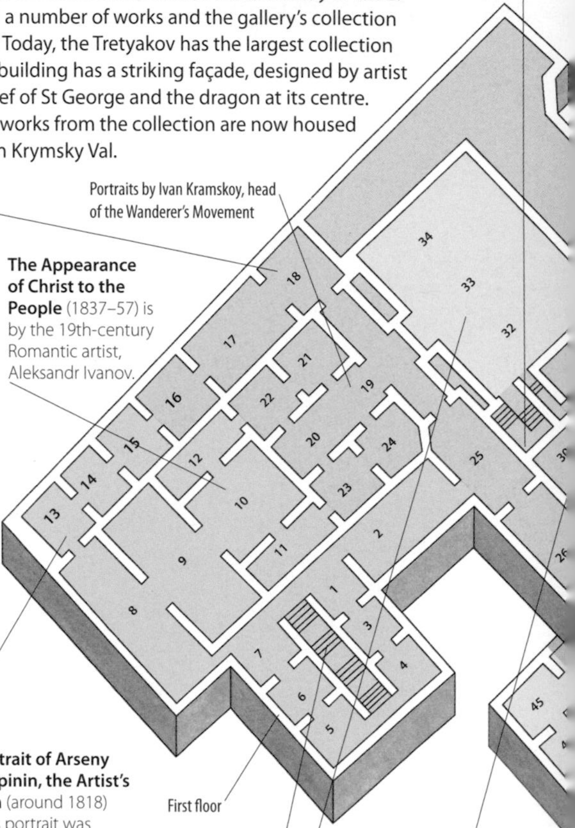

Stairs down to ground floor

Portraits by Ivan Kramskoy, head of the Wanderer's Movement

The Rooks Have Come (1871)
This bleak winter scene by Aleksey Savrasov contains a message of hope: rooks are taken by Russians as a sign of the coming spring.

The Appearance of Christ to the People (1837–57) is by the 19th-century Romantic artist, Aleksandr Ivanov.

Portrait of Arseny Tropinin, the Artist's Son (around 1818)
This portrait was painted by the renowned artist Vasily Tropinin. He was a serf for 47 years before gaining his freedom and finding commercial success.

First floor

Stairs from basement

Portraits by Ilya Repin

★ Demon (Seated) (1890)
This is one of several paintings by Mikhail Vrubel, who adopted a new, strikingly modern style. They are inspired by Mikhail Lermontov's Symbolist poem, *The Demon*, with which Vrubel became obsessed.

Gallery Guide

The gallery has 62 rooms on two main floors. On entering the museum, visitors first descend to the basement ticket office, then head straight up to the first floor. Paintings are hung in chronological order in rooms 1–48, while rooms 49–54 display drawings and engravings. The Russian Treasury is housed on the ground floor in room 55, while rooms 56–62 contain icons.

Ivan the Terrible and his Son Ivan on 16 November, 1581
Painted in 1885 by Ilya Repin, this intense painting depicts the mighty tsar's face fraught with guilt as he cradles the mortally wounded body of his son.

VISITORS' CHECKLIST

Practical information
Lavrushinskiy pereulok 10.
Map 4 D2.
Tel (495) 951 13 62.
tretyakovagallery.ru
Open 10am–6pm Tue, Wed, Sat & Sun (till 9pm Thu & Fri)

Transport
6, K, 25. Novokuznetskaya, Tretyakovskaya. 1, 4, 8, 33, 62.

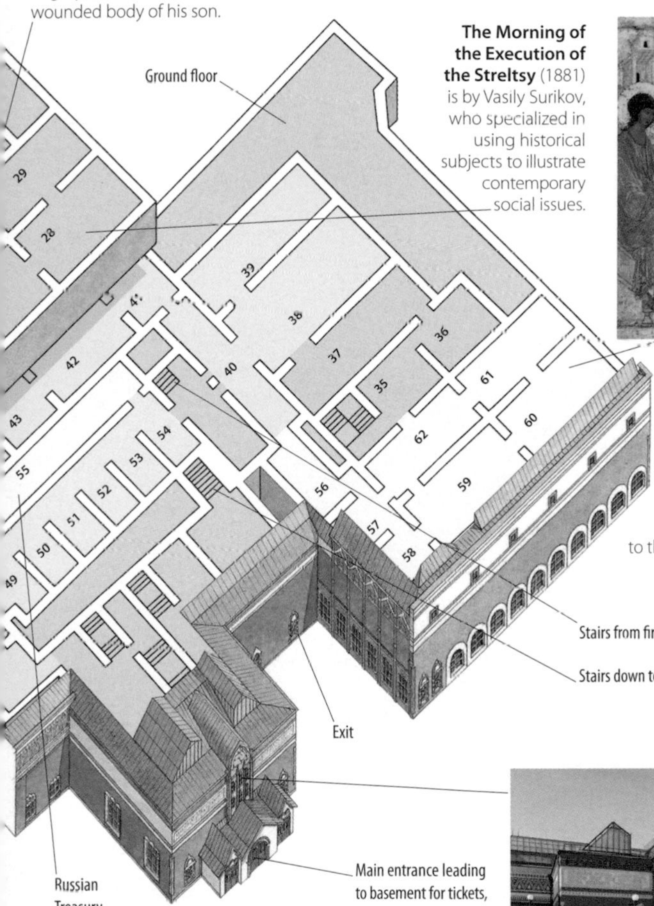

Ground floor

The Morning of the Execution of the Streltsy (1881) is by Vasily Surikov, who specialized in using historical subjects to illustrate contemporary social issues.

29 28 39 38 37 36 35 61 60 62 59 41 42 43 40 54 55 53 52 51 50 49 56 57 58

★ **The Trinity** (1420s)
This beautiful icon was painted by Andrei Rublev for the Trinity Monastery of St Sergius *(see p114)*, where he had been a novice monk. He dedicated the painting to the monastery's founder, St Sergius of Radonezh.

Stairs from first floor

Stairs down to basement

Exit

Russian Treasury

Main entrance leading to basement for tickets, information, toilets and cloakrooms

Key to Floorplan

- 18th and early 19th centuries
- Second half of the 19th century
- Late 19th and early 20th centuries
- Drawings and engravings of the 18th–20th centuries
- Icons and treasury
- Non-exhibition space

Main Façade
The gallery's façade was designed in 1902–04 by Viktor Vasnetsov. An example of the Russian-Revival style, it has a frieze inspired by medieval manuscripts.

❷ Church of the Resurrection in Kadashi

Храм Воскресения в Кадашах
Khram Voskreseniya v Kadashakh

2-oy Kadashevskiy pereulok 7. **Map** 4 D2. Ⓜ Tretyakovskaya. **Open** 8am–7pm daily. English, call (495) 953 22 91 to book in advance.

This five-domed church is a fine example of Moscow Baroque *(see p32)* and is thought to have been designed by Sergei Turchaninov. It was paid for by a wealthy guild of weavers who moved into the district of Kadeshevo in the 17th century.

The church was built around 1687, and a slender, tapering bell tower was added in 1695. Apart from the five gilded onion domes, the most notable features are the tiers of lace-like limestone balustrades just below the drums supporting the domes. In Soviet times, the church was turned into a furniture factory (hence the stream pipes that enter the compound), and it has stubbornly refused to vacate the building. A sign left by protestors reads, "Since 1992 we have sought the return of the Church of the Resurrection in Kadashi. Shame on you!"

❸ Church of the Consolation of All Sorrows

Церковь Богоматери Всех Скорбящих Радость
Tserkov Bogomateri Vsekh Skorbyashchikh Radost

Ulitsa Bolshaya Ordynka 20. **Map** 4 D3. Ⓜ Tretyakovskaya. **Open** 7am–8pm daily.

Both the Church of the Consolation of All Sorrows and the Neo-Classical mansion opposite belonged to the Dolgovs, a wealthy merchant family. After completion of their house in the 1770s, they commissioned the church from architect Vasiliy Bazhenov, a relation by marriage. He first built a new belfry and refectory and then replaced the existing medieval church – but his creation was destroyed in the

The Empire-style Church of the Consolation of All Sorrows

1812 Great Fire of Moscow. A new church was designed by Osip Bove, the architect in charge of Moscow's reconstruction after the fire. His Empire-style rotunda and dome were finished in 1833.

The interior is unusual for an Orthodox church due to its lavish Empire-style colonnade, theatrical iconostasis and exuberant sculpted angels. On display in the church's left aisle is the *Icon of Our Lady of Consolation of All Sorrows*. It is said to have miraculously cured the ailing sister of Patriarch Joachim in the 17th century.

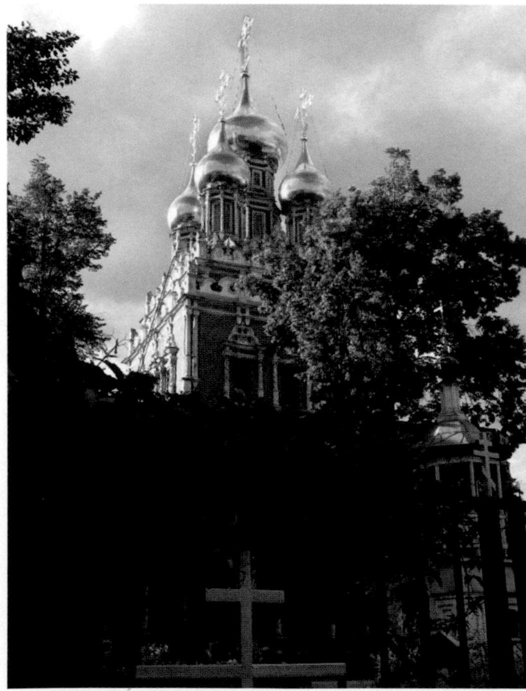

Spectacular view of the Church of the Resurrection in Kadashi

❹ Church of St Nicholas in Pyzhy

Церковь Николая в Пыжах
Tserkov Nikolaya v Pyzhakh

Ulitsa Bolshaya Ordynka 27a/8. **Map** 4 D3. **Tel** (495) 951 37 42. Ⓜ Tretyakovskaya. **Open** 7:30am–8pm daily.

Small crowns as well as the traditional crosses decorate the silver domes of this church, indicating that its construction (1670–72) was financed by the Streltsy, or royal guard. Some of these men were later executed by Peter the Great for their role in the 1682 Streltsy Revolt. The exterior decoration includes fretted cornices and a tiered bell tower. In 1934, the church was closed by the Communists and turned into a laboratory, only being returned to the Orthodox Church in 1990.

5 Convent of SS Martha and Mary

Марфо-Мариинская обитель

Marfo-Mariinskaya obitel

Ulitsa Bolshaya Ordynka 34. **Map** 4 D3. **Tel** (495) 951 11 39. M Tretyakovskaya, Polyanka. **Open** 7:30am–7:30pm daily.

A low archway leads from the street to this compound, containing what appear at first glance to be medieval buildings. In fact they date from 1908–12 and were designed by Aleksey Shchusev, who later built Lenin's Mausoleum.

The convent was conceived to house a dispensary, a clinic, a small women's hospital and a school. It was run by the Order of the Sisters of Charity, which was founded in 1908 by Grand Duchess Yelizaveta Fyodorovna, the sister-in-law of Tsar Nicholas II. She had turned to charitable work after her husband, Grand Prince Sergei (the tsar's uncle), was assassinated in a terrorist attack in the troubled year of 1905. Yelizaveta also met a violent death – the day after the shooting of Tsar Nicholas II and his family in 1918, the Bolsheviks pushed her down a mine shaft.

When designing the Church of the Intercession, the convent's main building, Shchusev carried out considerable research into Russian religious architecture, particularly that of the Pskov and Novgorod schools. His design juxtaposed a traditional style with Style-Moderne features such as boldly pointed gables, limestone carvings of mythical creatures and Slavonic script on the outer walls.

Convent of SS Martha and Mary, designed by Aleksey Shchusev

Set design by Mikhail Fokin, on show in the Bakhrushin Theatre Museum

The artist Mikhail Nesterov, a protegé of industrialist and art patron Savva Mamontov *(see p114)*, was commissioned to design and paint the frescoes in the interior of the church. He also designed the pale grey and white habits of the nuns.

After the Revolution, the Order of the Sisters of Charity was suppressed and the church was used as a workshop for restoring icons. The nuns have returned to staff the clinic since 1991, when the convent was restored to the Orthodox Church.

6 Bakhrushin Theatre Museum

Театральный музей имени А.А. Бахрушина

Teatralnyy muzey imeni AA Bakhrushina

Ulitsa Bakhrushina 31/12. **Map** 4 E4. **Tel** (495) 953 44 70. M Paveletskaya. **Open** noon–7pm Tue–Sun (last ticket 6pm). **Closed** last Fri of the month. English, book in advance.

Founded in 1894 by Aleksey Bakhrushin, a merchant and theatrical impresario, this museum contains probably the most important collection of theatre memorabilia in Russia. Spread over two floors, the exhibits range from sets and costumes to theatre tickets, programmes, advertisements and signed photographs.

The permanent exhibition begins in a study, where visitors can peruse a selection of Bakhrushin's belongings, as well as photographs and paintings depicting family life. From here, stairs lead down into the basement, which hosts temporary exhibitions on a variety of themes related to acting and the theatre.

Exhibits on 19th-century theatre include costumes and sets from the Ballets Russes. This company, formed by Sergei Diaghilev in 1909, revolutionized ballet. The sets include some designed by Mikhail Fokin, the company's inspired choreographer. A pair of ballet shoes belonging to Marie Taglioni, the renowned Swedish dancer, is also on show. She rose to fame when she featured in *La Sylphide* (1832), a ballet choreographed by her father.

The room on 20th-century avant-garde theatre includes stage models created for outstanding directors Konstantin Stanislavskiy and Vsevolod Meyerhold.

FURTHER AFIELD

Moscow's suburbs are generally rather bleak, but they conceal a surprising number of attractions, all accessible by metro. To the south of the centre lie a number of fortified monasteries, built to defend the city against the Mongols and the Poles. The most spectacular of them is the Novodevichiy Convent, a serene, fortified complex dating from the 16th century that boasts a glorious cathedral and a Baroque bell tower. Also worth a visit is the Donskoy Monastery with its ensemble of old and new cathedrals. The area is also known for the beauty and variety of its green spaces. Gorky and Izmaylovo parks are the perfect places to relax, while Sparrow Hills offers fantastic views. The city's best-kept secrets, however, are its grand estates situated away from the centre in what used to be countryside. Notable among these are the Neo-Classical summer residences of the Sheremetev family: Kuskovo and Ostankino. Both have beautifully preserved gardens and palaces full of fine paintings and period furnishings.

Sights at a Glance

Churches and Cathedrals

1 *Novodevichiy Convent pp104–105*
3 Church of St Nicholas of the Weavers
6 Donskoy Monastery

Museums

2 Tolstoy House-Museum
4 State Tretyakov Gallery on Krymsky Val
8 Kolomenskoe
12 Vasnetsov House-Museum

Historic Buildings

9 Tsaritsyno
10 Kuskovo

Parks

5 Gorky Park
7 Sparrow Hills
11 Izmaylovo
14 All-Russian Exhibition Centre (VVTs)

Palaces

13 Ostankino Palace

Key

Central Moscow
Motorway
Main road
Minor road
Railway

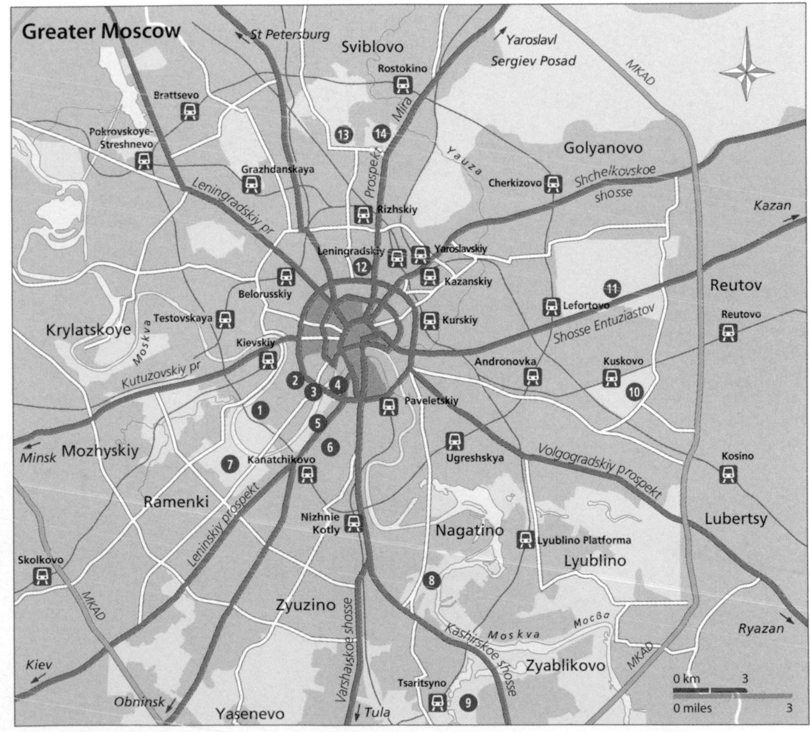

Picturesque view of the Novodevichiy Convent from across a verdant lake

For map symbols *see back flap*

❶ Novodevichiy Convent

Новодевичий монастырь

Novodevichiy monastyr

Probably the most beautiful of the semi-circle of fortified religious institutions to the south of Moscow is Novodevichiy Convent, founded by Basil III in 1524 to commemorate the capture of Smolensk from the Lithuanians. The only building to be built at this time was the Cathedral of the Virgin of Smolensk. Most of the other buildings were added in the late 17th century by Peter the Great's half-sister, the Regent Sophia. After Peter deposed her and reclaimed his throne in 1689, he confined her here for the rest of her life. In 1812, Napoleon's troops tried to blow up the convent but, according to a popular story, it was saved by the nuns, who snuffed out the fuses.

Gate Church of the Intercession
It is not known who designed this church, but it is believed to have been built in the second half of the 17th century.

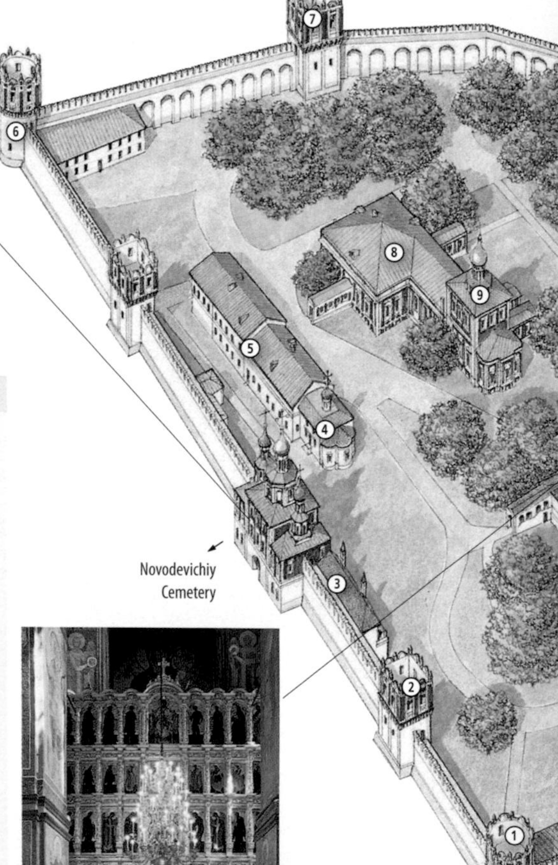

★ Cathedral of the Virgin of Smolensk
Built in 1524, this cathedral is the oldest building in the convent. The five-tier iconostasis, the rich frescoes and the onion domes all date from the 17th century.

0 metres 25
0 yards 25

KEY

① **Shoemaker's Tower**

② **Vorobeva Tower**

③ **Maria's Chambers** were used by the daughter of Tsar Alexis Mikhailovich, Maria.

④ **Church of St Ambrose**

⑤ **The Palace of Irina Gudunova** was home to the widow of Tsar Fyodor I.

⑥ **Setunskaya Tower**

⑦ **Faceted Tower**

⑧ **Refectory**

⑨ **The Church of the Assumption** and adjoining refectory were built in the 1680s on the orders of the Regent Sophia.

⑩ **Nuns' cells**

⑪ **Saviour's Tower**

⑫ **Naprudnaya Tower**

⑬ **The guard house** is where the Regent Sophia was imprisoned.

⑭ **Tsaritsa's Tower**

⑮ **St Nicholas's Tower**

⑯ **Tailor's Tower**

⑰ **Hospital**

Tomb of Boris Yeltsin, Novodevichiy Cemetery

Novodevichiy Cemetery

Many famous Russians are buried in this cemetery. Among the leading cultural figures are playwright Anton Chekhov, writer Nikolai Gogol, composers Sergei Prokofiev, Aleksandr Skryabin *(see p92)* and Dmitri Shostakovich and opera singer Fyodor Shalyapin *(see p93)*. The cemetery is also the final resting place for numerous military and political dignitaries from the Soviet era, including the former Russian premier Nikita Khrushchev *(see p45)* and the first President of the Russian Federation, Boris Yeltsin.

VISITORS' CHECKLIST

Practical information
Novodevichiy proezd 1.
Tel (499) 246 85 26.
Open 9am–5pm daily.
Closed Some public hols.
grounds only.
Cemetery: **Tel** (499) 246 66 14.
Open 9am–5pm daily.

Transport
64, 132. M Sportivnaya.
5, 15.

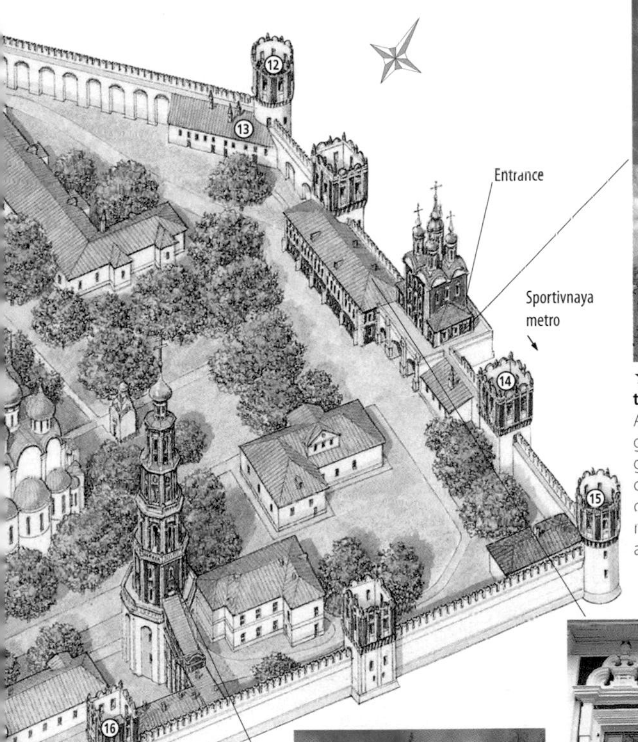

★ Gate Church of the Transfiguration
A cornice of scallop-shell gables, topped by five gilded domes and crosses, crowns this grand Baroque church. It stands over the main gate to the convent and was completed in 1688.

★ Bell Tower
Completed in 1690, this tower is one of the most exuberant examples of Baroque architecture in Moscow. The Church of St John the Divine occupies the second storey of the six-tiered, octagonal tower, which stands 72 m (236 ft) high.

Lopukhin Palace
This palace was built in 1687–9. After Peter the Great's death in 1725 his first wife, Yevdokiya Lopukhina, moved here from the Convent of the Intercession in Suzdal where she had been sent after Peter tired of her.

❷ Tolstoy House-Museum

Музей-усадьба ЛН Толстого
Muzey-usadba LN Tolstovo

Ulitsa Lva Tolstovo 21. **Tel** (499) 246 94 44. Ⓜ Park Kultury. **Open** 11am–6pm Tue, Wed & Fri–Sun, noon–8pm Thu. English, book in advance. **tolstoymuseum.ru**

The presence of one of Russia's greatest novelists can be felt in every corner of this evocative house. It was here that Leo Tolstoy (1828–1910) spent the winters between 1882 and 1901 with his long-suffering wife, Sofya Andreevna, and their nine surviving children. The summers were spent on the Tolstoy ancestral estate at Yasnaya Polyana *(see p116)*.

Their house in Moscow was turned into a museum in 1921 on Lenin's orders and has been preserved much as it would have been when Tolstoy and his family lived here.

On the ground floor, the large table in the dining room is still laid with crockery. The evening meal in the Tolstoy household always began promptly at 6pm at the summons of the cuckoo clock on the wall. Adjacent to the dining room is the "corner room" where, at one time, the elder sons, Sergei, Ilya and Lev, would retire to play Chinese billiards. The house exudes a sense of ordered, comfortable family life, but Tolstoy and his wife frequently quarrelled violently, largely on account of his wish to renounce society and live as simply as possible.

The simple desk in Tolstoy's study where he wrote his final novel, *Resurrection*

Leo Tolstoy

By the time Tolstoy was in his 50s, he was an author of international renown and had written his two masterpieces *War and Peace* (1863–9) and *Anna Karenina* (1873–7). He continued to write fiction, but later renounced his earlier books and the world they depicted. Instead Tolstoy concentrated on his highly individual brand of Christian Humanism, a doctrine that included non-violence, vegetarianism and sexual abstinence. It was in this period that he wrote the stories *The Death of Ivan Ilych* and the *Kreutzer Sonata* and his last great novel, *Resurrection*, which strayed so far from Orthodoxy that the Holy Synod excommunicated him in 1901. Tolstoy left Moscow the same year for Yasnaya Polyana, where he devoted himself to helping the poor and peasants on the estate.

The dining room with a painting of Tolstoy's favourite daughter Mariya

The couple were reconciled for a short time when Vanya, their youngest child, died from scarlet fever before reaching his seventh birthday. His memory is preserved in his bedroom near the scullery, where his high chair, rocking horse and books can be seen.

The bedroom of Tolstoy's second daughter, Tatyana, is crammed with ornaments and keepsakes. Her paintings and sketches are hung on the walls.

The stairs to the first floor open into the salon, a large hall where frequent guests were treated to supper. They included the young Sergei Rachmaninov who accompanied the opera singer, Fyodor Shalyapin, on the piano here; the artist Ilya Repin, whose bas-relief of Tatyana now hangs in the "corner room"; and the writer Maxim Gorky with whom Tolstoy would play chess. The drawing room next door was decorated by Sofya Andreevna herself.

The bedroom of Tolstoy's favourite child, Mariya, is rather spartan, testifying to her sympathy for her father's ideals and way of life.

At the far end of the upstairs passage is Tolstoy's study, a spacious room overlooking the garden. Reflecting his passion for austerity, the room is simply furnished in black leather. The plain, solid desk where he wrote his novel *Resurrection* is lit by candles. Rather than admit to being shortsighted, Tolstoy sawed off the ends of his chair legs to bring himself closer to his papers. In the adjoining washroom are dumbbells and a bicycle – evidence of his interest in keeping fit. Also on show are the tools he used for his hobby of shoe-making, with some of the pairs he made. The back stairs close by lead to the garden, which is only accessible to those taking a guided tour.

❸ Church of St Nicholas of the Weavers

Храм Святителя Николая в Хамовниках

Khram Svyatitelya Nikolaya v Khamovnikakh

Ulitsa Lva Tolstovo 2. **Tel** (499) 246 72 08. Ⓜ Park Kultury. **Open** 7:30am–8pm daily.

Dedicated to the patron saint of weavers, sailors and farmers, this church was founded in 1679 by *khamovniki* (local weavers). Their aim was to surpass the Church of the Resurrection in Kadashi that was built a few years before by rival weavers across the river.

While staying at their winter home nearby, Tolstoy and his family used to attend services here until his rift with the church authorities.

The church continued to function throughout the Soviet era. The exterior is decorated with vivid orange and green gables and topped with five golden domes, while the walls are decorated with beautiful patterned tiles.

Inside, the iconostasis features a 17th-century icon of St Nicholas. A separate icon of the Virgin, Helper of Sinners, is reputed to perform miracles.

Luxurious interior of the Church of St Nicholas of the Weavers

Church of St Nicholas of the Weavers, topped by golden domes

❹ State Tretyakov Gallery on Krymsky Val

Третьяковская галерея на Крымском Валу

Tretyakovskaya galereya na Krymskom Valu

Krymskiy val 10. **Tel** (499) 230 77 88. Ⓜ Park Kultury, Oktyabrskaya. **Open** 10am–7:30pm Tue–Sun. English. **tretyakov.ru**

This huge white box of a building is an annexe of the superb State Tretyakov Gallery *(see pp98–9)* in Zamoskvoreche. It is devoted to Russian art from the early 1900s to the present. Most of the canvases here belong to the official movement known as socialist realism and reflect the cultural strait-jacket imposed by Stalin. It had its roots in the Wanderers Movement of the 1860s, which was based on the principle that art has, first and foremost, a social role to play, which Stalin interpreted to mean that it must serve the state's interests and reflect socialist goals and achievements. A few examples of the titles given to the paintings say it all: *Life is Getting Better, Building New Factories* and *Unforgettable Meeting* (between Stalin and a spellbound young woman). Technological achievements were also immortalized in pictures such as *The First Russian Airship*.

Many people will find the Modernist paintings at the beginning of the exhibition more aesthetically pleasing. These include works by Futurist artists such as Kazimir Malevich's *Black Square* and also photomontages by Aleksandr Rodchenko.

Behind the gallery is the Muzeon, a mixture of discarded monuments from the Soviet era and contemporary sculptures. Pride of place belongs to the statue of the secret police chief, Feliks Dzerzhinskiy, which once stood outside the FSB headquarters on Lubyanka Square *(see p74)*. A striking addition to the view is the vast Monument to Peter the Great, which towers 95 m (312 ft) above the Moskva river. It was built in 1997 by the sculptor Zurab Tsereteli at a reputed cost of US $11 million.

Boating on the lake in the green, luxuriant surrounds of Gorky Park

❺ Gorky Park

Парк культуры и отдыха имени М. Горького

Park Kultury i otdykha imeni M. Gorkovo

Krymskiy val 9. **Tel** (495) 995 00 20. Ⓜ Park Kultury, Oktyabrskaya. **Open** 24 hrs daily.

Named in honour of the writer Maxim Gorky, but known locally as Park Kultury, this green space extends for more than 1 sq km (half a sq mile) along the banks of the Moskva river. Opened in 1928 as the Park of Culture and Rest, it incorporates the Golitsyn Gardens, laid out in the late 18th century, and a 19th-century pleasure park. During the Soviet era, loudspeakers delivered speeches by Communist leaders across the park. Today, visitors will find a skatepark, woodland walks, boating lakes, a 10,000-seat outdoor theatre and, in the winter months, an ice rink, which is the largest in Europe.

❻ Donskoy Monastery

Донской монастырь

Donskoy monastyr

Donskaya ploshchad 1–3. **Tel** (495) 952 14 81. Ⓜ Shabolovskaya. **Open** 7am–7pm daily. grounds only.

The Donskoy Monastery was founded in 1593 by Boris Godunov to honour *The Icon of the Our Lady of the Don*, credited with having saved Russia from the Mongols twice. The first time was in 1380 when Prince Dmitri Donskoy carried the icon into battle at Kulikovo. Boris Godunov also used it to rally his troops in 1591 against the army of Khan Kazy Girei, which retreated after minor skirmishes. The crescent moons, below the golden crosses on top of the monastery buildings, symbolize the church as a ship of salvation.

The modest scale of the original monastery is reflected in the beautifully understated Old, or Small Cathedral. The Orthodox prelate Archbishop Amvrosiy, killed by a mob during a riot in 1771, is buried within. The remains of Patriarch Tikhon, who was imprisoned by the Bolsheviks after the Revolution, were secretly buried here until 1992 when they were moved to the New, or Grand Cathedral.

The fortified outer walls and Grand Cathedral were added in the late 17th century when the monastery acquired greater prestige under the patronage of the Regent Sophia.

Donskoy Monastery's imposing 17th-century Grand Cathedral

Built in 1684–98 in the Moscow Baroque style, the Grand Cathedral is a towering brick building with five domes. Inside is a stunning seven-tiered iconostasis and frescoes, painted in 1782–5 by Italian artist Antonio Claudio. *The Icon of Our Lady of the Don* is now in the State Tretyakov Gallery *(see pp98–9)*, but a copy is on show in the Small Cathedral.

❼ Sparrow Hills

Воробьёвы горы

Vorobevy gory

Ⓜ Universitet.

The summit of this wooded ridge offers unsurpassed views across the city. There is an observation point on ulitsa Kosygina and newly wed couples traditionally come here to have their photograph taken against the panorama. It is also a favourite pitch for souvenir sellers.

The hills are dominated by the Moscow State University (MGU) building commissioned by Stalin, designed by Lev Rudnev and completed in 1953. With 36 floors, it is the tallest of the seven skyscrapers built in the Stalin-Gothic style in Moscow in the 1940s and 1950s.

On prospekt Vernadskovo, on the southeastern edge of the hills, is the silver-roofed New Moscow Circus and the Nataliya Sats Children's Musical Theatre.

8 Kolomenskoe

Коломенское

Kolomenskoe

Prospekt Andropova 39. **Tel** (499) 615 27 68. Kolomenskaya. Front Gate Museum: **Open** Jun–Aug: 11am–7pm Tue–Sun; Sep–May: 10am–6pm Tue–Sun. Church and Grounds: **Open** daily. English, book in advance. Grounds. **mgomz.com**

Set on the steep west bank of the Moskva river, Kolomenskoe was a favourite country estate of the tsars. The oldest surviving building is the soaring tent-roofed Church of the Ascension in 1532, erected by Vasiliy III to celebrate the birth of his son Ivan (later, the Terrible). Between 1667 and 1672, Peter the Great's father, Tsar Alexis Mikhailovich, built an astonishing wooden palace with barrel-shaped roofs, onion domes and carvings, that visiting diplomats described as the eighth wonder of the world. This was demolished by Catherine the Great, but a model was made, now on display in the **Front Gate Museum**.

In 1925, the park was designated a museum of wooden architecture, and historic buildings, such as Peter the Great's cabin from Archangel, were moved here from all over Russia. Folkloric festivals and historical pageants are staged here throughout the year.

9 Tsaritsyno

Царицыно

Tsaritsyno

Ulitsa Dolskaya 1. **Tel** (495) 321 63 66. Tsaritsyno, Orekhovo. **Open** Apr–Oct: 11am–6pm Tue–Fri (till 8pm Sat & 9pm Sun); Nov–Mar: 11am–6pm Wed–Fri (till 8pm Sat & 7pm Sun). Grounds: **Open** 6am–midnight daily. English, book in advance.

Catherine the Great bought this tract of land in 1775 and changed its name from Chyornaya Gryaz (Black Mud) to Tsaritsyno (Empress's Village). She commissioned architect Vasiliy Bazhenov to build a lavish imperial palace here. Bazhenov designed an innovative complex combining Gothic, Baroque and even Moorish styles, but when Catherine visited the site in 1785 she proclaimed herself dissatisfied. Bazhenov's young colleague Matvel Kazakov was told to rebuild the palace but, after a further decade of construction, lack of funds left it incomplete.

Model of the wooden palace, displayed in the Front Gate Museum

After centuries as a roofless shell, Kazakov's Great Palace has finally been completed and now serves as a museum of antique tapestries, Central Asian folk art, ceramics and contemporary glassware. Some of Bazhenov's smaller structures are equally impressive, such as the Figured Gate, with its Gothic-style towers and lancet windows, the Figured Bridge and the ornate two-storey Opera House, one of the few buildings Catherine approved. The extraordinary Bread Gate, with its arch of sharply pointed stone "teeth", leads to the kitchens, while the Octahedron was built as the servants' quarters.

10 Kuskovo

Кусково

Kuskovo

Ulitsa Yunosti 2. **Tel** (495) 370 01 60. 133, 208, 620. Ryazanskiy prospekt, Vykhino. **Open** mid-Apr–mid-Oct: 10am–6pm Wed–Sun; mid-Oct–mid-Apr: 10am–4pm Wed–Sun. **Closed** last Wed of the month. tickets sold at main entrance for individual sights. English, book in advance. Palace and grotto only.

For over 200 years before the Revolution, Kuskovo was the country seat of one of Russia's wealthiest aristocratic families, the Sheremetevs. The present buildings were commissioned by Count Pyotr Sheremetev after his marriage to the heiress Varvara Cherkasskaya in 1743. Among their 200,000 serfs were the architects Fyodor Argunov and Aleksey Mironov who played a major role in Kuskovo's construction, under the supervision of professional architect Karl Blank.

The Neo-Classical palace, made entirely of wood, has a magnificent ballroom. The gardens boast a shell-encrusted grotto, luxurious "cottages" and an orangery exhibiting paintings, ceramics and other treasures. Every year, Kuskovo hosts a US Independence Day party with rock bands and fireworks, on the Saturday nearest to 4 July.

Beautiful orangery in Kuskovo, now converted into a ceramics museum

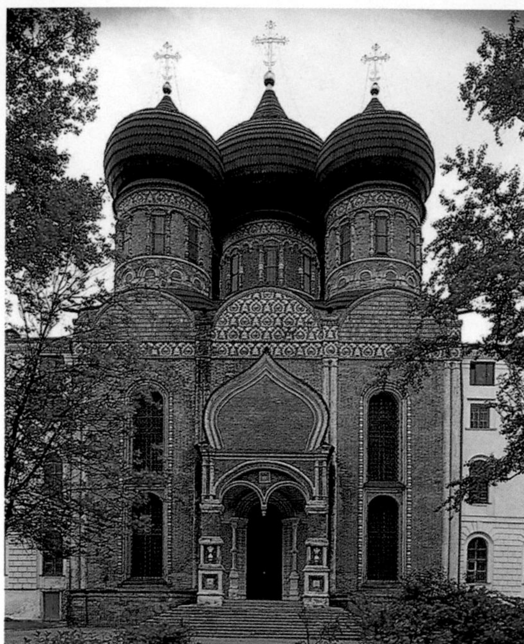

The stately 17th-century Cathedral of the Intercession, Izmaylovo

⓫ Izmaylovo

Измайлово

Izmaylovo

Gorodok Baumana 2. **Tel** (499) 165 13 36. Ⓜ Partizanskaya. **Open** 10am–6pm Tue–Sun.

One of Moscow's largest wooded areas, Izmaylovo park covers nearly 12 sq km (5 sq miles). Acquired by the Romanov family in the 16th century, it became one of their favourite hunting estates where, in 1663, Tsar Alexis built an enormous wooden palace and dedicated the land to experiments in animal and vegetable husbandry. His son, the future Tsar Peter the Great, spent an idyllic childhood here, secluded from palace intrigues as he learned to sail an old boat on a lake – the genesis of his lifelong fascination with the sea. The boat was later nicknamed the "grandfather of the Russian Navy".

The former royal estate is on an island, approached via the white, triple-arched Ceremonial Gate, to the northeast of Izmaylovsky Park metro station. While the wooden palace has long since disappeared (demolished by Catherine the Great in 1767), visitors can still see the royal estate's walls and the imposing 17th-century Cathedral of the Intercession, whose five black domes are tiled with metallic scales. The *zakomary* (arched) gables beneath them are beautifully decorated with "peacock's eye" tiles by Stepan Polubes, a Belorussian ceramicist working in Moscow.

To the cathedral's right is the Bridge Tower. Built in 1671, this tiered red-brick arch is all that remains of a 14-span bridge that once crossed the estate's waterways. The top tier of the bridge offers fine views of the estate.

The road northwards leads to the Izmaylovo flea market *(see p119)*. Known to Muscovites as the Vernissazh, it is a boisterous melange of stalls selling folk crafts and Soviet memorabilia. It is at its busiest at weekends, when buskers strum away on the stage-set medieval wooden palace just inside the market's entrance.

⓬ Vasnetsov House-Museum

Дом-музей ВМ Васнецова

Dom-muzey VM Vasnetsova

Pereulok Vasnetsova 13. **Tel** (495) 681 13 29. Ⓜ Sukharevskaya, Prospekt Mira. **Open** 10am–5pm Wed–Sun. **Closed** last Thu of the month. **W** **tretyakovgallery.ru**

A sculptor, painter, theatre designer and architect, Viktor Vasnetsov (1848–1926) was a member of the artists' colony at Abramtsevo *(see p114)*. He designed the façade of the State Tretyakov Gallery *(see pp98–9)* and also his own family home, where he lived until his death in 1926. An enthusiastic advocate of traditional Russian folk art and architecture, he employed peasant carpenters from Vladimir to build his log-cabin-like timber house with green roofs.

The ground-floor rooms display highly individual pieces of furniture, many designed by Vasnetsov and his similarly talented younger brother, Arkady (1856–1933). A spiral staircase hung with 17th-century chain mail and weaponry leads up to the artist's studio, which resembles a vaulted medieval hall. This is the perfect backdrop for Vasnetsov's arresting canvases that depict Russian legends such as the forest witch Baba Yaga stealing children. *The Sleeping Princess*, showing a scene from the classic fairy tale *Sleeping Beauty*, was painted in the last year of Vasnetsov's life, at a time when Stalin was tightening his grip on Russia.

Ornate roof of the wooden house designed by Viktor Vasnetsov

Theatre auditorium, Ostankino Palace, once home to Count Sheremetev's serf actors

⓭ Ostankino Palace

Московский музей-усадьба Останкино

Moskovskiy muzey-usadba Ostankino

1-ya Ostankinskaya ulitsa 5. **Tel** (495) 683 46 45. Ⓜ VDNKh. **Open** mid-May–Sep: 11am–8pm Wed–Sun. Grounds: **Open** 11am–9pm daily. English. gardens only.

Like the Sheremetev estate at Kuskovo *(see p109)*, Ostankino was built by the serf architects Pavel Argunov and Aleksey Mironov for Count Nikolai Sheremetev, a patron of the arts. He had the palace built around a theatre, where a company of 200 serf actors and actresses performed plays of his choosing. In 1800, he married Praskovia Zhemchugova-Kovaleva, one of the actresses, ignoring the censure of polite society. Praskovia died in childbirth three years later, whereupon the grief-stricken count abandoned the palace, which fell into disuse.

Built of wood skilfully plastered over to resemble brick and stone, the palace was completed in 1792–8. Its halls are a wonder of *trompe l'oeil* decor, with carved wooden mouldings painted to resemble bronze, gold and marble. The *pièce de résistance* is the ballroom, an elliptical hall whose floor can be lowered to transform it into a theatre, complete with ingenious devices to simulate the sound of rain and thunder. In the summer, concerts of classical music are held here.

The All-Russian Exhibiton Centre fronted by the Fountain of the Republics

⓮ All-Russian Exhibition Centre (VVTs)

Всероссийский Выставочный Центр (ВВЦ)

Vserossiyskiy Vystavochniy Tsentr (VVTs)

Prospekt Mira. **Tel** (495) 544 34 00. Ⓜ VDNKh. Grounds: **Open** May–Sep: 9am–9pm Mon–Fri (till 10pm Sat & Sun); Oct–Apr: 9am–8pm Mon–Fri (till 8pm Sat & Sun). Pavilions: **Open** May–Sep: 10am–7pm Mon–Fri (till 8pm Sat & Sun); Oct–Apr: 9am–8pm Mon–Fri (till 9pm Sat & Sun). Botanical Gardens: **Open** May–Oct: 10am–8pm daily. Space Museum: **Open** 11am–7pm Tue–Sun (till 9pm Thu). English.

W vvcentre.ru

One of Moscow's main tourist attractions in Soviet times, the former Exhibition of Economic Achievements of the USSR (VDNKh) has now become the All-Russian Exhibition Centre (VVTs), a vast exhibition site and shopping centre. The entrance is via a huge triumphal arch topped by the figures of a tractor driver and collective farmer, holding up a sheaf of corn. VVTs remains a fascinating place to visit, especially for lovers of Soviet architecture.

The centrepiece of the complex is the Fountain of the Republics, consisting of 16 gilded statues of maidens in national dress representing the former Soviet republics. They surround a basin from which jets of water are sprayed 24 m (79 ft) into the air, illuminated at night by 525 spotlights. Nearby is a 75-m (247-ft) high Ferris wheel that offers a superb view of northern Moscow. Beyond the VVTs is the entrance to the **Botanical Gardens**. Inside is a small Japanese Garden where tea is served.

Heading back towards VDNKh metro, it is hard to miss the titanium Space Obelisk. Over 100 m (328 ft) high, it represents a rocket blasting off, and was erected three years after Yuri Gagarin's historic flight in 1961. Underneath it is the **Space Museum**, containing models of Belka and Strelka, the two dogs who were the first creatures to come back alive from space, and Vostok 1, the tiny capsule in which Gagarin famously orbited the Earth.

BEYOND MOSCOW

Despite the numerous attractions of Moscow, the magnificence of some of the monasteries and historic sites in the surrounding region makes for rewarding day trips. To the north is the spectacular Trinity Monastery of St Sergius. Once a place of pilgrimage for the tsars, this huge complex has several superb cathedrals. To the west lies Borodino, site of the great battle between Napoleon's army and Russian forces in 1812. Located to the northeast are the towns of the Golden Ring, including Suzdal, Vladimir and Yaroslavl. Founded by Russians seeking shelter from invading tribes, these attractive settlements still have many historic buildings. Also situated outside Moscow are several country estates. Significant among them are Yasnaya Polyana, where Leo Tolstoy lived for many years; the house in Klin rented by Pyotr Tchaikovsky; and Abramtsevo Estate-Museum, a former artists' colony. Although parts of the landscape are unappealingly industrial, there are large tracts of wooded countryside dotted with villages of small wooden cottages or *dachas*, each with a small plot of land that is used for growing fruit and vegetables. One of the best ways to visit sights outside Moscow is on an organized tour since public transport can be erratic, but bus and train travel are perfectly feasible for those who prefer a taste of everyday local life.

Sights at a Glance

Churches and Cathedrals

2 Trinity Monastery of St Sergius

Museums

1 Abramtsevo Estate-Museum
3 Tchaikovsky House-Museum
5 Yasnaya Polyana

Historic Sites

4 Borodino
6 Vladimir
7 Suzdal
8 Yaroslavl

Key

Motorway
Main road
Minor road
Railway

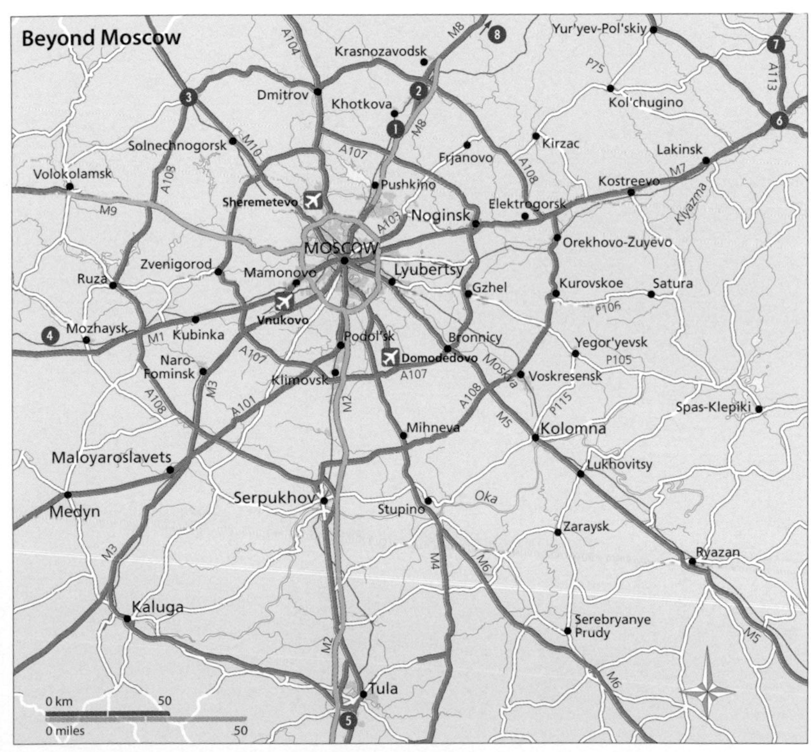

For map symbols *see back flap*

❶ Abramtsevo Estate-Museum

Музей-усадьба Абрамцево

Muzey-usadba Abramtsevo

60 km (35 miles) N of Moscow. **Tel** (495) 993 00 33. from Yaroslavskiy station to Abramtsevo. **Open** 10am–4pm Wed–Sun (till 6pm in summer). **Closed** last Thu of the month. **abramtsevo.net**

In the second half of the 19th century, this rural retreat became a hive of cultural activity after art patron Savva Mamontov established an artists' colony here. Viktor Vasnetsov, Mikhail Nesterov and others were inspired by the work of local peasant craftsmen, and used folk motifs and techniques in their art.

Dotted around the estate are a number of remarkable buildings. The Church of the Saviour Not Made by Human Hand is modelled on the medieval churches of Novgorod, its whitewashed brickwork enlivened by bands of painted majolica tiles. The *teremok* is a free improvization on the *izba* (typical peasant hut), with wooden furnishings and ornaments, and a tiled stove. Even more eye-catching is the House on Chicken Legs, which stands on stilts. In Russian folklore, the witch Baba Yaga lived in a house built on giant chicken legs.

The fortified Trinity Monastery of St Sergius as seen from the southeast

The superb 17th-century iconostasis in the Cathedral of the Assumption

❷ Trinity Monastery of St Sergius

Троице-Сергиева Лавра

Troitse-Sergieva Lavra

75 km (47 miles) N of Moscow. **Tel** (496) 540 53 34. from Yaroslavskiy station to Sergiev Posad. Monastery and Church of St Sergius: **Open** 5am–8pm daily. Cathedral of the Assumption: currently under renovation. Trinity Cathedral: **Open** 5am–9pm daily. Grounds: **Open** 5am–9pm daily. book in advance. grounds only. **stsl.ru**

Founded around 1335 by Sergius of Radonezh, the Trinity Monastery of St Sergius in Sergiev-Possad is one of Russia's most important religious centres and places of pilgrimage. Sergius persuaded Russia's princes to unite against the Mongol invaders, and the monastery later withstood a Polish siege during the Time of Troubles *(see p40)*. In the 1680s, the young Peter the Great found refuge here during the Streltsy Revolt *(see p41)*.

The huge complex is enclosed by white walls around 2 km (1 mile) in length, and its stunning churches are among the most beautiful in Russia.

The monks' refectory in the complex was built in 1686–92 using money donated by Peter the Great and his half-brother, Ivan V, in gratitude for the refuge given them by the monastery during the Streltsy Revolt. The exterior walls are divided into a series of panels, each painted so that it looks as though it has three-dimensional facets similar to those of the Faceted Chamber *(see p61)* in the Kremlin. The refectory's main façade features a covered terrace with a wealth of ornamentation. At the eastern end of the refectory is the **Church of St Sergius**.

The magnificent **Cathedral of the Assumption**, with its central golden cupola surrounded by four blue, star-spangled domes, lies at the heart of the monastery. It was commissioned by Ivan the Terrible in 1559 to celebrate his defeat of the Mongols at Kazan *(see p225)*, and completed

The reception area in the Tchaikovsky House-Museum, containing Pyotr Tchaikovsky's piano

26 years later to a design inspired by the Cathedral of the Assumption *(see pp58–9)* in the Kremlin.

The oldest stone building in the monastery, the exquisite white **Trinity Cathedral** is decorated with *kokoshniki* above a triple-banded frieze. It was built over the tomb of St Sergius in 1422, the year of his canonization. His remains, encased in a silver shrine inside, are a focus for visiting pilgrims. The iconostasis contains two icons by the renowned painter Simon Ushakov, *The Holy Face* and *Christ Enthroned*, plus a copy of Andrei Rublev's masterpiece *The Trinity*, the original of which is housed in the State Tretyakov Gallery *(see pp98–9)*.

Christ in Majesty (1425–7) in the Trinity Cathedral's iconostasis

❸ Tchaikovsky House-Museum

Дом-музей ПИ Чайковского

Dom-muzey PI Chaykovskovo

90 km (55 miles) NW of Moscow. Ulitsa Tchaikovskaya 48, Klin. **Tel** (496) 245 81 96. from Leningradskiy station to Klin. **Open** 10am–6pm Fri–Tue. **Closed** last Mon of the month. English. **cbook.ru/tchaikovsky**

In May 1892, Pyotr Tchaikovsky rented a house in Klin. Previous stays near Klin had inspired some of his best music, including the ballets *The Sleeping Beauty* and *The Nutcracker*. Tchaikovsky died in 1893, and his younger brother, Modest, opened the estate to visitors.

The walls of the reception area are covered with photos of family and fellow musicians. In the centre is a grand piano and on a shelf behind the piano is a Statue of Liberty inkpot, which Tchaikovsky brought back from his triumphant tour of the United States in 1891. The winner of the Tchaikovsky International Competition gives a recital here on 7 May, the composer's birthday. The bedroom is separated from the reception by a curtain. Tchaikovsky finished his *Sixth Symphony*, the *Pathétique*, at the table by the bedroom window.

Also open to visitors are the library and the study where Tchaikovsky worked as the Klin archivist until his death in 1916.

❹ Borodino

Бородино

Borodino

120 km (75 miles) W of Moscow. **Tel** (496) 385 15 46. from Belorusskiy station. **Open** May–Oct: 10am–6pm Wed–Sun; Nov–Apr: 9am–4:30pm Wed–Sun. **Closed** last Fri of the month. **borodino.ru**

One of the fiercest battles of the 19th century took place at Borodino on 7 September 1812. For over 15 hours Napoleon Bonaparte's Grande Armée and the Russian army, led by Field Marshal Mikhail Kutuzov, fought each other to a bloody impasse. The Russians were forced to abandon Moscow. However, their agents started a fire *(see p42)* that levelled the city. Faced with a Russian winter in the open, Napoleon's army was forced to retreat, vindicating Kutuzov's "scorched earth" strategy.

The battlefield covers over 100 sq km (40 sq miles), but the main places of interest are reasonably accessible. A museum, 1 km (half a mile) south of the village, recounts the story of the battle and a re-enactment takes place every 7 September. The nearby inn, where Tolstoy stayed to research for the novel *War and Peace*, is now a museum.

Monument to the fallen of Borodino

5 Yasnaya Polyana

Ясная Поляна

Yasnaya Polyana

200 km (125 miles) S of Moscow. **Tel** (487) 517 61 18. to Tula, then bus. **Open** 9am–5pm Tue–Sun. **Closed** last Tue of the month. English, book in advance.

The beloved country estate of Leo Tolstoy *(see p106)*, Yasnaya Polyana, is located in a peaceful valley surrounded by forests. Tolstoy was born on the estate in 1828. From the mid-1880s he spent summers here with his family, and moved here permanently in 1901. The house and its contents are much as they were in Tolstoy's day. The rooms on show include the study, where Tolstoy wrote *War and Peace* and *Anna Karenina*. The estate also includes the Volkonsky House, where the serfs lived, and a pavilion for guests. A literary museum is housed in the former peasants' school that Tolstoy established.

Tolstoy's study where he wrote *War and Peace* and *Anna Karenina*, Yasnaya Polyana

6 Vladimir

Владимир

Vladimir

170 km (106 miles) NE of Moscow. 360,000. daily.

Vladimir was founded on the Klyazma river by Prince Vladimir Svyatoslavich, the Baptizer of Russia, in the late 10th century. The city began to flourish under Prince Yuri Dolgorukiy's son Andrey Bogolyubskiy who made it the capital of the new principality of Vladimir-Suzdal. Had it not been for the Mongols who devastated Vladimir in 1238, the city might be Russia's capital today.

The 12th-century Cathedral of the Assumption in Vladimir

Today, Vladimir looks like any industrial city of the Soviet era, but fortunately its chemical plants and tractor and automobile appliance factories are away from the picturesque old part of the town.

Visitors arriving by train will see the town's landmarks arrayed along a ridge beside bolshaya Moskovskaya ulitsa, the road to Moscow. The most prominent among them is the **Cathedral of the Assumption**. It was built in 1158–60 and originally decorated with prodigious quantities of gold and silver, gems and majolica tiles. Craftsmen came from all over Russia, Poland and the Holy Roman Empire to contribute to what was then the tallest building in Russia, where the coronation of many princes, including Dmitri Donskoy *(see p40)* and Aleksandr Nevskiy, subsequently took place. Some superb frescoes by artists such as Andrei Rublev and Daniil Cherny are still visible under the choir's gallery on the west wall.

Nearby stands the **Cathedral of St Demetrius**, built in 1194–7 by Prince Vsevolod III. A single-domed church of white limestone, its exterior is covered by bas-reliefs featuring griffons, centaurs, birds and prancing lions as well as a portrait of Prince Vsevolod and his family.

A short stroll down bolshaya Moskovskaya ulitsa takes visitors past the 18th-century trading arcades and shops to the **Golden Gate**. Constructed in 1164, it combines the functions of a triumphal arch and defensive bastion. Over the centuries the gate has sunk 2 m (5 ft) into the ground due to its weight. Vladimir might have withstood the Mongol siege had not the young prince Vsevolod lost his nerve and ventured forth bearing gifts, whereupon Genghis Khan's grandson Batu Khan slew him on the spot and laid waste to the city. This is depicted by a diorama within the Golden Gate.

Cathedral of the Assumption
Bolshaya Moskovskaya 56. **Tel** (4922) 32 52 01. **Open** 1pm–4:45pm Tue–Sun.

Cathedral of St Demetrius
Bolshaya Moskovskaya 60. **Tel** (4922) 32 24 67. **Open** May–Oct: 11am–6pm Wed & Fri–Sun (till 5pm Mon & Thu); Nov–Apr: 10am–5pm Wed & Fri–Sun (till 4pm Mon & Thu).

7 Suzdal

Суздаль

Suzdal

200 km (124 miles) NE of Moscow. 12,100. to Vladimir, then bus or taxi. Sun.

Nestling on the banks of the Kamenka river, Suzdal is the best preserved of the Golden Ring towns. Its clusters of 17th- and 18th-century churches built by local merchants, and its low, wooden houses with traditional carved eaves and windows, make this the most attractive town in the Vladimir region.

The first records of Suzdal date from 1024, a century after which, Moscow's founder Prince Yuri Dolgorukiy built Suzdal's Kremlin on a grassy rampart above the river. Today, it is one of the several historic buildings that constitute the **Vladimir & Suzdal Museum of History, Art & Architecture**. The Kremlin's dominant building is the **Cathedral of the Nativity** with its blue, star-spangled domes. Although it was built in the 13th century, most of the current building dates from the 16th century. The south and west doors are of gilded copper, etched with biblical scenes.

Next door stands the former Archbishop's Palace, which now houses exhibitions devoted to the history of Suzdal. The main room of the palace, the magnificent Cross Chamber, is one of the largest unsupported vaults in Russia. Housed within the Annunciation Church in the western part of the palace is the Old Russian Painting Exhibition that features icons and ancient art from the 15th–17th centuries.

Suzdal also contains five important religious foundations, including the **Monastery of the Saviour and St Euphemius**. Once the richest monastery in the area, with more than 10,000 serfs at its disposal, it has a commanding position overlooking the town, behind fortified walls almost 6 m (20 ft) thick. The monks' cells and all the other buildings of the monastery contain impressive collections of exhibits, including religious paintings and jewellery.

To the south of the monastery is the **Aleksandrovskiy Convent**, founded in 1240 and rebuilt in the 17th century. Its Cathedral of the Ascension was built by Nataliya Naryshkina, mother of Peter the Great.

Across the river is the **Convent of the Intercession**, where Peter the Great incarcerated his first wife, Yevdokiya Lopukhina, following the example set by tsars Basil III, Ivan the Terrible and Boris Godunov.

Fifteenth-century icon of St Nicholas on display at the Old Russian Painting Exhibition

On the southwest edge of town is the **Museum of Wooden Architecture** – an open-air exhibition of wooden buildings brought from across the Vladimir region. Particularly impressive is the Church of the Transfiguration, built in 1756. With domes made with overlapping shingles, it was built without using metal nails.

Vladimir & Suzdal Museum of History, Art & Architecture
Ulitsa Lenina 22. **Tel** (4922) 32 42 63. **Open** call ahead of visit. **vladmuseum.ru**

Monastery of the Saviour and St Euphemius
Ulitsa Lenina. **Tel** (49231) 2 10 77. **Open** 10am–6pm Tue–Sun.

Museum of Wooden Architecture
Ulitsa Pushkarskaya. **Tel** (49231) 2 35 10. **Open** Thu–Tue daily.

8 Yaroslavl

Ярославль

Yaroslavl

250 km (155 miles) NE of Moscow. 592,000. from Yaroslavlsky station.

Founded in 1010 on the banks of the Volga river by Prince Yaroslav the Wise after he reputedly gained the trust of local villagers by slaying a bear with an axe, Yaroslavl later became a wealthy commercial and industrial town that rivalled Moscow until the 17th century. Yaroslavl's merchants endowed it with splendid churches, many of them within the **Monastery of Our Saviour and Transfiguration**. An annual festival of classical music is held here in late August.

A walk along the scenic Volga embankment leads to the **Museum of Music and Time**, a collection of antique clocks and musical instruments belonging to the eccentric magician and actor Ivan Mostoslavsky, who conducts tours in English if booked in advance.

Monastery of Our Saviour and Transfiguration
Bogoyavlenskaya ploshchad 25. **Tel** (4852) 230 40 72. Churches: **Open** Jun–Aug: 10am–5:30pm Tue–Sun. **Closed** first Wed of the month. **yarmp.yar.ru**

Museum of Music and Time
Volzhskaya naberezhnaya 33a. **Tel** (4852) 232 86 37. **Open** 10am–7pm daily. **music-and-time.narod.ru**

View of the Monastery of Our Saviour and Transfiguration, Yaroslavl

SHOPPING IN MOSCOW

In contrast to the long queues and shortages during the Soviet era, Moscow now boasts not just supermarkets and department stores stocking imported goods, but also exclusive boutiques selling international brands. Ulitsa Arbat and Tverskaya ulitsa are the main shopping hubs and are popular among shoppers visiting chic boutiques and other meccas of consumerism. However, high import duties, transportation costs and the relative lack of competition can make certain consumer goods more expensive than in the West. The colourful Russian arts and crafts available at many locations throughout the city are popular with visitors, as are exotic goods from the ex-Soviet Republics of Central Asia.

Opening Hours

Moscow's shops and businesses rarely open before 10am and often not until 11am. Most stay open until around 7pm. A few state-run stores close for an hour at lunchtime, either from 1pm to 2pm, or from 2pm to 3pm. Shops are usually open all day on Saturdays and most are also open on Sundays, although often for shorter hours. However, a large number of shops and services, from bookstores to beauty salons, are now open around the clock to cater for increasing consumer demands.

Outdoor markets are usually open from 10am to 4pm, but it is advisable to go in the morning to get the best choice of goods.

Food and Drink

Many Muscovites buy meat, cheese and fresh fruit and vegetables at one of the number of big food markets across the city. One of the biggest and most picturesque food markets is the **Danilovskiy Market**, which takes its name from the nearby Danilovskiy Monastery. The **Cheremushkinskiy Market** offers a wide variety of fresh produce; there is also sometimes a market across the road in which vendors from distant Russian regions sell produce and souvenirs. The **Dorogomilovsky Market**, located near Kievsky train station, displays a colourful selection of fresh produce from Russia and the former Soviet republics. The upmarket **Farmers' Market** on the fifth floor of Tsvetnoy Central Market is also worth a visit. Visitors can buy ingredients here and have them cooked at one of the restaurants nearby.

A variety of traditional *matryoshka* dolls on sale at a souvenir stall

Crafts and Souvenirs

The best place to buy crafts and souvenirs such as Soviet memorabilia and *matryoshka* dolls *(see p294)*, icons, samovars, fur hats and Central Asian rugs is the Izmaylovo Crafts Market, which is held on the edge of Izmaylovo Park *(see p110)*. Note that the crafts market is open on weekends only.

In the city centre, the Arbat Square *(see p89)* is the place to shop for crafts. Handmade lace and embroidery are sold at **Russkaya Vyshivka**; Russian jewellery and amber at **Samotsvety**; and lacquer trays and painted china at **Arbatskaya Lavitsa**. Elsewhere in the city, **Dom Farfora** sells hand-painted porcelain tea sets and crystal bowls. Art lovers can browse through whimsical sculptures at the **Salon of the Moscow Cultural Fund**, which also has old lamps and samovars. **Roza Azora**, a small art gallery, stocks Soviet bric-a-brac, including lamps, old biscuit tins and hats. Soviet posters and badges, amber and lacquer boxes can be bought at the superb souvenir shop in the Museum of Contemporary History *(see p85)*.

Antiques

Any item made before 1945 officially counts as an antique and can only be legally exported after being cleared. The duty is paid at the **Ministry of Culture**. The area around ulitsa Arbat has many of the best antique shops. **Eurasia Gallery**, one of the largest galleries of eastern antiques in Europe, specializes in Chinese and Japanese art, while **Ivan Tsarevich** has superb Soviet porcelain. For larger pieces and furniture, check out **Rokoko**.

Fashion and Accessories

Moscow's premier department store, GUM *(see p69)* is known around the world by its Cyrillic initials ГУМ. A beautiful edifice beside Red Square *(see p68)*, GUM contains three arcades of shops under a glass roof. It stocks a wide variety of designer brands of clothing, perfumes and cosmetics, besides many smaller, more exclusive labels from Italy, France and Scandinavia.

Wide variety of merchandise on display at the Izmaylovo Crafts Market

Another popular downtown arcade is **Petrovskiy Passage** that sells high-quality Russian fur hats and coats. The modern, three-storey **Gallery Aktyor** contains designer stores selling French perfumes, clothes and jewellery from Tiffany and Cartier.

Besides global brands, visitors will find works by Russian designers such as **Masha Tsigal**, who makes clothes, handbags and sunglasses. Both international and Russian designers are featured in the **Atrium** mall, which has boutiques, cafés, bars and a cinema.

Shoppers enjoying a meal at the café in the fashionable Atrium mall

Books and Music

For English-language books, **Dom Inostrannoy Knigi** is probably the best shop to visit. The enormous **Moscow House of Books** sells a good range of English-language books and also old icons and Soviet propaganda posters. **Biblio Globus** is another good book shop which you can browse. Both the Pushkin State Museum of Fine Arts *(see pp90–91)* and the State Tretyakov Gallery *(see pp98–9)* have shops selling art books with text in English.

The **Gorbushkin dvor** is a factory-size mart for CDs, DVDs and second-hand LPs, as well as video cameras and audio equipment. For vintage and specialist music, visit **Transylvania**.

Toys

The best children's shop is **Malenkiy Genii** (Little Genius), selling imported and Russian educational toys, audiotapes, cartoon books, puzzles and board games.

DIRECTORY

Food and Drink

Cheremushkinskiy Market
Prospekt Lomonosovskiy 1/64.

Danilovskiy Market
Mytnaya ulitsa 74.
Tel (495) 958 17 25.

Dorogomilovsky Market
Mozhaysky val 10.
Tel (499) 249 55 53.

Farmers' Market
Tsvetnoy blvd, 15, building 1.
Map 2 D3.
Tel (495) 737 77 73.

Crafts and Souvenirs

Arbatskaya Lavitsa
Ulitsa Arbat 27.
Map 3 B1.
Tel (495) 690 56 89.

Dom Farfora
Leninskiy prospekt 36.
Tel (495) 995 60 23.

Roza Azora
Nikitsky bulvar 14.
Map 1 B5.
Tel (495) 695 81 19.

Russkaya Vyshivka
Ulitsa Arbat 31.
Map 3 B1.
Tel (499) 241 28 41.

Salon of the Moscow Cultural Fund
Pyanitskaya ulitsa 16.
Map 4 E2.
Tel (495) 680 24 06.

Samotsvety
Ulitsa Arbat 35.
Map 3 A1.
Tel (495) 241 07 65.

Antiques

Eurasia Gallery
Nikitsky bulvar 12A.
Map 1 B5.
Tel (495) 690 05 49.

Ivan Tsarevich
Ulitsa Arbat 4.
Map 3 B1.
Tel (495) 691 74 44.

Ministry of Culture
Malyy Gnezdnikovskiy pereulok 7/6.
Map 1 C4.
Tel (495) 629 20 08.

Rokoko
Frunzenskaya naberezhnaya 54.
Map 3 A5.
Tel (499) 242 36 64.

Fashion and Accessories

Atrium
Zemlyanoy Val 33.
Tel (495) 970 15 55.
W atrium.su

Gallery Aktyor
Tverskaya ulitsa 16/1.
Map 1 C4.
Tel (495) 935 82 99.

Masha Tsigal
Ulitsa Yauzskaya 1/15.
Map 4 F1.
Tel (495) 660 56 44.

Petrovskiy Passage
Ulitsa Petrovka 10.
Map 2 D4.
Tel (495) 625 31 32.

Books and Music

Biblio Globus
Myasnitskaya ulitsa 6/3.
Map 2 E5.
Tel (495) 781 19 00.

Dom Inostrannoy Knigi
Kuznetskiy Most 18/7.
Map 2 D5.
Tel (495) 628 20 21.

Gorbushkin dvor
Bagrationovskiy proyezd 7/1.
Tel (495) 737 74 74.
W gorbushkin.ru

Moscow House of Books
Ulitsa Novyy Arbat 8.
Map 3 B1.
Tel (495)789 35 91.

Transylvania
Tverskaya ulitsa 6/1.
Map 1 C5.
Tel (495) 629 87 86.

Toys

Malenkiy Genii
Bolshoy Kozikhinskiy pereulok 6.
Map 1 B4.
Tel (495) 691 21 47.

ENTERTAINMENT IN MOSCOW

From great theatres hosting the gamut of acclaimed operas and ballets to umpteen bars and clubs offering thriving nightlife, Moscow boasts a myriad range of entertainment options. Attending a performance at the Bolshoi Theatre is considered by many to be the high point of a visit to the imperial city. Other theatres also put on an enormous range of productions, including musicals and shows for children. Many international artists frequently include the city on their tours, so visitors can enjoy performances by visiting reggae bands and DJs, orchestras and dance troupes, as well as local talent. In addition, there is plenty of lively entertainment from street performers.

A spectacular production of *Sleeping Beauty* at the Bolshoi Theatre

Information and Tickets

Moscow does not have any conventional tourist information offices. The English-language newspaper *The Moscow Times* has listings for clubs, concerts, plays and exhibitions in its Friday edition. Full listings of clubs, concerts and children's events also appear on Russian-language websites. Matinees start at noon and most evening performances at 7pm.

Tickets are available at any large hotel. However, this is often more expensive than buying directly from the venue. Visitors who speak Russian will be able to buy cheap tickets from theatre kiosks, found all over the city. Ticket-booking website **Parter.ru** charges 10 per cent commission on the face-value of tickets. Prices are lowest at the venue's box office. Opening hours are generally from 11am to 3pm and 4pm to 7pm, but may vary.

Ballet and Opera

The Bolshoi Theatre *(see pp82–3)* is the best venue to see ballet and opera. Best known abroad for performing Tchaikovsky's *Swan Lake* and *The Nutcracker*, its repertoire includes works such as *Boris Godunov* by Mussorgsky and European classics such as *Giselle*. Tickets can be booked by phone, online or at the box office.

Originally built as a convention hall for the Communist Party, the State Kremlin Palace *(see p56)* now hosts the Kremlin Ballet Company while the **Helikon Opera** specializes in risqué re-workings of obscure operas.

Music and Nightlife

Moscow's rich tradition of classical music is embodied in the **Tchaikovsky Concert Hall** and the Moscow Conservatory *(see p87)*. The annual December Nights held in the Pushkin State Museum of Fine Arts *(see pp90–91)* attract an array of talent, while the **Tchaikovsky International Competition** is a mecca for classical pianists. In summer both indoor and outdoor concerts are held at Kuskovo Palace *(see p109)* on Tuesday and Thursday evenings.

Moscow has a vibrant jazz scene. The city is now well used to hosting international stars, who perform at stadiums or on Red Square. The best in local talent play at clubs such as **B2** which has established itself as one of the capital's best live music venues, hosting a variety of acts from rock to ska. **Sixteen Tons** favours bands playing alternative and indie music. **Café Ekus**, a South American bar and restaurant, is a good bet for Latin American bands and hosts lively merengue and salsa nights, as does **Che**.

Russians like to party hard and long into the night. Entrance is usually cheaper or free before 11pm although the queues can be long. Most clubs do not close until 4am; some are open until 6am at weekends. **Propaganda** plays everything from the latest electronic sounds to classic disco. **Fabrique** is a huge split-level basement club, mostly playing house. **Cult** offers more urban grooves,

Indie band Race 7 performing at the Sixteen Tons club

including drum & bass and techno. "Art cafés" such as **Art Garbage** and **Bilingua** host live music one night, and an alternative fashion show or film screening the next.

The gay scene includes venues such as **Central Station**, a flamboyant club with nightly shows and karaoke. **Sharm** is set on two floors and offers a karaoke room and live shows.

Theatre and Film

Repertory theatres stage a different play every night. The **Moscow Arts Theatre** is best known for its productions of Anton Chekhov's plays. An excellent dramatization of *The Master and Margarita*, by Mikhail Bulgakov, is staged by the **Taganka Theatre**, while the **Mossoviet Theatre** presents alternative interpretations of Shakespearean dramas.

For English-language cinema, there are a few options within the city centre. **Pioneer** shows dubbed films as well as English-language screenings. **Dome** screens blockbusters, while **35mm** specializes in independent foreign films.

Children's Entertainment

The **Obraztsov Puppet Theatre** puts on matinee shows for children and evening performances for over 18s. The **Nataliya Sats Children's Musical Theatre** also stages fantastic shows.

Moscow's world-famous circus features clowns, acrobats, trapeze artists and performing animals. Visitors can attend shows at the **Old Circus** in the city centre, or the **New Circus** near Sparrow Hills.

The **Durov Animal Theatre** has performing cats and dogs as well as farm animals. Yuri Kuklachev's **Moscow Cats Theatre**, established in 1990, has a troupe of over a hundred feline actors performing all manner of tricks. Performances include *Cats of the Universe* and are a must-see for cat lovers.

Performing artist and clown rehearsing for a show at Moscow's Old Circus

DIRECTORY

Information and Tickets

Parter.Ru
W parter.ru

Ballet and Opera

Helikon Opera
Bolshaya Nikitskaya ulitsa 19. **Map** 1 B5
Tel (495) 690 09 71.

Music and Nightlife

Art Garbage
Starosadskiy pereulok 5/6.
Map 2 F5.
Tel (495) 628 87 45.

B2
Bolshaya Sadovaya ulitsa 8/1.
Map 1 A4.
Tel (495) 650 99 18.

Bilingua
Krivokolennyy pereulok 10/5. **Map** 2 E4.
Tel (495) 623 96 60.

Café Ekus
Bolshoi Sukharevsky pereulok 25/23.
Map 2 E3.
Tel (915) 106 64 66.

Central Station
Ulitsa Yuzhny proezd 4.
Tel (495) 988 35 85.

Che
Nikolskaya ulitsa 10/2.
Map 2 D5.
Tel (495) 621 74 77.

Cult
Yauzskaya ulitsa 5.
Map 4 F1.
Tel (495) 917 57 06.

Fabrique
Kosmodamianskaya naberezhnaya 2.
Map 4 F2.
Tel (495) 953 65 76.

Propaganda
Bolshoi Zlatoustinskiy pereulok 7.
Map 2 E5.
Tel (495) 624 57 32.

Sharm
Ulitsa Dubininskaya 69, Korpus 74.
Tel (495) 645 07 66.

Sixteen Tons
Ulitsa Presnenskiy Val 6.
Tel (499) 253 53 00.

Tchaikovsky Concert Hall
Triumfalnaya ploshchad 4/31.
Map 1 B3.
Tel (495) 232 53 53.

Theatre and Film

35mm
Ulitsa Pokrovka 47/24.
Map 2 F5.
Tel (495) 780 91 45.

Dome
Olympiysky prospekt 18/1.
Map 2 D1.
Tel (495) 931 98 73.

Moscow Arts Theatre
Kamergerskiy pereulok 3.
Map 1 C5.
Tel (495) 629 87 60.

Mossoviet Theatre
Ulitsa Bolshaya Sadovaya 16.
Map 1 B4.
Tel (495) 699 20 35.

Pioneer
Kutuzovsky prospekt 21.
Tel (499) 240 52 40.

Taganka Theatre
Ulitsa Zemlyanoy Val 76/21.
Tel (495) 915 12 17.

Children's Entertainment

Durov Animal Theatre
Ulitsa Durova 4.
Map 2 D2.
Tel (495) 631 30 47.

Moscow Cats Theatre
Kutuzovsky prospekt 25.
Tel (499) 243 40 05.

Nataliya Sats Children's Musical Theatre
Prospekt Vernadskovo 5.
Tel (495) 930 52 40.

New Circus
Prospekt Vernadskovo 7.
Tel (495) 930 03 00.

Obraztsov Puppet Theatre
Sadovaya-Samotechnaya ulitsa 3.
Map 1 A5.
Tel (495) 699 53 73.

Old Circus
Tsvetnoy bulvar 13.
Map 2 D3.
Tel (495) 625 89 70.

MOSCOW STREET FINDER

The map below shows the areas of Moscow covered by the Street Finder maps. The map references in the Moscow section for sights of interest, restaurants, hotels, shops and entertainment venues refer to the maps in this section. The symbols used to represent sights and useful information on the Street Finder maps are shown in the key. The first figure in the map reference indicates which Street Finder map to turn to, and the letter and number that follow refer to the map's grid. An index of key street names can be found on the following pages. The index lists street names in transliteration, followed by Cyrillics (on the maps, Cyrillics are only given for major roads).

Visitors strolling the busy Arbat Street, Moscow

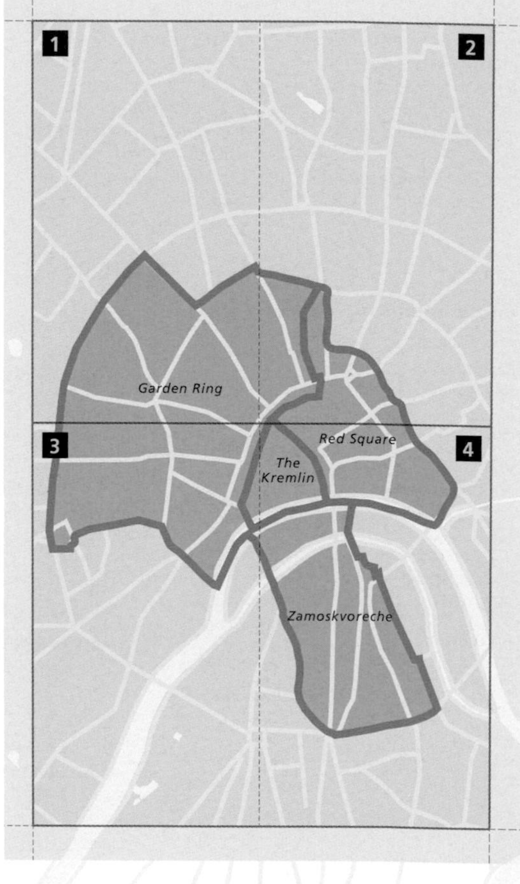

Key to Street Finder

- Major sight
- Place of interest
- Other building
- Train station
- Metro station
- Main tram stop
- Main trolleybus stop
- Main bus stop
- River boat pier
- Hospital
- Police station
- Orthodox church
- Non-Orthodox church
- Synagogue
- Mosque
- Railway line
- Pedestrian area

Scale of Maps 1–4

0 metres 400
0 yards 400

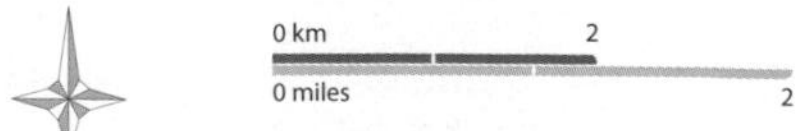

Street Finder Index

1-ya Brestskaya ulitsa
1-Я БРЕСТСКАЯ УЛИЦА **1A3**

1-ya Frunzenskaya ulitsa
1-Я ФРУНЗЕНСКАЯ УЛИЦА **3A5**

1-ya Miusskaya ulitsa
1-Я МИУССКАЯ УЛИЦА **1B2**

1-ya Tverskaya-Yamskaya ulitsa
1-Я ТВЕРСКАЯ-ЯМСКАЯ УЛИЦА **1A2**

1-ya Yamskovo Polya, ulitsa
1-Я ЯМСКОГО ПОЛЯ, УЛИЦА **1A2**

1-yy Kadashevskiy pereulok
1-ЫЙ КАДАШЕВСКИЙ ПЕРЕУЛОК **4D2**

1-yy Novokuznetskiy pereulok
1-ЫЙ НОВОКУЗНЕЦКИЙ ПЕРЕУЛОК **4E4**

1-yy Zachatevskiy pereulok
1-ЫЙ ЗАЧАТЬЕВСКИЙ ПЕРЕУЛОК **3B3**

2-oy Lesnoy pereulok
2-ОЙ ЛЕСНОЙ ПЕРЕУЛОК **1A2**

2-ya Tverskaya-Yamskaya ulitsa
2-Я ТВЕРСКАЯ-ЯМСКАЯ УЛИЦА **1A2**

3-iy Monetchikovskiy pereulok
3-ИЙ МОНЕТЧИКОВСКИЙ ПЕРЕУЛОК **4E4**

3-iy Samotechnyy pereulok
3-ИЙ САМОТЕЧНЫЙ ПЕРЕУЛОК **1C2**

3-ya Tverskaya-Yamskaya ulitsa
3-Я ТВЕРСКАЯ-ЯМСКАЯ УЛИЦА **1B3**

4-yy Dobryninskiy pereulok
4-ЫЙ ДОБРЫНИНСКИЙ ПЕРЕУЛОК **4D5**

A

Akademika Sakharova, prospekt
АКАДЕМИКА САХАРОВА, ПРОСПЕКТ **2E4**

Aleksandra Nevskovo, ulitsa
АЛЕКСАНДРА НЕВСКОГО, УЛИЦА **1A2**

Arbat, ulitsa
АРБАТ, УЛИЦА **3A1**

B

Bakhrushina, ulitsa
БАХРУШИНА, УЛИЦА **4E4**

Bersenevskaya naberezhnaya
БЕРСЕНЕВСКАЯ НАБЕРЕЖНАЯ **3C3**

Bolotnaya naberezhnaya
БОЛОТНАЯ НАБЕРЕЖНАЯ **3C2**

Bolotnaya ulitsa
БОЛОТНАЯ УЛИДА **4D2**

Bolshaya Bronnaya ulitsa
БОЛЬШАЯ БРОННАЯ УЛИЦА **1B5**

Bolshaya Dmitrovka, ulitsa
БОЛЬШАЯ ДМИТРОВКА, УЛИЦА **1C4**

Bolshaya Lubyanka, ulitsa
БОЛЬШАЯ ЛУБЯНКА, УЛИЦА **2D5**

Bolshaya Nikitskaya ulitsa
БОЛЬШАЯ НИКИТСКАЯ УЛИЦА **1A5**

Bolshaya Ordynka, ulitsa
БОЛЬШАЯ ОРДЫНКА, УЛИЦА **4D2**

Bolshaya Pereyaslavskaya ulitsa
БОЛЬШАЯ ПЕРЕЯСЛАВСКАЯ УЛИЦА **2F1**

Bolshaya Pionerskaya ulitsa
БОЛЬШАЯ ПИОНЕРСКАЯ УЛИЦА **4E5**

Bolshaya Polyanka, ulitsa
БОЛЬШАЯ ПОЛЯНКА, УЛИЦА **4D3**

Bolshaya Sadovaya ulitsa
БОЛЬШАЯ САДОВАЯ УЛИЦА **1A4**

Bolshaya Serpukhovskaya ulitsa
БОЛЬШАЯ СЕРПУХОВСКАЯ УЛИЦА **4D5**

Bolshaya Tatarskaya ulitsa
БОЛЬШАЯ ТАТАРСКАЯ УЛИЦА **4E3**

Bolshaya Yakimanka, ulitsa
БОЛЬШАЯ ЯКИМАНКА, УЛИЦА **3C4**

Useful words & abbreviations

	most	bridge
	podezd	entrance
	proezd	small street/passage/lane
	sad	garden
	shosse	road
	stroenie	building
	tupik	cul-de-sac
ul	**ulitsa**	street
pl	**ploshchad**	square
pr	**prospekt**	avenue
per	**pereulok**	small street/passage/lane

Bolshoi Kamennyy most
БОЛЬШОЙ КАМЕННЫЙ МОСТ **3C2**

Bolshoi Krasnokholmskiy most
БОЛЬШОЙ КРАСНОХОЛМСКИЙ МОСТ **4F4**

Bolshoi Levshinskiy pereulok
БОЛЬШОЙ ЛЕВШИНСКИЙ ПЕРЕУЛОК **3A3**

Bolshoi Moskvoretskiy most
БОЛЬШОЙ МОСКВОРЕЦКИЙ МОСТ **4D1**

Bolshoi Sergievskiy pereulok
БОЛЬШОЙ СЕРГИЕВСКИЙ ПЕРЕУЛОК **2E4**

Bolshoi Sukharevskiy pereulok
БОЛЬШОЙ СУХАРЕВСКИЙ ПЕРЕУЛОК **2E3**

Bolshoi Tolmachevskiy pereulok
БОЛЬШОЙ ТОЛМАЧЕВСКИЙ ПЕРЕУЛОК **4D3**

Bolshoi Ustinskiy most
БОЛЬШОЙ УСТЬИНСКИЙ МОСТ **4E2**

Bolshoi Vlasevskiy pereulok
БОЛЬШОЙ ВЛАСЬЕВСКИЙ ПЕРЕУЛОК **3A2**

Bolshoi Znamenskiy pereulok
БОЛЬШОЙ ЗНАМЕНСКИЙ ПЕРЕУЛОК **3D2**

Butyrskiy val, ulitsa
БУТЫРСКИЙ ВАЛ, УЛИЦА **1A2**

C

Chayanova, ulitsa
ЧАЯНОВА, УЛИЦА **1B2**

D

Delegatskaya ulitsa
ДЕЛЕГАТСКАЯ УЛИЦА **1C2**

Denezhnyy pereulok
ДЕНЕЖНЫЙ ПЕРЕУЛОК **3A2**

Dobryninskiy pereulok
ДОБРЫНИНСКИЙ ПЕРЕУЛОК **4D5**

Dolgorukovskaya ulitsa
ДОЛГОРУКОВСКАЯ УЛИЦА **1B2**

Donskaya ulitsa
ДОНСКАЯ УЛИЦА **3C5**

Dostoevskovo, ulitsa
ДОСТОЕВСКОГО, УЛИЦА **1C1**

Dubininskaya ulitsa
ДУБИНИНСКАЯ УЛИЦА **4E5**

Durova, ulitsa
ДУРОВА, УЛИЦА **2E2**

F

Fadeeva, ulitsa
ФАДЕЕВА, УЛИЦА **1B3**

Frunzenskaya naberezhnaya
ФРУНЗЕНСКАЯ НАБЕРЕЖНАЯ **3A5**

G

Gagarinskiy pereulok
ГАГАРИНСКИЙ ПЕРЕУЛОК **3A2**

Gasheka, ulitsa
ГАШЕКА, УЛИЦА 1A3

Gazetnyy pereulok
ГАЗЕТНЫЙ ПЕРЕУЛОК 1C5

Georgievskiy pereulok
ГЕОРГИЕВСКИЙ ПЕРЕУЛОК 1C5

Glinishchevskiy pereulok
ГЛИНИЩЕВСКИЙ ПЕРЕУЛОК 1C4

Gogolevskiy bulvar
ГОГОЛЕВСКИЙ БУЛЬВАР 3B2

Goncharnaya ulitsa
ГОНЧАРНАЯ УЛИЦА 4F2

Granatnyy pereulok
ГРАНАТНЫЙ ПЕРЕУЛОК 1A5

I

Ilinka, ulitsa
ИЛЬИНКА, УЛИЦА 4D1

K

Kadashevskaya naberezhnaya
КАДАШЕВСКАЯ НАБЕРЕЖНАЯ 4D2

Kalanchevskaya ulitsa
КАЛАНЧЕВСКАЯ УЛИЦА 2F2

Kamergerskiy pereulok
КАМЕРГЕРСКИЙ ПЕРЕУЛОК 1C5

Karetnyy ryad, ulitsa
КАРЕТНЫЙ РЯД, УЛИЦА 1C3

Khlebnyy pereulok
ХЛЕБНЫЙ ПЕРЕУЛОК 1A5

Kitaygorodskiy proezd
КИТАЙГОРОДСКИЙ ПРОЕЗД 4E1

Koroviy val, ulitsa
КОРОВИЙ ВАЛ, УЛИЦА 4D4

Kosmodamianskaya naberezhnaya
КОСМОДАМИАНСКАЯ НАБЕРЕЖНАЯ 4F2

Kotelnicheskaya naberezhnaya
КОТЕЛЬНИЧЕСКАЯ НАБЕРЕЖНАЯ 4F2

Kozhevnicheskaya ulitsa
КОЖЕВНИЧЕСКАЯ УЛИЦА 4F4

Krasina, ulitsa
КРАСИНА, УЛИЦА 1A3

Krasnoproletarskaya ulitsa
КРАСНОПРОЛЕТАРСКАЯ УЛИЦА 1C2

Kremlevskaya naberezhnaya
КРЕМЛЁВСКАЯ НАБЕРЕЖНАЯ 4D1

Krymskaya naberezhnaya
КРЫМСКАЯ НАБЕРЕЖНАЯ 3B4

Krymskiy most
КРЫМСКИЙ МОСТ 3B4

Krymskiy val, ulitsa
КРЫМСКИЙ ВАЛ, УЛИЦА 3C4

L

Lavrushinskiy pereulok
ЛАВРУШИНСКИЙ ПЕРЕУЛОК 4D2

Leninskiy prospect
ЛЕНИНСКИЙ ПРОСПЕКТ 3B5

Leontevskiy pereulok
ЛЕОНТЬЕВСКИЙ ПЕРЕУЛОК 1B5

Lesnaya ulitsa
ЛЕСНАЯ УЛИЦА 1A2

Letnikovskaya ulitsa
ЛЕТНИКОВСКАЯ УЛИЦА 4F5

Lva Tolstovo, ulitsa
ЛЬВА ТОЛСТОГО, УЛИЦА 3A3

Lyusinovskaya ulitsa
ЛЮСИНОВСКАЯ УЛИЦА 4D5

M

Malaya Bronnaya ulitsa
МАЛАЯ БРОННАЯ УЛИЦА 1A4

Malaya Dmitrovka, ulitsa
МАЛАЯ ДМИТРОВКА, УЛИЦА 1C3

Malaya Nikitskaya ulitsa
МАЛАЯ НИКИТСКАЯ УЛИЦА 1A5

Malaya Ordynka, ulitsa
МАЛАЯ ОРДЫНКА, УЛИЦА 4D4

Malaya Pionerskaya ulitsa
МАЛАЯ ПИОНЕРСКАЯ УЛИЦА 4E4

Malyy Gnezdnikovskiy pereulok
МАЛЫЙ ГНЕЗДНИКОВСКИЙ ПЕРЕУЛОК 1B5

Malyy Tolmachevskiy pereulok
МАЛЫЙ ТОЛМАЧЕВСКИЙ ПЕРЕУЛОК 4E4

Malyy Znamenskiy pereulok
МАЛЫЙ ЗНАМЕНСКИЙ ПЕРЕУЛОК 3B2

Manezhnaya ulitsa
МАНЕЖНАЯ УЛИДА 3C1

Maroseyka, ulitsa
МАРОСЕЙКА, УЛИЦА 2E5

Mira, prospekt
МИРА, ПРОСПЕКТ 2E2

Mokhovaya ulitsa
МОХОВАЯ УЛИЦА 3C1

Moskvoretskaya naberezhnaya
МОСКВОРЕЦКАЯ НАБЕРЕЖНАЯ 4E1

Myasnitskaya ulitsa
МЯСНИЦКАЯ УЛИЦА 2E5

Mytnaya, ulitsa
МЫТНАЯ, УЛИЦА 3C5

N

Nikitskiy bulvar
НИКИТСКИЙ БУЛЬВАР 3B1

Nikitskiy pereulok
НИКИТСКИЙ ПЕРЕУЛОК 1C5

Novaya ploshchad
НОВАЯ ПЛОЩАДЬ 2D5

Novokhokhlovskaya ulitsa
НОВОХОХЛОВСКАЯ УЛИЦА 1B1

Novokuznetskaya ulitsa
НОВОКУЗНЕЦКАЯ УЛИЦА 4E3

Novoslobodskaya ulitsa
НОВОСЛОБОДСКАЯ УЛИЦА 1B1

Novyy Arbat, ulitsa
НОВЫЙ АРБАТ, УЛИЦА 3A1

O

Olimpiyskiy prospekt
ОЛИМПИЙСКИЙ ПРОСПЕКТ 2D3

Orlikov pereulok
ОРЛИКОВ ПЕРЕУЛОК 2F3

Oruzheynyy pereulok
ОРУЖЕЙНЫИ ПЕРЕУЛОК 1B3

Ostozhenka, ulitsa
ОСТОЖЕНКА, УЛИЦА 3B3

Ovchinnikovskaya naberezhnaya
ОВЧИННИКОВСКАЯ НАБЕРЕЖНАЯ 4E2

Ozerkovskaya naberezhnaya
ОЗЕРКОВСКАЯ НАБЕРЕЖНАЯ 4E2

P

Pechatnikov pereulok
ПЕЧАТНИКОВ ПЕРЕУЛОК 2D4

Petrovka, ulitsa
ПЕТРОВКА, УЛИЦА 2D4

Petrovskiy bulvar
ПЕТРОВСКИЙ БУЛЬВАР 2D4

Petrovskiy pereulok
ПЕТРОВСКИЙ ПЕРЕУЛОК 1C4

Plotnikov pereulok
ПЛОТНИКОВ ПЕРЕУЛОК 3A2

Podgorskaya naberezhnaya
ПОДГОРСКАЯ НАБЕРЕЖНАЯ 4F2

Pokrovka, ulitsa
ПОКРОВКА, УЛИЦА 2F5

Street		Grid
Povarskaya ulitsa	ПОВАРСКАЯ УЛИЦА	1A5
Prechistenka, ulitsa	ПРЕЧИСТЕНКА, УЛИЦА	3A3
Prechistenskaya naberezhnaya	ПРЕЧИСТЕНСКАЯ НАБЕРЕЖНАЯ	3C2
Priyutskiy pereulok	ПРИЮТСКИЙ ПЕРЕУЛОК	1A1
Protopopovskiy pereulok	ПРОТОПОПОВСКИЙ ПЕРЕУЛОК	2E2
Pushkinskaya naberezhnaya	ПУШКИНСКАЯ НАБЕРЕЖНАЯ	3B5
Pyatnitskaya ulitsa	ПЯТНИЦКАЯ УЛИЦА	4D4

R

Street		Grid
Raushskaya naberezhnaya	РАУШСКАЯ НАБЕРЕЖНАЯ	4E1
Rozhdestvenskiy bulvar	РОЖДЕСТВЕНСКИЙ БУЛЬВАР	2D4

S

Street		Grid
Sadovaya-Karetnaya ulitsa	САДОВАЯ-КАРЕТНАЯ УЛИДА	1C3
Sadovaya-Kudrinskaya ulitsa	САДОВАЯ-КУДРИНСКАН УЛИЦА	1A5
Sadovaya-Samotechnaya ulitsa	САДОВАЯ-САМОТЕЧНАЯ УЛИЦА	2D3
Sadovaya Spasskaya ulitsa	САДОВАЯ-СПАССКАЯ УЛИЦА	2E3
Sadovaya-Sukharevskaya ulitsa	САДОВАЯ-СУХАРЕВСКАЯ УЛИЦА	2D3
Sadovaya-Triumfalnaya ulitsa	САДОВАЯ-ТРИУМФАЛЬНАЯ УЛИЦА	1B3
Sadovnicheskaya naberezhnaya	САДОВНИЧЕСКАЯ НАБЕРЕЖНАЯ	4E2
Sadovnicheskaya ulitsa	САДОВНИЧЕСКАЯ УЛИДА	4F3
Sadovnicheskiy proezd	САДОВНИЧЕСКИЙ ПРОЕЗД	4E2
Samotechnaya ulitsa	САМОТЕЧНАЯ УЛИЦА	2D2
Sandunovskiy pereulok	САНДУНОВСКИЙ ПЕРЕУЛОК	2D4
Seleznevskaya ulitsa	СЕЛЕЗНЕВСКАЯ УЛИЦА	1B2
Shabolovka, ulitsa	ШАБОЛОВКА, УЛИЦА	3C5
Sivtsev Vrazhek, pereulok	СИВЦЕВ ВРАЖЕК, ПЕРЕУЛОК	3B2
Skaternyy pereulok	СКАТЕРНЫЙ ПЕРЕУЛОК	1A5
Smolenskaya ploshchad	СМОЛЕНСКАЯ ПЛОЩАДЬ	3A2
Smolenskiy bulvar	СМОЛЕНСКИЙ БУЛЬВАР	3A2
Sofiyskaya naberezhnaya	СОФИЙСКАЯ НАБЕРЕЖНАЯ	3C2
Solyanka, ulitsa	СОЛЯНКА, УЛИЦА	4F1
Sovetskoy Armii, ulitsa	СОВЕТСКОЙ АРМИИ, УЛИЦА	2D2
Soymonovskiy prospekt	СОЙМОНОВСКИЙ ПРОСПЕКТ	3B2
Spiridonovka, ulitsa	СПИРИДОНОВКА, УЛИЦА	1A5
Sretenka, ulitsa	СРЕТЕНКА, УЛИЦА	2E5
Sretenskiy bulvar	СРЕТЕНСКИЙ БУЛЬВАР	2E4
Starokonyushennyy pereulok	СТАРОКОНЮШЕННЫЙ ПЕРЕУЛОК	3B2
Staromonetnyy pereulok	СТАРОМОНЕТНЫЙ ПЕРЕУЛОК	4D2
Stoleshnikov pereulok	СТОЛЕШНИКОВ ПЕРЕУЛОК	1C5
Strastnoy bulvar	СТРАСТНОЙ БУЛЬВАР	1C4
Stremyannyy pereulok	СТРЕМЯННЫЙ ПЕРЕУЛОК	4E5
Sushchevskaya ulitsa	СУЩЕВСКАЯ УЛИЦА	1B1

T

Street		Grid
Tatarskaya ulitsa	ТАТАРСКАЯ УЛИДА	4E3
Teatralnyy proezd	ТЕАТРАЛЬНЫЙ ПРОЕЗД	2D5
Timura Frunze, ulitsa	ТИМУРА ФРУНЗЕ, УЛИЦА	3A3
Troitskaya ulitsa	ТРОИЦКАЯ УЛИЦА	2D3
Tverskaya ulitsa	ТВЕРСКАЯ УЛИЦА	1B4
Tverskoy bulvar	ТВЕРСКОЙ БУЛЬВАР	1B5

U

Street		Grid
Uspenskiy pereulok	УСПЕНСКИЙ ПЕРЕУЛОК	1C3
Ustinskaya naberezhnaya	УСТЬИНСКАЯ НАБЕРЕЖНАЯ	4F2

V

Street		Grid
Valovaya, ulitsa	ВАЛОВАЯ, УЛИЦА	4E4
Varsonofevskiy pereulok	ВАРСОНОФЬЕВСКИЙ ПЕРЕУЛОК	2D4
Varvarka, ulitsa	ВАРВАРКА, УЛИЦА	4E1
Vasilevskaya ulitsa	ВАСИЛЬЕВСКАЯ УЛИЦА	1A3
Vishnyakovskiy pereulok	ВИШНЯКОВСКИЙ ПЕРЕУЛОК	4E3
Volkhonka, ulitsa	ВОЛХОНКА, УЛИЦА	3B2
Vozdvizhenka, ulitsa	ВОЗДНИЖЕНКА, УЛИЦА	3B1
Voznesenskiy pereulok	ВОЗНЕСЕНСКИЙ ПЕРЕУЛОК	1B5

Y

Street		Grid
Yakimanskaya naberezhnaya	ЯКИМАНСКАЯ НАБЕРЕЖНАЯ	3C3
Yauzskaya ulitsa	ЯУЗСКАЯ УЛИЦА	4F2
Yauzskiy bulvar	ЯУЗСКИЙ БУЛЬВАР	4F1

Z

Street		Grid
Zatsepa, ulitsa	ЗАЦЕПА, УЛИЦА	4E4
Zatsepskiy val, ulitsa	ЗАЦЕПСКИЙ, УЛИЦА	4E4
Zhitnaya, ulitsa	ЖИТНАЯ, УЛИЦА	3C4
Znamenka, ulitsa	ЗНАМЕНКА, УЛИЦА	3B1
Zoologicheskaya ulitsa	ЗООЛОГИЧЕСКАЯ УЛИЦА	1A4
Zubovskiy bulvar	ЗУБОВСКИЙ БУЛЬВАР	3A3
Zvonarskiy pereulok	ЗВОНАРСКИЙ ПЕРЕУЛОК	2D4

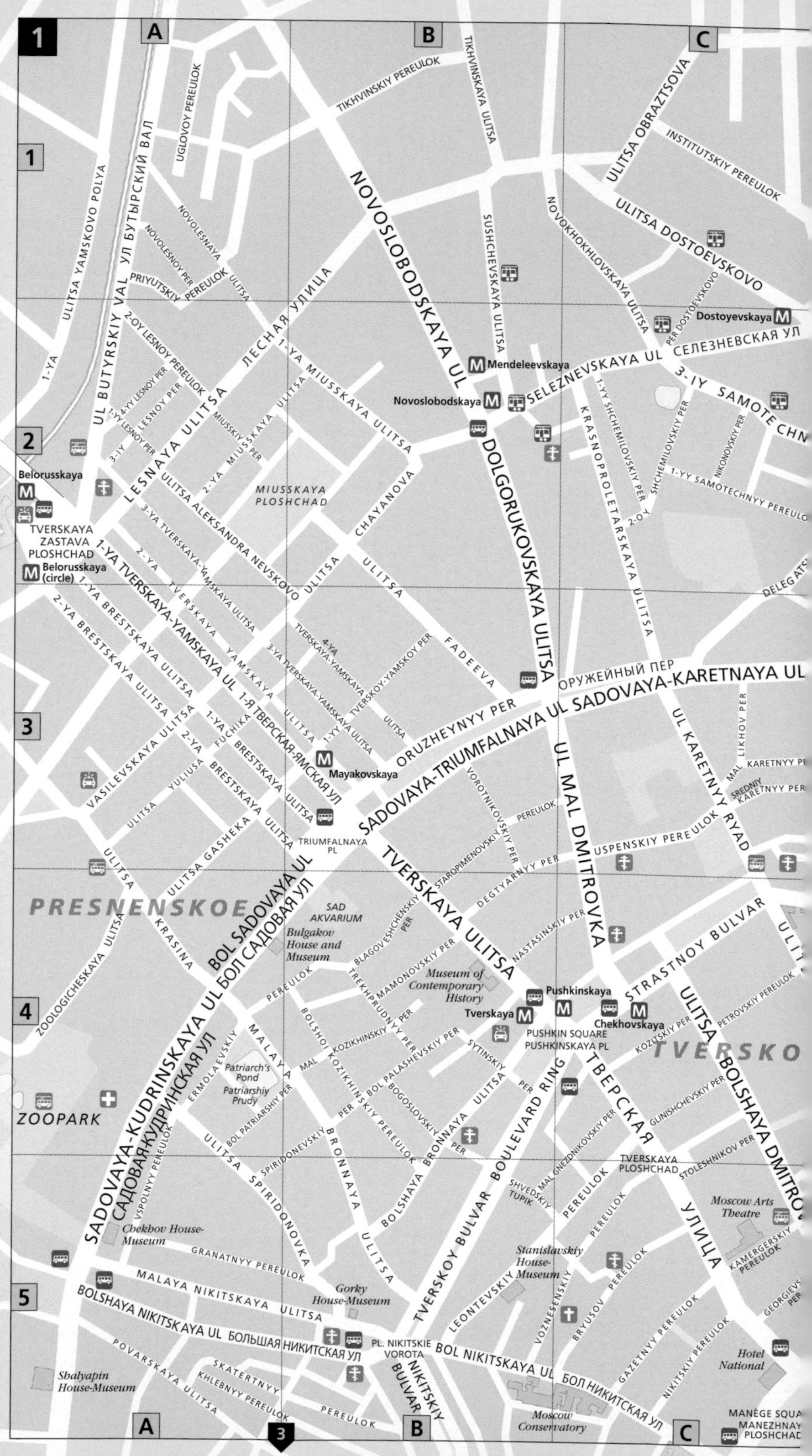
1
A
B
C
1
2
3
4
5
TIKHVINSKIY PEREULOK
TIKHVINSKAYA ULITSA
UGLOVOY PEREULOK
ULITSA OBRAZTSOVA
INSTITUTSKIY PEREULOK
ULITSA DOSTOEVSKOVO
NOVOSLOBODSKAYA UL
SUSHCHEVSKAYA ULITSA
NOVOKHOKHLOVSKAYA ULITSA
PER DOSTOEVSKOVO
Dostoyevskaya
ULITSA YAMSKOVO POLYA
1-YA
UL BUTYRSKIY VAL
УЛ БУТЫРСКИЙ ВАЛ
NOVOLESNAYA ULITSA
NOVOLESNOY PER
PRIYUTSKIY PEREULOK
ЛЕСНАЯ УЛИЦА
2-OY LESNOY PEREULOK
4-YY LESNOY PER
1-YY LESNOY PER
3-IY LESNOY PER
LESNAYA ULITSA
1-YA MIUSSKAYA ULITSA
MIUSSKIY PER
2-YA MIUSSKAYA ULITSA
MIUSSKAYA PLOSHCHAD
Mendeleevskaya
Novoslobodskaya
SELEZNEVSKAYA UL
СЕЛЕЗНЕВСКАЯ УЛ
3-IY SAMOTECHN
KRASNOPROLETARSKAYA ULITSA
1-YY SHCHEMILOVSKIY PER
2-OY SHCHEMILOVSKIY PER
NIKONOVSKIY PER
1-YY SAMOTECHNYY PEREULO
DOLGORUKOVSKAYA ULITSA
Belorusskaya
TVERSKAYA ZASTAVA PLOSHCHAD
Belorusskaya (circle)
ULITSA ALEKSANDRA NEVSKOVO
CHAYANOVA ULITSA
3-YA TVERSKAYA-YAMSKAYA ULITSA
2-YA TVERSKAYA YAMSKAYA
1-YA TVERSKAYA-YAMSKAYA UL
1-ЯЯ ТВЕРСКАЯ-ЯМСКАЯ УЛ
1-YA BRESTSKAYA ULITSA
2-YA BRESTSKAYA ULITSA
4-YA TVERSKAYA-YAMSKAYA ULITSA
3-YA TVERSKAYA-YAMSKAYA ULITSA
TVERSKOY-YAMSKOY PER
1-YY TVERSKAYA-YAMSKAYA ULITSA
FADEEVA
DELEGATS
ОРУЖЕЙНЫЙ ПЕР
ORUZHEYNYY PER
SADOVAYA-KARETNAYA UL
SADOVAYA-TRIUMFALNAYA UL
Mayakovskaya
VASILEVSKAYA ULITSA
FUCHIKA
YULIUSA FUCHIKA ULITSA
1-YA BRESTSKAYA ULITSA
2-YA BRESTSKAYA ULITSA
UL KARETNYY RYAD
LIKHOV PER
MAL KARETNYY PER
SREDNIY KARETNYY PER
VOROTNIKOVSKIY PEREULOK
STAROPIMENOVSKIY PER
UL MAL DMITROVKA
USPENSKIY PEREULOK
DEGTYARNYY PER
TRIUMFALNAYA PL
ULITSA GASHEKA
ULITSA KRASINA
PRESNENSKOE
BOL SADOVAYA UL
БОЛ САДОВАЯ УЛ
SAD AKVARIUM
Bulgakov House and Museum
BLAGOVESHCHENSKIY PER
TVERSKAYA ULITSA
NASTASINSKIY PER
STRASTNOY BULVAR
ZOOLOGICHESKAYA ULITSA
MAMONOVSKIY PER
Museum of Contemporary History
TREKHPRUDNYY PER
PEREULOK
Pushkinskaya
Tverskaya
Chekhovskaya
PUSHKIN SQUARE
PUSHKINSKAYA PL
KOZITSKIY PER
PETROVSKIY PEREULOK
TVERSKO
ULITSA BOLSHAYA DMITROV
SADOVAYA-KUDRINSKAYA UL
САДОВАЯ-КУДРИНСКАЯ УЛ
ERMOLAEVSKIY PER
MALAYA BRONNAYA ULITSA
BOLSHOI KOZIKHINSKIY PEREULOK
MAL KOZIKHINSKIY PER
BOL PALASHEVSKIY PER
SYTINSKIY PER
Patriarch's Pond
Patriarshiy Prudy
BOL PATRIARSHIY PER
ZOOPARK
BOGOSLOVSKIY PER
BOULEVARD RING
ТВЕРСКАЯ УЛИЦА
GLINISHCHEVSKIY PER
MAL GNEZDNIKOVSKIY PER
ULITSA SPIRIDONOVKA
SPIRIDONEVSKIY PER
BOLSHAYA BRONNAYA ULITSA
TVERSKAYA PLOSHCHAD
STOLESHNIKOV PER
VSPOLNYY PEREULOK
SHVEDSKIY TUPIK
PEREULOK
TVERSKOY BULVAR
Moscow Arts Theatre
Chekhov House-Museum
GRANATNYY PEREULOK
Stanislavskiy House-Museum
KAMERGERSKIY PEREULOK
MALAYA NIKITSKAYA ULITSA
Gorky House-Museum
LEONTEVSKIY PEREULOK
VOZNESENSKIY PEREULOK
BRYUSOV PEREULOK
GEORGIEVSKIY PER
BOLSHAYA NIKITSKAYA UL
БОЛЬШАЯ НИКИТСКАЯ УЛ
PL. NIKITSKIE VOROTA
BOL NIKITSKAYA UL
БОЛ НИКИТСКАЯ УЛ
GAZETNYY PEREULOK
NIKITSKIY PEREULOK
Hotel National
Shalyapin House-Museum
POVARSKAYA ULITSA
SKATERTNYY PEREULOK
KHLEBNYY PEREULOK
NIKITSKIY BULVAR
Moscow Conservatory
MANÈGE SQUA
MANEZHNAY PLOSHCHAD
3

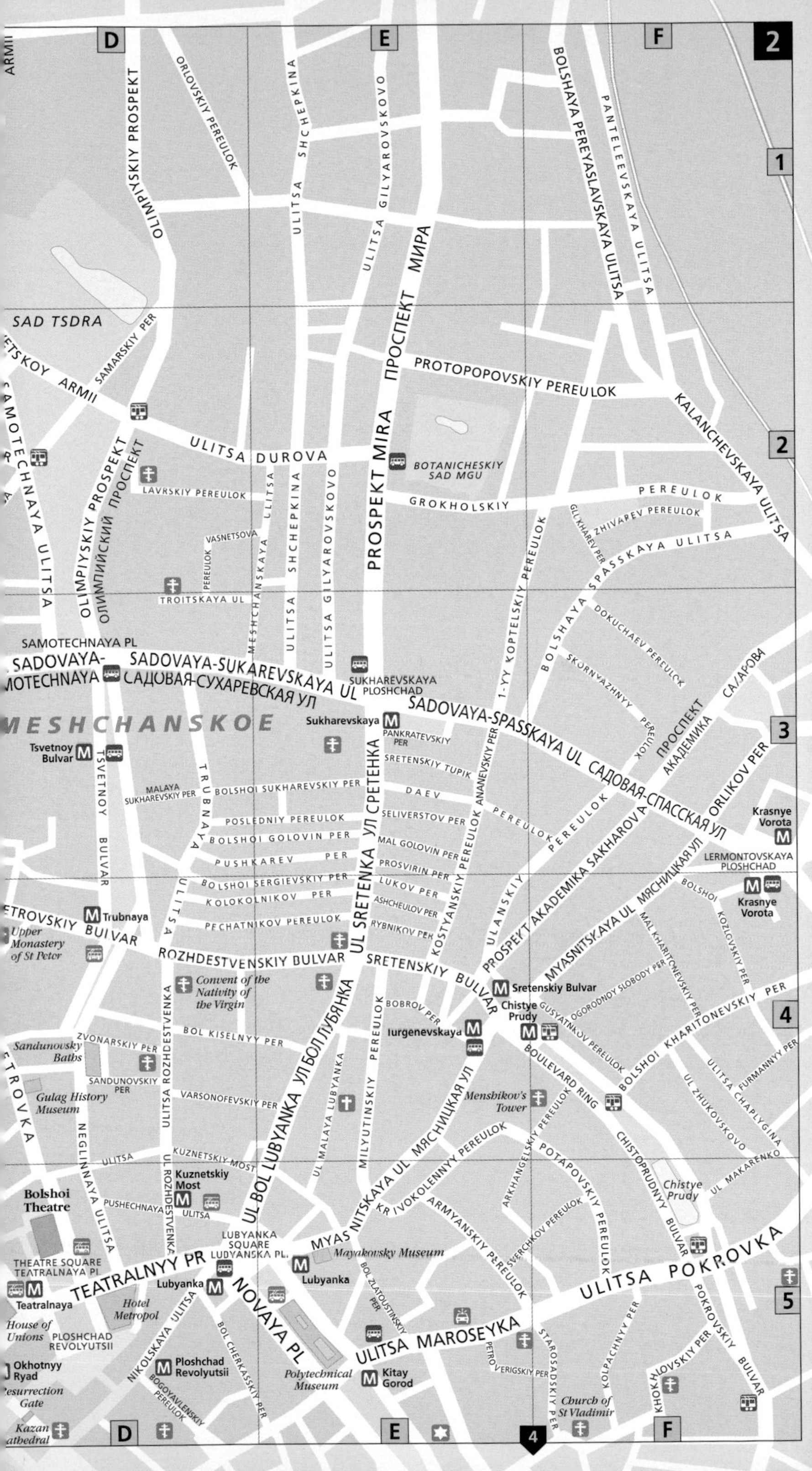
D
E
F
2
1
2
3
4
5
ARMII
OLIMPIYSKIY PROSPEKT
ORLOVSKIY PEREULOK
ULITSA SHCHEPKINA
ULITSA GILYAROVSKOVO
BOLSHAYA PEREYASLAVSKAYA ULITSA
PANTELEEVSKAYA ULITSA
ПРОСПЕКТ МИРА
SAD TSDRA
SAMARSKIY PER
SOVETSKOY ARMII
PROTOPOPOVSKIY PEREULOK
KALANCHEVSKAYA ULITSA
SAMOTECHNAYA ULITSA
ULITSA DUROVA
OLIMPIYSKIY PROSPEKT
ОЛИМПИЙСКИЙ ПРОСПЕКТ
PROSPEKT MIRA
BOTANICHESKIY SAD MGU
LAVRSKIY PEREULOK
GROKHOLSKIY PEREULOK
ZHIVAREV PEREULOK
GLUKHAREV PER
SPASSKAYA ULITSA
VASNETSOVA PEREULOK
MESHCHANSKAYA ULITSA
ULITSA SHCHEPKINA
ULITSA GILYAROVSKOVO
1-YY KOPTELSKIY PEREULOK
TROITSKAYA UL
BOLSHAYA SPASSKAYA
DOKUCHAEV PEREULOK
SKORNYAZHNYY PEREULOK
SAMOTECHNAYA PL
SADOVAYA-SAMOTECHNAYA
SADOVAYA-SUKAREVSKAYA UL
САДОВАЯ-СУХАРЕВСКАЯ УЛ
SUKHAREVSKAYA PLOSHCHAD
SADOVAYA-SPASSKAYA UL
САДОВАЯ-СПАССКАЯ УЛ
ПРОСПЕКТ АКАДЕМИКА САХАРОВА
ORLIKOV PER
MESHCHANSKOE
Sukharevskaya
Tsvetnoy Bulvar
TSVETNOY BULVAR
TRUBNAYA ULITSA
PANKRATEVSKIY PER
SRETENSKIY TUPIK
ANANEVSKIY PER
MALAYA SUKHAREVSKIY PER
BOLSHOI SUKHAREVSKIY PER
DAEV PEREULOK
POSLEDNIY PEREULOK
SELIVERSTOV PER
BOLSHOI GOLOVIN PER
MAL GOLOVIN PER
PUSHKAREV PER
PROSVIRIN PER
BOLSHOI SERGIEVSKIY PER
LUKOV PER
KOLOKOLNIKOV PER
ASHCHEULOV PER
PECHATNIKOV PEREULOK
RYBNIKOV PER
KOSTYANSKIY PEREULOK
ULANSKIY PEREULOK
PROSPEKT AKADEMIKA SAKHAROVA
Krasnye Vorota
LERMONTOVSKAYA PLOSHCHAD
Krasnye Vorota
BOLSHOI KOZLOVSKIY PER
MYASNITSKAYA UL
МЯСНИЦКАЯ УЛ
MAL KHARITONEVSKIY PER
Trubnaya
PETROVSKIY BULVAR
Upper Monastery of St Peter
ROZHDESTVENSKIY BULVAR
UL SRETENKA
УЛ СРЕТЕНКА
SRETENSKIY BULVAR
Sretenskiy Bulvar
Chistye Prudy
OGORODNOY SLOBODY PER
GUSYATNIKOV PEREULOK
BOLSHOI KHARITONEVSKIY PER
ULITSA ROZHDESTVENKA
Convent of the Nativity of the Virgin
BOBROV PER
Turgenevskaya
BOULEVARD RING
ULITSA CHAPLYGINA
FURMANNYY PER
UL BOL LUBYANKA
УЛ БОЛ ЛУБЯНКА
ZVONARSKIY PER
BOL KISELNYY PER
Sandunovsky Baths
SANDUNOVSKIY PER
PETROVKA
Gulag History Museum
VARSONOFEVSKIY PER
UL MALAYA LUBYANKA
MILYUTINSKIY PEREULOK
Menshikov's Tower
UL ZHUKOVSKOVO
UL MAKARENKO
NEGLINNAYA ULITSA
KUZNETSKIY MOST
Kuznetskiy Most
ARKHANGELSKIY PEREULOK
POTAPOVSKIY PEREULOK
CHISTOPRUDNYY BULVAR
Chistye Prudy
Bolshoi Theatre
PUSHECHNAYA ULITSA
UL ROZHDESTVENKA
MYASNITSKAYA UL
KRIVOKOLENNYY PEREULOK
ARMYANSKIY PEREULOK
SVERCHKOV PEREULOK
LUBYANKA SQUARE
LUBYANSKA PL
Mayakovsky Museum
THEATRE SQUARE
TEATRALNAYA PL
TEATRALNYY PR
Lubyanka
Lubyanka
NOVAYA PL
BOL ZLATOUSTINSKIY PER
ULITSA POKROVKA
Teatralnaya
Hotel Metropol
House of Unions
PLOSHCHAD REVOLYUTSII
NIKOLSKAYA ULITSA
BOL CHERKASSKIY PER
ULITSA MAROSEYKA
PETROVERIGSKIY PER
STAROSADSKIY PER
KOLPACHNYY PER
POKROVSKIY BULVAR
KHOKHLOVSKIY PER
Okhotnyy Ryad
Ploshchad Revolyutsii
Resurrection Gate
Polytechnical Museum
Kitay Gorod
Church of St Vladimir
BOGOYAVLENSKIY PEREULOK
Kazan Cathedral
4

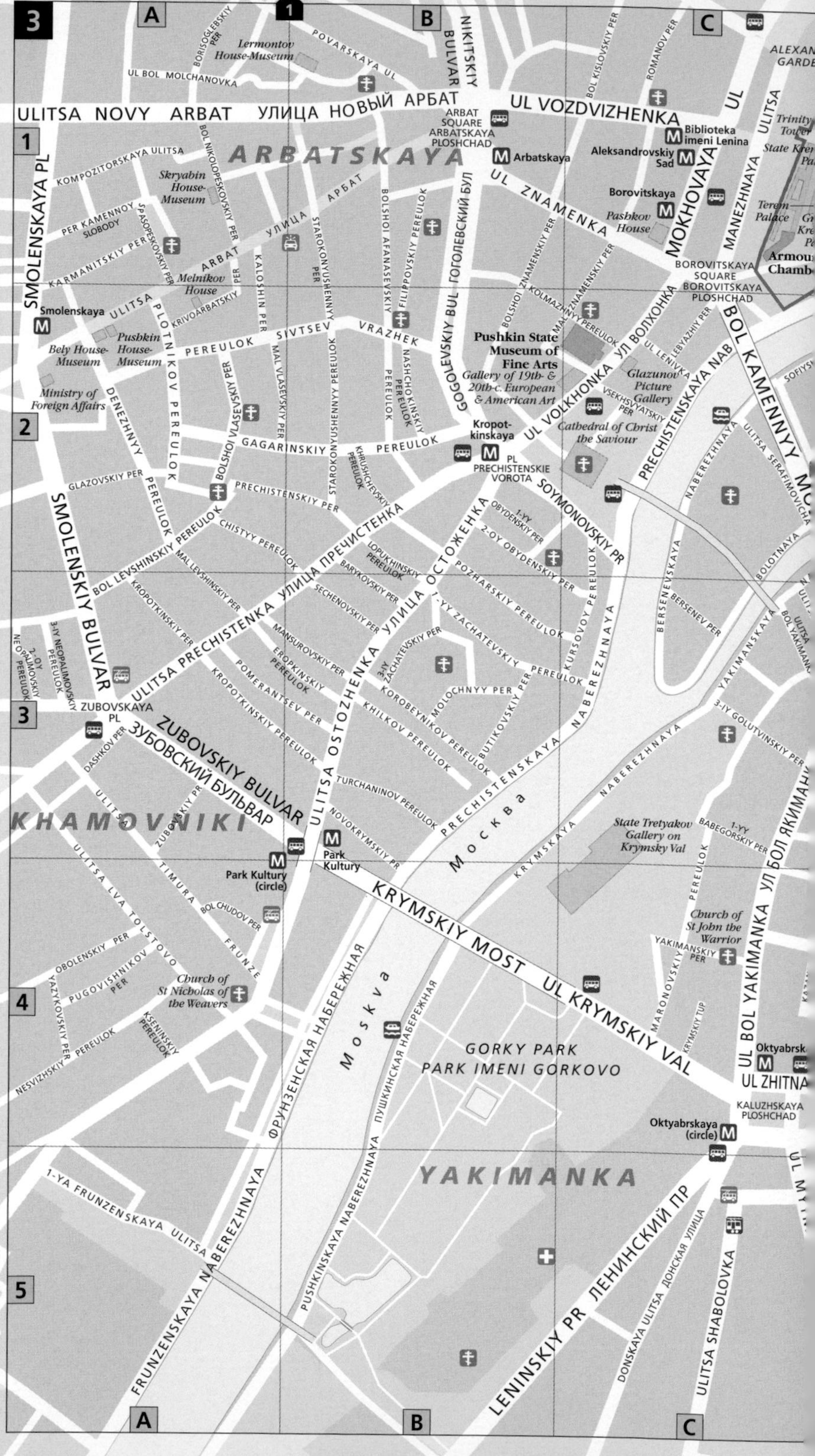

3
ULITSA NOVY ARBAT
УЛИЦА НОВЫЙ АРБАТ
UL VOZDVIZHENKA
ARBATSKAYA
Lermontov House-Museum
POVARSKAYA UL
UL BOL MOLCHANOVKA
NIKITSKIY BULVAR
Arbat Square
Arbatskaya Ploshchad
Arbatskaya
Biblioteka imeni Lenina
Aleksandrovskiy Sad
Borovitskaya
Pashkov House
MOKHOVAYA UL
UL ZNAMENKA
Skryabin House-Museum
Melnikov House
Smolenskaya
Bely House-Museum
Pushkin House-Museum
Ministry of Foreign Affairs
SMOLENSKAYA PL
ULITSA ARBAT
УЛИЦА АРБАТ
PEREULOK SIVTSEV VRAZHEK
GOGOLEVSKIY BUL
ГОГОЛЕВСКИЙ БУЛ
Pushkin State Museum of Fine Arts
Gallery of 19th- & 20th-c. European & American Art
Glazunov Picture Gallery
Cathedral of Christ the Saviour
UL VOLKHONKA
УЛ ВОЛХОНКА
Kropotkinskaya
PL PRECHISTENSKIE VOROTA
GAGARINSKIY PEREULOK
SOYMONOVSKIY PR
PRECHISTENSKAYA NAB
BOL KAMENNYY MOST
BOROVITSKAYA SQUARE
BOROVITSKAYA PLOSHCHAD
Trinity Tower
State Kremlin Palace
Terem Palace
Armoury Chamber
SMOLENSKIY BULVAR
ULITSA PRECHISTENKA
УЛИЦА ПРЕЧИСТЕНКА
ULITSA OSTOZHENKA
УЛИЦА ОСТОЖЕНКА
ZUBOVSKAYA PL
ZUBOVSKIY BULVAR
ЗУБОВСКИЙ БУЛЬВАР
KHAMOVNIKI
Park Kultury
Park Kultury (circle)
PRECHISTENSKAYA NABEREZHNAYA
Москва
State Tretyakov Gallery on Krymsky Val
KRYMSKAYA NABEREZHNAYA
KRYMSKIY MOST
UL KRYMSKIY VAL
Church of St John the Warrior
UL BOL YAKIMANKA
УЛ БОЛ ЯКИМАНКА
Oktyabrskaya
UL ZHITNAYA
KALUZHSKAYA PLOSHCHAD
Oktyabrskaya (circle)
Church of St Nicholas of the Weavers
ULITSA LVA TOLSTOVO
Moskva
ФРУНЗЕНСКАЯ НАБЕРЕЖНАЯ
ПУШКИНСКАЯ НАБЕРЕЖНАЯ
GORKY PARK
PARK IMENI GORKOVO
YAKIMANKA
1-YA FRUNZENSKAYA ULITSA
FRUNZENSKAYA NABEREZHNAYA
PUSHKINSKAYA NABEREZHNAYA
LENINSKIY PR
ЛЕНИНСКИЙ ПР
DONSKAYA ULITSA
ДОНСКАЯ УЛИЦА
ULITSA SHABOLOVKA

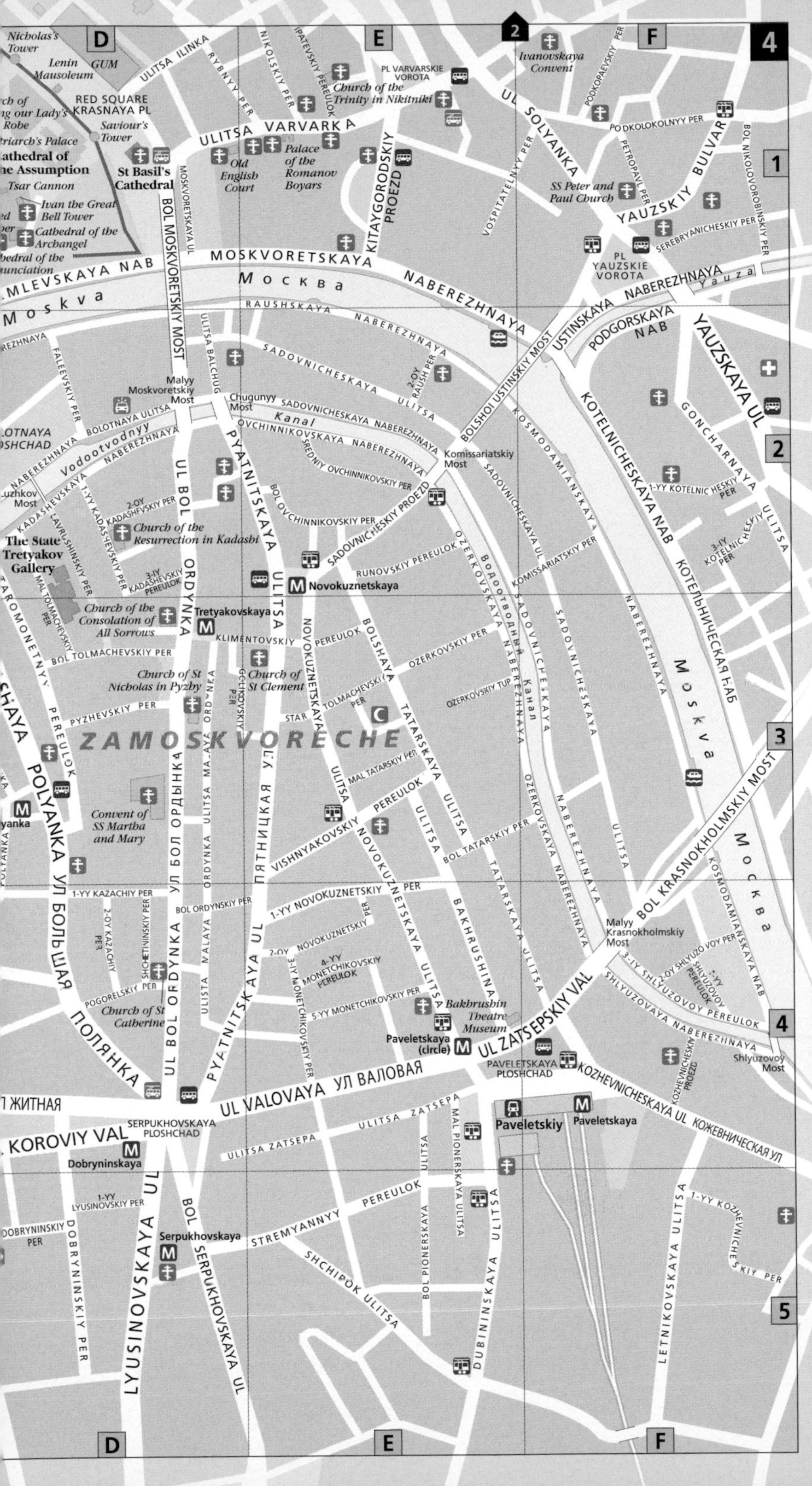

D
E
F
4
2
1
3
5
Nicholas's Tower
Lenin Mausoleum
GUM
RED SQUARE
KRASNAYA PL
Saviour's Tower
Cathedral of the Assumption
Tsar Cannon
Ivan the Great Bell Tower
Cathedral of the Archangel
St Basil's Cathedral
ULITSA ILINKA
RYBNYY PER
NIKOLSKIY PER
IPATEVSKIY PEREULOK
Church of the Trinity in Nikitniki
PL VARVARSKIE VOROTA
Ivanovskaya Convent
PODKOPAEVSKIY PER
UL SOLYANKA
PODKOLOKOLNYY PER
ULITSA VARVARKA
Old English Court
Palace of the Romanov Boyars
KITAYGORODSKIY PROEZD
MOSKVORETSKAYA UL
BOL MOSKVORETSKIY MOST
VOSPITATELNYY PER
PETROPAVL PER
SS Peter and Paul Church
YAUZSKIY BULVAR
BOL NIKOLOVOROBINSKIY PER
SEREBRYANICHESKIY PER
PL YAUZSKIE VOROTA
MOSKVORETSKAYA NABEREZHNAYA
Москва
Moskva
Yauza
RAUSHSKAYA NABEREZHNAYA
USTINSKAYA NABEREZHNAYA
PODGORSKAYA NAB
YAUZSKAYA UL
BOLSHOI USTINSKIY MOST
ULITSA BALCHUG
SADOVNICHESKAYA ULITSA
2-OY RAUSH PER
FALEEVSKIY PER
Malyy Moskvoretskiy Most
Chugunyy Most
BOLOTNAYA ULITSA
BOLOTNAYA PLOSHCHAD
Vodootvodnyy Kanal
SADOVNICHESKAYA NABEREZHNAYA
OVCHINNIKOVSKAYA NABEREZHNAYA
SREDNIY OVCHINNIKOVSKIY PER
Komissariatskiy Most
KOSMODAMIANSKAYA NAB
KOTELNICHESKAYA NAB
GONCHARNAYA ULITSA
1-YY KOTELNICHESKIY PER
3-IY KOTELNICHESKIY PER
Luzhkov Most
KADASHEVSKAYA NABEREZHNAYA
1-YY KADASHEVSKIY PER
2-OY KADASHEVSKIY PER
3-IY KADASHEVSKIY PEREULOK
LAVRUSHINSKIY PER
UL BOL ORDYNKA
PYATNITSKAYA ULITSA
BOL OVCHINNIKOVSKIY PER
SADOVNICHESKIY PROEZD
Church of the Resurrection in Kadashi
The State Tretyakov Gallery
RUNOVSKIY PEREULOK
KOMISSARIATSKIY PER
MAL TOLMACHEVSKIY PER
Church of the Consolation of All Sorrows
Tretyakovskaya
Novokuznetskaya
KLIMENTOVSKIY PEREULOK
NOVOKUZNETSKAYA ULITSA
BOLSHAYA TATARSKAYA ULITSA
OZERKOVSKAYA NABEREZHNAYA
SADOVNICHESKAYA NABEREZHNAYA
SADOVNICHESKAYA UL
Водоотводный канал
Москва
Котельническая наб
OZERKOVSKIY PER
OZERKOVSKIY TUP
BOL TOLMACHEVSKIY PER
Church of St Nicholas in Pyzhy
Church of St Clement
CHIKOVSKIY PER
TOLMACHEVSKIY PER
PYZHEVSKIY PER
STAR
ZAMOSKVORECHE
MAL TATARSKIY PER
VISHNYAKOVSKIY PEREULOK
BOL TATARSKIY PER
BOL KRASNOKHOLMSKIY MOST
BOL POLYANKA
POLYANKA
PEREULOK
Polyanka
Convent of SS Martha and Mary
ULITSA MALAYA ORDYNKA
УЛ БОЛ ОРДЫНКА
ПЯТНИЦКАЯ УЛ
1-YY KAZACHIY PER
2-OY KAZACHIY PER
BOL ORDYNSKIY PER
1-YY NOVOKUZNETSKIY PER
2-OY NOVOKUZNETSKIY PER
SHCHETININSKIY PER
4-YY MONETCHIKOVSKIY PEREULOK
3-IY MONETCHIKOVSKIY PER
5-YY MONETCHIKOVSKIY PER
BAKHRUSHINA ULITSA
TATARSKAYA ULITSA
NOVOKUZNETSKAYA ULITSA
KOSMODAMIANSKAYA NAB
Malyy Krasnokholmskiy Most
2-OY SHLYUZOVOY PER
3-IY SHLYUZOVOY PER
SHLYUZOVAYA NABEREZHNAYA
Shlyuzovoy Most
УЛ БОЛЬШАЯ ПОЛЯНКА
POGORELSKIY PER
Church of St Catherine
UL BOL ORDYNKA
PYATNITSKAYA UL
Bakhrushin Theatre Museum
Paveletskaya (circle)
UL ZATSEPSKIY VAL
PAVELETSKAYA PLOSHCHAD
KOZHEVNICHESKIY PROEZD
KOZHEVNICHESKAYA UL
КОЖЕВНИЧЕСКАЯ УЛ
UL VALOVAYA
УЛ ВАЛОВАЯ
УЛ ЖИТНАЯ
KOROVIY VAL
SERPUKHOVSKAYA PLOSHCHAD
Dobryninskaya
ULITSA ZATSEPA
MAL PIONERSKAYA ULITSA
Paveletskiy
Paveletskaya
1-YY LYUSINOVSKIY PER
DOBRYNINSKIY PER
DOBRYNINSKIY PER
LYUSINOVSKAYA UL
BOL SERPUKHOVSKAYA UL
Serpukhovskaya
STREMYANNYY PEREULOK
SHCHIPOK ULITSA
BOL PIONERSKAYA ULITSA
DUBININSKAYA ULITSA
LETNIKOVSKAYA ULITSA
1-YY KOZHEVNICHESKIY PER

ST PETERSBURG AREA BY AREA

St Petersburg at a Glance

Located at the head of the Gulf of Finland, St Petersburg covers an area of 605 sq km (235 sq miles). Founded by Tsar Peter the Great in 1703, this 300-year-old settlement has gradually evolved into a modern European city. Straddling a series of islands in the Neva delta, St Petersburg is justly known as the Venice of the North, thanks to its magnificent waterfront panorama of Baroque and Neo-Classical palaces, which are reflected in the waters of its canals. A network of bridges affords splendid views of the city, which can often seem like a gigantic stage set for real-life historical dramas.

Locator Map

Kunstkammer *(see p142)* was Russia's first museum, established by Peter the Great. Originally built to exhibit the intriguing collection of curios that the tsar purchased from anatomist Frederick Ruysch in 1717, the building now houses a Museum of Anthropology and Ethnography. Nearby are the red-coloured Rostral Columns.

The Islands
(see pp134–143)

Sennaya Ploshchad
(see pp170–177)

St Nicholas's Cathedral *(see p174)* is a superb example of Russian Baroque, and its ice-blue façade and gilded domes are a St Petersburg landmark. Founded as a sailors' church, it contains memorials to the victims of Russian naval battles and submarine disasters.

0 miles 600
0 yards 600

◀ A frozen canal overlooked by the giant bell tower of St Nicholas's Cathedral

Peter and Paul Fortress *(see pp136–7)* was originally built to secure Russia's hold on the Neva delta but later became a prison for generations of revolutionaries. It contains the Cathedral of SS Peter and Paul, where members of the Tsarist royalty were buried, and a prison museum.

The Islands
(see pp134–143)

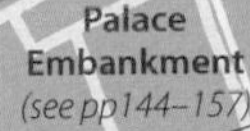

Palace Embankment
(see pp144–157)

The Hermitage *(see pp154–5)* houses a world-famous collection of art and antiquities, including prehistoric Scythian gold and Siberian mummies as well as Post-Impressionist works by Gauguin, Matisse and Picasso.

Gostlnyy Dvor
(see pp158–169)

Church on Spilled Blood *(see p162)* marks the spot where Tsar Alexander II was fatally wounded by "Nihilist" revolutionaries. This dramatically named church is recognized by its psychedelically painted onion domes and gilded mosaics.

THE ISLANDS

St Petersburg was founded in 1703 as a wooden fortress on an island in the Neva delta. Tsar Peter the Great envisaged a city on the northern shores of the Neva – later known as the Petrograd side – with an administrative centre on Vasilevskiy Island. However, lack of access and the hazards of floods and stormy crossings led to the abandonment of Peter's project, and the centre developed around the Admiralty instead. The Petrograd side remained a backwater until the Troitskiy Most (Trinity Bridge) made it accessible from the city centre. A penchant for Style-Moderne architecture in the 1900s endowed the area with many fine buildings such as the Kshesinskaya Mansion. The most notable structure, however, is the Peter and Paul Fortress with its golden-spired cathedral and grim history. The eastern end of Vasilevskiy Island, known as the Strelka, or "spit", is home to various museums.

Sights at a Glance

Churches and Cathedrals

3 Cathedral of SS Peter and Paul

Museums

2 Engineer's House
4 Commandant's House
6 Trubetskoy Bastion
7 Artillery Museum
10 Kirov Museum
11 Kshesinskaya Mansion
12 Cabin of Peter the Great
13 Cruiser Aurora
15 The Institute of Russian Literature (Pushkin House)
16 Zoological Museum
17 Kunstkammer
19 Menshikov Palace

Streets, Squares and Parks

8 Aleksandrovskiy Park
9 Kamennoostrovskiy Prospekt

Historic Buildings and Monuments

1 St Peter's Gate
5 Neva Gate
14 Rostral Columns
18 Twelve Colleges

Locator Map
See Street Finder, maps 1 & 2

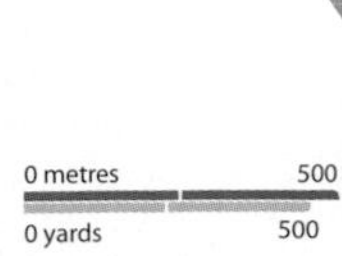

◄ Aerial view of the formidable Peter and Paul Fortress

For map symbols *see back flap*

Street-by-Street: Peter and Paul Fortress

The establishment of the Peter and Paul Fortress on 27 May 1703, on the orders of Peter the Great, is considered to mark the founding of St Petersburg. It was first built in wood and was later replaced, section by section, in stone by Domenico Trezzini. Its history is gruesome, since hundreds of forced labourers died while building the fortress and its bastions were later used to guard and torture many political prisoners, including Peter's own son Aleksey. The cells where prisoners were once kept are open to the public, along with a couple of museums and the magnificent cathedral, which houses the tombs of the Romanovs.

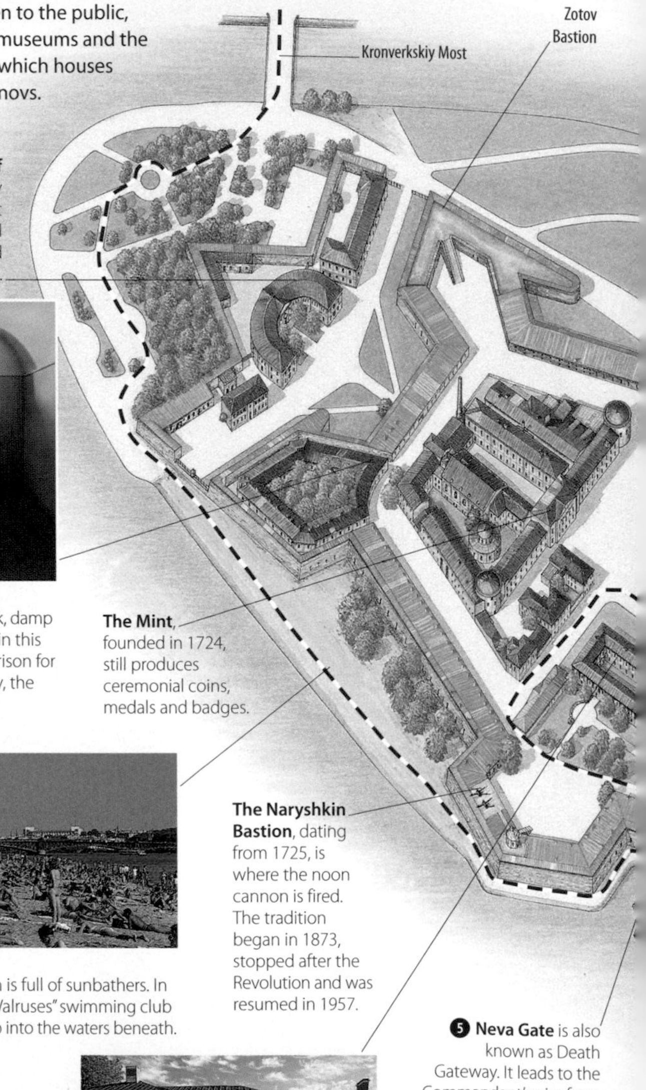

Kronverkskiy Most

Zotov Bastion

The Archives of the War Ministry occupy the site of the "Secret House", a prison for political criminals in the 18th and 19th centuries.

6 Trubetskoy Bastion
From 1872 to 1921, the dark, damp solitary-confinement cells in this bastion served as a grim prison for enemies of the state. Today, the bastion is open to visitors.

The Mint, founded in 1724, still produces ceremonial coins, medals and badges.

The Beach
During summer, the beach is full of sunbathers. In winter, members of "The Walruses" swimming club break through the ice to dip into the waters beneath.

The Naryshkin Bastion, dating from 1725, is where the noon cannon is fired. The tradition began in 1873, stopped after the Revolution and was resumed in 1957.

4 Commandant's House
For 150 years, this attractive Baroque house was the scene of interrogations and trials of political prisoners. It now houses a museum of local history.

5 Neva Gate is also known as Death Gateway. It leads to the Commandant's pier from which prisoners embarked on their journey to execution or exile. The Neva river's flood levels are recorded under the arch.

For restaurants in this area see pp283–4

3 ★ Cathedral of SS Peter and Paul
Marbled columns, glittering chandeliers and painted decor combine with Ivan Zarudnyy's carved and gilded iconostasis to create a magnificent setting for the tombs of the Romanov monarchs.

Area illustrated

The Boat House is now a ticket office and souvenir shop.

Golovkin Bastion

The Grand Ducal Mausoleum is the last resting place of several Grand Dukes shot by the Bolsheviks in 1919 and of Grand Duke Vladimir who died in exile in 1992.

1 St Peter's Gate
The entrance to the fortress was completed in 1718 and features the Romanov double eagle with an emblem of St George and the dragon.

Key

— Suggested route

0 metres 100
0 yards 100

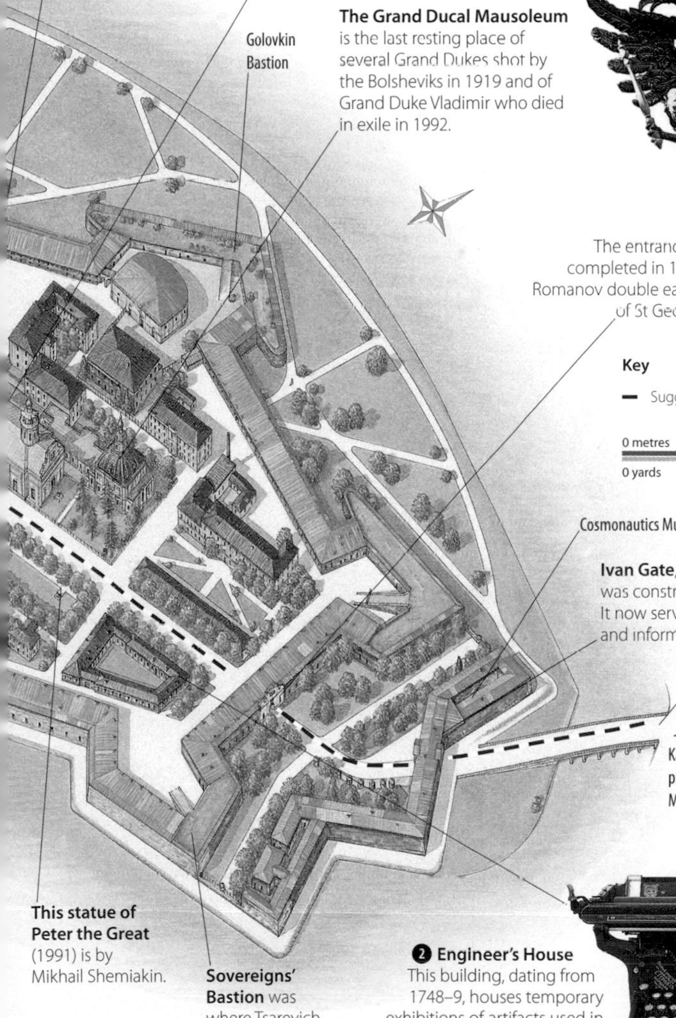

Cosmonautics Museum

Ivan Gate, in the outer wall, was constructed in 1731–40. It now serves as a ticket office and information centre.

Ioannovskiy Most

Kamennoostrovskiy prospekt, Gorkovskaya Metro and Troitskiy Most

This statue of Peter the Great (1991) is by Mikhail Shemiakin.

Sovereigns' Bastion was where Tsarevich Aleksey was tortured to death.

2 Engineer's House
This building, dating from 1748–9, houses temporary exhibitions of artifacts used in everyday life in St Petersburg before the Revolution.

❶ St Peter's Gate

Петровские ворота

Petrovskie vorota

Petropavlovskaya krepost. **Map** 2 D3. 46, 49, K-46, K-76, K-223. Ⓜ Gorkovskaya. 6, 40. Cosmonautics Museum: **Tel** (812) 230 64 31. **Closed** for renovation.

The main entrance to the Peter and Paul Fortress is through two contrasting arches. The sombre Ivan Gate, dating from the 1730s, leads to the more imposing St Peter's Gate. Built in 1708–18, it is a Baroque structure with scrolled wings and a rounded-gable pediment. Domenico Trezzini's redesign retained Karl Osner's carved bas-relief that depicts St Peter casting down the winged sorcerer Simon Magus. It allegorizes Peter the Great's victory over Charles XII of Sweden.

The rampart behind the Ivan Gate houses the **Cosmonautics Museum**, which traces the history of the Soviet space programme from Sputnik to the Mir orbital station, paying homage to the rocket-scientist Konstantin Tsiolkovskiy (1857–1935).

The impressive Baroque façade of St Peter's Gate

❷ Engineer's House

Инженерный дом

Inzhenernyy dom

Petropavlovskaya krepost. **Map** 2 D3. **Tel** (812) 230 64 31 Ⓜ Gorkovskaya. **Open** 11am–5pm Thu–Mon (till 4pm Tue). English. **spbmuseum.ru**

The Engineer's House, built in 1748–9, has a changing exhibition which gives a fascinating glimpse of daily life in St Petersburg before the Revolution. Architectural backdrops and historical paintings give way to an engaging miscellany of artifacts, ranging from model boats to duelling pistols and court costumes.

Style-Moderne furnishings in the Engineer's House

A section on vintage technology features Singer sewing machines, typewriters, Bakelite telephones and box cameras. In the child-friendly exhibition called the Street of Time, visitors can try writing with ink pens, and smell perfumes that were popular with Soviet women in the 1950s.

❸ Cathedral of SS Peter and Paul

Петропавловский собор

Petropavlovskiy sobor

Petropavlovskaya krepost. **Map** 2 D3. **Tel** (812) 230 64 31. Ⓜ Gorkovskaya. **Open** 10am–7pm Mon–Fri (till 5:45pm Sat), 11am–7pm Sun. English. **spbmuseum.ru**

Domenico Trezzini designed this magnificent church within the fortress in 1712. A Baroque masterpiece, it reflects Peter the Great's rejection of traditional Russian church architecture. The bell tower was completed first to test the foundations and this served as an excellent viewpoint from which Peter could oversee the construction of his new city. The cathedral was completed in 1733, but was badly damaged by fire in 1756 when the soaring 122-m (400-ft) spire was struck by lightning. The gilded needle spire, crowned by a weather-vane angel, remained the tallest structure in St Petersburg until the building of a TV transmitter in the 1960s.

The interior, with its dazzling chandeliers, pink and green Corinthian columns and overarching vaults, is a far cry from the traditional Russian Orthodox church. Even the iconostasis is a Baroque flight of fancy. This masterpiece of gilded woodcarving was designed by Ivan Zarudnyy and executed in the 1720s by craftsmen from Moscow.

After Peter's death in 1725, the cathedral became the last resting place of the tsars. The sarcophagi are all of a uniform white Carrara marble, except the tombs of Alexander II and his wife Maria Alexandrovna, which are carved from Altai jasper and Ural rhodonite. Peter the Great's tomb lies to the right of the iconostasis. In 1998, the remains of the

Cathedral of SS Peter and Paul, with the Dvortsovyy Most in the foreground

For restaurants in this area see pp283–4

last tsar, Nicholas II, his wife and children, and the servants who died with them in Yekaterinburg *(see p235)* were buried in a side chapel.

The Grand Ducal Mausoleum, where relatives of the tsars are buried, was added to the cathedral at the end of the 19th century.

❹ Commandant's House

Комендантский дом

Komendantskiy dom

Petropavlovskaya krepost. **Map** 2 D4. **Tel** (812) 230 64 31. Ⓜ Gorkovskaya. **Open** 11am–7pm Thu–Mon (till 6pm Tue) English.

Dating from the 1740s, the plain brick, two-storey Commandant's House served both as the residence of the fortress commander and as a courthouse. Over the years, political prisoners, including the Decembrist rebels, were brought here for interrogation and sentencing.

The house is now a museum, with a ground-floor exhibition on medieval settlements in the St Petersburg region. Upstairs, visitors can see a doll's-house-style model of a 1900s apartment block, and watch an animated video of the erection of the Alexander Column on Palace Square.

❺ Neva Gate

Невскце ворота

Nevskie vorota

Petropavlovskaya krepost. **Map** 2 D4. Ⓜ Gorkovskaya.

This austere river entrance to the fortress was once known as the Death Gate. Prisoners to be transported to Schlüsselburg Fortress on Lake Ladoga *(see p209)* for capital punishment, or to a "living death" in penal servitude, were led down the granite steps and taken away by boat. The appropriately dour, grey gateway (reconstructed in 1784–7) is unornamented apart from an anchor in the pediment. In the archway, brass plaques record flood levels. The catastrophic inundation of November 1824 is the one commemorated in Pushkin's poem, *The Bronze Horseman*.

Neva Gate leading from the river into the Peter and Paul Fortress

❻ Trubetskoy Bastion

Трубецкой бастион

Trubetskoy bastion

Petropavlovskaya krepost. **Map** 1 C4. **Tel** (812) 230 64 31. Ⓜ Gorkovskaya. **Open** 10am–7pm daily. English.

Peter the Great's son, Tsarevich Aleksey, was the first political prisoner to be detained in the grim fortress prison. Unjustly accused of treason in 1718 by his father, Aleksey escaped abroad only to be lured back to Russia with the promise of a pardon. Instead, he was tortured to death, almost certainly with Peter's consent and participation.

For the next 100 years prisoners were incarcerated in the much feared Secret House, since demolished. In 1872 a new prison block opened in the Trubetskoy Bastion which has existed as a museum since 1924. On the ground floor there is a small exhibition of period photographs, prison uniforms and a model of the guardroom. Upstairs are 69 isolation cells, while downstairs there are two unheated, unlit punishment cells where the recalcitrant were locked up for 48 hours at a time. Once every two weeks, all detainees were taken to the Bath House in the exercise yard for de-lousing. Here prisoners were chained before they were made to trek all the way to penal servitude in Siberia.

Political Prisoners

The fortress' sinister role as a prison for political activists continued until after the Revolution. Generations of rebels and anarchists were interrogated and imprisoned here, including Leon Trotsky in the wake of the 1905 Revolution. Other prominent detainees were the leading Decembrists in 1825, writer Fyodor Dostoevsky in 1849 and, in 1874–6, the anarchist Prince Pyotr Kropotkin. In 1917 it was the turn first of the tsar's ministers, then of members of the Provisional Government. Then, in the Civil War, the Bolsheviks held hostage four Romanov Grand Dukes who were executed in 1919.

Russian revolutionary Leon Trotsky (1879–1940)

Rocket launcher in the courtyard of the Artillery Museum

❼ Artillery Museum

Музей Артиллерии

Muzey Artillerii

Alexandrovskiy Park 7, Kronverkskaya Embankment. **Map** 1 C3. **Tel** (812) 232 02 96. Ⓜ Gorkovskaya. **Open** 11am–5pm Wed–Sun. **Closed** last Thu of the month. **W artillery-museum.ru**

This vast, horseshoe-shaped building in redbrick stands on the site of the Kronverk, the outer fortifications of the Peter and Paul Fortress. Designed by Pyotr Tamanskiy and constructed in 1849–60, the building was originally used as an arsenal.

There are more than 600 pieces of artillery and military vehicles, including tanks and the armoured car in which Lenin rode in triumph from Finland Station *(see p180)* to Kshesinskaya Mansion on 3 April 1917. There are uniforms, regimental flags, muskets and small arms dating to medieval times, as well as many rooms devoted to World War II.

❽ Aleksandrovskiy Park

Александровский парк

Aleksandrovskiy park

Kronverkskiy prospekt. **Map** 1 C3. Ⓜ Gorkovskaya.

The park's character as a centre of popular entertainment was established in the year 1900 with the inauguration of the Nicholas II People's House. This was where pantomime artists, magicians and circus acts entertained the crowds, while the more serious-minded were drawn to the lecture halls, reading galleries and tearooms. The *pièce de résistance* was the magnificent domed Opera House, built in 1911, where the legendary bass singer, Fyodor Shalyapin, sometimes gave performances.

Today, the Opera House offers less highbrow entertainment, as its change of name to Music Hall suggests. The adjoining 1930s buildings include the innovative Baltic House Theatre and a planetarium. The biggest draw, however, is the park's funfair.

Further west is the city zoo, which dates back to 1865. In winter visitors can see polar bears, sables, elk and deer when their fur is at its thickest.

Turreted House, built between 1913–15, Kamennoostrovskiy prospekt

❾ Kamennoostrovskiy Prospekt

Каменноостровский проспект

Kamennoostrovskiy prospekt

Map 1 C1. 46, K-30, K-76, K-223. Ⓜ Gorkovskaya or Petrogradskaya.

Laid out during the late 1890s, this elegant avenue is notable for its Style-Moderne architecture. The first house (No. 1–3), designed by Fyodor Lidval, epitomizes this Russian version of Art Nouveau, with its multitextured façade, windows of contrasting shapes and sizes, ornate iron balconies and fanciful carvings. The neighbouring house (No. 5) was once occupied by Count Sergei Witte, a leading industrialist who negotiated the peace treaty with Japan in 1905.

Just off the start of the avenue stands the city's only mosque, constructed in 1910–14. Its minarets, majolica tiling and rusticated granite walls are fully in keeping with the surrounding architecture, but were in fact modelled on the Mausoleum of Tamerlane in Samarkand.

Griffon, No. 1–3 Kamennoostrovskiy

At the intersection with ulitsa Mira, each house has individually designed turrets, spires, reliefs and iron balconies, forming a striking Style-Moderne ensemble. Other buildings of interest include No. 24, with its handsome redbrick majolica and terracotta façade; No. 26–28 where Sergei Kirov lived; and the Turreted House with its Neo-Gothic portal, on the corner of Bolshoi prospekt.

❿ Kirov Museum

Мүзей С. М. Кирова

Muzey S M Kirova

Kamennoostrovskiy prospekt 26–28, 4th floor. **Map** 1 C1. **Tel** (812) 346 02 17, (812) 346 02 89. Ⓜ Petrogradskaya. **Open** 11am–6pm Thu–Mon (till 5pm Tue). English. **W spb museum.ru**

From 1926 this apartment was home to Sergei Kirov, the charismatic first Secretary of the

Leningrad Communist Party. His popularity led Stalin to see in him a potential rival, and on 1 December 1934 Kirov was gunned down at the Smolnyy Institute *(see p182)* by a party malcontent. His assassination gave Stalin a pretext to launch the Great Terror *(see p45)*.

Although most historians believe that Stalin instigated his murder, Kirov was cynically elevated to the status of a Soviet martyr, with countless buildings named in his honour. His apartment, preserved as it was in his lifetime, is an example of the near cult status awarded to party leaders, with documents and photographs chronicling his political career, and an array of memorabilia.

Portrait of Sergei Kirov (1930s), in the Kirov Museum

⓫ Kshesinskaya Mansion

Особняк М. Кшесинской

Osobnyak M Kshesinskoy

Ulitsa Kuybysheva 4. **Map** 2 D3. **Tel** (812) 233 70 52. Ⓜ Gorkovskaya. **Open** 10am–6pm Fri–Tue (till 8pm Wed). **Closed** last Mon of the month. English. **polithistory.ru**

This Style-Moderne residence was built in 1904 for the prima ballerina Matilda Kshesinskaya, who was the mistress of the future Tsar Nicholas II at that time. Designed by court architect Von Gogen, the mansion is almost playfully asymmetric, with an octagonal tower and façades in contrasting bands of pink and grey granite and cream-coloured bricks ornamented with iron railings and majolica tiles.

An elegant recital hall in the Kshesinskaya Mansion

In March 1917 the mansion was commandeered by the Bolsheviks, and upon returning to Russia, Lenin addressed the crowds from its balcony. Formerly home to a museum glorifying the October Revolution, the mansion now houses the Museum of Russian Political History. The Bolshevik Party secretariat and Lenin's office on the first floor have been faithfully restored. Upstairs is a collection of revolutionary memorabilia, such as Communist posters, Nicholas II coronation mugs and a police file on Rasputin's murder *(see p176)*.

⓬ Cabin of Peter the Great

Музей-домик Петра I

Muzey-domik Petra I

Petrovskaya naberezhnaya 6. **Map** 2 E3. **Tel** (812) 232 45 76, (812) 314 03 74. Ⓜ Gorkovskaya. **Open** 10am–5:30pm Wed–Sun. **Closed** last Mon of the month.

This humble pine-log cabin was built for Peter the Great by his soldier-carpenters in just three days in 1703. Peter lived here for six years while overseeing the construction of his new city. Catherine the Great later had a protective brick shell built around the cabin.

There are only two rooms, both with period furnishings, and a hallway which doubled as a bedroom. Among Peter's possessions are a compass, a frock coat and his rowing boat. Outside are two statues of the Shih Tze lions, brought from Manchuria during the Russo-Japanese War (1904–5).

⓭ Cruiser Aurora

Крейсер Аврора

Kreyser Avrora

Petrogradskaya naberezhnaya 3. **Map** 2 F3. **Tel** 230 84 40. 🚌 49, K-30, K-183. 🚎 6, 40. **Open** 10:30am–4pm Tue–Thu, Sat & Sun. English, French or German, for a fee. Call to book.

According to the annals of the Revolution, at 9:40pm on 25 October 1917, the cruiser *Aurora* signalled the storming of the Winter Palace *(see pp156–7)*, by firing a single blank round from its bow gun.

The ship entered active service in 1903. It was later converted into a training ship and at the start of the Siege of Leningrad in 1941 it was sunk to protect it from German forces. The ship was raised in 1944 and has been a museum since 1956. The famous gun, bell and the crew's quarters can be viewed, along with an exhibition on the history of the *Aurora*.

The cruiser *Aurora*, moored in front of the Neo-Baroque Nakhimov Naval Academy

One of the two russet-coloured Rostral Columns on the Strelka

⓮ Rostral Columns

Ростральные колонны

Rostralnye kolonny

Birzhevaya ploshchad. **Map** 1 C5. 7, 10, 24, 47, 191, K-187, K-209, K-252. 1, 7, 10, 11.

Situated on the eastern end of Vasilevskiy Island, known as the Strelka, the twin russet-coloured Rostral Columns were designed as lighthouses by Thomas de Thomon in 1810. During the 19th century the oil lamps were replaced by gas torches, which are still lit on ceremonial occasions. The columns are decorated with protruding ships' prows in celebration of naval victories and the figures around the base represent four of Russia's rivers – the Neva, Volga, Dnieper and Volkhov.

⓯ The Institute of Russian Literature (Pushkin House)

Институт русской литературы (Пушкинский Дом)

Institut Russkoy Literatury (Pushkinskiy Dom)

Naberezhnaya Makarova 4. **Map** 1 B5. **Tel** (812) 328 05 02. 7, 10, 47, 187, K-209, K-252. 1, 7, 10, 11. **Open** 11am–4pm Mon–Fri. English, book in advance. **W** **pushkinskij dom.ru**

Founded at the beginning of the 20th century, this museum focuses on preserving the legacy of Russian literary culture from the distant past to the present. It houses numerous manuscripts and exhibits connected to Russia's greatest poet, Alexander Pushkin, as well as rare and unusual artifacts connected with some of Russia's eminent writers, including Gogol, Turgenev, Tolstoy and Dostoevsky.

Today, Pushkin House contains more than 3 million autographed manuscripts, including 12,000 pages from Pushkin alone. In addition to more than 700,000 books and print editions reflecting the history of Russian literature, the museum also preserves thousands of images, paintings, drawings and objects.

⓰ Zoological Museum

Зоологический музей

Zoologicheskiy muzey

Universitetskaya naberezhnaya 1/3. **Map** 1 C5. **Tel** (812) 328 01 12. 7, 10, 24, 47, 191, K-187, K-209, K-252. 1, 7, 10, 11. **Open** 11am–6pm Sat–Thu. free Thu. English. **W** **zin.ru**

One of the largest of its kind in the world, this museum contains more than 1.5 million specimens, and is renowned for its collection of prehistoric mammoths. One prized carcass was exhumed from the frozen wastes of Siberia in 1902 and is almost 44,000 years old.

Some of the stuffed animals on display belonged to Tsar Peter the Great's Kunstkammer collection, including the horse he rode at the Battle of Poltava. Dioramas re-create natural habitats for giant crabs, weasels, polar bears and blue whales.

⓱ Kunstkammer

Кунсткамера

Kunstkamera

Universitetskaya naberezhnaya 3. **Map** 1 B5. **Tel** (812) 328 08 12. 7, 10, 24, 47, 191, K-187, K-191, K-209, K-252. 1, 7, 10, 11. **Open** 11am–6pm Tue–Sun. **Closed** last Tue of the month. English. **W** **kunstkamera.ru**

Russia's first museum, the Baroque Kunstkammer (art chamber) was built in 1718–34 to exhibit Peter the Great's infamous collection of curios. While touring Holland in 1697, he attended the lectures of anatomist Frederik Ruysch (1638–1731) and was so impressed with Ruysch's collection of rarities that on a return visit in 1717, he purchased the entire collection of over 2,000 anatomical preparations.

It was transported to St Petersburg and was exhibited to a wide-eyed public. At the time, Peter's collection also included live exhibits of deformed or unusual people, including a hermaphrodite.

Today the Kunstkammer houses the Museum of Anthropology and Ethnography, with the remnants of Peter's bizarre collection on display on the first floor. Beside a cabinet of teeth extracted by the tsar (an amateur dentist) are pickled oddities such as a two-headed

Mammoth skeleton on display at the Zoological Museum

For restaurants in this area see pp283–4

The grandiose Baroque Menshikov Palace, built for nobleman Alexander Menshikov

sheep. The surrounding halls contain exhibitions on the peoples of the world. Often neglected by visitors, these marvellously old-fashioned displays present a wide range of artifacts, from an Inuit kayak to Javanese shadow puppets.

⓲ Twelve Colleges

Двенадцать коллегий

Dvenadtsat kollegiy

Universitetskaya naberezhnaya 7. **Map** 1 B5. 7, 24, 47, 129, K-187, K-209. 1, 10, 11. **Closed** to public.

This red-and-white Baroque building, almost 400 m (1,300 ft) in length, was intended for Peter the Great's newly streamlined administration of 12 colleges or ministries. The uninterrupted façade was designed to symbolize the government's unity of purpose. Its curious alignment, at right angles to the embankment, is supposedly due to Prince Menshikov changing the plan in Peter's absence so that the building would not encroach on his grounds.

The building's function gradually changed and in 1819 part of it was acquired by St Petersburg University. A string of revolutionaries, including Lenin, were educated here. Famous lecturers who taught here include the chemist Dmitri Mendeleev (1834–1907) and the physiologist Ivan Pavlov (1849–1936).

Outside the Twelve Colleges, overlooking the Neva, is an engaging bronze statue of the 18th-century polymath Mikhail Lomonosov. A fisherman's son, dubbed the "Russian Leonardo", Lomonosov wrote poetry, systematized Russian grammar, and explored mathematics and the physical sciences. His discoveries led to the introduction of porcelain, glass and mosaic production in Russia.

⓳ Menshikov Palace

Меншиковский дворец

Menshikovskiy dvorets

Universitetskaya naberezhnaya 15. **Map** 1 B5. **Tel** (812) 323 11 12. 7, 24, 47, 191, K-209. 1, 10, 11. **Open** 10:30am–6pm Tue–Sat (till 5pm Sun). compulsory, available in English, French and German.

Completed in 1720, the Menshikov Palace was one of the city's earliest stone buildings. It was built for Peter the Great's close friend, Alexander Menshikov, who rose from humble origins to the nobility,

A section of the detailed west façade of the Twelve Colleges

by helping Peter to crush the Streltsy Revolt of 1862 and defeat the Swedes at Poltava. Prince Menshikov entertained here on a lavish scale, often on the tsar's behalf. His palace is now a branch of the Hermitage with exhibitions on early 18th-century Russian culture, revealing the extent to which Peter's court was influenced by Western tastes.

The compulsory tour begins on the ground floor. Besides the kitchen there are displays of Peter's cabinet-making tools, period costumes, oak chests and ships' compasses. The hallway is adorned with marble statues from Italy; Menshikov and Peter's monograms are entwined on its grand stairway.

Upstairs, a secretariat decorated with engravings of Dutch cities is followed by a series of rooms lined with hand-painted blue-and-white 18th-century Dutch tiles. The bedroom of Menshikov's sister-in-law features a German-made four-poster bed and Flemish tapestry. Guests were often received in the Walnut Study, with its commanding views of the Neva. Paintings hang from coloured ribbons, as was the fashion then, while the mirrors were a novelty at that time, condemned by the Orthodox Church as vanity.

Balls and banquets were held in the Great Hall, decorated in gold and stucco, which once hosted a dwarfs' wedding that Menshikov arranged for Peter's amusement.

PALACE EMBANKMENT

In terms of sheer scale and grandeur, St Petersburg's magnificent southern waterfront has few equals. Its formidable granite quays, stretching over 2 km (1 mile) from the Senate building in the west to Peter the Great's Summer Palace in the east, and the surrounding area of stately aristocratic palaces and ornamental canal bridges are justly famous worldwide. Every aspect of the city's history is palpable in this atmospheric area. Etienne Falconet's statue of Peter the Great, The Bronze Horseman, is a testimony to imperial ambition while the square in which it stands was formerly named in honour of the Decembrist rebels who rose up against the Tsarist regime in 1825. Bartolomeo Rastrelli's Winter Palace evokes the opulence of imperial Russia whereas the Eternal Flame, flickering in the Field of Mars, is a sombre reminder of revolutionary sacrifice. Dominating St Petersburg's skyline are the splendid dome of St Isaac's Cathedral and the gilded spire of the Admiralty. Some of the best views can be appreciated by making a boat trip along the waterways, or by strolling through the delightful Summer Garden.

Sights at a Glance

Churches and Cathedrals

5 *St Isaac's Cathedral pp150–51*

Museums

9 *The Hermitage pp154–7*

Streets and Squares

2 Senate Square
6 St Isaac's Square
8 Palace Square
10 Millionaires' Street
12 Field of Mars

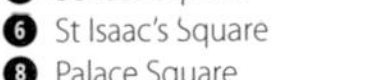

Historical Buildings and Monuments

1 The Admiralty
3 The Bronze Horseman
4 Horseguards' Manège
7 Angleterre Hotel

Palaces and Gardens

11 Marble Palace
13 Summer Garden
14 Summer Palace

Locator Map
See Street Finder, maps 1–4

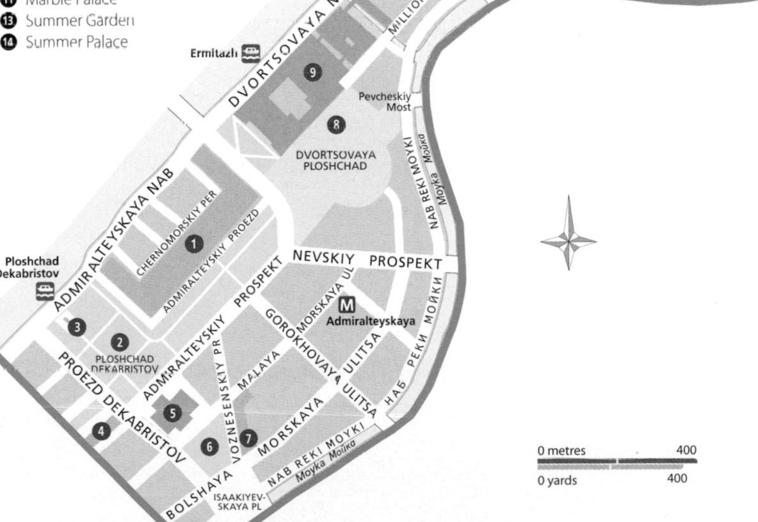

◀ The pretty central passageway of the Summer Garden, flanked by statues

For map symbols *see back flap*

Street-by-Street: St Isaac's Square

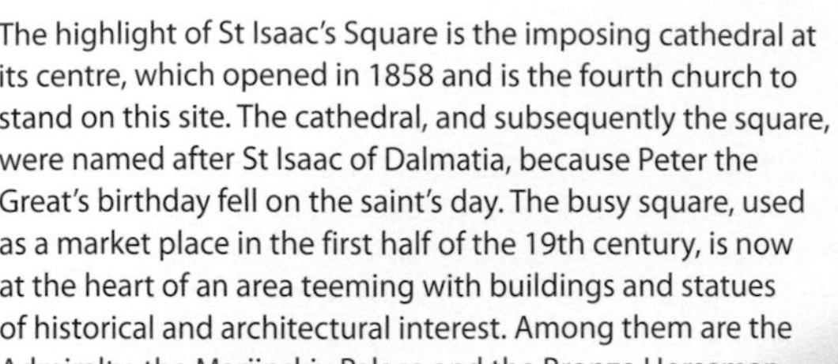

The highlight of St Isaac's Square is the imposing cathedral at its centre, which opened in 1858 and is the fourth church to stand on this site. The cathedral, and subsequently the square, were named after St Isaac of Dalmatia, because Peter the Great's birthday fell on the saint's day. The busy square, used as a market place in the first half of the 19th century, is now at the heart of an area teeming with buildings and statues of historical and architectural interest. Among them are the Admiralty, the Mariinskiy Palace and the Bronze Horseman.

4 Horseguards' Manège
was built in 1804–7 by Giacomo Quarenghi. It housed the Life Guards' Mounted Regiment.

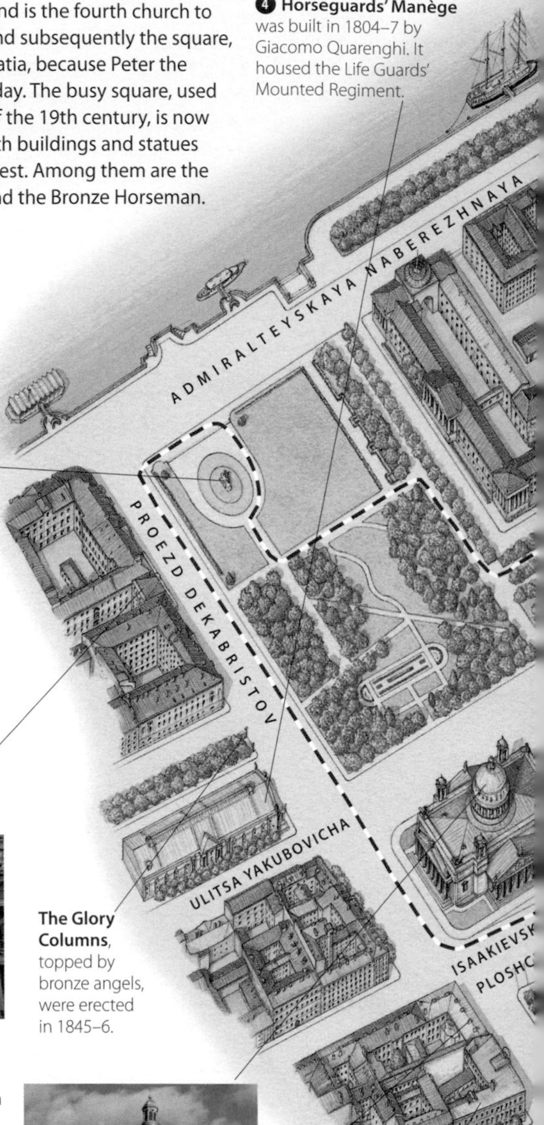

ADMIRALTEYSKAYA NABEREZHNAYA

PROEZD DEKABRISTOV

ULITSA YAKUBOVICHA

ISAAKIEVSK PLOSHC

BOLSHAYA

NAB MO

3 The Bronze Horseman
Etienne Falconet's impressive statue of Peter the Great, his horse trampling the serpent of treason, captures the spirit of the city's uncompromising and wilful founder.

2 Senate Square
Dominating the western side of the square are Carlo Rossi's monumental Senate and Synod buildings, linked by a triumphal arch.

The Glory Columns, topped by bronze angels, were erected in 1845–6.

Myatlev House

5 ★ St Isaac's Cathedral
The magnificent golden dome of the cathedral is visible all across the city. Its surface is covered with 100 kg (220 lb) of gold leaf.

The former German Embassy was designed by the German architect Peter Behrens in 1911–12.

For hotels and restaurants in this area see p268 and pp284–5

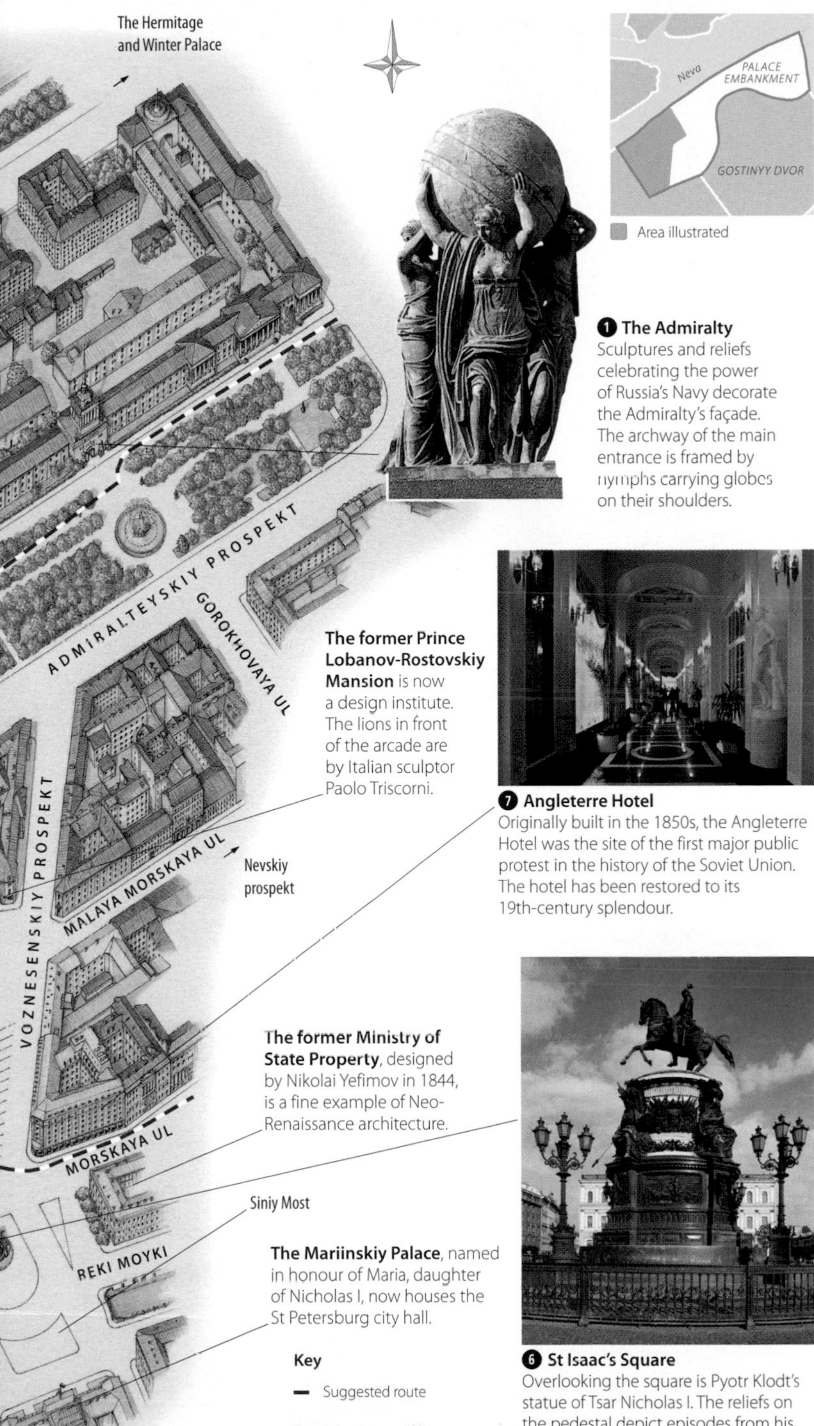

1 The Admiralty
Sculptures and reliefs celebrating the power of Russia's Navy decorate the Admiralty's façade. The archway of the main entrance is framed by nymphs carrying globes on their shoulders.

The former Prince Lobanov-Rostovskiy Mansion is now a design institute. The lions in front of the arcade are by Italian sculptor Paolo Triscorni.

7 Angleterre Hotel
Originally built in the 1850s, the Angleterre Hotel was the site of the first major public protest in the history of the Soviet Union. The hotel has been restored to its 19th-century splendour.

The former Ministry of State Property, designed by Nikolai Yefimov in 1844, is a fine example of Neo-Renaissance architecture.

The Mariinskiy Palace, named in honour of Maria, daughter of Nicholas I, now houses the St Petersburg city hall.

6 St Isaac's Square
Overlooking the square is Pyotr Klodt's statue of Tsar Nicholas I. The reliefs on the pedestal depict episodes from his reign. Significantly, two of them show the suppression of rebellions.

The gilded spire and detailed façade of the Admiralty

❶ The Admiralty

Адмиралтейство

Admiralteystvo

Admiralteyskaya naberezhnaya 2. **Map** 3 C1. 🚌 7, 10, 24, 100, 191, K-169, K-209, K-252. 🚎 1, 5, 7, 10, 11, 17, 22. **Closed** to public.

Having founded a city and built a fortress, Peter the Great's next priority was to create a Russian Navy. The Admiralty was built as a fortified shipyard in 1704–11, which soon employed some 10,000 men constructing the first battleships.

In 1806, Andrei Zakharov, one of Russia's most inspired architects, began to rebuild the Admiralty, creating a remarkable façade 407 m (1,335 ft) in length, adorned with an abundance of sculptures and reliefs symbolizing Russian naval glory. Zakharov retained some of the original features, including the central gate tower and spire which he recast in Neo-Classical style with columned porticos and pavilions. The heightened spire was gilded and topped with a model frigate. This has become a symbol of the city, just like the trumpet-blowing pair of angels on the portals of the façade overlooking the Neva.

In the 1840s, shipbuilding was moved downstream and the Admiralty was handed over to the Russian Navy. It has been occupied by the Naval Engineering School since 1925.

❷ Senate Square

Сенатская площадь

Senatskaya ploshchad

Map 3 B1. 🚌 3, 10, 22, 27, 71, 100, K-169, K-187, K-306. 🚎 5, 22.

The momentous Decembrist uprising took place in this square on 14 December 1825. During the inauguration of Tsar Nicholas I, army officers intent on imposing a constitutional monarchy attempted to stage a coup d'état. After a confused stand-off lasting several hours, the rebels were routed with grapeshot. Five of the ring-leaders were later executed and 121 others exiled to Siberia, thus effectively ending Russia's first revolution.

The imposing Neo-Classical buildings commanding the western side of the Senate Square were intended to harmonize with the Admiralty. Designed by Carlo Rossi between 1829 and 1834, they housed the headquarters of two important institutions originally created by Peter the Great: the Supreme Court, or Senate, and the Holy Synod that was responsible for the administration of the Orthodox Church. The two buildings, which now house historical archives, are linked to each other by a triumphal arch supported by Corinthian columns and decorated with a Neo-Classical frieze and a plethora of statuary.

❸ The Bronze Horseman

Медный Всадник

Mednyy Vsadnik

Senatskaya ploshchad. **Map** 3 B1. 🚌 3, 10, 22, 27, 71, 100, K-169, K-187, K-306. 🚎 5, 22.

Named after Alexander Pushkin's famous poem, this magnificent equestrian statue of Peter the Great was unveiled in Senate Square in 1782 as a tribute from Catherine the Great. The eminent French sculptor, Etienne Falconet, spent more than 12 years overseeing this ambitious project.

The pedestal alone weighs 1,625 tonnes (1,790 tons) and was hewn from a single block of granite hauled from the Gulf of Finland. It bears the inscription, "To Peter I from Catherine II". A serpent, underneath the horse's hooves, symbolizes treason.

❹ Horseguards' Manège

Конногвардейский манеж

Konnogvardeyskiy manezh

Isaakievskaya ploshchad 1. **Map** 3 B2. **Tel** (812) 312 22 43, (812) 571 41 57 (ticket office). 🚌 3, 22, 27, 71, 100, K-169, K-187, K-306. 🚎 5, 22. **Open** variable.

The enormous indoor riding school of the Life Guards' Cavalry was built by Giacomo Quarenghi in 1804–7 to resemble a Roman basilica.

Romanesque façade of Horseguards' Manège

For hotels and restaurants in this area see p268 and pp284–5

St Issac's Cathedral, statue of St Nicholas I and the Angleterre Hotel in St Issac's Square

Two clues to its original function are the frieze of a horse race beneath the pediment and the naked statues on either side of the portico, copied from the statues of the twin sons of Zeus reining in wild horses outside the Quirinale Palace in Rome. The statues were removed after the Holy Synod objected to this display of nudity so near to St Isaac's Cathedral, but were re-erected in 1954.

Like its namesake in Moscow, the Manège is now used as an exhibition hall.

❺ St Isaac's Cathedral

See pp150–51.

❻ St Isaac's Square

Исаакиевская площадь

Issakievskaya ploshchad

Map 3 C2. 3, 10, 22, 27, 71, 100, K-169, K-187, K-306. 5, 22.

Dominated by the majestic St Isaac's Cathedral, this square was created during the reign of Nicholas I, although a few buildings date from the 18th century. The tsar was posthumously honoured in 1859 by an equestrian monument sculpted by Pyotr Klodt, whose pedestal is embellished with allegorical sculptures of the tsar's wife and daughters, representing Faith, Wisdom, Justice and Might. The Holy Synod insisted that the horse's rump face away from the cathedral.

On the western side of the square, the Neo-Classical Myatlev House at No. 9 hosted the French encyclopedist Denis Diderot in 1773–4, following an invitation from Catherine the Great. In the 1920s, it became the premises of the State Institute of Artistic Culture where some of Russia's most influential avant garde artists, including Kazimir Malevich and Vladimir Tatlin, worked.

The impressive granite-faced building alongside is the former German embassy, which was looted by a frenzied crowd at the outbreak of war between Russia and Germany in 1914.

Across the 100-m (330-ft) wide Blue Bridge (Siniy Most), which was the site of a serf market until 1861, the Mariinskiy Palace dominates the southern end of the square.

❼ Angleterre Hotel

Гостиница Англетер

Gostinitsa Angleter

Malaya Morskaya ulitsa 24. **Map** 3 C2. **Tel** (812) 494 56 66. 3, 10, 22, 27, K-169, K-190, K-306. 5, 22.

The seven-storey Angleterre was designed in 1910–12 by Fyodor Lidval in the Style-Moderne form.

The American journalist, John Reed, author of the eyewitness account of the Revolution, *Ten Days that Shook the World*, was staying here when the Bolsheviks seized power in 1917.

In 1925, the poet Sergei Yesenin, husband of Isadora Duncan, hanged himself in the hotel's annexe, after daubing the walls of his room with a farewell verse in his blood, "To die is not new – but neither is it new to be alive".

The banqueting hall was to be the venue for Hitler's prematurely planned victory celebration, so sure was he that he would conquer Leningrad in 1941.

Style-Moderne foyer in the Angleterre Hotel

The Bronze Horseman by Alexander Pushkin

The famous statue of Peter the Great is brought to life in Alexander Pushkin's epic poem *The Bronze Horseman* (1833). In this haunting vision of the Great Flood of 1824, the hero is pursued through the mist-shrouded streets by the terrifying bronze statue. Pushkin's words evoke the domineering and implacable will for which the tsar was renowned, "How terrible he was in the surrounding gloom! … what strength was in him! And in that steed, what fire!"

5 St Isaac's Cathedral

Исаакиевский собор

Isaakievskiy sobor

One of the world's largest cathedrals, St Isaac's was designed in 1818 by the then unknown architect Auguste de Montferrand. The construction of the colossal building was a major engineering feat. Thousands of wooden piles were sunk into the marshy ground to support its weight of 300,000 tonnes (336,000 tons) and 48 huge columns were hauled into place. The cathedral opened in 1858 but was deconsecrated and became a museum of atheism during the Soviet era. Officially still a museum, the church is filled with hundreds of 19th-century works of art.

Angels with Torch
Ivan Vitali created many of the cathedral's sculptures, including the pairs of angels supporting gas torches that crown the four attic corners.

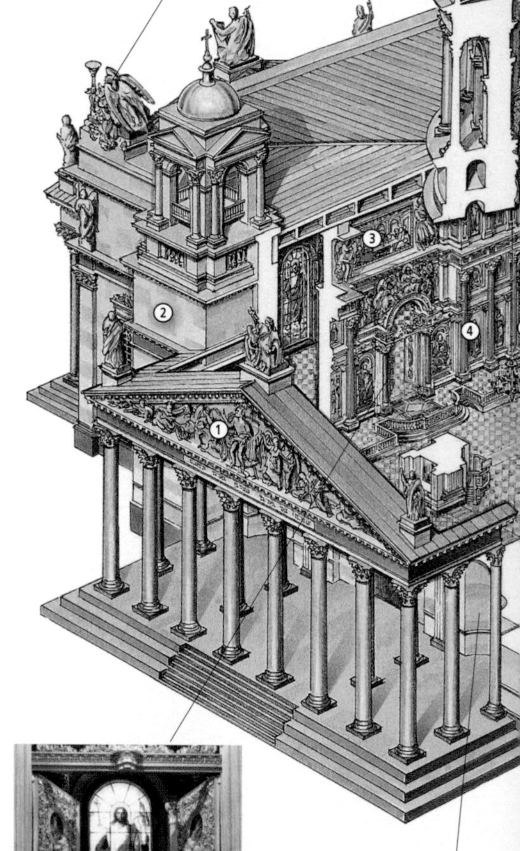

★ Iconostasis
Three rows of icons surround the royal doors through which a stained-glass window is visible. Above the doors is Pyotr Klodt's gilded sculpture, *Christ in Majesty*, dating from 1859.

KEY

① **The north pediment** is ornamented with a bronze relief of the Resurrection, designed by François Lemaire in 1842–4.

② **This chapel** honours Alexander Nevsky who defeated the Swedes in 1240.

③ **The mosaic icons** on the iconostasis are by Russian masters Bryullov, Neff and Zhivago.

④ **Malachite** and lapis lazuli columns frame the iconostasis. About 16,000 kg (35,280 lbs) of malachite decorate the cathedral.

⑤ **St Catherine's Chapel** has a white marble iconostasis, crowned by a sculpted Resurrection, built by Nikolai Pimenov in 1850–54.

⑥ **The silver dove** (1850) hanging in the cupola is a symbol of the Holy Spirit.

⑦ **Portraits of apostles and evangelists**

⑧ **Statue of St Matthew**

⑨ **The walls** are adorned with 14 coloured marbles and 43 other types of semi-precious stones and minerals.

⑩ **The relief of St Isaac** blessing the Roman Emperor Theodosius and his wife Flaccilla is by Ivan Vitali. On the extreme left, Montferrand is depicted clutching a model of his cathedral.

⑪ **Red granite columns**, each weighing 114 tonnes (116 tons), were transported from Finland in specially constructed ships.

⑫ **The vast interior** covers 4,000 sq m (43,000 sq ft).

VISITORS' CHECKLIST

Practical information
Isaakievskaya ploshchad 4.
Map 3 C1.
Tel (812) 315 97 32.
Open May–Sep: 10am–10:30pm Thu–Tue; Oct–Apr: 11am–7pm. religious festivals.

Transport
3, 10, 22, 27, 71, 100, K-169, K-190, K-289. M Nevskiy Prospekt, Sadovaya. 5, 22.

The Dome
From the dome there are panoramic views over the city, including the Admiralty *(see p148)* and the Hermitage *(see pp154–7)*. Adorning the gilded dome are angels sculpted by Josef Hermann.

7

8

9

10

11

12

★ Ceiling Painting
The celestial *Virgin in Majesty* by Karl Bryullov, dating to 1847, covers an area of 816 sq m (8,780 sq ft). It is ringed by exuberant gilded stucco mouldings and white marble.

The entrance is through the side doors on St Isaac's Square

South Doors
Three great doors of oak and bronze, built in 1841–6, are decorated with carved reliefs by Ivan Vitali. The exteriors of the doors show scenes from the life of Christ and saints, including Alexander Nevsky.

❽ Palace Square

Дворцовая площадь

Dvortsovaya ploshchad

Map 2 D5. 🚌 7, 10, 24, 191, K-209. 🚎 1, 7, 10, 11.

The Palace Square has played a unique role in Russian history. In January 1905, it was the site of the Bloody Sunday massacre, when troops fired on thousands of unarmed demonstrators. Then, on 7 November 1917, Lenin's Bolsheviks seized power by attacking the Winter Palace *(see pp156–7)* from the square. It remains a favourite venue for political meetings and cultural events such as rock concerts.

Designed by architect Carlo Rossi *(see p167)*, the resplendent square is dominated by the giant arc of the General Staff Building that was built in 1819–29. Its two curving wings are connected by a double arch leading through to Nevskiy prospekt. The arch is crowned by a sculpture of Victory in her chariot.

The Alexander Column in the centre of the square is dedicated to Tsar Alexander I. Designed by Auguste de Montferrand, the red-granite pillar is balanced by its own 600-tonne (661-tons) weight, making it the world's largest free-standing monument. It took 2,400 workmen two years to hew and transport the granite, but only 40 minutes to erect the column in 1834. Topped by a bronze angel, it is 47 m (154 ft) high.

❾ The Hermitage

See pp154–7.

❿ Millionaires' Street

Миллионная улица

Millionnaya ulitsa

Map 2 D5.

This street takes its name from the aristocrats and members of the imperial family who once inhabited its opulent residences.

No. 26, on the embankment, was the home of Grand Duke Vladimir Aleksandrovich, who ordered the shooting of peaceful demonstrators on Bloody Sunday. Putyatin's house, at No. 12, witnessed the end of the Romanov dynasty. It was here that Grand Duke Mikhail Aleksandrovich, Nicholas II's designated successor, signed the decree of abdication in March 1917.

The street crosses the tapering Winter Canal, providing a superb view of the Neva river through an archway between the Large Hermitage and the Hermitage Theatre.

⓫ Marble Palace

Мраморный дворец

Mramornyy dvorets

Millionnaya ulitsa 5 (entrance from the Field of Mars). **Map** 2 E4. **Tel** (812) 595 42 48. 🚌 46, 49, K-46, K-76. **Open** 10am–6pm Wed, Fri–Sun, 1pm–9pm Thu, 10am–5pm Mon. English. **W** **rusmuseum.ru**

The Marble Palace was a gift from Catherine the Great to her lover Grigori Orlov, who had helped her seize power in 1762. An early example of

The magnificent Gala staircase of the Marble Palace

Neo-Classical architecture, dating from 1768–85, it is considered to be Antonio Rinaldi's masterpiece.

The palace takes its name from the marbles used in its construction. Most of the interiors were reconstructed in the 1840s, although the gala staircase and the Marble Hall, with marbled walls in pastel hues and lapis lazuli, are Rinaldi's work.

Having housed a Lenin museum for 55 years, it is now a branch of the Russian Museum *(see pp164–5)*. It exhibits modern art bequeathed by two German collectors, including a Picasso and works by Andy Warhol and Roy Lichtenstein.

In the courtyard is an equestrian statue of Alexander III, which originally stood halfway down Nevskiy prospekt. Its sculptor said, "I simply depicted one animal on another".

The formidable red-granite Alexander Column in Palace Square

⑫ Field of Mars

Марсово Поле

Marsovo Pole

Map 2 E5. 🚌 46, 49, K-46, K-76.

Once a vast marshland, this area was drained during the 19th century and utilized for military manoeuvres and parades, fairs and other festivities. Named after Mars, the Roman god of war, the sandy expanse was nicknamed the "Petersburg Sahara". Following the Revolution, it was landscaped and transformed into a memorial to revolutionary martyrs (some of whom were buried here), and the Eternal Flame was added in 1957.

The western side is dominated by an imposing Neo-Classical edifice by Vasiliy Stasov, built in 1817–19 as the barracks of the Pavlovskiy Guards. The regiment's founder, Tsar Paul, is said to have only recruited guardsmen with snub noses like his own. Its soldiers were among the first to turn against the Tsarist government in the 1917 Revolution.

Today, the huge square is a popular spot for locals in the summer evenings, when the flowers are in full bloom.

The Eternal Flame, a memorial to martyrs at the Field of Mars

⑬ Summer Garden

Летний сад

Letniy sad

Map 2 E4. 🚌 46, 49, K-46, K-76, K-212. **Open** May–Oct: 10am–10pm daily; Nov–Apr: 10am–8pm daily.

In 1704, Peter the Great commissioned this beautiful formal garden, which was among the first in the city. Designed in the style of Versailles, it was planted with imported elms and oaks and adorned with fountains, pavilions and statues. A flood in 1777 destroyed most of the garden, and the English-style garden that exists today is the result of Catherine the Great's tastes. A lofty filigree iron grille along the Neva embankment gives the garden an air of seclusion.

Ivan Krylov's statue amidst pretty autumn foliage, Summer Garden

For a century the Summer Garden was reserved for the nobility, until Nicholas I opened it to "respectably dressed members of the public". Two Neo-Classical pavilions, the Tea House and the Coffee House were erected, which are now used for art exhibitions by local artists.

Nearby, the bronze statue of Ivan Krylov, Russia's most famous fabulist (one who invents fables) is a favourite with children. It has bas-reliefs on the pedestal depicting animals from his fables.

⑭ Summer Palace

Летний дворец

Letniy dvorets

Naberezhnaya Kutuzova. **Map** 2 F4. **Tel** (812) 595 42 48. 🚌 46, 49 K-46, K-76, K-212. **Closed** for renovation.

Peter the Great's two-storey Summer Palace is the oldest stone building in the city. Built in the Dutch style by Domenico Trezzini in 1714, it is grander than Peter's cabin but hardly comparable to the magnificent palaces of his successors. The tsar's bedroom has a four-poster bed and a ceiling painting showing the triumph of Morpheus, the god of sleep. Next door, the turnery contains Peter's lathes and a meteorological instrument connected to a weathervane on the roof.

The palace boasted the city's first plumbing system with water piped into the kitchen, which opened directly on to the dining room, so that dishes arrived hot at the table. This was only used for family gatherings; major banquets were held at the Menshikov Palace *(see p143)*.

On the first floor is the suite of Peter's wife, Catherine I, whose throne is ornamented with sea deities. The glass cupboards in the Green Room once displayed Peter's collection of curios, before it was transferred to the Kunstkammer *(see p142)*.

Peter the Great's original four-poster bed in the Summer Palace

9 The Hermitage

Эрмитаж

Ermitazh

One of the world's great museums, the Hermitage comprises a grand ensemble of buildings. The most impressive is the Winter Palace *(see pp156–7)*, to which Catherine the Great added the Small and Large Hermitages to house her collection of over 2,500 paintings, 10,000 drawings, gems, silver and porcelain. Her successors added to the collection, which was opened to the public in 1852. After the Revolution, the nationalization of private collections brought many more artworks, including Post-Impressionist masterpieces, into the Hermitage. In 1993 it became the first museum in Russia to admit possession of "trophy art" seized from Nazi Germany, kept hidden for decades.

★ **Litta Madonna** (around 1491)
One of two works by Leonardo da Vinci in the museum, this masterpiece was admired by his contemporaries and was frequently copied.

★ **Abraham's Sacrifice** (1635)
In the 1630s Rembrandt was painting religious scenes in a High Baroque style, using dramatic and striking gestures rather than detail to convey his message.

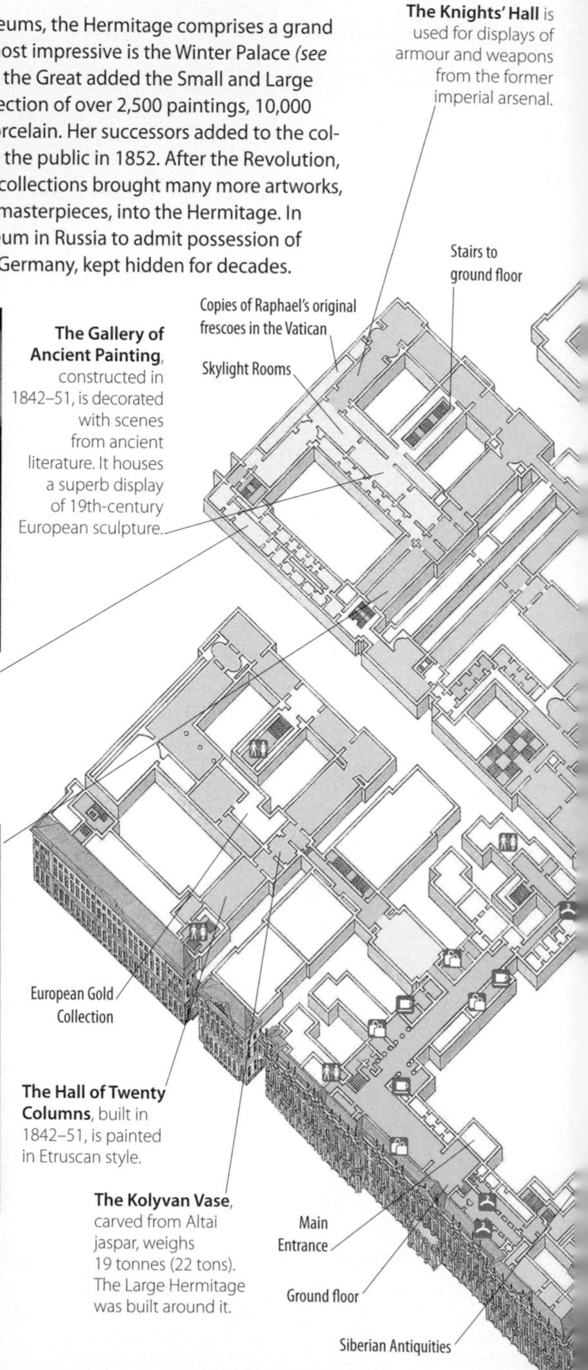

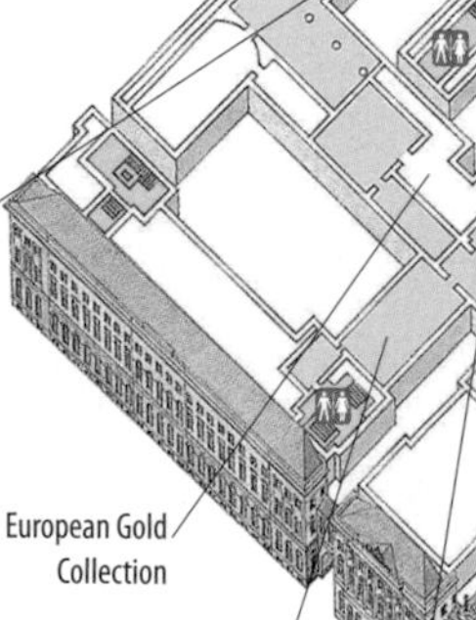

The Knights' Hall is used for displays of armour and weapons from the former imperial arsenal.

The Gallery of Ancient Painting, constructed in 1842–51, is decorated with scenes from ancient literature. It houses a superb display of 19th-century European sculpture.

The Hall of Twenty Columns, built in 1842–51, is painted in Etruscan style.

The Kolyvan Vase, carved from Altai jaspar, weighs 19 tonnes (22 tons). The Large Hermitage was built around it.

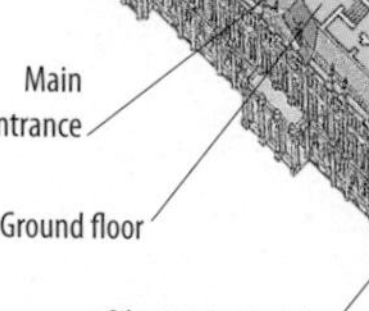

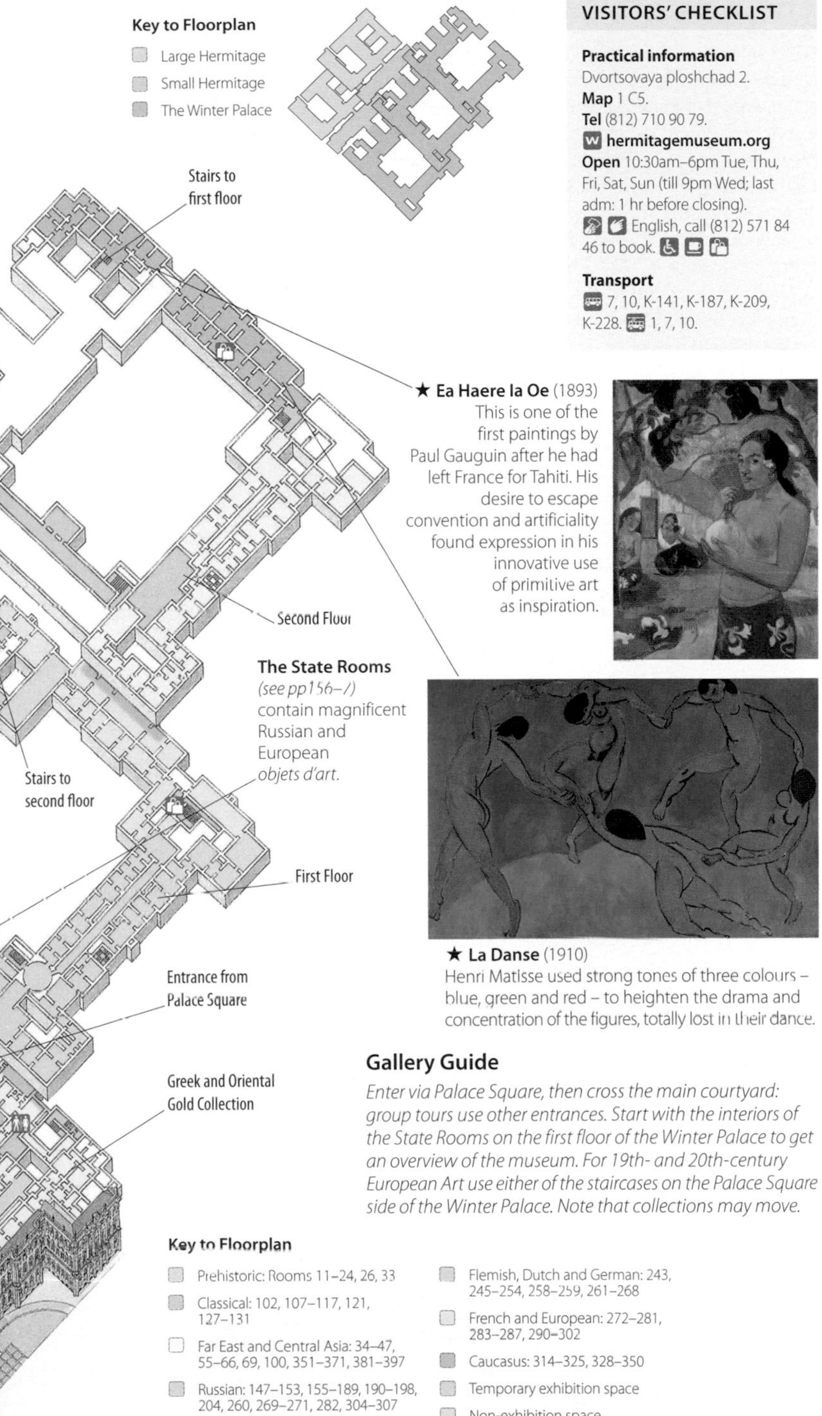

VISITORS' CHECKLIST

Practical information
Dvortsovaya ploshchad 2.
Map 1 C5.
Tel (812) 710 90 79.
hermitagemuseum.org
Open 10:30am–6pm Tue, Thu, Fri, Sat, Sun (till 9pm Wed; last adm: 1 hr before closing).
English, call (812) 571 84 46 to book.

Transport
7, 10, K-141, K-187, K-209, K-228. 1, 7, 10.

★ **Ea Haere Ia Oe** (1893)
This is one of the first paintings by Paul Gauguin after he had left France for Tahiti. His desire to escape convention and artificiality found expression in his innovative use of primitive art as inspiration.

The State Rooms *(see pp156–7)* contain magnificent Russian and European *objets d'art.*

★ **La Danse** (1910)
Henri Matisse used strong tones of three colours – blue, green and red – to heighten the drama and concentration of the figures, totally lost in their dance.

Gallery Guide

Enter via Palace Square, then cross the main courtyard: group tours use other entrances. Start with the interiors of the State Rooms on the first floor of the Winter Palace to get an overview of the museum. For 19th- and 20th-century European Art use either of the staircases on the Palace Square side of the Winter Palace. Note that collections may move.

Key to Floorplan

- Prehistoric: Rooms 11–24, 26, 33
- Classical: 102, 107–117, 121, 127–131
- Far East and Central Asia: 34–47, 55–66, 69, 100, 351–371, 381–397
- Russian: 147–153, 155–189, 190–198, 204, 260, 269–271, 282, 304–307
- Italian and Spanish: 207–223, 226–242
- Flemish, Dutch and German: 243, 245–254, 258–259, 261–268
- French and European: 272–281, 283–287, 290–302
- Caucasus: 314–325, 328–350
- Temporary exhibition space
- Non-exhibition space
- No access

The Winter Palace

Built for Tsarina Elizabeth in 1754–62, this opulent winter residence was considered to be the finest achievement of Bartolomeo Rastrelli. A superb example of Russian Baroque, the existing palace was preceded by three structures, all of them built within half a century of each other. Although the exterior has changed little, the interiors were altered by a number of architects and then largely restored after a fire gutted the palace in 1837. After the assassination of Alexander II in 1881, the imperial family rarely lived here. During World War I, a field hospital was set up in the Nicholas Hall and other state rooms. Then, in July 1917, the Provisional Government took the palace as its headquarters, which led to its storming by the Bolsheviks.

Small Throne Room
Dedicated to the memory of Peter the Great in 1833, this room houses a silver-gilt English throne, made in 1731.

KEY

① **North façade** overlooking the Neva.

② **The Nicholas Hall**, the largest room in the palace, was always used for the first ball of the season.

③ **The Field Marshals' Hall** (1833) was the reception room where the devastating fire of 1837 broke out.

④ **The Hall of St George** (1795) has monolithic columns and wall facings of Italian Carrara marble.

⑤ **The 1812 Gallery** (1826) has portraits of Russian military heroes of the Napoleonic War, most of them painted by English artist George Dawe.

⑥ **The Armorial Hall** (1839), with its vast gilded columns, covers over 800 sq m (8,600 sq ft). Hospital beds were set up here during World War I.

⑦ **The French Rooms**, designed by Bryullov in 1839, house a collection of 18th-century French art.

⑧ **South façade on Palace Square**

⑨ **The White Hall** retains decorations from the wedding of Alexander II in 1841.

⑩ **West wing**

⑪ **The Gothic Library** and other rooms in the northwestern part of the palace were adapted to suit Nicholas II's bourgeois lifestyle. This wood-panelled library was created by Meltzer in 1894.

⑫ **The rotunda** (1830) connected the private apartments on the west with the state apartments on the palace's north side.

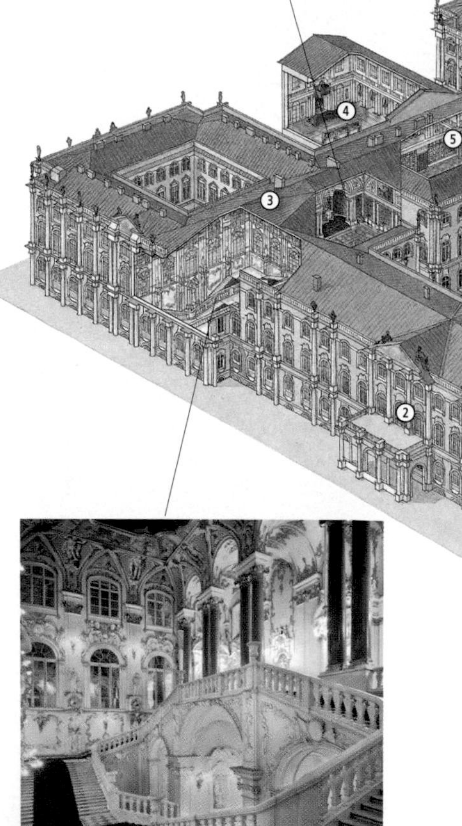

★ Main Staircase
This sweeping staircase built in 1762 was Rastrelli's masterpiece. It was from here that the imperial family watched the Epiphany ceremony of baptism in the Neva, which celebrated Christ's baptism in the Jordan.

For hotels and restaurants in this area see p268 and pp284–5

Alexander Hall
Architect Aleksandr Bryullov employed Gothic vaulting in this reception room dating from 1837. He combined it with Neo-Classical stucco bas-reliefs on military themes.

Bartolomeo Rastrelli

The Italian architect Rastrelli (1700–71) came to Russia with his father in 1716 to work for Peter the Great. His rich Baroque style became highly fashionable and he was appointed Chief Court Architect in 1738. During Elizabeth's reign, Rastrelli designed several buildings, including the Winter Palace, Tsarkoe Selo *(see pp188–9)* and Smolnyy Convent *(see p182)*. Unlike Elizabeth, Catherine the Great preferred classical simplicity and Rastrelli retired in 1763, after she came to power.

Dark Corridor
The French and Flemish tapestries here include *The Marriage of Emperor Constantine*, made in Paris in the 17th century to designs by Rubens.

★ Malachite Room
Over 2 tonnes (2.2 tons) of ornamental stone were used in this sumptuous room (1839), which is decorated with malachite columns and vases, gilded doors and a gilded ceiling, and rich parquet flooring.

★ Gold Drawing Room
Created in the 1850s, this room was given an extravagant all-over gilding covering the walls and ceiling in the 1870s. It houses a display of carved gems from Western Europe.

28

GOSTINYY DVOR

Dating from the earliest days of St Petersburg, Gostinyy Dvor, or the Great Bazaar, forms the commercial heart of the city. With modern shopping centres standing next to Tsarist-era churches, this vast square is also a major social and cultural hub of St Petersburg. Until the mid-19th century, shops in this area catered almost exclusively for the luxury end of the market, fulfilling the immense demand created by the royal and aristocratic households for gold and silverware, jewellery and haute couture. Increasing commercial and financial activity created a new middle class of business entrepreneurs. By the time of the Revolution, banks proliferated around Nevskiy prospekt, their imposing new offices introducing diverse architectural styles to a largely Neo-Classical setting. Today, the wheels of capitalism are turning again and Nevskiy prospekt continues to attract a wealthy clientele. In contrast to the bustling commercial atmosphere of much of the area is the peace and quiet of secluded Arts Square, with the Russian Museum and other institutions acting as a reminder of St Petersburg's rich cultural heritage.

Sights at a Glance

Churches and Cathedrals

1 *Church on Spilled Blood p162*
13 Cathedral of Our Lady of Kazan

Museums

2 Mikhaylovskiy Castle
3 *Russian Museum pp164–5*
16 Pushkin House-Museum

Streets, Square and Bridges

4 Arts Square
6 Malaya Sadovaya Ulitsa
7 Anichkov Bridge
9 Nevskiy Prospekt
11 Ostrovskiy Square
12 Ulitsa Zodchevo Rossi

Historic Buildings

5 Grand Hotel Europe
10 Gostinyy Dvor
15 Academic Capella
17 Imperial Stables

Palaces

8 Anichkov Palace
14 Stroganov Palace

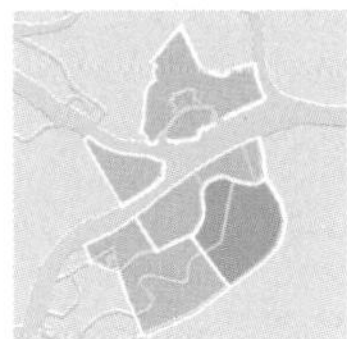

Locator Map
See Street Finder, maps 2 & 1

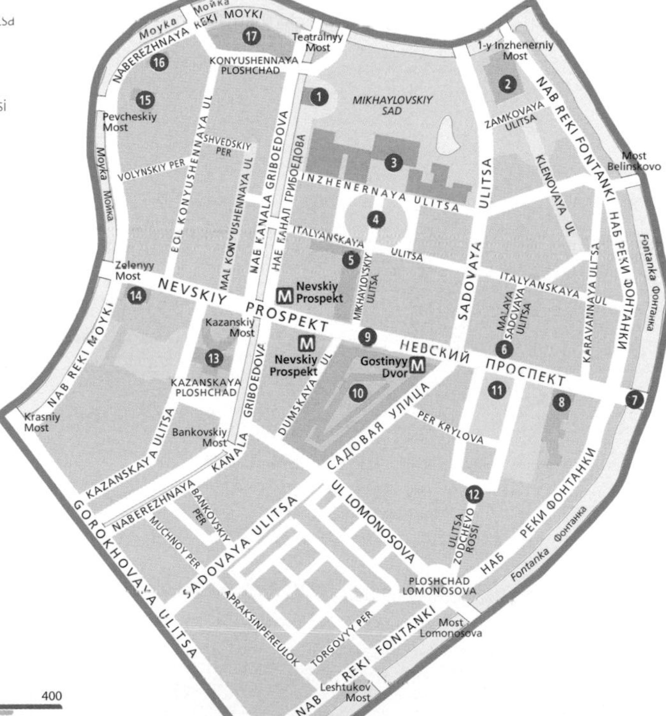

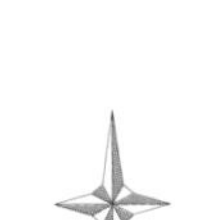

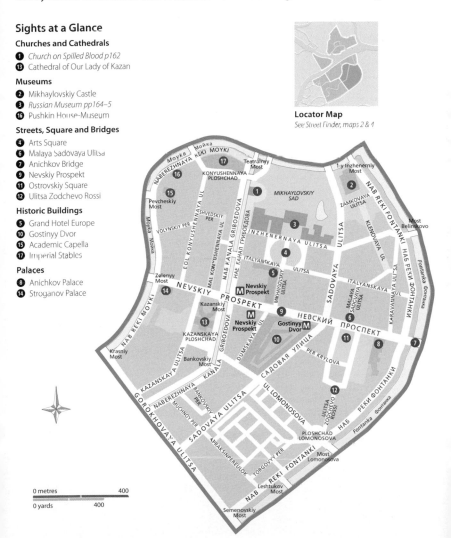

0 metres 400
0 yards 400

◀ Spectacular view of the façade of the Church on Spilled Blood

For map symbols *see back flap*

Street-by-Street: Around Arts Square

The aptly named Arts Square, one of Carlo Rossi's finest creations, is surrounded by buildings showcasing the city's impressive cultural heritage. The grand palace housing the Russian Museum is flanked by theatres and the Great Hall of the Philharmonia. Behind it is the leafy Mikhaylovskiy Garden, a haunt of St Petersburg's intellectuals. The gardens stretch down to the beautiful Moyka river, which together with two other waterways, the Griboedov and Fontanka, create a shimmering frame for this picturesque area.

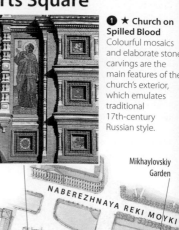

1 ★ Church on Spilled Blood
Colourful mosaics and elaborate stone carvings are the main features of the church's exterior, which emulates traditional 17th-century Russian style.

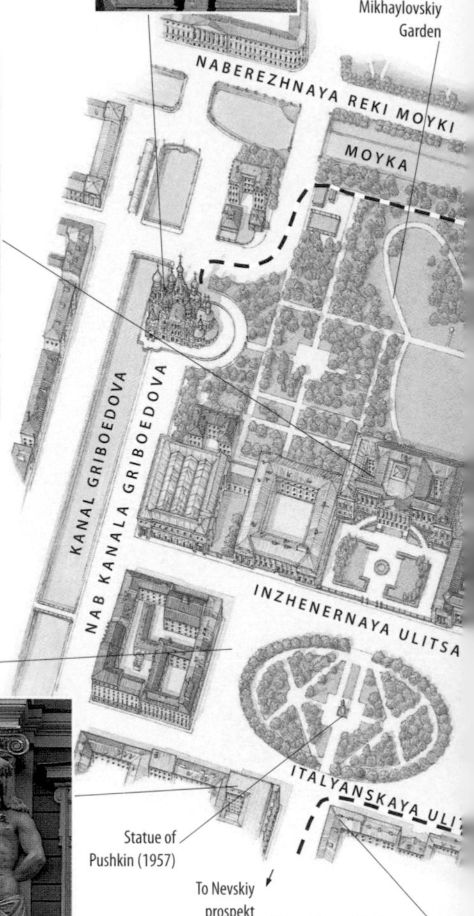

Mikhaylovskiy Garden

NABEREZHNAYA REKI MOYKI

MOYKA

KANAL GRIBOEDOVA

NAB KANALA GRIBOEDOVA

INZHENERNAYA ULITSA

ITALYANSKAYA ULI

3 ★ Russian Museum
Located in Rossi's Mikhaylovskiy Palace, this famous gallery boasts a fabulous collection of Russian painting, sculpture and applied art. The grand staircase and White Hall are original features.

4 Arts Square
The square's present name derives from the number of cultural institutions situated here. On the western side, the Mikhailovskiy Theatre opened in 1833 for opera performances.

Statue of Pushkin (1957)

To Nevskiy prospekt

The Great Hall of the Philharmonia is one of the major concert venues in St Petersburg.

5 Grand Hotel Europe
This famous St Petersburg hotel was constructed by Ludwig Fontana in 1873–5. Mighty atlantes adorn its eclectic façade, which stretches all the way down to Nevskiy prospekt.

For hotels and restaurants in this area see p268 and pp285–6

The Panteleymon Bridge
Rebuilt in 1907–08 to support a new tramway, this bridge retains its original Empire-style decor by Lev Ilyin.

Area illustrated

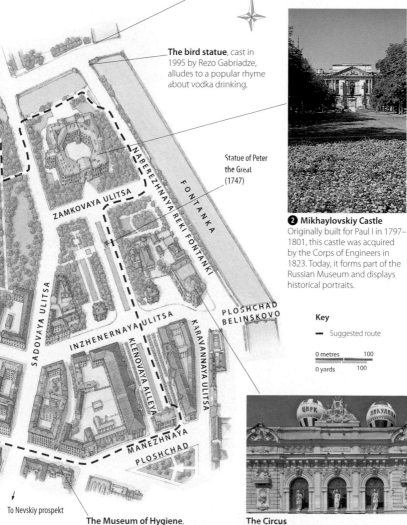

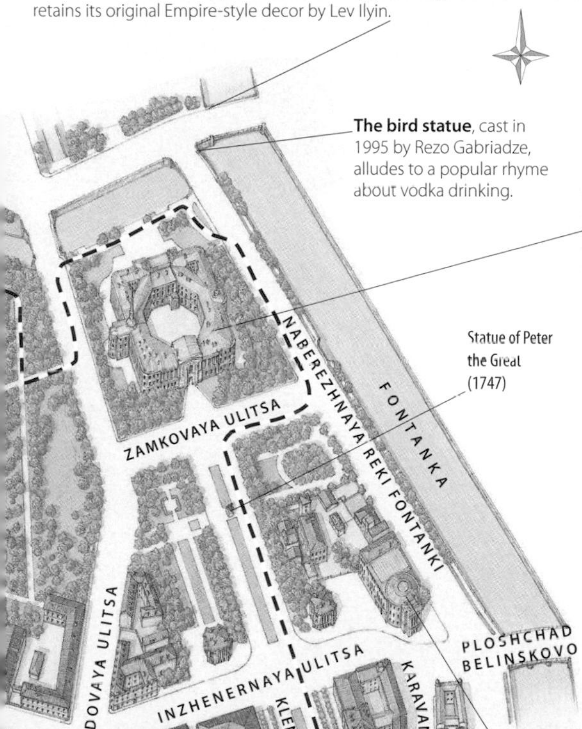

2 Mikhaylovskiy Castle
Originally built for Paul I in 1797–1801, this castle was acquired by the Corps of Engineers in 1823. Today, it forms part of the Russian Museum and displays historical portraits.

The bird statue, cast in 1995 by Rezo Gabriadze, alludes to a popular rhyme about vodka drinking.

Statue of Peter the Great (1747)

To Nevskiy prospekt

Key

Suggested route

0 metres 100

0 yards 100

The Museum of Hygiene, with macabre displays of preserved human organs, was set up in 1919 to teach the public about health and hygiene.

The Circus
The *tsirk* began performing in the 19th century when it was known as the Ciniselli Circus. It still offers traditional performances in this historic site by the Fontanka. The building's original façade was reinstated in 2003.

❶ Church on Spilled Blood

Храм Спаса-на-Крови

Khram Spasa-na-Krovi

Also known as the Resurrection Church of Our Saviour, this church was built on the spot where Tsar Alexander II was assassinated on 1 March 1881. In 1883, his successor, Alexander III launched a competition for a permanent memorial. The winning design, in the Russian-Revival style favoured by the tsar himself, was by Alfred Parland and Ignatiy Malyshev. The foundation stone was laid in 1883. A riot of colour, the overall effect of the church is created by the imaginative juxtaposition of materials. Inside, more than 20 types of minerals, including jasper, rhodonite, porphyry and Italian marble are used unsparingly on the mosaics of the iconostasis, icon cases, canopy and floor. The interior reopened in 1998 after more than 20 years of restoration.

VISITORS' CHECKLIST

Practical information

Kanala Griboedova 2b.

Map 2 E5.

Tel (812) 315 16 36.

Open May–Sep: 10am–11pm Thu–Tue; Oct–Apr: 11am–7pm Thu–Tue.

Transport

Ⓜ Gostinyy Dvor, Nevskiy Prospekt.

Mosaic Tympanum
Mosaic panels showing scenes from the New Testament adorn the exterior. They were based on designs by artists such as Viktor Vasnetsov and Mikhail Nesterov.

Jewellers' enamel was used to cover the 1,000 sq m (10,760 sq ft) surface of the five domes.

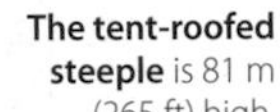

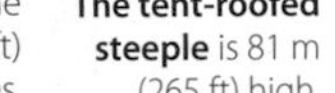

The tent-roofed steeple is 81 m (265 ft) high.

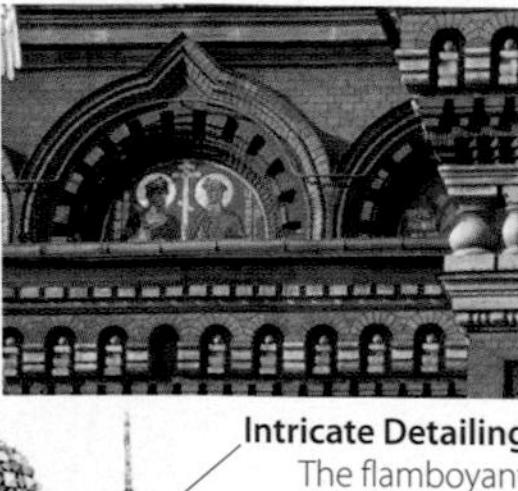

Coat of Arms
The 144 mosaic coats of arms on the bell tower represent the regions, towns and provinces of the Russian Empire. They were intended to reflect the grief shared by all Russians in the wake of Alexander's assassination.

Intricate Detailing
The flamboyant Russian-Revival style of the exterior provides a dramatic contrast to the Neo-Classical and Baroque architecture that dominates the centre of St Petersburg.

Glazed ceramic tiles enliven the façade.

Mosaic portraits of the saints are set in *kokoshniki* arches. Almost 7,000 sq m (75,300 sq ft) of mosaics embellish the church's extravagant exterior.

Twenty dark red plaques of Norwegian granite are engraved in gilt letters with the most outstanding events of Alexander II's reign (1855–81). Among the historic events recorded are the emancipation of the serfs in 1861 and the conquest of Central Asia in 1860–81.

Window Frames
The windows are flanked by carved columns of ornate Estonian marble. The casings are in the form of double and triple *kokoshniki*.

For hotels and restaurants in this area see p268 and pp285–6

South façade of Mikhaylovskiy Castle, with the statue of Peter the Great on horseback

❷ Mikhaylovskiy Castle

Михайловский замок

Mikhaylovskiy zamok

Sadovaya ulitsa 2. **Map** 2 F5. **Tel** (812) 595 42 48. 46, K-46, K-76, K 212. **Open** 10am–6pm Wed, Fri, Sat & Sun (till 5pm Mon), 1–9pm Thu. call to book.

This imposing fortified castle overlooking the Moyka and Fontanka rivers was commissioned by Tsar Paul shortly after his coronation in 1796. To clear the site, Paul had the wooden palace in which he had been born razed to the ground: a revealing act by a man plagued by rumours of illegitimacy and who blamed his mother, Catherine the Great, for murdering his father. Terrified of being assassinated himself, Paul ordered architects Vasiliy Bazhenov and Vincenzo Brenna to surround his new residence with moats and drawbridges, and construct a secret escape tunnel leading to the Field of Mars *(see p153)*. Unfortunately, all these precautions proved futile; after living here for just 40 days Paul was strangled in his bedroom by conspirators.

The castle was shunned by his successors and was acquired in 1823 by the Corps of Engineers as a training school known as the Engineers' Castle. Its most famous graduate was the writer Fyodor Dostoevsky. Today, the castle serves as a branch of the Russian Museum and is used to house temporary exhibitions.

The octagonal inner courtyard contains a statue of Paul, who also commissioned the bronze statue of Peter the Great on horseback on the castle's driveway. Its inscription "To great grandfather from great grandson" was intended to quell rumours of his illegitimacy.

❸ Russian Museum

See pp164–5.

❹ Arts Square

Площадь Искусств

Ploshchad Iskusstv

Map 4 E1. Ⓜ Nevskiy Prospekt, Gostinyy Dvor.

Several of the city's leading cultural institutions are located on this leafy Neo-Classical square – hence its name. The square was designed by Carlo Rossi in the early 19th century to harmonize with the splendid Mikhaylovskiy Palace (now the Russian Museum) which stands on its northern side.

On the opposite side of the square is the Great Hall of the Philharmonia, also known as the Shostakovich Hall. This is where the Philharmonic Orchestra has been based since the 1920s. Constructed by Paul Jacot over 1834–9, it started as a Nobles' Club where concerts were held. Works premiered here include Beethoven's *Missa Solemnis* in 1824 and Tchaikovsky's *Pathétique* in 1893.

On the square's western side is the Mikhailovskiy Theatre, rebuilt by Albert Kavos in the mid-19th century. In the centre of the square is a sculpture of one of Russia's greatest literary figures, Alexander Pushkin. The statue was executed by leading post-war Soviet sculptor, Mikhail Anikushin.

❺ Grand Hotel Europe

Гранд Отель Европа

Grand Otel Evropa

Mikhaylovskaya ulitsa 1/7. **Map** 4 E1. **Tel** (812) 329 60 00. Ⓜ Nevskiy Prospekt, Gostinyy Dvor.

One of Russia's most famous hotels (known locally as the Yevropeyskaya), the Grand Hotel Europe was built in the 1870s. However, it owes much of its character to alterations made in the 1910s by Style-Moderne architect Fyodor Lidval. Before the Revolution, the hotel's magnificent restaurant was a favourite rendezvous for diplomats and spies; later, the hotel became an orphanage.

Opulent Style-Moderne interiors of the Grand Hotel Europe

❸ Russian Museum

Русский музей

Russkiy Muzey

Built in 1819–25 for Grand Duke Mikhail Pavlovich, the Mikhaylovsky Palace – a fine Neo-Classical creation by Carlo Rossi – is home to one of Russia's most illustrious museums. Alexander III's plans to create a public museum were realized by his son, Nicholas II, when the Russian Museum opened here in 1898. Today, it holds what is arguably the greatest collection of Russian art in the world.

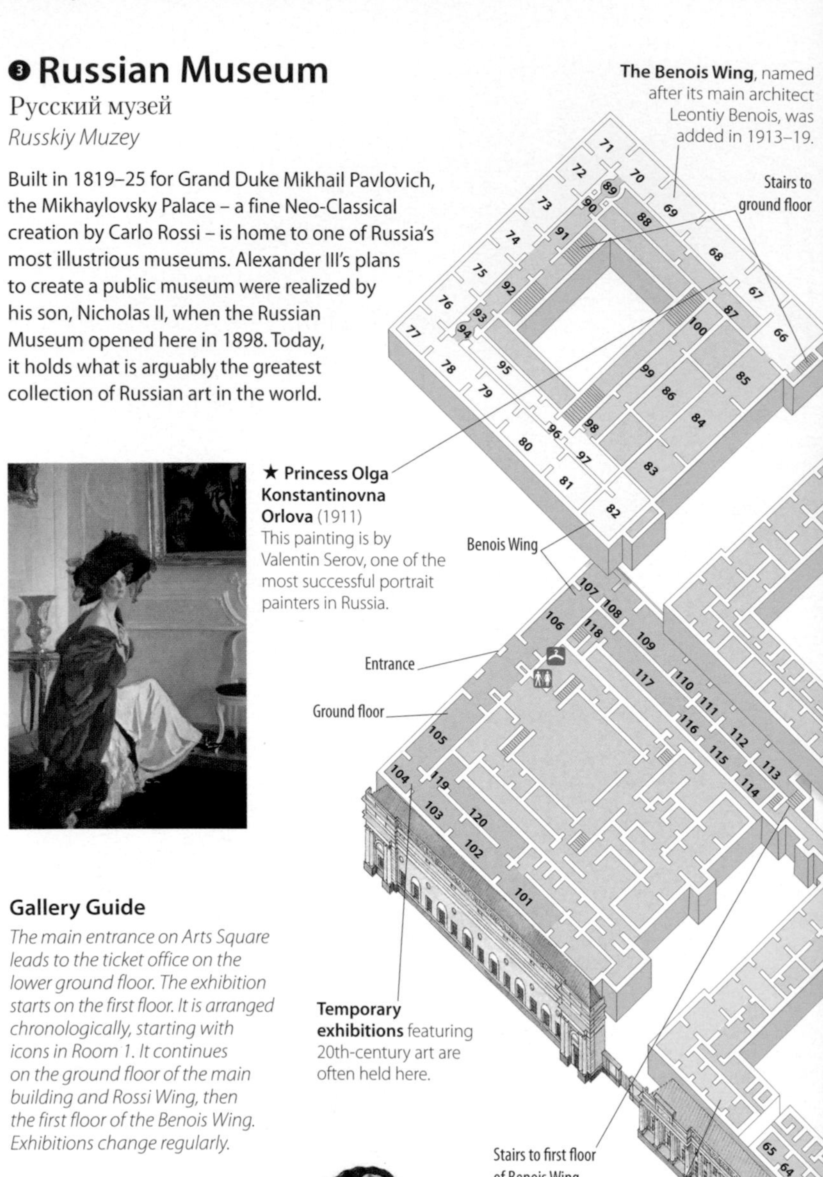

The Benois Wing, named after its main architect Leontiy Benois, was added in 1913–19.

★ Princess Olga Konstantinovna Orlova (1911)
This painting is by Valentin Serov, one of the most successful portrait painters in Russia.

Temporary exhibitions featuring 20th-century art are often held here.

Gallery Guide

The main entrance on Arts Square leads to the ticket office on the lower ground floor. The exhibition starts on the first floor. It is arranged chronologically, starting with icons in Room 1. It continues on the ground floor of the main building and Rossi Wing, then the first floor of the Benois Wing. Exhibitions change regularly.

Folk Art Toy (1930s)
This clay toy from Dykomovo is part of the colourful selection of folk art which also includes lacquer boxes, painted ceramics and textiles.

Key to Floorplan

- Old Russian art
- 18th-century art
- Early 19th-century art
- Late 19th-century art
- Late 19th–early 20th-century art
- 20th-century art
- 18th–20th-century sculpture
- Folk art
- Temporary exhibitions
- Non-exhibition space

For hotels and restaurants in this area see p268 and pp285–6

The Last Day of Pompeii (1833)
Karl Bryullov's Classical subject embodies the aesthetic principles of the Academy of Arts. This vivid depiction of the eruption of Mount Vesuvius won him the Grand Prix at the Paris Salon.

VISITORS' CHECKLIST

Practical information
Inzhenernaya ulitsa.
Map 4 E1. **Tel** (812) 595 42 48.
W rusmuseum.ru
Open 10am–5pm Mon, 10am–6pm Wed & Fri–Sun, 1–9pm Thu (last adm: an hour before closing).
English, (812) 314 34 48. English. call for details.

Transport
M Nevskiy Prospekt, Gostinyy Dvor. 3, 7, 22, 24, 27, 191, K-212, K-289. 1, 5, 7, 10, 11, 22.

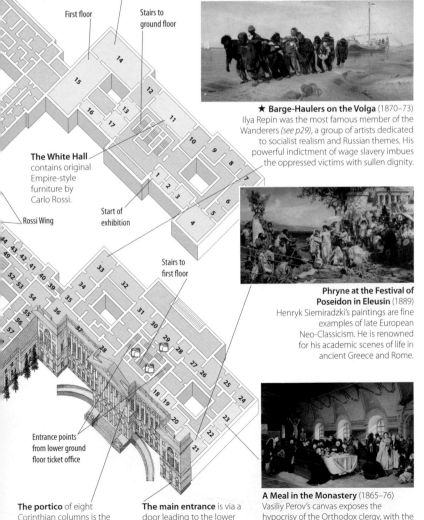

The White Hall contains original Empire-style furniture by Carlo Rossi.

★ **Barge-Haulers on the Volga** (1870–73)
Ilya Repin was the most famous member of the Wanderers *(see p29)*, a group of artists dedicated to socialist realism and Russian themes. His powerful indictment of wage slavery imbues the oppressed victims with sullen dignity.

Phryne at the Festival of Poseidon in Eleusin (1889)
Henryk Siemiradzki's paintings are fine examples of late European Neo-Classicism. He is renowned for his academic scenes of life in ancient Greece and Rome.

A Meal in the Monastery (1865–76)
Vasiliy Perov's canvas exposes the hypocrisy of the Orthodox clergy, with the juxtaposition of good and evil, rich and poor, false piety and true faith.

The portico of eight Corinthian columns is the central feature of Carlo Rossi's façade.

The main entrance is via a door leading to the lower ground floor with a ticket office, toilets and a café.

6 Malaya Sadovaya Ulitsa

Малая Садовая Улица

Malaya Sadovaya ulitsa

Map 4 F1. Ⓜ Gostinyy Dvor.

This pedestrianized side street is known for its many sculptures. Notable among these is a statue of the great photographer Karl Bulla (1853–1929) with his tripod camera, with which he captured life in St Petersburg before the Revolution. Beyond this, two sculpted cats watch each other from the second-floor ledges of buildings on opposite sides of the street. At the intersection of Malaya Sadovaya ulitsa and Nevskiy prospekt, a model of a loudspeaker recalls the public-address systems that broadcast air-raid warnings during the Siege of Leningrad.

7 Anichkov Bridge

Аничков мост

Anichkov most

Map 4 F2.

This bridge spanning the Fontanka river is named after Colonel Mikhail Anichkov, who set up camp on this site at the time of the founding of the city, and built a wooden drawbridge here. Today's bridge, built in the mid-19th century, is famous for the statues at its four corners, each portraying a near-naked youth taming a stallion. It is said that their sculptor Pyotr Klodt got so annoyed with repeated meddling by Tsar Nicholas I that he depicted the tsar's face in the groin of the horse nearest to the Anichkov Palace.

Bronze sculpture of a boy taming a stallion, Anichkov Bridge

Colonnaded wing overlooking the Fontanka river, Anichkov Palace

8 Anichkov Palace

Аничков дворец

Anichkov dvorets

Nevskiy prospekt 39. **Map** 4 F2. 🚌 3, 7, 22, 24, 27, 191. Ⓜ Gostinyy Dvor. 🚎 1, 5, 7, 10, 11, 22. **Closed** to public except for special events.

Built in 1741–50, the Anichkov Palace beside the Fontanka river was a gift from Tsarina Elizabeth to her lover Aleksey Razumovskiy. After his death, Catherine the Great in turn gave it to her own lover, Prince Potemkin. The palace became the traditional winter residence of the heir to the throne after 1817, although when Alexander III became tsar in 1881, he continued to live here rather than move to the Winter Palace as was customary. His widow Maria Fyodorovna stayed on until the Revolution.

The palace originally had large gardens to the west but these were truncated in 1816 when Ostrovskiy Square was created and two Neo-Classical pavilions were added. The elegant colonnaded wing overlooking the Fontanka river was built for storing goods from the imperial factories before they were distributed to various palaces. Later, the building was converted into government offices. It now houses the Palace of Youth Creativity.

9 Nevskiy Prospekt

Невский проспект

Nevskiy prospekt

Map 4 D1. Ⓜ Nevskiy Prospekt, Gostinyy Dvor.

Russia's most famous street, Nevskiy prospekt is also St Petersburg's main thoroughfare. In the 1830s, novelist Nikolai Gogol declared with great pride, "There is nothing finer than Nevskiy Avenue…in St Petersburg it is everything… is there anything more gay, more brilliant, more resplendent than this beautiful street of our capital?"

Laid out in the early days of the city, the street was originally named the Great Perspective Road, and ran 5 km (3 miles) from the Admiralty *(see p148)* to the Alexander Nevskiy Monastery *(see p183)*. Despite roaming wolves and periodic flooding, mansions such as the Stroganov Palace *(see p168)* were built, followed by shops and bazaars catering to the nobility, and inns for travelling merchants. A magnet attracting rich and poor alike, the avenue became the place to meet for gossip, business and pleasure.

Today, the theatres, shops, cinemas and eateries along the stretch between the Admiralty and Anichkov Bridge, and the many cultural landmarks in the vicinity, are a big draw for visitors.

10 Gostinyy Dvor

Гостиный двор

Gostinyy dvor

Nevskiy prospekt 35. **Map** 4 E2. **Tel** (812) 710 54 08. Ⓜ Gostinyy Dvor. **Open** 10am–10pm Fri–Tue (till 10:30pm Wed & Thu). **W** **bgd.ru**

The term *gostinyy dvor* originally meant a coaching inn, but as trade developed around the inns, with travelling merchants setting up their stalls, it later came to mean trading rows. The original wooden structure of this *gostinyy dvor* was destroyed by fire in 1736. It was replaced in 1761–85 by a huge brick structure designed by Vallin de la Mothe. The columned arcades of the building form an irregular quadrangle and the combined length of its façades is nearly 1,006 m (3,300 ft).

Serious damage during the Siege of Leningrad in 1941 led to major reconstruction, but even now, the original layout of "stalls" of individual trading units has been retained. The arcade offers a wide range of products and is the city's central supplier of basic goods and souvenirs.

Columned arcades at Gostinyy Dvor, St Petersburg's biggest department store

⓫ Ostrovskiy Square

Площадь Островского

Ploshchad Ostrovskovo

Map 4 F2. 🚌 3, 7, 22, 24, 27. 🚎 1, 5, 7, 10, 11, 22. Ⓜ Gostinyy Dvor. Russian National Library: **Tel** (812) 310 71 37. **Open** 9am–9pm Mon–Fri, 11am–9pm Sat & Sun. Theatre Museum: **Tel** (812) 571 21 95. **Open** 11am–6pm Thu–Mon, 1–7pm Wed. **Closed** last Fri of the month and public hols. **W theatremuseum.ru**

One of Russia's most brilliant architects, Carlo Rossi, created this early 19th-century square, now named in honour of the dramatist Aleksandr Ostrovskiy (1823–86). Its focal point is the elegant Alexandrinskiy Theatre, designed by Rossi in the Neo Classical style, with a six-columned portico crowned by a chariot of Apollo. Plays premiered here, and are still performed today, include Nikolai Gogol's *The Inspector General* (1836) and Anton Chekhov's *The Seagull* (1901).

Carlo Rossi

Architect Carlo Rossi (1775–1849) was one of the last great exponents of Neo-Classicism in St Petersburg. He found an ideal client in Alexander I, who shared his belief in the use of architecture to express the power of the ruling autocracy. Rossi created no fewer than 12 of St Petersburg's streets and 13 of its squares. His status as Alexander I's favourite architect encouraged rumours that Rossi was the tsar's illegitimate son.

The palatial Russian Museum, designed by Carlo Rossi

In the garden is a monument to Catherine the Great. Unveiled in 1873, it depicts her surrounded by generals and statesmen. On the west side of the square is a colonnade decorated with Classical sculptures, which Rossi designed as an extension of the **Russian National Library**. Founded in 1795, the library currently holds more than 28 million items, including the personal library of the French philosopher Voltaire, which Catherine the Great purchased to show her appreciation of her mentor and correspondent.

In the southeast corner of the square, at No. 6, the **Theatre Museum** traces the evolution of the Russian stage from its origins in mid-18th-century serf and imperial theatres. Amidst the eclectic array of playbills, photographs, costumes, set designs and other artifacts, there are also some set designs by one of the great innovators of modern theatre, the director Vsevolod Meyerhold (1874–1940).

⓬ Ulitsa Zodchevo Rossi

Улица Зодчего Росси

Ulitsa Zodchevo Rossi

Map 4 E2. Ⓜ Gostinyy Dvor.

There could be no better memorial to Carlo Rossi than the architectural ensemble of arcades and colonnades forming Architect Rossi Street. The 22-m (72-ft) high buildings stand precisely 22 m (72 ft) apart and stretch for 220 m (720 ft). Seen from ploshchad Lomonosova, the perspective coaxes the eye towards the Alexandriinskiy Theatre.

At No. 2 is the home of the former Imperial Ballet School, now named after the teacher Agrippina Vaganova. The school began in 1738 when Jean-Baptiste Landé began training the children of palace servants to take part in court entertainment. It has produced many famous dancers, including Anna Pavlova and Rudolf Nureyev.

Porticoed façade of Alexandrinskiy Theatre, Ostrovskiy Square

⓭ Cathedral of Our Lady of Kazan

Собор Казанской Богоматери

Sobor Kazanskoy Bogomateri

Kazanskaya ploshchad 2. **Map** 4 D1. **Tel** (812) 314 46 63. 3, 7, 22, 24, 27, 191. Ⓜ Nevskiy Prospekt. 1, 5, 7, 10, 11, 22. **Open** 9am–7:30pm daily.

Pink granite columns and mosaic floor in the main nave, Cathedral of Our Lady of Kazan

This majestic cathedral was commissioned by Tsar Paul and took over a decade to build. Completed in 1811, it is linked with the wars against Napoleon fought during the same period. In fact, Field Marshal Mikhail Kutuzov (1745–1813), who masterminded the strategic retreat from Moscow following the invasion of Napoleon's Grand Armeè in 1812, is buried here. His statue and that of his comrade-in-arms, Mikhail Barclay de Tolly (1761–1818), have stood outside the cathedral since 1837.

The cathedral is named after the miracle-working *Icon of Our Lady of Kazan*, kept within. Its design by serf architect Andrei Voronikhin was inspired by St Peter's Basilica in Rome. The 111-m (364-ft) long colonnade disguises the orientation of the building which runs parallel to Nevskiy prospekt, conforming to a religious stipulation that the main altar face east. The 80-m (262-ft) high dome and the pink Finnish granite columns with bronze capitals and bases are its most impressive features.

Occupied in the Soviet era by a Museum of Atheism, the cathedral was returned to religious use in 1999.

⓮ Stroganov Palace

Строгановский дворец

Stroganovskiy dvorets

Nevskiy prospekt 17. **Map** 4 D1. **Tel** (812) 571 82 38. 3, 7, 22, 24, 27, 191. Ⓜ Nevskiy Prospekt. 1, 5, 7, 10, 11, 17. **Open** 10am–6pm Wed, Fri–Sun (till 5pm Mon), 1–9pm Thu.

This Baroque masterpiece was designed in 1752–4 by Bartolomeo Rastrelli *(see p157)*, for the enormously wealthy Count Sergei Stroganov, whose descendants occupied the palace until the Revolution. The Stroganov fortune was amassed mainly through the monopoly the family held on salt, mined from their territories in Siberia.

The pink-and-white palace, overlooking both Nevskiy prospekt and the Moyka river, was one of the city's most impressive private residences. Its splendid façade overlooking the Moyka is decorated with Doric columns, cornices and pediments. The windows proffer stunning views across the river.

The Stroganovs were noted collectors of everything from Egyptian antiquities and Roman coins to icons and Old Masters. After the Revolution, the family's collection was expropriated by the state, and the palace was turned into a museum on the life of the decadent aristocracy. The building now belongs to the Russian Museum *(see pp164–5)* and features temporary exhibitions.

The Stroganov family chef is believed to have invented the dish beef stroganoff.

Detailed west façade of the Stroganov Palace overlooking the Moyka river

⓯ Academic Capella

Академическая капелла

Akademicheskaya kapella

Naberezhnaya Reki Moyki 20. **Map** 2 D5. **Tel** (812) 314 10 58. Ⓜ Nevskiy Prospekt. **Open** for concerts only.

Enclosed within a courtyard off the Moyka river is this ochre-coloured concert hall with a façade in the French Classical style of Louis XV. The Academic Capella was designed by Leontiy Benois in 1887–9 as the residence of the Imperial Court choir. Founded during the reign of Peter the Great, the choir is as old as the city itself. Its former directors have included the distinguished Russian composers Mikhail Glinka (1804–57) and Nikolai Rimsky-Korsakov (1844–1908).

With its superb acoustics, the Academic Capella claims to be one of the best concert halls in the world. Outside is the Singers' Bridge (Pevcheskiy Most), which was designed by Yegor Adam in 1837–40.

The main concert hall known for its excellent acoustics, Academic Capella

⓰ Pushkin House-Museum

Музей-квартира А. С. Пушкина

Muzey-kvartira AS Pushkina

Naberezhnaya Reki Moyki 12. **Map** 2 D5. **Tel** (812) 571 35 31. **Open** 10:30am–6pm Wed–Mon. **Closed** last Fri of the month and public hols.

Every year on the anniversary of Alexander Pushkin's death (29 January 1837), loyal devotees of Russia's greatest poet come to lay floral tributes outside his apartment. Pushkin was born in Moscow in 1799 but spent many years in St Petersburg. He settled in this fairly opulent apartment overlooking the Moyka, with his wife Natalya, their four children and Natalya's two sisters, from the autumn of 1836 until his death. It was here on the couchette in the study that he bled to death after his duel with d'Anthès *(see p93)*.

Pushkin's study, with his work desk and library carefully preserved, Pushkin House-Museum

Some half a dozen rooms on the first floor have been refurbished in the Empire style of the period. The most evocative of them is Pushkin's study, which is arranged exactly as it was when he died. On the writing table is an ivory paper knife given to the poet by his sister, a bronze handbell and a treasured inkstand. Embellished with the figure of an Ethiopian boy, the inkstand is a reminder of Pushkin's Ethiopian great-grandfather, Abram Hannibal. Bought by the Russian ambassador in Constantinople as a slave in 1706, Hannibal served as a general under Peter the Great and was the inspiration for the unfinished novel on which Pushkin was working at the time of his death.

On the wall in front of his desk is a Turkish sabre presented to Pushkin in the Caucasus, where he had been exiled in 1820 for his radical views, and spent some of his happiest years. It was there that he began his most famous work, *Eugene Onegin*, a novel in verse written in 1823–30. Pushkin's library contains more than 4,500 volumes in 14 European and Oriental languages, including works by Shakespeare, Byron, Heine, Dante and Voltaire.

⓱ Imperial Stables

Конюшенное Ведомство

Konyushennoe Vedomstvo

Konyushennaya ploshchad 1. **Map** 2 E5. Church: **Open** 10am–7pm daily.

The long, salmon-coloured building running parallel to the Moyka embankment is the former Imperial Stables. Originally built in the first part of the 18th century, the stables were reconstructed by Vasiliy Stasov in 1817–23.

The only part of the building open to the public lies behind the central section of the long south façade, crowned by a silver dome and cross. This is the church where Alexander Pushkin's funeral took place on 1 February 1837. Its Neo-Classical interior is in the form of a basilica and is decorated with yellow marble pillars. It is now a functioning Orthodox church.

North façade of the Imperial Stables

SENNAYA PLOSHCHAD

The western part of St Petersburg is an area of contrasts. While it boasts some of the city's wealthiest residences, the area is also home to poverty-stricken dwellings. The palatial 18th-century architecture along the Neva embankment is a world away from the decrepit living quarters around bustling Sennaya Ploshchad, which have changed little since Fyodor Dostoevsky described them in *Crime and Punishment*. In between these two areas lies the old maritime quarter. Once extending from the timber warehouses in New Holland to St Nicholas's Cathedral, it was inhabited by Peter the Great's shipwrights. This serene area, however, has much to offer. Its focal point is the marvellous Theatre Square, which has been a major entertainment hub since the mid-18th century. Dominated by the Mariinskiy Theatre and the Rimsky-Korsakov Conservatory, this is where many of Russia's greatest artists began their careers. Before 1917, many theatre directors, actors, ballerinas and musicians lived in the surrounding area. Today, artists are returning here, attracted by the tranquility of its tree-lined canal embankments.

Sights at a Glance

Churches and Cathedrals

2 St Nicholas's Cathedral

Museums

7 Railway Museum

Streets and Squares

8 Sennaya Ploshchad

Historic Buildings and Areas

3 Rimsky-Korsakov Conservatory
4 New Holland
6 Main Post Office

Theatres

1 Mariinskiy Theatre

Palaces

5 Yusupov Palace

See Street Finder, maps 3 & 4

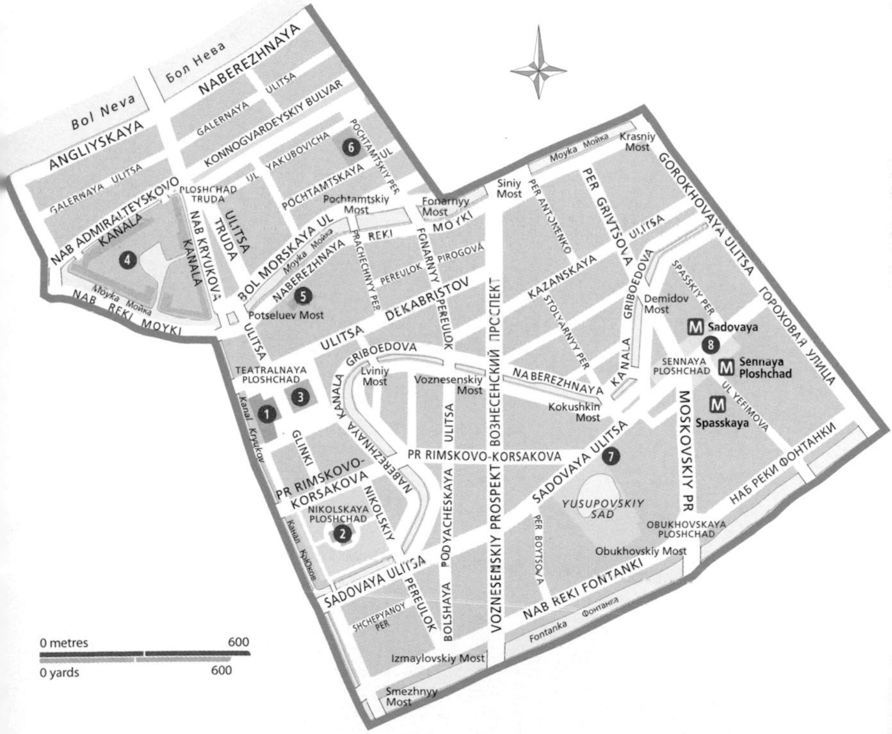

◀ Intricate mosaicked wall, interior of Yusupov Palace

For map symbols *see back flap*

Street-by-Street: Theatre Square

Known as Carousel Square till the 1780s, Theatre Square was frequently used as the site for fairs and festivals. During the 19th century when St Petersburg became the cultural capital of Russia, the Mariinskiy Theatre and Rimsky-Korsakov Conservatory were established and the neighbourhood became home to many artists. Today, the tradition of entertainment is still thriving and Theatre Square remains a focal point for theatrical and musical life. Nearby, the tree-lined canal embankments and the gardens surrounding the beautiful St Nicholas's Cathedral are enchanting places to explore.

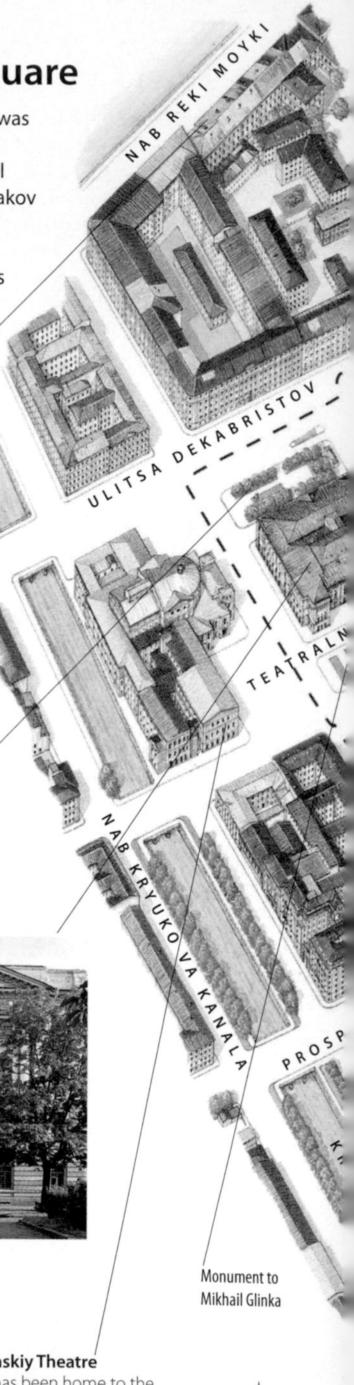

5 Yusupov Palace
Historic site of the gruesome murder of Rasputin, this grand palace belonged to the wealthy Yusupov family. Its opulent interiors include an Italian marble staircase and a tiny Rococo theatre.

Mariinsky Concert Hall

The monument to Rimsky-Korsakov, who taught at the Conservatory for 37 years, was designed by Veniamin Bogolyubov and Vladimir Ingal and erected here in 1952.

3 Rimsky-Korsakov Conservatory
Tchaikovsky, Prokofiev and Shostakovich were among the talents nurtured by Russia's first conservatory, founded in 1862 by pianist and composer Anton Rubinstein.

Monument to Mikhail Glinka

1 ★ Mariinskiy Theatre
This theatre has been home to the world-famous Mariinskiy (Kirov) Opera and Ballet Company since 1860. Hidden behind its imposing façade is the sumptuous auditorium where many of Russia's greatest dancers have performed.

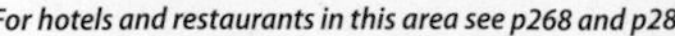

For hotels and restaurants in this area see p268 and p286

The Lion Bridge
This bridge is one of a number of quaint suspension bridges on the tree-lined Griboedov Canal. They are well-known meeting places, notably for romantic trysts.

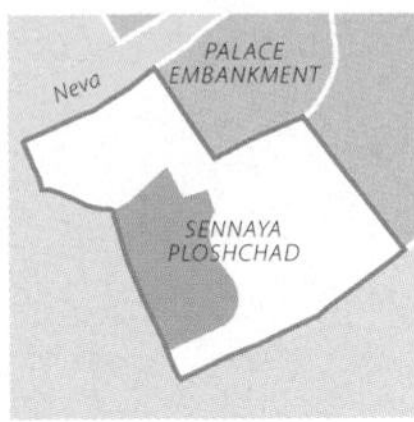

Area illustrated

The House of Mikhail Fokin at No. 109 is where the renowned ballet master and choreographer lived before the Revolution.

The Benois House belonged to an artistic dynasty that included the co-founder of the World of Art movement, Alexandre Benois.

The Belfry, an elegant four-tiered structure with a gilded spire, was built to mark the main entrance to St Nicholas's Cathedral.

2 St Nicholas's Cathedral
A fine example of 18th-century Russian Baroque, the lofty upper church is richly decorated with icons, gilding and this carved iconostasis. The lower church, beautifully lit with candles, is also open for worship.

The Former Nicholas Market
Characterized by its long arcade and steep roof, this building was constructed in 1788–9. In the 19th century, it became an unofficial labour exchange and many unemployed workers gathered here.

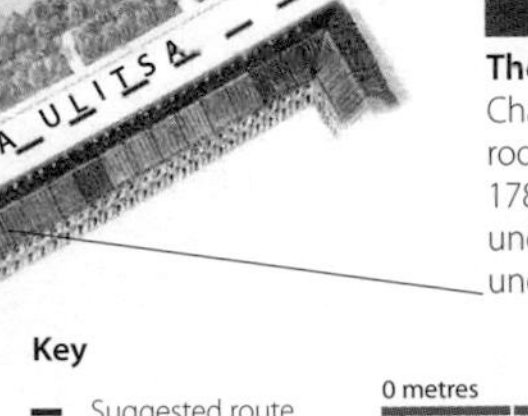

Key

Suggested route

0 metres 100

0 yards 100

The ornately decorated royal box in the Mariinskiy Theatre

❶ Mariinskiy Theatre

Мариинский театр

Mariinskiy teatr

Teatralnaya ploshchad 1 & ulitsa Dekabristov 37. **Map** 3 B3. **Tel** (812) 346 41 41. 2, 3, 6, 22, 27, 71, K-1, K-2, K-62, K-124, K-154, K-169, K-186, K-350. 5, 22. **Open** for performances. **mariinsky.ru**

Named in honour of Tsarina Maria Alexandrovna, wife of Alexander II, the Mariinskiy Theatre is still known abroad by its Soviet title, the Kirov, despite having reverted to its original name. A concert hall opened here in 2007 with plans to add more stages.

The building was erected in 1860 by the architect Albert Kavos, who designed the Bolshoi Theatre *(see pp82–3)* in Moscow. It stands on the site of an earlier theatre that was destroyed by fire. The Neo-Renaissance façade was remodelled by Viktor Schröter in 1883–96, who added a lot of ornamental detail to the exterior.

The pale blue-and-gold auditorium, where so many illustrious dancers have made their debut, creates a dazzling impression. Its architectural design comprising columns, atlantes, cherubs and cameo medallions has remained unchanged since the theatre's completion, and the imperial eagles have been restored to the royal box. The painting of dancing girls and cupids on the ceiling by Enrico Franchioli dates from around 1856, while the superb stage curtain was added during Russian ballet's golden age in 1914. Equally remarkable is the festive foyer, decorated with fluted pilasters, bas-reliefs of Russian composers and mirrored doors.

Imperial eagle on the royal box

Although the Mariinskiy Theatre is better known abroad for its ballet company, it is also one of the country's leading opera houses. Most of the great 19th-century Russian operas premiered here, including Mussorgsky's *Boris Godunov* (1874), Tchaikovsky's *Queen of Spades* (1890) and Shostakovich's controversial opera *Lady Macbeth of Mtsensk* (1934).

❷ St Nicholas's Cathedral

Никольский собор

Nikolskiy sobor

Nikolskaya ploshchad 1/3. **Map** 3 B4. **Tel** (812) 714 08 62. 2, 3, 22, 27, 49, 71, 181, K-2, K-19, K-154, K-212. **Open** 7am–7pm daily.

This stunning Baroque cathedral was built in 1753–62 by Savva Chevakinsky, one of Russia's great 18th-century architects. Founded for sailors and Admiralty employees housed in the neighbourhood, and named after St Nicholas, the patron saint of sailors, the cathedral came to be known as the "Sailors' Church".

The magnificent exterior is decorated with white Corinthian pilasters and surmounted by five gilded cupolas. Nearby, within the cathedral's leafy grounds and overlooking the intersection of the Kryukov and Griboedov canals, is a slender, four-tiered bell tower crowned by a spire.

Pale blue-and-white Baroque façade of St Nicholas's Cathedral

Following the Russian tradition, there are two churches within the cathedral. The lower church, intended for daily use, is lit by icon lamps, candles and chandeliers, creating a magical effect. Painted in 1755–7, the icons are the work of the brothers Fedot and Menas Kolokolnikov.

In total contrast, the upper church, used mainly on Sundays and for weddings, has a brighter, more airy feel and a typically Baroque exuberance, with gilt and stucco ornamentation and Italianate paintings. Its most impressive feature is the magnificent gilded iconostasis dating from 1755–60.

❸ Rimsky-Korsakov Conservatory

Консерватория Римского-Корсакова

Konservatoriya imeni Rimskovo-Korsakovu

Teatralnaya ploshchad 3. **Map** 3 B3. **Tel** (812) 571 85 74. 2, 3, 6, 22, 27, 71, K-1, K-2, K-62, K-124, K-154, K-169, K-186, K-350. 5, 22. **Open** for performances only. by appointment, call (812) 312 25 07.

Russia's oldest music school, the Rimsky-Korsakov Conservatory was founded in 1862 by Anton Rubinstein. The present building was designed in 1896 by Vladimir Nicolas.

Among those to graduate from the school before the Revolution were Pyotr Tchaikovsky *(see p115)* and Sergei Prokofiev. In the Soviet years, the school continued to flourish, and the greatest musical figure to emerge from this era was composer Dmitri Shostakovich (1906–75).

In the forecourt outside the school are two statues. On the left, a 1952 memorial honours the school's influential teacher, Nikolai Rimsky-Korsakov, after whom the conservatory is now named. On the right, the statue of Mikhail Glinka by Robert Bach is a reminder that the conservatory stands on the site where Russia's first opera, Glinka's *A Life for the Tsar*, was premiered in 1836 in the old Kamennyy (Stone) Theatre.

Vallin de la Mothe's impressive arch on the Moyka, leading into New Holland

❹ New Holland

Новая Голландия

Novaya Gollandiya

Admiral Teyskovo kanala 2. **Map** 3 A2. 3, 6, 22, 27, 70, 100, K-169, K-350. **Open** 11am–10pm Mon–Thu (till 11pm Fri–Sun).

Created when the Kryukov canal was constructed between the Moyka and Neva rivers in 1719, this island was originally used for storing flammable ship timber. It is named after Dutch shipbuilders who inspired Peter the Great's naval ambitions.

In 1765, the original wooden warehouses were rebuilt in redbrick by Savva Chevakinsky, while Vallin de la Mothe designed an austere but impressive arch facing the Moyka. Barges would pass through the arch and into a turning basin beyond, then return loaded with timber along the canals towards the Admiralty shipyards. A cultural complex is now open to visitors after years of reconstruction.

Russian Ballet

Admired throughout the world, Russian ballet traces its origins back to 1738 when a French dancing master, Jean-Baptiste Landé, established a school in St Petersburg to train the children of palace employees. The Imperial Ballet School, as it soon became known, flourished under a string of distinguished foreign teachers, culminating in Marius Petipa. Petipa first joined the school in 1847 as a principal dancer, and later choreographed over 60 ballets.

Vera Fokina and Mikhail Fokin in a production of *Scheherazade*

Following the 1905 Revolution, a reaction against Classicism led to numerous defections from the imperial theatres to Sergei Diaghilev's Ballets Russes, which took Europe by storm in 1909. Diaghilev's vision of a spectacle that would fuse music, ballet and decor in a seamless whole was shared by the choreographer Mikhail Fokin, and such talented costume and set designers as Léon Bakst and Alexandre Benois.

After the Bolsheviks seized power in 1917 many artists went into exile abroad. Fortunately for Soviet Russia, the prima ballerina Agrippina Vaganova remained to train the next generation of dancers. St Petersburg's Russian Ballet Academy now bears her name.

5 Yusupov Palace

Юсуповский дворец

Yusupovskiy dvorets

Naberezhnaya Reki Moyki 94. **Map** 3 B2. **Tel** (812) 314 98 83. 3, 22, 27. **Open** 11am–5pm daily. guided tours only. English. **yusupov-palace.ru**

Overlooking the Moyka river, this yellow, colonnaded building dating from the 1760s was designed by Vallin de la Mothe. The palace was acquired in 1830 by the Yusupov family to house their collection of paintings. Four generations of Yusupovs have lived here and, with the help of architects such as Andrei Mikhailov, Ippolito Monighetti and Andrei Vaitens, added their personal styles to the interiors.

The palace and its ceremonial rooms can be viewed by guided or audio tour. Notable rooms include the Moorish Room, with its fountain, mosaics and arches and the Turkish Study, built at the same time for Prince Nikolai Yusupov. His father, Prince Boris, commissioned the ballroom, and a Rococo-style family theatre that seats just 180. Today, it is a wonderful venue for concerts. Separate tickets are needed for the tour of the cellars, which house an exhibition on Grigori Rasputin, the infamous "holy man" who was murdered here by Prince Felix Yusupov.

6 Main Post Office

Главпочтамт

Glavpochtamt

Pochtamtskaya ulitsa 9. **Map** 3 B2. **Tel** (812) 314 23 71. 3, 22, 27, 70, 100, K-169, K-187, K-306. 5, 22. **Open** 24 hrs daily.

The main exterior feature of this building is the arched gallery spanning Pochtamtskaya ulitsa. Built as an extension to architect Nikolai Lvov's main building, the gallery was added by Albert Kavos in 1859. Under the "Pochtamt" (Post Office) sign on the arch is a clock showing the time in major cities around the world.

Inside the post office, behind Lvov's porticoed Neo-Classical façade built in 1782–9, is a splendid Style-Moderne hall. It is characterized by decorative ironwork and a glass ceiling over the vast, tiled floor space. The hall was created in the early 20th century when a roof was constructed over what had originally been the courtyard stables.

Porticoed façade and arched gallery, Main Post Office

The Grim Death of Rasputin

The Siberian peasant and mystic Grigori Rasputin (1869–1916) exercised an extraordinarily powerful influence over the court and government of Russia. The mysterious circumstances of his dramatic death on 17 December 1916 are legendary. Lured to Yusupov's palace on the pretext of a party, Rasputin was poisoned, then shot by Prince Felix Yusupov and left for dead. On returning to the scene, the prince found Rasputin still alive and a struggle ensued before Rasputin fled into the courtyard. He was pursued by the conspirators, shot another three times and brutally battered before being dumped in the Neva river. His corpse was found three days later, clinging to the supports of a bridge. Water in his lungs indicated death by drowning.

Islamic arches and coffered ceiling in the Moorish Room, Yusupov Palace

For hotels and restaurants in this area see p268 and p286

7 Railway Museum

Музей железнодорожного транспорта

Muzey zheleznodorozhnovo transporta

Sadovaya ulitsa 50. **Map** 3 C3. **Tel** (812) 315 14 76. M Sennaya ploshchad, Sadovaya, Spasskaya. **Open** 11am–5pm Sun–Thu. **Closed** last Thu of the month. English.

This museum houses more than 6,000 exhibits that illustrate the history of the Russian railway system since 1813. The most interesting sections of the museum deal with the earliest railways, including Russia's first railway line from Tsarskoe Selo *(see pp188–9)* to St Petersburg, which began running in 1837, and the 650-km (404-mile) line from Moscow to St Petersburg, which began operating in 1851.

Exhibits include models of the first Russian steam engine, built by the Cherepanovs in 1834, and an armoured train used in the defence of the city during the Civil War. The walk-through section of a first-class sleeping compartment offers an insight into luxury travel in the late Tsarist period. The compartment is furnished with Style-Moderne decoration.

Model of 1830s engine for the Tsarskoe Selo railway, Railway Museum

8 Sennaya Ploshchad

Сенная площадь

Sennaya ploshchad

Map 4 D3. M Sennaya Ploshchad, Sadovaya, Spasskaya.

One of the oldest squares in St Petersburg, Sennaya Ploshchad, meaning Haymarket, derives from the original market that opened here in the 1730s, where livestock, fodder and firewood were sold. A 10-minute stroll from Nevskiy prospekt, the area around the square was inhabited by the poor and the market was the cheapest and liveliest in the city. The oldest building at the centre of the square is the former guard-house. A Neo-Classical structure with a columned portico, it dates from 1818. By that time the neighbourhood had become synonymous with dirt, squalor, crime and vice. The guards' duties ranged from supervising traders to flogging serfs for misdemeanours. At No. 3 is the site of Vyazemskiy's Monastery, the nickname for a notorious tenement overrun with pubs, gambling dens and brothels in the 1850s and 1860s.

This was the squalid world so vividly evoked in Fyodor Dostoevsky's masterpiece *Crime and Punishment*. As the contemptuous hero of the novel, Raskolnikov, wanders around the market, he absorbs the "heat in the street… the airlessness, the bustle and the plaster, scaffolding, bricks and dust… that special St Petersburg stench… and the numerous drunken men" which "completed the revolting misery of the picture". The novel was completed in 1866 while Dostoevsky was living at Alonkin's House at No. 7 Przhevalskovo ulitsa to the west of the square.

During the Soviet era, the square was given a new image, stallholders were banished, trees were planted and it was optimistically renamed Peace Square (ploshchad Mira). The five-storey, yellow-and-white apartment blocks that surround the square today were also built then, in Stalin's version of Neo-Classicism. Sadly, in 1961, the square's most attractive monument, the Church of the Assumption, was pulled down to make way for one of the city's earliest metro stations. Today, there are numerous fast-food stalls and all-night shops here.

Fyodor Dostoevsky

One of Russia's greatest writers, Fyodor Dostoevsky was born in 1821 in Moscow but spent most of his adult life in St Petersburg, where many of his novels and short stories are set. A defining moment in his life occurred in 1849 when he was arrested and charged with revolutionary conspiracy. After eight months' solitary confinement in the Peter and Paul Fortress *(see pp136–7)*, Dostoevsky and 21 other "conspirators" from the socialist Petrashevsky Circle were subjected to a macabre mock execution before being exiled to hard labour in Siberia until 1859. The experience turned him from a socialist into an ardent supporter of autocracy and Orthodoxy. Unfortunately for him, the police continued to regard him as a subversive. He died of tuberculosis in 1881.

FURTHER AFIELD

While the majority of St Petersburg's sights are centrally located, the outlying areas of the city have a number of places of architectural, cultural and historical importance. To the east is the Smolnyy district, taking its name from the tar yard that supplied the city's ship-building industry in the 18th century. The highlight of this area is the dazzling Baroque Smolnyy Convent. Designed by Bartolomeo Rastrelli, the convent is a brilliant amalgamation of Western and Russian Baroque styles. Part of the same architectural complex, the Smolnyy Institute is famed for its historic role as the headquarters of the Bolshevik movement during the October Revolution. Southeast of the centre lies the Alexander Nevsky Monastery where many of Russia's celebrated artists, architects and composers are buried. The southern suburbs offer a different perspective of the city with rows of imperious-looking houses dating from the 1930s – a legacy of Stalin's urban planning. Other intriguing sights in the south are the stunning Chesma Church and the Victory Monument, a memorial to the victims of the Siege of Leningrad.

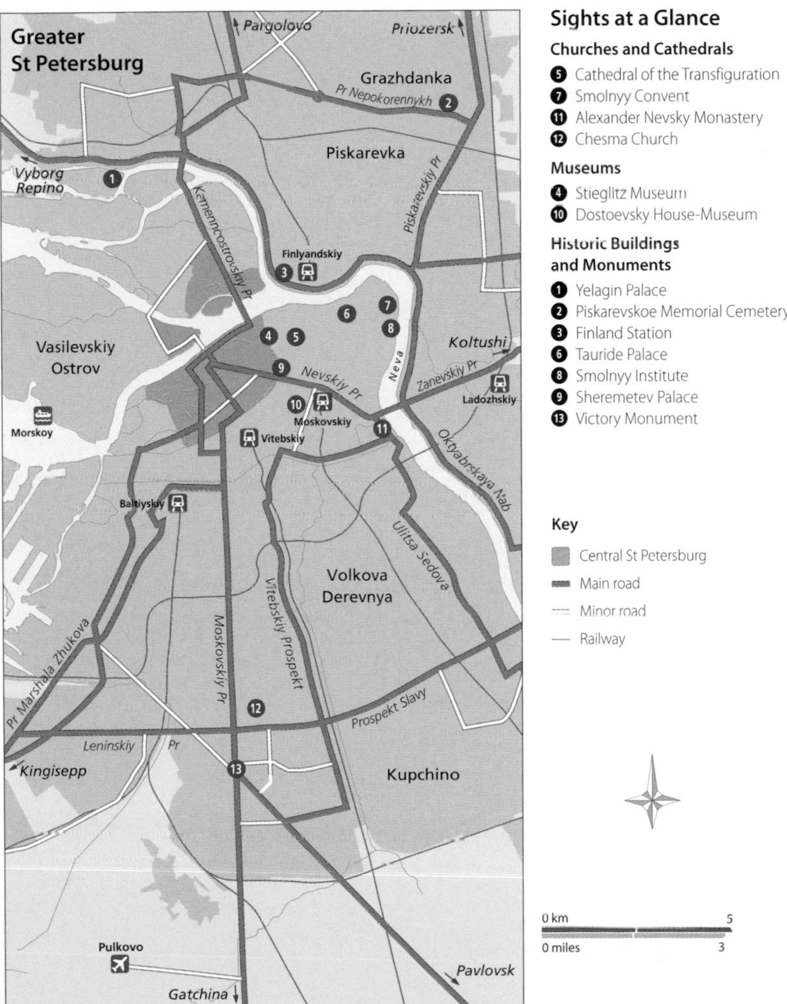

◀ Snow-covered monastic buildings, Alexander Nevsky Monastery

For map symbols *see back flap*

The Neo-Classical Yelagin Palace and its spacious grounds, designed by Carlo Rossi

❶ Yelagin Palace

Елагин дворец

Yelagin dvorets

Yelagin ostrov 1. **Tel** (812) 430 11 31. Ⓜ Krestovskiy ostrov. **Open** 10am–6pm Tue–Sun. **Closed** last Tue of month. ground floor.

One of the northernmost islands of St Petersburg, Yelagin Island is named after a court official who built a palace here at the end of the 18th century. Alexander I then bought the island in 1817 for his mother, Maria Fyodorovna, and commissioned Carlo Rossi to rebuild the palace. The magnificent Neo-Classical edifice, constructed in 1818–22, is part of an ensemble that includes an orangery, a horseshoe-shaped stable block and porticoed kitchens.

The palace interior was destroyed by fire during World War II but has now been restored to its former glory. The Oval Hall is resplendent with statuary and *trompe l'oeils* while the rooms leading from it are exquisitely decorated with stucco, *faux marbre* (false marble) and painted friezes, executed by gifted artists and craftsmen.

In the Soviet era, the island became the Central Park of Culture and Rest. Today, it is a venue for festivals and public entertainment, and there is an exhibition of decorative art in the palace's former stables.

Statue of Mother Russia at the Piskarevskoe Memorial Cemetery

❷ Piskarevskoe Memorial Cemetery

Пискаревское мемориальное кладбище

Piskarevskoe memorialnoe kladbishche

Prospekt Nepokorennykh 72–74. **Tel** (812) 297 57 16. 80, 123, 138, 178. Ⓜ Akademicheskaya. **Open** 24 hrs daily. Memorial Halls: **Open** 10am–6pm daily.

This vast, bleak cemetery is a memorial to the two million people who died during the Siege of Leningrad *(see p45)*. With little food and no electricity, water or heating, the citizens of Leningrad perished from starvation, cold and disease. Corpses were dragged on sledges to collection points from where they were taken for burial to mass cemeteries on the outskirts of town. Piskarevskoe was the largest, with 490,000 burials.

Today, the cemetery is a place of pilgrimage. The memorial complex opened in 1960, on the 15th anniversary of the end of the war. Two memorial halls, one of which contains an exhibition on the siege, flank the stairs down to a 300-m (984-ft) long avenue, which culminates in a towering, heroic bronze statue of Mother Russia. On the wall behind are verses composed by Olga Bergholts – a survivor of the siege. The funereal music broadcast over the whole cemetery adds to the sombre atmosphere.

On either side of the avenue are 186 grassy mounds, each with a granite slab marking the year and indicating, with a red star or hammer and sickle, whether those interred were soldiers or civilians.

❸ Finland Station

Финляндский вокзал

Finlyandskiy vokzal

Ploshchad Lenina 6. Ⓜ Ploshchad Lenina.

On the night of 3 April 1917, the exiled Vladimir Lenin and his Bolshevik companions arrived at Finland Station after travelling from Switzerland on a sealed train. A triumphant reception awaited them, and on leaving the station, Lenin spoke to cheering crowds from the turret of an armoured car. A statue erected outside the station in 1926 depicts Lenin delivering his speech.

The modern terminal at Finland Station was opened in the 1960s. On platform 5 there is a huge glass case containing Locomotive 293 in which Lenin fled the capital for a second time in July 1917, disguised as an engine stoker. After spending the summer as a fugitive in Russian Finland, Lenin returned on the same train and spurred on the October Revolution.

❹ Stieglitz Museum

Музей Штиглица

Muzey Shtiglitsa

Solyanoy pereulok 13–15. **Tel** (812) 273 32 58. 46, K-76, K-100, K-217. **Open** Sep–Jul: 11am–4:30pm Tue–Sat. **Closed** last Fri of month.

The millionaire industrialist Baron Aleksandr Stieglitz founded the Central School of Industrial Design in 1876. His aim was to provide a top quality collection of original works for the use of Russian students of applied arts and design.

With a large budget and the good taste of Stieglitz's son-in-law, the collection soon outgrew the school and in 1896 a Museum of Applied Arts opened next door. This building, designed by Maximilian Messmacher, was inspired by Italian Renaissance palaces. Inside, the halls and galleries were decorated in a variety of national and period styles, echoing French and German Baroque and Italian Renaissance monuments, such as St Mark's Library in Venice and the Raphael Loggias of the Vatican.

Situated on the ground floor, the exhibition features opulent displays of glassware, ceramics and majolica, as well as porcelain from all the great European manufacturers. One room, decorated in the style of the medieval Terem Palace *(see p60)* in the Kremlin, provides a superb backdrop for a collection of embroidered dresses and headgear made by Russian peasant women. The workmanship seen on the wooden furniture is breathtaking. A Neo-Gothic cabinet with finely inlaid doors, depicting church naves in perspective, opens to reveal sculpted biblical scenes.

A last look at the Grand Exhibition Hall with its curving staircase of Italian marble and magnificent glass roof is a fine way to end the visit.

Dolls in 17th–19th-century Russian folk costumes, Stieglitz Museum

❺ Cathedral of the Transfiguration

Спасо-Преображенский собор

Spaso-Preobrazhenskiy sobor

Preobrazhenskaya ploshchad 1. **Tel** (812) 579 60 10. 46, K-46, K-76, K-90, K-177, K-258. M Chernyshevskaya. **Open** 8am–8pm daily.

Despite its monumental Neo-Classicism and the surrounding fence made of guns captured during the Russo Turkish wars, Vasiliy Stasov's church has an intimate air, nestled in its leafy square. The original church on this site was built by Tsarina Elizabeth to honour the Preobrazhenskiy Guards, but it was rebuilt after a fire in 1825. Today, the church is famous for its excellent choir – second only to that in the Alexander Nevsky Monastery *(see p183)*.

Tauride Palace nestled among abundant gardens on the banks of a quiet lake

❻ Tauride Palace

Таврический дворец

Tavricheskiy dvorets

Shpalernaya ulitsa 47. M Chernyshevskaya. 46, 136. **Closed** to public.

This finely proportioned palace by Ivan Starov was built in 1783–9 as a present from Catherine the Great to her influential lover Prince Grigori Potemkin. Having successfully annexed the Crimea (Tauris) to Russia in 1783, Potemkin was given the title of Prince of Tauris, hence the palace's name. The building, with its austere yellow façade and distinctive six-columned portico, was one of Russia's first Neo-Classical structures.

Despite its magnificent interiors having been ruined by Catherine's son, Paul, who turned the palace into barracks after 1799, it went on to play a vital role in 20th-century political life. After the 1905 Revolution forced Tsar Nicholas II to permit a Russian parliament, or State Duma, the palace became the seat of parliament. Following the overthrow of the monarchy after the February Revolution of 1917, it became the headquarters of the Provisional Government, and later, the Petrograd Soviet of Workers' and Soldiers' Deputies, in 1918. Today, it is still a government building.

The palace's gardens, with winding streams, bridges and an artificial lake, are among the city's most popular parks.

Façade of the cathedral with adjacent buildings, Smolnyy Convent complex

7 Smolnyy Convent

Смольный монастырь

Smolnyy monastyr

Ploshchad Rastrelli 3/1. **Tel** (812) 710 31 59. 46, 136. **Open** May–Sep: 10am–7pm Thu–Tue; Sep–Apr: 11am–7pm Thu–Tue. English.

In 1748, Tsarina Elizabeth commissioned Bartolomeo Rastrelli to design a convent for the education of young noblewomen. He conceived a brilliant fusion of Russian and Western Baroque styles and incorporated it into the design of this architectural ensemble, whose centrepiece is the stunning cathedral. Work advanced very slowly; 50,000 wooden piles had to be sunk into the marshy soil before construction could begin.

When Catherine the Great came to power in 1762, funding stopped, and it was only in 1835 that Nicholas I commissioned Vasiliy Stasov to complete the cathedral. His austere white interior contrasts dramatically with the florid exterior.

Exhibitions and weekly concerts are now held here.

8 Smolnyy Institute

Смольный Институт

Smolnyy Institut

Smolnyy proezd 1. **Tel** (812) 710 31 59, (812) 710 31 43. 46, 54, 74, 136, K-15, K-76, K-136. 5, 7, 11, 15, 16. Smolnyy Museum: **Open** 11am–4pm Mon–Fri, by appointment only. English.

As the school for noblewomen outgrew its premises at the Smolnyy Convent, Giacomo Quarenghi built an adjacent Neo-Classical structure in 1806–8, which came to be known as the Smolnyy Institute.

It was from here, in October 1917, that Lenin directed the Bolshevik coup d'état against the Provisional Government. The Smolnyy Institute remained Lenin's seat of government until March 1918, after which it became the headquarters of the Leningrad Communist Party. On 1 December 1934, the First Secretary of the party, Sergei Kirov *(see p141)* was murdered here, providing the pretext for Stalin's great purges *(see p45)*.

The rooms where Lenin lived and worked can be viewed by appointment. The rest of the institute is now the Mayor's Office. The imperial eagle has replaced the hammer and sickle, but the statue of Lenin has survived.

Painting of Vladimir Lenin, Smolnyy Institute Assembly Hall

9 Sheremetev Palace

Шереметевский дворец

Sheremetevskiy dvorets

Naberezhnaya Reki Fontanki 34. 15, 22, 27, K-15, K-90, K-187, K-258. Mayakovskaya, Gostinyy Dvor. 1, 5, 7, 10, 22. Museum of Musical Life: **Tel** (812) 272 44 41. **Open** 11am–7pm Wed–Mon. **Closed** last Wed of the month. Anna Akhmatova Museum: **Tel** (812) 579 72 39. **Open** 10:30am–6:30pm Tue–Sun. English.

Also known as the "Fountain House" after the fountains that once adorned its grounds, this palace was the home of the Sheremetev family from 1712 until the Revolution. The family were great artistic patrons, and the palace is now home to the **Museum of Musical Life**. Exhibits include period instruments and several scores, some composed by the Sheremetevs themselves.

The great poetess Anna Akhmatova (1889–1966) lived in one of the service blocks from 1933 to 1941 and then between 1944 and 1954. Her flat is now the **Anna Akhmatova Museum** and is reached through the courtyard of No. 53 Liteynyy prospekt. Visitors can see some of her personal possessions, and listen to recordings of the poetess reading her poems. Her most famous poem, *Requiem*, relating her experiences during the purges when both her son and her lover were arrested, was written in fragments in 1935–61 and distributed among friends.

10 Dostoevsky House-Museum

Музей Достоевского

Muzey Dostoevskovo

Kuznechnyy pereulok 5/2. **Tel** (812) 571 40 31. Vladimirskaya. 49. **Open** 11am–6pm Tue–Sun. English.

This evocative museum was the final home of Russian author Fyodor Dostoevsky, who lived here from 1878 until his death in 1881. It was here that he completed his last great novel, *The Brothers Karamazov*, in 1880. Although his public image was dour and humourless, he was a devoted and affectionate husband and father. The delightful nursery contains a rocking horse, silhouettes of his children and the book of fairy tales that he read aloud to them. In Dostoevsky's study are his writing desk and a reproduction of his favourite painting, Raphael's *Sistine Madonna*.

⓫ Alexander Nevsky Monastery

Александро-Невская лавра

Aleksandro-Nevskaya lavra

Ploshchad Aleksandra Nevskovo. **Tel** (812) 274 17 02. 8, 27, 46, 55, 58, 191, K-156, K-187, K-209. Ⓜ Ploshchad Aleksandra Nevskovo. 1, 14, 16, 22. 7, 65. Church of the Annunciation: **Tel** (812) 274 17 02. **Open** 9:30am– 5pm Tue, Wed & Fri–Sun (till 6pm in summer). Holy Trinity Cathedral: **Open** 6am–8pm daily. Cemeteries & Church of the Annunciation:

Founded by Peter the Great in 1710, this monastery is named after Prince Alexander Nevsky of Novgorod, who defeated the Swedes in 1240. From the entrance, a path runs between two walled cemeteries into the monastic complex. Many leading cultural figures are buried in these cemeteries. The Lazarus Cemetery, to the east, contains the graves of the polymath Mikhail Lomonosov and Carlo Rossi *(see p167)*. Clustered together along the northern wall of the Tikhvin Cemetery, to the west, are the tombs of some of Russia's most famous composers; many of the tombs

Reliquary with Alexander Nevsky's remains, Holy Trinity Cathedral

are inscribed with musical motifs. Fyodor Dostoevsky is buried here, to the right of the entrance.

The oldest building in the monastery complex is the **Church of the Annunciation**, built in 1717–25. Non-ruling members of the royal family are buried here. However, the Neo Classical **Holy Trinity Cathedral**, constructed in 1776–90 by Ivan Starov, dominates the complex. To the right of the iconostasis is a silver reliquary containing the remains of Alexander Nevsky, who has been venerated as a saint in Russia since the mid-16th century.

⓬ Chesma Church

Чесменская церковь

Chesmenskaya tserkov

Ulitsa Lensoveta 12. 16, 34, 50, 64. Ⓜ Moskovskaya. **Open** 10am–7pm.

There is hardly anything Russian about the Chesma Church built by Yuri Velten in 1777–80. Its "pastry Gothic" façade is decorated with vertical stripes which direct the eye upwards to its zig-zagged crown and cupolas. The name commemorates the Russian naval victory over the Turks at Chesma in the Aegean in 1770.

Across the street is the Chesma Palace that served as a staging post for Catherine the Great en route to Tsarskoe Selo *(see pp188–9)*. Rasputin's body lay in state here after his murder. The palace now serves as a home for the elderly.

⓭ Victory Monument

Монумент Защитникам Ленинграда

Monument Zashchitnikam Leningrada

Ploshchad Pobedy. **Tel** (812) 371 29 51, (812) 373 65 63. 3, 11, 13, 39, 59, 90, 150, 187, K-13, K-100, K-350. Ⓜ Moskovskaya. 27, 29, 45. Memorial Hall: **Open** 11am–6pm Thu & Sat–Mon (till 5pm Tue & Wed). **Closed** last Tue of the month. book by phone.

Erected in 1975 to coincide with the 30th anniversary of the end of World War II, this monument commemorates the victims of the Siege of Leningrad. A red granite obelisk rises beside a circular enclosure, which symbolizes the grip of the siege, fronted by statues of soldiers, nurses and grieving mothers.

An underpass leads to the subterranean **Memorial Hall**, where solemn music gives way to the beat of a metronome, the wartime radio signal that represented the city's heartbeat. Among the artifacts on display is a morsel of bread, which was many people's daily ration.

The vertically-striped façade of the Chesma Church, designed by Yuri Velten

BEYOND ST PETERSBURG

Before St Petersburg was founded in 1703, the surrounding landscape was a marshy, inhospitable wilderness. When Russia was victorious in the Great Northern War, Peter the Great celebrated by building a summer residence on the shore of the Gulf of Finland. Known as the "Russian Versailles", Peterhof is dominated by water; the Gulf and the fountains mirror Peter's maritime interest. Yet, the Great Palace remains the centrepiece of the estate and owes much of its opulence to Peter's daughter, Tsarina Elizabeth, who commissioned Bartolomeo Rastrelli to redecorate its interiors. Wilfully extravagant, she also created her own stunning residence at Tsarskoe Selo, with a Baroque palace for hosting legendary costume balls. Her successor Catherine the Great added private apartments and secluded pavilions to the palace. Catherine's son Paul had his own estate at Pavlovsk, not far away, but due to his untimely death its Neo-Classical decor largely reflected the tastes of his wife, Maria Fyodorovna, who outlived him by 28 years. These magnificent palaces suffered extensive damage during World War II, and it has taken 50 years of painstaking restoration to return them to their former glory. All three sights are easily accessible from the city, on organized excursions or by public transport.

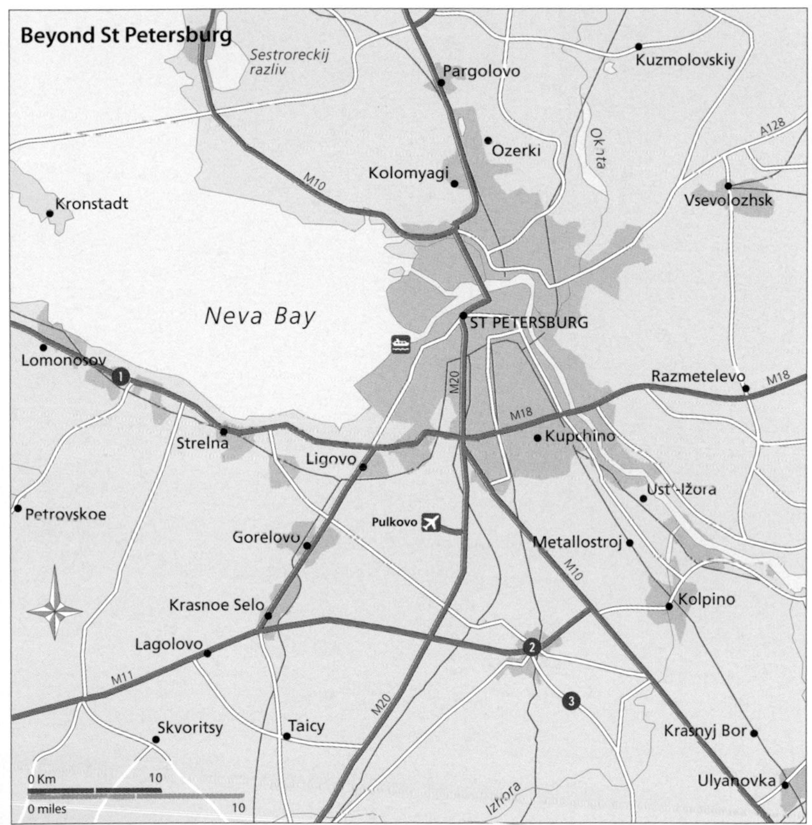

Sights at a Glance

Palaces

1. Peterhof
2. Tsarskoe Selo
3. Pavlovsk

Key

- Main road
- Minor road
- Railway

◀ The famous Visconti bridge over the Slavyanka river, Pavlovsk

For map symbols *see back flap*

❶ Peterhof

Петергоф

Petergof

With its commanding views of the Baltic, Peterhof is a perfect expression of triumphalism. Originally designed by Jean Baptiste Le Blond in 1714–21, the Great Palace was transformed during the reign of Tsarina Elizabeth when Bartolomeo Rastrelli added a third storey and wings with pavilions at either end. He tried to preserve Le Blond's early Baroque exterior, but redesigned the interiors, which demonstrate his love for gilded Baroque decoration. Peterhof stands at the centre of a magnificent landscaped park, with both French and English gardens.

View from the palace of the Grand Cascade leading down to the Gulf of Finland

The Imperial Suite

Situated in the palace's eastern wing, the Imperial Suite comprises several rooms. Peter's Oak Study is one of the few rooms to have survived unaltered from Le Blond's design. Some of the oak panel motifs are originals by Nicholas Pineau, designed in 1718–21.

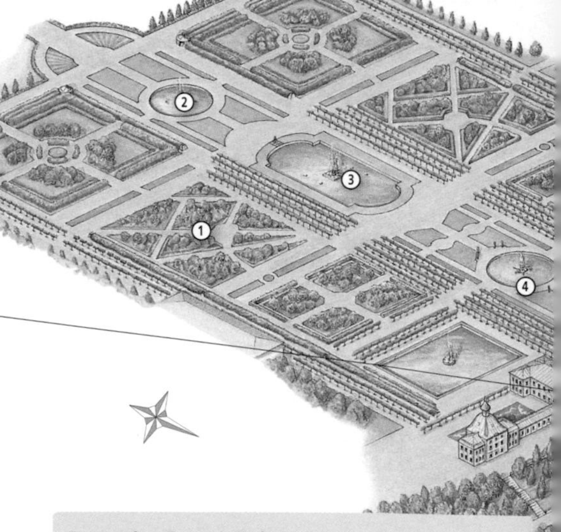

KEY

① **The Upper Gardens** are framed by borders and hedges and punctuated with ornamental ponds.

② **Mezheumnyy Fountain**

③ **Neptune Fountain**

④ **Oak Fountain**

⑤ **Samson Fountain**

⑥ **The Marine Canal** enabled the tsars to sail from the Gulf of Finland up to the Great Palace.

⑦ **Eve Fountain**

⑧ **Adam Fountain**

Peter the Great's Palace

After his victory over the Swedes at Poltava in 1709, Peter the Great decided to build a palace "befitting to the very highest of monarchs". A visit to Versailles in 1717 furthered Peter's ambitions and he employed more than 5,000 labourers, serfs and soldiers, supported by architects, water-engineers, landscape gardeners and sculptors. Work proceeded at a frenetic pace from 1714 until Peterhof was officially opened in 1723. Le Blond's Great Palace was completed in 1721 and has changed considerably over the decades. Catherine the Great commissioned Yuri Velten to redecorate some of Rastrelli's interiors in the 1770s, including the Throne Room and the Chesma Room.

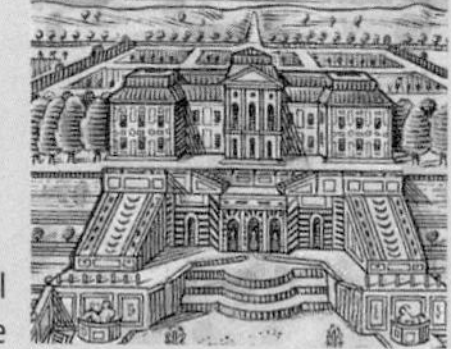

Jean Baptiste Le Blond's original two-storey Great Palace

★ **Main Staircase**
Caryatids and gilded carvings adorn Rastrelli's glittering staircase. The fresco on the ceiling depicts Aurora and Genius chasing away the night.

VISITORS' CHECKLIST

Practical information
Petrodvorets, 30 km (19 miles) W of St Petersburg.
Tel (812) 450 52 87.
Great Palace: **Open** 10:30am–5pm Tue–Sun. **Closed** last Tue of the month. Other Pavilions: **Open** May–Sep: 11am– 5pm Tue–Sun; Oct–Apr: 11am–5pm Sat & Sun. Fountains: **Open** May–early Oct: 10:30am–5pm.

Transport
from Baltiysky station to Novyy Petergof. Hermitage (May–Oct).

★ **State Rooms**
The highlight of the State Rooms is the opulent Throne Room, redesigned by Yuri Velten in 1770. The relatively restrained stucco ornamentation, red velvet hangings and parquet floor provide an exquisite setting for portraits of Russia's imperial family.

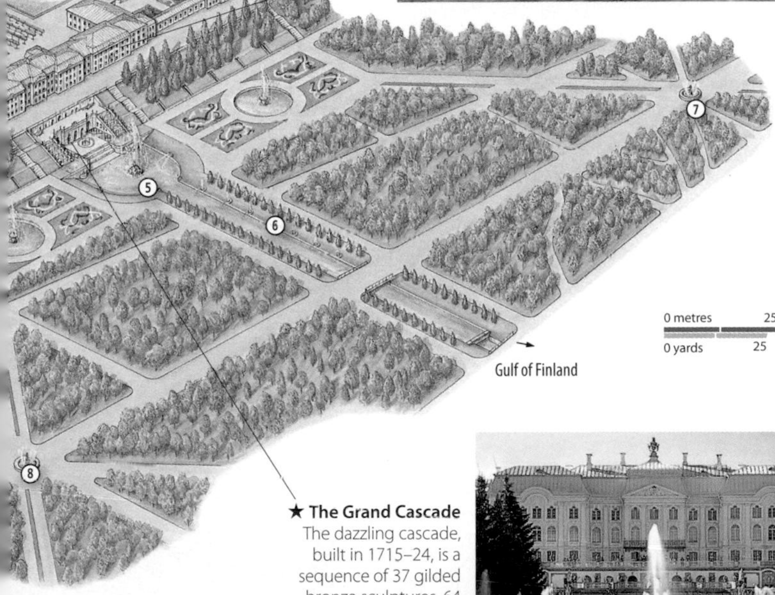

5
6
7
8

0 metres 25
0 yards 25

Gulf of Finland

★ **The Grand Cascade**
The dazzling cascade, built in 1715–24, is a sequence of 37 gilded bronze sculptures, 64 fountains and 142 water jets, descending from the terraces of the Great Palace to the Marine Canal and the sea.

❷ Tsarskoe Selo

Царское Село

Tsarskoe Selo

The imperial palace at Tsarskoe Selo was designed by Bartolomeo Rastrelli in 1752 for Tsarina Elizabeth. She named it the Catherine Palace in honour of her mother, Catherine I, who originally owned the estate. The next ruler to leave a mark on the palace was Catherine the Great, and during her reign she commissioned the Scotsman Charles Cameron to redesign the Baroque interiors according to her Neo-Classical taste. Cameron also designed a two-storey ensemble – as a summer pavilion – comprising the Agate Rooms, the Imperial Baths and the Cameron Gallery. The Amber Room, looted by the Nazis, has been reconstructed.

★ The Great Hall
Light streams into Rastrelli's glittering hall illuminating the mirrors, gilded carvings and the vast ceiling painting, *The Triumph of Russia* (around 1755), by Giuseppe Valeriani.

★ Atlantes
The stunning 300-m (980-ft) long Baroque façade is adorned with a profusion of atlantes, columns, pilasters and ornamented window framings.

The Cavaliers' Dining Room
The table is laid for Tsarina Elizabeth's gentlemen-in-waiting, in the refined gold-and-white room created by Rastrelli.

KEY

① **The Cameron Gallery** was part of Catherine's private apartments.

② **The Agate Rooms** are part of the Imperial Baths and faced with semi-precious stones from the Urals. (Temporarily closed)

③ **The Great Staircase**, designed by Ippolito Monighetti in 1860, leads to the state rooms on the first floor.

④ **Small Enfilade** are unrestored rooms that exhibit a varied selection of furniture and *objets d'art*. Chinese lacquer furniture and Oriental rugs were among the treasures used to furnish the palace in the 19th century.

⑤ **The Picture Gallery** displays canvases by Italian, French, Dutch and Flemish masters of the 17th and 18th centuries.

⑥ **The Royal Chapel** is decorated in dark blue and gold. Built by Chevakinskiy in the 1740s, it contains an elaborate six-tiered iconostasis.

⑦ **The French-style formal gardens** were laid out in the 1740s. Their formality and symmetry contrasts with the naturalistic English-style landscaping of the park, created in 1768.

For hotels and restaurants in this area see p269 and p288

★ **Amber Room**
The original amber panels by Andreas Schlüter, dating from 1709, were a gift from Friedrich Wilhelm I of Prussia to Peter the Great. The room has been recreated from photographs, with carved reliefs and panels in Florentine mosaic.

VISITORS' CHECKLIST

Practical information
Tsarskoe Selo, 25 km (16 miles) S of St Petersburg.
Palace: **Tel** (812) 465 20 24 **Open** 10am–6pm Wed–Mon, May–Sep: noon–2pm & 4–6pm only for individuals. **Closed** last Mon of the month.
Grounds: **Open** 7am–9pm daily.
May–Oct: 9am–6pm.
Agate Rooms & Cameron Gallery: **Closed** for renovation.

Transport
from Vitebskiy station to Detskoe Selo, then bus 371 or 382.

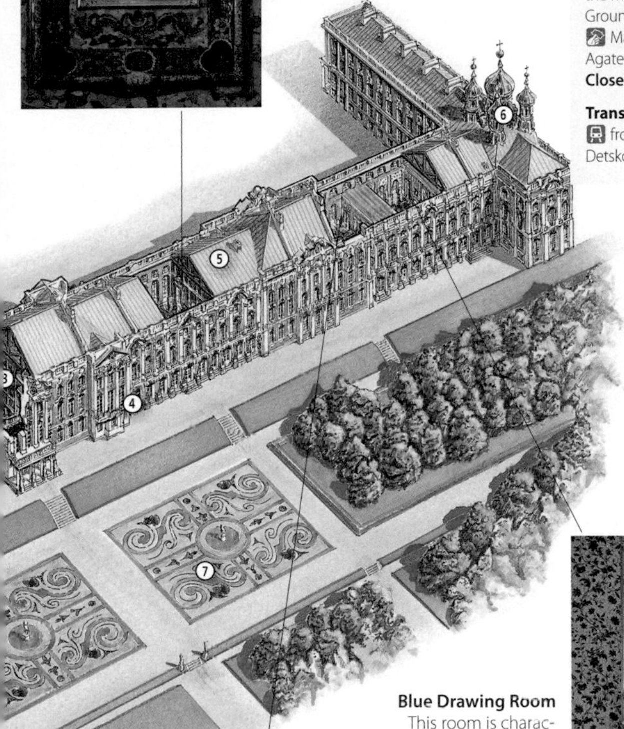

Blue Drawing Room
This room is characterized by blue floral motifs painted on silk. Among the royal portraits hanging here is a painting of Peter the Great by Ivan Nikitin, dating from around 1720.

★ **Green Dining Room**
Cameron's restrained Neo-Classical style contrasts with the Baroque flamboyance of Rastrelli's work. The exquisite stucco bas-reliefs, sculpted by Ivan Martos, were based on motifs from frescoes discovered in Pompeii.

❸ Pavlovsk

Павловск

Pavlovsk

To celebrate the birth of his heir, Grand Duke Paul was presented this land by Catherine the Great in 1777. She also "gave" him their favourite architect, Charles Cameron, to design both the palace and park. Work at Pavlovsk (from Pavel or Paul) began in 1780 and was continued by Paul's grieving widow, Maria Fyodorovna, long after his death. "English gardens" were at the height of fashion and inspired Cameron's design of a seemingly natural landscape dotted with pavilions (used for informal parties), romantic ruins and attractive vistas around the Slavyanka river.

The Apollo Colonnade
Cameron's colonnade, built in 1782–83, encircles a copy of the Apollo Belvedere above a romantically dilapidated cascade.

★ Pavlovsk Palace
Cameron's elegant Palladian mansion, built in 1782–6, forms the central block of today's palace, with wings added in 1789 by Paul's favoured architect, Vincenzo Brenna.

★ Temple of Friendship (1780)
This Doric temple was the first building to use the Greek form of architecture in Russia.

KEY

① **Cameron's Dairy** (1782) housed both a milking shed and a salon.

② **Aviary**

③ **Three Graces Pavilion**

④ **The Centaur Bridge** by Voronikhin (1805) nestles in a bend of the Slavyanka river.

⑤ **The Cold Baths** were built by Charles Cameron in 1799. This austere pavilion was used as a summer swimming pool, complete with an elegant vestibule, paintings, furniture and rich wall upholstery.

⑥ **Green Woman Alley**

⑦ **The Beautiful Valley** was the favourite spot of Elizabeth, wife of Alexander I.

⑧ **Paul's Mausoleum** bears the inscription "To my beneficient consort".

⑨ **The Rose Pavilion** was the favourite haunt of Maria Fyodorovna from 1812. She held many concerts and literary evenings in this cottage.

For hotels and restaurants in this area see p269 and p288

VISITORS' CHECKLIST

Practical information
Pavlovsk, 26 km (16 miles) SE of St Petersburg.
Tel (812) 452 15 36.
Palace: **Open** 10am–6pm Sat–Thu. **Closed** Oct–Apr: first Mon of the month.
English.
Grounds: **Open** May–Nov: 10am–6pm.

Transport
from Vitebskiy, Kupchino or Moscovskay stations to Pavlovsk, then bus 370, 383, 383a, 493, K-286, K-299.

Visconti Bridge
One of the most famous bridges that cross the winding Slavyanka, it was designed by Andrei Voronikhin in 1807.

Pavlovsk Railway Station

6

7

8

9

The Étoile
The earliest landscaped area in the park, L'Étoile, was laid out by Cameron in 1780. The circle of statues represents the nine Muses, protectors of the arts and sciences.

0 metres 200

0 yards 200

Pil Tower and Bridge
Brenna's tower, constructed in 1795–97, contained a spiral staircase, lounge and library. The bridge was a later addition made in 1808.

ST PETERSBURG STREET FINDER

The map below shows the areas of St Petersburg covered by the Street Finder maps. The map references given in the St Petersburg section for sights of interest, restaurants, hotels, shops and entertainment venues refer to the maps in this section. The symbols used to represent sights and useful information on these maps are listed below in the key. The first figure in the map reference indicates which Street Finder map to turn to, and the letter and number that follow refer to the map's grid. An index of street names can be found on the following pages. The index lists street names in transliteration, followed by Cyrillics (on maps, Cyrillics are only given for major roads).

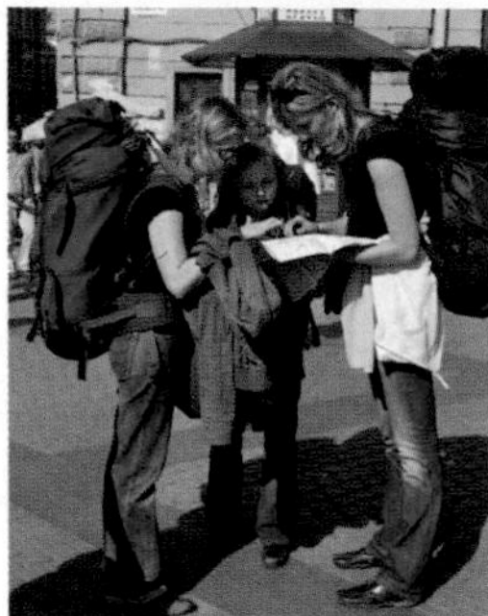

Backpackers referring to a map in order to get around St Petersburg

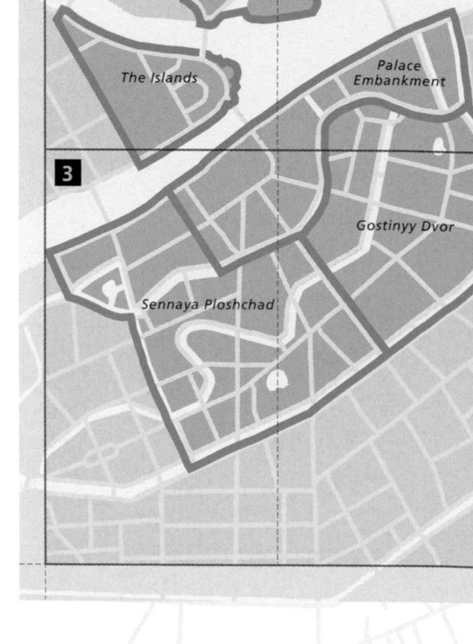

Key

- Major sight
- Place of interest
- Other building
- Train station
- Metro station
- Main tram stop
- Main trolleybus stop
- Main bus stop
- River boat pier
- Hospital
- Police station
- Orthodox church
- Non-Orthodox church
- Synagogue
- Mosque
- Railway line
- Pedestrian area

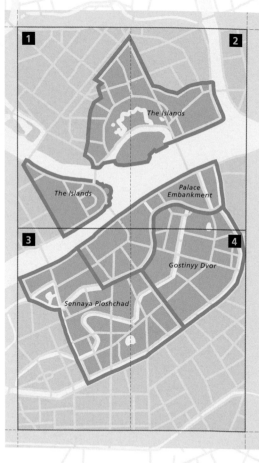

Scale of Maps 1–4

0 metres 300
0 yards 300

0 kilometres 2
0 miles 1

Street Finder Index

A

B

Useful words & abbreviations

	most	bridge
	podezd	entrance
	proezd	small street/passage/lane
	sad	garden
	shosse	road
	stroenie	building
	tupik	cul-de-sac
ul	**ulitsa**	street
pl	**ploshchad**	square
pr	**prospekt**	avenue
per	**pereulok**	small street/passage/lane

C

D

E

F

G

I

Inzhenernaya Ulitsa
ИНЖЕНЕНАЯ УЛИЦА 4E1
Italyanskaya Ulitsa
ИТАЛЬЯНСКАЯ УЛИЦА 4E1
Izmaylovskiy Prospekt
ИЗМАЙЛОВСКИЙ ПРОСПЕКТ 3C5

K

Kadetskaya 1-ya Liniya
Кадетская и 1-я Линия 1A4
Kamennoostrovskiy Prospekt
КАМЕННООСТРОВСКИЙ ПРОСПЕКТ 1C1
Kanonerskaya Ulitsa
КАНОНЕРСКАЯ УЛИЦА 3A4
Karavannaya Ulitsa
КАРАВАННАЯ УЛИЦА 4F1
Kazachiy pereulok
КАЗАЧИЙ ПЕРЕУЛОК 4E4
Kazanskaya Ulitsa
КАЗАНСКАЯ УЛИЦА 3C3
Kirpichnyy Pereulok
КИРПИЧНЫЙ ПЕРЕУЛОК 4D1
Klimov pereulok
КЛИМОВ ПЕРЕУЛОК 3B4
Klinskiy Prospekt
КЛИНСКИЙ ПРОСПЕКТ 4D5
Konnogvardeyskiy Bulvar
КОННОГВАРДЕЙСКИЙ БУЛЬВАР 3A2
Konnogvardeyskiy Per
Конногвардейский переулок 3B2
Konnyy Pereulok
КОННЫЙ ПЕРЕУЛОК 2D2
Korpusnaya Ulitsa
КОРПУСНАЯ УЛИЦА 1A1
Kotovskovo, ulitsa
КОТОВСКОГО, УЛИЦА 2E1
Krasnovo Kursanta, ulitsa
КРАСНОГО КУРСАНТА, УЛИЦА 1A2
Kronverkskaya Naberezhnaya
КРОНВЕРКСКАЯ НАБЕРЕЖНАЯ 1C3
Kronverkskaya, Ulitsa
КРОНВЕРКСКАЯ, УЛИЦА 1C1
Kronverkskiy Prospekt
КРОНВЕРКСКИЙ ПРОСПЕКТ 1C2
Kropotkina, ulitsa
КРОПОТКИНА, УЛИЦА 1C2
Kryukova Kanala, naberezhnaya
КРЮКОВА КАНАЛА, НАБЕРЕЖНАЯ 3B4
Kutuzova, naberezhnaya
КУТУЗОВА, НАБЕРЕЖНАЯ 2E4
Kuybysheva, ulitsa
КУЙБЫШЕВА, УЛИЦА 2D3

L

Labutina, ulitsa
ЛАБУТИНА, УЛИЦА 3A5
Lazaretnyy pereulok
ЛАЗАРЕТНЫЙ ПЕРЕУЛОК 4E4
Lebyazhevo Kanala, naberezhnaya
ЛЕБЯЖЬЕГО КАНАЛА, НАБЕРЕЖНАЯ 2E4
Lenina, ulitsa
ЛЕНИНА, УЛИЦА 1C2
Lermontovskiy Prospekt
ЛЕРМОНТОВСКИЙ ПРОСПЕКТ 3A3
Levashovskiy Prospekt
ЛЕВАШОВСКИЙ ПРОСПЕКТ 1A1
Lizy Chaykinoy, ulitsa
ЛИЗЫ ЧАЙКИНОЙ, УЛИЦА 1B2
Lomonosova, ulitsa
ЛОМОНОСОВА, УЛИЦА 4E2
Lva Tolstovo, ulitsa
ЛЬВА ТОЛСТОГО, УЛИЦА 1C1

M

Makarenko, pereulok
МАКАРЕНКО, ПЕРЕУЛОК 3B4
Makarova, naberezhnaya
МАКАРОВА, НАБЕРЕЖНАЯ 1A4
Malaya Konyushennaya ulitsa
МАЛАЯ КОНЮШЕННАЯ УЛИЦА 4D1
Malaya Monetnaya Ulitsa
МАЛАЯ МОНЕТНАЯ УЛИЦА 2D1
Malaya Morskaya ulitsa
МАЛАЯ МОРСКАЯ УЛИЦА 3C1
Malaya Posadskaya ulitsa
МАЛАЯ ПОСАДСКАЯ УЛИЦА 2E3
Malaya Pushkarskaya ulitsa
МАЛАЯ ПУШКАРСКАЯ УЛИЦА 1C2
Malaya sadovaya ulitsa
МАЛАЯ САДОВАЯ УЛИЦА 4F1
Malodetskoselskiy Prospekt
МАЛОДЕТСКОСЕЛЬСКИЙ ПРОСПЕКТ 4D5
Malyy Prospekt
МАЛЫЙ ПРОСПЕКТ 1B1
Malyy ProspeKT
МАЛЫЙ ПРОСПЕКТ 1A3
Marata, ulitsa
МАРАТА, УЛИЦА 4E4
Markina, ulitsa
МАРКИНА УЛИЦА 1C2
Masterskaya Ulitsa
МАСТЕРСКАЯ УЛИЦА 3A3
Matveeva, pereulok
МАТВЕЕВА ПЕРЕУЛОК 3A3
Mendeleevskaya Liniya
МЕНДЕЛЕЕВСКАЯ УЛИЦА 1B5
Michurinskaya Ulitsa
МИЧУРИНСКАЯ УЛИЦА 2E2
Millionaires Street
МИЛЛИОННАЯ УЛИЦА 2D5
Minskiy pereulok
МИНСКИЙ ПЕРЕУЛОК 3A3
Mira, ulitsa
МИРА, УЛИЦА 1C2
Moskatelnyy pereulok
МОСКАТЕЛЬНЫЙ ПЕРЕУЛОК 4D2
Moskovskiy prospekt
МОСКОВСКИЙ ПРОСПЕКТ 4D3
Mozhayskaya Ulitsa
МОЖАЙСКАЯ УЛИЦА 4E4
Muchnoy pereulok
МУЧНОЙ ПЕРЕУЛОК 4D2
Mytninskaya naberezhnaya
МЫТНИНСКАЯ НАБЕРЕЖНАЯ 1B4
Mytninskiy pereulok
МЫТНИНСКИЙ ПЕРЕУЛОК 1B3

N

Nesterova, pereulok
НЕСТЕРОВА, ПЕРЕУЛОК 1B3
Nevskiy Prospekt
НЕВСКИЙ ПРОСПЕКТ 4D1
Nikolskiy Pereulok
НИКОЛЬСКИЙ ПЕРЕУЛОК 3B3

O

Obvodnovo Kanala, naberezhnaya
ОБВОДНОГО КАНАЛА, НАБЕРЕЖНАЯ 4E5
Ofitserskiy pereulok
ОФИЦЕРСКИЙ ПЕРЕУЛОК 1A3
Orenburgskaya Ulitsa
ОРЕНБУРГСКАЯ УЛИЦА 2F2

P

Penkovaya Ulitsa
ПЕНЬКОВАЯ УЛИЦА 2E3
Pestelya, ulitsa
ПЕСТЕЛЯ, УЛИЦА 2F5

Petrogradskaya Naberezhnaya
ПЕТРОГРАДСКАЯ НАБЕРЕЖПАЯ **2E1**

Petrovskaya naberezhnaya
ПЕТРОВСКАЯ НАБЕРЕЖПАЯ **2E3**

Pevcheskiy Pereulok
ПЕВЧЕСКИЙ ПЕРЕУЛОК **2D2**

Pinskiy pereulok
ПИНСКИЙ ПЕРЕУЛОК **2E3**

Pionerskaya ulitsa
ПИОНЕРСКАЯ УЛИЦА **1A2**

Pirogova, pereulok
ПИРОГОВА, ПЕРЕУЛОК **3B2**

Pirogovskaya naberezhnaya
ПИРОГОВСКАЯ НАБЕРЕЖПАЯ **2F1**

Pisareva, ulitsa
ПИСАРЕВА, УЛИЦА **3A3**

Pochtamtskaya Ulitsa
ПОЧТАМТСКАЯ УЛИЦА **3B2**

Pochtamtskiy pereulok
ПОЧТАМТСКИЙ ПЕРЕУЛОК **3B2**

Podezdnoy Pereulok
ПОДЪЕЗДНОЙ ПЕРЕУЛОК **4E4**

Podolskaya Ulitsa
ПОДОЛЬСКАЯ УЛИЦА **4D5**

Prachechnyy Pereulok
ПРАЧЕЧНЫЙ ПЕРЕУЛОК **3B2**

Pravdy, ulitsa
ПРАВДЫ, УЛИЦА **4F4**

Pryadilnyy pereulok
ПРЯДИЛЬНЫЙ ПЕРЕУЛОК **3A5**

Pushkarskiy pereulok
ПУШКАРСКИЙ ПЕРЕУЛОК **1C2**

R

Reki Fontanki, naberezhnaya
РЕКИ ФОНТАНКИ, НАБЕРЕЖНАЯ **4F1**

Reki Moyki, naberezhnaya
РЕКИ МОЙКИ, НАБЕРЕЖНАЯ **3A3**

Rentgena, ulitsa
РЕНТГЕНА, УЛИЦА **2D1**

Repina, ulitsa
РЕПИНА, УЛИЦА **1A5**

Revelskiy Per
РЕВЕЛСКИЙ ПЕРЕУЛОК **3A5**

Rimskovo-Korsakova, prospekt
РИМСКОГО-КОРСАКОВА, ПРОСПЕКТ **3B3**

Rizhskiy Prospekt
РИЖСКИЙ ПРОСПЕКТ **3A5**

Rubinshteyna, ulitsa
РУБИНШТЕЙНА, УЛИЦА **4F3**

Ruzovskaya Ulitsa
РУЗОВСКАЯ УЛИЦА **4E4**

Rybatskaya ulitsa
РЫБАЦКАЯ УЛИЦА **1B2**

S

Sablinskaya Ulitsa
САБЛИНСКАЯ УЛИЦА **1C2**

Sadovaya ulitsa
САДОВАЯ УЛИЦА **2F5**

Saratovskaya Ulitsa
САРАТОВСКАЯ УЛИЦА **2F3**

Serpukhovskaya Ulitsa
СЕРПУХОВСКАЯ УЛИЦА **4D5**

Sezzhinskaya Ulitsa
СЪЕЗЖИНСКАЯ УЛИЦА **1B3**

Shchepyanoy pereulok
ЩЕПЯНОЙ ПЕРЕУЛОК **3B4**

Shvedskiy pereulok
ШВЕДСКИЙ ПЕРЕУЛОК **4D1**

Sovetskiy Pereulok
СОВЕТСКИЙ ПЕРЕУЛОК **3C5**

Soyuza Pechatnikov, ulitsa
СОЮЗА ПЕЧАТНИКОВ, УЛИЦА **3A4**

Spasskiy pereulok
СПАССКИЙ ПЕРЕУЛОК **4D2**

Sredniy Prospekt
СРЕДНИЙ ПРОСПЕКТ **1A4**

Srednyaya Podyacheskaya Ulitsa
СРЕДНЯЯ ПОДЬЯЧЕСКАЯ УЛИЦА **3B3**

Stolyarnyy pereulok
СТОЛЯРНЫЙ ПЕРЕУЛОК **3C3**

Sytninskaya Ulitsa
СЫТНИНСКАЯ УЛИЦА **1C2**

T

Tatarskiy pereulok
ТАТАРСКИЙ ПЕРЕУЛОК **1B3**

Telezhnaya ulitsa
ТЕЛЕЖНАЯ УЛИЦА **1B5**

Torgovyy pereulok
ТОРГОВЫЙ ПЕРЕУЛОК **4E3**

Troitskiy Prospekt
ТРОИЦКИЙ ПРОСПЕКТ **3B5**

Truda, ulitsa
ТРУДА, УЛИЦА **3A2**

Tuchkov Pereulok
ТУЧКОВ ПЕРЕУЛОК **1A4**

U

Universitetskaya naberezhnaya
УНИВЕРСИТЕТСКАЯ НАБЕРЕЖНАЯ **1B5**

V

Vereyskaya Ulitsa
ВЕРЕЙСКАЯ УЛИЦА **4D4**

Volkhovskiy pereulok
ВОЛХОВСКИЙ ПЕРЕУЛОК **1A5**

Volynskiy pereulok
ВОЛЫНСКИЙ ПЕРЕУЛОК **4D1**

Voskova, ulitsa
ВОСКОВА, УЛИЦА **1C2**

Voznesenskiy prospekt
ВОЗНЕСЕНСКИЙ ПРОСПЕКТ **3C2**

Vvedenskaya Ulitsa
ВВЕДЕНСКАЯ УЛИЦА **1B2**

Vvedenskovo kanala, naberezhnaya
ВВЕДЕНСКОГО КАНАЛА, НАБЕРЕЖНАЯ **4D4**

Y

Yablochkova, ulitsa
ЯБЛОЧКОВА, УЛИЦА **1B3**

Yakobshtadtskiy pereulok
ЯКОБШТАДТСКИЙ ПЕРЕУЛОК **3C5**

Yakubovicha, ulitsa
ЯКУБОВИЧА, УЛИЦА **3B2**

Yefimova, ulitsa
ЕФИМОВА, УЛИЦА **4D3**

Z

Zagorodnyy Prospekt
ЗАГОРОДНЫЙ ПРОСПЕКТ **4D5**

Zamkovaya Ulitsa
ЗАМКОВАЯ УЛИЦА **2F5**

Zhdanovskaya Ulitsa
ЖДАНОВСКАЯ УЛИЦА **1A3**

Zodchevo Rossi, ulitsa
ЗОДЧЕГО РОССИ, УЛИЦА **4E2**

Zvenigorodskaya Ulitsa
ЗВЕНИГОРОДСКАЯ УЛИЦА **4F4**

Zverinskaya Ulitsa
ЗВЕРИНСКАЯ УЛИЦА **1A3**

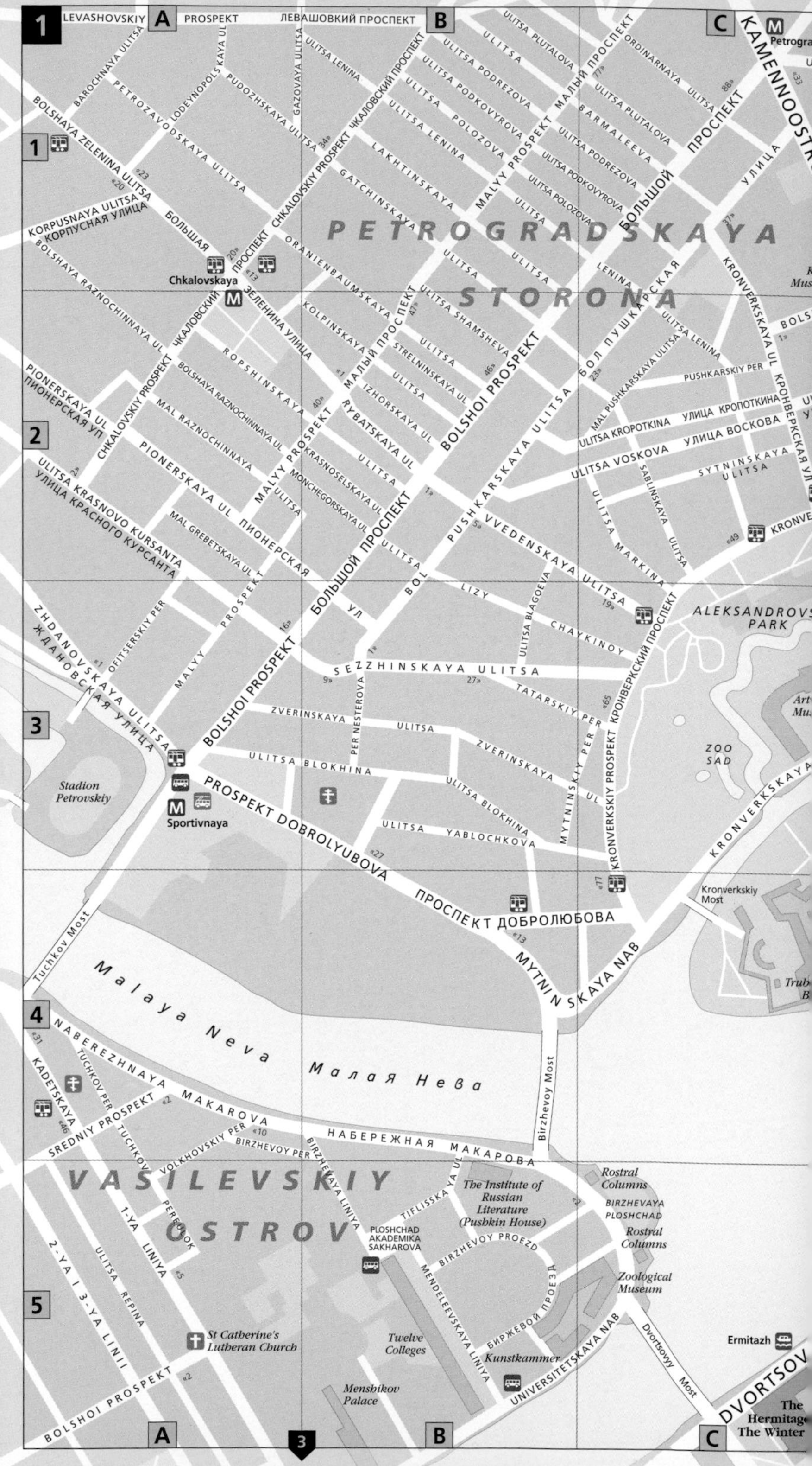

1
LEVASHOVSKIY PROSPEKT
ЛЕВАШОВКИЙ ПРОСПЕКТ
A
B
C
Petrograd
KAMENNOOSTR
BAROCHNAYA ULITSA
PETROZAVODSKAYA ULITSA
LODEYNOPOLSKAYA UL
PUDOZHSKAYA ULITSA
GAZOVAYA ULITSA
ULITSA LENINA
ULITSA PLUTALOVA
ORDINARNAYA ULITSA
BOLSHAYA ZELENINA ULITSA
БОЛЬШАЯ
КОРПУСНАЯ УЛИЦА
KORPUSNAYA ULITSA
BOLSHAYA RAZNOCHINNAYA UL
Chkalovskaya
CHKALOVSKIY PROSPEKT
ЧКАЛОВСКИЙ ПРОСПЕКТ
ЗЕЛЕНИНА УЛИЦА
ORANIENBAUMSKAYA
LAKHTINSKAYA
GATCHINSKAYA
ULITSA LENINA
ULITSA PODKOVYROVA
ULITSA POLOZOVA
ULITSA PODREZOVA
BARMALEEVA
MALYY PROSPEKT
МАЛЫЙ ПРОСПЕКТ
БОЛЬШОЙ ПРОСПЕКТ
PETROGRADSKAYA
STORONA
KRONVERKSKAYA UL
KOLPINSKAYA
ULITSA SHAMSHEVA
STRELNINSKAYA UL
ROPSHINSKAYA
IZHORSKAYA UL
RYBATSKAYA UL
BOLSHOI PROSPEKT
БОЛ ПУШКАРСКАЯ
BOL PUSHKARSKAYA ULITSA
ULITSA LENINA
PUSHKARSKIY PER
MAL PUSHKARSKAYA ULITSA
ULITSA KROPOTKINA
УЛИЦА КРОПОТКИНА
ULITSA VOSKOVA
УЛИЦА ВОСКОВА
SYTNINSKAYA ULITSA
КРОНВЕРКСКАЯ УЛ
PIONERSKAYA UL
ПИОНЕРСКАЯ УЛ
MAL RAZNOCHINNAYA
ULITSA KRASNOVO KURSANTA
УЛИЦА КРАСНОГО КУРСАНТА
KRASNOSELSKAYA UL
MONCHEGORSKAYA UL
VVEDENSKAYA ULITSA
SABLINSKAYA ULITSA
ULITSA MARKINA
MAL GREBETSKAYA UL
ALEKSANDROVS PARK
ULITSA LIZY
ULITSA BLAGOEVA
CHAYKINOY
ZHDANOVSKAYA ULITSA
ЖДАНОВСКАЯ УЛИЦА
OFITSERSKIY PER
SEZZHINSKAYA ULITSA
TATARSKIY PER
KRONVERKSKIY PROSPEKT
КРОНВЕРКСКИЙ ПРОСПЕКТ
ZVERINSKAYA ULITSA
PER NESTEROVA
ULITSA BLOKHINA
MYTNINSKIY PER
ZOO SAD
Stadion Petrovskiy
Sportivnaya
PROSPEKT DOBROLYUBOVA
ULITSA YABLOCHKOVA
ПРОСПЕКТ ДОБРОЛЮБОВА
KRONVERKSKAYA
Kronverkskiy Most
MYTNINSKAYA NAB
Tuchkov Most
Malaya Neva
Малая Нева
Birzhevoy Most
NABEREZHNAYA MAKAROVA
НАБЕРЕЖНАЯ МАКАРОВА
KADETSKAYA
TUCHKOV PER
SREDNIY PROSPEKT
VOLKHOVSKIY PER
BIRZHEVOY PER
BIRZHEVAYA LINIYA
VASILEVSKIY
OSTROV
1-YA LINIYA
PEREULOK
TIFLISSKAYA UL
The Institute of Russian Literature (Pushkin House)
Rostral Columns
BIRZHEVAYA PLOSHCHAD
PLOSHCHAD AKADEMIKA SAKHAROVA
BIRZHEVOY PROEZD
БИРЖЕВОЙ ПРОЕЗД
Zoological Museum
MENDELEEVSKAYA LINIYA
2-YA I 3-YA LINII
ULITSA REPINA
St Catherine's Lutheran Church
Twelve Colleges
Kunstkammer
UNIVERSITETSKAYA NAB
Dvortsovy Most
Ermitazh
DVORTSOV
Menshikov Palace
BOLSHOI PROSPEKT
The Hermitage
The Winter
3

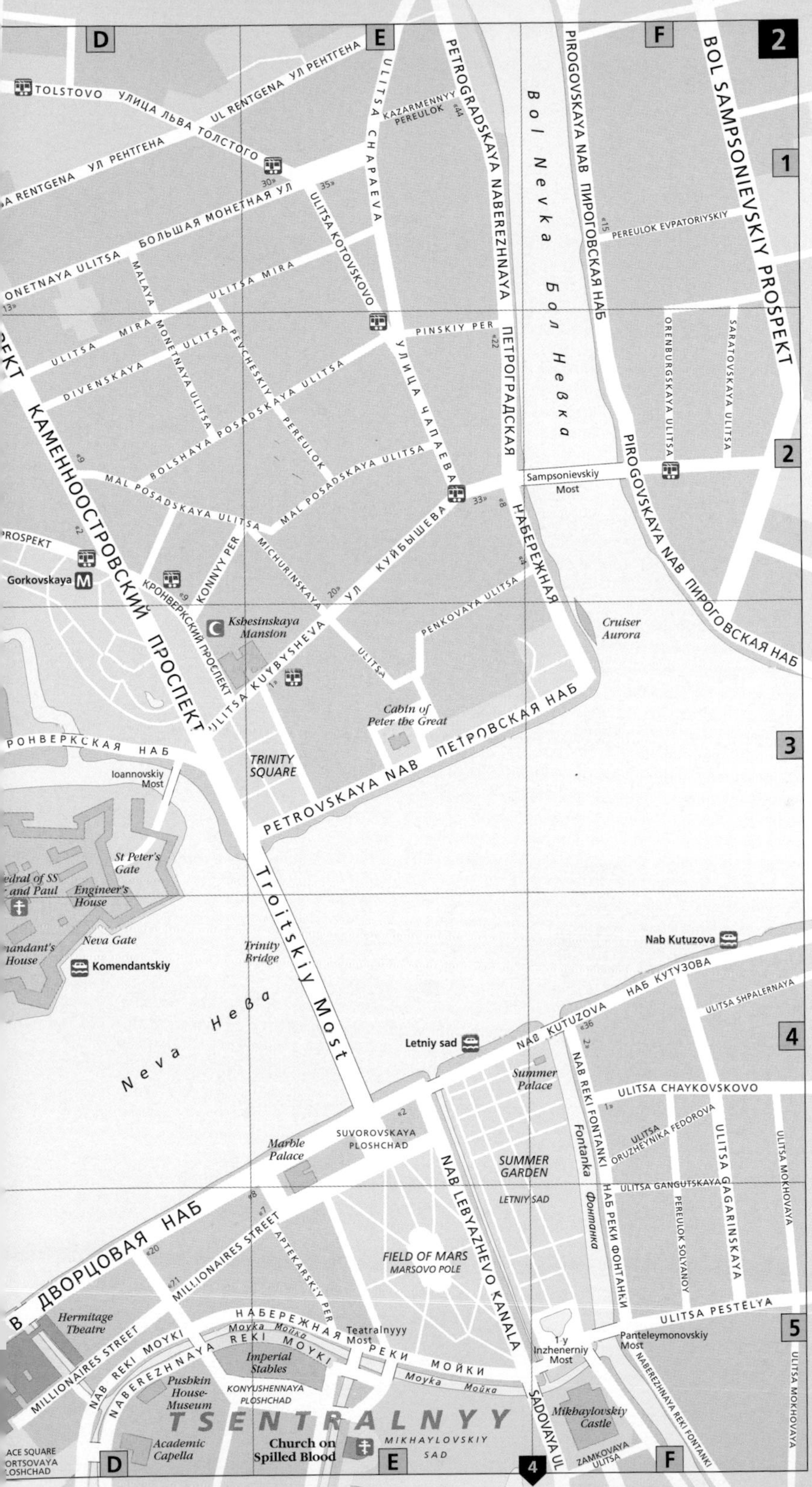

D
E
F
2
1
2
3
4
5
4
TOLSTOVO
Bol Nevka
Бол Невка
Sampsonievskiy Most
Gorkovskaya
Kshesinskaya Mansion
Cruiser Aurora
Cabin of Peter the Great
TRINITY SQUARE
Ioannovskiy Most
St Peter's Gate
Engineer's House
Neva Gate
Komendantskiy
Trinity Bridge
Troitskiy Most
Neva
Нева
Nab Kutuzova
Letniy sad
Summer Palace
SUMMER GARDEN
LETNIY SAD
Marble Palace
SUVOROVSKAYA PLOSHCHAD
FIELD OF MARS
MARSOVO POLE
Hermitage Theatre
Imperial Stables
Teatralnyyy Most
Pushkin House-Museum
KONYUSHENNAYA PLOSHCHAD
TSENTRALNYY
Academic Capella
Church on Spilled Blood
MIKHAYLOVSKIY SAD
Mikhaylovskiy Castle
1 y Inzhenerniy Most
Panteleymonovskiy Most
Fontanka
Фонтанка
Moyka
Мойка
PETROGRADSKAYA NABEREZHNAYA
ПЕТРОГРАДСКАЯ НАБЕРЕЖНАЯ
PIROGOVSKAYA NAB
ПИРОГОВСКАЯ НАБ
BOL SAMPSONIEVSKIY PROSPEKT
PEREULOK EVPATORIYSKIY
ORENBURGSKAYA ULITSA
SARATOVSKAYA ULITSA
ULITSA CHAPAEVA
УЛИЦА ЧАПАЕВА
KAZARMENNYY PEREULOK
UL RENTGENA
УЛ РЕНТГЕНА
УЛИЦА ЛЬВА ТОЛСТОГО
БОЛЬШАЯ МОНЕТНАЯ УЛ
MONETNAYA ULITSA
ULITSA KOTOVSKOVO
ULITSA MIRA
MALAYA MONETNAYA ULITSA
DIVENSKAYA
PINSKIY PER
BOLSHAYA POSADSKAYA ULITSA
PEVCHESKIY PEREULOK
MAL POSADSKAYA ULITSA
КАМЕННООСТРОВСКИЙ ПРОСПЕКТ
PROSPEKT
KONNYY PER
КРОНВЕРКСКИЙ ПРОСПЕКТ
MICHURINSKAYA ULITSA
УЛ КУЙБЫШЕВА
ULITSA KUYBYSHEVA
PENKOVAYA ULITSA
ПЕТРОВСКАЯ НАБ
PETROVSKAYA NAB
КРОНВЕРКСКАЯ НАБ
НАБ КУТУЗОВА
ULITSA SHPALERNAYA
NAB REKI FONTANKI
НАБ РЕКИ ФОНТАНКИ
ULITSA CHAYKOVSKOVO
ULITSA ORUZHEYNIKA FEDOROVA
ULITSA GAGARINSKAYA
ULITSA GANGUTSKAYA
PEREULOK SOLYANOY
ULITSA MOKHOVAYA
ULITSA PESTELYA
NABEREZHNAYA REKI FONTANKI
NAB LEBYAZHEVO KANALA
ДВОРЦОВАЯ НАБ
MILLIONAIRES STREET
APTEKARSKIY PER
НАБЕРЕЖНАЯ РЕКИ МОЙКИ
NAB REKI MOYKI
SADOVAYA UL
ZAMKOVAYA ULITSA

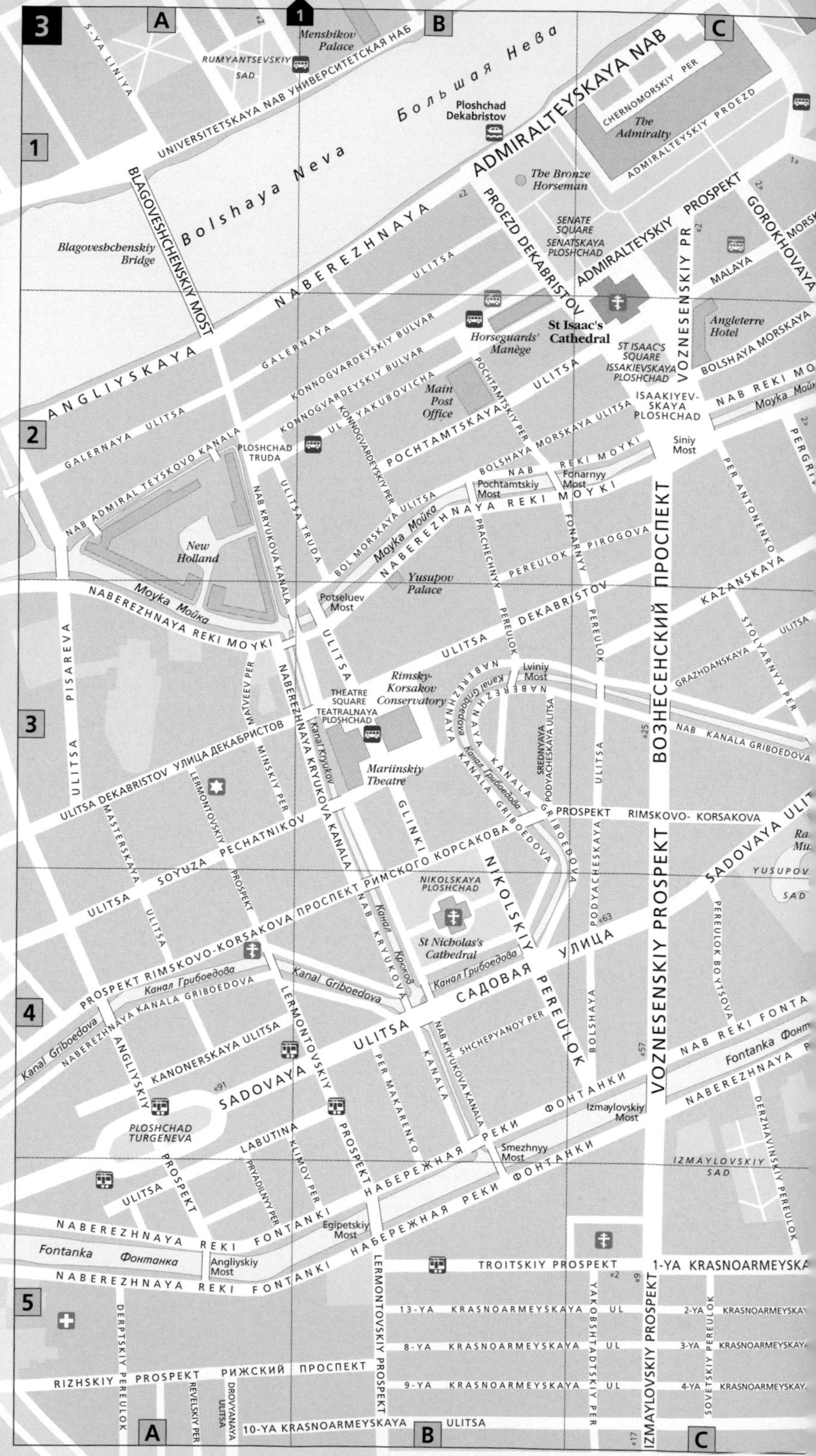
3
A
B
C
1
2
3
4
5
5-YA LINIYA
Menshikov Palace
RUMYANTSEVSKIY SAD
UNIVERSITETSKAYA NAB УНИВЕРСИТЕТСКАЯ НАБ
Большая Нева
Bolshaya Neva
Ploshchad Dekabristov
ADMIRALTEYSKAYA NAB
CHERNOMORSKIY PER
The Admiralty
ADMIRALTEYSKIY PROEZD
The Bronze Horseman
BLAGOVESHCHENSKIY MOST
Blagoveshchenskiy Bridge
ADMIRALTEYSKAYA NABEREZHNAYA
PROEZD DEKABRISTOV
SENATE SQUARE
SENATSKAYA PLOSHCHAD
ADMIRALTEYSKIY PROSPEKT
GOROKHOVAYA
VOZNESENSKIY PR
MALAYA
MORSK
St Isaac's Cathedral
Angleterre Hotel
BOLSHAYA MORSKAYA
ANGLIYSKAYA
ULITSA
GALERNAYA
KONNOGVARDEYSKIY BULVAR
Horseguards' Manège
ST ISAAC'S SQUARE
ISSAKIEVSKAYA PLOSHCHAD
ISAAKIYEVSKAYA PLOSHCHAD
NAB REKI MOYKI
Moyka Мойка
UL YAKUBOVICHA
KONNOGVARDEYSKIY PER
Main Post Office
POCHTAMTSKIY PER
POCHTAMTSKAYA ULITSA
BOLSHAYA MORSKAYA ULITSA
Siniy Most
PERGRI
GALERNAYA ULITSA
PLOSHCHAD TRUDA
NAB ADMIRAL TEYSKOVO KANALA
Pochtamtskiy Most
Fonarnyy Most
NABEREZHNAYA REKI MOYKI
PER ANTONENKO
ВОЗНЕСЕНСКИЙ ПРОСПЕКТ
NAB KRYUKOVA KANALA
ULITSA TRUDA
BOL MORSKAYA ULITSA
PRACHECHNYY PEREULOK
FONARNYY PEREULOK
PEREULOK PIROGOVA
New Holland
Yusupov Palace
Potseluev Most
KAZANSKAYA
NABEREZHNAYA REKI MOYKI
ULITSA DEKABRISTOV
ULITSA PISAREVA
STOLYARNYY PER
GRAZHDANSKAYA ULITSA
Lviniy Most
Rimsky-Korsakov Conservatory
THEATRE SQUARE
TEATRALNAYA PLOSHCHAD
MATVEEV PER
NABEREZHNAYA KRYUKOVA KANALA
Kanal Kryukov
NABEREZHNAYA KANALA GRIBOEDOVA
Канал Грибоедова
SREDNYAYA PODYACHESKAYA ULITSA
NAB KANALA GRIBOEDOVA
ULITSA DEKABRISTOV УЛИЦА ДЕКАБРИСТОВ
LERMONTOVSKIY PROSPEKT
MINSKIY PER
Mariinskiy Theatre
GLINKI
PROSPEKT RIMSKOVO-KORSAKOVA
MASTERSKAYA
ULITSA SOYUZA PECHATNIKOV
NIKOLSKIY PEREULOK
SADOVAYA ULITSA
YUSUPOV SAD
PROSPEKT RIMSKOVO-KORSAKOVA ПРОСПЕКТ РИМСКОГО КОРСАКОВА
NIKOLSKAYA PLOSHCHAD
St Nicholas's Cathedral
NAB KRYUKOVA
Канал Крюков
PODYACHESKAYA
PEREULOK BOYTSOVA
САДОВАЯ УЛИЦА
Kanal Griboedova
NABEREZHNAYA KANALA GRIBOEDOVA
BOLSHAYA
ANGLIYSKIY PROSPEKT
KANONERSKAYA ULITSA
SHCHEPYANOY PER
NAB KRYUKOVA KANALA
NAB REKI FONTANKI
Fontanka Фонтанка
NABEREZHNAYA
VOZNESENSKIY PROSPEKT
SADOVAYA ULITSA
PER MAKARENKO
НАБЕРЕЖНАЯ РЕКИ ФОНТАНКИ
Izmaylovskiy Most
PLOSHCHAD TURGENEVA
LABUTINA ULITSA
KLIMOV PER
PRYADILNYY PER
Smezhnyy Most
IZMAYLOVSKIY SAD
DERZHAVINSKIY PEREULOK
Egipetskiy Most
NABEREZHNAYA REKI FONTANKI
Fontanka Фонтанка
Angliyskiy Most
TROITSKIY PROSPEKT
1-YA KRASNOARMEYSKAYA
YAKOBSHTADTSKIY PER
IZMAYLOVSKIY PROSPEKT
13-YA KRASNOARMEYSKAYA UL
2-YA KRASNOARMEYSKAYA
8-YA KRASNOARMEYSKAYA UL
3-YA KRASNOARMEYSKAYA
9-YA KRASNOARMEYSKAYA UL
4-YA KRASNOARMEYSKAYA
SOVETSKIY PEREULOK
DERPTSKIY PEREULOK
RIZHSKIY PROSPEKT РИЖСКИЙ ПРОСПЕКТ
REVELSKIY PER
DROVYANAYA ULITSA
10-YA KRASNOARMEYSKAYA ULITSA

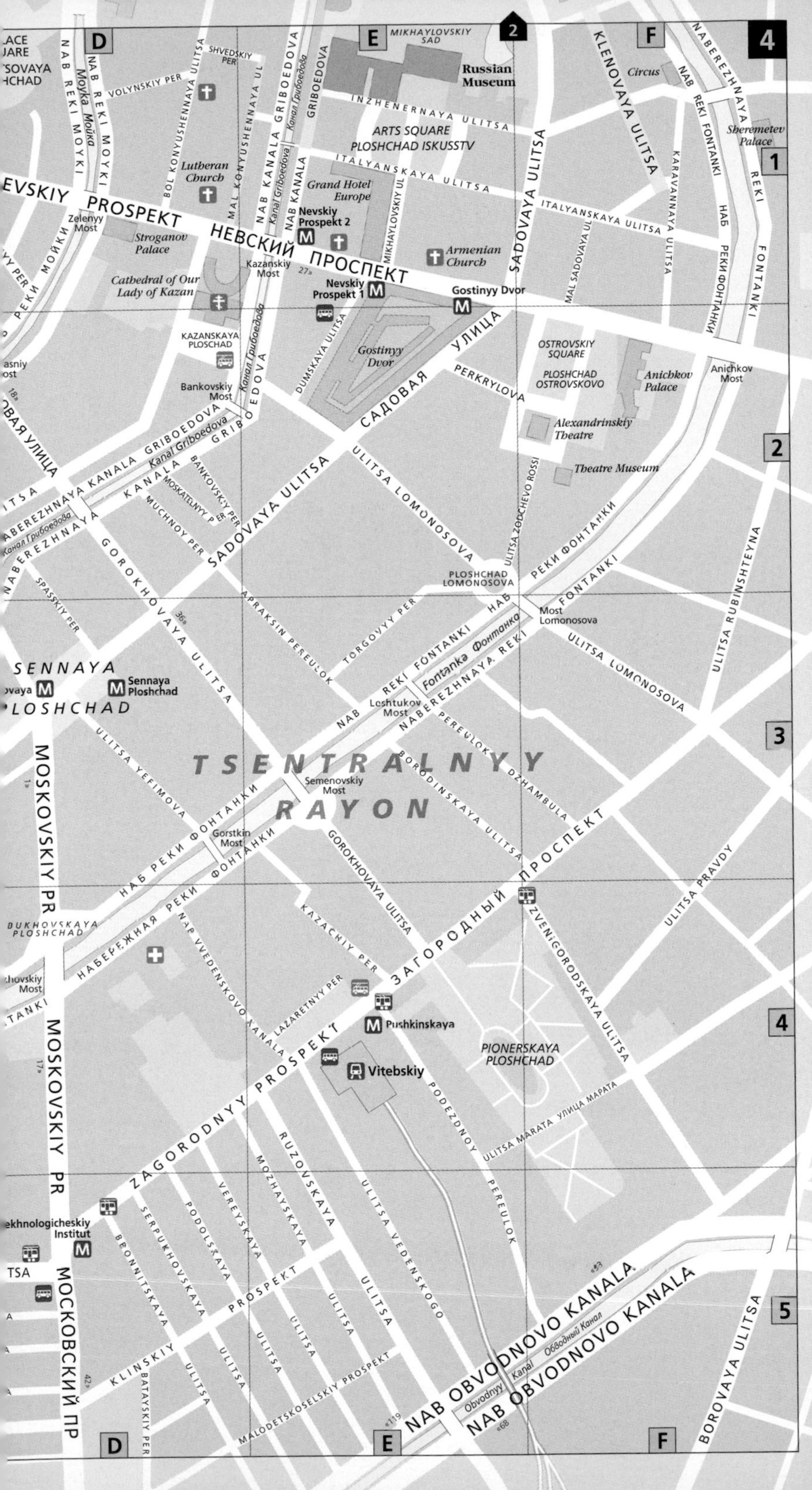
4
2
D
E
F
1
2
3
4
5
Russian Museum
Mikhaylovskiy Sad
Circus
Sheremetev Palace
Arts Square
Ploshchad Iskusstv
Lutheran Church
Grand Hotel Europe
Nevskiy Prospekt 2
Nevskiy Prospekt
Невский проспект
Zelenyy Most
Stroganov Palace
Armenian Church
Kazanskiy Most
Cathedral of Our Lady of Kazan
Nevskiy Prospekt 1
Gostinyy Dvor
Kazanskaya Ploschad
Ostrovskiy Square
Ploshchad Ostrovskovo
Anichkov Palace
Anichkov Most
Bankovskiy Most
Alexandrinskiy Theatre
Theatre Museum
Sadovaya Ulitsa
Садовая улица
Ploshchad Lomonosova
Most Lomonosova
Ulitsa Lomonosova
Ulitsa Rubinshteyna
Sennaya Ploshchad
Leshtukov Most
Fontanka Фонтанка
Tsentralnyy Rayon
Semenovskiy Most
Gorstkin Most
Moskovskiy Pr
Московский пр
Zagorodnyy Prospekt
Загородный проспект
Ulitsa Pravdy
Pushkinskaya
Vitebskiy
Pionerskaya Ploshchad
Ulitsa Marata улица Марата
Tekhnologicheskiy Institut
Nab Obvodnovo Kanala
Obvodnyy Kanal Обводный Канал
Borovaya Ulitsa
Malodetskoselskiy Prospekt

ПРОЛИѦША КРОВЬ ИХЪ ѦКѠ ВОДꙊ ѠКРЕСТЪ

RUSSIA REGION BY REGION

Russia at a Glance

Dominating the eastern end of Europe and all of northern Asia, Russia's longitudinal extent is phenomenal and its topography incredibly varied. The country's fascinating cultural heritage is manifested in its many ancient towns and cities, of which Moscow and St Petersburg are foremost with their wealth of historical and architectural attractions. Beyond the Urals to the east, the Trans-Siberian Railway traverses the epic tracts of dense forest and featureless steppe that lie between Siberia's reassuringly civilized cities. Intrepid visitors can venture north to the desolate city of Magadan and beyond to the mesmerizing volcanic peninsula of Kamchatka, so remote that helicopters are often the only means of transport.

Kizhi *(see pp208–209)*, with its magnificent pair of 18th-century wooden churches topped with a profusion of tiny onion domes, has long attracted both pilgrims and tourists.

Curonian Spit *(see p218)* is a spectacular landform created by sand deposition millions of years ago. This strip of sandy wilderness stretches for almost 100 km (60 miles) between Kaliningrad and Lithuania and has some of the best beaches in the region. Known as Kurshkaya Kosa locally, it is also a UNESCO World Heritage Site.

Volga Delta

Sochi National Park *(see p242)* runs parallel to the Black Sea coast. The densely forested park encompasses mountains, canyons, rivers and caves, and is home to diverse wildlife.

◀ Magnificent view of the front of the Church on the Blood, Yekaterinburg

Volga Delta *(see p233)*, a picturesque labyrinth of waterways and islands sheltering an abundance of wildlife, lies at the end of the great Volga river where it meets the Caspian Sea.

Kamchatka *(see p259)* is a remote volcanic peninsula that offers unforgettable vistas of brown bears roaming the pristine natural landscapes dotted with mighty geysers and rumbling volcanoes.

Lake Baikal *(see p253)* is the oldest and deepest lake on earth, containing an astonishing 20 per cent of the planet's unfrozen freshwater supplies. Its largely unspoilt shoreline offers numerous opportunities for hiking and camping.

NORTHERN RUSSIA

Sharing a 1,000-km (621-mile) border with Finland and a tiny sliver of Norway in the Arctic far north, much of Northern Russia's lake-covered wilderness resembles the terrain of its Scandinavian neighbours and lies within the Russian Republic of Karelia. With its potent blend of rugged nature, complex medieval history and rich cultural heritage, the region is a treasure-trove of attractions that is only just beginning to be appreciated by locals and foreigners alike.

To the north of St Petersburg lie vast stretches of rocky wilderness strewn with dense coniferous forests and myriad rivers once used as trade routes into Russia by the Vikings. Dotted with 100,000 glacial lakes, the northern region includes two of Europe's largest lakes: Ladoga and Onega. The island of Valaam on Lake Ladoga has been home to a monastic community for hundreds of years, while Kizhi island on Lake Onega features the iconic wooden churches that were built by god-fearing farmers who settled here in the 16th century.

With temperatures dropping as low as -40°C (-40°F) in some parts during winters, Northern Russia is popular among visitors in search of dazzling frozen landscapes. The northwestern region, by contrast, has a more hospitable climate. This, combined with the region's proximity to Western Europe, made it the obvious location for some of Russia's earliest settlements.

Founded around the 10th century, the towns of Pskov and Veliky Novgorod prospered from the lucrative trade in furs and developed into powerful city-states that rivalled Moscow. Both built mighty kremlins to withstand frequent aggression from their hostile neighbours.

Today, crumbling kremlin walls have been rebuilt and the once splendid churches and monasteries that were woefully neglected during the Soviet era are being painstakingly restored. Infrastructure has improved over the years and despite the numbing temperatures there is access to plenty of adventure activities, from snowmobiling to ice-hole swimming.

Detail of one of the panels in an iconostasis on display in the Pskov Museum of History, Architecture and Art

◀ The spectacular Transfiguration Church and the hexagonal bell tower at Kizhi

Exploring Northern Russia

Dominated by lush wilderness and lakes, Northern Russia is a sparsely populated area. Although the landscape is punctuated by sleepy villages of faded wooden cottages and log cabins hemmed in by vegetable gardens, a vast majority of the population is concentrated around St Petersburg. Located up north, Petrozavodsk serves as the gateway to Kizhi, which is famous for its striking wooden churches. The grand cathedrals on the island of Valaam are another architectural attraction. South of St Petersburg, the impressive kremlins and medieval churches of Veliky Novgorod and Pskov are well worth an overnight trip. Alexander Pushkin's picturesque ancestral estate at Mikhaylovskoye makes for a superb day trip by bus from Pskov. Hiking and cycling trails in the region are poorly marked; it is advisable to register with one of the several travel agencies in Petrozavodsk to arrange organized trips.

Sights at a Glance

1 Petrozavodsk
2 Kizhi
3 Valaam
4 Veliky Novgorod
5 Pskov
6 Mikhaylovskoye

Key

- Major road
- Minor road
- Major railway
- Minor railway
- International border
- Federal border

0 km 100
0 miles 100

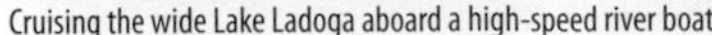

Cruising the wide Lake Ladoga aboard a high-speed river boat

For map symbols *see back flap*

Austere façade of the bell tower of Trinity Cathedral within the Kremlin, Pskov

Getting Around

Russia's extensive rail network connects St Petersburg with most of the major cities in Northern Russia such as Petrozavodsk, Sortavala, Pskov and Veliky Novgorod as well as with settlements further north. Buses run throughout the region, although poor road surfaces often make for a rough ride. During winter, road conditions can be extremely hazardous due to snow and ice. Kizhi and Valaam are well connected to the mainland by hydrofoil services between June and September. These islands can also be reached on a cruise from St Petersburg.

Picturesque view of the redbrick Kremlin watchtowers, Veliky Novgorod

For hotels and restaurants in this region see p270 and pp288–9

1 Petrozavodsk

Петрозаводск

Petrozavodsk

410 km (255 miles) NE of St Petersburg. 260,000. Ulitsa Kuybushev 5, (8142) 76 48 35. **ticrk.ru**

Surprisingly attractive for an industrial city, Petrozavodsk, meaning Peter's Factory, is the capital of the Republic of Karelia, a vast area of largely untouched wilderness bordering Finland. Petrozavodsk's boulevards and Neo-Classical city centre lie on the gently sloping shore of Lake Onega, Europe's second largest lake. In summer the city is a popular stop for visitors on their way to Kizhi island; in winter, when the temperature drops as low as -40°C (-40°F) it is mostly visited by the locals.

Petrozavodsk was established by Peter the Great in 1703 to process local iron ore deposits into munitions for the Great Northern War with Sweden *(see p41)*. The foundry was later used during the Russo-Turkish Wars in the 18th and 19th centuries. The munitions factory has since been replaced by a tractor plant, but an 1873 statue of Peter the Great still marks the spot near the hydrofoil station where the city was founded. A short walk southwest through the park from here leads up to ploshchad Kirova, dominated by the colonnaded **Music and Drama Theatre**. Facing the theatre on one side is the **Kizhi Museum** whose two halls feature rotating exhibitions about Kizhi island, while on the opposite side is the **Fine Arts Museum**, with a collection of modern works by regional artists. From ploshchad Kirova, Karl Marx prospekt passes the tractor factory before reaching ploshchad Lenina, with an imposing statue of Lenin.

Statue of Peter the Great on the embankment of Lake Onega, Petrozavodsk

Music and Drama Theatre
Ploshchad Kirova 4. **Tel** (8142) 78 44 42. **Open** 11am–8pm Mon–Fri, 10am–6pm Sat & Sun (ticket office).
mrteatr.onego.ru

Kizhi Museum
Ploshchad Kirova 10A. **Tel** (8142) 78 35 43. **Open** 10am–6pm daily.
kizhi.karelia.ru

Fine Arts Museum
Prospekt Marksa 8. **Tel** (8142) 78 37 13. **Open** 10am–6pm Tue–Sun.
artmuseum.karelia.ru

2 Kizhi

Кижи

Kizhi

68 km (42 miles) NE of Petrozavodsk. from Petrozavodsk. Ploshchad Kirova 10a, Petrozavodsk, (8142) 76 70 91. **kizhi.karelia.ru** Note: The island is icebound between Oct and May; the only access is by helicopter, snowmobile or hovercraft. In summer, a hydrofoil from Petrozavodsk provides daily connections.

With its profusion of medieval wooden churches and homesteads set amidst lakeside scenery, Kizhi island is the highlight of a visit to Northern Russia.

One of over a thousand islands on Lake Onega, this island's main attraction is the Kizhi *pogost*, which is part of the **Kizhi State Open-Air Museum**. A UNESCO World Heritage Site, the *pogost* (enclosure) comprises an iconic pair of multi-domed wooden churches that date from the 18th century. The stunning Transfiguration Church with its 22 cascading onion domes was built in 1714 and was used as a summer church, while the heated nine-domed Intercession Church was used in winter. The Transfiguration Church has been closed to the public since restoration work began in 1980, but the smaller Intercession Church is open to visitors. A hexagonal bell tower from 1862 stands between the two churches. A short walk south is the tiny **Resurrection of Lazarus**

Spectacular view of the Transfiguration Church (left), the Intercession Church (centre) and the bell tower (right), Kizhi

Church, built in the 14th century and considered one of Russia's oldest wooden buildings.

Populated by peasant farmers as early as the 16th century, Kizhi island once supported 14 small settlements of which only two, Yamka and Vasilyevo, remain. These two restored villages now form part of the "living museum" where visitors can see traditional craft making and observe members of the Old Believer community going about their daily life.

Kizhi State Open-Air Museum
Tel (8142) 53 57 22. **Open** year-round; see website for timings. **kizhi.karelia.ru**

Resurrection of Lazarus Church
Tel (8142) 53 57 22. **Open** year-round; call ahead for timings.

Façade of the Valaam Monastery with the bell tower rising in the background

❸ Valaam

Валаам

Valaam

239 km (148 miles) SW of Kizhi. (812) 902 86 11. **valaam.ru**
Note: Daily hydrofoil connections from Jun–Aug. Icebound from late Jan–Apr, when the only access is by helicopter, or, between Jan and Mar, by hovercraft.

A trip across Lake Ladoga, Europe's largest lake, to Valaam Monastery is another highlight of a tour to Northern Russia.

Churches and chapels belonging to the monastery are scattered throughout the Valaam archipelago, which has been inhabited by monks since the 10th century. Its heyday was in the late 19th century under the perspicacious abbotship of Father Damaskin (1795–1881).

A hydrofoil ferrying visitors across Lake Ladoga to Valaam

Valaam was then part of Russian Finland and home to a thriving monastic community replete with its own brickworks, tannery and farm. The **Transfiguration Cathedral**, Valaam's spiritual centre, dates from 1887 to 1896. Following over half a century of neglect after the Soviets took over the territory in 1940, the cathedral was fully restored in 2005. Its splendid pale blue domes and a gold-tipped bell tower can be seen from afar.

The islands of the Valaam archipelago are home to a number of *sketes* (settlements of monks). One of the most famous is the Resurrection Skete, located not far from the cruise ship quay. A simple redbrick affair, it was consecrated in 1906. Nearby are the pretty tent-roofed Gethsemane Skete and the Konevsky Skete, close to which is the refuge where Father Damaskin spent seven years in solitude before he was made abbot. All Saints Skete is closer and makes for an idyllic one-hour walk through the woods. Built in the late 18th century, it stands within a walled compound and is renowned for its strict monastic rules, which allow women to enter for only one day a year.

Transfiguration Cathedral
Tel (812) 902 85 72. **Open** 10am–7pm Mon–Fri. **valaam.ru**

White Sea Canal

The White Sea Canal was built between 1931 and 1933 to connect the Baltic Sea with the White Sea through Lake Onega. It was an early pet project of Stalin's for which there was little need at the time. The construction was assigned to the thousands of political prisoners who were pouring into Gulag prison camps in the region. The project also provided the Soviet regime with the opportunity to portray the gruelling prison labour as necessary for "reforging" these "class enemies".

Prisoners at the construction site of the White Sea Canal

Stalin wanted the canal completed within 20 months and infamously demanded that it be built cheaply and quickly. As many as 170,000 convict labourers were put to work, but without mechanized equipment. Instead, shovels and picks were used to hack out the canal in appalling conditions, which led to an estimated 100,000 deaths. Terrified of failing to meet Stalin's impossible deadline, the construction chiefs had the canal dug shallower than necessary, which allowed them to complete the project four months early to great Soviet acclaim. However, as it wasn't deep enough to transport most seagoing ships, larger vessels had to have their cargo unloaded and transported by barge.

4 Veliky Novgorod

Великий Новгород

Velikiy Novgorod

508 km (315 miles) SW of Petrozavodsk. 220,000. Ploshchad Sennaya 5, (8162) 77 30 74. **visitnovgorod.com**

Thought to be Russia's oldest city, Veliky Novgorod celebrated its 1,150th anniversary in 2009 despite the exact date of its foundation being a matter of academic dispute. However, less contentious is the assertion that Novgorod was the birthplace of Russian democracy. It was here, between the 12th and 15th centuries, that a citizens' assembly had the power to make laws and to select or dismiss their leaders. Novgorod's historic centre, dominated by the walled Kremlin, dates back to the period when the city was a partner of the Hanseatic League and profited handsomely from exporting Russian furs to the West. As the capital of an independent state, Novgorod was powerful enough to rival Moscow, but Ivan the Terrible brought its supremacy to an end when his troops slaughtered 60,000 Novgorodians in 1570.

The restored **Kremlin**, on the left bank of Volkhov river, remains Veliky Novgorod's central feature, but the city's power has long since ebbed. It is a peaceful place with numerous churches, well-kept parks and a leisurely air. In summer, locals gather by the river to swim or sunbathe and to promenade across the footbridge.

Built within the Kremlin in 1045, the **Cathedral of St Sophia** is one of Russia's oldest surviving church buildings. Typical of church construction from that period, the lavish iconostasis, giant chandeliers and bright frescoes were intended to inspire awe, while the almost windowless exterior and thick walls were designed to resist attack. Next to the cathedral is a 15th-century belfry that can be climbed for views over the river. The multiple arches that house bells are known as *zvonitsa* and are characteristic of the region's church architecture. The 17th-century **Kokuy Tower** that rises 41 m (134 ft) above the Kremlin's redbrick walls offers sweeping views of the city.

Kokuy Tower, one of the major attractions within the Kremlin in Veliky Novgorod

Nearby is the **Museum of History, Architecture and Art** whose collection includes a chronological display of hundreds of icons dating from the 12th century and over a thousand medieval letters written on birch bark that were excavated in the 1950s.

Opposite the museum is the grand **Millennium Monument**, erected in 1862 to commemorate the city's 1,000th anniversary. Cast from 65 tonnes (71 tons) of bronze, it resembles a bell adorned with sculptures of famous Russian figures from bygone years. An ensemble of pretty medieval churches known as **Yaroslav's Court**, once the city's main square, lies across the footbridge east of the Kremlin.

Cathedral of St Sophia
Tel (8162) 77 35 56. **Open** 8am–8pm daily.

Museum of History, Architecture and Art
Tel (8162) 77 36 08. **Open** 10am–6pm Wed–Mon. **Closed** last Thu of the month. **novgorodmuseum.ru**

5 Pskov

Псков

Pskov

211 km (131 miles) SW of Veliky Novgorod. 200,000. Ploshchad Lenina 3, (953) 242 57 00. **tourism.pskov.ru**

Pskov benefited hugely from trade between the East and West in medieval times, becoming

Millennium Monument, celebrating Novgorod's 1,000 years of history

For hotels and restaurants in this region see p270 and pp288–9

Splendid interior of the Trinity Cathedral in Pskov's Kremlin

Pokrovskaya Tower, a part of Pskov's outer ring of fortifications

a member of the powerful Hanseatic League and gaining independence from Veliky Novgorod, its overbearing neighbour, in the 14th century. This led to frequent attacks and sieges, but the heavily fortified city famously withstood all barring a few.

Following the region's belated acceptance of Christianity in the 12th century, churches were erected throughout Pskov. Many of these were destroyed during the course of World War II and those that survived were neglected during the Soviet era. Efforts have been made in recent years to restore them.

The **Kremlin** lies at the heart of Pskov, opposite ploshchad Lenina. Ensconced within its mighty walls is **Trinity Cathedral**, founded in the 10th century and rebuilt several times since; the current building was consecrated in 1699. Its austere, defensive exterior belies the stunning iconostasis within, which rises some 20 m (65 ft) to the base of the central dome, and gleams with multiple rows of bright gilt-framed icons. South of the Kremlin, on the opposite bank of the Velikaya river, **Mirozhky Monastery** shelters the pretty turquoise-domed Transfiguration Cathedral whose interior walls are covered with well-preserved 12th-century frescoes that have earned it a place on the UNESCO World Heritage List. Facing the monastery across the river is the massive **Pokrovskaya Tower**, the southernmost point of Pskov's fortifications. It bore the brunt of 31 Polish and Lithuanian attacks during their unsuccessful siege of the city from 1581–2.

Nearby is the **Pskov Museum of History, Architecture and Art**, which consists of several buildings. Foremost is the imposing 17th-century **Pogankin's Chambers**, built for a wealthy merchant and now home to a comprehensive display of 14th- to 17th-century Pskov icon painting and an impressive collection of antique silverware. The adjoining museum has an exhibition devoted to Pskov's involvement in World War II.

Mirozhky Monastery
Mirozhskaya Naberezh 2. **Tel** (8112) 57 64 06. **Open** 11am–6pm Tue–Sun. **mirozhsky-monastery.ru**

Pskov Museum of History, Architecture and Art
Ulitsa Nekrasova 7. **Tel** (8112) 66 33 11. **Open** 11am–6pm Tue–Sun. **museums.pskov.ru**

❻ Mikhaylovskoye

Михайловское

Mikhaylovskoye

130 km (81 miles) S of Pskov. **Tel** (81146) 2 23 21. **Open** 10am–5pm Tue–Sun. **Closed** last Tue of the month

This idyllic lakeside country estate in the settlement of Pushkinskie Gory belonged to Alexander Pushkin's mother. It was here amidst lush meadows, lakes and dense forest that the revered author and poet spent several happy summers during his childhood. After the authorities intercepted a letter in which Pushkin had expressed support for atheism, he was exiled to Mikhaylovskoye from Odessa. From 1824–6, he lived in the family's small wooden house on the estate as a virtual prisoner but found the inspiration to complete several of his literary masterpieces. The house has been rebuilt several times since and was wholly restored in time for his 200th anniversary in 1999.

Pushkin was killed in a duel at the age of 37 and was buried beside his mother in the nearby Svyatagorsky Monastery.

Façade of the family house at Mikhaylovskoye where Pushkin spent two years in exile

KALININGRAD

Dotted with tumbledown castles where Teutonic knights once engaged in bloody battles, this isolated piece of Russia with its half-forgotten history, vast deposits of amber and expanses of desolate sea-bound dunes exudes a strong sense of romance. The regional capital Kaliningrad, formerly Königsberg, has awakened from its Soviet slumber and is emerging as a vibrant city replete with great museums, historic monuments and a thriving social scene.

Known as Eastern Prussia and ruled by the Teutonic knights during the Middle Ages, this region had been coveted by many for centuries before it fell to the Soviet Union. To resist the Poles in the south and Lithuanians in the north and east during the 15th-century Teutonic wars, castles and fortresses were built throughout the region. The province was reorganized within the Kingdom of Prussia in 1773 and Königsberg became the seat of government. Prussian kings had successive defensive rings of massive fortresses constructed around the city in the 18th and 19th centuries. However, these were no match for the relentless Allied bombardments in 1944–5 that razed most of Königsberg's historic buildings; a massive Soviet offensive in 1945 brought the territory to its knees. As the Soviet Union's westernmost point, the Kaliningrad region gathered immense strategic value. It became a militarized zone that was completely off limits to foreigners, and was only opened to visitors in 1991 when the Union collapsed.

Although the symbols of Kaliningrad's Prussian heritage have long been neglected, the ruined architecture still evinces the region's glorious past. The Insterburg and Georgenburg castles are gradually being restored by enthusiastic local volunteers. The region's other attractions include the charming Baltic Sea resorts of Svetlogorsk, Yantarny and Zelenogradsk as well as the Curonian Spit, a UNESCO-listed strip of shifting dunes that stretches for 98 km (60 miles) between Kaliningrad and Lithuania.

A stretch of sandy beach against the calm waters of the Baltic Sea, Zelenogradsk

◀ The ancient water tower in the town of Svetlogorsk, an example of the region's impressive architecture

Exploring Kaliningrad

Separated from the Russian mainland by Lithuania and Poland, and fringed by the Baltic coast, Kaliningrad *oblast* (region) is Russia's smallest territory. Most of the region comprises low-lying land dotted with patches of forest, and enjoys a temperate climate. Kaliningrad, the region's capital, sits to the west and boasts architecture redolent of its Prussian past. The city is punctuated by captivating museums and leafy avenues, and has the best choice of shops, restaurants, bars and clubs. Easily accessible from Kaliningrad are the northwestern seaside towns of Zelenogradsk, Yantarny and Svetlogorsk. Yantarny is particularly delightful with its golden sand beach and incredible amber reserves. Further north lies the enigmatic Curonian Spit – a 5,000-year-old landform that has been recognized as a UNESCO World Heritage Site. Chernyakhovsk, the region's second-largest city, lies to the east and makes a good base for exploring the haunting castle ruins of nearby Insterburg and Georgenburg.

Sights at a Glance

1. *Kaliningrad pp216–17*
2. Zelenogradsk
3. Curonian Spit
4. Svetlogorsk
5. Yantarny
6. Chernyakhovsk

Key

- Major road
- Minor road
- Major railway
- Minor railway
- International border

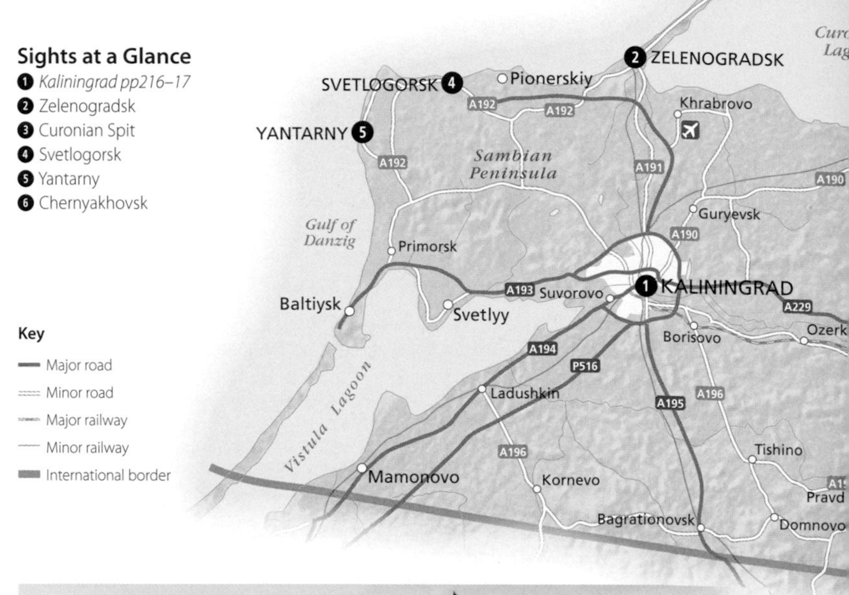

The Gothic Königsberg Cathedral with its towering steeple, on the waterfront in Kaliningrad

For map symbols *see back flap*

The golden domes of the Cathedral of Christ the Saviour towering above Kaliningrad's skyline

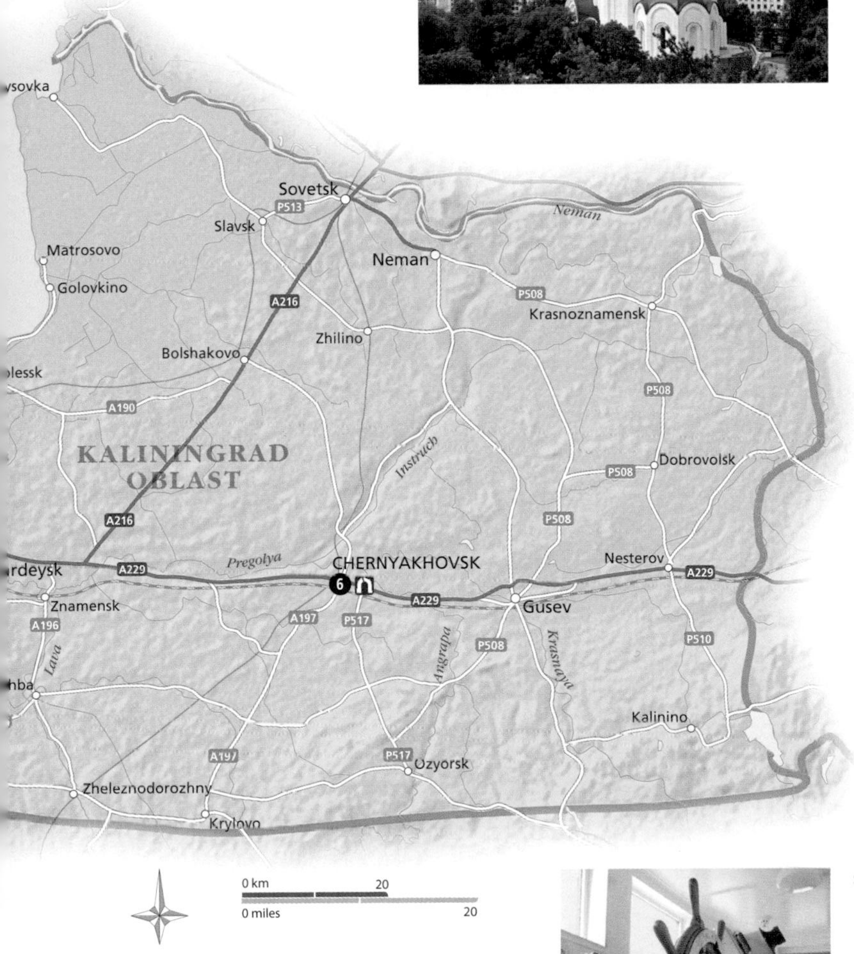

Getting Around

Regular bus and train services connect the city of Kaliningrad with coastal and inland towns, but roads are often single-lane highways so traffic can be slow. Tours of the Curonian Spit can be arranged in either Kaliningrad or Zelenogradsk. It is advisable to check the final departure times of return buses and trains when planning day trips. Taxis are plentiful but drivers will often overcharge tourists. Car hire is best arranged in Kaliningrad.

Exhibit of a ship's steering mechanism at the Museum of the World Ocean, Kaliningrad

For hotels and restaurants in this region see p270 and p289

❶ Kaliningrad

Калининград

Kaliningrad

Capital of Eastern Prussia in the 13th century, Kaliningrad – then known as Königsberg – took great pride in its architecture, which was as exquisite as Prague's. However, the Allied bombardments and Soviet occupation in 1945 devastated its rich heritage. Renamed in 1946, Kaliningrad was closed to foreigners under the Soviet regime. After the collapse of the Soviet Union in 1991, the city struggled through a decade of economic uncertainty before its transformation into today's buzzing regional capital. Kaliningrad 750th anniversary in 2005 saw the restoration of many historic buildings – a sign that the city is coming to terms with its traumatic past.

Königsberg Cathedral

Кафедральный собор Кенигсберга

Kafedralniy sobor Kjonigsberga

Kneiphof Island. **Tel** (4012) 63 17 05. **Open** 9am–5pm daily. **W sobor-kaliningrad.ru**

The striking redbrick Gothic cathedral with its 60-m (197-ft) steeple has dominated the city's skyline for centuries. Built in the early 1300s shortly after Prussia's conquest by the Teutonic knights, it was virtually destroyed during the Soviet bombardments of Königsberg in 1944. The ruined cathedral barely escaped total annihilation in the Soviet era by those intent on eradicating symbols of the city's German past. Its Gothic grandeur was restored in the 1990s with the aid of German and Russian funding.

Today, the cathedral has an Orthodox and a Lutheran chapel and two museums dedicated to its history and to the philosopher Immanuel Kant (1724–1804), who is buried under the edifice's northeastern wall. The cathedral also houses Russia's largest organ.

Museum of the World Ocean

Музей Мирового Океана

Muzey Mirovogo Okeana

Petra Velikogo Embankment 1. **Tel** (4012) 52 17 44. **Open** 10am–6pm Wed–Sun. **W world-ocean.ru**

Aquariums packed with all manner of oceanic creatures, the remains of an 18th-century shipwreck and a 16-m (53-ft) long sperm whale skeleton are among the exhibits to be found within this quayside museum.

Its main draw, however, is the chance to board the exhibition vessels moored nearby, including the B143 diesel-electric submarine, built in 1968 and operational throughout the Cold War. Its cramped crew quarters jammed with instruments, a working periscope and torpedo tubes emblazoned with Soviet stars provide a fascinating glimpse of life on board. Alongside is the *Vityaz*, a research ship famed for using a cable to measure the ocean's maximum depth for the first time. It is now home to dozens of exhibit-filled rooms. Representing Kaliningrad's booming fishing industry during the Soviet era is the German-built SRT-129 trawler, capable of carrying up to 110 tonnes (123 tons) of herring in its hold. It has since been converted into an exhibition space.

Giant sperm whale skeleton on display in the Museum of the World Ocean

Art Gallery

Галерея

Khudozhestvennaya Galereya

Moskovskiy prospekt 60. **Tel** (4012) 46 71 43. **Open** 10am–6pm Tue–Sun. **W artgallery-klgd.ru**

The gallery has a collection of contemporary works by both Russian and international artists. There are a number of socialist realism pieces as well as a small display of early 20th-century paintings by artists from pre-Soviet Königsberg. Temporary exhibitions are held regularly.

Museum of History and Art

Историко-Художественный Музей

Istonko-Khudozhestvenniy Muzey

Ulitsa Klinicheskaya 21. **Tel** (4012) 45 38 44. **Open** 10am–6pm Tue–Sun. **W westrussia.org**

Housed in a beautifully restored building that served as the city hall from 1912 until World War II, this museum has exhibits from the pre-war, wartime and post-war periods with an emphasis on the Soviet era. Archaeological findings from local Viking settlements and early Prussian villages are also on display.

Bunker Museum

Музей Блиндаж

Muzey Blindazh

Ulitsa Universitetskaya 3. **Tel** (4012) 53 65 93. **Open** 10am–5pm Tue–Sun.

Tucked away in a park off the main street is the nondescript entrance to the bunker built in February 1945 for the German commander Otto von Lasch. It was from here that he directed the defence of the city before surrendering Königsberg to the Soviet Army in April 1945 after days of relentless bombardments. One of the rooms re-creates the scene of Lasch signing the surrender document.

For hotels and restaurants in this region see p270 and p289

The steep towers of the Cathedral of Christ the Saviour, ploshchad Pobedi

Cathedral of Christ the Saviour
Собор Христа Спасителя
Sobor Khrista Spasitelya
Ploshchad Pobedi. **Open** 8am–6:30pm.

Facing Kaliningrad's main square and with its brilliant white marble façade and golden domes, this cathedral is testament to the bold resurgence of the Orthodox faith in Russia. Built in 2006, it is one of the largest cathedrals in the country.

Amber Museum
Музей Янтаря
Muzey Yantarya
Ploshchad Marshala Vasilevskogo 1. **Tel** (4012) 46 68 88. **Open** Summer: 10am–7pm Tue–Sun; Winter: 10am–6pm Tue–Sun
ambermuseum.ru

Ninety per cent of the world's amber reserves are buried underneath the Kaliningrad region from where the "sun stone" has been mined for thousands of years. Opened in 1979 and housed in the Dona Tower, the Amber Museum has displays devoted to the history of amber extraction and processing along with a splendid array of amber artworks. Besides intriguing Soviet-era pieces such as "Epoch", a clock stand depicting technological achievements, there are numerous copies of 17th- and 18th-century amber artworks. The museum also exhibits replicas of the 4,000-year-old carved amber figures found near Juodkrante on the Curonian Spit and boasts a superb array of rare "inclusions": nuggets of amber with prehistoric insects trapped inside.

King's Gate
Королевские Ворота
Korolevskie Vorota
Ulitsa Frunze 112. **Tel** (4012) 58 12 72. **Open** Wed–Sun 11am–6pm.

Built in the 1840s as part of the city's second defensive ring, this mighty redbrick gate has 2 m (7-ft) thick walls and features statues of Frederick I, Prussia's first king; Ottokar II, the king of Bohemia and Duke Albert, the last Grand Master of the Teutonic Order. It weathered the Soviet bombardment of 1944 and the damage was not repaired until 2005. Since then it has been used as a cultural centre and has a small museum dedicated to Peter the Great's visit to Königsberg in 1697.

VISITORS' CHECKLIST

Practical information
950 km (590 miles) SW of St Petersburg.
431,000.
Prospekt Mira 4. **Tel** (4012) 55 52 00. **visit-kaliningrad.ru**

Transport

Friedland Gate
Музей Фридландские Ворота
Muzey Fridlandskie Vorota
Ulitsa Dzerzhinskogo 30. **Tel** (4012) 64 40 20. **Open** 10am–6pm daily.

One of the last gates of the defensive ring to be constructed, Friedland Gate has the same redbrick Gothic structure as King's Gate. A statue of Siegfried von Feuchtwangen, a Grand Master of the Teutonic Order, that originally adorned its outer wall was restored in 2005 and the gate is now home to a museum exhibition dedicated to the history of pre-war Königsberg, from 1862–1945.

Imposing redbrick façade of King's Gate

Sights at a Glance

1. Königsberg Cathedral
2. Museum of the World Ocean
3. Art Gallery
4. Museum of History and Art
5. Bunker Museum
6. Cathedral of Christ the Saviour
7. Amber Museum
8. King's Gate
9. Friedland Gate

0 metres 800
0 yards 800

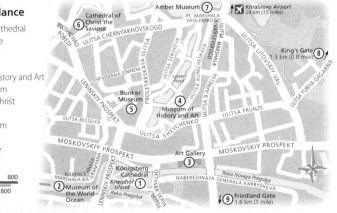

For map symbols *see back flap*

Holidaymakers enjoying the beach at Zelenogradsk

❷ Zelenogradsk

Зеленоградск

Zelenogradsk

30 km (19 miles) N of Kaliningrad. 13,000.

Just half an hour by train from Kaliningrad, Zelenogradsk is the closest seaside resort to the region's capital. Originally an unassuming fishing village called Cranz, the area first attracted tourists in the 19th century owing to its dune-backed beach that stretches for kilometres along the Curonian Spit. The village was soon overrun by wealthy Prussians who built wooden villas and guesthouses here. Renamed by the Russians, Zelenogradsk was neglected during the Cold War *(see p45)* and its status as a prime destination was usurped by Svetlogorsk.

Today, a new generation of middle-class Russians are replacing Zelenogradsk's German-era buildings with characterless modern villas, yet the resort's palpable sense of faded glory remains.

❸ Curonian Spit

Куршская Коса

Kurshskaya Kosa

1 km (half a mile) NE of Zelenogradsk. from Zelenogradsk. No. 402, Ulitsa Sergeeva 2, Kaliningrad, (4012) 53 29 07. **park-kosa.ru**

Split equally between Lithuania and Russia, this intriguing land formation, known locally as Kurshskaya Kosa, was created around 5,000 years ago when retreating glaciers deposited a strip of glacial rubble off the shore of the Baltic Sea. Sand gradually accumulated along the 98-km (60-mile) long spit to form a natural barrier between the Baltic Sea and the freshwater Curonian Lagoon.

A single road runs the entire length of the spit, which is just 400 m (1,312 ft) wide at its narrowest point and 4 km (2 miles) at its widest. Its landscape consists largely of pine forests and sandy beaches, from which Europe's largest drifting sand dunes rise to a height of up to 60 m (197 ft).

Although the region is home to just three small villages today, it was relatively densely inhabited in the past. However, deforestation in the 18th century damaged the ecosystem as a result of which the sand dunes began to shift dramatically, burying entire villages. The spit was saved by the Prussian government's reforestation initiative in the 19th century, when a vast number of trees were planted in the area. It now enjoys national park status in Russia and UNESCO recognized it as a World Heritage Site in 2000.

❹ Svetlogorsk

Светлогорск

Svetlogorsk

33 km (21 miles) W of Zelenogradsk. 11,000. Ulitsa Karla Marksa 7a, (40153) 2 20 98. **svetlogorsk-tourism.ru**

Up until the early 19th century, Svetlogorsk was a humble Prussian fishing village called Rauschen. However, once a path had been cut through its steep wooded hills to access the narrow strip of sandy beach below, it soon evolved into a pleasant summer resort. A promenade and short pier were built to make the beach accessible to public, and several quirky sculptures and mosaics were added by resident sculptor Hermann Brachert (1890–1972). Installed on Svetlogorsk's promenade is one of his most famous works, *Nymph* (1938), a mosaic clam shell sheltering a life-size bronze statue of Venus.

The town's characterful 19th-century architecture includes the Water Tower, which offers mud baths and sea water therapies. In recent years, an open cable car has been installed to save holidaymakers the walk between the town centre and the beach below.

Environs

About 2 km (1 mile) west of Svetlogorsk is the village of Otradnoe – home to the cosy

The busy promenade and beach on a summer's day, Svetlogorsk

Impressive ruins of the Insterburg Castle – bastion of the Teutonic knights

Hermann Brachert House-Museum. The charming garden here features works by the sculptor, along with other pieces by contemporary artists.

Hermann Brachert House-Museum
Ulitsa Tokareva 7. **Tel** (40153) 2 11 66.
Open 10am–5pm Sat–Thu.

5 Yantarny

Янтарный
Yantarnyy

21 km (13 miles) SW of Svetlogorsk.
6,400

Meaning "amber" in Russian, Yantarny is an appropriate name for a town that sits upon 90 per cent of the world's amber reserves. The town also boasts a breathtaking beach that is considered by many to be the best in the Kaliningrad region. Holidaymakers can make a day out of gathering small chunks of amber that are washed up onto the beach or found floating in the sea.

A shop in Yantarny selling luminous amber souvenirs

Amber, or "sun stone", has been fashioned into jewellery for millennia. In fact, an open-cast mine just outside Yantarny has been industrially extracting the precious fossilized tree resin since 1861. It currently produces around 200 tonnes (224 tons) of raw amber every year. Visitors can watch the extraction process from a viewing platform.

6 Chernyakhovsk

Черняховск
Chernyakhovsk

116 km (72 miles) SE of Zelenogradsk.
40,500.

Renamed after General Ivan Chernyakhovsky who led the Soviet forces against East Prussia in 1945, Chernyahovsk started life as Insterburg, an isolated settlement that developed around the 14th-century Teutonic castle of the same name. The town was heavily bombed by the Allies during World War II, but a number of historic buildings have since been restored. Among them are the bright yellow house on ulitsa Pionerskaya where Napoleon stayed in 1812, a crenellated 14th-century mill and a three-tiered church built in 1883 for the Lutherans, which now functions as St Michael's Orthodox Church.

Built by Teutonic knights in the 14th century, the redbrick **Insterburg Castle**, located just outside town, now stands in ruins. The castle houses a gallery of local artworks and a small museum with a collection of donated antique exhibits. Several informative displays outline the exploits of the Teutonic knights who defended their order against Lithuanian attacks from here. A team of local volunteers runs the castle and organizes popular medieval-themed events throughout the summer.

Another formidable 14th-century Teutonic relic is the nearby **Georgenburg Castle**. Standing on a steep hillside above the Insterburg river, its façade still dominates the landscape, but the interior is in need of urgent restoration for which locals are attempting to raise funds. Next door is the Georgenburg Stud Farm whose origins can be traced back to the 18th century when Trakehner horses were first bred here.

Insterburg Castle
Ulitsa Zamkovaya. **Tel** 8 906 233 78 63.
Open 11am–6pm daily.

Georgenburg Castle
Ulitsa Centralnaya 10. **Tel** 8 911 473 26 58. **Open** by prior arrangement only.

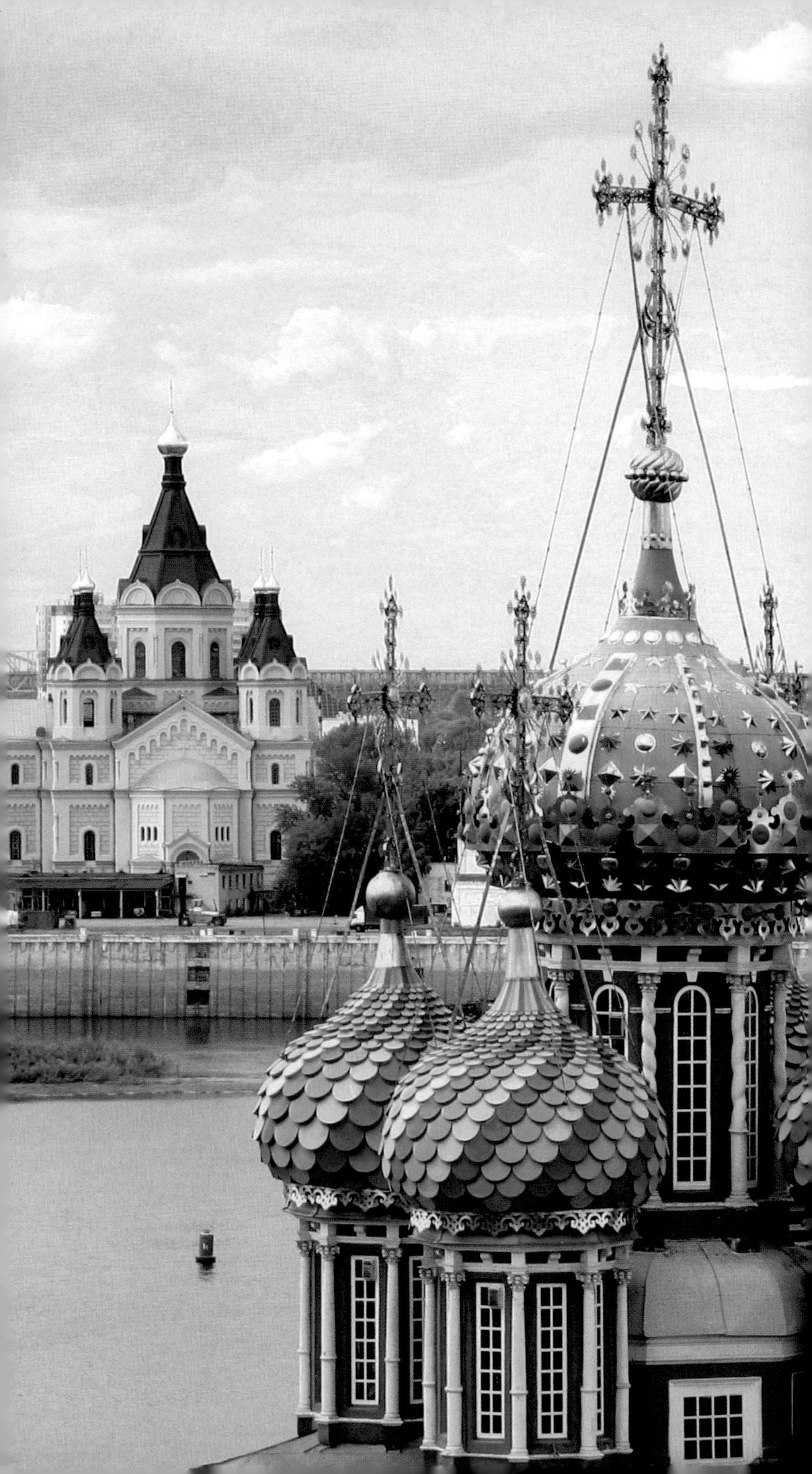

CENTRAL AND SOUTHERN RUSSIA

Colossal kremlins, gleaming golden-domed cathedrals, majestic mosques and monolithic Soviet-era buildings welcome visitors to this historic heartland of Russia. Winding its course through the region, the Volga river has played a crucial role in Russia's history. A vital trade and transport route, its banks are home to some of the country's finest cities.

Locally known as Mother Volga, Europe's largest river meanders for 3,219 km (2,000 miles) through Central Russia's fertile grasslands before reaching the lush wetlands of the Volga Delta where it drains into the Caspian Sea. For centuries, the river nurtured medieval citadels and trading posts, which came to be established along its course during Ivan the Terrible's forceful expansion of the Russian Empire in the 16th century. Fortified by kremlins and enriched by trade along the river, the settlements developed into glorious cities adorned with grand mansions, churches and state buildings.

Religion in all its forms was repressed during the Soviet era, but most religious buildings have since been returned to their communities. The cultural revival that began after the collapse of the Soviet Union in 1991 is in full swing. Since Russia's selection as host of the 2018 FIFA World Cup™, massive investment is being made in infrastructure projects to modernize the region.

A melting pot of cultures, the central and southern regions are inhabited by numerous ethnic groups, notably the Tatars, whose roots can be traced back to the 10th century when Islam was first adopted in Bolgar. The mosques and churches of Astrakhan and Kazan are a testament to the harmonious relations between the various cultures here.

Although tourism is still in its infancy, the cities across the region are a joy to explore. Today, the Volga is a source of summer leisure for locals who stroll along well-kept embankments or sunbathe on the riverside beaches. In winter, when the river freezes over, ice-hole fishing is a popular pastime.

Locals watching jugglers perform at Samara Embankment

◀ Multicoloured domes of the Church of the Blessed Virgin, Nizhny Novgorod

Exploring Central and Southern Russia

Packed with sites of both historical and natural interest, the central and southern regions form the heart of Russia, although it covers only a fraction of the country's territory. Located along the Volga river, the cities of Kazan, Astrakhan and Nizhny Novgorod boast immaculate kremlins. Kazan also makes an excellent base to visit the ruins of Sviyazhsk and Bolgar that are currently being restored. The region is home to several cities famous for their historic quarters of wooden houses. Some of the best examples can be seen in Ulyanovsk and Yekaterinburg, where many have been converted into house-museums. West of Yekaterinberg, Perm is a draw among art enthusiasts for its contemporary art scene. A must-visit for history lovers, Volgograd's attractions include striking war monuments and museums. Astrakhan is the obvious base for trips into the Volga Delta, which delights with labyrinthine waterways that are home to lotus flowers, flamingoes and some of the country's largest sturgeon.

Area illustrated

Sights at a Glance

1. Nizhny Novgorod
2. Kazan
3. Staroye Arakchino
4. Sviyazhsk
5. Bolgar
6. Ulyanovsk
7. Saransk
8. *Samara pp228–9*
9. Volgograd
10. Astrakhan
11. Volga Delta
12. Perm
13. Perm-36 Memorial Centre of Political Repression
14. Kungur Ice Cave
15. Yekaterinburg

Key

- Major road
- Minor road
- Major railway
- Trans-Siberian Railway
- Minor railway
- International border
- Federal border
- Peak

Buildings in the Old Tatar Quarter in Kazan

For additional map symbols *see back flap*

Wooden house with brightly painted shutters, Sviyazhsk

Getting Around

Regular bus services connect most of the region's settlements. Road conditions, however, range from good to poor and tend to get worse in winter. Trains are a safe and efficient means of getting around; the Trans-Siberian route passes through Perm, Yekaterinburg and Nizhny Novgorod. Visitors seeking a quicker means of transportation can fly between the major cities in the region. A long-distance cruise on the Volga river is worth considering, although it is relatively slow and expensive.

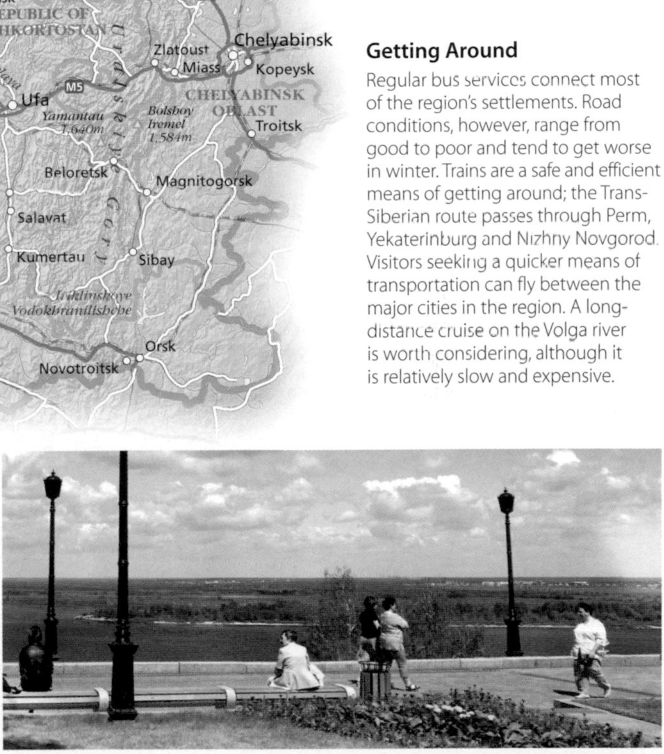

The well-kept promenade overlooking the Volga river, Nizhny Novgorod

For hotels and restaurants in this region see pp270–71 and pp289–90

The splendid Annunciation Monastery overlooking the picturesque riverside, Nizhny Novgorod

1 Nizhny Novgorod

Нижний Новгород

Nizhniy Novgorod

430 km (267 miles) NE of Moscow. 1,250,000. **admgor.nnov.ru**

This refreshingly upbeat city with its robust **Kremlin**, elegant 19th-century architecture and a sprinkling of golden-domed churches sits on a hilltop above the confluence of two great rivers: the Volga and the Oka.

Nizhny Novgorod was founded in 1221 by Grand Prince Yuri II to defend the northeastern frontier of the Vladimir-Suzdal Principality that later merged with Muscovy. The city's first Kremlin was razed by the Crimean Tatars in 1408. A century later, a redbrick Kremlin, the region's strongest, was built to protect Muscovy's eastern border from the Tatars of Kazan. By the 19th century, the city had developed into a wealthy centre of commerce due to its port on the Volga river. Many of its elegant buildings, especially those that line the pedestrianized ulitsa Pokrovskaya, date from that period. During the Soviet era, it was renamed Gorky after Maxim Gorky, Stalin's favourite Soviet writer, who grew up here.

Today, the Kremlin's reconstructed towers and walls give a definite sense of past glory. But the grounds within lack the atmosphere of other walled cities as many of the original churches were demolished to make way for 19th-century and Soviet-era administration buildings. The view of the Volga river from within the Kremlin, however, never fails to disappoint. The early 16th-century Dmitri Tower, the Kremlin's main gate, was rebuilt between 1949 and 1969.

A museum within the tower tells the story of its reconstruction. The pretty tent-roofed **Archangel Mikhail Cathedral**, dating from 1628, houses the tomb of Nizhny Novgorod's most celebrated son, Kuzma Minin, a butcher who famously raised an army of local volunteers with Prince Dmitri Pozharskiy to rescue Moscow from Polish invaders in the early 17th century *(see p41)*. An obelisk near the cathedral commemorates their heroism. The arsenal building running along the wall to the right of Dmitri Tower houses the National Centre of Contemporary Art, which regularly hosts exhibitions by Russian and international artists. A short walk northwest is the **State Art Museum**, with a collection of Russian and Western European works.

Below the Kremlin, on the banks of the Oka river, is the 18th-century **Church of the Blessed Virgin** with its wedding-cake structure and multicoloured domes. Equally impressive is the nearby **Annunciation Monastery** that was founded in 1229. On the other side of the city is the AM Gorky Museum-Apartment, one of the three museums dedicated to the life of Maxim Gorky. Another of the city's attractions is the open-air **Museum of Volga People's Architecture**, which lies south of the city centre. The museum contains 18th- and 19th-century wooden houses and churches that have been moved here from around the Volga region.

State Art Museum
Kreml, Korpus 3. **Tel** (831) 439 13 73. **Open** 11am–6pm Wed & Fri–Mon, noon–8pm Thu.
artmuseumnn.ru

Annunciation Monastery
Melnichny pereulok. **Tel** (831) 430 07 97. call ahead to book.

Museum of Volga People's Architecture
Shchelokovsky Kutor Park. **Tel** (831) 422 10 88. **Open** 10am–5pm Tue–Sun.
ngiamz.ru

The imposing Dmitri Tower, Nizhny Novgorod

❷ Kazan

Казань

Kazan'

387 km (240 miles) SE of Nizhny Novgorod. 1,160,000. Ulitsa Kremlovskaya 15, (843) 292 30 10. **gokazan.com**

A thriving, progressive city, Kazan has invested massively in modernization programmes yet has deep historic roots. Originally part of the ancient Volga Bulgaria kingdom, it was not until the 15th century that the Kazan khanate was formed, with Kazan as its powerful Islamic capital. Trade along the Volga river brought immense wealth to the khanate. Soon this attracted the attention of Russia's Ivan the Terrible who laid siege to the city before capturing it in 1552. Under Russian rule, the white-stone **Kremlin** was constructed and onion-domed churches were built alongside Kazan's ancient mosques. But Soviet rule after 1917 stifled the city's multiculturalism by razing many of its religious buildings. Since the collapse of the Soviet Union, Kazan has emerged as a city proud of its mixed faith heritage. Officially recognized as Russia's third capital, the city is also known as the country's sporting capital.

Kazan's focal point is its imposing hilltop Kremlin, overlooking the confluence of the Kazanka and Volga rivers. The 16th-century Spasskaya Tower is the main entrance to the Kremlin.The Cadet School now houses the Hermitage Centre, a branch of the Hermitage in St Petersburg. The pencil-thin minarets of the grand **Kul Sharif Mosque** rise behind the Cadet School. Built in 2005 for Kazan's millennium celebrations, this huge mosque has an observation balcony on the third floor. The six-tiered Suyumbike Tower, which leans at a rather alarming angle, was named after the last queen of Kazan and stands at the heart of the Kremlin alongside the presidential palace and the **Annunciation Cathedral**, commissioned by Ivan the Terrible in 1552.

Empress Catherine I's carriage in the National Museum of the Republic of Tatarstan, Kazan

Across from the Kremlin's main entrance is the **National Museum of the Republic of Tatarstan**. Housed in a palatial 19th-century building, the museum's exhaustive collection covers the region's history in great detail. Among the notable exhibits is Empress Catherine I's carriage, which was used during her visit to Kazan in 1767. Nearby, the **St Peter and Paul's Cathedral** is one of the city's finest buildings. Decorated with lacy floral plasterwork and topped with a blue-and-white tiled dome, it was built to commemorate Peter the Great's visit to Kazan in 1722.

The far end of pedestrianized ulitsa Bauman, Kazan's central street, is dominated by the red-brick Epiphany Bell Tower that was erected in 1897 to accompany the modest 18th-century Epiphany Church to its rear.

South of the city centre lies the Old Tatar Quarter. Sadly, most of its characterful wooden buildings have since been replaced with modern blocks. Of the quarter's surviving mosques, Nurallah Mosque, built in 1849, is Kazan's oldest working mosque. The late 19th-century **Azimov Mosque**, with its elaborate decorative brickwork, is considered the city's most beautiful.

Annunciation Cathedral
Open 9am–6pm daily.

National Museum of the Republic of Tatarstan
Ulitsa Kremlenskaya 2. **Tel** (843) 292 89 84. **Open** 10am–6pm Tue–Sun (till 5pm Fri). **tatar.museum.ru**

St Peter and Paul's Cathedral
Ulitsa Musy Dzhalilya 21.
Open 9am–6pm daily.

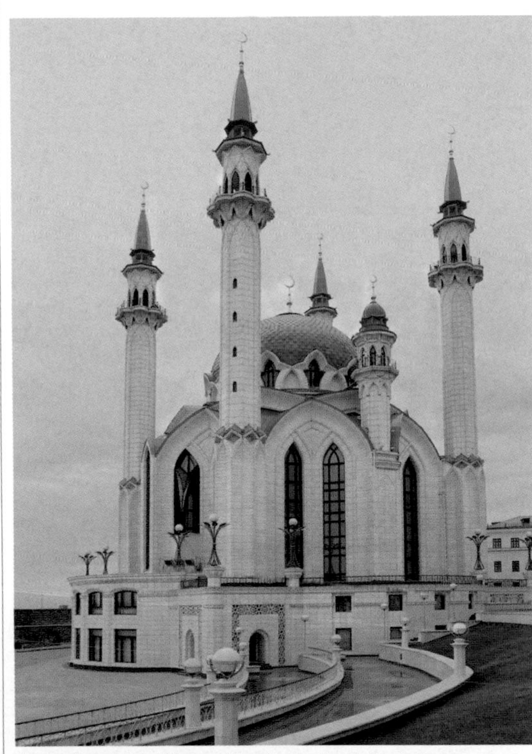

The magnificent Kul Sharif Mosque with soaring blue-tipped minarets, Kazan

❸ Staroye Arakchino

Старое Аракчино

Staroe Arakchino

10 km (6 miles) W of Kazan. Ulitsa Kremlovskaya 15/25, (843) 292 30 10. **gokazan.com**

A small suburb of Kazan until 1994, Staroye Arakchino has since been put on the map by sculptor and healer Ildar Khanova's inspiration to build the **Temple of All Religions** beside the local railway station. Relying on donations and volunteer labour has meant slow progress, but the unusual structure is finally nearing completion. A gloriously eclectic blend of colours, styles and shapes, the temple has a tower, dome, minaret or spire for each of the world's 12 major religions.

The striking Temple of All Religions, Staroye Arakchino

❹ Sviyazhsk

Свияжск

Sviyazhsk

60 km (37 miles) SW of Kazan. 300. from Kazan. Ulitsa Kremlovskaya 15, Kazan, (843) 292 30 10.

The settlement of Sviyazhsk has been considered an island since the Kuybyshev Reservoir, a hydroelectric dam, raised water levels in 1957, but is still accessible by a strip of road. Ivan the Terrible chose the spot in 1551 to build a base after his attempt to conquer Kazan ended with a humiliating retreat. His troops turned the barren hilltop into a fortress larger than Moscow's before laying siege to Kazan and finally taking the city in 1552. In a curious historical parallel, the Bolshevik Red Army used Sviyazhsk as a base from which to defeat their White Army foes at Kazan in 1918.

Following massive local government investment, Sviyazhsk's decaying collection of ancient ruins has recently been transformed into a major tourist attraction. The restored 16th-century church and cathedral within the walled **Assumption Monastery** are the island's oldest buildings and contain fragments of frescoes painted during the reign of Ivan the Terrible. Typically for the period, both are simple structures that were built with defence in mind. Across from these are the Monastery Stables, where local craftsmen demonstrate their traditional skills and children can ride horses in the yard.

Further inland is the **John the Baptist Monastery** with its red-brick Church of Our Lady from 1898 and a replica 16th-century wooden church. At the opposite end of the island, the town square overlooks the river port.

Assumption Monastery

Ulitsa Uspenskaya. **Tel** (917) 265 65 47. **Open** 10am–5pm daily. **ostrovgrad.org**

John the Baptist Monastery

Ulitsa Troitskaya. **Tel** (917) 265 65 47. **Open** 10am–5pm daily. **ostrovgrad.org**

Stunning view of the island town of Sviyazhsk on the frozen Volga river

❺ Bolgar

Болгар

Bolgar

198 km (123 miles) S of Kazan. 8,300. from Kazan. from Kazan. from Kazan. Ulitsa Kremlovskaya 15, Kazan, (843) 292 30 10.

The ancient riverside capital of Volga Bulgaria is of great significance to Russia's Muslims as it was here in AD 922 that Islam was first accepted on what is now Russian soil. Bolgar's historic ruins are part of the open-air **Great Bulgar Museum**, just outside modern Bolgar. Although they were neglected during the Soviet era, the region's influential Muslim community has since attracted local government investment to enhance the site.

Of the ruins spread over a vast expanse of grassland, the 13th-century Main Mosque forms the centrepiece. Its restored minaret is the focus of annual celebrations to mark Bolgar's acceptance of Islam. Nearby are the restored 14th-century Eastern and Northern Mausoleums and the 18th-century Assumption Church, which is seen as a symbol of the region's harmonious interfaith relations. To the north is the small minaret that offers great views from its balcony, and the Black Chamber that served as a courtroom in the 14th century before its use as a smokehouse blackened the interior.

Opposite the museum stands the Monument to the Adoption of Islam that houses Kazan's Great

Koran, the largest printed one in the world. Near the southern gate to the museum is the splendid **White Mosque**, next to which is the **Museum of Bread**, which focuses on agricultural cycles and bread-making techniques.

Great Bulgar Museum
Ulitsa Nazarovyk 67. **Tel** (843) 473 94 14. **Open** 8am–5pm daily.

❻ Ulyanovsk

Ульяновск

Ulyanovsk

231 km (143 miles) SW of Kazan.
610,000.
welcometoulyanovsk.com

Named after one of the 20th century's most influential figures, Ulyanovsk is the birthplace of Vladimir Ilyich Ulyanov (1870–1924), better known as Lenin. Known as Simbirsk when the city was founded, it was here that Lenin, the mastermind of the October Revolution, spent his first 17 years. The various houses that his wealthy middle-class family rented or owned have been preserved; two of them form the core of the **Lenin Memorial Centre**. Built in 1970 to commemorate his 100th anniversary, the museum is packed with Lenin-related memorabilia.

Ulyanovsk's position above the vast expanse of the Volga river affords superb views and many of its 19th-century wooden houses in the peaceful leafy suburbs are in remarkably good condition. Lined with pretty wooden houses is ulitsa Lenina, one of Simbirsk's oldest streets. **Melochnaya Lavka** at number 78 is a small museum that has re-created the interior of a 19th-century general store. On the next street, the **Simbirsk Museum of Architecture** is housed in a wooden building, with elaborately decorated eaves and window frames.

One of the many wooden houses on ulitsa Lenina, Ulyanovsk

Façade of the Military Museum, Saransk

Lenin Memorial Centre
Ploshchad 100-Letiya Lenina 1. **Tel** (8422) 44 11 55. **Open** 10am–5pm Tue–Sun.

Melochnaya Lavka
Ulitsa Lenina 76. **Open** 10am–5pm Tue–Sun.

Simbirsk Museum of Architecture
Ulitsa L Tolstogo 24. **Tel** (8422) 42 04 63. **Open** 10am–5pm Tue–Sun.

❼ Saransk

Саранск

Saransk

229 miles (142 km) SW of Ulyanovsk.
295,500.

The capital of the Russian Republic of Mordovia, Saransk is home to a significant minority of ethnic Mordovians who speak either Moksha or Erzya. Both languages have Finno-Ugric roots and are listed as endangered by UNESCO. Mordovian culture can be traced back to the 6th century, but Saransk was founded only in 1641 as a fortress to protect Russia's eastern frontier. Although fires in the 19th century and decades of Soviet city planning left Saransk with little architectural heritage, in recent years the city has invested heavily in a reconstruction programme timed for completion before it hosts the FIFA World Cup™ in 2018. The city's new centrepiece is the golden-domed **Theodore Ushakov Cathedral**, consecrated in 2006 and fronted by immaculate flowerbeds. Just behind is the War Memorial dedicated to Mordovian soldiers who died in World War II, and the circular **Military Museum**, which tells the stories of Russia's 20th-century wars. The **Mordovian Museum of Visual Arts**, to the northeast, houses works by internationally acclaimed Mordovian sculptor Stepan Erzia (1876–1959).

Theodore Ushakov Cathedral
Ulitsa Bolshevistskaya. **Open** 7am–9pm daily.

Military Museum
Ulitsa Sovetskaya 34. **Tel** (8342) 47 50 00. **Open** 10am–5pm Tue–Sun.

Mordovian Museum of Visual Arts
Ulitsa Kommunisticheskaya 61. **Tel** (8342) 47 56 38. **Open** 9am–6pm Tue–Sun. **erzia-museum.ru**

View of the splendid Theodore Ushakov Cathedral, Saransk

❽ Samara

Самара

Samara

Founded as a fortress in the 16th century to protect Russia's eastern border, Samara soon developed into a bustling city because of its location along the Volga trading route. Known as Kuybyshev in 1935 after Stalin's key economic advisor, Valerian Vladimirovich Kuybyshev, the city was chosen as the Soviet Union's alternative capital should Moscow fall to the Germans during World War II. The city regained its original name in 1991 when it was also fully opened to foreigners. Today, the charming historic centre and the lovely embankment, with sweeping views of the Volga river, make Samara a pleasant city to visit.

Regional Art Museum

Самарский Областой Художественный Музей

Samarskiy Oblastoy Khudozhestvenniy Muzey

Ulitsa Kuybysheva 92. **Tel** (846) 333 46 50. **Open** 10am–6pm Wed–Mon. **artmus.ru**

A short walk north of the Lenin Statue that dominates ploshchad Revolyutsii, this museum is worth visiting for a glimpse of the magnificent interior alone. Its large collection includes a significant number of pieces from the Soviet era such as the evocative *Lenin on Red Square* (1934) by Boris Yohansen, a leading Soviet painter in the 1930s. In addition, the museum contains Russian 18th- to 19th-century and avant-garde paintings, along with an impressive collection of exhibits from the Middle East and Asia.

Children's Art Gallery

Детская картинная галерея

Detskaya Kartinnaya galereya

Ulitsa Kuybysheva 139. **Tel** (846) 332 43 98. **Open** 9am–5:30pm daily.

Dedicated to exhibiting and encouraging children's art since 1991, this unique gallery has a delightful collection of art. The museum occupies a fantastic 19th-century mansion that was built for a wealthy merchant who made his fortune by importing Edison's electric light bulbs. The mansion's combination of Russian and German architectural styles, replete with a fairy-tale turret, make it one of the city's most iconic buildings.

Alabin Museum

Музей Им П.В. Алабина

Muzey IM PV Alabina

Ulitsa Leninskaya 142. **Tel** (846) 332 28 89. **Open** 10am–6pm Tue–Sun. **alabin.ru**

One of the region's oldest, the Alabin Museum was founded by city mayor Petr Alabin in 1886. Although the museum has a somewhat uninviting, concrete exterior, its collection of over 180,000 exhibits are worth visiting. The wide range of displays include weapons dating back to the 14th century, ancient coins and clothes as well as dinosaur fossils.

The austere façade of Alabin Museum

Stalin's Bunker

Бункер Сталина

Bunker Stalin

Ulitsa Frunze 167. **Tel** (846) 333 35 71. **Open** 11am–3pm Mon–Fri.

A well-guarded secret until 1990, this 34-m (116-ft) deep bunker was constructed between February and December 1942. It was intended to accommodate Stalin and his State Defence Committee in the event of their evacuation from Moscow as German troops advanced towards the capital. But Stalin stayed in Moscow and never made use of the bunker. Now open as a museum, visitors need to descend five floors to the lowest level to see a 70-sq m (753-sq ft) copy of the Kremlin's meeting hall as well as the private office intended for Stalin's use.

Zhiguli Brewery

Жигулевский Пивоваренный Завод

Zhigulevskiy Pivovarenniy Zavod

Volzhsky prospekt 4. **Tel** (846) 332 41 75. **samarabeer.ru**

This imposing redbrick brewery was built on the bank of the Volga river in 1881 by an Austrian entrepreneur. Within a few years, his award-winning Vienna Beer was being distributed throughout Russia and was regarded as one of the country's best. During the Soviet era, the beer's bourgeois name was changed to Zhiguli, after the Zhiguli Hills nearby. It became the country's most popular beer following its production in vast quantities at hundreds of breweries across Russia. Zhiguli beer remains hugely popular and Samara is considered the best place to sample it. Locals can be seen queuing outside the brewery through the year to buy fresh draught beer from its shop.

A bottle of Zhiguli Beer

Monument of Glory

Монумент Славы

Monument Slavy

Ploshchad Slavy.

This striking monument features a tapering 40-m (131-ft) high pedestal upon which a gleaming

For hotels and restaurants in this region see pp270–71 and pp289–90

The magnificent Monument of Glory dedicated to aviation workers

statue of a worker holds aloft a pair of silver wings. It was erected in 1971 to celebrate the heroic achievements of Samara's aviation workers who produced the IL-4 bomber and over 36,000 IL-2 ground attack planes during World War II. The neighbouring War Memorial and eternal flame were also built in 1971. In the northeastern corner of the square stands the golden domed St George's Cathedral, which was added in 1997 to commemorate the 55th anniversary of the Soviet Union's victory in World War II.

Samara Embankment

Самарская набережная

Samarskaya naberezhnaya

With a sandy beach stretching for several kilometres along the shore of the Volga river, the Samara embankment is the city's most attractive feature during summer. The embankment has a raised promenade, which is thronged with locals walking, roller-skating, cycling and jogging past a seemingly endless succession of cafés and bars. The beach below is a major draw for sunbathers.

Summer crowds at the beach along Samara Embankment

VISITORS' CHECKLIST

Practical information

352 km (219 miles) S of Kazan.

1,165,000.

city.samara.ru

Transport

Samara Space Museum

Самара Космическая

Samara Kosmicheskaya

Prospekt Lenina 21. **Tel** (846) 263 39 35. **Open** 10am–6pm Tue–Sat.

samaracosmos.ru

The highlight of this museum's exterior is the awe-inspiring 50-m (164-ft) high Soyuz rocket that seems to puncture the skyline like a modern-day church spire. Opened in 2007, the museum's well-presented exhibits cover the Russian space industry's recent history. Samara has a long history of involvement in the space industry. In 1961, Yuri Gagarin was brought to rest in the city after successfully orbiting the Earth in his Vostok 1 spacecraft, which along with the later Soyuz rockets was designed and built here.

Sights at a Glance

1. Regional Art Museum
2. Children's Art Gallery
3. Alabin Museum
4. Stalin's Bunker
5. Zhiguli Brewery
6. Monument of Glory
7. Samara Embankment
8. Samara Space Museum

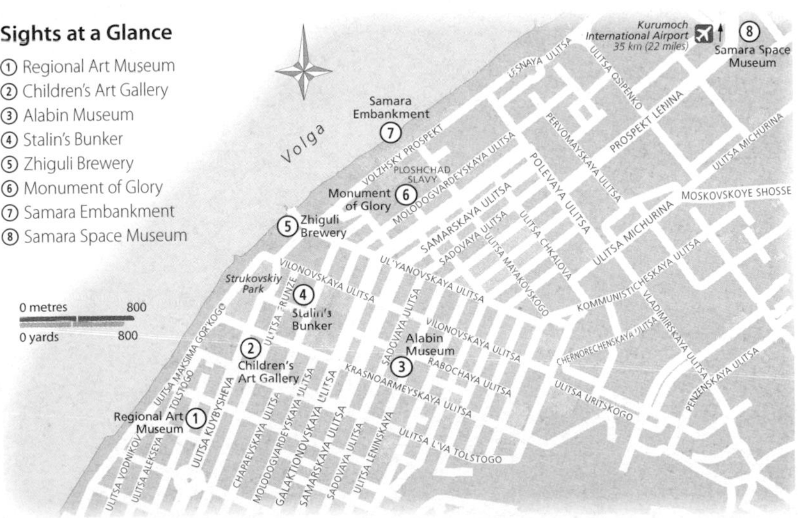

For map symbols *see back flap*

The splendid Kul Sharif Mosque, iconic of Kazan's multicultural heritage ▶

A tank on display in the Battle of Stalingrad Panorama Museum

9 Volgograd

Волгоград
Volgograd

810 km (503 miles) SW of Samara. 1,020,200.

Built to defend Russia's southern border, Volgograd was founded in the 16th century as a fortress called Tsaritsyn. It did not bear witness to major warfare until 1918 when the Russian Red and White armies clashed here repeatedly *(see p44)*. But it was in August 1942 that the city, renamed Stalingrad, saw the Soviet Union fight the invading Axis armies in the landmark Battle of Stalingrad. By February 1943, the battle had claimed around two million lives and the city was in ruins. Renamed Volgograd in 1961, the city has since been rebuilt, but the horrors of war are unlikely to be forgotten.

Mamayev Kurgan

Мамаев Курган
Mamaev Kurgan

Mamayev Kurgan hill. **Open** 24 hrs daily.

A strategic location that witnessed intense fighting during the Battle of Stalingrad, Mamayev Kurgan hill is now the site of a remarkable memorial complex to all who perished in the battle. Broad flights of steps, flanked by relief sculptures of battle scenes, lead visitors to the centrepiece – a mighty statue of Mother Russia wielding a 27-m (88-ft) sword. Built in 1967, it is one of the largest freestanding statues in the world. Just below is the cylindrical Hall of Glory, with a huge statue of a hand holding an eternal flame in the centre. A guard of honour keeps constant vigil.

Battle of Stalingrad Panorama Museum

Музей-панорама Сталинградская Битва
Muzey-panorama Stalingradskaya bitva

Ulitsa Chuykova 47. **Tel** (8442) 23 72 72. **Open** check website for timings. **stalingrad-battle.ru**

A visit to this enthralling museum is an absolute must. Halls on the ground floor show the stages of the Battle of Stalingrad chronologically, from the German advance during Operation Barbarossa to the eventual Soviet victory. The fascinating exhibits include mangled weapons found on the battlefield, a General's greatcoat riddled with bullet holes, military vehicles and battle plans. Another of the museum's highlights can be viewed by climbing the central spiral staircase that culminates in a model of Mamayev Kurgan hill surrounded by a panoramic painting of the battle. The war-damaged flour-mill building outside the museum has been left untouched as a monument to the horrors of war.

View of the grand arch on the Volga-Don Canal right opposite the Volga-Don Canal Museum

Regional Museum

Краеведческий Музей
Kraevedcheskiy Muzey

Prospekt Lenina 7. **Tel** (8442) 38 04 54. **Open** 10am–6pm Wed–Mon.

This museum offers a glimpse of life in pre-Soviet Tsaritsyn. Scale models and maps of the old town are on display alongside some big-barrelled flintlock muskets and pistols from the 18th century. Peter the Great's felt cap and cane, which he donated to the museum during a visit to the town, hold pride of place. A copy of his death mask can also be seen.

Old Sarepta Ethnographic Museum

Музей этнографический "Старая Сарепта"
Muzey-Zapovednik "Staraya Sarepta"

Ulitsa Izobilnaya 10. **Tel** (8442) 67 33 02. **Open** 9am–5pm Tue–Sun. **altsarepta.ru**

Located far enough from the battle scene to have survived World War II relatively unscathed, this small cluster of 18th- and 19th-century buildings was built by Germans invited to the region by Catherine the Great. The Ethnographic Museum has a fine display of agricultural tools, traditional outfits, early medical instruments and household objects used by the Volga German community.

Volga-Don Canal Museum

Музей Истории Волго-Донского канала-
Muzey Istorii Volgo-Donskogo Kanala

Ulitsa Fadeeva 35A. **Tel** (8442) 69 57 44. **Open** 10am–noon & 1–4:30pm Tue, Wed & Fri. **volgodon-museum.ru**

Located opposite the Volga-Don Canal, this museum features impressive exhibits on the history of the canal's construction. After two failed attempts by Peter the Great in the early 18th century, the 101-km (63-mile) canal was finally completed by Soviet political prisoners between 1948 and 1952. This connection between the two great rivers, Volga and Don, was the final link in the European waterway ring that served to shorten shipping routes.

⑩ Astrakhan

Астрахань

Astrakhan'

424 km (263 miles) SE of Volgograd. 520,000.

The immaculate 16th-century **Kremlin** in Astrakhan is one of Russia's best, but most visitors flock to this "capital of the Caspian Sea" to see the region's diverse flora and fauna. The city makes for a pleasant visit with its riverside embankment, an atmospheric old quarter of mosques and weathered wooden houses as well as the splendid Kremlin.

Although Astrakhan today is mainly populated by ethnic Russians, the city also has a significant minority of Tatars whose roots date back to the once powerful Astrakhan khanate that fell to Ivan the Terrible in 1552. Construction of the Kremlin began soon after, with walls measuring up to 5 m (16 ft) wide in places designed to withstand the heaviest of bombardments. The Russian defenders knew that, in the event of an attack, there would be no chance of reinforcements from Moscow. Of its seven towers, only three – the Zhitnaya, Crimean and Artillery towers – were part of the original complex. East of the Kremlin, the Prechistensky Gate serves as the main entrance. It is topped with an 80-m (262-ft) high bell tower that was built in 1912 to complement the adjacent 18th-century **Assumption Cathedral**. Its lower church is heated for winter use, while the glorious upper cathedral, with its 30-m (98-ft) columns and marble-clad walls, is used in summer. Opposite lies the 17th-century **Trinity Monastery**. Currently under renovation, it is one of the Kremlin's oldest buildings.

Exterior of the three-storey Dogadin Art Gallery, Astrakhan

A short walk east of the Kremlin along ulitsa Sovetskaya is the **Regional Museum**. A collection of exquisite Sarmatian gold jewellery from the 4th and 5th centuries is among the museum's highlights. Further east is the **Dogadin Art Gallery** with an absorbing display of mostly Russian works that include paintings by Kazimir Maleevich (1879–1935) and Vasily Kandinsky (1866–1944) and by Astrakhan-born painter Boris Kustodiev (1878–1927). The best of Kustodiev's artworks can be seen at the **Kustodiev House Museum** northeast of the city centre.

South of the May 1st Canal lies the old Kirushi Quarter. Part of former Tatar and Persian suburbs, it is dotted with dilapidated wooden residences. Several of the quarter's mosques have been renovated in recent years, but it is still in dire need of restoration.

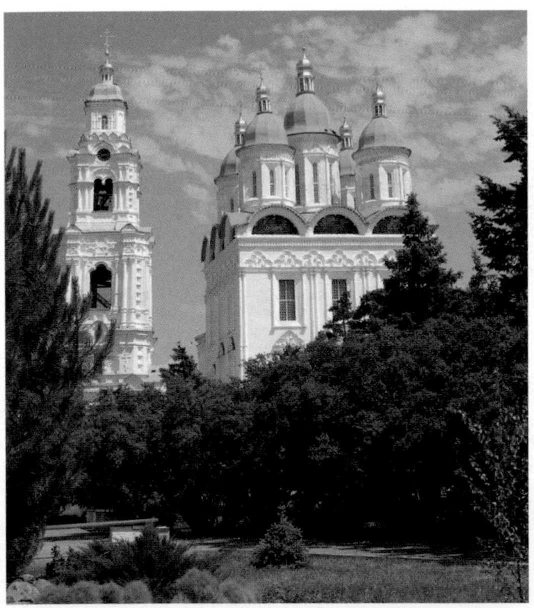

Spectacular view of the Prechistensky Gate and the adjacent Assumption Cathedral, Astrakhan

Assumption Cathedral
Ulitsa Trediakovskogo 2, Kreml. **Open** 8am–7pm daily. **astrsobor.ru**

Regional Museum
Ulitsa Sovetskaya 15. **Tel** (8512) 51 18 22. **Open** 10am–5pm Sat–Thu.

Dogadin Art Gallery
Ulitsa Sverlova 81. **Tel** (8512) 51 11 21. **Open** 10am–6pm Tue–Sun. **agkg.narod.ru**

⑪ Volga Delta

Астрахань

Astrakhan

70 km (43 miles) S of Astrakhan. from Astrakhan. Note. A permit is required to enter the delta. Several tour agencies in Astrakhan organize trips to the delta.

Europe's largest river delta is a labyrinth of lakes and water channels formed from sediment dumped by the Volga river as it drains into the Caspian Sea. Although hunting and fishing are big business here, the wetlands also attract bird watchers and nature-lovers in search of pristine beauty.

The star attraction of the Volga Delta is the **Astrakhan Biosphere Reserve**. Established in 1919, the huge reserve is home to a variety of exotic species of birds, fish and plants. The Museum of Nature within the reserve details its history and provides an insight into scientific studies.

⓬ Perm

Пермь

Perm'

663 km (412 miles) NE of Kazan. 990,000. Ulitsa Lenina 58 (entry from Komsomolsky prospekt), (342) 218 60 21. Jun: White Nights Summer Festival. **visitperm.ru**

Exhibits on display at the Perm Museum of Contemporary Art

Perm is blighted by its typically unappealing Soviet architecture, but progressive local policies have given a new lease of life to the city – it hopes to become Russia's first European Capital of Culture in 2020. Dotted with modern artworks and some lovely 19th-century buildings, the city centre has a Green Line, a walking and cycling route that links all the city's sights. A regular feature of the city's cultural calendar, the White Nights Summer Festival features dance shows and exhibitions.

An industrial centre since its foundation by Vasily Tatishchev in 1723, Perm was a centre of weapons production during World War II. Many west Russian factories were relocated to the city when Nazi armies threatened the Soviet capital. The city was subsequently rendered off-limits to foreigners until 1991.

Recent excavations suggest that the area has been inhabited since the Paleolithic Era. Related artifacts are on display at the **Perm Regional Museum**, housed in a palatial 19th-century mansion overlooking the Kama river. Among the museum's other intriguing exhibits are the "Perm animal-style" bone ornaments carved with animal motifs that date back to the 5th century BC; copies are sold as souvenirs throughout the city. Opposite the museum is the former building of the River Boat Station, which is now occupied by **Perm Museum of Contemporary Art (PERMM)**. A capacious contemporary art gallery, it regularly hosts rotating exhibitions and is the hub of the city's thriving modern art scene. West of PERMM along the river bank is the **Perm State Art Gallery** located in the grand Transfiguration Cathedral since 1922. Among its huge collection of Russian and West European artworks are numerous crude wooden figures, which were made for local churches but were often venerated as pagan idols in the 17th and 18th centuries. The gallery is due to be relocated to a building next to the Transfiguration Cathedral.

Perm Regional Museum
Ulitsa Monastyrskaya 11. **Tel** (342) 257 18 06. **Open** 10am–7pm Tue, Wed & Fri–Sun, noon–9pm Thu.

Perm Museum of Contemporary Art (PERMM)
Ulitsa Monastyrskaya 2. **Tel** (342) 219 91 72. **Open** noon–9pm daily. **permm.ru**

Perm State Art Gallery
Komsomolsky prospekt 4. **Tel** (342) 212 22 50. **Open** check website for timings. **gallery.permonline.ru**

Permian wooden sculptures at the Perm State Art Gallery

⓭ Perm-36 Memorial Centre of Political Repression

Пермь-36 музей истории политических репрессий

Muzey Istorii politicheskikh repressiy

120 km (74 miles) NE of Perm; Kutchino, (342) 212 61 29. **Open** 10am–5pm Tue–Sun. call in advance. **perm36.ru**

Of the numerous brutal Gulag prison camps set up during Stalin's repressive regime, Perm-36 is the only one to have survived. Now a memorial and museum, it was built in a remote forest in 1946. Unlike other camps that were relocated once they had served their purpose, Perm-36 remained in operation until 1987, when most political prisoners were pardoned.

One of the camp's original timber huts has been preserved and many buildings, including the punishment block, bathhouse and infirmary, have been restored. The on-site museum details the daily life of prisoners who were woken at 6am for a meagre breakfast before a 90-minute march to work in temperatures as low as -40°C (-40°F).

For hotels and restaurants in this region see pp270–71 and pp289–90

⓮ Kungur Ice Cave

Кунгурская ледяная пещера
Kungurskaya Ledyanaya Peshchera

98 km (61 miles) SE of Perm, Kungur District. **Tel** (342) 716 26 10. **Open** 10am–5pm daily. **kungurcave.ru**

Located 5 km (3 miles) northeast of the town of Kungur and accessible by taxi, the Kungur Ice Cave is one of Russia's most famous caves. Its 6-km (4-mile) long subterranean passages were first mapped in the 18th century. Legend has it that the Cossack leader Yermak (1532–84) hid his looted treasure here. The cave is best visited in February and March when the underground temperature averages -12ºC (10ºF) and the stalactite icicles and frozen stalagmites reach up to 2 m (6 ft) in length. There is an 80-minute tour that passes through a series of caverns and a 90-minute tour that ends with a laser show loosely based on the cave's mythological past.

Frozen stalagmites in the fascinating Kungur Ice Cave

⓯ Yekaterinburg

Екатеринбург
Ekaterinburg

357 km (222 miles) SE of Perm. 1,400,000. (343) 222 24 45. **ekburg.ru**

Situated on the eastern slopes of the Ural Mountains, Yekaterinburg straddles the border between Europe and Asia. The city was named after Peter the Great's wife and, like Perm, was founded in the early 18th century during the tsar's drive to industrialize the Ural region. As many as 50 factories were moved here from the west of the country during World War II. Despite being a major industrial zone, the city has retained much of its Classical architecture and exudes an air of cultural sophistication.

The splendid Church on the Blood, Yekaterinburg

Among the city's notable attractions is the **Fine Arts Museum**. Founded in 1936, this museum houses the excellent Kasli Iron Pavilion, which showcases the Urals' traditional Kasli iron sculptures. The museum also contains a great collection of 16th–19th-century Russian paintings. Northeast of the museum lies the pleasant **Literary Quarter**. The city had a lively literary scene in the 19th century, and several local authors' wooden houses have since been turned into house-museums that constitute the quarter. Nearby is the golden-domed **Church on the Blood** that is built on the spot where Tsar Nicholas II and his family were executed under orders from the Bolshevik Party after the tsar's abdication in 1918 *(see p43)*. The cellar in which they were shot is now a shrine along with memorial stones to the tsar, his wife, and their five children who have recently been canonized by the Orthodox Church.

Fine Arts Museum
Ulitsa Voevodina 5. **Tel** (343) 371 06 26. **Open** 11am–6pm Wed–Sun.

Church on the Blood
Ulitsa Tolmachev 34. **Open** 9am–9pm daily.

The Demise of the Romanovs

The Romanov family's 300-year rule of Russia came to an abrupt end following the February Revolution of 1917 when Tsar Nicholas II abdicated. Kept under house arrest in St Petersburg until July 1917, the tsar and his family were then exiled to Tobolsk in Siberia. Their comfortable living conditions deteriorated after the October Revolution of 1917, but Nicholas II maintained his spirit by teaching Russian history to his children. The Bolsheviks moved them to Yekaterinburg in April 1918 where they were accommodated in a house owned by Nikolai Ipatiev, a local engineer. Fearful of the Romanovs being rescued by White Russian forces that were approaching the region, the Bolsheviks hastily ordered their execution, gunning them down in the basement of Ipatiev House on the night of 17 July 1918.

Tsar Nicholas II (1868–1918) with his wife Alexandra and their five children

THE CAUCASUS

With the enchanting open steppe to its north, the indomitable Caucasus Mountains at its heart and the sea and lush forests to the south, the Caucasus is a geographically diverse region that has long attracted settlers in search of fertile lands. Although it has been inhabited by a succession of native groups since ancient times, the northern Caucasus region is associated most strongly with its relatively recent and culturally rich Cossack past.

First colonized by the Greeks in the 6th century BC, the Black Sea coast was the scene of the Russo-Turkish wars in the 17th–19th centuries when Russia and the Ottoman Empire fought for political control over the region. The native Slavic people, or Cossacks, helped realize the Russian tsars' dream and Russia eventually gained the territory through the 1829 Treaty of Adrianople. Over the next few decades, the coast's fishing villages were developed into resorts with sanatoriums providing specialist treatments. Concerned for their own health after Lenin's early death in 1924, Stalin and other high-ranking party members chose Sochi as the place for ministerial summer recuperation. This boosted the resort's popularity, earning it the title of Russia's summer capital. However, after destructive occupation of the region by Axis forces during World War II, it was many years before the region returned to a state of normality.

Since the fall of the Soviet Union, the coast has drawn an ever-increasing number of wealthy Russian and foreign tourists. The selection of Sochi to host the 2014 Winter Olympics has attracted huge investments to update the coast's ageing infrastructure, while simultaneously developing its winter sports facilities. Sochi also makes a good base for exploring the region. Day trips to the picturesque Sochi National Park or the ski resort of Krasnaya Polyana are a must on any itinerary. The quintessentially Cossack settlements of Krasnodar and Rostov-na-Don are other favoured destinations.

Tranquil seaside promenade of Gelendzhik, with the hazy promontory jutting out into the Black Sea

◀ Hikers soaking up views of the pristine Caucasus Mountains

Exploring The Caucasus

Sandwiched between the Black Sea and the Caspian Sea, this region derives its name from the mighty Caucasus mountain range that is considered to be a natural border between Europe and Asia. The southern Caucasian republics are politically unstable and hence unsuitable for tourism but the north remains rather tourist friendly. Set against the tropical backdrop of the Black Sea coast, Sochi is a bustling resort city. Famed for its restorative santoriums, it is one of the host cities for the 2014 Winter Olympics. It also serves as a gateway to the expansive Sochi National Park, the ski-resort of Krasnaya Polyana and other provincial towns along the palm tree-lined coast. Watered by the Don and Kuban rivers after which the local Cossack groups were named, Krasnodar and Rostov-na-Don are steeped in Cossack history that is best explored by a visit to their regional museums.

Area illustrated

Sights at a Glance

1. *Sochi pp240–41*
2. Sochi National Park
3. Adler
4. Krasnaya Polyana
5. Gelendzhik
6. Anapa
7. Krasnodar
8. Rostov-na-Don
9. Starocherkassk

Key

- Major road
- Minor road
- Major railway
- Minor railway
- International border
- Federal border

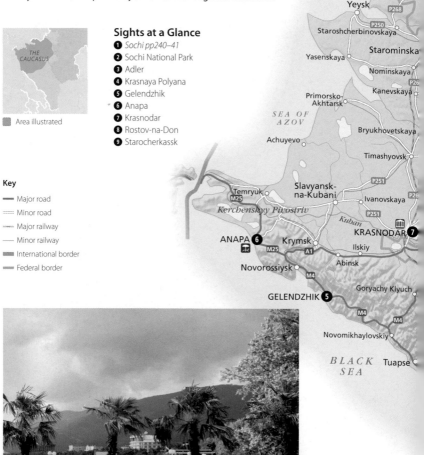

Sochi's elegant tree-fringed promenade, against the backdrop of the Caucasus mountain range

For map symbols *see back flap*

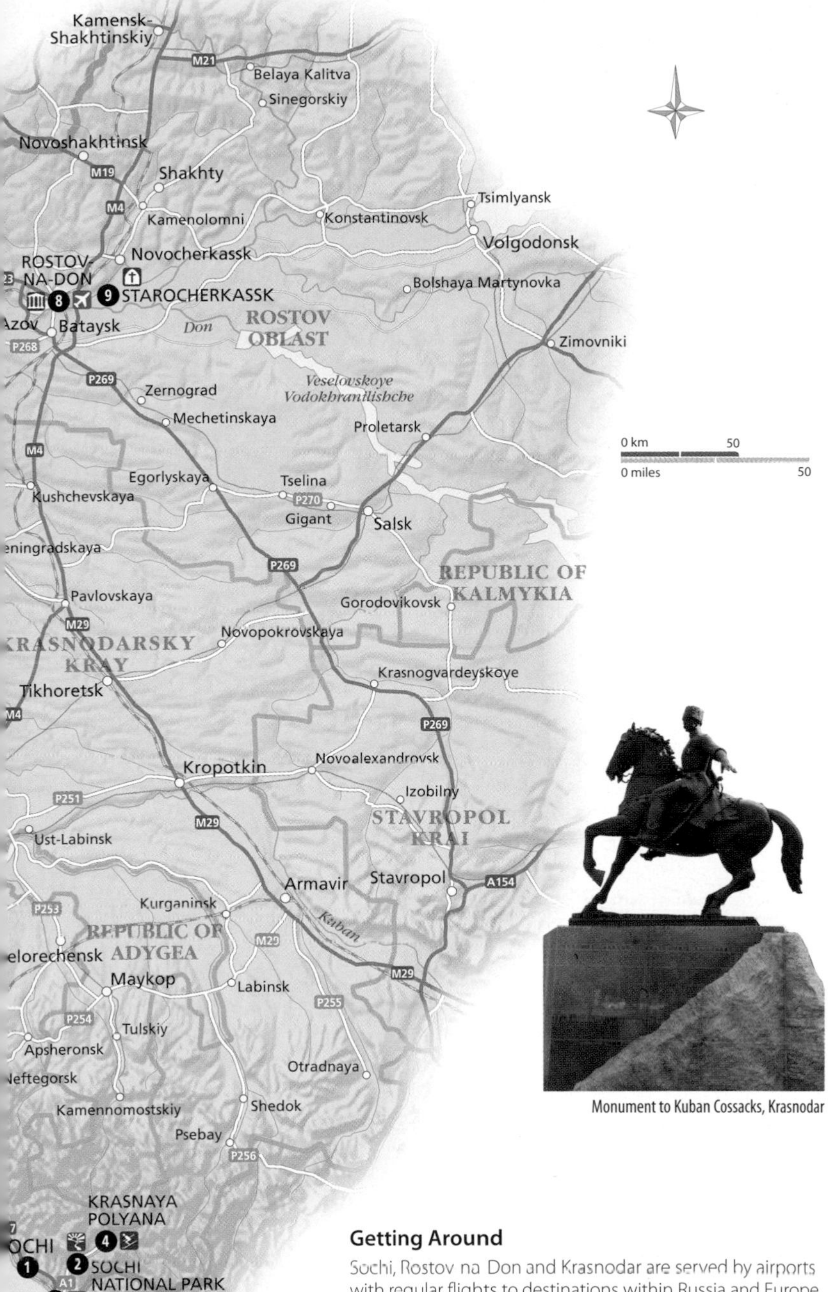

Monument to Kuban Cossacks, Krasnodar

Getting Around

Sochi, Rostov na Don and Krasnodar are served by airports with regular flights to destinations within Russia and Europe. Trains link all the major towns and cities and also run along the Black Sea coast connecting Gelendzhik and Adler. An efficient bus network covers the entire region and road conditions are generally good. However, construction work for the Winter Olympics 2014 has been causing severe traffic jams around Sochi. Car hire is the quickest way to get around and can be arranged by hotels or travel agencies.

For hotels and restaurants in this region see pp271–2 and p290

❶ Sochi

Сочи

Sochi

Nestling beneath the forested foothills of the Caucasus Mountains, Russia's summer capital is as popular as ever despite frenetic refurbishment for the impending Olympic games in 2014. Controlled by a succession of mountain peoples until it was ceded to Russia in 1829, Sochi was transformed into a sprawling health resort during the Soviet era after Stalin and his top ministers built their summer *dachas* here. Since then the balmy seaside city has prospered and the massive Olympic investment in infrastructure and facilities is likely to further enhance its reputation.

Train Station

Железнодорожная станция

Vokzal

Ulitsa Gorkogo.

Conceived by renowned Soviet architect Alexei Dushkin (1904–77), the Sochi Train Station is a grandiose example of Stalinist-era architecture and design. Built between 1950 and 1952 from local sandstone and polished granite, the station is a complex architectural composition. Its huge arches, stately columns and high-ceilinged halls are based around a 55-m (180-ft) high clock tower that is adorned with zodiac symbols and topped with a gleaming red star.

History Museum

Музей истории

Muzey Istorii

Ulitsa Vorovskogo 54/11. **Tel** (862) 264 23 26. **Open** Summer: 9am–7:30pm Tue–Sun; Winter: 9am–5:30pm Tue–Sun.

The museum's chronologically-arranged exhibition space boasts an engaging series of mock-ups that include a prehistoric cave dwelling, a typical peasant cottage and the interior of a 19th-century ship. Early agricultural tools are also on display along with Greek and Roman finds from the region. Black-and-white photographs tell the story of Sochi's architectural heritage being replaced by concrete blocks during the development of the city in the Soviet era. There is also a section devoted to the cosmonauts who have recu-perated at Sochi's sanatoriums between space missions.

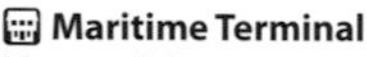

Maritime Terminal

Морской Вокзал

Morskoy Vokzal

Kurortny prospekt 74.

Built in 1955, the Maritime Terminal's elegant design was influenced by Sochi's earlier Neo-Classical buildings. Centred upon a tapering 73-m (240-ft) tower topped with the Soviet Union's ubiquitous red star, the terminal's vaulted upper floor is decorated with murals. An exclusive restaurant catering to luxury yacht owners has lovely views of the harbour.

Elegant façade of Sochi's History Museum

Sochi's beaches

Пляжи

Plyazhi

Sochi's narrow pebble beaches and murky sea are not its most alluring features, but tourists flock to them nonetheless and sun umbrellas and plastic deckchairs clog the limited beach space in summer. Centrally located restaurants and hotels often have private sections of beach reserved for clientele. However, for a more relaxing seaside experience, it is well worth travelling north of Sochi to access several cleaner and less crowded beaches.

Neo-Classical Maritime Terminal building topped by a steeple

Winter Theatre

Зимний Театр

Zimniy Teatr

Teatralnaya ulitsa. **Open** 10am–5:30pm Tue–Sun. June: Kinotavr Film Festival. **kinotavr.ru**

Another of Sochi's Neo-Classical Soviet-era buildings, the Winter Theatre's imposing colonnaded façade supports a portico topped with sculptures of Terpsichore, Melpomene and Thalia – the Greek muses of singing, dancing and comedy. Opened in 1938, it still hosts regular theatre performances as well as Kinotavr, one of Russia's major film festivals.

Dendrarium

Дендрарий

Dendrariy

Kurortny prospekt 74. **Tel** (862) 262 18 42. **Open** Summer: 8am–8pm daily; Winter: 8am–5pm daily.

The delightful arboretum dotted with fountains and monuments is among the city's highlights. Its 48 ha (120 acres) of lush grounds are home to over 2,000 plants and trees collected from around the world since its foundation

For hotels and restaurants in this region see pp271–2 and p290

in 1892. A cable car runs to the top of the arboretum, affording superb views.

Art Museum

Художественный музей

Khudozhestvenniy muzey

Kurortny prospekt 51. **Open** 10am–5:30pm Tue–Sun.

The Art Museum is housed in a grand building with elaborate Neo-Classical motifs typical of Sochi's Stalinist-era architecture. Its interior is equally impressive with three floors of high-ceilinged halls that are packed with works by Russian and foreign artists from the 19th and 20th centuries. Notable among the numerous seascapes on display is *Heroic Landscape*, a gigantic work in pastel hues painted by Konstantin Bogaevski in 1930. Other artworks include a dramatic depiction of a sea battle by Viktor Samorezov and an image of a tumbledown seaside cottage painted in 1890 by Vyacheslav Korenev.

Riviera Park

Парк Ривьера

Park Riv'era

Kurortny prospekt. **Open** 10am–1am.

Hugely popular with children and promenading locals since it was opened in 1898, Riviera Park's expanse of woods and gardens that runs along the seafront is packed with play areas, eateries and fairground rides that stay open till dusk. Among the attractions is Cosmonaut Alley where 45 Magnolia trees have been planted by American and Russian astronauts who have recuperated in Sochi since Yuri Gagarin started the tradition in 1961.

Environs

Camouflaged by green paint that renders it virtually invisible from the surrounding countryside, Stalin's unpretentious summer *dacha*, **Zelenaya Roscha** *(see p273)*, is tucked away on a steep forested hill just outside the city. Built in 1937 for the infamous dictator, and featuring oak panelled interiors through-out, the quadrangular villa is in remarkably good condition despite having been neglected for decades. The vaulted conference hall with its floor-to-ceiling windows and broad terrace with sweeping coastal view is open to the public, as is the hall where Stalin personally vetted every new Soviet film before its release.

Zelenaya Roscha

Green Grove, Kurortny prospekt 120. **Tel** (862) 269 56 00. **Open** by prior arrangement only.

VISITORS' CHECKLIST

Practical Information

1,600 km (995 miles) S of Moscow.

1,000,000.

Transport

Welcoming entrance to the lush Riviera Park

Sights at a Glance

1. Train Station
2. History Museum
3. Maritime Terminal
4. Sochi's beaches
5. Winter Theatre
6. Dendrarium
7. Art Museum
8. Riviera Park

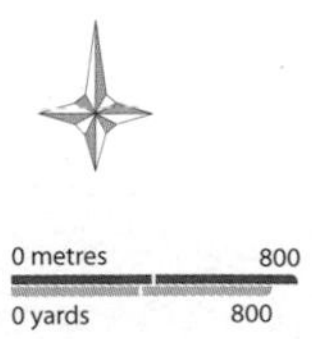

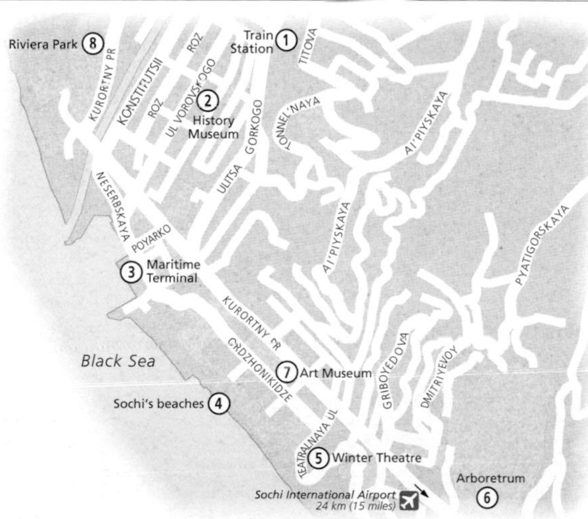

For map symbols *see back flap*

Spectacular karst topography in the Vorontsovskaya cave, Sochi National Park

2 Sochi National Park

Сочиский Национальный Парк

Sochinskiy Natsionalnyy Park

4 km (2 miles) NE of Sochi. **Tel** (8622) 64 52 37. from Sochi. Ulitsa Moskovskaya 21, 9am–5pm Mon–Fri. **sochinp.ru**

Established in 1983, this vast 1,940-sq km (749-sq mile) expanse of protected area is one of Russia's first national parks. All industrial activity in the region was halted when it was first created and strict planning laws were implemented to preserve the area's lumber.

Stretching from the sub-alpine meadows of the Caucasus Mountains through beech- and fir-covered foothills to the oak and chestnut forests that extend along the Black Sea coast, Sochi National Park has a diverse ecosystem. It is home to an enormous number of rare and endemic plants and animals that include several species of eagle, vulture and falcon besides wolves, bears, Persian squirrels and the endangered Caucasian otter. Numerous trails link its wealth of canyons, rivers, waterfalls and karst caves, including Vorontsovskaya, the largest in the Caucasus region. The park attracts thousands of wildlife enthusiasts every year.

3 Adler

Адлер

Adler

7 km (4 miles) SE of Sochi. 76,000.

Far more relaxed than its upmarket neighbour Sochi, this Black Sea resort boasts cleaner and more easily accessible beaches – a combination that appeals to young families and elderly tourists in particular. Restaurants and shops liven up its seaside promenade, which is the town's main attraction.

Although Adler is one of the host towns for the 2014 Winter Olympics, the acres of purpose-built accommodation are being constructed just beyond its suburbs. The impact of the games on the town is limited to initiatives to spruce up the seafront.

4 Krasnaya Polyana

Красная Поляна

Krasnaya Polyana

43 km (27 miles) NE of Adler. 4,600.

Since the day Sochi was chosen as the venue for the 2014 Winter Olympics, Krasnaya Polyana has rapidly transformed from an unassuming mid-range ski resort into a vast construction site. A new road and rail link provides direct connections to Sochi Airport, state-of-the-art ski lifts are in place and the newly constructed town centre is beginning to resemble a high-end Alpine ski resort.

However, the area comes within the purview of Sochi National Park and environmentalists have raised concerns about the expansion's impact on the park's unique eco-systems. Developers have pressed on regardless with the full support of the Russian government as well as President Putin's encouragement.

A brand-new commercial complex in Krasnaya Polyana

Sparsely populated beach with a pier extending into the Black Sea, Adler

For hotels and restaurants in this region see pp271–2 and p290

Crowds strolling down the pleasant promenade, Gelendzhik

❺ Gelendzhik

Геленджик

Gelendzhik

310 km (193 miles) NW of Krasnaya Polyana. 55,000.

A charming seaside resort, Gelendzhik is overlooked by densely forested hills sporting a huge sign that once spelt "Lenin is with us" and has since been replaced by "Gelendzhik". It combines pleasant nightlife with child-friendly water parks and play areas, and is a laid-back alternative to busy Anapa.

Bronze-Age tribes left dolmen scattered throughout the forests surrounding Gelendzhik. However, records of the first settlement date from the 6th century BC when the Greeks established a trading port here. During the Middle Ages, Genoese traders followed suit and maintained an outpost in the bay area. The town was occupied by the Ottomans from the 15th century until its annexation to Russia under the Treaty of Adrianople in 1829.

Gelendzhik welcomed its first tourists in the early 20th century and gradually evolved into today's bustling resort town with its fetching tree-shaded promenade. The **Regional Museum** has displays related to its role as a Soviet base during World War II as well as re-created interiors of local homes in the 1950s.

Regional Museum
Ulitsa Ostrovska 1. **Tel** (86141) 352 87. **Open** 9am–6pm daily.

Dolmen dating from the Bronze Age in the forests surrounding Gelendzhik

❻ Anapa

Анапа

Anapa

93 km (58 miles) NW of Gelendzhik. 59,000.

Popular with Russian tourists since the first sanatoriums were built here in the late 19th century, Anapa is an attractive family resort. Its wooded parks and neat flowerbeds provide the perfect backdrop for a central beach that is gridlocked with sun umbrellas throughout the busy summer season.

First settled by the Greeks and named Gorgipia in the 6th century BC, the area was later colonized by the Genoese before it fell to the Ottoman Empire in 1475. After the Russo-Turkish War of 1828–9, it was formally annexed to Russia and gradually developed into a thriving resort, but was totally destroyed during its occupation by German and Romanian troops during World War II.

Today, modern hotels, bars, discos and restaurants line the seafront and the town throngs with Russian holidaymakers. The reconstructed ruins of Gorgipia are on display at the central **Archaeological Museum** along with various ancient Greek artifacts from the region.

Archaeological Museum
Ulitsa Naberezhnaya 4. **Tel** (86133) 569 37. **Open** 9am–6pm Tue–Sun.

Sanatoriums

An extensive network of sanatoriums, or wellness centres, was established in Russia in the 1930s. The Caucasus region especially abounds in them, owing to its curative mineral water springs. These relics of the Soviet era prove to be good alternatives to hotels. Seaside resorts such as Sochi have sanatoriums offering traditional and modern spa therapies for just about any ailment imaginable. Visitors traditionally stay for a three-week cure, but shorter treatments are also available.

The sanatorium at Zelenaya Roscha, Sochi

❼ Krasnodar

Краснодар

Krasnodar

170 km (106 miles) E of Anapa.
832,000.

A welcoming city, Krasnodar enjoys an almost Mediterranean climate that fuels an appealing outdoor culture. Locals promenade through its parks and along its boulevards until late into the night during the long hot summers.

Granted to the Kuban Cossacks by Catherine the Great in 1792 for defending Russia's southern border against the Circassians, the settlement was originally named Yekaterinodar – meaning Catherine's Gift. Initially a fort town, it developed into a major transport and trading hub with the arrival of the railway in the late 19th century. Many Cossacks remained loyal to the tsar during the Civil War and held the town against the Red Army until 1920 when it was annexed by the Bolsheviks and renamed Krasnodar or Gift of the Reds.

The German occupation between 1942 and 1943 saw the extermination of an estimated 13,000 locals in gas chambers by the Nazis. A memorial in Chistyakovskaya Roscha park denotes the mass grave where the victims are buried. A short walk from the park is the Aurora Cinema, a superb example of Soviet architecture from the 1960s. It marks one end of ulitsa Krasnaya, a boulevard that stretches for 7 km (4 miles) through the city centre. The street is adorned with statues, fountains and monuments to the Cossacks and Catherine the Great.

Alexander's Triumphal Arch and St Martyr Catherine Memorial, Krasnodar

The city's **Regional Museum** has a collection of artifacts that recount the area's Cossack past as well as its natural history, archaeology and ancient roots. The nearby **Art Museum** exhibits 19th-century paintings by Russian artists.

Regional Museum
Ulitsa Gimnazicheskaya 67. **Tel** (861) 262 40 86. **Open** 10am–6pm Tue–Sun.

Art Museum
Ulitsa Krasnaya 13. **Tel** (861) 268 09 00. **Open** 10am–6pm Tue–Sat (till 5pm Sun).

Golden domes of the Nativity of the Blessed Virgin Cathedral, Rostov-na-Don

❽ Rostov-na-Don

Ростов-на-Дону

Rostov-na-Donu

280 km (174 km) N of Krasnodar.
1,100,000.

Spread out along the northern banks of the great Don river lies the modern city of Rostov-na-Don with its appealing blend of 19th- and-20th-century architecture interspersed by parks and broad squares.

Empress Elizabeth established a customs post here in the late 18th century to control trade with Turkey and the settlement soon evolved into a thriving commercial centre. Owing to its unique riverside location between European Russia and the Caucasus region, it came to be known as the "gateway to the Caucasus".

The area's fascinating history is documented by the **Regional Museum** where Scythian and Sarmatian golden ornaments dating back to the 3rd century BC are on display. Additionally, Don Cossack outfits replete with fur hats and jewel embroidery from the 18th and 19th centuries can be found upstairs alongside Cossack uniforms and weaponry from World War II. The museum is flanked by parks on both sides. To the east is the Revolutsii Park that is dotted with monuments and fountains, while Gorky Park, to the west, is popular for its fairground rides and bustling eateries. The two parks lie between the city's parallel thoroughfares – ulitsa Sadovaya, a traffic-clogged street, and ulitsa Pushkinskaya, a much calmer tree-lined boulevard.

The splendid **Nativity of the Blessed Virgin Cathedral**, built in 1860, stands on the northern slopes of the steep riverbank. Its striking golden domes and neighbouring bell tower are surrounded by the city bazaar, a maze of open market stalls selling pungent spices, fresh fish from the Don and local produce. Downhill is the great river itself. Lined with floating bars and restaurants, the city side of the river is a popular hangout, but locals frequent the opposite side, known as the Left Bank, where a number of good restaurants and bars abut the sandy beaches.

Rostov-na-Don is also slated to act as one of Russia's host cities for the 2018 FIFA World Cup™. A brand new football stadium is under construction, with a seating capacity of 43,700.

Regional Museum
Ulitsa Bolshaya Sadovaya 79. **Tel** (863) 240 93 04. **Open** 10am–6pm Tue–Sun. **rostovmuseum.ru**

Nativity of the Blessed Virgin Cathedral
Ulitsa Stanislavskogo 58. **Open** 8am–7pm daily.

Tree-lined ulitsa Pushkinskaya running the length of Rostov-na-Don

9 Starocherkassk

Старочеркасск

Starocherkassk

35 km (22 miles) NE of Rostov-na-Don. 5,000.

It is hard to believe that this tranquil museum village, formerly known as Cherkassk, used to be the fortified island capital of the Don Cossacks between the 17th and 19th centuries. Peter the Great visited the area several times during his attempts to conquer the fortress at nearby Azov. Held by the Turks, the fortress prevented Russian access to the Black Sea. When it was eventually captured by Russian troops in 1696, it was in Cherkassk that

Ataman Palace and its lovely gardens, Starocherkassk

Peter the Great celebrated his victory with Russia's first ever fireworks display.

Starocherkassk's **Historical and Architectural Museum Reserve** was established in 1970 on the initiative of Mikhail Sholokhov – author of the classic Cossack novel *And Quiet Flows the Don* – and has since developed into one of the region's principal tourist attractions. It is a unique complex with over 30 architectural monuments that reflect the life and customs of the Don Cossacks. Just down the road from the museum is the **Resurrection Cathedral**, which dates back to 1706 and boasts an incredible iconostasis flanked by balconies decorated with vivid depictions of biblical scenes. Displayed nearby are the hefty iron gates known as the Azov Trophies that were captured by local Cossacks during their first occupation of Azov between 1637 and 1641. Another draw is the impressive Ataman Palace – an 18th-century mansion – that houses exhibits relating to the Cossack culture. From May to September, the village hosts lively Cossack fairs.

Historical and Architectural Museum Reserve
Ulitsa Pochtovaya. **Tel** (863) 502 97 49. **Open** 9am–5pm daily. **siamz-ro.ru**

Resurrection Cathedral
Open 9am–5pm daily.

The Turbulent South

The South Caucasian republics have struggled bitterly for independence since the break up of the Soviet Union in 1991. Chechnya finally submitted to Russia's authority in 2009 after the Second Chechen War; Azerbaijan fought over territory with neighbouring Armenia until 1994; Dagestan has remained a Russian republic but suffers from internal Islamic tensions; and Abkhazia is recognized by Russia as an independent state yet is considered part of neighbouring Georgia by much of the international community. Most recently, Russia's brief war with Georgia in 2008 confirmed Russian control of South Ossetia. Although the region has been comparatively calm for the past few years, mutual mistrust and simmering tensions between the neighbouring states have created a volatile climate that has resulted in occasional attacks and kidnappings of Russian and foreign citizens by minority groups. Travel in the region is currently considered dangerous and potential visitors are advised to consult their embassies for the latest security information.

Ramzan Kadyrov, President of the Chechen Republic

SIBERIA AND THE FAR EAST

A land of enormous proportions, this region offers stunning landscapes, fascinating museums and exciting adventures. The architecture and culture of the cities are similar yet each has its own unique gems to be discovered. Beyond these urban centres lies a vast wilderness where indigenous peoples, some of whom still practice shamanism, can sometimes be found.

Stretching from the Ural Mountains in the West to the Pacific Ocean in the east, the Siberia and Far East region shares its border with China, Mongolia and Central Kazakhstan. Russia began exploring the region in the 16th century when pioneering Cossacks forced local tribes to pay regular tributes in furs to the tsar or face annihilation. By the 18th century, Siberia had become a prime location for imprisonment and exile, a convenient way to populate the unappealing region.

The construction of the Trans-Siberian Railway in the late 19th century had a massive social and economic impact on the region. It not only boosted trade and shortened travel time between cities across the country, but also led to the settlement of remote areas in Siberia. The 20th century saw the Soviet government establish thousands of Gulag prison camps across the region to run factories, mines and logging operations; these became an integral part of the Soviet economy.

Rich in natural resources, the region has attracted heavy investment from energy companies all over the world since the collapse of the Soviet Union in 1991. The region is also emerging as a major tourist destination. Cities such as Tomsk and Irkutsk have made efforts to restore and preserve their pre-Soviet architectural heritage. Much of the eastern part offers fantastic mountain scenery and a host of thrilling adventure sports. Reached via Irkutsk, Lake Baikal is not just famous for scenic views, but also for amazing hiking and trekking trails.

A shepherd with reindeer in a typical Siberian snow-covered landscape

◀ Spectacular view of conifers lining the banks of a meandering mountain river in the Altai Republic

Exploring Siberia and the Far East

Extending across seven time zones from the Ural Mountains in the west to Kamchatka in the east, this region has plenty in store for the relatively few foreign visitors it receives. Still largely unpopulated, a vast majority of its inhabitants live in the cities lining the route of the Trans-Siberian Railway, so wilderness is seldom far away. While the stunning Altai Mountains are accessible from Krasnoyarsk, the utterly remote landscapes of Sakhalin Island in the Far East can be explored from Yuzhno-Sakhalinsk. Most Siberian cities were greatly changed during the Soviet era, but several cities such as Tobolsk, Tomsk and Irkutsk have preserved the remnants of their architectural heritage. Irkutsk is the obvious base for excursions to Lake Baikal, a natural gem. East of Lake Baikal lies the Buryat (an ethnic minority group in Siberia) capital of Ulan-Ude, from where there are bus links to Ivolginsky Datsan, the most important Buddhist monastery in Russia.

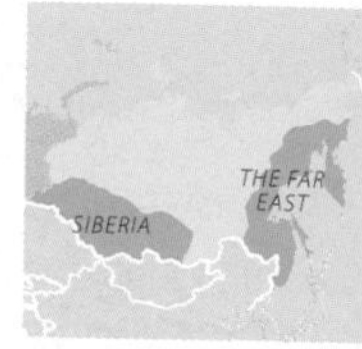

Areas illustrated

Sights at a Glance

1. Omsk
2. Tobolsk
3. Novosibirsk
4. Tomsk
5. Krasnoyarsk
6. Barnaul
7. Irkutsk
8. Taltsy Museum of Wooden Architecture
9. Lake Baikal
10. Ulan-Ude
11. Ivolginsky Datsan
12. Vladivostok
13. Khabarovsk
14. Komsomolsk-na-Amur
15. Sakhalin Island
16. Magadan
17. Kamchatka

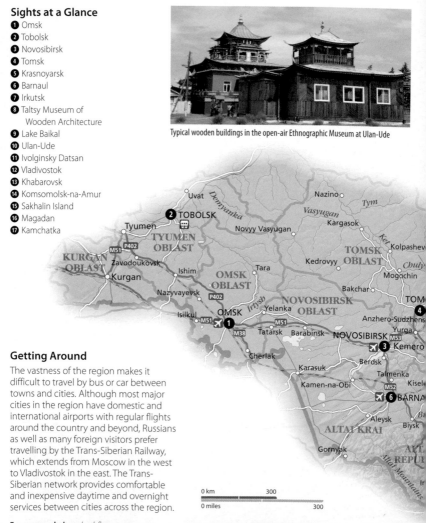

Typical wooden buildings in the open-air Ethnographic Museum at Ulan-Ude

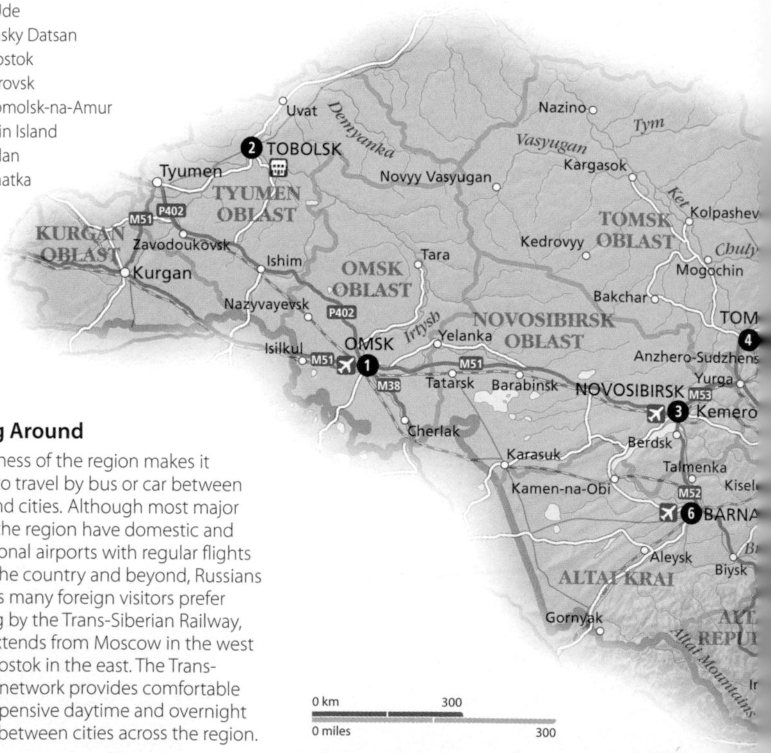

Getting Around

The vastness of the region makes it difficult to travel by bus or car between towns and cities. Although most major cities in the region have domestic and international airports with regular flights around the country and beyond, Russians as well as many foreign visitors prefer travelling by the Trans-Siberian Railway, which extends from Moscow in the west to Vladivostok in the east. The Trans-Siberian network provides comfortable and inexpensive daytime and overnight services between cities across the region.

For map symbols *see back flap*

A herd of reindeer crossing a river in northern Kamchatka

Key

- Major road
- Minor road
- Major railway
- Trans-Siberian Railway
- Minor railway
- International border
- Federal border

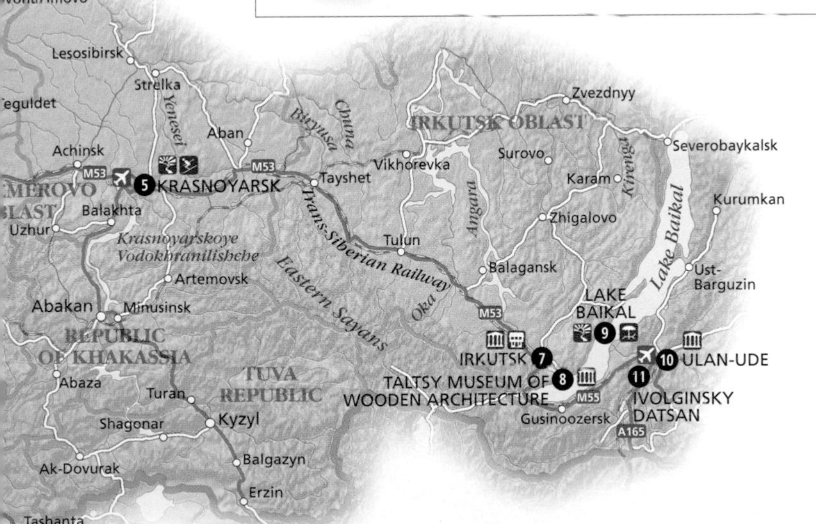

For hotels and restaurants in this region see pp272–3 and pp290–91

The Assumption Cathedral crowned by a massive onion dome, Omsk

❶ Omsk

Омск

Omsk

2,724 km (1,700 miles) NE of Moscow. 1,150,000. **Tel** (3812) 27 06 20. **admomsk.ru**

Stretching along the banks of the Irtysh river at its confluence with the Om river, Omsk is a lively city packed with restaurants, bars and clubs. It was founded in 1716 during the reign of Peter the Great to protect Russia's southern border from hostile Kazakh tribes. With the construction of the Trans-Siberian Railway in the 1890s, the city evolved into a prosperous trading outpost.

The **Assumption Cathedral**, the city's most central landmark, dominates ploshchad Sobornaya. Distinctive for its bulbous onion dome, it was built in 2007 to replace the original cathedral pulled down by the Soviets in 1935. A short distance south is the **Regional Museum** with artifacts related to the history and culture of the region. Nearby, the **MA Vrubel Regional Museum of Fine Arts** houses a superb collection of decorative and applied art.

Regional Museum
Ulitsa Lenina 23A. **Tel** (3812) 31 22 86.
Open 10am–6pm Tue–Sun.
sibmuseum.ru

MA Vrubel Regional Museum of Fine Arts
Ulitsa Lenina 3. **Tel** (3812) 20 00 47.
Open 10am–7pm Tue–Sun.

❷ Tobolsk

Тобольск

Tobolsk

862 km (536 miles) NW of Omsk. 100,000. **admtobolsk.ru**

Founded in 1587 by Cossacks intent on expanding the Russian Empire eastwards, Tobolsk became Siberia's first capital. It was inhabited by wealthy merchants who built churches and wooden mansions all over the city. The merchants refused to allow the Trans-Siberian Railway to be routed through the city, fearing it would ruin their trade monopolies. However, Tobolsk's fortunes declined anyway when the railway was built.

Situated atop the high bank of the Irtysh river, Tobolsk's magnificent stone Kremlin overlooks the old town's wooden buildings. Restored during the Soviet era, it contains the elegant 17th-century **Cathedral of St Sofia**. To the right of the Kremlin is the Governor's Palace, which houses the **Regional Museum**.

Cathedral of St Sofia
Tobolsk Kremlin. **Open** 8am–8pm daily.

Regional Museum
Dvorets Namestnika, ploshchad Krasnaya 1. **Tel** (345) 622 37 13.
Open 10am–6pm Tue–Sun.

❸ Novosibirsk

Новосибирск

Novosibirsk

652 km (405 miles) E of Omsk. 1,500,000. **novo-sibirsk.ru**

Russia's third-largest city was founded in 1893 as a small settlement of workers engaged in building a bridge across the Ob river for the Trans-Siberian Railway. Named Novonikolaevsk in honour of Tsar Nicholas, the town attracted local traders who capitalized on its river and rail connections to amass small fortunes. In due course the town expanded into a bustling city.

Despite the reluctance of the wealthier citizens to embrace Communism, Novonikolaevsk fell to the Bolsheviks in 1919 and was renamed Novosibirsk in 1926. The Soviet era saw an influx of huge industrial enterprises accompanied by the construction of monolithic state buildings and four-lane roads throughout the city. In spite of the fall of Communism, a great statue of Lenin dominates ploshchad Lenina, the city's central square. Just behind is the grand **Opera and Ballet Theatre**, which was completed in 1944 and is larger than the Bolshoi Theatre in Moscow. Opposite the Lenin Statue is the excellent **Regional Museum** whose

Statue of Lenin at the city centre, Novosibirsk

Crowds outside the impressive white stone Kremlin, Tobolsk

absorbing collection includes a section devoted to shamanism, which is still practiced in some parts of the Altai Republic.

Opera and Ballet Theatre
Krasny prospekt 36. **Tel** (383) 227 15 37. **Open** check website for schedule. **opera-novosibirsk.ru**

Regional Museum
Ulitsa Lenina 23. **Tel** (383) 222 51 73. **Open** 10am–6pm Mon–Fri. **museum.nsk.ru**

One of the few well-preserved wooden mansions, Tomsk

❹ Tomsk

Томск

Tomsk

270 km (168 miles) NE of Novosibirsk. 525,000.

Founded in 1604 atop the Voskresenskaya Gora (Resurrection Hill), Tomsk is a lively university city dotted with parks and monuments. The city is famous for its intricately decorated wooden buildings that date back to the early 19th century. Though many of Tomsk's wooden houses are in a state of decay, some of the best examples of wooden architecture can be seen along ulitsa Krasnoarmeiskaya. The **Tomsk City History Museum** houses fascinating exhibits on the history of the city. Within the museum grounds is a wooden lookout tower. Once used for spotting fires, the tower offers sweeping views of the city. The nearby **Voskresenskaya Church** was first constructed from wood in 1622 and replaced by the current stone building in 1789.

Tomsk City History Museum
Ulitsa Bakunina 3. **Tel** (382) 265 72 55. **Open** 10am–7pm Tue–Sun.

❺ Krasnoyarsk

Красноярск

Krasnoyarsk

582 km (362 miles) E of Tomsk. 1,000,000.

Described by Anton Chekhov as a picturesque and cultured town in 1890, Krasnoyarsk is located along both banks of the broad Yenisei river beneath the craggy rock formations of the Stolby Nature Reserve. The city's central thoroughfares are lined with an eclectic mix of architectural styles and the thousands of students at its numerous universities lend a youthful vibrancy, which finds expression in quirky contemporary artworks on display around the city.

Krasnoyarsk was founded in 1627 by pioneering Cossacks and the **Regional Museum** contains fascinating displays devoted both to the city's recent history and to the lifestyles of indigenous peoples that have inhabited the region for millennia. Overlooking the Yenisei river is the Modernist **Museum of Culture and History** that combines dated exhibitions of city history with impressive contemporary art installations over its several floors.

Environs

About 10 km (6 miles) west of the Yenisei river's south bank is the **Stolby Nature Reserve**, known for striking rock formations and outdoor activities such as hiking and rock climbing. The **Bobrovy Log Ski Resort**, 30 minutes by car from Krasnoyarsk and on the northeastern edge of the nature reserve, is popular for winter sports.

Regional Museum
Ulitsa Dubrovinskogo 84. **Tel** (391) 265 34 81. **Open** 10am–6pm Tue–Sun. **kkkm.ru**

Museum of Culture and History
Ploshchad Mira. **Tel** (391) 212 46 63. **Open** 11am–7pm Tue–Sun. **mira1.ru**

Bobrovy Log Ski Resort
Tel (391) 256 86 86. **Open** 10am–10pm daily. **bobrovylog.ru**

Yellow autumn foliage in the taiga forests of Stolby Nature Reserve near Krasnoyarsk

Trans-Siberian Railway

A marvellous feat of late 19th-century engineering, the world's longest railway connects Moscow with the Sea of Japan at Vladivostok over a distance of 9,288 km (5,771 miles). During the week-long journey the train passes through vast forests, crosses immense rivers and trundles across seemingly endless vistas of steppes. A Trans-Siberian train journey is surprisingly easy to arrange and conditions on board are comfortable and well organized. The Trans-Siberian line runs from Moscow to Vladivostok; the Trans-Mongolian line connects Moscow with Ulan Bator, and the Trans-Manchurian line terminates in Beijing.

A section of the Trans-Siberian Railway near Lake Baikal

6 Barnaul

Барнаул

Barnaul

241 km (150 miles) S of Novosibirsk.
621,700.

The industrial city of Barnaul was founded in the mid-18th century and was once home to Russia's largest silver-smelting factory. The city serves as an excellent base for touring the mountainous Altai Republic. Although the region's wild landscape has attracted visitors since the early 20th century and popular sights are easily accessible, travelling deeper into the mountains is best arranged through a local tour operator. The **Altai Museum of Regional Studies and History** in Barnaul provides an absorbing overview of the region's past.

Altai Museum of Regional Studies and History
Ulitsa Polzunova 46. **Tel** (385) 263 47 58. **Open** 10am–5:30pm Wed–Sun.

7 Irkutsk

Иркутск

Irkutsk

2,090 km (1,300 miles) SE of Barnaul.
600,000.
Ulitsa F Engels 21, (395) 220 50 18.
itsirkutsk.com

Dubbed "the Paris of Siberia" by Anton Chekhov in the late 19th century, Irkutsk is a delightful city dotted with well-preserved wood and stone buildings. Largely unspoiled by concrete Soviet architecture, the city centre features tree-lined avenues, punctuated with well-kept parks, and an elegant embankment promenade that follows the curve of the Angara river.

Brightly painted façade of the Epiphany Cathedral, Irkutsk

Established around 1661 on the right bank, Irkutsk profited from its proximity to Mongolia by importing tea, silk and porcelain into Russia. The discovery of gold and diamonds in the region attracted a surge of fortune-seekers who were accompanied in almost equal numbers by exiled criminals. Among the exiles were the Decembrists *(see p43)* whose arrival enhanced the city's cultural life, which soon revolved around the mansions of Prince Volkonsky (1788–1865) and Prince Trubetskoy (1790–1860); both mansions have been preserved as house-museums. Between the two mansions stands the late 18th-century Transfiguration Church where the aristocrats worshipped.

A short distance away is a restored complex of lovely mansions that house the **Museum of City Life**, which showcases how a typical 19th-century merchant-class family lived. Overlooking the Angara river, the city's oldest churches in ploshchad Kirova have been meticulously restored in recent years. The brightly painted Epiphany Cathedral was built in 1718, while the more sombre **Church of Our Saviour** dates back to 1706. From ploshchad Kirov, ulitsa Lenina runs south past the **Sukachev Regional Art Museum**, whose superb collection includes Mongolian religious paintings and Russian Impressionist artworks. Further south, ulitsa Lenina connects with Irkutsk's main street, ulitsa Karla Marksa. This street leads to a pretty riverside square where a statue of Tsar Alexander III commemorates the construction of the Trans-Siberian Railway. Nearby, the **Regional Museum** contains a great collection of ethnographic exhibits and displays from the 20th century.

Museum of City Life
Ulitsa Frank Kamenetskogo 16A. **Tel** (3952) 20 48 84. **Open** 10am–6pm Wed–Mon.

Church of Our Saviour
Ploshchad Kirov. **Open** 7:30am–8:30pm daily.

Sukachev Regional Art Museum
Ulitsa Dekabrski Sobiti 112. **Tel** (3952) 53 12 24. **Open** 10am–6pm Wed–Mon. **sukachoff.ru**

Spectacular mountains surrounding a lake, Altai Republic

❽ Taltsy Architectural and Ethnographic Museum

Музей Тальцы

Muzey Taltsy

47 km (29 miles) SE of Irkutsk. **Tel** (3952) 76 83 23. from Irkutsk. **Open** 10am–5pm daily. **talci.ru**

This fascinating outdoor museum is tucked away in the woods on the right bank of the Angara river. Established in 1966, its exhibits were collected from flooded local villages in an attempt to preserve Siberia's traditional folk architecture.

The exhibition trail begins with a *chum*, a traditional house covered in pine-tree bark that was used by the north Siberian Evenk tribe. The hollowed out logs perched on trees nearby are examples of the Evenk's aerial graves. A 19th-century water mill consisting of three huts stands on a nearby hillside; stream water was channelled down through the huts to power the mills within. A series of Cossack homes lie beyond alongside a part of a stockade with the main watch-tower; there is also a pretty wooden church that dates from the end of the 17th century. Both the tower and church were rescued from the village of Ust-Ilimsk before it was flooded by a hydroelectric dam project in 1974. Traditional crafts are sold from stalls in a meadow setting surrounded by forested hills.

Tour boats moored along the beach at Listvyanka

❾ Lake Baikal

Озеро Байкал

Ozero Baikal

69 km (43 miles) S of Irkutsk. from Irkutsk. Ulitsa Narodnaya 10 Olkhon, Khuzhir, (3952) 65 06 52. **discoverbaikal.ru**

Sandwiched between the Baikal and Barguzin mountains to the north, Lake Baikal is the deepest and oldest lake in the world. A natural wonder, the lake was considered a living entity by local tribes who revered it for thousands of years. It contains around 20 per cent of the planet's unfrozen fresh water and is home to around 2,000 animal and plant species of which more than half are endemic. Its 3,219-km (2,000-mile) shoreline is scarcely populated and the majority of its few settlements are located along the southern shores.

Running right beside the lake between the villages of Sludyanka and Port Baikal, the Circum-Baikal Railway is a great way to experience the lake. Built between 1911 and 1915 to connect the eastern and western Trans-Siberian lines, the route was an incredible feat of engineering as it involved hacking a rail bed into the sheer cliffs rising from the lake. The Circum-Baikal Railway has since been bypassed by the faster Irkutsk–Sludyanka line, although there is still a twice-daily service used by locals and tourists.

Train on the Circum-Baikal Railway at Port Baikal station

Located at the mouth of the Angara river opposite Port Baikal, Listvyanka is the most popular of Baikal's villages. Fronted by shingle beaches, it stretches along the shore beneath steep forested hills. The village is the best spot to sample smoked Omul, a delicious fish endemic to Baikal, and to learn more about the lake at the **Baikal Museum**.

Northeast of Listvyanka, Olkhon Island is Baikal's largest island and has long been a place of pilgrimage for the local Buryat shamans. Pretty wooden guesthouses scattered around the island provide bases to explore Olkhon's hills, rocky bays and shamanic monuments.

Baikal Museum

Ulitsa Akademicheskaya 1. **Tel** (3952) 45 31 46. **Open** 9am–7pm daily.

Visitors aboard a horse-drawn carriage, Taltsy Architectural and Ethnographic Museum

A magnificent rock projection rising above the tranquil waters of Lake Baikal ▶

The magnificent Odigitria Cathedral with gold-tipped spires, Ulan-Ude

⑩ Ulan-Ude

Улан-Уде

Ulan-Ude

450 km (280 miles) SE of Irkutsk. 400,000.

Best known for the world's largest statue of Lenin's head, which dominates the bleak Soviet-era upper end of the city, Ulan-Ude is steeped in history. Long before a group of Cossack soldiers erected a fort here in 1666, the indigenous Buryats considered the place to be sacred. Closely related to the Mongols, Buryats were originally nomadic herders. Today, they make up around 30 per cent of the city's population and Ulan-Ude has been the capital of the autonomous Buryatia Republic since its creation in 1992. The simple Buryat tepees and yurts can be seen at the **Ethnographic Museum**, 5 km (3 miles) east of the city centre. A short walk southeast of ploshchad Sovetov, the **Buryat History Museum** has a great collection of relics rescued from the region's Buddhist monasteries before they were demolished by the Soviets.

Ulan-Ude's pleasant old town lies at the city's lower end on the banks of the Selenga and Uda rivers. A pedestrianized section of ulitsa Lenina, locally known as the Arbat, runs through the city centre where souvenir shops flank the small City Museum. A short distance southeast is the Fine Arts Museum, filled with fascinating paintings of Buryat culture. A little further south is the Odigitria Cathedral, which was consecrated in 1785 and is the city's oldest stone building.

Ethnographic Museum
Verchnyaya Berezovka. **Tel** (3012) 33 25 10. **Open** 9:30am–6:30pm Tue–Fri, 9:30am–7:30pm Sat & Sun.

Buryat History Museum
Ulitsa Profsoyuznaya 29. **Tel** (3012) 21 06 53. **Open** 11am–7pm Tue–Sun.

⑪ Ivolginsky Datsan

Иволгинский Датцан

Ivolginskiy Datsan

23 km (14 miles) S of Ulan-Ude. **Tel** (9021) 69 81 08. from Ulan-Ude. **Open** 8am–7pm daily

Russia's spiritual centre of Buddhism occupies a remote piece of windswept steppe beneath the Khamar Daban mountains. After having systematically destroyed the region's Buddhist temples throughout the 1930s, the Soviet government granted a plot of land to Buryatia's Buddhist community in 1945 as part of its postwar policy of easing the pressure on Russia's religious communities.

Ivolginsky Datsan has since developed into a thriving complex of temples, prayer wheels and souvenir stalls that attracts as many pilgrims as tourists, yet remains peaceful. Its most intriguing asset is the body of Ivolginsky's 12th Lama, Dashi-Dorzho Itegelov, who foresaw both his own death in 1927 and the fact that his corpse would never decay. His remains are exhibited to the public each year to mark Buddhist holidays.

Striking façade of one of the temples within the monastery complex, Ivolginsky Datsan

For hotels and restaurants in this region see pp272–3 and pp290–91

Models of animals on display at the Regional Museum, Vladivostok

⓬ Vladivostok

Владивосток

Vladivostok

3,345 km (2,078 miles) SE of Ulan-Ude.
620,000.

The final destination of the Trans-Siberian Railway, Vladivostok is Russia's largest Pacific port. The charming city sits on a hilly peninsula at the head of the Golden Horn Bay and offers superb sea views in every direction.

The Far East was loosely under Chinese control for centuries, but there was little resistance when Russia established Vladivostok, meaning Owner of the East, in 1860. During the Russian Civil War *(see p44)*, thousands of foreign troops landed here to support the White Army, but the Bolsheviks' eventual triumph at Vladivostok in 1922 signalled the end of the war. Closed until 1991, the city has since flourished and massive investment was made to upgrade the city's infrastructure prior to the 2012 Asia-Pacific Economic Cooperation (APEC) summit.

The **Regional Museum** in the city centre provides a visual overview of Vladivostok's history. Its huge collection of artifacts includes sections on natural history, archaeology, trade with China and Japan, and a fascinating collection of Soviet statues and propaganda posters. A short distance north of the museum lies the pedestrianized **ulitsa Fokina**. Lined with small shops and cafés, this pretty street overlooks the Amur Gulf and is known as Vladivostok's Arbat *(see p89)*. A 10-minute walk northwest of the street leads to the cannons of the **Fortress Museum**. The fort was built in the early 20th century to protect Vladivostok against any military threat.

At the heart of Vladivostok next to the harbour lies ploshchad Bortsov Revolutsii and the grand Monument to the Fighters for Soviet Power in the Far East. The adjacent street runs along the seafront past a memorial to Vladivostok's founders before reaching the World War II S-56 Submarine on the grass verge. Inside the submarine is a fascinating museum replete with torpedo tubes, cramped sleeping quarters and the personal effects of its crew.

Vintage car at the Antique Automobile Museum, Vladivostok

The funicular railway, about 15 minutes east of the city centre, takes passengers up to an observation point that offers brilliant views of the Golden Horn Bay on a clear day. A 30-minute bus ride from the city centre, the **Antique Automobile Museum** has a superb collection of Soviet limousines and motorcycles.

Regional Museum
Ulitsa Svetlanskaya 20. **Tel** (4232) 41 11 73. **Open** 9:30am–6pm daily.

Antique Automobile Museum
Ulitsa Sakhalinskaya 2. **Tel** (4232) 21 24 77. **Open** 10am–6pm daily.
automotomuseum.vl.ru

⓭ Khabarovsk

Хабаровск

Khabarovsk

762 km (473 miles) NE of Vladivostok.
594,000.

Named after the Cossack explorer Yerofey Khabarov (1603–71), whose heroic attempts to expand the Russian Empire into the Far East caused a series of conflicts with China, Khabarovsk sits on three hills beside the vast Amur river. The territory was not granted to Russia until the Treaty of Aguin in 1858, which established an official border with China and saw the construction of a Russian military fort here.

Khabarovsk is an upbeat city with boulevards connecting the several vast squares that were laid out during the Soviet era. In summer, locals flock to the City Park on the river bank where sandy beaches allow for sunbathing and swimming. Behind the park is the superb **Regional Museum**, which has a wide range of interesting exhibits devoted to the region's history. The **Far Eastern Arts Museum**'s absorbing collection of Russian artworks stands next door in a grand early 20th-century building opposite the Military Museum.

Just uphill is ploshchad Sobornaya that is dominated by the **Dormition Cathedral**, whose tiny onion domes perch on an unusual high-rise structure.

Regional Museum
Ulitsa Shevchenko 11. **Tel** (4212) 31 63 44. **Open** 10am–6pm Tue–Sun

Far Eastern Arts Museum
Ulitsa Shevchenko 7. **Tel** (4212) 31 48 71. **Open** 10am–6pm Tue–Sun.
dvhm.ru

Steps leading to the splendid Dormition Cathedral, Khabarovsk

Impressive stone sculptures of the World War II Memorial, Komsomolsk-na-Amur

⓮ Komsomolsk-na-Amur

Комсомольск-на-Амуре

Komsomolsk-na-Amur

399 km (248 miles) NE of Khabarovsk.

 268,000.

Built in remote, swampy taiga by a workforce of *Komsomol* (Communist Young League) volunteers and prison labour in 1932, Komsomolsk-na-Amur was a result of the Soviet regime's defensive policy to industrialize the Far East. The city was chosen as the location of a shipyard and an aircraft factory; the aviation industry continues to be the region's largest employer today.

Komsomolsk-na-Amur has progressed greatly since the days of canvas tents for shelter in winter, but living conditions here remain tough due to long, bitter winters and brief hot summers. The city is laid out according to typical Stalin-era town planning, with grandiose pastel-coloured buildings lining four and six-lane streets. The dilapidated River Terminal lies at the heart of Komsomolsk-na-Amur's summer social scene, which sees open-air bars strung out along the river bank. North-west of the river terminal lies the stunning **World War II Memorial** featuring superb stone sculptures. Nearby, the small **Regional Museum** on prospekt Mira houses exhibits ranging from traditional clothing such as fish-skin jackets to a stuffed Amur tiger. Just north is the **Art Museum**, which showcases a selection of paintings by local artists. Although the city offers attractions worth a day's visit, it is also well known for rafting tours in the region that can be arranged by local travel agents.

Regional Museum
Prospekt Mira 8. **Tel** (4217) 54 14 40. **Open** 9:30am–5pm Tue–Fri, 11:30am–6pm Sat & Sun.

Art Museum
Prospekt Mira 16. **Tel** (4217) 59 08 50. **Open** 10am–6pm Tue–Fri (till 5pm Sat & Sun).

⓯ Sakhalin Island

Сахалин

Sakhalin

354 km (220 miles) NE of Komsomolsk-na-Amur.

Home to an abundance of diverse wildlife, this mountainous island draws nature enthusiasts from around the world. Rich in oil and gas reserves, the region is a magnet for international energy companies.

Inhabited since the Stone Age, Sakhalin Island is still occupied by three indigenous tribes who share the territory with ethnic Russians and a large number of international workers based in Yuzhno-Sakhalinsk, the island's main city. Following a series of bitter territorial disputes, Japan occupied the southern half of the island from 1905 until the end of World War II when the Soviets took control. A number of Japanese buildings have survived from that period, one of which in Yuzhno-Sakhalinsk now houses the excellent **Museum of Local Lore**. Exhibitions cover the island's indigenous tribes, the Japanese occupation, and the Soviet era, when the island was used primarily as a penal colony. The Soviet era saw Gulag prisoners forced to dig a 10-km (6-mile) tunnel using hand tools from the mainland to the island. The project cost thousands of lives and was abandoned shortly after Stalin's death.

While it is possible to explore Sakhalin Island independently, it is more convenient to join an organized tour to access the island's natural beauty. Popular summer trips to the island include hiking up Mount Legushka and fishing in its vast lakes.

Museum of Local Lore
Kommunisticheskiy prospekt 29. **Tel** (4242) 72 75 55. **Open** 11am–6pm Tue–Sun (till 8pm Sat). **sakhalinmuseum.ru**

Elegant whooper swans at the coast of Sakhalin Island

Dramatic rock formations on the Sea of Okhotsk coast of Sakhalin Island

For hotels and restaurants in this region see pp272–3 and pp290–91

Concrete buildings lining a street winding through the city, Magadan

⓰ Magadan

Магадан

Magadan

2,225 km (1, 382 miles) NE of Sakhalin Island. 95,000.

Built in a region of permafrost by prison labour, the remote city of Magadan is rarely visited by tourists. The few who make the effort to visit the city do so not for its dreary Soviet-era architecture, but to experience what life was like at this former Gulag town. Winters in Magadan stretch over six months, with temperatures dropping below -35°C (-31°F), making living conditions harsh in the city.

The discovery of gold and platinum in the region inspired the Soviets to establish a port in the city in 1929. During the 1930s and 40s, thousands of prisoners were sent by ship via Magadan to the Kolyma region beyond, where Gulag camps had been set up to mine gold and platinum in appalling conditions. The prisoners were also assigned the task of building the infamous Kolyma Highway by using hand tools to connect Magadan with Yakutsk, 2,025 km (1,258 miles) away. Later, the highway came to be known as the Road of Bones due to the countless lives that were lost while building it. An imposing concrete memorial to the Gulag victims, the **Mask of Sorrow** was erected on the hillside above Magadan in 1996. A decade later, the huge **Holy Trinity Cathedral** was built on the site of the unfinished House of the Soviets as an Orthodox memorial to the victims of Stalin's repression.

Holy Trinity Cathedral
Sobornaya ploshchad. **Open** 7:30am–8pm daily.

⓱ Kamchatka

Камчатка

Kamchatka

400 km (248 miles) NE of Magadan. 320,000.

The landscape of this mountainous peninsula is an intriguing mix of geographical features, ranging from rolling plains to geysers and glaciated volcanoes. Brown bears roam freely across the peninsula, frolicking and foraging beneath a horizon of blunt-topped volcanoes, some of which belch sulphurous vapours. Thrilling helicopter flights over wide craters and jagged mountains are the only way to reach many parts of this remote territory, which was closed to non-Russians until 1991.

Among Kamchatka's many highlights is a visit to the **Valley of the Geysers**. A UNESCO World Heritage Site, the valley is a vast expanse of steam fields and spouting geysers. Lying in an ancient volcano crater, **Lake Kurilskoe** is a popular daytrip option; it is a great spot for bear and bird watching. **Mount Mutnovskaya**, a stunning 2,323-m (7,621-ft) active volcano that last erupted in 2000, is also a must see. Visitors can stand atop its two colossal craters and gaze at the volcanic activity below; in winter, it is possible to heli-ski down the volcano's side.

Kamchatka's largest city, Petropavlovsk-Kamchatsky is the starting point for most tours. Founded by Vitus Bering (1681–1741) on behalf of the Russians in 1740, the city boasts dramatic mountain scenery overlooked by drab Soviet buildings.

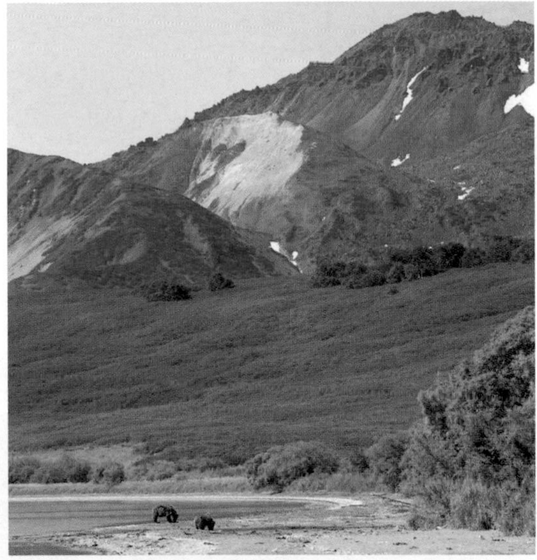

Brown bears foraging by a lake surrounded by majestic mountains, Kamchatka

атриум
Hamleys

TRAVELLERS' NEEDS

WHERE TO STAY

From luxury hotels in outstanding locations to wonderfully atmospheric bed and breakfast accommodation (B&Bs), Russia offers a range of places to stay to suit every budget. While Moscow abounds in high-end hotels, with cities such as St Petersburg not far behind, the provinces offer limited options. Out of the cities, hotels are mostly concrete blocks from the Soviet era where every floor is guarded by a *dezhurnaya* (concierge) who not only dispenses keys but also controls room service. Travellers visiting on a package tour are usually housed in large, somewhat anonymous hotels outside the city centre. These hotels provide reasonable service and full amenities such as bars, restaurants and fitness facilities. Travelling in off season cuts costs and offers the opportunity to book one of the many excellent deals available at the city-centre hotels. However, during peak season bookings for accommodation at all price levels should be made well in advance.

Where to Look

Independent travellers should consider the location, price and facilities before making a reservation. Large, usually expensive hotels can be easily spotted in most city centres. But mini-hotels, as they are commonly known, and B&Bs may be tucked away in the courtyards of residential blocks, often with only a nameplate by the doorbell to identify them, whether they are located in the centre or in the suburbs. If they are in the suburbs, be sure to enquire about local transport links to the centre before making a booking.

Façade of the Fifth Corner Business Hotel, a popular hotel in St Petersburg's city centre

How to Book

Most hotels can be booked online or by fax. Some of the smaller hotels, which cannot be booked by email or phone, can be reserved through accommodation agencies such as **All Hotels Russia**, **All Russian Hotels** and **Lodging.ru**. Guests are required to supply a credit card number, and money will be debited if a cancellation is made less than 72 hours in advance. A number of hotels and agencies provide visa support. Be sure that the establishment where you are staying can register you with the authorities within 7 working days, otherwise you may face problems if asked to present this document by the police or authorities.

Sign for a hotel on a quiet street off the city centre, Veliky Novgorod

Hotels

Hotels in Russia can be broadly divided into luxury hotels, mid-price hotels and the plainer ex-Soviet hotels, which were formerly run by the state. Rooms in most places have a shower, a TV and a telephone at the minimum and possibly air conditioning. Luxury hotels have comfortable rooms and offer modern facilities such as mini-bars. There is usually a luggage room for storing baggage after the midday check-out time. Bars are generally open until late at night, and fitness and sauna facilities are more or less standard in bigger establishments. A number of smaller, more modern hotels are emerging in the mid-price category. Rooms are generally clean and amenities include air conditioning and even sauna facilities. The cheaper ones in this category are mostly low-rises with small rooms, often without en-suite facilities. Ex-Soviet hotels are frequently lacklustre, with nondescript decor and poor-quality furniture. But the rooms are usually clean and of a good size.

The Russian word for hotel is *gostinitsa*, but some establishments may use the English

The reception desk at Park Inn, Astrakhan

◀ Stylish interior of a shopping mall selling international brands in Moscow

The fine dining restaurant in Dvor Podznoeva, a luxury hotel in Pskov

term, which is pronounced "khotyel". Taxi drivers should be able to understand either term.

Price

The big city-centre hotels nearly all fall into the luxury category, offering everything from exclusive single rooms to imperial suites costing several thousand dollars a day. However, staying at a smaller but centrally located hotel or B&B costs less money.

Prices are often stated in euros or US dollars, but all cash transactions must be made in Russian roubles. Note that many small hotels and hostels do not accept credit cards. It is important to be prepared to pay in cash.

Accommodation costs rise considerably during events such as Stars of the White Nights (late May–early Jul) in St Petersburg, any major sports tournament, or even locally specific events such as during the summer season in Sochi. Christmas and New Year (by both the Western and Orthodox calendars) is another period during which hotel rates tend to soar across the country. Prices return to normal during "mid-season" (usually from April to May and late July to late September), with good deals available from October to November and February to March.

Hidden Extras

Upmarket hotels that provide visa support and obligatory passport registration for free may not include local taxes or breakfast in their quoted prices, and these can be a significant addition to the final bill. In smaller hotels, breakfast is usually included in the price, but expect to pay extra for the initial visa support. Phone calls made from hotels are usually far more expensive than those from public or cell phones.

Tipping

A tip is expected if a hotel bellman or porter carries your bags to your room, but is not customary otherwise. However, in hotels that have a *dezhurnaya* on each floor, a small tip (as per your discretion) will ensure that room service is efficient and any requests or problems are attended to swiftly.

Taxes

Local taxes vary from region to region. They usually range from 1.5 to 15 per cent. Tax is generally included in the cost of a room quoted on hotel websites or on tariff-boards at reception desks.

Security

Many high-end hotels have metal detectors and bag searches at entrances, while smaller hotels have a doorman who may ask to see a visitor's card or identification. Most business-class hotels have a safe in the room or security deposit boxes at the front desk, where it is advisable to store large sums of money or valuables.

Disabled Travellers

Due to the thick snow in winter, most hotels have steps up to their entrances, making access difficult for disabled visitors. Only a few of the elite hotels are fully wheelchair accessible, with staff trained to be of assistance, although other hotels are increasingly adding ramps, widening doors and trying to adapt to meet the needs of disabled travellers. Travellers with special requirements should contact their preferred hotel before booking.

Travelling with Children

Few hotels in Russia cater specifically for families. Large hotels, however, provide babysitting facilities. Most hotels will charge an additional fee for an extra bed in the room. It is worth checking this before making a reservation. Visitors are advised not to expect extensive facilities for children or favourable room rates for families.

Elegantly decorated lobby in Radisson Hotel, Kaliningrad

Mini-hotels

St Petersburg and Moscow have by far the widest range of mini-hotels, ranging from basic to boutique. Other cities may have only a handful, sometimes squeezed into unlikely premises such as office blocks.

Not always a budget option considering some are extremely luxurious, mini-hotels can have anything from four to 15 or 20 rooms. In St Petersburg and Moscow, rooms may be elaborately furnished and decorated, but in the provinces the decor may be rather "Soviet", or garish in the "New Russian" style.

Many of St Petersburg's mini-hotels belong to the **Nevsky Hotels Group**, **Filippov Hotels** and **Rinaldi** networks. Mini-hotels elsewhere in the country can be booked through online agencies such as All Hotels Russia, Lodging.ru and All Russian Hotels.

A simply furnished room in Filippov Hotel, St Petersburg

Budget Accommodation

Truly cheap accommodation is hard to find in Russia. If hostels are not for you but your budget is tight, choose one of the more modest mini-hotels, which may describe themselves as a B&B. These establishments offer a small number of rooms in a converted flat in a residential building, with a housekeeper who makes breakfast. There may be a shared toilet rather than separate facilities.

Agencies such as **Apartment Reservation Network** and **Enjoy Moscow** offer short-term apartment rental. Note that the price drops considerably if more people share an apartment. Centrally located and refurbished, the apartments have one or more bedrooms, as well as satellite TV. In many cases, although the apartment has been refurbished, the communal staircase to the building may be on the grubby side, which can be off-putting at first.

Couchsurfing is another option, where you can find places to stay for free with Russian hosts. Travelling during off season is also a good idea.

Hostels

For budget travellers seeking decent accommodation in a reasonably central location, there are hostels in most major cities. Guests can choose from private, double and dormitory-style rooms. Several hostels offer kitchen facilities and free Wi-Fi. Almost all hostels offer visa support and registration and are quite friendly. Few are "youth" hostels as such, although young people do tend to dominate in the summer months. In the off season, it is not uncommon to see guests in the over-forty age range.

There are many hostels in Moscow, St Petersburg and Novgorod that are affiliated to the **Russian Youth Hostel Association**. In addition, **Hostelling International** and **HostelWorld** feature hostels in Russia on their websites. However, no single booking site covers all hostels and some may not be on any network at all.

Plush reception area of a Nevsky Moyka mini-hotel

Homestays

For an insight into Russian culture, staying with a family can be a worthwhile option, especially for visitors who plan to stay for a month or more. The system of homestays is similar to that of B&Bs in Europe, with prices including breakfast but no other meals. Extra meals can usually be provided at a small cost.

International Homestay Agency and **Worldwide Homestay** are good for booking homestays in Moscow and St Petersburg, while **OstWest** and **HOFA (Host Families Association)** are two reliable agencies covering a wide range of locations across Russia. OstWest focuses on St Petersburg and Lake Baikal, while HOFA also offers Moscow, Irkutsk, Kazan, Khabarovsk, Nizhny Novgorod, Veliky Novgorod, Novosibirsk, Omsk, Perm, Rostov-na-Don, Samara, Saratov, Suzdal, Vladivostok, Volgograd, Yaroslavl and Yekaterinburg as homestay destinations. The host families are likely to be extremely hospitable. Many are well educated, speak several languages and are keen to talk to guests about life in Russia.

Many apartments are reached through scruffy entrance halls or courtyards, but do not let this act as a deterrent, as it gives little indication of the quality of the accommodation inside.

Dachas and Camping

Russians love visiting the countryside for walks, swimming and mushroom gathering in warmer months. It is possible to do these on day trips, but finding accommodation out of town is difficult. Many Russians own *dachas* (country cottages), but these are seldom rented out except to people known to the owner. In fact, the demand for *dachas* located within 100 km (62 miles) from the city outstrips the supply. Be sure to book as early as February to ensure accommodation for the summer.

Uncle Pasha is an agency that can arrange *dacha* stays and horse-riding in a picturesque village beside the Volga river between Moscow and St Petersburg. The agency also recommends campsites.

Russia's climate means that camping is only feasible during summertime or until early autumn in temperate southern regions. Most campsites are geared towards travellers with cars, with motel-style rooms and guarded parking spots. Organized campsites are few and far between except around St Petersburg and Lake Baikal, but many people enjoy "wild" camping in the Altai Mountains, the Caucasus or even in the forests of Northern Russia.

Cosy interior of a *dacha* listed on Uncle Pasha

Extended Stays

Those intending to stay in any city for a month or more will find renting an apartment far cheaper than a hotel. This can be arranged by a number of agencies, such as HOFA (Host Families Association), OstWest, the Apartment Reservation Network or Enjoy Moscow. However, be sure to enquire about registration formalities.

Recommended Hotels

The hotels listed in this guide have been carefully selected and are among the best in Russia in their categories: business/chain, historic, hostel, guesthouse and luxury. From guesthouses in picturesque settings to luxurious hotels in bustling city centres, accommodation in Russia can be found at all price levels. Befitting its rich history, the country also boasts a host of splendid historic hotels. The hotels labelled "DK Choice" have been highlighted for their stunning location, spectacular interiors, or inviting atmosphere.

DIRECTORY

Accommodation Agencies

All Hotels Russia
Tel (495) 956 06 59.
W all-hotels.ru

All Russian Hotels
Pyatnitskaya ulitsa 3/4, Moscow. **Map** 4 E2.
Tel (495) 225 50 12.
W allrussianhotels.com

Lodging.ru
W lodging.ru

Mini-hotels

Filippov Hotels
St Petersburg.
Tel (812) 579 71 52.
W filippovhotel.ru

Nevsky Hotels Group
St Petersburg.
Tel (812) 703 38 60.
W hon.ru

Rinaldi
St Petersburg.
Tel (812) 325 41 88.
W rinaldi.ru

Budget Accommodation

Apartment Reservation Network
Tel (495) 225 50 12.

Couchsurfing
W couchsurfing.org

Enjoy Moscow
Tel (495) 741 76 06.
W enjoymoscow.com

Hostels

Hostelling International
W hihostels.com

HostelWorld
W hostelworld.com

Russian Youth Hostel Association (RYHA)
W hostelling-russia.ru

Homestays

HOFA (Host Families Association)
Tavricheskaya ulitsa 5, Apartment 25, St Petersburg.
Tel (7911) 766 54 64.
W hofa.ru

International Homestay Agency
W homestay agency.com

OstWest
Ligovsky prospekt 10, Office 2133, St Petersburg.
Tel (812) 327 34 16.
W ostwest.com

Worldwide Homestay
W worldwidehome stay.com

Dachas and Camping

Uncle Pasha
Ovchinnikovskaya naberezhnaya 8, Flat 508, Moscow.
Map 4 E2.
Tel (985) 217 32 41.
W unclepasha.com

Where to Stay

Moscow
Red Square and Kitay Gorod

DK Choice

Hotel Metropol
Метрополь ®®®
Luxury **Map** 2 D5
Teatralnyy proezd 2
Tel *(499) 501 78 00*
W metmos.ru
A wonderful example of Style-Moderne, the Metropol boasts spectacular interiors adorned with mosaics, golden chandeliers and stained glass. Many of the rooms are similarly lavish.

Hotel Savoy Савой ®®®
Luxury **Map** 2 D5
Ulitsa Rozhdestvenka 3/6
Tel *(495) 620 85 00*
W savoy.ru
Stylish hotel with rich furnishings, artworks, soft lighting and all modern facilities.

Garden Ring

Marco Polo Presnya Hotel
Марко Поло Пресня ®®
Business/chain **Map** 1 B4
Spiridonevskiy pereulok 9
Tel *(495) 660 06 06*
W presnja.ru
Quiet and comfortable hotel in a lovely residential area, a short walk from Red Square.

Peking Hotel Пекин ®®
Historic **Map** 1 A3
Ulitsa Bolshaya Sadovaya 5
Tel *(495) 650 09 00*
W hotelpeking.ru
Towering Empire-style building with rooms ranging from basic to luxurious. Free Wi-Fi.

DK Choice

Ararat Park Hyatt Moscow™
Арарат Парк Хаятт ®®®
Luxury **Map** 2 D5
Neglinnaya ulitsa 4
Tel *(495) 783 12 34*
W moscow.park.hyatt.com
Housed in a former Stalinist ministry, the Ararat offers superb views of the Bolshoi Theatre and the Kremlin from its terrace. The hotel has a health club with lounging areas, a sauna and a big Roman bath. Restaurants on site serve Armenian, Japanese and European cuisines.

Hotel Arbat Арбат ®®®
Business/chain **Map** 3 A2
Plotnikov pereulok 12
Tel *(499) 271 28 01*
W president-hotel.ru/arbat
Quiet hotel with large rooms and a nice veranda. Centrally located.

Hotel Marriott Grand Moscow
Марриотт Грандъ ®®®
Business/chain **Map** 1 B4
Tverskaya ulitsa 26/1
Tel *(495) 937 00 00*
W marriott.com
Ultra-luxury establishment with all modern amenities. Great service.

Hotel National Националь ®®®
Historic **Map** 1 C5
Mokhovaya ulitsa 15/1
Tel *(495) 258 70 00*
W national.ru
Lenin stayed here before moving into the Kremlin. Rooms are well-appointed. Free Wi-Fi.

The Ritz-Carlton
Ритц Карлтон ®®®
Business/chain **Map** 1 C5
Tverskaya ulitsa 3
Tel *(495) 225 88 88*
W ritzcarlton.com
Indulge in the spa and pool at this grand hotel opposite Red Square.

Zamoskvoreche

DK Choice

Hotel Baltschug Kempinski
Балчуг Кемпински ®®®
Business/chain **Map** 4 D2
Ulitsa Balchug 1
Tel *(495) 287 20 00*
W kempinski-moscow.com
Located by the Moskva river, this elegant yet modern hotel offers magnificent views of the Kremlin and St Basil's Cathedral from its rooms on the riverside. Facilities include a business centre, a spa and a beauty centre. Taxi and transfer services are available from the hotel's fleet of luxury cars.

Exterior of the stately Peking Hotel in Moscow

Price Guide
Prices are based on one night's stay in high season for a standard double room, inclusive of service charges and taxes.

®	up to ®3,000
®®	®3,000 to 6,500
®®®	over ®6,500

Further Afield

Godzillas Hostel
Годзиллас Хостел ®
Hostel **Map** 2 D3
Bolshoy Karetnyy pereulok 6
Tel *(495) 699 42 23*
W godzillashostel.com
Comfortable rooms and dorms in this amusingly named hostel. Kitchens available for guest use. Friendly staff.

Danilovskaya Даниловская ®®
Business/chain
Bolshoy Starodanilovskiy pereulok 5
Tel *(495) 954 05 03*
W danilovsky.ru
Run by the Orthodox Church, Danilovskaya offers clean, quiet rooms. Portraits of patriarchs and icons adorn the hotel's walls.

Domodedovo AirHotel
Аэротель ®®
Business/chain
Domodedovo Airport
Tel *(495) 795 38 68*
W airhotel.ru
Lacks character but is well equipped with modern facilities, such as free Wi-Fi and conference rooms for business travellers.

Holiday Inn Vinogradovo
Холидей Инн Виноградово ®®
Business/chain
Dmitrovskoe shosse 171
Tel *(495) 937 06 70*
W himv.ru
Lakeside hotel, a 5-minute drive from Sheremetevo airport, with comfortably furnished rooms. Good sports and fishing facilities.

Hotel Belgrade Белград ®®
Business/chain **Map** 3 A2
Smolenskaya ulitsa 8
Tel *(499) 248 27 14*
W hotel-belgrad.ru
Ex-Soviet budget hotel near the city centre. The restaurant serves good Eastern European food.

Hotel Sherston Шерстон ®®
Business/chain
Gostinichniy proezd 8/1
Tel *(495) 580 90 90*
W sherston.ru
Clean, simple rooms at this hotel. Far from the city centre but easily accessible by metro.

Hotel Yunost Юность ®®
Business/chain
Khamovnicheskiy val 34
Tel *(499) 242 48 61*
W hotelyunost.ru
Once connected to the Soviet youth organization, *Komsomol*, Yunost has bright, airy rooms.

Izmailovo Gamma-Delta
Измайлово Гамма-Дельта ®®
Business/chain
Izmaylovskoe shosse 71
Tel *(495) 737 70 70*
W izmailovo.ru
Simple, comfortable and well-appointed rooms. Very close to Izmaylovo Market.

Maxima Irbis Hotel Гостиница Максима Ирбис ®®
Business/chain
Gostinichnaya ulitsa 1
Tel *(495) 788 72 72*
W maximahotels.ru
Well-equipped hotel near the All-Russian Exhibition Centre. Friendly staff. Free Wi-Fi.

Maxima Zarya
Максима Заря ®®
Business/chain
Gostinichnaya ulitsa 4/9
Tel *(495) 788 72 72*
W maximahotels.ru
Zarya offers a wide range of accommodation options, from budget to luxurious studios.

Novotel Новотель ®®
Business/chain
Sheremetevo 2 Airport
Tel *(495) 626 59 00*
W novotel.com
Clean and bright airport hotel. Great on-site restaurant.

Sovietskiy Советский ®®
Historic
Leningradskiy prospekt 32/2
Tel *(495) 960 20 00*
W sovietsky.ru
Grand Stalinist decor with period furniture and a mirrored restaurant. Night club and lounge on site.

Tourist Турист ®®
Hostel
Ulitsa Selskokhozyaystvennayav 17
Tel *(495) 980 60 50*
W www.turist-hotel-moscow.ru
Five separate blocks offering an authentic Soviet experience. Rooms are basic but clean.

Plush waiting area at the Katerina City Hotel, Moscow

Art Hotel Арт Отель ®®®
Business/chain
3-ya Peschanaya ulitsa 2
Tel *(495) 725 09 05*
W arthotel.ru
Just 20 minutes from the city centre by car. Cosy rooms, sauna and a beer garden.

Crowne Plaza Краун Плаза ®®®
Business/chain
Krasnopresnenskaya naberezhnaya 12
Tel *(495) 258 22 22*
W crowneplaza.ru
A huge complex of rooms, offices, shops and restaurants in the riverside World Trade Center.

Golden Apple Boutique Hotel
Голден Еппл Бутик ®®®
Luxury **Map** 1 C3
Ulitsa Malaya Dmitrovka 11
Tel *(495) 980 70 00*
W goldenapple.ru
A homage to design in wood, marble and slate. Rooms are much cheaper at weekends.

Golden Ring Hotel Отель Золотое Кольцое ®®®
Business/chain **Map** 3 A2
Smolenskaya ulitsa 5
Tel *(495) 725 0100*
W hotel-goldenring.ru
Disabled-friendly hotel. Restaurants serve a wide variety of cuisines.

DK Choice

Hilton Leningradskaya
Хилтон Ленинградская ®®®
Historic
Ulitsa Kalanchevskaya 21/40
Tel *(495) 627 55 50*
W moscow.hilton.com
With marble columns and bronze chandeliers, this hotel is one of the most famous in the city. Its elegant interiors and opulent rooms belie the modern amenities on offer. Well-equipped fitness room and pool for guests.

Katerina City Hotel
Катерина Сити ®®®
Business/chain **Map** 4 F4
Shluzovaya naberezhnaya 6
Tel *(495) 795 24 44*
W katerinahotels.com
Contemporary Swedish styled hotel with two relaxing bars and restaurants. Non-smoking.

Kebur Palace Кебур Палас ®®®
Guesthouse **Map** 3 B3
Ulitsa Ostozhenka 32
Tel *(495) 733 90 70*
W keburpalace.ru
Near the Cathedral of Christ the Saviour, with some rooms overlooking a pretty cobbled patio.

Korston Hotel Корстон ®®®
Business/chain
Ulitsa Kosygina 15
Tel *(495) 939 88 88*
W korston.ru
Comfortable retro rooms, multi-cuisine restaurants and karaoke at this hotel in the Sparrow Hills.

Moscow Country Club Москоу Кантри Клаб ®®®
Luxury
Nakhabino, Krasnogorsky District
Tel *(495) 626 59 11*
W moscowcountryclub.ru
A favourite weekend retreat for the city's elite. Boasts Russia's only 18-hole championship golf course.

President Президент ®®®
Historic **Map** 3 C3
Ulitsa Bolshaya Yakimanka 24
Tel *(495) 271 28 58*
W president-hotel.ru
Communist-era haven for party leaders, with stately rooms, kitsch decor and tight security.

Proton Hotel Протон ®®®
Business/chain
Novozavodskaya ulitsa 22
Tel *(495) 797 33 00*
W protonhotelmoscow.com
Well-equipped business hotel with comfortable rooms and excellent service.

Radisson Slavyanskaya
Радиссон Славянская ®®®
Business/chain
Ploshchad Europa 2
Tel *(495) 941 80 20*
W radisson.com
Panoramic views and well-furnished contemporary rooms.

Renaissance Ренессанс ®®®
Business/chain **Map** 2 D1
Olimpiyskiy prospekt 18/1
Tel *(495) 931 90 00*
W renaissancehotels.com
Small but comfortable rooms with all modern amenities. There is a swimming pool for guests.

For more information on types of hotels *see p265*

DK Choice

Swissôtel Krasnye Holmy
Красные Холмы ®®®
Luxury **Map** 4 F4
Kosmodamianskaya naberezhnaya 52/6
Tel *(495) 787 98 00*
W swissotel.com
One of Moscow's best hotels, with stunning river-facing views and two excellent restaurants. Plush interiors and floor-to-ceiling windows make for a luxurious experience. Relax in the heated indoor pool or unwind at the hotel spa.

St Petersburg

Palace Embankment

Petro Palace Hotel
Петро палас ®®
Business/chain **Map** 3 C1
Malaya Morskaya ulitsa 14
Tel *(812) 571 28 80*
W petropalacehotel.com
Grand interiors and extensive facilities, including a gym, a sauna and a Jacuzzi, at competitive prices.

Prestige Hotel Centre
Престиж Центр ®®
Business/chain **Map** 3 C1
Gorokhovaya ulitsa 5
Tel *(812) 312 83 26*
W prestige-hotels.com
Simply furnished rooms, a bistro and a café. Tucked away near the gardens fronting the Admiralty.

Angleterre Hotel
Отель Англетер ®®®
Historic **Map** 3 C2
Malaya Morskaya ulitsa 24
Tel *(812) 494 56 66*
W angleterrehotel.com
Stylishly refurbished hotel with views of St Isaac's Cathedral from some rooms. Relax at the indoor pool, spa or the turbo-solarium.

DK Choice

Casa Leto ®®®
Historic **Map** 3 C2
Bolshaya Morskaya ulitsa 34
Tel *(812) 600 10 96*
W casaleto.com
This ultra-chic family-owned boutique hotel – reached by a grand stairwell – boasts light-filled rooms and a superb central location. Completely non-smoking, with many complimentary extras such as fresh fruit and refreshments. Airport transfer facilities available upon request. Free Wi-Fi.

Comfort Hotel Комфорт ®®®
Business/chain **Map** 3 C1
Bolshaya Morskaya ulitsa 25
Tel *(812) 560 67 00*
W comfort-hotel.org
Simple, airy rooms in the heart of the historic centre. Basic facilities, but helpful staff.

Gostinyy Dvor

Polikoff Поликофф ®
Guesthouse **Map** 4 F1
Karavannya ulitsa 11/64, apt 24–26
Tel *(812) 995 34 88*
W polikoff.ru
Mini-hotel with bright, cosy rooms. Centrally located. Buffet breakfast.

DK Choice

Grand Hotel Europe Гранд Отель Европа ®®®
Historic **Map** 4 E1
Mikhaylovskaya ulitsa 1/7
Tel *(812) 329 60 00*
W grandhoteleurope.com
With a superb location beside Nevskiy prospekt, the Europe is close to all the main sights. It boasts a wonderful decor, especially the Art Nouveau Caviar Bar. Suites are furnished with antiques.

Kempinski Hotel Moika 22
Кемпински Мойка 22 ®®®
Luxury **Map** 2 D5
Naberezhnaya Reki Moyki 22
Tel *(812) 335 91 11*
W kempinski.com
Great views of the Hermitage from some rooms. Restaurant offers international cuisine. Indulge in the Turkish bath.

Pushka Inn
Отель Пушка ИНН ®®®
Guesthouse **Map** 2 D5
Naberezhnaya Reki Moyki 14
Tel *(812) 312 09 13*
W pushkainn.ru
Chic modern rooms in a historic building right on the Moyka river.

Outdoor café at the Grand Hotel Europe, St Petersburg

Sennaya Ploshchad

DK Choice

B&B Randhouse ®
Guesthouse **Map** 4 D3
Pereulok Grivtsova 11, apt 83
Tel *(812) 310 70 05*
W randhouse.ru
Named after Ayn Rand, this loft-based mini-hotel has open fireplaces, bare brick walls and king-size duvets. Some rooms have private bathrooms, others share facilities. Great location.

Hotel Columb
Отель Колумб ®®
Guesthouse **Map** 3 C2
Kazanskaya ulitsa 41
Tel *(812) 315 70 93*
W columbhotel.com
Quiet, comfortable hotel near the metro. Free parking and Wi-Fi.

Ambassador Амбассадор ®®®
Luxury **Map** 3 C3
Prospekt Rimskogo-Korsakova 5–7
Tel *(812) 331 88 44*
W ambassador-hotel.ru
Plush rooms with city views. Gym and beauty services available.

Further Afield

Andersen Hotel
Андерсен отель ®®
Business/chain
Ulitsa Chapygina 4
Tel *(812) 740 51 40*
W andersenhotel.ru
Pleasantly furnished rooms. Hotel arranges tours of the city centre.

AZIMUT Hotel St Petersburg
АЗИМУТ Отель Санкт-етербург ®®
Business/chain **Map** 3 B5
Lermontovskiy prospekt 43/1
Tel *(812) 740 26 40*
W azimuthotels.com
Over 1,000 budget rooms with stunning views of Fontanka river.

Baltic Star Hotel Отель Балтийская Звезда ®®
Luxury
Berezovaya alleya 3, Strelna
Tel *(812) 438 57 00*
W balticstar-hotel.ru
A superb retreat for those seeking elegance and comfort. Cottages are available for greater privacy.

Brothers Karamazov Братя Карамазовы ®®
Guesthouse **Map** 4 F4
Sotsialisticheskaya ulitsa 11a
Tel *(812) 355 11 86*
W karamazovhotel.ru
Hotel with airy rooms named after heroines in Dostoyevsky's novels.

Fifth Corner Business Hotel
Пятый угол ®®
Business/chain **Map** 4 F3
Zagorodnyy prospekt 13
Tel *(812) 380 81 81*
W 5ugol.ru
Simple rooms at this eco-friendly hotel. Mini-bar and safe in all rooms.

German Club Немецкий клуб ®®
Business/chain
Ulitsa Gastello 20
Tel *(812) 371 51 04*
W hotelgermanclub.com
Provides personalized services, from arranging guided tours to advice on where to eat.

Kronverk Кронверк ®®
Business/chain **Map** 1 B3
Ulitsa Blokhina 9
Tel *(812) 703 36 63*
W kronverk.com
Very close to Peter and Paul Fortress, this place offers rooms with kitchenettes. Free Wi-Fi.

Moskva Москва ®®
Business/chain
Ploshchad Aleksandra Nevskogo 2
Tel *(812) 333 24 44*
W hotel-moscow.ru
Centrally located package-tour establishment with good facilities.

Okhtinskaya Охтинская ®®
Business/chain
Bolsheokhtinskiy prospekt 4
Tel *(812) 318 00 40*
W okhtinskaya.com
Contemporary hotel, with airy rooms overlooking the Neva river near the Smolnny Cathedral.

Park Inn Pribaltiyskaya Парк Инн Прибалтийская ®®
Business/chain
Korablstroiteley ulitsa 14
Tel *(812) 329 26 26*
W parkinn.com
Vast hotel looking out on to the Gulf of Finland. Free shuttle bus service to the city centre.

Park Inn Pulkovskaya
Парк Инн Пулковская ®®
Business/chain
Ploshchad Pobedy 1
Tel *(812) 740 39 00*
W parkinn.com
Good selection of bars and restaurants, with great views of Victory Monument. Close to the airport.

Rossiya Россия ®®
Business/chain
Ploshchad Chernyshevskogo 11
Tel *(812) 329 39 01*
W rossiya-hotel.ru
Refurbished Soviet-era hotel amidst the Stalinist buildings of Moskovskiy prospekt.

Brightly lit reception area at the Fifth Corner Business Hotel, St Petersburg

DK Choice

Hotel Shelfort Шелфорт ®®
Historic **Map** 1 A5
3-ya liniya 26, Vasilevskiy Island
Tel *(812) 328 05 55*
W shelfort.ru
With lovely tiled stoves in elegantly minimalist rooms, Shelfort will charm guests with its understated beauty. It also offers two luxury suites with log fireplaces, one of them with a balcony. There is no lift.

St Petersburg Hotel
Санкт-Петербург ®®
Business/chain **Map** 2 F2
Pirogovskaya naberezhnaya 5/2
Tel *(812) 380 19 19*
W hotel-spb.ru
Splendid views from rooms on the south side. Healthy breakfast spread. Free Wi-Fi.

Stony Island Hotel
Стоуни Айлэнд ®®
Business/chain
Kamennoostrovskiy prospekt 45
Tel *(812) 337 24 34*
W stonyisland.ru
Housed in a historic building, with a relaxed American bar and restaurant. Non-smoking.

Corinthia Nevskij Palace
Коринтия Невский Палас ®®®
Business/chain
Nevskiy prospekt 57
Tel *(812) 380 20 01*
W corinthia.com
Popular with celebrities. Has a DJ in the lobby at weekends. Excellent on-site restaurant.

Grand Hotel Emerald
Гранд Отель Эмеральд ®®®
Business/chain
Suvorovskiy prospekt 18
Tel *(812) 740 50 00*
W grandhotelemerald.com
Modern hotel with opulent rooms and plush decor. It also has a great fitness centre, sauna and Turkish bath.

Holiday Inn St Petersburg
Холидэй Инн ®®®
Business/chain
Moskovskiy prospekt 97a
Tel *(812) 448 71 71*
W holidayinn.com
Comfortable, well-equipped and minimalist rooms. Great location.

Hotel Dostoevsky Отель Достоевский ®®®
Business/chain
Vladimirskiy prospekt 19
Tel *(812) 331 32 03*
W dostoevsky-hotel.ru
Vibrant, modern hotel wrapped around a shopping mall. Airport shuttle available.

Radisson Royal Hotel
Рэдиссон Роял Отель ®®®
Business/chain
Nevskiy prospekt 49/2
Tel *(812) 322 50 00*
W radissonblu.com
Opulent rooms. The café offers fine views of Nevskiy prospekt.

Beyond St Petersburg

Hotel Natali Натали ®®
Guesthouse
Malaya ulitsa 56a, Pushkin
Tel *(812) 466 27 68*
W hotelnatali.ru
Cosy rooms, an excellent spa and a bowling alley for guests to unwind. Free Wi-Fi.

DK Choice

New Peterhof
Новый Петергоф ®®®
Business/chain
Sankt-Peterburgskiy prospekt 34, Petrodvorets
Tel *(812) 319 10 10*
W new-peterhof.com
Rooms at this award-winning hotel are stylish, spacious and comfortable – many rooms offer great views of Peterhof's Upper Park. The hotel's amenities include a spa and excellent on-site restaurants serving Russian and Bavarian cuisines.

For more information on types of hotels *see p265*

Northern Russia

Petrozavodsk: Petrozavodsk
Петрозаводск ®
Hostel
Ulitsa Krasnaya 28, 2nd floor
Tel *(8142) 77 98 77*
W petrohostel.ru
Pleasant budget option with smartly furnished dorms and doubles. Central location.

Petrozavodsk: Zarechnaya
Заречная ®®
Business
Naberezhnaya Lososinskaya 7A
Tel *(8142) 59 22 20*
W zarekoy.ru
Decent hotel with comfortable rooms and a café-restaurant. Friendly and helpful staff.

DK Choice

Pskov: Dvor Podznoeva
Двор Подзноева ®®
Historic
Ulitsa Nekrasova 1B
Tel *(8112) 79 70 00*
W dvorpodznoeva.ru
Enjoy all modern facilities within an ensemble of renovated 17th-century buildings. Located in the old town, this extremely atmospheric hotel is a short walk from the Kremlin.

Pskov: Rizhskaya Рижская ®®
Business
Rizhskiy prospekt 25
Tel *(8112) 56 22 23*
W rijskaya.ru
A vast Soviet-era hotel, recently renovated, but still exuding period charm. Great service.

Valaam: Zimnaya Зимняя ®®
Historic
Valaam Monastery
Tel *(921) 629 33 11*
W valaam.ru
Comfortably furnished rooms in a functional hotel on the island.

Veliky Novgorod: Voyage
Вояж ®
Guesthouse
Ulitsa Dvortsovaya 1
Tel *(8162) 66 41 66*
W hotel-voyage.ru
Centrally located with big rooms, some with four-poster beds.

Veliky Novgorod: Park Inn (Radisson) Парк Инн ®®
Business
Ulitsa Studencheskaya 2
Tel *(8162) 94 09 10*
W parkinn.ru
High-end hotel with tennis courts, jogging trails and barbecue areas.

Kaliningrad

Kaliningrad: Amigos Hostel
Амигос Хостел ®
Hostel
Ulitsa Yablonevaya 34
Tel *911 485 2157 (mobile)*
W amigoshostel.ru
Cosy dorm rooms in a modern house amidst the leafy suburbs of Kaliningrad.

Kaliningrad: Hotel Kaliningrad
Гостиница Калининград ®
Business/chain
Leninsky prospekt 81
Tel *(4012) 53 60 21*
W hotel.kaliningrad.ru
Authentic Soviet-era building, but modern interiors. Features a billiards room. Central location.

DK Choice

Kaliningrad: Hotel Kaiserhof
Кайзерхоф ®®
Business
Ulitsa Oktyabrskaya 6A
Tel *(4012) 59 22 22*
W heliopark.ru
This stylish business hotel overlooks the Pregolya river and has splendid views of Königsburg Cathedral. Highlights include a lovely spa centre to unwind in and a fitness studio with sweeping views of the river. Helpful and professional staff.

Kaliningrad: Radisson Hotel
Радисон Отель ®®
Business/chain
Ploshchad Pobedy 10
Tel *(4012) 59 33 44*
W radisson.ru
State-of-the-art facilities in a superb central spot overlooking the main square. Efficient service.

Entrance to the ultra-chic Hotel Kaiserhof, Kaliningrad

Svetlogorsk: Dom Skazochnika
дом Сказочника ®
Guesthouse
Pereulok Gofmana 2
W hoffmanhouse.ru
Tel *(4015) 32 23 96*
A budget option set in well-kept wooded gardens. Ten minutes walk to the beach.

Central and Southern Russia

Astrakhan: Park Inn
Парк Инн ®®
Business
Ulitsa Anri Barbusa 29
Tel *(8512) 29 01 20*
W parkinn.ru
A 14-storey hotel with classy rooms. Excellent standards of service. Close to the railway station.

Astrakhan: Victoria Palas
Виктория Палас ®®
Business
Ulitsa K Naberezhnaya 3
Tel *(8512) 39 48 01*
W victoriapalas.ru
Plush hotel on the banks of the Volga river. Amenities include a spa centre and a piano bar.

Kazan: Vhostele Вхостеле ®
Hostel
Ulitsa Volkova 54A
Tel *(843) 238 06 93*
W vhostele.com
Budget-friendly hostel with air-conditioned dorms. All rooms non-smoking. Located near a bus stop.

Kazan: Giuseppe Джузеппе ®®
Historic/luxury
Ulitsa Kremliovskaya 15/25
Tel *(843) 292 69 34*
W giuseppe.ru
Set in a historic building exuding character. Spacious rooms. The on-site restaurant serves Italian and Mediterranean cuisines.

Kazan: Shalyapin Palace
Шаляпин Палас ®®
Luxury
Ulitsa Universitetskaya 7
Tel *(843) 231 10 00*
W shalyapin-hotel.ru
Recently refurbished hotel with elegantly furnished rooms. Helpful staff. Central location.

Nizhny Novgorod: Naberzhny Hostel Чабержный Хостел ®
Hostel
Naberezhnaya Nizhne-Volzhskaya 7/2
Tel *(831) 230 13 15*
W bereghostel.ru
Great location, low prices, spacious dorms and all the usual hostel facilities.

Key to Price Guide *see p266*

Nizhny Novgorod: Sergievskaya Сергиевская ®®
Historic
Ulitsa Sergievskaya 12
Tel *(831) 433 00 10*
W hotel-sergievskaya.ru
Discover a delightful blend of the old and new in this atmospheric 19th-century mansion.

Perm: Ural Урал ®
Business
Ulitsa Lenina 58
Tel *(342) 218 62 61*
W hotel-ural.com
Colossal Soviet-era hotel dominating the city centre. Modern business and wellness centres.

Perm: Hilton Garden Inn Хилтон Гарден Инн ®®
Business
Ulitsa Mira 45B
Tel *(342) 227 67 87*
W hiltongardeninn3.hilton.com
The Hilton offers predictably high standards and smart decor. Suites feature a whirlpool bath.

Samara: JK Hostel Хостел Джей Кей ®
Hostel
Studencheskiy pereulok 7, 3rd floor
Tel *(8469) 22 83 92*
W jk-hostel.com
Comfortably furnished place boasting a huge living room and a large country-style kitchen.

DK Choice

Samara: Bristol-Zhiguly Бристоль Жигули ®®
Historic/luxury
Ulitsa Kuybyscheva 111
Tel *(846) 331 65 55*
W bristol-zhiguly.ru
A lovely historic hotel that has been in business since the late 18th century. Pleasant, spacious and well-appointed rooms offer all modern amenities. The 24-hour restaurant serves European cuisine. Warm and friendly staff.

Samara: Rossiya Россия ®®
Business
Ulitsa M Gorkogo 82
Tel *(846) 339 03 11*
W hotel-rossia.ru
An ex-Soviet hotel with reasonable service standards. Most rooms come with fantastic river views.

Saransk: Hotel Saransk Саранск ®®
Business
Ulitsa Kommunisticheskaya 35
Tel *(8342) 47 88 82*
W hotelsaransk.ru
A fully renovated hotel with comfortable rooms and a Turkish bath.

Façade of Park Inn, a modern hotel in the heart of Yekaterinburg

Saransk: Park Hotel Парк Отель ®®
Guesthouse
Ulitsa Krasnaya 4
Tel *(8342) 23 29 19*
W parkhotel-saransk.ru
Pleasant hotel, resembling a chateau from the outside. Tucked away in a quiet residential area.

Ulyanovsk: Venets Венец ®®
Business
Ulitsa Spasskaya 19/9
Tel *(8422) 44 18 70*
W venets-hotel.ru
Towering Soviet-era block with modern interiors, a rooftop restaurant and views of the Volga river

Volgograd: Flamingo Motel Фламинго Мотель ®
Guesthouse
Ulitsa Rokossovskogo 63
Tel *937 725 9960 (mobile)*
Popular budget option. Comprises several clean en suites located above a car wash.

Volgograd: Hotel Volgograd Волгоград ®®
Business/luxury/historic
Ulitsa Mira 12
Tel *(8442) 55 19 55*
W hotelvolgograd.ru
Housed in a grand 19th-century building with tastefully decorated rooms. Spa treatments available.

Yekaterinburg: Domino Hostel Домино Хостел ®
Hostel
Ulitsa Chelyuskintsev 60
Tel *(343) 361 54 60*
W dominohotel.ru
Basic apartments with clean dorms and doubles. Free Wi-Fi.

Yekaterinburg: Park Inn Ekaterinburg Парк Ин ®®
Business/chain
Ulitsa Mamina-Sibiryaka 98
Tel *(343) 216 60 00*
W parkinn.ru
Spacious hotel with well-furnished rooms. Popular with business travellers. Convenient location.

Yekaterinburg: Viz' Avi Виз' Ави ®®
Business
Ulitsa Tatischeva 86
Tel *(343) 381 50 27*
W vizavi-hotel.ru
Uninspiring decor but good-sized rooms at this modern hotel.

The Caucasus

Adler: Ekodom Екодом ®®
Guesthouse
Ulitsa Prosveshcheniya 160B
Tel *(8622) 47 37 13*
W ekodom-hotels.ru
Recently built with all mod cons. Superb breakfast spread.

Adler: Flamingo Фламинго ®®
Guesthouse
Ulitsa Prosveshcheniya 15B
Tel *(8622) 40 87 70*
W adler-flamingo.ru
Comfortable hotel just a few minutes from the beach. Friendly atmosphere. Efficient service.

DK Choice

Anapa: Starinnaya Старинная ®®®
Luxury
Ulitsa Naberezhnaya 2
Tel *(86133) 405 04*
W starinnaya-anapa.ru
The Starinnaya is a grand, colonnaded affair with plush carpets, polite staff and a fantastic array of spa treatments. Most rooms have superb sea views. Both indoor and outdoor pools available

Gelendzhik: White House Белый Дом ®
Guesthouse
Ulitsa Lunacharskogo 127
Tel *(86141) 320 08*
W whitehouse.azur.ru
A calm alternative to the bustling city centre, with an outdoor pool and lovely sea views.

For more information on types of hotels *see p265*

Gelendzhik: Gelendzhik Геленджик ®®
Guesthouse
Ulitsa Khersonskaya 1
Tel *(86141) 211 45*
W gelhotel.ru
Charming all-inclusive place right in the centre of the city, a short distance from the seafront.

Krasnaya Polyana: Piramida Пирамида ®
Guesthouse
Ulitsa Berezovaya 157
Tel *918 401 1478 (mobile)*
Pleasant family-run guesthouse located near the ski slopes.

Krasnaya Polyana: Tulip Inn Rosa Farm Тюлип Инн Роза Хутор ®®
Luxury
Rosa Khutor Alpine Ski Resort
Tel *(8622) 43 00 00*
W tulipinnrosakhutor.com
Brand-new hotel in the heart of the Olympic ski resort.

Krasnodar: Intourist Интурист ®®
Business
Ulitsa Krasnaya 109
Tel *(861) 255 88 97*
W int-krd.ru
Centrally located ex-Soviet hotel with rooms decorated in warm colours. High standards of service.

Krasnodar: Lux-Platan Люкс-Платан ®®
Business/luxury
Ulitsa Rashpilevskaya 4/1
Tel *(861) 262 86 84*
W platanhotel.ru
Popular with visiting rock stars. Boasts big rooms, a sauna and a well-equipped fitness centre.

Rostov-na-Don: Don-Plaza Дон-Плаза ®®
Business
Ulitsa Bolshaya Sadoyova 115
Tel *(863) 263 90 52*
W don-plaza.ru
Stylish place with an impressive open-plan lobby and spa centre.

Rostov-na-Don: Pushkinskaya Пушкинская ®®
Business/historic
Ulitsa Pushkinskaya 121
Tel *(863) 299 92 70*
W hotel-pushkinskaya.ru
Characterful 19th-century mansion with graceful interiors. Free Wi-Fi.

Sochi: Villa Svetlana Вила Светлана ®
Guesthouse
Ulitsa Chernomorskaya 12/2
Tel *918 200 3794 (mobile)*
Small guesthouse in a peaceful suburb. Close to the beach.

A contemporary-style room in Tulip Inn Rosa Farm, Krasnaya Polyana

Sochi: Sochi Breeze Сочи Бриз ®®
Guesthouse
Kurortny prospekt 72
Tel *(8622) 66 38 00*
W sochibreeze.ru
Smart hotel with a great spa and an outdoor pool overlooking the Dendrarium.

Sochi: Marins Park Маринс Парк ®®®
Business/luxury
Morskoy pereulok 2
Tel *(8622) 69 30 00*
W parkhotel-sochi.ru
Swanky, central hotel with spacious rooms. Private beach for guests. Excellent breakfast spread.

Sochi: Zelenaya Roscha Зеленая Роща ®®®
Historic
Kurortny prospekt 120
Tel *(8622) 269 53 33*
W rosha-sochi.ru
Cavernous oak-panelled guest rooms at Stalin's camouflaged *dacha*, set in the forested hills just outside Sochi.

Siberia and the Far East

Irkutsk: Baikaler Hostel Байкалер Хостел ®
Hostel
Ulitsa Lenina 9, apt 11
Tel *(3952) 33 62 40*
W baikaler.com
Hugely popular hostel with an affable owner who arranges trips throughout the region for guests.

Irkutsk: Courtyard Marriott Кортъярд Марриотт ®®
Business
Ulitsa Chkalova 15
Tel *(3952) 48 10 00*
W courtyardirkutsk.ru
One of the city's best hotels offering rooms adapted for guests with disabilities. Elegant ballroom.

Irkutsk: Irkutsk Иркутск ®®
Business
Bulvar Gagarina 44
Tel *(3952) 25 01 68*
W irkutsk-hotel.ru
Huge riverfront hotel with superb views from most of its rooms.

Khabarovsk: Intour Интур ®®
Business
Amurskiy Bulvar 2
Tel *(4212) 31 23 13*
W intourist-khabarovsk.ru
Towering ex-Soviet hotel with renovated rooms decorated in elegant European style.

Komsomolsk-na-Amur: Amur Амур ®
Guesthouse
Prospekt Mira 15
Tel *(4217) 59 09 84*
Constructed in the 1930s, this place offers all the basic amenities. Friendly and helpful staff.

Komsomolsk-na-Amur: Voskhod Восход ®®
Business
Prospekt Pervostroiteley 31
Tel *(4217) 53 51 31*
W hotel-voskhod.ru
Soviet-era hotel with elegantly furnished suites. Home to one of the city's top restaurants.

Krasnoyarsk: SibTourGuide Hostel СибТурГид ®
Hostel
Prospekt Mira 85, apt 72
Tel *(391) 251 26 54*
W sibtourguide.com
Centrally located hostel run by a tour guide who organizes excursions for guests around the city.

Krasnoyarsk: Metelitsa Метелица ®®
Business
Prospekt Mira 14/1
Tel *(391) 227 60 60*
W hotel-metelica.ru
Classy, upmarket hotel offering opulent rooms with luxurious furnishings. Excellent multi-cuisine restaurant on site.

Key to Price Guide *see p266*

DK Choice

Listvyanka: Eco Hostel
Эко Хостел ®
Hostel
Ulitsa Chapaeva 77A
Tel *983 243 3280 (mobile)*
W baikaler.com
Huddled amidst pine trees, a short distance from the shores of Lake Baikal, the solar-powered eco cabins at Eco Hostel offer cosy and atmospheric accommodation. Try the Russian *banya*.

Magadan: Golden House
Голден Хаус ®®
Business
Ulitsa Transportnaya 1
Tel *(4132) 20 11 11*
W hotel-goldenhouse.ru
Refreshingly modern and comfortable rooms at this hotel.

Novosibirsk: Zokol Hostel
Цоколь Хостел ®
Hostel
Ulitsa Schetinkina 34
Tel *(383) 223 36 11*
W zokolhostel.ru
Stylish dorms and doubles at this inviting hostel. Outstanding facilities and great location.

Novosibirsk: Double Tree Hilton Даблтри Хилтон ®®®
Business/luxury
Ulitsa Kamenskaya 7/1
Tel *(383) 223 01 00*
W doubletree3.hilton.com
Offers chic and well-appointed rooms. Relax in the spa or unwind in big whirlpool baths.

Omsk: Ibis Sibir Omsk
Ибис Сибирь Омск ®®
Business
Ulitsa Lenina 22
Tel *(3812) 31 15 51*
W ibis-sibir-omsk.com
Classy hotel with bright, modern interiors set in an imposing 19th-century building.

Omsk: Shato Шато ®®
Luxury
Ulitsa 1ya Severnaya 95
Tel *(3812) 38 32 82*
W hotel.shato55.ru
Palatial place with elaborate decor and excellent service. Great on-site restaurant.

Petropavlovsky-Kamchatsky: Avacha Авача ®®
Business
Ulitsa Leningradskaya 61
Tel *(4152) 42 72 01*
W avacha-hotel.ru
Soviet-era hotel with comfortable rooms and mountain views.

Petropavlovsky-Kamchatsky: Idelveis Эдельвейс ®®
Business
Prospekt Pobedy 27
Tel *(4152) 29 50 00*
W idelveis.com
Basic but clean and comfortable rooms in the town centre. Helpful multi-lingual staff.

Sakhalin: Pacific Plaza
Пацифик Плаза ®®
Business
Prospect Mira 172
Tel *(4242) 45 50 00*
W sakhalinpacificplaza.ru
Popular upmarket hotel with restaurants and conference facilities.

Sakhalin: Sakhalin Sapporo
Сахалин Саппоро ®®
Business
Ulitsa Lenina 181
Tel *(424) 272 15 60*
W sakhsapporo.ru
Spacious well-appointed rooms with contemporary furnishings at this hotel. Good service.

Tobolsk: Georgievska
Георгиевская ®®
Business
Ulitsa Lenskaya 35
Tel *(3456) 22 09 09*
W hotel-georgievskaya.ru
A centrally located hotel with cosy rooms and adequate facilities. Warm and personable staff.

Tobolsk: Sibir Сибирь ®®
Business
Ploshchad S Remezova 1
Tel *(3456) 25 13 53*
W hotel-siberia.com
Although in dire need of refurbishment, the Sibir offers decent rooms. Close to the Kremlin.

Tomsk: Yoko Йоко ®
Business
Ulitsa Altayskaya 149
Tel *(3822) 20 02 20*
W yoko.tomsk.ru
Delightful Japanese-themed mini-hotel with ultra-stylish interiors. Great sushi bar.

Tomsk: Toyan Тоян ®®
Luxury
Ulitsa Obrub 2
Tel *(3822) 51 01 51*
W toyan.ru
Stunning hotel with cutting-edge design features that include stone- and marble-clad room interiors.

Ulan-Ude: Traveller's House
Трэвелерс Хаус ®
Hostel
Ulitsa Lenina 63, apt 18
Tel *950 391 6325 (mobile)*
W uuhostel.com
Popular hostel in a converted central apartment with views of the city's famed statue of Lenin's head.

Ulan Ude: Buryatiya Бурятия ®®
Business
Ulitsa Kommunisticheskaya 47A
Tel *(3012) 21 48 88*
W buryatiahotel.ru
Soviet-era hotel with great views of the city and beyond. Good value for money.

Vladivostok: Optimum Hostel
Оптимум Хостел ®
Hostel
Ulitsa Aleutskaya 17
Tel *(423) 272 91 11*
Budget-friendly hostel with bright, funky design offering singles, doubles and dorms.

Vladivostok: Sibirskoe Podvorie
Сибирское подворье ®®
Guesthouse
Okeansky prospekt 26
Tel *(4232) 51 81 32*
W otelsp.com
Centrally located hotel with wooden floors and imaginatively designed rooms.

Vladivostok: Hyundai
Хёндэ ®®®
Business
Ulitsa Semenovskaya 29
Tel *(423) 240 22 33*
W hotelhyundai.ru
Sleek hotel with high standards of services and facilities. Features a restaurant serving Korean cuisine.

Neatly arranged beds in a dorm at the Zokol Hostel, Novosibirsk

WHERE TO EAT AND DRINK

Eating out in Russia was a rare privilege during the Soviet era, and a luxury for most people in the years immediately after *perestroika*. However, the country has seen a phenomenal boom in restaurants, cafés and bars since the 1990s. From cheap student cafés to staggeringly expensive eateries, Russia has it all. Restaurants in Moscow, St Petersburg and other major cities offer the world's leading cuisines, including French, Italian, Japanese, Indian, Chinese and Thai. Restaurants serving cuisines of former Soviet Republics such as Georgia, Armenia and Uzbekistan provide a wide selection of vegetarian dishes. In provincial towns, non-Russian cuisine may be limited, but the standards of cooking and level of service has vastly improved since Soviet times.

The bustling outdoor dining area of McDonald's, Moscow

Places to Eat

Restaurants located in the city centre tend to be more expensive than those situated in the outer streets. However, a variety of dining options can be found outside the centre to suit most pockets and tastes.

Upmarket restaurants serve a mix of European and Russian dishes, with some Asian elements. Style and fashion can overshadow the cuisine in some restaurants, but other eateries manage to combine food, decor and service in fine Russian style. Trends include "imperial Russian" in a historic interior, themed (Retro-Soviet style or based on characters in novels or films) and hybrid (Italian, Thai and Japanese under one roof).

In addition to individual restaurants and cafés, there are plenty of international and home-grown fast-food chains to choose from. Sit-down cafés serve traditional Russian dishes while street kiosks sell *blinis* (pancakes) to take away.

Department stores, theatres and major museums offer a stand-up buffet serving open sandwiches with salami, pickled herring, caviar or other nibbles.

Reading the Menu

Restaurants specializing in international cuisine usually have menus in Russian and English; the menu might be separately available in English. But in local eateries, knowledge of the Cyrillic alphabet will help to decipher the menu, as many ingredients are phonetic versions of their English equivalents. Most restaurants geared towards non-Russians usually have an English-speaking staff.

Dickens Bar, a typical English pub in St Petersburg

Types of Cuisine

Much of the best Russian food is either wholesome dishes and soups from recipes passed down over generations, or cured and salted fish as well as caviar, for which preparation is more important at its source, as opposed to in restaurants.

Georgian or Armenian cooking, both of which are delicious and relatively inexpensive, are a better option. Mediterranean and other Western European restaurants, especially Italian ones, are very popular in most cities, but Chinese and Indian food is generally a bit bland and of variable quality. However, there are a few excellent Asian restaurants, particularly Japanese, with sushi being the most fashionable dish of the last decade.

What to Drink

Vodka is the alcoholic drink most often associated with Russia, but beer is usually preferred as an accompaniment to meals. Most restaurants now offer imported and local beer on tap, along with a variety of bottled beers; Russian beer is light and generally very good. The better European restaurants have commendable wine lists, although good imported wine tends to be quite expensive. Be sure to sample a bottle of Georgian wine *(see p279)*, which is the perfect accompaniment to Georgian food. However, it can at times overpower the subtler flavours of European cuisine.

Payment and Tipping

Prices vary widely – while a meal in a cheap *stolovaya* (local cafeteria) might cost 120 roubles, it could cost well over 2,500 roubles in classy restaurants.

Many restaurants in Russia, especially those outside of the big cities, accept payment only in cash. This is gradually changing, but it is still a consideration when deciding where to eat. It is advisable to call ahead and check which cards (if any) are accepted and whether there is a surcharge.

Tipping is not as ingrained in Russia as elsewhere. Service is rarely included in the bill. It is appropriate to tip between 10 to 15 per cent if satisfied with the quality of service. However, it is unnecessary to leave more than a few hundred roubles regardless of the amount spent in a restaurant.

Opening Times

In major cities, most restaurants are open from noon–11pm. Many eateries in big cities have adopted the concept of the business lunch. These often take the form of a fixed-price menu and can be excellent value. They are usually served from noon to 4pm. Most restaurants start serving dinner at around 6pm and stop taking orders at 10:30pm; some family-run Georgian establishments close their kitchens as early as 9pm. Increasingly though, restaurants are staying open until the early hours of the morning and some are even open around the clock.

Making a Reservation

Most international and tourist-oriented restaurants accept reservations and some of the more popular ones require them. It is best to book ahead whenever possible. However, some of the well-known Georgian and Caucasian restaurants do not take reservations and these can be busy, particularly at weekends.

Dress Code

Casual or semi-formal dress is acceptable in the majority of restaurants, but formal dress is *de rigueur* at fashionable upmarket restaurants. Trainers and tracksuits are acceptable in the less expensive cafés.

Sign for a Japanese restaurant

Children

On the whole, Russians love children, and will rarely refuse them entry to restaurants. Family-friendly restaurants are growing in number and most Western or Russian fast-food chains provide children's menus.

Vegetarians

Much of Russian cuisine consists of meat dishes. Salads generally contain meat, so the best option for vegetarians is often a beetroot or tomato platter. Georgian cuisine, featuring a number of excellent bean and aubergine dishes, is usually a better choice. Restaurants are increasingly taking into account the demands of vegetarian visitors. European, Chinese and Japanese restaurants usually have some dishes suitable for vegetarians. For those who eat fish, however, there is always plenty of choice.

Disabled Access

Besides expensive eateries and bars, few restaurants in Russia have facilities for disabled visitors, although waiters and doormen can at times be very helpful. It is best to check beforehand if there is full disabled access.

Recommended Restaurants

The restaurants in this guide have been selected across a wide price range for their value, good food, ambience and location. Diners can look forward to a variety of cuisines, ranging from international to that of ex-Soviet republics and even home cooking. Fusion cuisine blends elements of European and Asian cooking, while Oriental usually offers Caucasian and Central Asian fare, rather than Indian, Chinese or Japanese cuisine. Note that the establishments labelled "DK Choice" have been highlighted in recognition of an exceptional feature – a celebrity chef, exquisite food or inviting atmosphere.

Diners at a formal Retro-Soviet-style restaurant in Moscow

The Flavours of Russia

The Tsarist and Soviet empires stretched from Poland in the west to the Pacific Ocean in the east, leaving behind a legacy of multi-cultural cuisines. Aubergine and tomatoes, from the Caucasus in the south, bring in the flavours of the Mediterranean, while spices from Central Asia lend an exotic touch. The stalls in farmers' markets sell caviar and crayfish alongside honey from Siberia and melons and peaches from Georgia. Yet, Russia's culinary reputation centres on warming stews full of wintry vegetables such as cabbage, beetroot and potatoes.

Wild mushrooms

Black caviar, or sturgeon roe, on lightly toasted slices of bread

Russian Countryside

Many Russians have *dachas* (country cottages) within easy reach of the city, where they spend weekends from spring to early winter tending their immaculate vegetable gardens, or combing the countryside for wild berries and mushrooms. Much of this bountiful harvest is made into preserves and pickles. Restaurant menus regularly feature pickled mushrooms in sour cream along with a variety of fresh berry juices. Pickled cucumbers impart a delicious salty taste to a refreshing soup known as *solyanka*.

Very little is wasted in a country where food shortages remain a fairly recent memory. *Kvas*, a popular, mildly alcoholic drink is frequently made in homes by fermenting stale black or rye bread with sugar and a scattering of fruit. Summer visitors should make a point of trying the delicious cold soup *okroshka*, which is based on *kvas*.

Russia is also a land with hundreds of rivers and lakes, and has a long tradition of fish-based dishes. These range from

A range of cold appetizers, commonly known as *zakuski*

Russian Dishes and Specialities

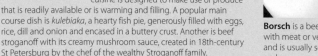

Beetroot

Borsch (beetroot soup) and *blinis* (buttery pancakes) served with caviar are perhaps two of the most famous Russian dishes. The former is a peasant dish, which varies with the availability of ingredients, while the latter is a staple for the week leading up to Lent, when rich food is eaten to fatten up for the forty days of fasting prior to Easter. Much of Russia's cuisine is designed to make use of produce that is readily available or is warming and filling. A popular main course dish is *kulebiaka*, a hearty fish pie, generously filled with eggs, rice, dill and onion and encased in a buttery crust. Another is beef stroganoff with its creamy mushroom sauce, created in 18th-century St Petersburg by the chef of the wealthy Stroganoff family.

Borsch is a beetroot soup made with meat or vegetable stock and is usually served with dill and sour cream.

A wealth of fresh vegetables and herbs at a market, Moscow

simple soups, such as *ukha*, to caviar and sturgeon and salmon cooked in a bewildering variety of ways.

The Caucasus

The former Soviet states of the Caucasus – Georgia, Azerbaijan and Armenia – are renowned for their legendary banquets, where tables are laden with an enormous quantity and variety of food and drink. They still supply Russia's cities with a tempting array of fine sub-tropical produce. Limes, figs, lemons, oranges, walnuts, pomegranates, peaches, beans, salty cheeses and herbs are all shipped in season to city markets and Georgian restaurants. The cuisine of Georgia, with its focus on freshly grilled meats, pulses, vegetables, yogurt, herbs and nut sauces, including *satsivi* (the hallmark walnut sauce), is famously healthy, and Georgians are known for their longevity.

Central Asia

The Central Asian republics of the former Soviet Union contributed a range of culinary traditions to Russian cuisine, which were based on the nomadic lifestyles of Russia's one-time overlords – the Mongol or Tartar Hordes. The meat of fat-tailed sheep, which thrive in the dry desert air, is used to make communal piles of *plov* (pilaf) around which guests sit, eating in the traditional manner with their hands.

Plov, a typical Uzbek dish prepared with rice, vegetables and lamb

In addition to *plov*, the menus in Uzbek restaurants also offer delicious flat breads, spicy noodle soups, *manti* (tasty dumplings reminiscent of Chinese cuisine) and a variety of melons and grapes, which proliferate in the desert oases, as well as apricots and nuts, grown in the mountains.

ZAKUSKI

A traditional Russian meal generally begins with *zakuski*, which is a selection of cold appetizers. These may include *griby* (pickled mushrooms), *ogurtsy* (gherkins), *seliodka* (salted herrings), an assortment of smoked fish, *blinis* topped with caviar, various vegetable pâtés (sometimes known as vegetable caviars), *yaitsa farshirovanniye* (stuffed eggs), *brinza* (spiced feta cheese), *salat iz svyokly* (beetroot salad) and *pirozhki* (small meat pies) accompanied by rye bread and washed down with shots of vodka. A bowl of steaming soup often follows, before the main course reaches the table.

Kulebiaka, a rich, buttery puff pastry, is wrapped around a mixture of fish, hard-boiled eggs, rice, onion and chopped dill.

Pelmeni are meat-stuffed dumplings that are served in a clear broth, or with tomato sauce or sour cream.

Kissel, a soft fruit-based jelly, is made from a mixture of red berries and presented with a swirl of fresh cream on top.

What to Drink

Russian vodka is famous throughout the world and distilled in many cities across the country. Vodka first appeared in Russia sometime in the 14th or 15th century. Peter the Great was particularly fond of anise or pepper-flavoured vodkas and devised modifications to the distillation process that improved the quality of the finished product. Tea is Russia's other national drink. Traditionally made using a samovar and served black, tea has been popular in Russia since the end of the 18th century when it was first imported from China.

Merchants from Nizhny Novgorod drinking tea at a pub

Stolichnaya   Russian Standard   Stolichnaya Cristall

Clear Vodka

Gzhelka vodka

Vodka is produced from grain, usually wheat, although some rye is also used. The 80° proof (40° ABV) standard was set by Tsar Alexander III, based on a formula by the famous scientist Dmitri Mendeleev. Russia's principal distilleries are St Petersburg's Liviz, whose best brands are Diplomat, Five Star and Russian Standard; Moscow's Cristall with brands such as Cristall, Gzhelka and Stolichnaya; and Flagman, official purveyor of vodka to the Kremlin. The range of vodkas available these days is overwhelming, but illegal bootlegging is still a problem. There is one golden rule: if it is under US$10 for half a litre, do not drink it.

Vodka is always served with food, most often with *zakuski* *(see p276)*. It is not always served ice cold, but it should be chilled.

Flavoured Vodka

The practice of adding various flavours to vodka has entirely practical origins. When vodka was first produced commercially in the Middle Ages, the techniques and equipment were so primitive that it was impossible to remove all the impurities. This left unpleasant aromas and flavours, which were disguised by adding honey together with aromatic oils and spices. Over time distillation techniques improved and flavoured vodkas became a speciality in their own right. *Limonnaya*, which derives its taste from lemon zest, is one of the most traditional vodkas, as is *Pertsovka*, flavoured with red chilli pepper pods. *Okhotnichya* (hunter's vodka) has a wider range of flavourings including juniper, ginger and cloves. *Starka* (old vodka) is distilled from rye with an infusion of apple and pear leaves, aged in oak barrels. Some of the best flavoured vodkas are made at home by soaking peach stones or whole berries in alcohol for months.

Pertsovka

Limonnaya   Okhotnichya   Starka

Wine

The Soviet Union was one of the world's largest producers of *vino* (wine), but many of the major wine regions are now republics in their own right. Several indigenous types of grape are cultivated in the different regions, along with many of the more familiar international varieties.

Georgia and Crimea (in southeastern Ukraine) have traditionally produced the best wines, although Georgian wines may be difficult to find in Russia due to frosty relations between the two countries. Wines such as Gurdzhaani are made from the Rkatsiteli grape, which imparts a unique, slightly bitter taste, and the Mtsvane grape that adds a subtle, fruity flavour and floral aroma. Among Georgia's best red wines is the smooth Mukuzani. Moldova produces white, sparkling wines and a sweet, champagne-like wine called "Soviet Sparkling", widely known as *shampanskoe*.

Georgian wines *Shampanskoe*

Other Alcoholic Drinks

Konyak (brandy) was originally a by-product of winemaking, and commercial production only began in Russia in the 19th century. Armenian brandy is one of the finest with a distinctive vanilla fragrance, a result of its ageing in 70–100-year-old oak barrels. Georgia and Dagestan also produce good brandies. Baltika, Vena and Stepan Razin make a full range of beers in bottles and on draught. In addition, Iver beers such as Afanasy are well worth trying. Various imported beers are also available.

Baltika beer

Armenian brandy

Mineral water

Kvas

Mors

Other Drinks

Made from barley and rye, *kvas* is a sweet, mildly alcoholic drink consumed by adults and children alike. Less commonly found but also traditional are *myod* (honey mead) and *sbiten*, a version flavoured with herbs. Russia's vast range of *mineralnaya voda* (mineral water) includes many with unusually high mineral contents. Those from the Caucasus, Siberia and Georgia are especially prized. Also available are *sok* (fruit juices), and *kompot* (sweetened drinks made by boiling fruit with sugar and water). The cranberry version is called *mors*.

Tea

Russian tea is served black with a slice of lemon and may be drunk from tall glasses or cups. Sweetened with *varenye* (jam) instead of sugar, *chay* (tea) is an ideal accompaniment to rich cakes and pastries. The boiling water for tea traditionally comes from a samovar. The water is used to brew a pot of tea, from which a little is poured into a cup then it is diluted with more hot water.

Tall glass of tea with jam

The Samovar

Made from brass or copper and heated by coals in the central chimney, samovars traditionally provided boiling water for a wide variety of domestic purposes and were an essential wedding gift. Modern electric ones are made of stainless steel and are used mainly for boiling water to make tea. The word samovar comes from *samo* meaning "itself" and *varit* meaning "to boil".

Where to Eat and Drink

Moscow

Red Square and Kitay Gorod

Jagannath Джаганнат ®
Vegetarian **Map** 2 D4
Ulitsa Kuznetskiy Most 11
Tel *(495) 628 35 80*
Stylish café serving tasty Indian, Mexican, Thai, Chinese and European vegetarian dishes. No alcohol is served but the ginger beer is divine.

Maharaja Махараджа ®
Indian **Map** 2 F5
Ulitsa Pokrovka 2/1
Tel *(495) 621 98 44*
Go for delicious Indian food at Maharaja, which offers a modern interior and a relaxed atmosphere.

Dissident Диссидент ®®
Mediterranean **Map** 2 D5
Nikolskaya ulitsa 25
Tel *(495) 500 27 67*
The focus is on French specialities at this restaurant-wine bar. Good selection of Italian and French pâtés. Excellent wine list.

DK Choice

Khodzha Nasreddin v Khive
Ходжа Насреддин в Хиве ®®
Uzbek **Map** 2 F5
Ulitsa Pokrovka 10
Tel *(495) 917 04 44*
One of several restaurants in Moscow named after Hodja Nasreddin, the popular hero of Central Asian folklore. Get the taste of delectable Uzbek cuisine amidst stunning decor evoking the ancient Uzbek city of Khiva. Clowns keep children entertained on weekend afternoons.

Tastefully decorated interior of Maharaja, Moscow

Noev Kovcheg Ноев Ковчег ®®
Armenian **Map** 4 F1
Malyy Ivanovskiy pereulok 9
Tel *(495) 917 07 17*
Savour Armenian delights at "Noah's Ark". Their bean stew and grilled cheese appetizers are excellent, as is the acclaimed Armenian cognac.

Nostalgie Ностальжи ®®®
French/fusion **Map** 2 F5
Chistoprudnyy bulvar 12a
Tel *(495) 258 56 68*
French haute cuisine with a Japanese touch and a wine cellar boasting 5,000 bottles should be reason enough to try this place. Reservation recommended.

Garden Ring

Book Café Бук Кафе ®
International **Map** 1 C4
Glinishchevskiy pereulok 3
Tel *(495) 692 97 31*
An eclectic menu of quality French, Italian and Russian dishes served in a tasteful, minimalist setting. Booking recommended at weekends.

Bublik Бублик ®
International **Map** 1 B4
Tverskoy bulvar 24
Tel *(495) 629 13 42*
Located on one of the city's most historic boulevards, this deli-style restaurant features an extensive sandwich and brunch menu.

Montalto Монтальто ®
Pizzeria **Map** 1 A4
Ulitsa Sadovaya-Kudrinskaya 20
Tel *(495) 234 34 87*
Thick-crust pizzas cooked in a wood-fired oven. Toppings come with an original twist – try the pear, goat's cheese, fennel and pistachio or spicy sausage.

Price Guide
Prices are based on a three-course meal per person, with an alcoholic beverage, including tax but not service.

®	under ®1,000
®®	®1,000 to 2,000
®®®®®	over ®2,000

5-Spice Пять Специй ®®
Chinese **Map** 3 B2
Pereulok Sivtsev Vrazhek 3/18
Tel *(495) 697 12 83*
Chinese restaurant specializing in Cantonese food and dishes from the northern provinces. Pleasant interiors and good service.

Akademiya Академия ®®
Italian **Map** 1 C5
Kamergerskiy pereulok 2
Tel *(495) 692 96 49*
Dark-panelled pizzeria that is a great place for delectable Italian food and people-watching.

Baba Marta Баба Марта ®®
Bulgarian **Map** 3 B2
Gogolevskiy bulvar 8
Tel *(495) 232 92 09*
A family-run restaurant serving diverse meat and vegetable dishes, including mouthwatering *banitsa* (pies with spinach, meat, cheese, pumpkin and walnuts).

Champagne Café
шампанское кафе ®®
European **Map** 1 C5
Bolshaya Nikitskaya ulitsa 12
Tel *(495) 629 59 13*
Set in Venetian-style halls, this eatery serves dishes such as *foie gras* with berry sauce and beef stroganoff.

Clumba Club Клумба Клаб ®®
International **Map** 1 A5
Novinskiy bulvar 31
Tel *(495) 644 96 69*
Clumba Club is home to Europe's largest oyster bar. The menu is international with an emphasis on seafood. Extensive wine list.

DoDo ДоДо ®®
International **Map** 1 C4
Ulitsa Petrovka 21/2
Tel *(903) 105 10 10*
Enjoy European dishes with a dash of the exotic in this laid-back restaurant with outdoor seating.

Khachapuri Хачапури ®®
Georgian
Bolshoi Gnezdnikovskiy pereulok 10
Tel *(495) 629 66 56*
This inexpensive restaurant serves eight types of *khachapuri* (bread stuffed with cheese), and wonderful *khinkali* (dumplings).

Mayak Маяк ®®
Russian/European **Map** 1 B5
Bolshaya Nikitskaya ulitsa 19
Tel *(495) 691 74 49*
Popular meeting place for actors and artists, with a wonderfully bohemian atmosphere. Good selection of wines. Do not miss the roast beef salad.

Noor Нур ®®
International **Map** 1 C5
Tverskaya ulitsa 23
Tel *(903) 136 76 86*
More of a cocktail bar than a restaurant, Noor serves classic cocktails accompanied by dishes such as shrimps in filo pastry.

Sisters Grimm Сёстры Гримм ®®
International **Map** 1 C4
Stoleshnikov pereulok 11
Tel *(495) 628 89 75*
Decorated like a country cottage, this restaurant offers a range of international dishes, including Dagestani lamb burgers.

Vostochnaya komnata
Восточная комната ®®
Indian/Georgian **Map** 3 A2
Smolenskaya ploshchad 3
Tel *(495) 937 84 23*
Located above a French café, the "Eastern Room" is popular for its tasty curries and *dal* as well as lots of vegetarian options.

Ararat Арарат ®®®
Armenian **Map** 2 D5
Neglinnaya ulitsa 4
Tel *(495) 783 12 34 (ext 5208)*
Relish Armenian specialities based on authentic recipes, plus a wide selection of vintage Armenian brandies and wines at the Ararat.

Barashka Баращка ®®®
Azerbaijani **Map** 3 B1
Ulitsa Novyy Arbat 21
Tel *(495) 228 37 31*
An understated restaurant with minimalist decor serving Azeri dishes such as lamb *dolma* in grape leaves and sturgeon *shashlik*.

Café Mart Кафе Март ®®®
International **Map** 1 C4
Ulitsa Petrovka 25
Tel *(495) 231 3661*
Café Mart offers a selection of light, international dishes, as well as tempting Georgian specialities.

Central House of Writers
Центральный Дом Литераторов ®®®
Russian **Map** 1 A5
Ulitsa Bolshaya Nikitskaya 53
Tel *(495) 691 15 15*
This eatery features carved-oak wood decor, fireplaces, live music and tasty traditional dishes. Uniquely atmospheric, especially for devotees of Russian literature.

Neatly arranged tables in Noor, a popular restaurant in Moscow

Cutty Sark
Катти Сарк ®®®
Seafood **Map** 1 A5
Novinskiy bulvar 12
Tel *(495) 691 33 50*
Designed to resemble the British clipper ship, Cutty Sark serves fresh seafood from all over the world, and has separate oyster and sushi bars.

DK Choice

Godunov Годунов ®®®
Russian **Map** 1 C5
Teatralnaya ploshchad 5
Tel *(495) 698 44 80*
Named after Tsar Boris Godunov and housed in a former monastic outbuilding, this restaurant serves excellent *borsch* and other rich soups, delicious game, *pirozhki* and a good choice of vegetarian main dishes. There is traditional Russian entertainment in the evenings.

Classy decor at Barashka, an Azerbaijani eatery in Moscow

Mari Vanna Мари Ванна ®®®
Russian **Map** 1 B4
Spiridonevskiy pereulok 10
Tel *(495) 650 65 00*
Designed to replicate a 1930s Soviet flat, this restaurant offers delicious home cooking. Limited vegetarian options.

Moskovskiy Московский ®®®
Russian/European **Map** 1 C5
Mokhovaya ulitsa 15
Tel *(495) 258 70 68*
Besides offering stunning views of the Kremlin, Moskovskiy serves a mix of Russian aristocratic, French and Mediterranean fare.

Polo Club Поло Клуб ®®®
Steakhouse/seafood **Map** 2 D4
Ulitsa Petrovka 11
Tel *(495) 937 10 00*
This renowned steakhouse also offers a good seafood menu and a large selection of sinful desserts. Superb wine list.

Pushkin Пушкин ®®®
Russian/French **Map** 1 B4
Tverskoy bulvar 26a
Tel *(495) 739 00 33*
An aristocratic café with elegant decor, Pushkin offers an extensive menu and a rooftop terrace for dining in the summer.

Scandinavia
Скандинавия ®®®
European **Map** 1 B4
Malyy Palashevskiy pereulok 7
Tel *(495) 937 56 30*
A Swedish-run restaurant with quality European cuisine. Excellent steaks and desserts. Dine under chestnut trees in a pretty courtyard in fine weather.

Shekhtel Шехтель ®®®
International/Russian **Map** 1 C5
Tverskoy bulvar 18, Bldg 1
Tel *(495) 629 11 50*
An exciting mix of international and reinvented Russian dishes. Live jazz music in the evenings.

Zamoskvoreche

DK Choice

Suliko Сулико ®®
Georgian **Map** 4 D4
Ulitsa Bolshaya Polyanka 42/1
Tel *(499) 238 28 88*
With its mini-fountains, figurines and fake plants, and evening entertainment from a choir, Suliko is a fun place to enjoy high-quality Georgian cuisine. There are no Georgian wines on the menu, but you can try Georgian *chacha* (grape vodka).

Discovery Дискавери ®®®
Mediterranean **Map** 4 E4
Novokuznetskaya ulitsa 24/2
Tel *(495) 953 38 63*
Located in an old merchant's townhouse, Discovery offers a relaxed atmosphere. The second floor was designed to resemble a luxury yacht.

Dorian Gray Дориан Грей ®®®
Italian **Map** 4 D2
Kadashevskaya naberezhnaya 6/1
Tel *(499) 238 64 01*
A riverside restaurant with splendid views of the Kremlin, chic Italian decor and a traditional menu.

Oblomov Обломов ®®®
French/Russian **Map** 4 E4
1-y Monetchikovskiy pereulok 5
Tel *(495) 953 68 28*
While the café on the first floor serves home-roasted coffee, the Eastern Room on the third floor has *hookah* and live belly dancing.

Further Afield

Addis Abeba Аддис Абеба ®
Ethiopian
Ulitsa Zemlyanoy Val 6
Tel *(495) 916 24 32*
Authentic Ethiopian fare, including vegetarian dishes and spicy dishes, most of which are eaten from "plates" of *injera* (sourdough bread).

Avocado Авокадо ®
Vegetarian **Map** 2 F4
Christoprudnyy bulvar 12, Bldg 2
Tel *(495) 621 77 19*
This eatery is famed for its vegetarian versions of world cuisine, from *pelmeni* to pasta to curries.

U Giuseppe У Джузеппе ®
Italian **Map** 2 D2
Samotechnaya ulitsa 13
Tel *(495) 681 13 26*
A welcoming *osteria* (Italian wine and food joint) serving good home-made pasta. Caters to kids with board games and toys.

Art Clumba Арт Клумба ®®
International/fusion
Nizhnyaya Syromyatnicheskaya 5/7, Bldg 10
Tel *(499) 678 02 25*
The menu at Art Clumba featues Uzbek dishes such as *plov* and *lagman* (lamb and noodle soup).

Bar Strelka Бар Стрелка ®®
International **Map** 3 C2
Bersenevskaya naberezhnaya 14, Bldg 5
Tel *(495) 771 74 16*
Enjoy a bistro-style international menu, featuring dishes from New Zealand, Asia, Europe and Russia.

Black Market Блэк Маркет ®®
American/fusion
Ulitsa Usacheva 2, Bldg 1
Tel *(495) 989 04 45*
Savour modern American fusion cuisine at this restaurant where the decor evokes a black market warehouse. Great pancakes.

Corner Burger Корнер Бургер ®®
American
Bolshaya Gruzinskaya ulitsa 76
Tel *(499) 926 83 98*
Dig in to burgers made from beef, turkey, chicken or pork. Or try the vegetarian soups and salads.

Delicatessen Деликатессен ®®
International **Map** 1 C3
Sadovaya-Karetnaya ulitsa 20, Bldg 2
Tel *(495) 699 39 52* **Closed** *Sun, Mon*
Family-run restaurant offering delicious home cooking and a good selection of wines and cocktails.

Italianets Итальянец ®®
Italian **Map** 2 D2
Samotechnaya ulitsa 13
Tel *(495) 688 56 51*
Try a range of macrobiotic Italian dishes, prepared using fresh produce flown in from Italy.

Osteria Numero Uno Остерия Нумеро Уно ®®
Italian **Map** 2 D4
Tsvetnoy bulvar 2
Tel *(495) 507 73 74*
Reminiscent of a seaside eatery, the interiors of this place are in marine blue and white. Seasonal menu and a varied wine list.

Ragout Рагу ®®
European
Bolshaya Gruzinskaya ulitsa 69
Tel *(495) 728 64 58*
Spacious interiors and a menu that leans towards British and French dishes, including shepherd's pie and Sunday roast.

Skazka Vostoka Сказка Востока ®®
Middle Eastern **Map** 3 A5
Frunzenskaya naberezhnaya 22D
Tel *(499) 242 85 10*
Spicy Georgian and Azeri food served aboard a floating restaurant on the Moskva river.

High-ceiling dining area with beige furnishings at Art Clumba, Moscow

Key to Price Guide *see p280*

Tapa de Comida
Тапа Де Комида ®®
Spanish **Map** 2 D3
Trubnaya ulitsa 20/2, Bldg 3
Tel *(495) 608 20 07*
Spanish decor throughout this eatery, with Moorish tiles and rustic furniture. The menu includes a decent selection of tapas.

U Pirosmani У пиросмани ®®
Georgian
Novodevichiy proezd 4
Tel *(499) 255 79 26*
Come here for delicious vegetable starters and meat dishes such as *chanahi* (lamb with aubergine, tomatoes, potatoes and spices).

Yapona Mama Япона Мама ®®
Japanese **Map** 3 A3
Smolenskiy bulvar 4
Tel *(499) 246 99 67*
"Japanese Mother" offers good service in a stylish environment, and some of the finest sushi in Moscow. Business lunch recommended.

Carre Blanc Карре Блан ®®®
French **Map** 1 C2
Seleznevskaya ulitsa 19/2
Tel *(495) 258 44 03*
An ever-evolving menu and a beautiful summer courtyard, makes this arguably the best French restaurant in Moscow. Excellent seafood. Great service.

DK Choice

Chestnaya Kuhnya
Честная Кухня ®®®
European/Russian
Ulitsa Sadovaya-Chernogryazskaya 10
Tel *(495) 607 50 90*
A cosy restaurant in the heart of the city, Chestnaya Kuhnya offers superb home cooking. The wide-ranging menu includes meats cooked on open fire, fresh salads, home-made pasta and delicious desserts. Extensive wine list. Good service.

China Garden
Китайский Сад ®®®
Chinese
Krasnopresnenskaya naberezhnaya 12
Tel *(495) 967 05 86*
Relish tasty Szechwan, Peking and Cantonese dishes at China Garden. Most staff can speak English.

Ermak Ермак ®®®
Russian
Ulitsa Nizhniye Mnevniki 41
Tel *(499) 191 25 23*
Built in the style of a Cossack log cabin, Ermak offers delicacies such as Siberian river fish.

Well-stocked bar at Chestnaya Kuhnya, Moscow

Genatsvale VIP
Генацвале VIP ®®®
Georgian **Map** 3 B2
Ulitsa Ostozhenka 14/2
Tel *(495) 695 03 93*
Enjoy delicious *khachapuri*, *lobio* (beans with walnuts and spices), and vintage Georgian wines.

Isola Pinocchio
Изола Пиноккио ®®®
Mediterranean
Naberezhnaya Tarasa Schevchenko 23a
Tel *(495) 730 44 00*
Enjoy river views through stained-glass windows while savouring Mediterranean cuisine and Spanish wines at Isola Pinocchio.

Kavkazskaya Plenitsa
Кавказская пленница ®®®
Georgian **Map** 2 E2
Prospekt Mira 36
Tel *(495) 680 51 11*
This restaurant offers Georgian favourites and a summer terrace facing a lovely garden.

Market Маркет ®®®
Asian/seafood **Map** 2 D3
Ulitsa Sadovaya-Samotechnaya 18
Tel *(495) 650 37 70*
Dine on the special oyster that the restaurant prepares for certain national holidays.

Traditional Chinese lion statue at the entrance to China Garden, Moscow

There is a heated veranda for outdoor eating. Efficient and friendly service.

Shinok Шинок ®®®
Ukrainian
Ulitsa 1905 Goda 2a
Tel *(495) 651 81 01*
A rustically themed restaurant, Shinok serves the best Ukrainian food in Moscow. Efficient service.

Simple Pleasures
Симпл Плэжерс ®®®
International **Map** 2 E3
Ulitsa Sretenka 22/1
Tel *(495) 607 15 21*
Sample an eclectic menu, from Mediterranean to South American, in a chic minimalist setting. Extensive wine list. Live music on Thursday evenings.

Sky Lounge Скай Лаунж ®®®
Asian/European
Leninskiy prospekt 32a
Tel *(495) 781 57 75*
Situated on the top floor of a 22-storey building, Sky Lounge offers spectacular views and a wide range of Asian and European cooking. Lounge music by DJs at weekends.

Tinatin Тинатин ®®®
Georgian
Ulitsa Plyushchikha 58, Bldg 1A
Tel *(985) 761 66 36*
This elegant restaurant offers fine Georgian cuisine and an extensive selection of Russian and European wines. There are secluded balconies for private dining.

Vanil Ваниль ®®®
Fusion **Map** 3 B2
Ulitsa Ostozhenka 1
Tel *(495) 637 10 82*
Inventive blending of French and Japanese cuisine, fine wines and elegant interiors. There is also a summer veranda with fine views.

For more information on types of restaurants *see p275*

Provincial cottage-style decor at Gosti, St Petersburg

St Petersburg

The Islands

Casa del Мясо ®
Steakhouse **Map** 1 B5
Birzhevoy proezd 6
Tel *(812) 320 97 46*
A short walk west of the Rostral Columns and the Kunstkammer, this cellar restaurant is squarely aimed at carnivores, with a wide variety of meat dishes on the menu.

Demyanova Ukha
Демьянова уха ®
Russian/seafood **Map** 1 C3
Kronverkskiy prospekt 53
Tel *(812) 232 80 90*
"Demyanova's Fish Soup", the city's oldest specialist fish restaurant, serves traditional Russian dishes. Enjoy live music in the evenings.

Imperator Император ®
International **Map** 1 B5
Tamozhennyy pereulok 2
Tel *(812) 323 30 31*
Imperator serves the usual mix of European and Caucasian cuisine, with the addition of spicy Mexican dishes.

Yakitoriya Якитория ®
Japanese **Map** 2 E2
Petrovskaya naberezhnaya 4
Tel *(812) 970 48 58*
One of the best sushi restaurants in St Petersburg, Yakitoriya serves high-quality sushi and sashimi. The Peter and Paul Fortress is located nearby.

Okean Океан ®®
Seafood **Map** 1 B4
Prospekt Dobrolyubova 14a
Tel *(812) 986 86 00*
With floor-to-ceiling windows overlooking the Neva, this light-filled barge offers cocktails and modern interpretations of traditional seafood dishes.

DK Choice

Salkhino Салхино ®®
Georgian **Map** 1 D2
Kronverkskiy prospekt 25
Tel *(812) 232 78 91*
Generous home cooking is offered at this eatery run by two Georgian women. The *khachapuri* is the best in town. Gorge on aubergines stuffed with walnuts, bite into roast beef or try the delicious fish in white sauce. The restaurant features paintings by Georgian artists.

Tbiliso Тбилисо ®®
Georgian **Map** 1 C2
Sytninskaya ulitsa 10
Tel *(812) 232 93 91*
The authentic menu at Tbiliso includes dishes such as *mamalyga* (ground corn with salted cheese) and *khachapuri*.

Volna Волна ®®
Fusion **Map** 2 E3
Petrovskaya naberezhnaya 4
Tel *(812) 322 53 83*
One of the cheaper fusion restaurants in town, the Volna has Japanese minimalist interiors. Try the Italian lettuce with salmon tempura, or grilled white salmon with mint and prawn sauce.

Zver Зверь ®®
Steakhouse **Map** 2 D3
Aleksandrovskiy park 5b
Tel *(812) 232 20 62*
Every hunter's catch, from wild boar to hare, is available at this rustic steakhouse. Wooden tables, and hearty portions.

Austeria Аустерия ®®®
Russian **Map** 2 D4
Peter and Paul Fortress
Tel *(812) 716 13 73*
Impressive Dutch-style decor, and a menu of 17th-century Russian dishes. Choose from a wide range of flavoured vodkas.

Flying Dutchman
Летучий Голландец ®®®
International **Map** 1 C4
Mytninskaya naberezhnaya, Birzhevoy most
Tel *(812) 336 37 37*
Savour European and Latin American dishes and also try the sushi and salad bars.

New Island Нью Айленд ®®®
International **Map** 3 B1
Universitetskaya naberezhnaya 15
Tel *(812) 320 21 00*
Much loved by the elite, this floating restaurant has played host to Bush and Putin. It sails four times daily from April to October.

Old Customs House
Старая таможня ®®®
International **Map** 1 B5
Tamozhennyy pereulok 1
Tel *(812) 327 89 80*
This eatery serves mainly French meat or seafood dishes, accompanied by French wines.

Palace Embankment

Baltika Brew Балтика Брю ®
International **Map** 4 D1
Bolshaya Morskaya ulitsa 3/5
Tel *(812) 921 09 12*
This restaurant and brewery serves a selection of international dishes to accompany nearly a dozen home-made beers.

Da Albertone ®
Italian **Map** 2 D5
Millionnaya ulitsa 23
Tel *(812) 315 86 73*
Ideal for those with children, Da Albertone offers a kids' menu, a playroom and 40 types of pizza and various pasta dishes.

Gastronom Гастроном ®
Italian/Japanese **Map** 2 E5
Naberezhnaya Reki Moyki 1/7
Tel *(812) 314 38 49*
Try the horseradish and mustard at Gastronom, which is equally popular with locals and tourists.

Gosti Гости ®
Italian/Serbian **Map** 3 C1
Malaya Morskaya ulitsa 13
Tel *(812) 312 58 20*
Casual and cosy, Gosti serves Italian classics alongside Serbian specialities, including pies with sweet and savoury fillings.

Krokodil Крокодил ®
International **Map** 3 B1
Galernaya ulitsa 18
Tel *(812) 314 94 37*
A small and intimate restaurant featuring fresh salads, great vegetarian dishes, a non-smoking room and board games for diners.

Key to Price Guide *see p280*

Park Giuseppe Парк Джузеппе ®
Italian **Map** 4 E1
Naberezhnaya kanala Griboedova 2b
Tel *(812) 571 73 09*
Park Giuseppe is the place for eating Neapolitan pizzas baked in a wood-burning stove and sipping Italian wine as the sun sets.

DK Choice

1913 ®®
Russian **Map** 3 C3
Voznesenskiy prospekt 13
Tel *(812) 315 51 48*
Named after the last year of Russian imperial greatness, 1913 serves delicious regional dishes such as *draniki* (potato pancakes) with bacon and sorrel soup. Warm atmosphere and excellent service. Artists perform Russian songs in the evenings.

Borsalino Борсалино ®®
Italian **Map** 3 C2
Malaya Morskaya ulitsa 24
Tel *(812) 494 51 15*
Situated within the Angleterre Hotel, Borsalino's fabulous decor and excellent Italian food attracts locals as well as tourists. Live jazz in the bar on most evenings.

Canvas Канвас ®®
European **Map** 3 B2
Pochtamtskaya ulitsa 4
Tel *(812) 380 40 00*
This elaborate breakfast room in the Renaissance Hotel turns into a restaurant later in the day serving fine European cuisine.

T-Lounge ®®
International **Map** 3 B2
Pochtamtskaya ulitsa 4
Tel *(812) 380 40 00*
The T-Lounge within Renaissance Hotel offers delicious sandwiches, salads and pastries. Live music in the evenings.

Gostinyy Dvor

Aragvi Арагви ®
Georgian **Map** 2 F5
Naberezhnaya Reki Fontanki 9
Tel *(812) 570 56 43*
Take in enchanting views of the Fontanka river while savouring yummy *satsivi* (walnut sauce), *khachapuri* and pork *shashlik*.

Fasol Фасоль ®
Fusion **Map** 4 D2
Gorokhovaya ulitsa 17
Tel *(812) 571 09 07*
Conveniently located on the corner of the Moyka river, Fasol offers healthy dishes. Service is speedy and the decor modern.

Literary Café Литературное кафе ®
Russian **Map** 4 D1
Nevskiy prospekt 18
Tel *(812) 312 60 57*
The former Wolff and Beranger Café serves rather delicious meat dishes in rich sauces.

Mama Roma Мама Рома ®
Italian **Map** 4 F1
Karavannaya ulitsa 3/35
Tel *(812) 314 03 47*
One of the city's first authentic Italian restaurants, Mama Roma has light, airy interiors. There is a children's menu and toys.

Suliko Сулико ®
Georgian **Map** 4 D2
Kazanskaya ulitsa 6
Tel *(812) 314 73 73*
Tucked away behind the Kazan Cathedral, Suliko is popular with Georgians. Plenty of options for meat lovers.

Erivan Эривань ®®
Armenian **Map** 4 F2
Naberezhnaya Reki Fontanki 51
Tel *(812) 703 38 20*
Furnished in Armenian style, with rugs and brightly coloured tablecloths. Traditional dishes with lots of mutton and veal.

Kalinka-Malinka Калинка-Малинка ®®
Russian **Map** 4 E1
Italyanskaya ulitsa 5
Tel *(812) 314 26 81*
Rustic, wooden-hut interior and classic Russian meals. Folk music on most evenings. Popular with tour groups.

Kavkaz-Bar Кавказ-бар ®®
Caucasian **Map** 4 F1
Karavannaya ulitsa 18
Tel *(812) 312 16 65*
Sink your teeth into the best vegetarian kebabs in town. Excellent wines and brandies on offer.

Ket Кэт ®®
Georgian **Map** 4 F1
Karavannaya ulitsa 24
Tel *(812) 315 38 00*
A comfortable no-frills basement restaurant serving authentic Georgian food. Great place to mingle with the locals.

St Petersburg Санкт-Петербург ®®
Russian **Map** 4 E1
Naberezhnaya kanala Griboedova 5
Tel *(812) 314 49 47*
Generous portions of standard Russian fare are served at this eatery. Live music begins at 8pm.

Baku Баку ®®®
Caucasian/European **Map** 4 F1
Sadovaya ulitsa 12/23
Tel *(812) 941 37 56*
A Central Asian delight, Baku features a menu that is a mix of Continental and Caucasian cuisine.

Barbaresco Барбареско ®®®
Italian **Map** 4 E1
Konyushennaya ploshchad 2
Tel *(812) 647 82 82*
Sample classic Italian dishes at this intimate restaurant accompanied by wine from the north of Italy.

Bellevueh Brasserie Бельвью Брассери ®®®
European **Map** 2 D5
Naberezhnaya Reki Moyki 22
Tel *(812) 335 91 11*
The Bellevueh in the Kempinski Hotel offers superlative city views and great salads. Do not miss the grilled king prawns.

Caviar Bar and Restaurant Икорный Бар ®®®
Russian **Map** 4 E1
Mikhaylovskaya ulitsa 1/7
Tel *(812) 329 60 00*
Dine on elegantly served caviar and fish at this bar-restaurant in Grand Hotel Europe. The interior is tiny, with a fountain, like a grotto in an 18th-century park.

Stylish interior of Barbaresco, St Petersburg

For more information on types of restaurants *see p275*

L'Europe Европа ®®®
European/Russian **Map** 4 E1
Mikhaylovskaya ulitsa 1/7
Tel *(812) 329 60 00*
Lobster soup and steak tartare are served in an Art Nouveau hall with a stained-glass ceiling at this restaurant in Grand Hotel Europe.

DK Choice

Tsar Царь ®®®
Russian **Map** 4 F1
Sadovaya ulitsa 12
Tel *(812) 640 19 00*
Housed within a former noble's palace, Tsar offers diners a sumptuous setting in which to enjoy first-rate Russian classics. Be it the stylish decor or cut crystal glassware, everything exudes opulence. The menu is elaborate and features excellent meat and fish dishes.

Sennaya Ploshchad

Apsheron Апшерон ®
Azerbaijani **Map** 3 C2
Kazanskaya ulitsa 39
Tel *(812) 312 72 53*
Authentic Azeri dishes are served in three warm, colourful dining rooms at Aspheron.

Entrée Антрэ ®
French **Map** 3 B4
Nikolskaya ploshchad 6
Tel *(812) 572 52 01*
This French bistro serves well-prepared food such as beef, duck and salmon carpaccio. The pastries here are noted as the best in town.

Wasabi Васаби ®
Japanese **Map** 4 D3
Ulitsa Yefimova 3
Tel *(812) 244 73 03*
This chain restaurant has a wide selection of freshly prepared sushi and hot meals.

Model market stall selling fresh fruits and nuts at Baklazhan, St Petersburg

Elegantly laid out table at Tsar, an upmarket restaurant in St Petersburg

Mozzarella Bar
Моцарелла Бар ®®
Italian/Japanese **Map** 3 C3
Naberezhnaya kanala Griboedova 64
Tel *(812) 310 64 54*
The menu here offers something for everyone – ideal for a group of diners with different tastes.

Russkaya Ryumochnaya No.1
Русскя Рюмочная No. 1 ®®
Russian **Map** 3 B2
Konnogvardeiskiy bulvar 4
Tel *(812) 570 64 20*
An old world-style dining room serving modern interpretations of classic Russian dishes. Offers over 100 vodkas; many are flavoured.

DK Choice

Bella Vista Белла Виста ®®®
Italian **Map** 3 B2
Angliyskaya naberezhnaya 26
Tel *(812) 312 32 38*
Bella Vista is the perfect place for a romantic pre- or post-theatre dinner. Indulge in tasty Italian food in an elegant atmosphere. A summer-only terrace and superb views across the Neva river add to the restaurant's delights.

Further Afield

Baklazhan Баклажан ®
Oriental
Ligovskiy prospekt 30
Tel *(812) 677 73 72*
The menu at Baklazhan offers tasty renditions of Georgian and Asian classics. The home-made noodles and baked goods are a must-try.

Beer House Бир Хаус ®
International
Ulitsa Nekrasova 25
Tel *(812) 273 71 01*
Beer lovers can revel at the extensive beer selection here. The meat dishes are great too.

Bufet Буфет ®
Russian
Pushkinskaya ulitsa 7
Tel *(812) 764 78 88*
A cosy eatery near Nevskiy prospekt with framed photographs and mementos on the walls. Serves simple Russian fare.

Fartuk Фартук ®
Mediterranean **Map** 4 F2
Ulitsa Rubinshteyna 15–17
Tel *(812) 764 52 56*
Relaxed outdoor dining at a communal country kitchen-style table. Delicious home-made lemonades. Reserve in advance.

Gulchatay Гульчатай ®
Oriental **Map** 4 D5
Zagorosnyy prospekt 70
Tel *(812) 575 07 90*
Enjoy fantastic belly dances, live music and a game of backgammon. Excellent food and service.

Jean-Jacques Rousseau
Жан-Жак Руссо ®
French
Ulitsa Marata 10
Tel *(812) 315 49 03*
A stylish bistro, Jean-Jacques serves breakfast, lunch and dinner. Extensive wine list. Friendly staff.

Khochu Kharcho Хочу Харчо ®
Georgian **Map** 3 C3
Sadovaya ulitsa 39/41
Tel *(812) 310 32 36*
Enjoy authentic *kharcho* (beef-walnut soup) and *khachapuri* at this homely eatery. One of the best places in town to meet up with friends.

Kompot Компот ®
International
Ulitsa Zhukovskovo 10
Tel *(812) 719 65 42*
Among the city's haute cuisine establishments, Kompot offers Italian, Mexican and Asian cuisines. Superb wine list.

Key to Price Guide *see p280*

Kvartirka Квартирка ®
Russian **Map** 4 F2
Nevskiy prospekt 51
Tel *(812) 315 55 61*
A Soviet-era themed café that packs in locals hungry for rustic cooking as well as tourists in the know. Brusque service.

Lagidze Лагидзе ®
Georgian
Ulitsa Belinskovo 3
Tel *(812) 579 11 04*
Lagidze serves Georgian food in a modest but modern setting. Try the *lodka* (hot cheese-filled bread with egg) and *satsivi*, and finish the meal with Georgian brandy.

Palermo Палермо ®
Italian **Map** 4 F2
Naberezhnaya Reki Fontanki 50
Tel *(812) 764 37 64*
A good family restaurant offering a classic Sicilian menu, plus a few Russian favourites – mainly heavy meat dishes.

Staraya Derevnya
Старая деревня ®
Russian
Ulitsa Savushkina 72
Tel *(812) 431 00 00*
The decor at Staraya Derevnya resembles an old-fashioned apartment. Do not miss the cabbage pie and aubergine rolls.

Sunduk Сундук ®
European/Russian
Furshtatskaya ulitsa 42
Tel *(812) 272 31 00*
A trendy art café with Russian and European dishes and an extensive wine list. Live jazz in the evenings.

Tres Amigos ®
Latin American **Map** 4 F3
Ulitsa Rubinshteyna 25
Tel *(812) 572 26 85*
Tres Amigos is notable for its bizarre decor inspired by Aztecs and beer halls. It has a children's room with slides and swings.

Troitskiy Most
Троицкий мост ®
Vegetarian
6-ya liniya 27
Tel *(812) 327 46 22*
The emphasis is on vegetables at this no-smoking café-restaurant. Try the cheese and spinach salad or tagliatelle with mushroom sauce.

Xren Хрен ®
European **Map** 4 F3
Zagorodnyy prospekt 13
Tel *(812) 347 88 50*
Xren comprises three dining rooms, each with a different decor. Go for *gazpacho* (cold Spanish soup), duck and couscous. DJs perform at weekends.

Demidov Демидов ®®
Russian **Map** 2 F5
Naberezhnyaya Reki Fontanki 14
Tel *(812) 272 91 81*
This touristy restaurant has an interesting menu that features quail's eggs, delectable pancakes and caviar. Enjoy gypsy music from 8pm onwards.

Marcelli's Марчелли's ®®
Italian
Ulitsa Vosstaniya 15
Tel *(812) 986 91 11*
Casual and spacious, Marcelli's is the place for Italian food lovers. Affordable lunch specials.

Na zdorovye! На здоровье! ®®
Russian **Map** 1 B3
Bolshoi prospekt 13, Petrograd Side
Tel *(812) 232 40 39*
With garish 19th-century decor, gypsy cabaret and boisterous clientele, this is the place to revel in Russian kitsch and relish vodka.

Novaya Istoriya
Новая история ®®
Seafood/Russian
Ulitsa Belinskogo 8
Tel *(812) 579 85 50*
Feast on Kamchatka crab, oysters, and delicious meat dishes at this chic restaurant. Sophisticated but friendly atmosphere.

Brightly painted wall panels at Na Zdorovye, St Petersburg

Pirosmani Пиросмани ®®
Georgian **Map** 1 A3
Bolshoi prospekt 14, Petrograd Side
Tel *(812) 235 46 66*
Set out like a Georgian hill village, Pirosmani serves Georgian classics such as *lobio* (beans in spicy sauce).

Povari Повари ®®
Italian **Map** 1 B2
Bolshoi prospekt 38/40, Petrograd Side
Tel *(812) 233 70 42*
Specializes in all kinds of freshly made pasta such as fettuccini with mushrooms and truffle sauce.

Probka Пробка ®®
Italian
Ulitsa Belinskovo 5
Tel *(812) 273 49 04*
This chic wine bar's minimalist decor complements its Italian cuisine – fine sauces give the dishes great flavour.

Ruskaya Charka
Русская Чарка ®®
Russian **Map** 4 E3
Naberezhnaya Reki Fontanki 92
Tel *(812) 495 55 58*
Enjoy a selection of traditional game dishes such as Siberian venison at this restaurant.

Russian Fishing
Русская рыбалка ®®
Fish
Yuzhnaya doroga 11, Krestovskiy Island
Tel *(812) 323 98 13*
A stylized fisherman's hut with a pond where guests can catch their own fish and watch it being cooked. Great for families.

Russian Kitsch Русский китч ®®
Russian **Map** 3 A1
Universitetskaya naberezhnaya 25
Tel *(812) 325 11 22*
The menu here is a mix of fusion cuisine and sushi rather than *pelmeni* and cabbage. Enjoy the very Russian dance floor.

Sherbet Шербет ®®
Uzbek
Ulitsa Vosstaniya 26
Tel *(812) 716 08 74*
Laid-back ambience with charming, candlelit tables. The menu combines Oriental cooking with some Turkish dishes.

Shinok Шинок ®®
Ukrainian **Map** 4 F3
Zagorodnyy prospekt 13
Tel *(812) 571 82 62*
Elegant minimalism has no place at Shinok, which offers hearty food with three kinds of *salo* (salted pork belly), and Ukrainian vodka that hits the spot.

For more information on types of restaurants *see p275*

Shurpa Шурпа ®®
Oriental
Engelsa prospekt 27, 2nd floor
Tel *(812) 600 25 75*
Shurpa ffers an elaborate range of Oriental dishes such as *plov*, flat cakes and aromatic soups. Superb wine list to accompany the food.

Dickens Restaurant
Диккенс ®®®
British **Map** 4 D4
Naberezhnaya Reki Fontanki 108, 2nd floor
Tel *(812) 702 62 63* **Closed** *Sun*
This cosy restaurant specializes in steaks and game dishes. A selection of fine cigars are offered in the lounge. Fantastic views of the Fontanka river.

Karl & Friedrich
Карл и Фридрих ®®®
International
Yuzhnaya doroga 15, Krestovskiy Island
Tel *(812) 320 79 78*
Aimed at families, this place has a nanny on weekdays and children's entertainment at weekends. There is a strong meat orientation to the menu. Great selection of beer.

DK Choice

Matrosskaya Tishina
Матросская тишина ®®®
Seafood/French
Ulitsa Marata 54/34
Tel *(812) 764 44 13*
This restaurant features a real trawler cut into pieces, aquariums stuffed with live lobsters, oysters and crayfish; tiger prawns and sea scallops. And all this with just the right wines for company. Everything is delivered fresh and kept cool on ice.

Façade of La Parisienne, a modern café-restaurant in Petrozavodsk

Ryba Рыба ®®®
Italian/Asian
Ulitsa Akademika Pavlova 5
Tel *(812) 234 50 60*
Diners can choose from a wide selection of pizzas, or try the delectable Asian wok-based dishes.

SunDay Ginza Сандей Гинза ®®®
European/Japanese
Yuzhnaya doroga 15
Tel *(812) 900 33 31*
One of the best restaurants in the area, SunDay Ginza is the ideal place to try sushi or grilled dishes.

Troika Тройка ®®®
Russian **Map** 4 F3
Zagorodnyy prospekt 27
Tel *(812) 407 53 43*
Enjoy circus acrobatics, folk songs, Russian dancing, glitz and glamour. The menu may not offer much variety but the food is good.

Beyond St Petersburg

Krapiva Крапива ®
Russian
Sankt-Peterburgskoe shosse 111, Shuvalovka
Tel *(812) 450 53 93*
Set in a stylized Russian tower, Krapiva is a good place to try traditional rural dishes.

Vena Вена ®
European/Russian
Sankt-Peterburgskiy prospekt 30, Petrodvorets
Tel *(812) 427 94 47*
A Viennese-themed restaurant near the upper garden of Peterhof Palace, Vena serves Weiner schnitzel, goulash, delicious chicken Kiev, pancakes and other central European favourites.

DK Choice

Sofia София ®®
European
Pavlovskoye shosse 7
Tel *(812) 451 98 02*
Not far from the main attractions of Pushkin and Pavlovsk, Sofia offers a charming ambience and excellent service standards. It has two exquisitely decorated banquet rooms for large groups. Savour the delicious cream of cauliflower soup or try the scrumptious salmon on the grill. There are plenty of meat dishes as well.

Podvorie Подворье ®®®
Russian
Filtrovskoe shosse 16, Pavlovsk
Tel *(812) 466 85 44*
Situated within a re-creation of a 17th-century wooden house, Podvorie offers plenty of meaty soups and vodkas. Sample traditional fare such as *pelmeni* and pancakes with caviar or sink your teeth into a juicy beef stroganoff. Great desserts.

Northern Russia

Petrozavodsk: La Parisienne
Парижанка ®
European/Russian
Prospekt Lenina 2
Tel *(8142) 79 56 71*
This rapidly expanding chain has 12 branches scattered throughout the centre. All are smart French-style café-restaurants offering reliable pizza, sandwiches, soups and pancakes. Try the banana tempura.

Well-manicured gardens fronting the landmark windmill at Karl & Friedrich, St Petersburg

Pskov: Rus Русь ®
Russian
Vlasevskaya Vashni
Tel *(8112) 72 26 05*
Relish rabbit fillet and stewed mutton while sitting at cosy alcove tables overlooking the river.

Veliky Novgorod: Horoshie Ludi Хорошие Люди ®
European
Ulitsa Meretskova-Volosova 1/1
Tel *(8162) 73 08 79*
Diners can make their own salads and slice their own freshly baked bread here. Go for the home-made sausages in cowberry sauce.

Veliky Novgorod: Teplo Тепло ®
International
Ulitsa Meretskova-Volosova 7/1
Tel *(8162) 90 98 62*
A smart yet casual place with rustic styling and excellent service. Delectable desserts.

DK Choice

Veliky Novgorod: Dom Berga Дом Берга ®®
Russian
Ulitsa Bolshaya Moskovskaya 24
Tel *(8162) 94 88 38*
Housed in a historic 19th-century mansion, this restaurant serves traditional Russian dishes such as Boyarsky *borsch*, stewed rabbit and home-made gingerbread. Wash it all down with locally produced mead.

Kaliningrad

Kaliningrad: Solnechni Kamen Солнечный Камень ®
Russian
Ploshchad Vasilevskogo 3
Tel *(4012) 53 91 06*
An atmospheric restaurant near the Amber Museum, this place offers dishes such as pike stuffed with eel and Siberian fried pork.

Kaliningrad: Fish Club Рыбный Клуб ®®
Seafood
Oktyabrskaya ulitsa 4a
Tel *(4012) 30 71 50*
Popular restaurant serving a range of tasty fish dishes. The summer terrace offers fine river views.

DK Choice

Kaliningrad: Khmel Хмель ®®
Russian
Ploshchad Pobedy 10a
Tel *(4012) 59 33 77*
Bare brick walls and industrial piping provide a stylish backdrop for this popular eatery. The menu covers most Russian specialties from Kaliningrad quail to Kamchatka crab. There is even smoked Omul from Lake Baikal. Excellent service.

Exterior of Rus, a medieval-themed restaurant in Pskov

Central and Southern Russia

Astrakhan: Shollie Шоли ®
Uzbek
Ulitsa Uritskogo 3
Tel *(8512) 51 28 88*
Lovely Oriental-style restaurant specializing in delicious Uzbek cuisine and other appetizing dishes. Splendid river views.

Kazan: Dom Tatarskoy Kulinarii Дом Татарской Кулинарии ®®
Tatar/Russian
Ulitsa Baumana 31
Tel *(843) 292 70 70*
One of Kazan's best restaurants, Dom Tatarskoy is a great place to sample traditional Tatar dishes – do not be surprised if horsemeat is on the menu.

Nizhny Novgorod: Pyatkin Пяткинь ®®
Russian
Ulitsa Rozhdestvenskaya 25
Tel *(831) 430 91 83*
The grand furnishings in Pyatkin re-create the setting of a 19th-century mansion. Great spot to try Russian staples such as beef stroganoff.

Perm: Nairi Наири ®
Armenian/Russian
Ulitsa Sovetskaya 67
Tel *(342) 257 05 51*
A charming Armenian restaurant offering excellent food and a superb wine list. Live music and traditional Armenian dancing on most evenings.

DK Choice

Samara: Staraya Kvartira Старая Квартира ®
Russian
Ulitsa Samarskaya 51/53
Tel *(846) 332 22 60*
Dine at this fabulous retro restaurant that rustles up period dishes from all over the ex-Soviet Union. Ensconced in a warren like cellar, it features dining tables in the re-created rooms of a Soviet-era apartment replete with elegant decor that adds to the charm.

Samara: U Vakano У Вакано ®
Russian
Volzhskiy prospekt 4
Tel *(846) 332 60 73*
Delightful Soviet-era restaurant with dining booths and a menu featuring lots of meat options and plenty of local fish.

Sviyazhsk: Trapeznaya Трапезная ®
Russian
Konechny Dvor
Tel *(8422) 44 18 80*
A medieval-themed eatery with vaulted ceilings. First-rate three-course menu that changes daily.

The elegantly furnished Dom Berga, Veliky Novgorod

The stylish glass-and-concrete exterior of Ris, Sochi

Ulyanovsk: Karl Marx Strasse Карл Маркс Штрассе ®
German/Russian
Ulitsa Karla Marksa 13
Tel *(8422) 24 91 09*
A pub-restaurant serving standard Russian fare along with German sausages and beer. The apple strudel is divine.

Ulyanovsk: Olymp Олимп ®
International
Ulitsa Spasskaya 19/9
Tel *(8422) 44 11 44*
Olymp offers European dishes, such as grilled salmon, and stunning views of the Volga.

Volgograd: Shafran Шафран ®
Uzbek
Ulitsa Gvardeyskaya
Tel *(8442) 23 57 52*
Plush Oriental-themed restaurant serving plenty of grilled meat options. Excellent *baklava* (sweet pastry filled with chopped nuts) and Armenian wine.

Volgograd: Moliere Мольер ®®
Traditional Russian
Hotel Volgograd, Ulitsa Mira 12
Tel *(8442) 55 12 55*
A classy restaurant dishing out exquisite fare with a pianist playing in the background.

Yekaterinburg: Dacha Дача ®®
Russian/European
Prospekt Lenina 20A
Tel *(343) 379 35 69*
Sample traditional Russian cuisine at this popular eatery. Charming country house-inspired interiors.

The Caucasus

Adler: Café Mayak Кафе Маяк ®
Russian
Ulitsa Prosvyasheniya
Tel *(8622) 44 41 86*
Fresh fish and dishes such as pancakes with red caviar feature on Mayak's menu. Pleasant open seafront terrace with comfortable furniture shaded by palms and umbrellas.

Anapa: Evrasia Евразия ®
Asian/Russian
200 m (656 ft) east of the sea port of Anapa
Located right on the beach, Evrasia serves a reasonable range of sushi and Russian cuisine. Friendly staff.

Gelendzhik: Sea House Си Хаус ®
International
Ulitsa Mira 21
Tel *(909) 450 60 20*
Sample sushi, pizza, panini and other Russian dishes. Wonderful sea views from the shaded terrace.

Krasnodar: Zharovnya Жаровня ®
Russian
Ulitsa Mira 40
A simple buffet restaurant offering huge portions of hearty Russian food in modern surroundings. Good place to try *okroshka*.

Rostov-na-Don: Mein Herz Мейн Герц ®®
Russian/European
Ulitsa Bolshaya Sadova 115
Tel *(8632) 63 90 52*
Savour high-quality dishes such as Argentinian beef steak or Russian specialties such as *kurnik* (chicken pie) at this restaurant in Don Plaza Hotel.

Sochi: Akhun Ахун ®
Russian
Mount Bolshoi Akhun
A cavernous, castle-like eatery where grilled meat permanently sizzles over a huge barbeque.

Sochi: Ris Рис ®
International
Kurortny prospekt 16
Tel *(8622) 64 38 73*
This restaurant serves a good range of international cuisine with an emphasis on rice-based dishes and sushi.

DK Choice

Sochi: Vostochny Kvartal Восточный квартал ®®
Uzbek/Russian
Ulitsa Primorskaya 7
Tel *(8622) 66 10 99*
Wonderfully atmospheric Uzbek restaurant with glorious sea views. Diners can relax on the cushions beneath the wood panelled canopy and enjoy delicious Uzbek food served in traditional ceramic dishes. Lamb is roasted on spits at weekends.

Sochi: Chayka Чайка ®®®
International
Voykova ulitsa 1
Tel *(8622) 41 81 64*
A swanky restaurant within the Maritime Terminal building. Diners can sample delicious home-made pasta and locally caught fish.

Siberia and the Far East

Irkutsk: Bier Haus ®
European
Ulitsa Karla Marksa
Tel *(3952) 55 05 55*
A German tavern-style restaurant, "Beer House" offers a selection of draft Czech, German and Irish beer and delicious beer sausages and pork shank to go with it.

Irkutsk: Kochevnik Кочевник ®®
Mongolian
Ulitsa Gorkogo 19
Tel *(3952) 20 04 59*
The best place to sample Mongolian cuisine in Irkutsk, Kochevnik offers *pozi* (Mongolian dumplings) and plenty of horse-meat dishes.

Khabarovsk: Telegraph Телеграф ®
European/Russian
Ulitsa Sheronova 10
Tel *(4212) 31 66 83*
Smart English-themed pub and restaurant with a cosy wood-panelled interior that is popular with locals and business diners. Serves a good range of Russian and Western dishes that includes steak and braised ribs.

Bier Haus, a classy Bavarian-style beer hall in Irkutsk

Charming wooden building housing Ladeyni, Tobolsk

Komsomolsk-na-Amur: Escher Эшер ®®
International
Prospekt Pervostroiteley 31
Tel *(4217) 53 51 31*
This restaurant in Hotel Voskhod boasts modern design, excellent service and an international menu with dishes such as duck breast salad and Munich sausage platter.

Krasnoyarsk: Kalinka Malinka
Калинка Малинка ®
Russian
Propekt Mira 91a
Tel *(391) 211 50 81*
Vaguely Soviet-themed establishment with Russian staples such as *blini* and *pelmeni* plus a good selection of salads.

Novosibirsk: People's Bar and Grill
Гриль-бар Пиплс ®
International
Krasnyy prospekt 22
Tel *(383) 209 25 90*
TV screens line the walls and Thai noodles, sausages and steaks are among the international offerings at this lively basement spot in the heart of the city.

Novosibirsk: Paris
Пэрис ®®
International/Russian
Ulitsa Kamenskaya 7/1
Tel *(383) 223 01 00*
Exclusive à la carte fine dining restaurant in Doubletree by Hilton Hotel serving exquisite international and locally inspired dishes. Wide range of innovative cocktails. Good wine list.

Omsk: Pertsi
Перцы ®
Italian
Ulitsa Partizanskaya 2
Tel *(3812) 20 20 65*
Excellent range of pizza and pasta dishes feature on the menu of this ultra-modern restaurant. Do not miss the locally renowned lasagne. Efficient service.

DK Choice

Omsk: Kolchak Колчак ®®
International
Ulitsa Broz Tito 2
Tel *(3812) 45 99 99*
An extraordinary establishment within a stunning Art Deco building, Kolchak has an Irish pub on the ground floor, an Italian restaurant on the second floor and an Uzbek restaurant on the third. There is even a comfortable and cosy cocktail lounge and an elaborate banquet hall. Personable and friendly staff.

Petropavlovsk-Kamchatskiy: Yamato Ямото ®
Japanese/Russian
Ulitsa Lukashevskogo 5
Tel *(4152) 26 77 00*
A pleasant, central restaurant that serves a mixture of Japanese and Russian dishes prepared with fresh local ingredients.

Tobolsk: Ladeynyi
Ладейный ®
Russian
Ulitsa Revolutsionnaya 2
Tel *(3456) 22 21 11*
Lovely eatery in a reconstructed wooden building facing the Kremlin. Dishes include "Cucumbers for Vodka", several tongue options and *vareniki* (Ukrainian stuffed dumplings).

Tomsk: Vechny Zov
Вечный зов ®®
Siberian/Russian
Ulitsa Sovetskaya 47
Tel *(3822) 52 81 67*
An award-winning restaurant where diners can choose from a broad range of enticing Siberian dishes or Russian classics.

Ulan-Ude: Kailash
Кайлаш ®®
Buryat/international
Ulitsa Strelets 1
Tel *(3012) 20 00 28*
Frequented by well-heeled locals, this modern restaurant has a hill-top location. Offers both European and Mongolian cuisine.

Vladivostok: Ukh Ty Blin!
Ух ты, блин! ®
Russian
Ulitsa Fokina 9
Tel *(4232) 51 56 71*
The perfect place to try Russia's most popular dish – *blini* (pancakes cooked to order with every conceivable filling from gooey sweet cream to seafood).

Vladivostok: Michelle
Мишель ®®
International
Ulitsa Uborevicha 5A, 8th floor
Tel *(4232) 30 81 16*
Worth visiting just for the panoramic sea and city views. Choose from a wide selection of fresh local seafood dishes.

Yuzhno-Sakhalinsk: Cippolini
Чипполини ®®
International
Ulitsa Chekhova 78
Tel *(4242) 46 84 01*
A popular expat hangout offering dishes such as Angus beef tenderloin and grilled lamb chops.

Impressive façade of the Art Deco edifice housing Kolchak, Omsk

For more information on types of restaurants *see p275*

SHOPPING IN RUSSIA

Shopping in Russia is easier and more rewarding today than it was in Soviet times, when queues and shortages were the norm. However, there is one thing reminiscent of the Communist era and that is the country's export restrictions that cover a broad range of categories. Today, department stores offer everything from souvenirs to furs and supermarkets overflow with a variety of fresh produce. Most malls and boutiques stock apparel and accessories by international brands as well as little-known Italian and Scandinavian designers. In recent years imported goods have pushed out many local products, but Russian linen, chocolates and crafts and toys are still much sought after by tourists. Shoppers can head to specialist shops and flea markets to buy these wonderful gifts.

A typical flea market selling a collection of samovars

Opening Hours

Shops across Russia are usually open from 10am until at least 7pm, although upmarket outlets may open later. A few small stores, especially inexpensive food shops, close for lunch. Department stores and large shops remain open on Sundays. However, smaller places are generally open for shorter hours and closed on weekends during summer. Most cities and towns have 24-hour food shops.

How to Pay

Credit cards are accepted at many big stores, but cash is the preferred mode of payment in cities and towns across the country. The only legal currency in Russia is the rouble and paying in non-Russian currency amounts to a criminal offence. While most shops in Moscow now use the one-stop cashier system, the Soviet *kassa* system of visiting several separate cashiers' desks is still common outside Moscow.

Self-service shopping is generally confined to supermarkets and retail chains. Shop assistants are usually helpful; they will write down the prices for you to hand to the cashier. Defective goods can be returned provided they are accompanied by a receipt.

The price of all goods includes Value Added Tax (VAT), which is mostly 18 per cent, with a reduced rate of 10 per cent on basic food items, medical products and children's clothing. Note that there is no tax-free shopping for foreign visitors.

Export Restrictions

All outgoing luggage is X-rayed by customs officials to check for items subject to export restrictions. The **Federal Customs Service** has set limits on the amount of caviar and alcohol that can be taken out of Russia.

Under Russian law, all objects made before 1956, and all objects made from valuable materials such as gold, silver, precious stones and fur, are subject to export controls. Contemporary art and books published before 1946 also fall under this ruling. Permission to export these can be obtained from the **Ministry of Culture** in Moscow or St Petersburg. Applications take about two weeks to process and entail paying an export tax of 50 per cent of the item's value according to the ministry's assessment.

It is best to buy items less than 50 years old and be able to prove their age. Books, medals and porcelain are all inscribed with a manufacturing date. For undated objects, ask for receipts from the vendor. The gallery from which art is purchased should assist with the paperwork.

Export restrictions are, however, not applicable to mass-produced paintings, icons, amber, porcelain, books and clothing.

Bargaining

Avoid bargaining if a set price is displayed at markets. In all other cases, you can usually get some reduction if you haggle, especially since non-Russian visitors are likely to be quoted a higher price than locals. However, bargaining in Russia is a serious matter; do not negotiate unless you genuinely intend to buy.

A dazzling variety of merchandise on sale at the Souvenir Market, St Petersburg

Department Stores and Shopping Malls

Known as *univermag* (universal shop), Russian department stores evolved from Tsarist "trading rows" of kiosks owned by different merchants. After GUM *(see p69)* in Moscow, the most atmospheric of these shopping emporia is Gostinyy Dvor *(see pp166–7)* in St Petersburg. Other high-end shopping arcades include **Passazh** in St Petersburg and the **Pokrovskiy Passage** in Yekaterinburg.

Modern shopping malls are present in all big cities, often in residential suburbs or on the outskirts. One of the largest shopping centres in the Ural region, **Dirzhabl** stocks a wide variety of apparel, footwear and perfumes.

GUM, one of the most popular shopping malls in Moscow

Markets and Bazaars

Large indoor food markets, or *rynoks*, selling flowers, fruit, vegetables, home-made cream cheese, sausages and other delicacies can be found in every city. Visitors can buy jars of organic honey and sticks of sera, a traditional Siberian "chewing gum" at markets in the Altai Region. All kinds of food shopping can be done at **Andreevskiy Market** in St Petersburg, stacked high with Russian specialities.

Crafts and souvenir markets can be found in some towns and cities. In St Petersburg, the **Souvenir Market** offers a wide variety of *matryoshka* dolls and Soviet memorabilia. Flea markets such as **Unona** and the Friday- and Saturday-morning market at Udelnaya metro are worth visiting in St Petersburg. Shoppers are advised to be aware of pickpockets.

Museum Shops

Museum shops are an excellent place to find reproduction prints, Soviet memorabilia (including ceramics), silk scarves and books on the museum's collection of exhibits, its home city as well as Russia in general. Besides Moscow, St Petersburg has the best museum shops in the Hermitage *(see pp154–5)* and the Russian Museum *(see pp164–5)*. In Kaliningrad, amber jewellery can be bought at the city's Amber Museum *(see p168)* or from vendors outside.

Specialist Shops

Devoted to a local craft or product, specialist shops are popular in larger cities. In St Petersburg, the **Imperial Porcelain Factory** has two downtown outlets that stock wonderful tea sets and dinner services. **Slavyanskiy Stil** specializes in fine linen products such as skirts, shirts and duvet covers. The **Chocolate Museum** sells chocolates moulded into unusual shapes, such as busts of Lenin or chess sets.

DIRECTORY

Export Restrictions

Federal Customs Service
w russian-customs.org

Ministry of Culture
Malaya Morskaya ulitsa 17, St Petersburg. **Map** 3 C1.
Tel (812) 571 03 02.

Department Stores and Shopping Malls

Dirzhabl
Ulitsa Akademika Shvartsa, Yekaterinburg.
Tel (343) 278 09 89.

Passazh
Nevskiy prospekt 48, St Petersburg.
Map 4 E1.
Tel (812) 315 52 09.
w passage.spb.ru

Pokrovskiy Passage
Ulitsa Rosy Lyuksemburg 4, Yekaterinburg.
Tel (343) 365 87 87.
w pokrovskiy passage.ru

Markets and Bazaars

Andreevskiy Market
Bolshoi prospekt 18, St Petersburg.
Map 1 A3.
Tel (812) 323 66 87.

Souvenir Market
Naberezhnaya kanala Griboedova, by Church on Spilled Blood, St Petersburg. **Map** 4 E1.

Unona
Ulitsa Marshala Kazakova 35, St Petersburg.
Tel (812) 747 02 00.
w spb-unona.ru

Specialist Shops

Chocolate Museum
Nevskiy prospekt 17, St Petersburg.
Map 4 D1.
Tel (812) 315 13 48.
w muzeyshokolada.ru

Imperial Porcelain Factory
Vladimirskiy prospekt 7, St Petersburg.
Tel (812) 713 15 13.
Nevskiy prospekt 160, St Petersburg.
Tel (812) 717 48 38.
w ipm.ru

Slavyanskiy Stil
Pushkinskaya ulitsa 3, St Petersburg.
Tel (812) 325 85 99.

What to Buy

It is easy to find interesting and beautiful souvenirs in Moscow and St Petersburg. They range in price from small, enamelled badges, which sell for very little, through to hand-painted Palekh boxes and samovars which can be very expensive. Traditional crafts were encouraged by the state in the old Soviet Union and many items, such as lacquered boxes and bowls, *matryoshka* dolls, wooden toys and chess sets, are still made by craftsmen and women using age-old methods. Memorabilia from the Soviet era also make good souvenirs and Russia is definitely the best place to buy the national specialities, vodka and caviar.

Samovar Used to boil water to make tea *(see p279)*, samovars come in all shapes and sizes. A permit is needed to export a pre-1945 samovar.

Flavoured vodka

Clear vodka

Vodka and Caviar An enormous variety of both clear and flavoured vodkas (such as lemon and pepper) is available *(see p278)*. They make excellent accompaniments to *ikra* (black and red caviar), which are often served with *blini (see p276)*.

Red caviar

Black caviar

Malachite egg

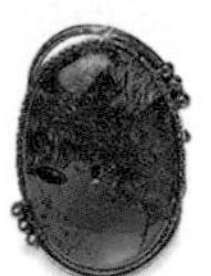

Amber ring

Semi-precious Stones Malachite, amber, jasper and a variety of marbles from the Ural Mountains are used to make a wide range of items – everything from jewellery and chess sets to inlaid table tops.

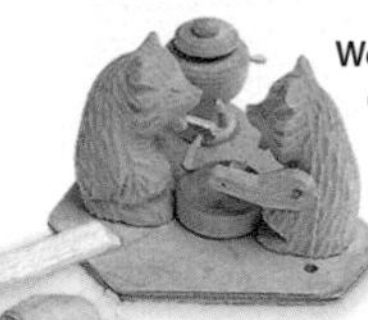

Wooden Toys These crudely carved wooden toys usually have moving parts. They are known as Bogorodskiye toys and make charming gifts.

Chess Sets Attractive chess sets made from all kinds of beautiful materials, including malachite, are widely available. This wooden chess set is painted in the same style as the *matryoshka* dolls.

Matryoshka Dolls These dolls fit one inside the other and come in a wide range of styles. The traditional dolls are the prettiest, but those painted as Russian, Soviet and world leaders are also very popular.

Lacquered Artifacts

Painted wooden or papier-mâché artifacts make popular souvenirs and are sold all over the city. The exquisite hand-painted, lacquered Palekh boxes can be very costly, but the eggs decorated with icons and the typical red, black and gold bowls are more affordable.

Palekh Box The art of miniature painting on papier-mâché items originated in the late 18th century. Artists in the four villages of Palekh, Fedoskino, Mstera and Kholui still produce these hand-painted marvels. The images are based on Russian fairy tales and legends.

Painted wooden egg

Bowl with Spoon The brightly painted bowls and spoons, generally known as *Khokhloma*, have a lacquer coating, forming a surface which is durable, but not resistant to boiling liquids.

Russian hand-painted tray

Musical Instruments Russian folk music uses a wide range of musical instruments. This *gusli* is similar to the Western psaltery and is played by plucking the strings with both hands. Also available are brightly painted balalaika and *bayan* (accordion).

Russian Scarf These brilliantly coloured traditional woollen shawls are good for keeping out the cold. Mass-produced polyester versions are also available, mostly in big department stores, but these are not so warm.

Gzhel Ceramics With a distinctive blue and white pattern, this style of ceramics takes its name from Gzhel, a village near Moscow. Ranging from figurines and vases to household crockery, they are popular with Russians and visitors alike.

Soviet Memorabilia An eclectic array of memorabilia from the Soviet era is on sale. Old banknotes, coins, pocket watches and Red Army kits, including belt buckles, badges and other items from uniforms, can be found alongside watches with cartoons of KGB agents on their faces.

Pocket watch

Badge with Soviet symbols

Red Army leather belt

ENTERTAINMENT IN RUSSIA

Russia is a vibrant country where both mainstream and eclectic forms of entertainment have flourished. The range of cultural events and recreation here is wide and richly varied. Both Moscow and St Petersburg have an impressive choice of entertainment and their ballet, opera, classical music and theatre are among the best in the world. Moreover, both cities have a crowded cultural calendar since international artistes, bands, soloists and conductors frequently come to visit. Additionally, Russia's great musical culture is manifested by the many music festivals that happen across the country throughout the year. Circuses remain an extremely popular form of entertainment. The Russian versions are highly stylized and elaborate, with a variety of impressive acts.

Ballerina warming up for a performance at the Mariinskiy Theatre

Information and Tickets

There is never a dearth of things to do in Russia. St Petersburg can be quite a difficult city to keep up with as both official and unofficial events are organized at short notice. To keep abreast of what is on in the city, check out the weekly *St Petersburg Times* and the monthly magazine *Pulse*. Visitors who can read Russian can refer to two bi-weekly magazines, *Afisha* and *Time Out*, for detailed listings.

St Petersburg's Mariinskiy Theatre has an English-language website on which tickets can be bought. Ticket booking website **Artis** offers similar services for other theatres. Elsewhere, visitors can buy tickets in person from local ticket kiosks or the venue's box office, or online.

Ballet, Opera and Classical Music

Russia's musical tradition has been upheld in its major cities. St Petersburg rivals, and occasionally surpasses, Moscow in the quality of its ballet, opera and classical music. The Mariinskiy Theatre *(see p174)* boasts some of the world's finest dancers, such as the prima ballerinas Ulyana Lopatkina and Diana Vishneva. The company tours abroad over summer, returning for the opening of the autumn season. One of the highlights of the year is the Christmas production of *The Nutcracker*, performed by children from the Vaganova Ballet School *(see p167)*. The Mariinskiy Concert Hall, near the theatre, is one of the main venues for the Stars of the White Nights Festival *(see p34)*.

While the Mariinskiy and the **Mikhailovskiy Theatre** are St Petersburg's main operatic venues, the **Great and Small halls of the Philharmonia** and the Academic Capella *(see p169)* are the city's best-known concert halls where classical music is performed. The former is the home of the St Petersburg Philharmonic Orchestra. All are used during the city's annual International Early Music Festival *(see p36)*.

In Yekaterinburg, the local **Philharmonic** is home to the acclaimed Urals Academic Orchestra and often hosts visiting directors and soloists. The city's **Opera and Ballet Theatre**, with its Baroque auditorium, is a lovely place to see the Russian classics. Novosibirsk's silver-domed **Opera and Ballet Theatre** is bigger than Moscow's Bolshoi, with a grand interior to match.

Cinema, Theatre and Circus

Russia's cinematic culture is showcased during film festivals, such as St Petersburg's **Festival of Festivals** held during the White Nights and **Open Cinema** (August), an acclaimed forum for short films. **The Russian International Film Fair** held in March has two venues – St Petersburg's **Dom Kino** cinema and Sochi's **Winter Theatre**.

After Moscow, St Petersburg is the second home of Russian drama. The **Bolshoi Dramatic Theatre** has a repertory that includes Chekhov, Gogol and other Russian classics. Plays by Shakespeare and Molière are staged at the **Theatre on Liteynyy**, the city's only wheelchair-accessible theatre.

Japanese pianist and composer Nobuyuki Tsujii performing at the Stars of the White Nights

A host of talented companies attend the **Festival of Russian Theatres** (mid-April) and the **Baltic House Festival** (October).

Circuses are popular with people of all ages. The **Bolshoi St Petersburg State Circus** is the oldest in Russia, having been based at its present site since 1877. Its shows include performing animals.

Rock, Jazz and Folk Music

Russia boasts a unique pop culture. Every April, St Petersburg rock clubs such as **Kosmonavt** play host to SKIF, a three-day festival of DJs, performance artists and bands from all over Russia and abroad. Other events include the **White Nights Swing** and Autumn Rhythms, jazz festivals held in early July and mid-November respectively.

In the Siberian city of Perm, a **White Nights Festival** in June with rock and folk bands, street theatre, circuses and bonfires beside the Kama river, is followed in late July or early August by Kamwa, an ethno-futuristic celebration of ancient Ugric culture and contemporary art, which brings together DJs, fashion designers and bands.

Other festivals include Ferma, a techno picnic festival with designer tents for hire, held at Tarusa in the Kaluga region in the first week of July, and **Nashestvie** (8–10 July) in the Tver region.

Traditional folk festivals include the Sadko Folklore Festival, held in Veliky Novgorod, and the Kizhi Volost Festival *(see p35)*.

Children's Entertainment

Most big cities have theatres specializing in plays for children based on Russian fairy tales. In St Petersburg, the best-known are **Zazerkalye** and the **Large Puppet Theatre**. Shows are in Russian, but often transcend the language barrier.

Attending a dolphin show at St Petersburg's **Dolphinarium** is a must. By bringing a bathing costume, children may play and be photographed with the dolphins after the show. For a "real" Russian winter experience, try a *troika* (horse-drawn sleigh) ride.

Awe-inspiring performance of trapeze artists, Bolshoi St Petersburg State Circus

These are offered at **Shuvalovka**, a reproduction Russian village located 30 km (19 miles) south-west of St Petersburg. Open throughout the year, it includes 17th-century-style wooden houses, a museum of peasant life, a working smithy, a skating rink and ice slides. Take a minibus from Avtovo metro towards Peterhof and ask to stop at Shuvalovka.

DIRECTORY

Information and Tickets

Artis
W artis.spb.ru

Ballet, Opera and Classical Music

Great Hall of the Philharmonia
Mikhaylovskiy ulitsa 2, St Petersburg. **Map** 4 E2.
Tel (812) 710 42 57

Mikhailovskiy Theatre
Ploshchad Iskusstv 1, St Petersburg. **Map** 4 E2.
Tel (812) 595 43 05.

Opera and Ballet Theatre
Krasnyy prospekt 36, Novosibirsk.
Tel (383) 227 15 37.

Opera and Ballet Theatre
Prospekt Lenina 46A, Yekaterinburg.
Tel (343) 350 32 07.

Small Hall of the Philharmonia
Nevskiy prospekt 30, St Petersburg. **Map** 4 E2.
Tel (812) 571 83 33.

Yekaterinburg Philharmonic
Ulitsa Karla Libknekhta 38a, Yekaterinburg.
Tel (343) 371 46 82.

Cinema, Theatre and Circus

Baltic House Festival
Aleksandrovsky Park 4, St Petersburg. **Map** 1 C3.
Tel (812) 232 35 39.

Bolshoi Dramatic Theatre
Naberezhnaya Reki Fontanki 65, St Petersburg.
Map 4 E3.
Tel (812) 310 92 42.

Bolshoi St Petersburg State Circus
Naberezhnaya Reki Fontanki 3, St Petersburg.
Map 4 F1.
Tel (812) 570 53 90.

Dom Kino
Ulitsa Karavannaya 12, St Petersburg. **Map** 4 F1.
Tel (812) 314 56 14.

Festival of Festivals
W filmfest.ru

Open Cinema
W opencinemafest.com

Theatre on Liteynyy
Liteynyy prospekt 51, St Petersburg.
Tel (812) 273 53 35.

Winter Theatre
Ulitsa Teatralnaya 2, Sochi.
Tel (862) 262 96 16.

Rock, Jazz and Folk Music

Kosmonavt
Ulitsa Bronnitskaya 24, St Petersburg. **Map** 4 D5.
Tel (812) 303 33 33.

Nashestvie
W nashestvie.ru

White Nights Festival
W permfest.com

White Nights Swing Festival
W jazz-hall.ru

Children's Entertainment

Dolphinarium
Konstantinovskiy prospekt 19, St Petersburg.
Tel (812) 235 46 31.

Large Puppet Theatre
Ulitsa Nekrasova 10, St Petersburg.
Tel (812) 273 66 72.

Shuvalovka
Sankt-Peterburgskoe shosse 111.
Tel (812) 450 53 93.

Zazerkalye
Ulitsa Rubinshteyna 13, St Petersburg. **Map** 4 F2
Tel (812) 712 43 93.

OUTDOOR ACTIVITIES

Russia's varied terrain offers a wide range of outdoor activities. From trekking in the Caucasus and the Altai Mountains and rafting in the Siberian rivers to volcano-watching in Kamchatka and pony trekking in the Urals, the country is an adventure-sports enthusiast's dream destination. In addition, those seeking more unusual experiences will find living in a nomad's yurt, dog-sledding in the Urals or visiting a *banya* especially rewarding. Specialist tour operators offering a variety of tour packages can be easily found in most big cities. However, for activities such as trekking and climbing, tourists can also contact local guides who usually have detailed knowledge of the area. Visitors must always check the safety gear before setting out for particularly risky adventure sports such as climbing and rafting.

Exploring a grotto in the spectacular Kungur Ice Cave

Banya

The Russian steam bath or *banya* (баня) has been an integral part of the country's culture for many centuries. Its origins are rooted in village life, when peasants cleansed themselves communally once a week before spending Saturday drinking and Sunday in church. Today, well-equipped *banya*, such as **Kruglye Bani** and Sandunovskiy Baths *(see p75)*, can be found in cities and towns across the country.

Some *banya* have separate floors for men and women, while others operate on different days for each sex. Regardless of the set up, men and women do not bathe in the same area.

Towels, flip-flops and felt halts to protect your hair from the intense heat can be rented at any *banya*. Many bathers buy a *venik*, a bunch of leafy birch twigs, with which they fan and flail themselves in the *parilka* (steam room) to open up the pores of the skin and enhance blood circulation.

In the countryside, visitors can experience a Siberian *banya* – a riverside log-built sweat lodge – from which bathers emerge to plunge into the icy water of the river. Russians believe the difference between the temperature inside and the weather outside makes the body stronger.

Caving

The Kungur Ice Cave *(see p235)* in the Perm region of the Urals is the most accessible of Russia's many caves. The numerous grottoes and lakes inside the cave can be explored on three different tour routes of varying duration and difficulty. Trips can be arranged by **Krasnov**.

Climbing and Volcano-watching

The Caucasus in the south offers superb trekking and climbing opportunities. Here, one of the best places to climb is the 5,642-m (18,510-ft) Mount Elbrus, the highest peak in Europe. Although it is popular with Russian climbers, foreign governments advise their citizens against going there due to ongoing separatist terrorism. It is far safer to go climbing in the Altai Mountains of Siberia. The area's snow-capped peaks, alpine meadows and pristine lakes provide some of the most picturesque trekking trails.

In the Far East, Kamchatka offers thrilling climbing opportunities, including the chance to climb Klyuchevskaya Sopka, Eurasia's highest active volcano at 4,750 m (15,584 ft). Expeditions are only allowed when the local volcano-monitoring station judges it safe.

LenAlpTours offers a variety of volcano-watching and climbing tour packages.

Ethnographic Tourism

Visitors can experience the culture and traditions of ethnic minority groups in the Buryatia, Tuva and Altai regions of Siberia. In addition to living in a yurt, herding on horseback and sampling *kumis*, a mildly alcoholic beverage made of fermented mare's milk, tourists can also learn about the Buddhist and shamanic rituals practiced around these parts. Sayan Ring

Breathtaking views reward hikers in the Caucasus

(see p315) is one of the several Siberian travel companies that offers such tour packages.

Kayaking and Rafting

With its great rivers swollen by snowmelt in early summer, Russia offers plenty of kayaking and rafting opportunities. In southern Russia, thousands of locals raft the Samara Bend in an annual event called the *Zhigulyovskaya krugosvetka* (Zhiguli Circuit). Samara Intour *(see p315)* arranges 10-day rafting trips in this area.

In the Altai Mountains, the Katun river offers high-speed rafting, where enthusiasts can test their skills in catamaran kayaks, rubber dinghies and other craft. The US-based tour company **Bio Bio Expeditions** offers a tour package that includes rafting, camping, fishing and a Siberian *banya* experience. **Kayak USSR**, Krasnov and LenAlpTours also organize kayaking trips on the Katun and other Siberian rivers.

Pony Trekking and Dog-sledding

Pony trekking is a great way to explore the rugged terrain of the Altai Mountains and visit settlements where traditional Altai culture, a fusion of Turkic, Mongol and indigenous shamanism, is still practiced. LenAlpTours can arrange multi-day pony treks during the summer months.

A visitor dog-sledding in the Urals

From mid-December to mid-March, **Ural Expeditions & Tours** and **Visit Ural** offer dog-sledding in the Urals. The one-day excursion includes instructions on how to manage a sledge and feed a team of dogs, as well as a barbecue with vodka.

Military Experiences

Since the collapse of the Soviet Union, Russia's Defence Ministry and arms factories have capitalized on their military equipment and expertise by offering a variety of sanitized military experiences. **Go Russia** offers package holidays with high-altitude aerobatics and supersonic flights to the edge of space in MiG-29 and MiG-31 jet fighters from airbases outside Moscow and Nizhny Novgorod. Visitors are required to undergo a medical examination before the flight.

Spectator Sports

Football is the most popular spectator sport in the country. The Russian Championship runs from spring to autumn. It is dominated by four Moscow clubs and Zenit St Petersburg. Zenit's current home ground is the 21,000-seat **Petrovskiy Stadium**. Visitors can find a schedule of the year's matches on the **Russian Football Union**'s website.

Ice hockey runs a close second in popularity. The season starts in September and culminates in the annual world championships that are held in summer. In St Petersburg, **Ice Palace** and **Yubileynyy Sports Palace** host ice hockey matches.

Russia is set to host major international sporting events this decade, including the 2014 Winter Olympics in Sochi and the 2018 FIFA World Cup™ in a number of cities across the country.

DIRECTORY

Banya

Kruglye Bani
Karbysheva ulitsa 22A, St Petersburg.
Tel (812) 550 09 85.

Caving

Krasnov
Ulitsa Borchaninova 4, Perm.
Tel (342) 238 35 20.
W uraltourism.com

Climbing and Volcano-watching

LenAlpTours
Ulitsa Vosstania 9–4, St Petersburg.
W russia-climbing.com

Kayaking and Rafting

Bio Bio Expeditions
Tel (1800) 246 72 38.
W bbxrafting.com

Kayak USSR
Novosibirsk.
Tel (909) 50 89 23.
W kayakussr.com

Pony Trekking and Dog-sledding

Ural Expeditions & Tours
Posadskaya ulitsa 23A, Yekaterinburg.
Tel (343) 253 57 75.
W welcome-ural.ru

Visit Ural
Ulitsa Radishcheva 28, Level 13, Yekaterinburg.
Tel (343) 377 77 25.
W visitural.com

Military Experiences

Go Russia
Boundary House, Boston Rd, London W7 2QE.
Tel (020) 3355 77 17.
W justgorussia.co.uk

Spectator Sports

Ice Palace
Prospekt Pyatiletok 1, St Petersburg.
Tel (812) 718 66 20.
W newarena.spb.ru

Russian Football Union
W rfs.ru

Petrovskiy Stadium
Petrovskiy ostrov 2, St Petersburg.
Map 1 A3.
Tel (812) 232 16 22.
W petrovsky.spb.ru

Yubileynyy Sports Palace
Prospekt Dobrolyubova 18, St Petersburg.
Map 1 A3.
Tel (812) 498 60 33.
W yubi.ru

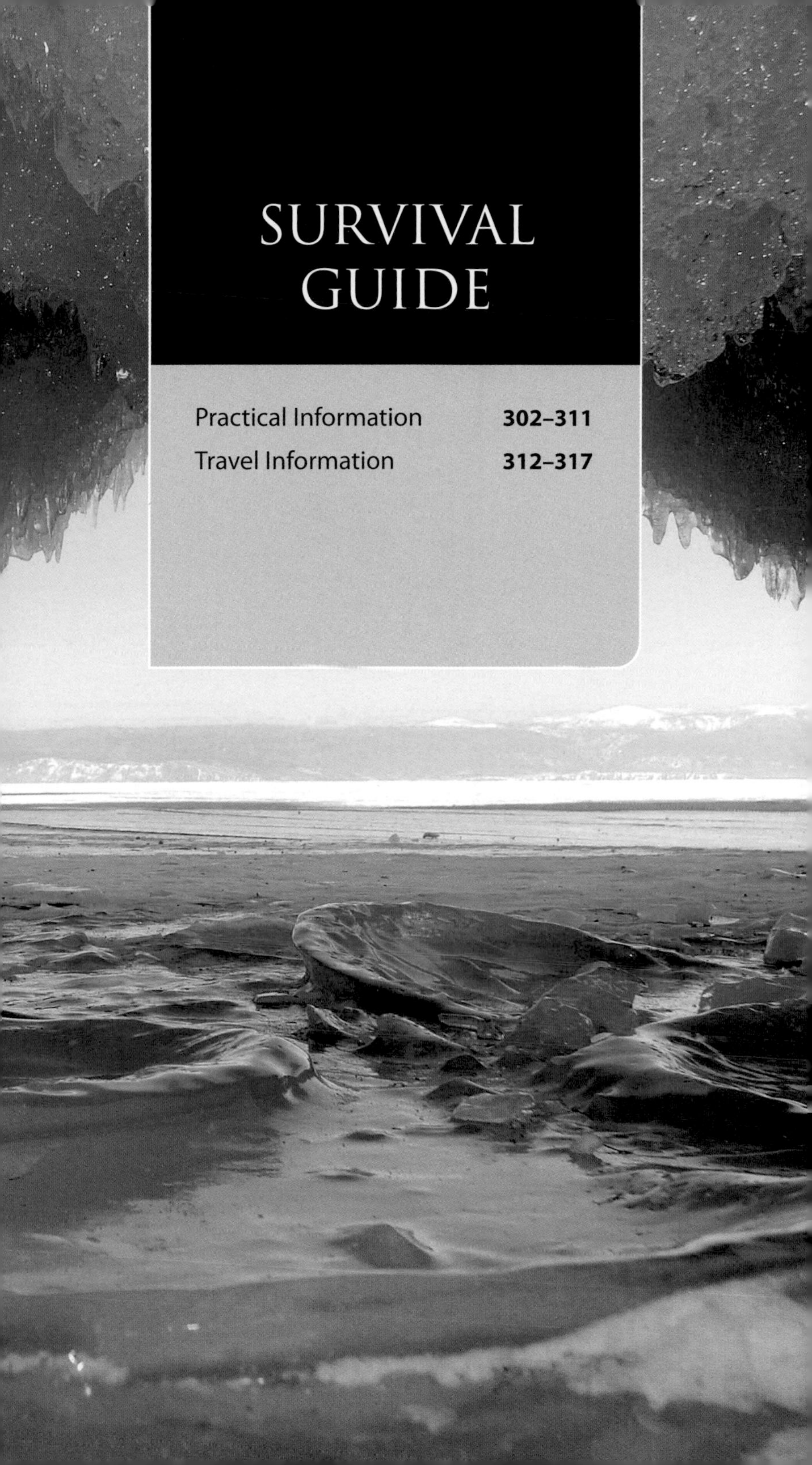

SURVIVAL GUIDE

PRACTICAL INFORMATION

Russia can be a bewildering country for visitors. Besides the downtown areas of Moscow and St Petersburg, most street names and signs are only in Cyrillic, although bilingual signage can be occasionally found in other cities or at major tourist sights in the country. Staff at hotels, restaurants and in all service sectors, as well as passers-by are usually helpful to foreigners. However, it is a good idea for visitors to familiarize themselves with the Cyrillic alphabet in order to decipher signs. Conventional tourist offices are hard to find in Russia, but a number of cities now have online information portals. Hotels, restaurants and theatre tickets can be expensive; check the price carefully before booking something. Public transport is generally cheap and efficient.

When to Go

Visitors should not be daunted by Russia's long, harsh winters. Temperatures fall to around -8°C, or even -31°C, between November and late March across the country. However, most big cities are well equipped with an army of snow ploughs and street cleaners to deal with the ice and snow. Note that sturdy footwear, warm layers of clothing and hats are a must.

The height of the tourist season is from May to September, especially during Stars of the White Nights *(see p34)* in June and July, when prices are at their highest. Although fewer tourists visit during the low season, from October to April, it is the best time for skiing and visiting museums and galleries.

Visitors dressed in winter clothes and boots playing in the snow

Visas and Passports

Citizens of almost all countries will need a visa to visit Russia. Be sure to verify entry requirements with the Russian embassy in your country several weeks ahead of departure; visitors arriving by train from Europe will also need a transit visa for Belarus. Note that visas can be obtained only from a Russian consulate in a country where you have right of residence. However, EU citizens can apply from any EU country.

For travellers on a package tour, visas will be organized by the tour companies. Independent travellers can pay a modest fee and get a specialist agent, such as **Real Russia** or **Visa Express**, based in the UK, or **Peace Travel Services** in the US, to arrange it for you. Moscow-based **Visa House** can also arrange visas for visitors of any nationality.

Alternatively, apply to the Russian embassy. All visa applications must be accompanied by a letter of invitation, which is often referred to as a "visa support letter". This can be provided by your hotel (if booked in advance) or a tourist or accommodation agency in Russia, the UK or the US.

Visas take around 10 days to process. However, all specialist agents offer an express service for an extra fee. Overstaying your visa can lead to a hefty fine or having to remain until an extension is obtained.

A Russian Railways Service office functioning as a tourist information centre, Kaliningrad

Customs Information

Passports and visas are thoroughly checked at immigration desks. On arrival, visitors are given an immigration card by immigration officials; it must be retained while in the country and presented upon departure. If you lose the exit half of your immigration card, you will need to visit the Immigration Service offices in the airport terminal to request a replacement card.

There are no limitations on the amount of foreign currency that can be brought in to Russia, but visitors carrying more than US$10,000 in cash will be expected to fill in a customs declaration form. Departure customs are generally stricter than in other countries, particularly in regard to art and antiques.

Registration

All foreign nationals must register with the Federal Migration Service (FMS) within seven days of arrival. Hotels and hostels can do this for their guests. If travelling independently on a business visa, the agency that provided

◀ Striking view of people standing next to their cars on frozen Lake Baikal

the visa support should register you at a local police station or FMS office. Non-registration can lead to on-the-spot fines by local police of up to US$160.

Embassies and Consulates

Every country that has diplomatic relations with Russia has an embassy or consulate in Moscow; some also have consulates in St Petersburg, Vladivostok or Yekaterinburg. Travellers intending to reside in Russia for longer than three months are advised to register with their consulate or embassy. If a visitor is robbed, hospitalized, imprisoned or otherwise rendered helpless, the embassy or consular officials will help make arrangements, find an interpreter or at least offer advice. They can also re-issue passports and, in some cases, provide a loan to get visitors home.

Visitor Information

Walk-in tourist information centres can rarely be found in cities across Russia; there are walk-in offices in Kazan, Veliky Novgorod and St Petersburg. However, many Russian cities such as Königsberg have online "information portals". The **Moscow Tourist Helpline** provides information about the city's sights and public transportation in English.

In other cities, local tourist agencies and hotels are the main source of information. In addition, monthly or weekly publications, which are distributed at hotels and restaurants, and online media (often in Russian only) are useful too.

Opening Hours

Most sights open from 10 or 10:30am to 6pm and close one day a week. A number of sights also close one day each month for cleaning. Last tickets are usually sold about an hour before closing. All museums remain open on Sundays. Some cathedrals and churches are always open, but others open only for services.

Visitors outside a tourist information centre in Listvyanka

Admission Charges

Many museums and theatres charge foreigners considerably higher admission fees than Russians, although well within European and North American norms. Such places include the State Tretyakov Gallery *(see pp98–9)*, the Armoury Chamber *(see pp62–3)*, the Pushkin State Museum of Fine Arts *(see pp90–91)* and the Bolshoi Theatre *(see pp82–3)* in Moscow as well as the Hermitage *(see pp154–5)*, the Russian Museum *(see pp164–5)* and the Mariinskiy Theatre *(see p174)* in St Petersburg. However, schoolchildren and students *(see p305)* are entitled to discounts. Credit cards are only accepted at some sights. A good option is to buy a Tourist Card from tourist information offices. It offers free entry to many state museums as well as discounts in some restaurants.

The *kassa* (ticket office) is often located at some distance from the entrance to the sight. It can be recognized by the "KACCA" sign; staff at the entrance will point you in its direction.

Women entering the Cathedral of St Sophia in Tobolsk wearing headscarves

Visiting Churches and Mosques

The most important Orthodox church services take place on Saturday evenings and Sunday mornings as well as on religious holidays. In general, services run for several hours. It is acceptable for visitors to drop in on a service for a while, but certain dress codes must be observed: shorts are not acceptable; men must remove their hats; women should cover their chest and shoulders and preferably wear a headscarf or hat. Although acceptable in town churches, women wearing trousers might be refused entry to monasteries.

Visitors should always seek permission before entering mosques. Besides observing the dress code specified for Orthodox churches, be sure to remove your shoes before entering the mosque premises.

Language

Cyrillic, the alphabet used in the Russian language, is named after the 9th-century monks Cyril and Methodius who invented it. Various systems for transliterating Cyrillic into Roman characters exist, but they do not differ enough to cause confusion.

Many Russians who regularly come into contact with visitors can speak some English. However, knowledge of a few Russian words will be much appreciated and taken as a sign of respect.

An outdoor café where debit and credit cards are accepted, Krasnodar

Addresses

Russian addresses are given in reverse order: post code, city, street name, *dom* (house) number, *kvartira* (apartment) number and finally the person's name.

Buildings on the corner of two streets are denoted by two numbers separated by a slash, the first referring to the larger street and the second to the smaller one.

If a flat is part of a complex, a *korpus (k)* or *stroinie (str)* number will also be given to indicate which block it is in.

Social Etiquette

On public transport, young men are expected to give up their seats to women with young children or the elderly.

Smoking is prohibited in museums, cinemas, theatres and public transport. Special areas are usually reserved for smoking in restaurants. When invited to a private home, be sure to toast *za khozyayku* (the hostess) or *za khozyaina* (the host).

Photographing metro stations, official-looking buildings and any type of military structure is prohibited, and may lead to detention by the police. In some museums, visitors must buy a ticket to photograph or video.

Travelling with Children

Russians adore children, and those accompanying visitors to Russia are likely to attract plenty of compliments. Children under six travel free on public transport, but over this they pay the full price. While museums are free for toddlers and babies, schoolchildren pay a reduced price.

Gay and Lesbian Travellers

Russian society is not in general very tolerant of homosexuality and its "promotion" is a criminal offence. Any public displays of affection will almost always be frowned upon. Despite hostility, the gay and lesbian scene continues to thrive in major cities. The **Russian LGBT Network** provides general information on gay and lesbian life in the country.

Disabled Travellers

There are few facilities for the disabled in Russia. Public transport is difficult to access, entrances have steps and narrow doors and public lifts are rare. However, the Russian Museum and the Hermitage in St Petersburg, as well as the State Tretyakov Gallery in Moscow, all have wheelchair access. **Liberty**, a tour company in St Petersburg, specializes in wheelchair-accessible tours in and around the city and can even book hotels with suitable facilities. Travel advice can also be obtained abroad, from **RADAR** in the UK and **SATH** in the US.

A day out with children at one of Saransk's many museums

Student Travellers

An ISIC (International Student Identity Card) entitles its holder to discounts in museums and on rail and air tickets booked through **STAR Travel**.

Paying and Tipping

The rouble is the only valid currency in Russia *(see p308)*. Some hotels and agencies may display prices in US dollars or euros, but all cash payments must be in roubles. Debit and credit cards are accepted in some restaurants and most hotels, as well as in large retail stores in major cities.

Tipping is a matter of choice, but baggage handlers at airports and train stations may ask exorbitant sums. Visitors should simply pay what they consider to be appropriate.

Public Toilets

Most cafés and bars have toilet facilities, but public toilets on the street are not pleasant. It is often best to find the nearest large hotel or McDonald's, or a pay toilet in a department store, where fees may range from 10 to 30 roubles. Although the lady who takes the money also hands out toilet paper rations, it is a good idea to carry your own.

Electricity

The electrical current in Russia is 220 V. Two-pin plugs are required, but some of the old Soviet two-pin sockets do not take modern European plugs, which have thicker pins. US appliances need a 220:110 volt current adaptor. Adaptors are best bought before travelling.

Time

Since Russia abolished winter daylight saving in 2011, Moscow time has been four hours ahead of Greenwich Mean Time (GMT).

Moscow time is the standard for Russia's nine time zones. Note that Trans-Siberian Railway schedules express Moscow time, not local time zones.

Conversion Table

Imperial to Metric
1 inch = 2.54 centimetres
1 foot = 30 centimetres
1 mile = 1.6 kilometres
1 ounce = 28 grams
1 pound = 454 grams
1 pint = 0.6 litres

Metric to Imperial
1 centimetre = 0.4 inches
1 metre = 3 feet, 3 inches
1 kilometre = 0.6 miles
1 gram = 0.04 ounces
1 kilogram = 2.2 pounds
1 litre = 1.8 pints

Responsible Travel

Despite the efforts of Greenpeace and other NGOs, Russia has a regrettably poor record in environmental issues. State funding to develop 12 nature reserves for eco tourism has been greeted with scepticism: activists fear it will open them to property developers, as at Krasnaya Polyana, which is set to host Winter Olympics.

Tourists can support local communities by opting for homestays or B&Bs *(see p264)* over chain hotels. While Moscow is not renowned as a green city, there are a few eco-friendly, but expensive, hotels such as Ararat Park Hyatt Moscow *(see p266)* and Swissôtel Krasnye Holmy *(see p268)*, which employ energy-saving systems and recycle much of their waste. The centrally located Dorgomilovsky Market *(see p118)* is one of the city's largest farmers' markets selling fresh produce from regional farms. At local markets across Russia, the older women on the fringes often sell organic produce grown at their own *dachas*. Visitors can also buy organic fruits, vegetables and honey from the numerous markets in the Altai Republic.

Adventure travel agencies in the Urals and Siberia offer itineraries involving a variety of eco-friendly activities, such as rafting, dog sledding and pony-trekking. Based in Moscow, **Astravel** supports conservation projects through tours that include activities such as volcano-watching and surveying snow leopards.

Rafting, a popular environment-friendly activity in the Urals

DIRECTORY

Visas and Passports

Peace Travel Services
848 North Rainbow Blvd #1224, Las Vegas, 89107.
W **go-russia.com**

Real Russia
3, The Ivories, Northampton St, Islington, London, N1 2HY.
W **realrussia.co.uk**

Visa Express
Parnell House, 25 Wilton Rd, London, SW1V 1LW.
W **visaexpress.co.uk**

Visa House
22/2 Bolshaya Nikitskaya, Office 18, Moscow.
Map 1 B5.
Tel (495) 721 10 21.
W **visahouse.com**

Embassies and Consulates

Australia
10A/2 Podkolokolny pereulok, Moscow.
Map 4 F1.
Tel (495) 956 60 70.
W **russia.embassy.gov.au**

Canada
Starokonyushenny pereulok 23, Moscow.
Map 3 B2.
Tel (495) 925 60 00.
W **russia.gc.ca**

United Kingdom
Smolenskaya naberezhnaya 10, Moscow.
Tel (495) 956 72 00.
W **ukinrussia.fco.gov.uk**

United States
Bolshoy Deviatinsky pereulok 8, Moscow.
Tel (495) 728 50 00.
W **moscow.usembassy.gov**

Visitor Information

City Tourist Information Centre
Sadovaya ulitsa 14/52, St Petersburg. **Map** 4 D1.
Tel (812) 310 28 22.

Kazan Tourist Information Centre
Chernyshevskogo 27A, Kazan.
Tel (843) 292 97 77.
W **gokazan.com**

Königsberg.ru
Kaliningrad.
W **konigsberg.ru/eng**

Moscow Tourist Helpline
Tel (800) 220 00 02.

Red Izba
Sennaya ploshchad 5, Veliky Novgorod.
Tel (816) 277 30 74.
W **visitnovgorod.com**

Gay and Lesbian Travellers

Russian LGBT Network
Ligovsky prospekt 87, office 509, St Petersburg.
Tel (812) 454 64 52.
W **lgbtnet.ru**

Disabled Travellers

Liberty
Ulitsa Polozova 12, Office 1, St Petersburg.
Map 1 B1.
Tel (812) 232 81 63
W **libertytour.ru**

RADAR
W **disabilityrights.org**

SATH
347 Fifth Ave, Suite 605, New York, 10016.
W **sath.org**

Student Travellers

STAR Travel
Novoslobodskaya ulitsa 3, Moscow.
Map 1 B2.
Tel (495) 797 95 55.

Responsible Travel

Astravel
Novoslobodskaya ulitsa 31, Moscow. **Map** 1 B2.
W **astravel.ru**

Personal Security and Health

Despite lurid worldwide reporting on the Russian mafia, most visitors to Russia encounter little if any serious crime. Hazards such as pickpocketing and car-thefts are common, but they can usually be avoided by taking sensible precautions. Due to language reasons, it is a good idea to have a card with your Russian address written on it for use in taxis or emergencies. Medical insurance is essential, as local health care compares poorly with Western standards and English-speaking services and medical evacuation are expensive. Many medicines are readily available, but it is best to bring specific medicines if needed.

Bright red fire engine with the distinctive white stripe

What to be Aware of

Visitors to Russia are advised to take out travel insurance. Once in the country, tourists can prevent trouble by following some simple measures. Pickpockets can be avoided by not carrying money in open pockets or displaying large sums of money in public; bags should be kept closed and roubles kept apart from foreign currency and credit cards. It is advisable to carry a small sum of money for purchases, and to keep the rest in the hotel safe.

Downtown areas are often frequented by "gypsies", ostensibly begging but often engaged in pickpocketing. If approached, hold tight to valuables and walk on without aggression.

Traveller's cheques are insured against loss or theft. However, if they are stolen report it immediately to the issuing company as they can easily be "laundered" in Russia.

It is essential to report thefts to the police in order to obtain certificates for insurance claims. Since the police station is unlikely to have an interpreter, contact your hotel security staff for assistance. Embassies generally deal with more serious situations.

In an Emergency

The emergency services can be reached by dialling 01 for the fire department, 02 for police and 03 for an ambulance. There is also a combined number, 112. If at all possible, seek help first from your embassy or consulate.

Personal Safety

The greatest danger faced by travellers is posed by thieves who might become violent if they encounter resistance. It is advisable to hand over belongings that are demanded with menace.

Although widespread, the mafia has scant contact with foreigners, particularly tourists, who are generally less wealthy than Russian businessmen.

Women on their own may be approached by kerb crawlers or may be propositioned in bars and restaurants. It is best to ignore such advances and take responsibility for your own security.

At night, it is safer to use taxis booked in advance rather than hailed on the street. The metro is usually safe.

Racism is unfortunately rampant in Russia. It is advisable to be vigilant on the streets, especially around Hitler's birthday on 20th April and National Unity Day on 4th November, when bands of neo-Nazi thugs usually roam the streets.

Police

Several kinds of police operate in Russia. They change uniforms according to the weather, with the necessary addition of fur hats and big coats in winter. The *politsiya* (street officers), who always carry guns, can be frequently spotted on the streets. The riot police or OMON, who dress in blue camouflage fatigues, are seldom seen on the streets, except during demonstrations and football matches.

Separate from both these are the traffic police, whose uniforms carry the logo ДПС (DPS) on the chest and shoulder. They have the authority to stop any vehicle to check documents.

Both the *politsiya* and traffic police supplement their income by fining people for minor infringements of the law, and have unfortunately been known to stop tourists for document checks. Carry a photocopy of your passport and visa, and try to avoid handing over your original passport to the police.

Pharmacies

Apteka (pharmacies) in Russia can be recognized by the "Аптека" sign and a green cross hanging

A police car patrolling a city street

outside. Although pharmacies in cities are well stocked with imported and locally made products, small-town pharmacies usually have limited stock. Prescriptions are not necessary for any purchase, and antibiotics and other strong medications can be purchased over the counter. All assistants are trained pharmacists and can suggest a Russian alternative to visitors who name the drug they are seeking. However, visitors with specific requirements, particularly insulin, should bring enough supplies to last the length of their stay. Every city has several all-night pharmacies, whose addresses can be obtained from hotel receptionists.

Façade of a 24-hour city pharmacy stocking both local and imported medicines

Medical Treatment

Most large hotels have their own doctor and this should be the first port of call for anyone who falls ill. Public health care is based on local polyclinics and hospitals, where the standard of care is variable. Since few physicians and nurses speak English, visitors generally prefer private companies such as the **European Medical Centre**, the **American Medical Clinic** and **Euromed**. These companies provide a wide range of facilities, from basic treatment to dental care and X-rays, ultrasound scans and even medical evacuation. **US Dental Care** offers a full range of dental treatment. Although expensive, they are experienced in dealing with foreign insurance policies.

Brightly painted kiosk selling bottled water and other beverages

Most of these companies are in Moscow and St Petersburg, but some can be found in other major cities. If you are taken to a local hospital and require further treatment, contact either your consulate or an international private facility. Hospital bills tend to be rather stiff, so it is best to have a comprehensive health insurance policy. However, most travel insurance policies cover medical treatment as well.

Health Precautions

Visitors should not drink tap water in Russia as it contains heavy metals and giardia, a parasite that causes stomach ailments. Stick to bottled water and avoid fruit and raw vegetables that may have been washed in tap water. Avoid eating *pirozhki* sold on the streets.

With an increasing incidence of diphtheria, and a low risk of rabies, polio and hepatitis A and B, visitors intending to spend much time in remote areas are advised to be inoculated against these. Sexually-transmitted diseases are on the rise, so all due caution must be exercised.

Komari (mosquitoes) are rife from June to late September. Plug-in chemical mosquito coils are available and are good at night. Alternatives are sprays, or citronella oil repellents used in vaporizers.

A more serious issue is warding off encephalitis-bearing ticks, found in the taiga forests. Visitors planning to trek in the taiga from May to June are recommended to have encephalitis vaccinations, and should always wear insect repellent as well as cover exposed skin. If you find a tick, remove it carefully with tweezers; should any part remain, it can still infect you.

DIRECTORY

In an Emergency

Ambulance *(skoraya pomoshch)*
Tel 03.

All emergencies
Tel 112.

Fire *(pozhar)*
Tel 01.

Police *(politsiya)*
Tel 02.

Medical Treatment

American Medical Clinic
Naberezhnaya Reki Moyki 78, St Petersburg.
Map 3 C2.
Tel (812) 740 20 90.
W amclinic.com

Euromed
Suvorovskiy prospekt 60, St Petersburg.
Tel (812) 327 03 01.
W euromed.ru

European Medical Centre
Spiridonievskiy pereulok 5, Building 1, Moscow.
Tel (495) 933 66 55.
W emcmos.ru

US Dental Care
Ulitsa Bolshaya Dmitrovka 7/5, Buillding 2, Moscow.
Map 1 C4.
Tel (495) 933 86 86.

Banking and Local Currency

The official currency of Russia is the rouble. Major European debit and credit cards can be used to pay at hotels, restaurants and large retail stores across Russia, but cash is still the norm in some cities as well as in provincial towns and villages. Exchange bureaux and banks are widespread where visitors can change their currency to roubles. Money should never be changed on the street, where apparently better offers from individuals will lead to visitors being cheated.

An automatic cash dispenser

Banks and Exchange Bureaux

Roubles can be obtained outside Russia, but rates are usually better once in the country. There are numerous exchange bureaux in cities and towns, some of which are open 24 hours. They can be identified by the Обмен валюты (obmen valyutiy) sign. US dollars and euros are widely accepted, but other currencies may be difficult or impossible to exchange.

A passport has to be shown when changing money. Any defect on foreign banknotes, especially vertical tears or ink or water stains, can make them difficult to exchange. Make sure that all banknotes brought into Russia are in good condition and that any US dollars were issued after 1990.

There are few foreign banks in Russia and they rarely offer over-the-counter services. However, most Russian banks will exchange US dollars, euros and sometimes other currencies. They also offer cash advances on credit cards. **Alfa-Bank** and **Sberbank** offer the best rates, although this can vary across Russia. Master Bank and Bank Moskvy also offer money transfer and accept American Express traveller's cheques.

ATMs

Recognized by the Банкомат (bankomat) sign, ATMs, or cash dispensers, can be easily found in cities. If unsure of where to find one, head to a big hotel. Visa and MasterCard are accepted in all ATMs while American Express is taken at Sberbank and Russkiy Standart. Maestro and Diners Club cards, however, are rarely accepted. Prepaid currency cards can be used to withdraw cash at many ATMs. As always, it is advisable to be alert when withdrawing cash and to cover the keypad when entering your PIN, to avoid becoming the victim of credit card fraud.

Western Union is widely used for international money transfers, which can be made through almost any bank. Note that commissions are exorbitant (US$40 to transfer US$300).

A money changing office displaying exchange rates

Credit Cards and Traveller's Cheques

Credit cards can be used to obtain cash, both roubles and US dollars, through the larger banks and from ATMs in some banks or hotels. Although the local commission is only 1 per cent (or zero), the credit card company will charge a fee for the transaction.

The most commonly accepted cards are Visa and MasterCard. Diners Club and American Express, however, are less widely recognized. Less commission is charged for cash in roubles.

Lost or stolen cards should be reported immediately to the credit card company in Moscow or St Petersburg.

Banks charge 1–3 per cent commission to refund or cash traveller's cheques. Note that only large banks, such as Alfa-Bank and Sberbank, offer this service. American Express cheques are most widely accepted, followed by Thomas Cook. Traveller's cheques can only be used as payment for goods or services in a few large hotels and are acceptable only in US dollars and euros. Recent customs regulations make it necessary to declare traveller's cheques on arrival in Russia.

DIRECTORY

Banks and Exchange Bureaux

Alfa-Bank
W alfabank.com/russia

Sberbank
W sberbank.ru

ATMs

Western Union
W westernunion.co.uk

Credit Cards and Traveller's Cheques

American Express
Moscow.
Tel (495) 933 84 00.
St Petersburg.
Tel (812) 329 60 60.

Visa, MasterCard and Diners Club
Tel (866) 654 01 64.

Local Currency

The Russian currency is the rouble (or ruble), written as рубль and abbreviated to р or руб. While the higher denominations are currently available in banknotes, all of which bear images of well-known Russian cities, the lower denominations are in coins. The kopek is issued in coins as well. Traditionally, the rouble always consisted of 100 kopeks. Today, however, kopeks have virtually no purchasing power.

Banknotes

There are six denominations of banknotes, with face values of 10, 50, 100, 500, 1,000 and 5,000 roubles. When changing money check that the notes correspond to those pictured here.

10 roubles

50 roubles

100 roubles

500 roubles

1,000 roubles

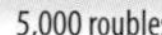

5,000 roubles

Coins

The revaluation of the Russian rouble in 1998 led to the revival of the long-redundant kopek. Any coins issued before 1997 are essentially valueless. Visitors should therefore always examine change they receive and refuse to accept any old coins.

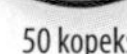

50 kopeks

10 kopeks

10 roubles

5 roubles

2 roubles

1 rouble

Communications

Telecommunications is one of the most dynamic sectors of Russia's economy. Cafés and restaurants in big cities have a Wi-Fi connection, which is usually free. Mobile phone shops can be found across cities, where a local SIM can be purchased upon presentation of a passport. The abundance of newspapers, magazines and TV channels on offer includes some in English. Russia's postal system has improved, but remains slow and unreliable.

International and Local Telephone Calls

Phone calls can be made from one of the public phone boxes on the streets and in metro stations. A prepaid *telefonnaya karta* (phonecard), which is available from kiosks, telecom shops or Sberbank branches, is required to make a call. Some of the popular phonecards include Zebra, which can also be used for dial-up Internet access, MTU-Net, Matrix and Access. Cards come in 25, 50, 100, 120, 200, 400 and 1,000 units. However, you will need at least 100 units to call internationally. Note that international and inter-city calls are cheaper 10pm–8am all through the week.

In cities and towns, it may be cheaper to call abroad through a *peregovorniy punkt* (public communications centre). Here, you give the clerk the number you want to call, pay a deposit and then go to your assigned booth to make the call, paying the difference afterwards.

Visitor at MTS office, one of the biggest telecom operators in Russia

Mobile Phones

MTS, **Megafon** and **Beeline** are the main mobile network operators in Russia. They cover most cities and also areas along the Trans-Siberian Railway, but due to the size of the country remote areas may lack coverage.

Most visitors from the EU can use their mobile phones in Russia if "roaming" is activated, but those from the US and Australia, who do not have a GSM phone, may not be able to. It is advisable to contact your local service provider to enable your "roaming" access before travelling to the country. Bear in mind that "roaming" in Russia is expensive.

A cheaper option is to buy prepaid Russian SIM cards if your phone is unlocked. A passport is required for registration when buying a SIM. Offered by service providers and usually priced at 300 roubles, these SIMs give you a local telephone number and a sum of credit that can be topped up by prepaid cards sold in phone shops, ATMs and top-up points in city underpasses. Two reliable phone shop chains are **Euroset** and **Svyaznoy**. Call charges are low within networks. Since roaming charges across Russia are high, it may be worth changing SIM cards when crossing regional telecom boundaries.

Useful Dialling Codes

- To call Russia from abroad, dial the international access code, followed by Russia's country code (7), the city code, and finally the individual number.
- To call Moscow, dial 495 followed by the individual number.
- To call St Petersburg, dial 812 followed by the individual number.
- To make an inter-city call, dial 8, followed by the city code and the individual number.
- To call Moscow, dial 495 followed by the individual number.
- To make a call from a landline to a mobile number, dial 8, then the city code, and finally the mobile number.
- To use an international calling card, dial the local access number followed by the card number and the PIN, then dial the number along with the country code.
- To make an international call from a domestic phone, dial 8, then dial the international access number (10), followed by the country code.
- To call Moscow, dial 495 followed by the individual number.
- For Moscow or St Petersburg directory enquiries, dial 09.

Internet, Email and Fax

Major cities have 4G (mobile broadband Internet access) coverage. Internet cafés can be found in every city and town, and sometimes even in villages. They provide access for around 100 roubles per hour.

Wi-Fi coverage is widely available in hotels as well as at the airport. It is generally free, but some hotels may charge, where Internet is available only in a specific area. Wi-Fi hotspots can also be found in stations, malls, cafés and bars. It has been introduced on the circle line of Moscow metro as well.

Fax services are available at post offices, communications centres and hotel business

Façade of a Svyaznoy outlet, Russia's leading mobile phone retailer

centres. Some hotels and travel agencies still require reservations or documentation for visa support, to be transmitted by fax.

Postal Services

The state-run postal service has offices everywhere, even in villages. However, the service is very slow, and is best avoided except for sending postcards. Ordinary post offices, and those in hotels, sell normal and commemorative Russian stamps, postcards and envelopes. Russian postoffices are marked Почта (pochta) and can be found across cities.

For important documents, use a courier service such as **DHL**, **FedEx** or **TNT**, which have offices in Moscow, St Petersburg and other cities. Anything other than paper, especially computer discs, is checked by customs, which can delay despatch by an extra day or so.

TV and Radio

Almost every hotel room in Russia has a television equipped to receive a variety of local, national, cable or satellite channels, including CNN, BBC World Service TV and Eurosport. Russian-language television is dominated by detective shows, soap operas and talk shows. Russia Today, the state-run English-language channel widely viewed as a mouthpiece for the Kremlin, is available in most hotels.

Since the BBC World Service stopped transmitting in Russia, there has been no regular English language radio station, but online radio stations from around the world are easily accessible. Local pop stations include Europa Plus (106.2 FM), Radio Maximum (103.7) and Russkoe Radio (105.7 FM). Radio Orfey (72.14 FM) plays classical music.

A streetside kiosk selling a variety of newspapers and magazines

Newspapers and Magazines

Quality national papers include *Izvestiya*, *Nezavisimaya Gazeta* and *Kommersant*, as well as the twice-weekly *Novaya Gazeta*, known for its investigative journalism. *Pravda* and *Komsomolskaya Pravda* (the former Communist Party and Communist Youth papers) are mass-market tabloids.

The Moscow Times is one of the best English-language newspapers. It is published from Tuesday to Saturday and includes event listings in its Friday edition. *The St Petersburg Times* comes out every Wednesday and provides detailed cultural listings and reviews, as well as national Russian news. Both newspapers are available free of charge from hotels, cafés and bars. *Moscow In Your Pocket* is a free listings guide published every two months.

DIRECTORY

Mobile Phones

Beeline
1ya Tverskaya-Yamskaya ulitsa 2, Moscow.
Map 1 B3.
Tel (495) 974 88 88.
W beeline.ru

Euroset
Tverskaya ulitsa 4, Moscow.
Map 1 C5.
Tel (495) 771 73 12.
W euroset.ru

Megafon
Myasnitskaya ulitsa 48, Moscow.
Map 2 F4.
Tel (495) 50 77 77.
Artilleriyskaya ulitsa 1, St Petersburg.
Tel (800) 300 05 00.
W english.megafon.ru

MTS
Sadovaya-Karetnaya ulitsa 2, Moscow.
Map 1 C3.
Tel (495) 766 0166.
Kazanskaya ulitsa 45, St Petersburg.
Map 3 C3.
Tel (800) 380 00 00.
W vis.mtsgsm.com

Svyaznoy
Ulitsa Arbat 1, Moscow.
Map 3 A2.
Tel (495) 788 52 55.
W svyaznoy.ru

Postal Services

DHL
1ya Tverskaya-Yamskaya ulitsa 11, Moscow.
Map 1 B3.
Tel (495) 956 10 00.
Nevskiy prospekt 10, St Petersburg.
Map 4 D1.
Tel (812) 326 64 00.
W dhl.ru

FedEx
Sokolnicheskiy val 1L, Moscow.
Tel (495) 737 52 23.
Nevskiy prospekt 30, St Petersburg.
Map 4 E1.
Tel (812) 325 88 25.
W fedex.com.ru

TNT
Ulitsa Svobody 31, Moscow.
Tel (495) 797 27 77.
Sofiyskaya ulitsa 14, St Petersburg.
Tel (812) 718 33 30.
W tnt.com

Newspapers and Magazines

Pravda
W english.pravda.ru

St Petersburg Times
W sptimes.ru

The Moscow Times
W themoscowtimes.com

TRAVEL INFORMATION

Flying remains the easiest way of travelling to Russia from Europe or the US, although many Australasians from China take the famous Trans-Siberian Railway. Travelling overland, especially by road, can be difficult and often involves crossing many borders and negotiating road networks and pot-holed roads. However, if cost is a priority, arriving by train or coach are cheaper alternatives, especially for visitors from neighbouring countries such as Ukraine or Belarus. Ferries are an increasingly popular form of transport to reach cities such as St Petersburg, Sochi and Vladivostok. Irrespective of the route chosen, it is worth shopping around to find the best deal as flight prices fluctuate greatly throughout the year. Many companies also offer package deals.

View of the three-level air terminal complex at Sochi International Airport

Arriving by Air

Direct flights run from London to Moscow on **British Airways** and the Russian airlines **Aeroflot** and **Transaero**, while British Airways as well as the Russian carrier **Rossiya** fly to St Petersburg. The two cities can also be reached by inexpensive indirect flights such as **Finnair** via Helsinki, **SAS** via Stockholm or **Austrian Airlines** via Vienna.

Direct flights from the US to Moscow are limited to Aeroflot, Transaero and **Delta Air Lines**. There are very few direct flights to other Russian cities from the US, Ireland, Canada, South Africa or Australia. The usual route from these places is to fly via a European city (often Helsinki) or via Moscow.

Scott's Tours in London and **Visit Russia** in New York are good for budget fares. Some agencies only sell flights, while others also book hotels or offer package deals, which can be cheaper than booking flights and accommodation separately.

Main Airports

Moscow has three international airports: **Domodedovo**, **Sheremetyevo** and **Vnukovo**. Each of the airports is linked by **Aeroexpress** trains to railway stations in the city centre and metro stations on the circle line. A one-way ticket costs 320 roubles and trains depart every 30 minutes from 6am to midnight.

There are also buses to outlying metro stations between 6am and midnight. However, traffic congestion often causes delays. Official airport taxis can be pre-booked by your hotel or at the terminal. Meters are rarely used; be sure to negotiate a price beforehand.

St Petersburg has two airports, both 17 km (11 miles) south of the centre. International flights arrive at **Pulkovo 2**, although Rossiya flights mostly land at the domestic airport, **Pulkovo 1**. Both airports have a regulated taxi system with stands near the exit of the arrivals terminals. Visitors should expect to pay about 1,000 roubles to reach the city centre. A cheaper alternative is to take bus 13 from Pulkovo 2 or bus 39 from Pulkovo 1 to Moskovskaya metro station. Minibuses travel the same route but charge twice as much.

The **Sochi International Airport** in Adler is linked to the central train station by buses and minibuses. The ski resort of Krasnaya Polyana can also be reached by bus from the airport. Taxi fares are negotiable; they start around 500 roubles. The main airport for Yekaterinburg is **Koltsovo**. It is connected to the central train station by buses and minibuses.

Arriving by Train

From Paris, Brussels, Berlin, Prague or Warsaw, it takes at least 24 hours to reach Moscow and 48 hours to reach St Petersburg. Note that a transit visa is required for Belarus. **Seat 61** contains full details of all rail routes to Russia.

Trains from Western Europe, Poland and Belarus arrive in Moscow at Belorusskaya station; from the Baltic States at Rizhskaya station and from Eastern Europe at Kievskaya station. Yaroslavskiy and Kazanskiy serve domestic routes only. Komsomolskaya is the terminus for trains arriving from Finland and St Petersburg. Paveletskaya and Kurskaya stations handle trains from southern Russia and Ukraine.

In St Petersburg, trains from Helsinki arrive at Finlyandskiy station; from Tallinn and Riga

A Trans-Siberian train travelling on a route along Lake Baikal

at Baltiskaya station; and from Germany, Poland and Belarus at Vitebskiy station. The most central terminus is Moscow station, where trains from the capital and most other parts of Russia arrive.

There are two rail routes to Russia from China and Mongolia. Starting from Beijing, the Trans-Mongolian route runs via the Mongolian capital, Ulan Bator, while the Trans-Manchurian route runs via the Chinese city of Harbin. The routes converge at Ulan-Ude and head west across Siberia following the Trans-Siberian Railway.

Arriving by Sea

From May to September, UK operators such as **Fred Olsen Cruises**, **P&O Cruises** and **Virgin Holidays** offer luxury cruises to St Petersburg. Cruise boats dock in the Neva basin in the heart of the city or at the Marine Facade Terminal on Vasilievskiy Island, linked to the centre by trolleybus 10 and bus 7. From February to December, there are regular **St Peter Line** ferries from Helsinki, Stockholm and Tallinn. On all these cruises, passengers may travel visa-free for up to 72 hours in St Petersburg.
In summer, Sochi can be reached by hydrofoil or ferry from the Black Sea port of Trabzon in Turkey. Hydrofoils take 4–5 hours and tickets cost 4,000 roubles; ferries take 12 hours. Note that services may be upgraded for the Winter Olympics; contact **Abdullah CAKIR** for details.

Visitors from Asia can reach Vladivostok by a **DBS Cruise** boat that sails once a week from the Japanese port of Sakamintao via Donghae in South Korea.

One of Lux Express's luxury Wi-Fi-enabled coaches

Arriving by Coach

Coach travel is suitable for visitors travelling on a very tight budget. There are **Eurolines** routes to Moscow from Germany, the Czech Republic, Slovakia, Poland and Hungary, Latvia and Estonia. All these routes usually terminate at the **Moscow Central Bus Station**.

For visitors to St Petersburg, **Finnord** runs a daytime and an overnight service from Helsinki, which drops off passengers at several locations. The journey takes around 8 hours. **Ecolines** and **Lux Express** run services from the Baltic States, terminating at the Baltiskaya train station near Baltiyskaya metro. One-way fares cost as little as 560 roubles from Tallinn, 520 roubles from Riga and 1,280 roubles from Vilnius.

Green Travel

Travelling to Russia by train reduces the high ecological impact of flying. As green initiatives are limited in the country, an easy way to reduce your carbon footprint is by choosing a centrally located hotel for ease of access to the main sights. Cycle hire is possible and is also one of the most eco-friendly ways to get around a city. The public transport system in most cities is good enough to make travelling by car unnecessary.

However, if you do not hike or cycle, exploring the remoter regions without your own vehicle will be difficult, as buses are slow and infrequent.

DIRECTORY

Arriving by Air

Aeroflot
W aeroflot.ru

Austrian Airlines
W austrian.com

British Airways
W britishairways.com

Delta Air Lines
W delta.com

Finnair
W finnair.com

Rossiya
W rossiya-airlines.com

SAS
W flysas.com

Scott's Tours
W scottstours.co.uk

Transaero
W transaero.com

Visit Russia
W visitrussia.com

Main Airports

Aeroexpress
W aeroexpress.ru

Domodedovo
W domodedovo.ru

Koltsovo
W koltsovo.ru

Pulkovo 1/Pulkovo 2
W pulkovoairport.ru

Sheremetyevo
W svo.aero

Sochi International Airport
W sochi-airport.com

Vnukovo
W vnukovo.ru

Arriving by Train

Seat 61
W seat61.com

Arriving by Sea

Abdullah CAKIR
W al-port.com.

DBS Cruise
W dbsferry.com/eng/main/main.asp

Fred Olsen Cruises
W fredolsencruises.com

P&O Cruises
W pocruises.com

St Peter Line
W stpeterline.com

Virgin Holidays
W virginholidays.co.uk

Arriving by Coach

Ecolines
W ecolines.ru

Eurolines/Lux Express
W luxexpress.eu

Finnord
Tel (812) 314 89 51.

Moscow Central Bus Station
W busmow.ru

Travelling around Russia

The railway network is the mainstay of long-distance travel in Russia. Although European discount passes provide little or no reduction in fares, trains are still cheaper than internal flights, and also much safer. Inter-city buses are suitable only for short trips, while travelling around by car can be difficult due to the unpredictable weather and the vagaries of the traffic police. For a leisurely tour through Russia's heartland, a river cruise on the Volga or the northern lakes is a good idea.

Aeroflot airplanes docked at the Sheremetyevo Airport

Travelling by Air

Flying is not only the fastest form of transport between cities, but often the only way to get to some Siberian cities during the winter months or spring thaw. However, domestic aviation in Russia does not have a great safety record, especially among the smaller carriers known as "Babyflots".

All airports in Moscow handle domestic flights. Aeroflot uses Sheremetyevo's Terminal D; the low-cost airlines Transaero and **S7** use Teminal B at Domodedovo, and the Siberian **UTair Aviation** flies from Terminal A at Vnukovo. In St Petersburg, all domestic flights arrive at Pulkovo 1.

Aeroflot, Transaero and Rossiya run regular 50–90-minute flights between Moscow and St Petersburg. Prices range from 2,700 roubles for an economy class one-way ticket to 4,200 roubles for business class. Tickets are sold online at airports, or through hotels and travel agencies.

Passengers need to show their passport on departure despite the fact that they will not be leaving the country.

Travelling by Train

Russia's rail network is one of the longest in the world and provides reliable service.

Russian Railways' (RZD) Russian-language website covers the entire network and has a journey planner, unlike the English version. Full instructions on how to use this feature can be found on Seat 61 *(see p313)*. Tickets can be booked online through either of these websites, or agencies specializing in rail travel such as **Russiantrains** and **RussianRail.com**. Be sure to buy tickets in advance; tickets are not sold on trains.

Owing to the long distances covered, the majority of trains are overnight sleepers, but some standard trains operate on shorter routes. Trains fall into four categories: *ekspressy* (express) trains, which travel between Moscow and St Petersburg only; *skorye* (fast) trains, which operate on long journeys and stop at only a few stations; *passazhirskie* (passenger) trains, which also operate on long routes, but stop at most or all stations; and suburban trains *(see p317)*. Sleepers offer a choice of *spalny vagon* (two-bed cabins), *kupe* (four-person compartments), or *platzkart* (dormitory-style carriages), which is a good option for travellers on a tight budget.

Trains are the most popular form of transport between Moscow and St Petersburg; there are ten or more trains daily. The fastest is the Sapsan train, which covers the distance in less than 4 hours at speeds of up to 250 kmph (150 mph).

Prices vary depending on class and services included. There is a choice between *sidyashchyy* (sitting) tickets and more expensive sleeper options. One-way prices for standard trains range from 2,500 roubles for *kupe* to 400 roubles for *sidyashchyy*, while Sapsan tickets start at 3,300 roubles. Prices do not always include bed linen, for which there is an additional small charge. On cheaper trains, the *provodnik* (carriage attendant) will issue and charge for bed linen.

Travelling by Bus

Buses are much less comfortable than trains and are worth taking only occasionally. They are useful for travelling to sights such as Vladimir *(see p116)* or Veliky Novgorod *(see p210)* rather than big cities. Elsewhere, the

The high-speed Sapsan train running between Moscow and St Petersburg

rail network may not reach certain attractions, making buses the only option for travellers.

Travelling by Boat

In summer, river cruises are an enjoyable way to see more of Russia. Volga cruises between Moscow and St Petersburg stop at several historic towns, on 5- to 7-day itineraries. From both cities, there are longer river cruises to Kazan *(see p225)*, Samara *(see pp228–9)* or Nizhny Novgorod *(see p224)*, and cruises on Lake Ladoga to Valaam *(see p209)* and Kizhi *(see p208)*.

All cruises can be booked through **Noble Caledonia** or **Voyages Jules Verne** in the UK, and through Visit Russia *(see p313)* in the US, often as part of a package deal including flights. Cruises can also be booked within Russia at a fairly short notice, through agencies such as **Infoflot**. Note that some boats are less modern than others, and the standard of meals can vary.

In St Petersburg, cruises depart from the *Rechnoy Vokzal* (River Terminal), which is a 10-minute walk from Proletarskaya metro. Boats in Moscow depart from *Severnoy Rechnoy Vokzal* (Northern River Terminal), a 10-minute walk from Rechnoy Vokzal metro station, or from the *Yuzhniy Rechnoy Vokzal (Southern River Terminal)*. The routes to both termini are well-signposted.

Travelling by Car

Driving in Russia can be gruelling and is not advisable for the uninitiated. Major cities suffer from chronic traffic congestion, with cars travelling in disorderly lanes, veering dangerously to avoid pot holes. Road signs mostly follow international conventions but are rarely bilingual, so drivers should familiarize themselves with the names of places in advance.

Russia's traffic police *(see p306)*, have the right to stop drivers and ask for documents. They can issue fines on the spot for infringements such as not having a fire extinguisher or first-aid kit and not wearing seat belts. It is compulsory for both drivers and front-seat passengers to wear seat belts, although many people do not. Drivers are not allowed to drink any alcohol at all and fines for drunk driving can be very high.

Priority is given to traffic approaching from the right unless a yellow, diamond-shaped sign indicates otherwise. Buying driving licences, rather than obtaining them through legitimate means, is common, so not all road users are qualified and responsible.

Driving is dangerous during winter and not advisable unless drivers have had experience in other northern climes. Drivers must use studded tyres as roads are icy and covered with snow. Car rental is possible in all cities, with **Avis**, **Europcar** and **Hertz** offices at international airports.

Traffic congested roads during rush hour, St Petersburg

Guided Tours and Excursions

Local tourist agencies such as **Patriarshy Dom Tours**, **Baikaler**, **Peter's Walking Tours**, **Intourist Delta Volga**, **Sayan Ring** and **Samara Intour** offer a wide range of tours and day trips around Russia. Many of the agencies can arrange visa support and accommodation too. Tours should generally be booked at least 48 hours in advance.

DIRECTORY

Travelling by Air

S7 Airlines
Tel (495) 777 99 99 or (8800) 200 00 07.
W s7.ru

UTair Aviation
W utair.ru/en

Travelling by Train

General enquiry
Tel 055.

Russian Railways
W rzd.ru
W eng.rzd.ru

RussianRail.com
W russianrail.com

Russiantrains
W russiantrains.com

Travelling by Boat

Infoflot
W infoflot.com

Noble Caledonia
W noble-caledonia.co.uk

Voyages Jules Verne
W vjv.com

Travelling by Car

Avis
W avis.com

Europcar
W europcar.com

Hertz
W hertz.com

Guided Tours and Excursions

Baikaler
Ulitsa Lenina 9, Apartment 11, Irkutsk.
Tel (395) 292 96 86.
W baikaler.com

Intourist Delta Volga
Ulitsa Zhelyabova 33, Astrakhan.
Tel (8512) 73 22 20.
W deltavolgy.narod.ru

Patriarshy Dom Tours
Vspolniy pereulok 6, Moscow.
Tel (495) 795 09 27.
W toursinrussia.com

Peter's Walking Tours
St Petersburg.
Tel (812) 943 12 29.
W peterswalk.com

Samara Intour
Ulitsa Samarskaya 51/53, Samara.
Tel (846) 279 20 40.
W samaraintour.ru

Sayan Ring
Ulitsa Uritskogo 41, Krasnoyarsk.
Tel (391) 245 4646.
W sayanring.com

Travelling in the Cities

Public transport in Russian cities is abundant, efficient and cheap. In major cities, the metro has stops close to many sights, but it can get extremely crowded during peak hours. Buses, trams and trolleybuses are useful for travelling to areas beyond the metro network. Knowledge of the Cyrillic alphabet will help with reading signs on these services, although signs in English can be found in some cities. Taxis are the most flexible, but also the most expensive, way of getting around.

Lavish decoration on the metro system in Moscow

Metro

Efficient, relatively inexpensive and usually safe, metro systems are possibly the best way to get around cities in Russia.

Moscow's 305-km (190-mile) metro network has 185 stations on 11 lines, and is one of the busiest in the world. The circle line, which follows the Garden Ring road, intersects with other metro lines and main railway stations. Intended by Stalin to be "palaces for the people", many metro stations are adorned with statuary, murals and mosaics.

St Petersburg's metro system is one of the deepest in the world due to the city's swampy subsoil. The 110-km (68-mile) network has 65 stations on five lines.

The metro network of Novosibirsk has two lines with 13 stations and a metro bridge over the Ob river, while Nizhny Novgorod's is confined to the west bank where two lines meet beside the main railway terminus.

Volgograd's **Metrotram** has 22 stations on a single line that runs along the Volga river for 17 km (11 miles) and is mostly overground beyond the city centre. Yekaterinburg's metro – the last built in the Soviet Union – has a single line with eight stations decorated with semi-precious stones from the Urals.

Kazan's metro is Russia's most advanced, with automated, driverless trains on a single line with seven stations. All signs are bilingual in Russian and Tatar.

Using the Metro

Metro stations at street level are usually indicated by a large "M" sign and use Cyrillic signage for directions. Bilingual signs in Russian and English are at present limited to Moscow and St Petersburg, but are likely to be rolled out in all cities hosting Olympic or World Cup events.

Most metro systems operate from 6am to midnight, with trains every 2 to 5 minutes. All have flat fares, whether the journey is a couple of stops or the length of the network. Travellers with large items of luggage will be asked to pay a surcharge.

In some metro systems, the stations where it is possible to change between metro lines often have two or more separate names, according to the line they serve. When changing lines, it is, therefore, vital to know the name of the station on the other line. It is then easy to reach the right platform by following the "interchange" or *perekhod* signs indicating this name. Exits are marked выход *(vykhod)*.

It is advisable to buy enough rides for your stay in any city at the outset, to avoid queuing at the *kassa*. In Moscow, visitors can buy a smart card for 1, 2, 5, 10, 20 or 60 rides, or a travel pass that allows unlimited travel for three months. Any number of people can travel on the same card. When the card is swiped at the barrier, the number of journeys left will be reduced by one. The number of remaining journeys will then flash up on the barrier display.

In St Petersburg, travellers pay for rides with a *zheton* (plastic token) or magnetic cards that can be topped up with as many strips as needed. Monthly magnetic cards are valid for 70 metro journeys during a calendar month. Cards valid for 35 journeys for a two-week period can be bought between the 5th and 16th of each month. Note that all cards are valid from the 1st to the 15th of each month.

Buses and Minibuses

In major cities, buses are useful for travelling to outlying suburbs. Bus stops are often shared with trolleybus stops and marked by a white and yellow sign showing the Cyrillic letter "A".

Bus routes are often duplicated by *marshrutki* (minibuses) serving the city centre, outlying suburbs and malls. Minibuses can be

A tram passing through Irkutsk en route to suburban areas

Double-decker boat cruising down the Moskva river

hailed or requested to stop anywhere along the route. Fares are fixed, usually 30 to 100 roubles, and are paid to the driver.

Trolleybuses and Trams

Trolleybuses are an environmentally friendly way of travelling around towns and cities. The stops are marked by a sign with a bus symbol on a white background and the Cyrillic letter "T".

Trams remain the country's most traditional means of transport. Although services have been cut back over the years, the remaining services run frequently, especially in the suburbs, providing links to metro stations and apartment blocks. Stops are marked by a sign labelled "Tp" in Cyrillic with a tram symbol on a white background.

Tickets and Travel cards

Tickets valid for 1, 2, 5, 10, 15, 20 or 60 local journeys can be bought in cities across Russia. The same tickets can be used on all buses, trolleybuses and trams for a single ride without changes. Tickets are bought from kiosks next to bus stops or from the vehicle's driver. In St Petersburg, visitors can also buy a monthly or a half-monthly travel card for all forms of transport.

Taxis

For safety reasons, it is best to travel by official taxis that should at least have a taxi light on the roof and some kind of chequered markings. However, in provincial cities, travellers rely on rides from local moonlighters, which can mean travelling in a private car for a negotiable sum. But this is best avoided if you are travelling alone at night. Visitors speaking little or no Russian should stick to pre-ordered cabs from firms such as **Taxi956** in Moscow or **Six Million** in St Petersburg. Fares must be negotiated in advance. It is easier to ask the hotel or restaurant staff to book a taxi by phone.

Boat Trips

From May to October, some cities offer a variety of superb boat trips, which should not be confused with cruises on Russia's great waterways. The commentary is usually in Russian only.

In Moscow, the boat trips cover a long stretch of the Moskva river, offering a fantastic view of the Kremlin. **Capital Shipping Company** runs such trips from May to October. You can hop on or off at 10 locations, including the Novodevichiy Convent and the Uritskiy Bridge.

In St Petersburg, large covered boats depart from the Anichkov Bridge on Nevskiy prospekt *(see p166)*. A 60-minute trip for about 500 roubles takes in the Moyka and Fontanka rivers, and sometimes the Griboedov Canal. For 100 roubles more, you can get a guided tour in English from **Anglotourismo**.

Suburban Trains and Buses

Prigorodnye poezda (suburban trains) depart from an annexe to mainline stations. Popularly known as *elecktrichki*, they are busy at weekends when Russians head for their *dachas*.

All cities have a network of *prigorodnye marshruty* (suburban buses) and one or more terminals for *mezhdugorodnye avtobusy* (inter-city buses). These buses are useful where trains are too slow or do not allow access to sights you might want to visit.

Cycling

Traffic congested roads make most cities far from ideal for cycling. Cyclists are advised to wear brightly coloured clothing – drivers will generally take care to avoid cyclists if they notice them.

In Moscow, **Kruti-Pedali** offers bikes and equipment for hire costing around 500–600 roubles. In St Petersburg, daily rental costs 600–800 roubles from **Rentbike**, **Skatprokat** or **Velotour**, who also deliver on request. Elsewhere in Russia, adventure-travel companies offer cycling tours of the great outdoors.

DIRECTORY

Metro

Metrotram Volgograd
W volgograd.metro.ru

Moscow
W engl.mosmetro.ru

St Petersburg
W metro.spb.ru

Taxis

Six Million
W 6-000-000.ru

Taxi956
W taxi956.ru

Boat Trips

Anglotourismo
W anglotourismo.com

Capital Shipping Company
W cck-ship.ru

Cycling

Kruti-Pedali
W kruti-pedali.ru

Rentbike
W Rentbike.org

Skatprokat
W skatprokat.ru

Velotour
W velotour-spb.ru

General Index

Page numbers in **bold** refer to main entries.

D

E

Q

R

Acknowledgments

Dorling Kindersley would like to thank the following people whose help and assistance contributed to the preparation of this book.

Main Contributors

Daniel Richardson was born in England. Before joining Rough Guides, he worked as a sailor on the Red Sea and lived in Peru. Since then he has authored or co-authored guidebooks to Moscow, St Petersburg, Hungary, Romania, Budapest, Bulgaria and Egypt. He has also lectured at the Foreign Office and been a volunteer aid worker in Albania. When not abroad, he lives in London.

Matt Willis is a widely published travel writer whose fascination with Russia can be traced back to an early obsession with the country's literary greats. Tentative trips to Moscow soon evolved into a period of residence during which he produced the *DK Eyewitness Top 10 Moscow* guide. Based for the past decade in Russia and Eastern Europe, Matt has also written *DK Eyewitness Top 10 Turkey's Southwest Coast*, and co-authored DK Eyewitness guides to Bulgaria and Central and Eastern Europe.

Additional Photography

Jonathan Buckley; Demetrio Carrasco; Andy Crawford; Steve Gorton; John Heseltine; Nigel Hicks; Dave King; William Reavell; Rough Guides/Jonathan Smith; Jon Spaull; Clive Streeter; James Young; Leandro Zoppe.

Fact Checkers Andrei Bogdanov, Kiki Deere

Proofreader Sandhya Iyer

Indexer Helen Peters

Editorial Consultant Scarlett O'Hara

Design and Editorial

Publishing Director Claire Currie
Publisher Vivien Antwi
List Manager Kate Berens
Senior Editors Michelle Crane, Georgina Palffy
Managing Art Editor Mabel Chan
Designer Tracy Smith
Senior Cartographic Editor Casper Morris
Senior DTP Designer Jason Little
Senior Picture Researcher Ellen Root
Production Controller Rita Sinha

Special Assistance

Dorling Kindersley would like to thank the following for their assistance:

Kiki Deere; Public Relationship Office at Russian Museum; Public Relationship Office at The State Academic Bolshoi Theatre of Russia; Nikita Anikin at State Central Museum of Contemporary History of Russia; Elena Obuhovich & Olga Novoseltseva at The State Hermitage Museum; Lara Bobkova at The State Tretyakov Gallery; Alex Dmitriev at Tsarskoye Selo State Museum.

Photography Permissions

Dorling Kindersley would like to thank all the museums, galleries, churches and other sights that allowed us to photograph at their establishments:

16 Tons Club; Battle of Stalingrad Panorama Museum; Museum of the World Ocean; National Museum of the Repulic of Tatarstan; Perm State Art Gallery; Regional Museum, Vladivostok; Samara Cosmos Museum; Zoological Museum.

Works of art have been reproduced with the kind permission of the following copyright holders:
La Danse © Succession H Matisse/DACS 2013 155crb.

Picture Credits

a = above; b = below/bottom; c = centre; f = far; l = left; r = right; t = top

The publisher would like to thank the following for their kind permission to reproduce their photographs:

Works of art have been reproduced with the permission of the following copyright holders:

Akg-images: 63tl; Russian Picture Service 63cr.
Alamy Images: Sergey Bogomyako 76; The Bridgeman Art Library Ltd. 91tl; Caro 202cl; Joeri De Rocker 34bl; Ekaterinburg 200–201; Bernie Epstein 27tr; Pavel Filatov 246; imagebroker 259tl; ITAR-TASS Photo Agency 21br, 62bl, 116cl, 130–131, 184, 278cr, 312cl; Frans Lemmens 59tc; Yadid Levy 108t; Steve Morgan 23tr; Joanne Moyes 292br; Andrey Nekrasov 300–301; Sergey Nezhinkiy 212; North Wind Picture Archives 41tl; 42clb; Prisma Bildagentur AG 2–3; RIA Novosti 35bl, 55cr, 62cl, 83cr, 91crb, 117br, 167tr, 209crb, 218br, 297tr; Russ Images 178; Peter Russian 148br; Helen Sessions 1c; Alexey Solodov 144; Travel Pictures 18; Universal Images Group/DeAgostini 121cr; Ivan Vdovin 203tl, 205b; ZUMA Press, Inc. 296br.
Archives H. Matisse: 155crb.
Art Clumba: 282b.
AWL Images: Amar Grover 236.
Baklazhan Restaurant: 286bl.
Barashka Restaurant: 281bc.
Barbaresco Restaurant: 285br.
Bier Haus Restaurant: 290br.
Capital Shipping Company: 317tl.
Corbis: 93br; Adoc-photos 106tr; The Art Archive/Alfredo Dagli Orti 41cb; Morton Beebe 37cl; Bettmann 43bc, 45cb, 45bl, 46tc; Alan Carey 25tr; Dean Conger 61tl; Fridmar Damm 149tl; Design Pics/Keith Levit 13tr; DPA/Agentur Voller Ernst/Evgeny Khaldei 45tl; The Gallery Collection 42tc; Global Look/Serguei Fomine 226bl; Jon Hicks 133tr, 133br, 260–261; Hulton-Deutsch Collection 83br, 176cr; ITAR-TASS Photo/Mudrats

Alexander 29t;/Korotayev Artyom 12bl,/Katayev Igor 298cl,/ Shemetov Maxim 35crb,/ Shamukov Ruslan 4br, 22bc, 28tr,/ Krasilnikov Stanislav 28br,/ Rodionov Vladimir 46br,/ Belinsky Yuri 36tr; JAI/Walter Bibikow 94, 158/Jane Sweeney 112,/ Katie Garrod 173cr; Braham Nowitz 89t; Diego Lezama Orezzoli 54cl; Steve Raymer 296cl; Robert Harding World Imagery/ Graham Lawrence 68c; Sygma/ Antoine Gyori 34cra; Peter Turnley 46clb.

Dom Berga Restaurant: 289br.

Dreamstime.com: 2bears 51cr; Alex_us 230–231; Alexsol 26tr; Alexvu 57tc; Andytv 244bl; Atovot 24c; Catthesun 202br, 242tl; Count 180bl; Definedtalent 52; Demian1975 211tl; Doroo 88tl; Ir717 24cl; Jackf 36cl; Larshinksten 254–255; Lenikovaleva 220; Limp 20br; Loonara 276cl; Lvenok1968 177br; Markovskiy 15tr, 32bl, 208b; Mgrushin 119tr; Mil 21tl; Nebesnaya 56cl; Nobilior 35tl; Ortodoxfoto 314br; Photoniles 151cr; Pingvin121674 51br; Pokec 25bc; Ppl5806 245cl; Psv 102; Rogkoff 250tl; Roumyantseva 315c; Rudolft 55tc; Sborisov 10cl; Shap1964 258br; Silentiger 27br; Sportfoto 24cra; Stevart 46bl; Symphoni 252bl; Uralla 24tr; Valerii 24cb, 25cla; Vas177 26bc; Vitalyfoto 20t; Voltan1 146cl, 180t; Vovez 170, 172cl; Wrangel 251br; Yuryz 314cl; Zanskar 277br.

Dvor Podznoeva Restaurant: 263tl.

Fotolia: Alz 25cra; M. Bolot 203br; Evgeniy_golovko 243c; Gl0ck 214b; Donkey IA 13bl; Iva 163tl; JackF 14br; Mikhail Markovskiy 202tr; Maxximmm 44bl; Neirfy 111c; Nikolny 259br; OlegDoroshin 132cl; Pavel Parmenov 40bc; RedTC 258crb; Maksim Shebeko 277c; WithGod 24crb.

Getty Images: 26–27c, 45crb; AFP/Gerard Julien 31tc,/ Stringer 47tr, 69br, 245crb; Age fotostock/Gonzalo Azumendi 58c; AWL Images/Gavin Hellier 215tr,/ Ken Scicluna 302c; The Bridgeman Art Library/Boris Mihajlovic Kustodiev 44tl,/ Carl Faberge 62tr,/ Russian School 44cb,/ Vladimir Egorovic Makovsky 43tr; Danita Delimont 5tr, 249t; Epsilon 47bc; Hemis.fr/Perousse Bruno 48–49; Hulton Archive 8–9,/ Apic 31br,/ Imagno 28cla,/ Stringer 30tr, 41bc, 42bl, 175crb, 278tr,/ Topical Press Agency 139bc; The Image Bank/Frans Lemmens 55br,/ Bruno Morandi 312br; Lonely Planet Images/Jane Sweeney 26clb,/ Jonathan Smith 80tr,/ Richard I'Anson 50bl, 64; Mordolff 12tr; Moviepix/Keith Hamshere 30bl; New York Public Library/Wu Swee Ong 251crb; Photo Researchers 235br; Popperfoto/Bob Thomas 40clb; Robert Harding World Imagery/Gavin Hellier 217tl; Kevin Schafer 25cb; Slow Images 19b; Stone/Paul Harris 247b; Stringer/Oleg Nikishin 90cla; Time & Life Pictures 39bc,/ Mansell 38; Universal Images Group 63crb.

Gosti Restaurant: 284tl.

Lux Express Group: 313tr.

Maharaja Restaurant: 280bl.

Masterfile: Robert Harding Images 74tl.

Nevsky Hotel: 264bl.

Noor Restaurant: 281tr.

Park Inn by Radisson Astrakhan: 262br.

Park Inn by Radisson Ekaterinburg: 271tr.

Photoshot: DeAgostini/UIG 134, Shamukov Ruslan 11br.

Radisson Hotel: 263br.

Roses & Filippov Hotels: 264tr.

The State Academic Bolshoi Theatre of Russia: Damir Yusupov 22t, 50cl, 82br, 83tc, 83bc, 120cl.

State Central Museum of Contemporary History of Russia: 85b.

The State Hermitage Museum, St Petersburg: 5cl, 154cl, 154bl, 155cr, 156tr, 156bc, 157tl, 157tr, 157cra, 157bl, 157br.

© 2013, State Russian Museum, St Petersburg: 164cl, 164bc, 165tl, 165cra, 165cr, 165br.

The State Tretyakov Gallery: 98cl, 98clb, 98bc, 99tl, 99cr, 99br.

SuperStock: age fotostock 14cl, 204, imagebroker.net 24cla, NaturePL 203tr.

Tourist Information Centre of Perm Region: 235cl.

Tsar Restaurant: 286tr.

Tsarskoye Selo State Museum: 189tl, 189crb.

Tulip Inn Rosa Khutor Hotel: 272tr.

Uncle Pasha: 265tr.

Ural Expeditions & Tours: 298br, 299tr.

Zokol Hostel: 273br.

Front Endpaper

Alamy Images: Pavel Filatov fbr, Sergey Nezhinkiy cl; **AWL Images**: Amar Grover bl; **Dreamstime**.com: Lenikovaleva br; **Getty Images**: Lonely Planet Images/ Richard I'Anson bc; **Photoshot**: DeAgostini/UIG tc; **SuperStock**: age fotostock tr.

Jacket Images

Front: Corbis: Abraham Nowitz bl; **SuperStock**: Kaehler, Wolfgang c.

Spine

SuperStock: Kaehler, Wolfgang t.

Phrase Book

In this guide the Russian language has been transliterated into Roman script following a consistent system used by the US Board on Geographic Names. All street and place names, and the names of most people, are transliterated according to this system. For some names, where a well-known English form exists, this has been used – hence, Leo (not Lev) Tolstoy. In particular, the names of Russian rulers, such as Peter the Great, are given in their anglicized forms. Throughout the book, transliterated names can be taken as an accurate guide to pronunciation. The Phrase Book also gives a phonetic guide to the pronunciation of words and phrases used in everyday situations, such as when eating out or shopping.

Guidelines for Pronunciation

The Cyrillic alphabet has 33 letters, of which only five (а, к, м, о, т) correspond exactly to their counterparts in English. Russian has two pronunciations (hard and soft) of each of its vowels, and several consonants without an equivalent.

The right-hand column of the alphabet, below, demonstrates how Cyrillic letters are pronounced by comparing them to sounds in English words. However, some letters vary in how they are pronounced according to their position in a word. Important exceptions are also noted below.

On the following pages, the English is given in the left-hand column, with the Russian and its transliteration in the middle column. The right-hand column provides a literal system of pronunciation and indicates the stressed syllable in bold. The exception is in the Menu Decoder section, where the Russian is given in the left-hand column and the English translation in the right-hand column, for ease of use. Because of the existence of genders in Russian, in a few cases both masculine and feminine forms of a phrase are given.

The Cyrillic Alphabet

А а	*a*	**a***limony*
Б б	*b*	**b***ed*
В в	*v*	**v***et*
Г г	*g*	**g***et (see note 1)*
Д д	*d*	**d***ebt*
Е е	*e*	**ye***t (see note 2)*
Ё ё	*e*	**yo***nder*
Ж ж	*zh*	*lei***s***ure (but a little harder)*
З з	*z*	**z***ither*
И и	*i*	*s***ee**
Й й	*y*	*bo***y** *(see note 3)*
К к	*k*	**k***ing*
Л л	*l*	**l***oot*
М м	*m*	**m***atch*
Н н	*n*	**n***ever*
О о	*o*	*r***o***b (see note 4)*
П п	*p*	**p***ea*
Р р	*r*	**r***at (rolling, as in Italian)*
С с	*s*	**s***top*
Т т	*t*	**t***offee*
У у	*u*	*b***oo***t*
Ф ф	*f*	**f***ellow*
Х х	*kh*	**kh** *(like loch)*
Ц ц	*ts*	*le***ts**
Ч ч	*ch*	**ch***air*
Ш ш	*sh*	**sh***ove*
Щ щ	*shch*	*fre***sh sh***eet (as above but with a slight roll)*
ъ		*hard sign (no sound, but see note 5)*
Ы ы	*y*	*l***i***d*
ь		*soft sign (no sound, but see note 5)*
Э э	*e*	**e***gg*
Ю ю	*yu*	**you***th*
Я я	*ya*	**ya***k*

Notes

1) Г Pronounced as *v* in endings -ого and -его.
2) Е Always pronounced *ye* at the beginning of a word, but in the middle of a word sometimes less distinctly (more like *e*).
3) Й This letter has no distinct sound of its own. It usually lengthens the preceeding vowel.
4) О When not stressed it is pronounced like *a* in **a**cross.
5) ъ, ь The hard sign (ъ) is rare and indicates a very brief pause before the next letter. The soft sign (ь, marked in the pronunciation guide as ') softens the preceeding consonant and adds a slight *y* sound: for instance, *n'* would sound like *ny* in 'ca**ny**on'.

In an Emergency

Help!	Помогите! *Pomogite!*	*pamag***ee***tye!*
Stop!	Стоп! *Stop!*	*Stop!*
Leave me alone!	Оставьте меня в покое! *Ostavte menya v pokoe!*	*ast***a***vt'ye myen***ya** *v pak***o***ye!*
Call a doctor!	Позовите врача! *Pozovite vracha!*	*pazav***ee***tye vrach***a***!*
Call an ambulance!	Вызовите скорую помощь! *Vyzovite skoruyu pomoshch!*	*vizav***ee***tye sk***o***ru-yu p***o***mash'!*
Fire!	Пожар! *Pozhar!*	*pazh***a***r!*
Call the fire brigade!	Вызовите пожарных! *Vyzovite pozharnykh!*	*vizav***ee***tye pazh***a***rnikh!*
Police!	Милиция! *Militsiya!*	*meel***ee***tseeya!*
Where is the nearest…	Где ближайший… *Gde blizhayshiy…*	*gdye bleezh***a***ysheey…*
…telephone?	…телефон? *…telefon?*	*…tyelyef***o***n?*
…hospital?	…больница? *…bolnitsa?*	*…bal'n***ee***tsa?*
…police station?	…отделение милиции? *…otdelenie militsii?*	*…atdyel***ye***nye meel***ee***tsee-ee?*

Communication Essentials

Yes	Да *Da*	*da*
No	Нет *Net*	*nyet*
Please	Пожалуйста *Pozhaluysta*	*pazh***a***lsta*
Thank you	Спасибо *Spasibo*	*spas***ee***ba*
You are welcome	Пожалуйста *Pozhaluysta*	*pazh***a***lsta*
Excuse me	Извините *Izvinite*	*eezveen***ee***t-ye*
Hello	Здравствуйте *Zdravstvuyte*	*zdr***a***stvooyt-ye*
Goodbye	До свидания *Do svidaniya*	*da sveed***a***nya*
Good morning	Доброе утро *Dobroe utro*	*d***o***bra-ye* **oo***tra*
Good afternoon/day	Добрый день *Dobryy den*	*d***o***bree dyen'*
Good evening	Добрый вечер *Dobryy vecher*	*d***o***bree v***ye***chyer*
Good night	Спокойной ночи *Spokoynoy nochi*	*spak***o***ynay n***o***chee*
Morning	утро *utro*	**oo***tra*
Afternoon	день *den*	*dyen'*
Evening	вечер *vecher*	*v***ye***chyer*
Yesterday	вчера *vchera*	*fchyer***a**
Today	сегодня *sevodnya*	*syev***o***dnya*
Tomorrow	завтра *zavtra*	*z***a***ftra*
Here	здесь *zdes*	*zdyes'*
There	там *tam*	*tam*

What?	Что? *Chto?*	*shto?*
Where?	Где? *Gde?*	*gdye?*
Why?	Почему? *Pochemu?*	*pachyem**oo**?*
When?	Когда? *Kogda?*	*kagd**a**?*
Now	сейчас *seychas*	*seych**a**s*
Later	позже *pozzhe*	*p**o**zhe*
Can I…?	можно? *mozhno?*	*m**o**zhna…?*
It is possible/allowed	можно *mozhno*	*m**o**zhna*
It is not possible/allowed	нельзя *nelzya*	*nyelz**ya***

Useful Phrases

How are you?	Как дела? *Kak dela?*	*kak dyel**a**?*
Very well, thank you	Хорошо, спасибо *Khorosho, spasibo*	*kharash**o**, spas**ee**ba*
Pleased to meet you	Очень приятно *Ochen priyatno*	***o**chen' pree-**ya**tna*
How do I get to…?	Как добраться до…? *Kak dobratsya do…?*	*kak dabr**a**t'sya da…?*
Would you tell me when we get to…?	Скажите, пожалуйста, коеда мы приедем в…? *Skazhite, pozhaluysta, kogda my priedem v…?*	*skazh**ee**t-ye, pazh**a**lsta, kagd**a** mi pree-**ye**dyem v…?*
Is it very far?	Это далеко? *Eto daleko?*	***e**ta dalyek**o**?*
Do you speak English?	Вы говорите по-английски? *Vy govorite po-angliyski?*	*vi gavar**ee**t-ye po-angleesk**ee**?*
I don't understand	Я не понимаю *Ya ne ponimayu*	*ya nye paneem**a**-yoo*
Could you speak more slowly?	Говорите медленнее *Govorite medlennee*	*gavar**ee**t-ye m**ye**dlyenye-ye*
Could you say it again please?	Повторите, пожалуйста *Povtorite, pozhaluysta*	*paftar**ee**t-ye, pazh**a**lsta*
I am lost	Я заблудился (заблудилась) *Ya zabludilsya (zabludilas)*	*ya zablood**ee**lsya (zablood**ee**las')*
How do you say… in Russian?	Как по русски...?	*kak pa r**oo**skee…?*

Useful Words

big	большой *bolshoy*	*bal'sh**oy***
small	маленький *malenkiy*	*m**a**lyen'kee*
hot (water, food)	горячий *goryachiy*	*gar**ya**chee*
hot (weather)	жарко *zharko*	*zh**a**rka*
cold	холодный *kholodnyy*	*khal**o**dnee*
good	хорошо *khorosho*	*kharash**o***
bad	плохо *plokho*	*pl**o**kha*
okay/fine	нормально *normalno*	*narm**a**l'na*
near	близко *blizko*	*bl**ee**zka*
far	далеко *daleko*	*dalyek**o***
up	наверху *naverkhu*	*navyerkh**oo***
down	внизу *vnizu*	*fneez**oo***

early	рано *rano*	*r**a**na*
late	поздно *pozdno*	*p**o**zdna*
vacant (unoccupied)	свободно *svobodno*	*svab**o**dna*
free (no charge)	бесплатно *besplatno*	*byespl**a**tna*
cashier/ticket office	касса *kassa*	*k**a**sa*
avenue	проспект *prospekt*	*prasp**ye**kt*
bridge	мост *most*	*most*
embankment	набережная *naberezhnaya*	*n**a**byeryezhnaya*
highway/motorway	шоссе *shosse*	*shass**e***
lane/passage	переулок *pereulok*	*pyerye**oo**lak*
square	площадь *ploshchad*	*pl**o**shat'*
street	улица *ulitsa*	***oo**leetsa*
flat/apartment	квартира *kvartira*	*kvart**ee**ra*
floor	этаж *etazh*	*et**a**sh*
house/block	дом *dom*	*dom*
entrance	вход *vkhod*	*fkhot*
exit	выход *vykhod*	*v**i**khot*
river	река *reka*	*ryek**a***
summer country house	дача *dacha*	*d**a**cha*
swimming pool	бассейн *basseyn*	*basy**ey**n*
town	город *gorod*	*g**o**rat*
toilet	туалет *tualet*	*tooal**yet***

Making a Telephone Call

Can I call abroad from here?	Можно отсюда позвонить за границу? *Mozhno ostyuda pozvonit za granitsu?*	*mozhn**a** ats**yoo**da pazvan**ee**t' za gran**ee**tsoo?*
I would like to speak to…	Позовите, пожалуйста… *Pozovite, pozhaluysta*	*pazav**ee**t-ye, pazh**a**lsta…*
Could you leave him/her a message?	Вы можете передать ему/ей? *By mozhete peredat emy/ey?*	*vi m**o**zhet-ye pyeryed**a**t' yem**oo**/yay?*
My number is…	Мой номер… *Moy nomer…*	*moy n**o**myer…*
I'll ring back later	Я позвоню позже *Ya pozvonyu pozzhe*	*ya pazvany**oo** p**o**zhe*

Sightseeing

castle	замок *zamok*	*z**a**mak*
cathedral	собор *sobor*	*sab**o**r*
church	церковь *tserkov*	*ts**e**rkaf'*
circus	цирк *tsirk*	*tseerk*
closed for cleaning "cleaning day"	санитарный день *sanitarnyy den*	*saneet**a**rnee dyen'*
undergoing restoration	ремонт *remont*	*rem**o**nt*
exhibition	выставка *vystavka*	*v**i**stafka*
fortress	крепость *krepost*	*kr**ye**post'*
gallery	галерея *galereya*	*galer**ye**ya*
garden	сад *sad*	*sad*

island	остров *ostrov*	***o**straf*
kremlin/fortified stronghold	Кремль *kreml*	*kryeml'*
library	бибдиотека *biblioteka*	*beeblee-at**ye**ka*
monument	памятник *pamyatnik*	*p**a**myatneek*
mosque	мечеть *mechet*	*myech**ye**t'*
museum	музей *muzey*	*moozy**ey***
palace	дворец *dvorets*	*dvar**ye**ts*
park	парк *park*	*park*
parliament	дума *duma*	*d**oo**ma*
synagogue	синагога *sinagoga*	*seenag**o**ga*
tourist information	пункт информации для туристов *punkt informatsii dlya turistov*	*poonkt eenfarm**a**tsee-ee dlya toor**ee**staf*
zoo	зоопарк *zoopark*	*zapa**r**k*

Shopping

open	открыто *otkryto*	*atkri**t**a*
closed	закрыто *zakryto*	*zakri**t**a*
How much does this cost?	Сколько зто стоит? *Skolko eto stoit?*	*sk**o**l'ka **e**ta st**o**eet?*
I would like to buy…	Я хотел (хотола) бы купить**…** *Ya khotel (khotela) by kupit…*	*ya khat**ye**l (khat**ye**la) bi koop**ee**t'…*
Do you have…?	У вас есть...? *U vas yest…?*	*oo vas yest'…?*
Do you take credit cards?	Кредитные карточки вы принимаете? *Kreditnye kartochki vy prinimaete?*	*kryed**ee**tnye k**a**rtachkee vy preeneem**a**yetye?*
What time do you open/close?	Во сколько вы открываетесь/ закрываетесь? *Vo skolko vy otkryvaetes/ zakryvaetes?*	*Va sk**o**l'ka vy atkriv**a**yetyes'/ zakriv**a**yetyes'?*
This one	этот *etot*	***e**tat*
expensive	дорого *dorogo*	*d**o**raga*
cheap	дёшево *deshevo*	*dyosh**ye**va*
size	размер *razmer*	*razm**ye**r*
white	белый *belyy*	*b**ye**lee*
black	чёрный *chernyy*	*ch**yo**rnee*
red	красный *krasnyy*	*kr**a**snee*
yellow	жёлтый *zheltyy*	*zh**o**ltee*
green	зелёный *zelenyy*	*zyel**yo**nee*
dark blue	синий *siniy*	*s**ee**nee*
light blue	голубой *goluboy*	*galoob**oy***
brown	коричневый *korichnevyy*	*kar**ee**chnyevee*

Types of Shop

bakery	булочная *bulochnaya*	*b**oo**lachna-ya*
bookshop	книжный магазин *knizhnyy magazin*	*kn**ee**zhnee magaz**ee**n*
butcher	мясной магазин *myasnoy magazin*	*myasn**oy** magaz**ee**n*
camera shop	фото-товары *foto-tovary*	*f**o**to-tav**a**ri*
chemist	аптека *apteka*	*apt**ye**ka*
delicatessen	гастроном *gastronom*	*gastran**o**m*
department store	универмаг *univermag*	*ooneevyerm**a**g*
florist	цветы *tsvety*	*tsvyet**i***
grocer	бакалея *bakaleya*	*bakal**ye**-ya*
hairdresser	парикмахерская *parikmakherskaya*	*pareekm**a**khyerskaya*
market	рынок *rynok*	***r**inak*
newspaper stand	газетный киоск *gazetniy kiosk*	*gaz**ye**tnee kee-**o**sk*
post office	почта *pochta*	*p**o**chta*
record shop	грампластинки *gramplastinki*	*gramplast**ee**nkee*
shoe shop	обувь *obuv*	***o**boof'*
travel agent	бюро путешествий *byuro puteshestviy*	*byoor**o** pootyesh**e**stvee*
bank	банк *bank*	*bank*

Staying in a Hotel

Do you have a vacant room?	У вас есть свободный номер? *U vas yest svobodnyy nomer?*	*oo vas yest' svab**o**dnee n**o**myer?*
double room with double bed	номер с двуспальной кроватью *nomer s dvuspalnoy krovatyu*	*n**o**myer s dvoosp**a**l'noy krav**a**t'-yoo*
twin room	двухместный номер *dvukhmestnyy nomer*	*dvookhm**ye**stnee n**o**myer*
single room	одноместный номер *odnomestnyy nomer*	*adnam**ye**stnee n**o**myer*
bath	ванная *vannaya*	*v**a**na-ya*
shower	душ *dush*	*doosh*
porter	носильщнк *nosilshchik*	*nas**ee**l'sheek*
key	ключ *klyuch*	*klyooch*

Eating Out

A table for two, please	Стол на двоих, пожалуйста	*stol na dva-**ee**kh, pazh**a**lsta*
I would like to book a table	Я хочу заказать стол *Ya khochu zakazat stol*	*ya khach**oo** zakaz**at'** stol*
The bill, please	Счёт, пожалуйста *Schet, pozhaluysta*	*shyot, pazh**a**lsta*
I am a vegetarian	Я вегетерианец (вегетерианка) *Ya vegeterianets (vegeterianka)*	*ya vyegyetaree**a**nyets (vyegyetaree**a**nka)*
breakfast	завтрак *zavtrak*	*z**a**ftrak*
lunch	обед *obed*	*ab**ye**t*
dinner	ужин *uzhin*	***oo**zheen*
waiter!	официант! *ofitsiant!*	*afeetsee-**a**nt!*
waitress!	официантка! *ofitsiantka!*	*afeetsee-**a**ntka!*
dish of the day	фирменное блюдо *firmennoe blyudo*	*f**ee**rmenoye bly**oo**da*
appetizers/starters	закуски *zakuski*	*zak**oo**skee*
main course	второе блюдо *vtoroe blyudo*	*ftar**o**ye bly**oo**da*
meat and poultry dishes	мясные блюда *myasnye blyuda*	*m**ya**sniye bly**oo**da*
fish and seafood dishes	рыбные блюда *rybnye blyuda*	*ribniye blyooda*
vegetable dishes	овощные блюда *ovoshchnye blyuda*	*avashshn**i**ye bly**oo**da*
dessert	десерт	*dyes**ye**rt*

drinks	напитки *desert*	*nap**ee**tkee*
vegetables	овощи *napitki*	***o**vashshee*
bread	хлеб *ovoshchi*	*khlyeb*
wine list	карта вин *khleb*	*k**a**rta veen*
rare (steak)	недожаренный *karta vin*	*nyedazh**a**renee*
well done (steak)	прожаренный *nedozharennyy*	*prozh**a**renee*
glass	стакан *prozharennyy*	*stak**a**n*
bottle	бутылка *stakan*	*boot**i**lka*
knife	нож *butylka*	*nosh*
fork	вилка *nozh*	*v**ee**lka*
spoon	ложка *vilka*	*l**o**shka*
plate	тарелка *lozhka*	*tar**ye**lka*
napkin	салфетка *tarelka*	*salf**ye**tka*
salt	соль *salfetka*	*sol*
pepper	перец *sol*	*p**ye**ryets*
butter/oil	масло *perets*	*m**a**sla*
sugar	сахар *maslo*	*s**a**khar*

Menu Decoder

абрикос *abrikos*	*abreek**o**s*	*apricot*
апельсин *apelsin*	*apyel's**ee**n*	*orange*
апельсиновый сок *apelsinovyy sok*	*apyels**ee**navee sok*	*orange juice*
арбуз *arbuz*	*arb**oo**z*	*water melon*
белое вино *beloe vino*	*b**ye**laye veen**o***	*white wine*
бифштекс *bifshteks*	*beefsht**ye**ks*	*steak*
блины *bliny*	*bleen**i***	*pancakes*
борщ *borshch*	*borshsh*	*borsch (beetroot soup)*
варенье *varene*	*var**ye**n'ye*	*Russian syrup-jam*
варёный *varenyy*	*var**yo**nee*	*boiled*
ветчина *vetchina*	*vyetcheen**a***	*ham*
вода *voda*	*vad**a***	*water*
говядина *govyadina*	*gav**ya**deena*	*beef*
грибы *griby*	*greeb**i***	*mushrooms*
груша *grusha*	*gr**oo**sha*	*pear*
гусь *gus*	*goos*	*goose*
джем *dzhem*	*dzhem*	*jam*
жареный *zharenyy*	*zh**a**ryenee*	*roasted/grilled/fried*
икра *ikra*	*eekr**a***	*black caviar*
икра красная/кета *ikra krasna-ya/keta*	*eekra krasna-ya/ k**ye**ta*	*red caviar*
капуста *kapusta*	*kap**oo**sta*	*cabbage*
картофель *kartofel*	*kart**o**fyel'*	*potato*
квас *kvas*	*kvas*	*kvas (sweet, mildly alcoholic drink)*
клубника *klubnika*	*kloobn**ee**ka*	*strawberries*
колбаса *kolbasa*	*kalbas**a***	*salami sausage*
кофе *kofe*	*k**o**fye*	*coffee*
красное вино *krasnoe vino*	*kr**a**snoye veen**o***	*red wine*
креветки *krevetki*	*kryev**ye**tkee*	*prawns*
курица *kuritsa*	*k**oo**reetsa*	*chicken*
лук *luk*	*look*	*onion*
малина *malina*	*mal**ee**na*	*raspberries*
минеральная вода *mineralnaya voda*	*miner**a**l'naya vad**a***	*mineral water*
мороженое *morozhenoe*	*marozhena-ye*	*ice-cream*
мясо *myaso*	*m**ya**sa*	*meat*
огурец *ogurets*	*agoor**ye**ts*	*cucumber*
осетрина *osetrina*	*asyetr**ee**na*	*sturgeon*
пельмени *pelmeni*	*pyel'm**ye**nee*	*meat or fish dumplings*
персик *persik*	*p**ye**rseek*	*peach*
печенье *pechene*	*pyech**ye**n'ye*	*biscuit*
печёнка *pechenka*	*pyech**yo**nka*	*liver*
печёный *pechenyy*	*pyech**yo**nee*	*baked*
пиво *pivo*	*p**ee**va*	*beer*
пирог *pirog*	*peer**o**k*	*pie*
пирожки *pirozhki*	*peerashk**ee***	*small parcels with savoury fillings*
помидор *pomidor*	*pameed**o**r*	*tomato*
продукты моря *produkty morya*	*prad**oo**kti mor**ya***	*seafood*
рыба *ryba*	*r**i**ba*	*fish*
салат *salat*	*sal**a**t*	*salad*
свинина *svinina*	*sveen**ee**na*	*pork*
сельдь *seld*	*sye'ld'*	*herring*
сосиски *sosiski*	*sas**ee**skee*	*sausages*
сыр *syr*	*sir*	*cheese*
сырой *syroy*	*sir**oy***	*raw*
утка *utka*	***oo**tka*	*duck*
фасоль *fasol*	*fas**o**l'*	*beans*
форель *forel*	*far**ye**l'*	*trout*
чай *chay*	*chai*	*tea*
чеснок *chesnok*	*chyesn**o**k*	*garlic*
шашлык *shashlyk*	*shashl**i**k*	*kebab*
яйцо *yaytso*	*yayts**o***	*egg*
слива *sliva*	*sl**ee**va*	*plum*
фрукты *frukty*	*fr**oo**kti*	*fruit*
яблоко *yabloko*	***ya**blaka*	*apple*

Transport

north	север *sever*	*s**ye**ver*
south	юг *yug*	*yook*
east	восток *vostok*	*vast**o**k*
west	запад *zapad*	***za**pat*
airport	аэропорт *aeroport*	*aerap**o**rt*
aeroplane	самолёт *samolet*	*samal**yot***

traffic police	ГАИ *GAI*	*Ga-ee*
bus	автобус *avtobus*	*aft**o**boos*
bus station	автобусная станция *avtobusnaya stantsiya*	*aft**o**boosna-ya st**a**ntsee-ya*
bus stop	остановка автобса *ostanovka avtobusa*	*astan**o**fka aft**o**boosa*
car	мащина *mashina*	*mash**ee**na*
flight	рейс *reys*	*ryeys*
metro (station)	(станция) метро *(stantsiya) metro*	*(st**a**ntsee-ya) myetr**o***
no entry	нет входа *net vkhoda*	*nyet fkh**o**da*
no exit	нет выхода *net vykhoda*	*nyet v**i**khada*
parking	автостоянка *avtostoyanka*	*aftosto**ya**nka*
petrol	бензин *benzin*	*byenz**ee**n*
railway	железная дорога *zheleznaya doroga*	*zhel**ye**zna-ya dar**o**ga*
railway station	вокзал *vokzal*	*vagz**a**l*
return ticket	обратный билет *obratniy bilet*	*obr**a**tnee beel**ye**t*
seat	место *mesto*	*m**ye**sta*
suburban train	пригородный поезд *prigorodniy poezd*	*pr**ee**garadnee p**o**-yezd*
straight on	прямо *pryamo*	*pr**ya**ma*
taxi	такси *taksi*	*taks**ee***
ticket	билет *bilet*	*beel**ye**t*
token (for a single metro journey)	жетон *zheton*	*zhet**o**n*
to the left	налево *nalevo*	*nal**ye**va*
to the right	направо *napravo*	*napr**a**va*
train	поезд *poezd*	*p**o**-yezd*
tram	трамвай *tramvay*	*tramv**ay***
trolleybus	троллейбус *trolleybus*	*tral**ey**boos*

Numbers

1	один/одна/одно *odin/odna/odno*	*ad**ee**n/adn**a**/adn**o***
2	два/две *dva/dve*	*dva/dvye*
3	три *tri*	*tree*
4	четыре *chetyre*	*chyet**ir**-ye*
5	пятъ *pyat*	*pyat'*
6	шестъ *shest*	*shest'*
7	семь *sem*	*syem'*
8	восемъ *vosem*	*v**o**syem'*
9	девятъ *devyat*	*d**ye**vyat'*
10	десятъ *desyat*	*d**ye**syat'*
11	одиннадцатъ *odinnadtsat*	*ad**ee**natsat'*
12	двенадцатъ *dvenadtsat*	*dvyen**a**tsat'*
13	тринадцатъ *trinadtsat*	*treen**a**tsat'*
14	четырнадцатъ *chetyrnadtsat*	*chyet**i**rnatsat'*
15	пятнадцатъ *pyatnadtsat*	*pyatn**a**tsat'*
16	щестнадцатъ *shestnadtsat*	*shestn**a**tsat'*
17	семнадцатъ *semnadtsat*	*syemn**a**tsat'*
18	восемнадцатъ *vosemnadtsat*	*vasyemn**a**tsat'*
19	девятнадцатъ *devyatnadtsat*	*dyevyatn**a**tsat'*
20	двадцатъ *dvadtsat*	*dv**a**tsat'*
21	двадцатъ один *dvadtsat odin*	*dv**a**tsat' ad**ee**n*
22	двадцатъ два *dvadtsat dva*	*dv**a**tsat' dva*
23	двадцатъ три *dvadtsat tri*	*dv**a**tsat' tree*
24	двадцатъ четыре *dvadtsat chetyre*	*dv**a**tsat' chyet**ir**-ye*
25	двадцатъ пятъ *dvadtsat pyat*	*dv**a**tsat' pyat'*
30	тридцатъ *tridtsat*	*tr**ee**tsat'*
40	сорок *sorok*	*s**o**rak*
50	пятъдесятъ *pyatdesyat*	*pyadyes**ya**t'*
60	щестъдесят *shestdesyat*	*shes' dyes**ya**t*
70	семъдесят *semdesyat*	*s**ye**m'dyesyat*
80	восемъдесятъ *vosemdesyat*	*v**o**syem'dyesyat*
90	девяносто *devyanosto*	*dyevyan**o**sta*
100	сто *sto*	*sto*
200	двести *dvesti*	*dv**ye**stee*
300	триста *trista*	*treest**a***
400	четыреста *chetyresta*	*chyet**i**ryesta*
500	пятьсот *pyatsot*	*pyat's**o**t*
1,000	тысяча *tysyacha*	*t**i**syacha*
2,000	две тысяч *dve tysyach*	*dvye t**i**syach*
5,000	пятъ тысяч *pyat tysyach*	*pyat' t**i**syach*
1,000,000	миллион *million*	*meelee-**o**n*

Time and Days

one minute	одна минута *odna minuta*	*adn**a** meen**oo**ta*
one hour	час *chas*	*chas*
half an hour	полчаса *polchasa*	*polchas**a***
day	денъ *den*	*dyen'*
week	неделя *nedelya*	*nyed**ye**l-ya*
Monday	понеделъник *ponedelnik*	*panyed**ye**l'neek*
Tuesday	вторник *vtornik*	*ft**o**rneek*
Wednesday	среда *sreda*	*sryed**a***
Thursday	четверг *chetverg*	*chyetv**ye**rk*
Friday	пятница *pyatnitsa*	*p**ya**tneetsa*
Saturday	суббота *subbota*	*soob**o**ta*
Sunday	воскресенъе *voskresene*	*vaskryes**ye**n'ye*

Moscow Metro Map

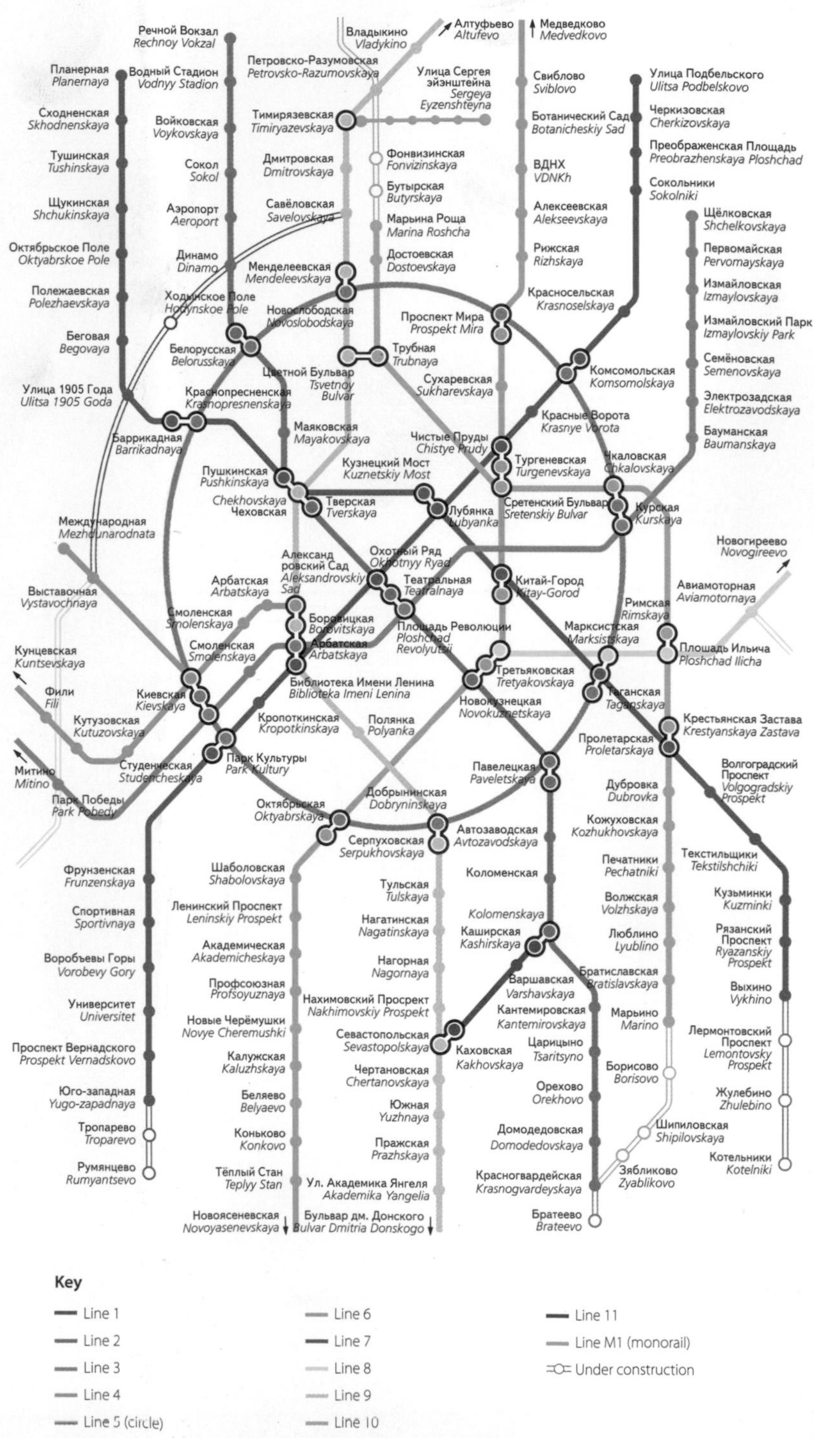

Алтуфьево
Altufevo
Медведково
Medvedkovo
Владыкино
Vladykino
Речной Вокзал
Rechnoy Vokzal
Петровско-Разумовская
Petrovsko-Razumovskaya
Улица Сергея Эйзенштейна
Sergeya Eyzenshteyna
Свиблово
Sviblovo
Улица Подбельского
Ulitsa Podbelskovo
Планерная
Planernaya
Водный Стадион
Vodnyy Stadion
Тимирязевская
Timiryazevskaya
Ботанический Сад
Botanicheskiy Sad
Черкизовская
Cherkizovskaya
Сходненская
Skhodnenskaya
Войковская
Voykovskaya
Преображенская Площадь
Preobrazhenskaya Ploshchad
Фонвизинская
Fonvizinskaya
Тушинская
Tushinskaya
Сокол
Sokol
Дмитровская
Dmitrovskaya
ВДНХ
VDNKh
Сокольники
Sokolniki
Бутырская
Butyrskaya
Щукинская
Shchukinskaya
Аэропорт
Aeroport
Савёловская
Savelovskaya
Марьина Роща
Marina Roshcha
Алексеевская
Alekseevskaya
Щёлковская
Shchelkovskaya
Октябрьское Поле
Oktyabrskoe Pole
Динамо
Dinamo
Менделеевская
Mendeleevskaya
Достоевская
Dostoevskaya
Рижская
Rizhskaya
Первомайская
Pervomayskaya
Полежаевская
Polezhaevskaya
Ходынское Поле
Hodynskoe Pole
Новослободская
Novoslobodskaya
Красносельская
Krasnoselskaya
Измайловская
Izmaylovskaya
Проспект Мира
Prospekt Mira
Измайловский Парк
Izmaylovskiy Park
Беговая
Begovaya
Белорусская
Belorusskaya
Трубная
Trubnaya
Семёновская
Semenovskaya
Цветной Бульвар
Tsvetnoy Bulvar
Сухаревская
Sukharevskaya
Комсомольская
Komsomolskaya
Улица 1905 Года
Ulitsa 1905 Goda
Краснопресненская
Krasnopresnenskaya
Электрозаводская
Elektrozavodskaya
Красные Ворота
Krasnye Vorota
Маяковская
Mayakovskaya
Бауманская
Baumanskaya
Баррикадная
Barrikadnaya
Чистые Пруды
Chistye Prudy
Тургеневская
Turgenevskaya
Чкаловская
Chkalovskaya
Пушкинская
Pushkinskaya
Кузнецкий Мост
Kuznetskiy Most
Chekhovskaya
Чеховская
Тверская
Tverskaya
Лубянка
Lubyanka
Сретенский Бульвар
Sretenskiy Bulvar
Курская
Kurskaya
Международная
Mezhdunarodnata
Александ ровский Сад
Aleksandrovskiy Sad
Охотный Ряд
Okhotnyy Ryad
Новогиреево
Novogireevo
Арбатская
Arbatskaya
Театральная
Teatralnaya
Китай-Город
Kitay-Gorod
Авиамоторная
Aviamotornaya
Выставочная
Vystavochnaya
Смоленская
Smolenskaya
Боровицкая
Borovitskaya
Площадь Революции
Ploshchad Revolyutsii
Римская
Rimskaya
Марксистская
Marksistskaya
Площадь Ильича
Ploshchad Ilicha
Кунцевская
Kuntsevskaya
Смоленская
Smolenskaya
Арбатская
Arbatskaya
Третьяковская
Tretyakovskaya
Библиотека Имени Ленина
Biblioteka Imeni Lenina
Фили
Fili
Киевская
Kievskaya
Новокузнецкая
Novokuznetskaya
Таганская
Taganskaya
Кутузовская
Kutuzovskaya
Кропоткинская
Kropotkinskaya
Полянка
Polyanka
Крестьянская Застава
Krestyanskaya Zastava
Пролетарская
Proletarskaya
Митино
Mitino
Студенческая
Studencheskaya
Парк Культуры
Park Kultury
Павелецкая
Paveletskaya
Волгоградский Проспект
Volgogradskiy Prospekt
Парк Победы
Park Pobedy
Добрынинская
Dobryninskaya
Дубровка
Dubrovka
Октябрьская
Oktyabrskaya
Автозаводская
Avtozavodskaya
Кожуховская
Kozhukhovskaya
Серпуховская
Serpukhovskaya
Фрунзенская
Frunzenskaya
Шаболовская
Shabolovskaya
Печатники
Pechatniki
Текстильщики
Tekstilshchiki
Тульская
Tulskaya
Коломенская
Kolomenskaya
Спортивная
Sportivnaya
Ленинский Проспект
Leninskiy Prospekt
Волжская
Volzhskaya
Кузьминки
Kuzminki
Нагатинская
Nagatinskaya
Каширская
Kashirskaya
Люблино
Lyublino
Рязанский Проспект
Ryazanskiy Prospekt
Академическая
Akademicheskaya
Воробьевы Горы
Vorobevy Gory
Нагорная
Nagornaya
Варшавская
Varshavskaya
Братиславская
Bratislavskaya
Выхино
Vykhino
Профсоюзная
Profsoyuznaya
Университет
Universitet
Нахимовский Просрект
Nakhimovskiy Prospekt
Кантемировская
Kantemirovskaya
Марьино
Marino
Лермонтовский Проспект
Lemontovsky Prospekt
Новые Черёмушки
Novye Cheremushki
Севастопольская
Sevastopolskaya
Царицыно
Tsaritsyno
Проспект Вернадского
Prospekt Vernadskovo
Калужская
Kaluzhskaya
Каховская
Kakhovskaya
Борисово
Borisovo
Чертановская
Chertanovskaya
Орехово
Orekhovo
Жулебино
Zhulebino
Юго-западная
Yugo-zapadnaya
Беляево
Belyaevo
Южная
Yuzhnaya
Тропарево
Troparevo
Коньково
Konkovo
Домодедовская
Domodedovskaya
Шипиловская
Shipilovskaya
Пражская
Prazhskaya
Котельники
Kotelniki
Румянцево
Rumyantsevo
Тёплый Стан
Teplyy Stan
Ул. Академика Янгеля
Akademika Yangelia
Зябликово
Zyablikovo
Красногвардейская
Krasnogvardeyskaya
Новоясеневская
Novoyasenevskaya
Бульвар дм. Донского
Bulvar Dmitria Donskogo
Братеево
Brateevo
Key
Line 1
Line 2
Line 3
Line 4
Line 5 (circle)
Line 6
Line 7
Line 8
Line 9
Line 10
Line 11
Line M1 (monorail)
Under construction